21.95

PRODUCTION/OPERATIONS MANAGEMENT

Concepts and Situations

ROGER W. SCHMENNER

Graduate School of Business Administration, Duke University

SCIENCE RESEARCH ASSOCIATES, INC.
Chicago, Palo Alto, Toronto, Henley-on-Thames, Sydney

A Subsidiary of IBM

Acquisition Editor	Michael Zamczyk
Project Editor	Gretchen Hargis
Designer	Judith Olson
Technical Art	House of Graphics
Composition	Computer Typesetting Services, Inc.

Library of Congress Cataloging in Publication Data

Schmenner, Roger W.   1947–
    Production/operations management.

    Includes bibliographical references and index.
    1. Production management — Case studies.
I. Title.
TS155.S322   658.5   80-15627
ISBN 0-574-19500-9

The author wishes to thank the following companies for reviewing the relevant manuscript pages and authorizing use of the process descriptions: International Paper Company, Norcen Industries, Jung Products, Inc., Jos. Schlitz Brewing Company, General Motors Corporation (GM Assembly Division), Burger King Corporation, and Giant Food Inc.

Pages 91, 92: Reprinted by permission of the Harvard Business Review. Excerpts from "Quality of Work Life — Learning from Tarrytown" by Robert H. Guest (July–August 1979). Copyright © 1979 by the President and Fellows of Harvard College. All rights reserved.
Pages 159–60: List adapted from "QWL Indicators — Prospects and Problems" by Richard E. Walton in *Studies in Personnel Psychology* 6, no. 1 (Spring 1974). Used by permission.
Pages 186–99: Courtesy of Savage Arms Division, Emhart Industries, Inc.
Pages 417–18: Reprinted by permission from Fortune Magazine; © 1978 Time Inc.

Table 9-1: Reprinted with permission from the *Industrial and Labor Relations Review*, vol. 32, no. 2 (January 1979). © 1979 by Cornell University. All rights reserved.

Table 9-2: Reprinted with permission of the author from *The Public Interest*, no. 57 (Fall 1979), p. 75. © 1979 by National Affairs, Inc.
Table 12-12: Reprinted by permission of the Harvard Business Review. Exhibit from "Before You Build a *Big* Factory" by Roger W. Schmenner (July–August 1976). Copyright © 1976 by the President and Fellows of Harvard College. All rights reserved.
Table 15-1: Reprinted by permission of the Harvard Business Review. Exhibit from "How Should You Organize Manufacturing?" by Robert H. Hayes and Roger W. Schmenner (January–February 1978). Copyright © 1978 by the President and Fellows of Harvard College. All rights reserved.

Figure 9-2: Reprinted by permission of the Harvard Business Review. Exhibit from "Work Innovation in the United States" by Richard E. Walton (July–August 1979). Copyright © 1979 by the President and Fellows of Harvard College. All rights reserved.
Figure 13-5: Reprinted from "Patterns of Industrial Innovation" by William J. Abernathy and James M. Utterback in *Technology Review* (June–July 1978). © 1978 Technology Review. Used by permission.

10 9 8 7 6 5 4 3

Contents

Foreword

The slow growth in productivity over the past decade has been a concern for many people, and some would tie it to the recent round of inflation and the relative decline in the U.S. international competitive position. Productivity is a complex phenomenon, and reversing the trend requires a variety of actions. One of the proven approaches is more effective performance of the production/operations management function—the primary focus of this book.

This book effectively integrates the techniques approach and the case method approach to the study of production/operations management. In clear, readable style the first six chapters take the reader on a series of plant tours of actual organizations with a variety of production processes, problems, and opportunities. These examples encourage the reader to appreciate the various techniques and strategies for improving operations. Professor Schmenner emphasizes the application of analytical techniques rather than their study as theoretical abstractions. The book works through a multitude of problems facing operations managers. It deals with typical issues occurring at the operating level, regardless of the industry or the type of product or service involved.

The sequence of topics flows logically, concentrating on smaller problems at the beginning and working toward larger, more strategic problems at the end. Although its coverage of analytical techniques is excellent, the book does not stop at this level. It integrates such technical material with broader issues and topics not generally covered in P/OM texts, such as quality of work life, managing technology, operations strategy, labor relations, and government regulations.

With the increasing emphasis on improving productivity, the production/operations management field has taken on renewed interest and importance. Professor Schmenner has successfuly captured the excitement and intellectual challenge facing this field in a format and style that is interesting and stimulating for the reader.

Fremont Kast
James Rosenzweig

Preface

Like many broad fields of inquiry, production/operations management has spawned a number of distinct teaching styles, some of which pull in very different directions. At the risk of oversimplifying this diversity, let me outline what I view as the two leading schools of thought on the teaching of P/OM: the techniques school and the case method school.

From the days of Frederick Taylor, the Gilbreths, Henry Gantt, and others early in this century and the "scientific management" they pioneered, much of the development of production/operations management has been associated with the creation and refinement of tools and techniques for improving operations. The development of time and motion studies, scheduling charts and algorithms, inventory control models, statistical sampling, and a bushelful of other techniques, many very sophisticated, has been a triumph of the discipline. These techniques are indeed a rich lode, and for many teachers of production/operations management, the teaching of P/OM is primarily the mining of these techniques.

While widely practiced, this school of thought has not gone without criticism. One line of criticism cautions that the techniques school sometimes becomes wedded to the techniques themselves and not to the problems they were developed to help solve; what becomes paramount are the intricacies of the techniques and not their range and usefulness in actual operational situations. These critics worry that the techniques school has lost its "roots."

At the other pole of teaching style lies the case method school of thought. This school emphasizes the problems faced by operating managers. Its adherents assume that the managers of the future are better served by an understanding of the situations they will face than by a rigorous and complete understanding of the techniques that have been developed over the years.

Although critics of the case method concede that it can provide wonderful motivation and some managerial insight for the student, they argue that it sometimes forsakes the recognized tools and techniques altogether, letting the student flounder unnecessarily. Casebooks traditionally have given the student little overarching theory and structure and next to no help in analyzing the case material. This lack puts tremendous pressure on the instructor to provide the structure and analysis, and to link one case with another so that the course is more than a series of vignettes.

This textbook has been designed to combine and unify the best elements of both of these schools of thought. To provide the kind of appreciation for managerial problems characteristic of the case method, this textbook introduces many of the tools, techniques, and concepts of P/OM through 22 small case examples (termed "situations"). A realistic management situation is described where a decision must be made quickly. The text then walks the student through an analysis of the situation and suggests some ways by which the manager involved might resolve the dilemma. This analysis often utilizes the tools and techniques that have been developed through the years, and, where appropriate, explains them in depth in what are termed "asides." By this format, the text seeks to relate the concepts and techniques of P/OM to the problems that operating managers face every day.

As a further means of unifying the techniques and case method schools of thought on P/OM, the text is grounded in the study and appreciation of different types of production processes. Each of the first six chapters describes and discusses the actual operations of some distinctly different processes—a General Motors assembly plant, an International Paper pulp and paper mill, a Burger King restaurant, a Schlitz brewery, a small machine shop (Norcen Industries), and a maker of elastic knit products (Jung Products, Inc.). These "plant tours" give the student some basic information and understanding that are built upon in successive chapters. These true-to-life plant tours are supplemented by (1) a description of technological change at Giant Food Inc., the Washington, D.C.-based grocery chain that has pioneered in laser beam scanning at the checkout counter and (2) excerpts from the labor-management agreement between Savage Arms (division of Emhart) and the Machinists union.

By unifying pedagogic schools of thought in this way, this book is designed for use by instructors of either the technical or the case method persuasion. Because appropriate concepts and techniques are presented in conjunction with the management situations, technical method instructors can draw upon their own expertise in particular techniques and not have to spend extra time and effort first putting the technique into context. Case method instructors may want to concentrate on the small case examples, perhaps using them as practice runs for longer, more involved cases.

After the plant tour segment, the material follows much the same sequence as the careers of many operating managers, rising from smaller, more specific problems to larger, more general ones. The first concepts and techniques deal with improving existing operations—breaking bottlenecks, managing the workforce, managing materials, planning and controlling production. Only then are the longer term issues of deciding future operations broached—changing capacity, dealing with technological change, deciding about vertical integration. Finally, operations strategy and the impact of government regulation are discussed. Throughout all of these segments, care is taken to include discussion of both manufacturing and non-manufacturing operations and to highlight their similarities and differences.

We are all the products of our training and associations; I am no different. This textbook owes much to the influence of a number of people on my understanding of production/operations management. In particular I would like to express my gratitude to Robert H. Hayes, Wickham Skinner, Paul W. Marshall, Robert A. Leone, Steven C. Wheelwright, Jeffrey G. Miller, W. Earl Sasser, William J. Abernathy, John R. Meyer, D. Daryl Wyckoff, James J. Healy, and James L. Heskett for sharing their time and insights with me over the years.

I would also like to thank the following reviewers for their many helpful suggestions: Joseph R. Biggs (University of Wyoming), Thomas E. Callarman (Arizona State University), Edwin Duerr (San Francisco State University), Dale Flowers (Texas Tech University), Robert Hall (Indiana University), Fremont E. Kast (University of Washington), Dennis McLeavey (University of Rhode

Island), Jill Mellick (Golden Gate University), Joseph Monks (Gonzaga University), and James E. Rosenzweig (University of Washington).

Particular chapters of this text owe much as well to the cooperation of numerous companies. While I cannot acknowledge the contributions of everyone in those companies who helped me, I would like to make special mention of several of them: Errol Savoie of International Paper, Joseph B. Gehret of Norcen Industries, Robert A. Conway of Jung Products, Peter Stammberger of Schlitz, Thomas Pilkington of General Motors, Charles Kanan of Burger King, and Barry F. Scher and Donald R. Buchanan of Giant Food.

Textbooks are not written in a day. I especially value the understanding of my wife, Barbie, during the months when this book was created. I hope she may one day find the time and courage to pick up this text and read it.

I have been aided as well by Elaine Ciccarelli Mossmann, who typed and reviewed all of the manuscript, and Gretchen Hargis, who edited it. Almost all of the questions for discussion and review, found at the end of each chapter, are attributable to Jill Mellick. Almost all of the problems and all of the situations for study are the work of Joseph R. Biggs of the University of Wyoming and Thomas E. Callarman of Arizona State University. These are important contributions that have both improved this text and reduced the burden of its writing for me. I am most grateful to them. Lastly, I would like to thank William J. Bruns, Jr., for calling my bluff on this project. Without his nudging and David Bruce Caldwell's fortuitous timing, this text might still be merely a twinkle in my mind's eye.

Roger W. Schmenner

INTRODUCTION

Operations. For many people mentioning the word brings on a rush of disagreeable feelings and sensations. Details. Pressure. Long hours. Inhospitable working conditions. Dull colleagues. For these people, a company's operating managers—usually typed as engineers who could not hack it in the "more creative" design aspects of the business—lead very unromantic careers. Moreover, operations is viewed as a dead-end job with no future in the upper layers of management.

This description is an exaggeration, of course, but it conveys some of the impressions that people hold about operations. This text is a crusade against that kind of stereotype of the operations manager. In fact, operations offers an exciting and dynamic management challenge that is as absorbing and rewarding as any marketing or finance can offer. After all, for the typical company, most of its assets and people are devoted to the production function. Moreover, a badly run operation can be a staggering drain on corporate profits and morale, as a number of even large corporations can attest; conversely, a well-run operation can be a competitive weapon every bit as potent as any in the corporate arsenal.

For many senior managers, the path to the top snaked through manufacturing—even for those whose climb has been in so-called "marketing companies." Many others would admit that a tour of duty in operations was an important part of their general management education and background.

The point is that operations is and rightly should be a key concern for most companies and one that all students of business who aspire to general management responsibilities ought to know about.

What makes for an outstanding operating manager is an elusive concept that no doubt will be debated for years to come. One recent thoughtful analysis, however, was made by Wickham Skinner and Earl Sasser.[1] Citing a study of a number of managers thrust into some very different situations, they suggest that the managers who are real achievers demonstrate four distinct characteristics:

- They employ analytical tools with discipline and consistency and are careful to keep information and data flowing.
- They truly motivate their subordinates and know what satisfies their own superiors.
- They manage themselves—their time, their temper, their clout, their thinking.
- They focus on one task of prime importance at a time.

This text cannot hope to teach you, the reader, how to manage yourself or all the subtleties in the interpersonal interactions that abound in business organizations. It can, however, open the doors to some useful ways of looking at operations, of identifying and analyzing their problems, and of judging what merits chief concern and attention as well as to possible means of solving problems. Instilling this awareness is the goal of this text.

THIS TEXT'S PHILOSOPHY
AND ORGANIZATION

This text approaches operations management from the bottom up. I am convinced that a sound grounding in the nitty-gritty of existing operations is a prerequisite to a fuller understanding of what it means to alter a production system or to design a new one. Therefore, Segment I of this text describes in detail six production processes that differ from one another in important ways and represent the entire spectrum of process choice. Each process is analyzed in turn, and then all of them are compared and contrasted against one another, so as to highlight the particular features that define a production process. The remainder of the text builds on the foundation provided by these six processes.

Segment II considers some of the typical problems of ongoing operations and how these operations can be improved over the short run. The areas of management concern addressed in Segment II include breaking production bottlenecks, managing the workforce (including a unionized workforce), managing materials (purchasing, inventories, and logistics), and planning, scheduling, and controlling production over the near term (say, 6 to 18 months).

Segment III takes operations one step further, by considering more drastic changes to the production process — capacity change, technological change, change in the span of process undertaken (vertical integration) — all of which require advance planning and, usually, a year or more to implement.

Segment IV then ties together Segments I, II, and III by focusing on the broad issue of operations strategy and organization. It is only here that the design of a production system — its facilities, technology, policies, and organization — is discussed in full. It is here too that the use of operations as a competitive weapon can be appreciated most keenly, even in the face of government regulation.

It has been my experience that nothing serves better to stimulate interest in a problem or topic than seeing it come to life in a real world situation. With this in mind, Segments II through IV of this book are liberally sprinkled with production and operations situations demanding management decisions and derived from the travails of managers in a host of industries; these situations supplement and reinforce the process descriptions in Segment I. They are like small case studies that make very specialized points about operations. They serve as a touchstone for both the reader's understanding of the nature and importance of a particular concept and the text's ensuing discussion of possible resolutions of the problems and opportunities exposed by each situation. Thus, much of the format of this text consists of a particular situation followed by discussion of that situation and its more general implications.

For the situations that initiate the discussion of operations concepts, this text draws on both manufacturing and nonmanufacturing company experience. One of the six process discussions that anchor this text deals with a Burger King restaurant, and six of the 22 small case study situations used in Segments II, III, and IV are from nonmanufacturing industries. Thus, at regular intervals throughout the text the similarities and differences between manufacturing and nonmanufacturing industry operations are highlighted.

With this as a prologue, let us begin our exploration of various production processes.

REFERENCE NOTE

1. Wickham Skinner and W. Earl Sasser, "Managers with Impact: Versatile and Inconsistent," *Harvard Business Review* 55, no. 6 (November-December 1977): 140–48.

I

PLANT TOURS

Each of the following six chapters introduces a particular kind of production process. All six processes described are different in important respects; together they span the entire range of process choice. Included in these "plant tours" are the following types of processes:

- Job shop
- Batch flow process
- Worker-paced line flow process
- Machine-paced line flow process
- Continuous flow process
- Hybrid process (part batch and part continuous flow)

The models for each of these process types are drawn from actual operations as they were functioning in the summer of 1978. Naturally, I am greatly indebted to the cooperating companies for spending a good deal of time with me discussing their production processes and walking me around them, and also for reviewing and correcting my written descriptions of their operations.

Each chapter consists of a process description followed by a discussion of the salient features of the process. The sequence of chapters highlights the differences among the processes. For example, the description of a continuous flow process (Chapter 1) is followed immediately by the description of a job shop, which lies at the opposite extreme of the process spectrum. By playing up these contrasts, the unique features of each process may be kept more clearly in mind.

The seventh and concluding chapter of this segment compares and contrasts all six processes and in so doing pinpoints the key realms of management choice and concern in each.

These seven chapters anchor this text. They introduce few, if any, techniques of analysis since they are essentially descriptive. Rather, they provide the background against which the usefulness of the concepts and techniques discussed in Chapters 8 through 16 can best be seen. Aspects of these seven chapters are referred to on numerous occasions elsewhere in the text. The plant tours taken in this segment are a constant reminder of the diversity, complexity, and challenge of the operations decisions faced by managers every day in hosts of industries.

1

A CONTINUOUS FLOW PROCESS
International Paper Company, Androscoggin Mill
Jay, Maine

The Androscoggin Mill, situated along the Androscoggin River in central Maine, was one of 28 pulp and paper mills which the International Paper Company operated worldwide. It was one of the largest and most modern, having been built originally in 1965 with significant additions in 1968 and 1977. The plant occupied 478 acres of land, had 20 acres under roof, and represented a book value investment of over $300 million.

The mill, part of International Paper's White Papers Group, produced three distinctly different

kinds of paper: (1) forms bond, envelope, tablet, and offset paper for office or computer use; (2) paper tissue for use as carbon paper in business forms; and (3) publication gloss for magazine printing.

Androscoggin was a fully integrated mill; that is, it produced all the wood pulp it needed to make its paper. The mill was laid out to receive logs or chips of wood at one end and, about a mile farther down, to ship packaged "logs" of paper from the other end. (See Figure 1-1 for a layout of the mill; the production flow is from left to right.)

PART ONE
PROCESS DESCRIPTION

A BRIEF AND SIMPLIFIED DESCRIPTION OF PAPERMAKING

The paper we use today is created from individual wood fibers that are first suspended in water and then pressed and dried into sheets. The process of converting the wood to a suspension of wood fibers in water is known as pulpmaking, while the manufacture of the dried and pressed sheets of paper is formally termed papermaking. The process of making paper has undergone a steady evolution, and

larger and more sophisticated equipment and better technology continue to improve it.

THE WOODYARD AND WOODROOMS

The process at Androscoggin began with the receiving of wood in the form of chips or of logs 4 or 8 feet in length. From 7 A.M. to dusk a steady

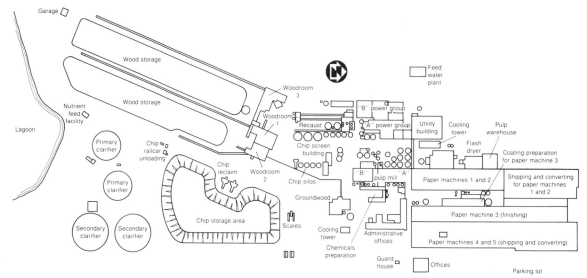

FIGURE 1-1   Layout of International Paper Company's Androscoggin Mill.

stream of trucks and railroad cars were weighed and unloaded. About 40 percent of the deliveries were of wood cut from International Paper's own land (over 1.25 million acres in Maine), while the other 60 percent was supplied by independents who were paid by weight for their logs. The mill also received wood chips from lumber mills in the area. The chips and logs were stored in mammoth piles with separate piles for wood of different species (e.g., pine, spruce, hemlock).

When needed, logs were floated in flumes from the woodyard into one of the mill's three woodrooms. There bark was rubbed off in long, ribbed debarking drums by tumbling the logs against one another. The logs then fell into a chipper; within seconds a large log was reduced to a pile of chips approximately 1 inch by 1 inch by ¼ inch. The wood chips were then sorted through screens in a large agitator. Too large chips were rechipped, and too small ones were collected for burning in the power house. (The mill provided approximately 50 percent of all its own steam and electricity needs from burning waste. An additional 50 percent of total electricity needs was produced by harnessing the river for hydroelectric power.)

The chips were then stored in silos. There were separate silos for spruce and fir, pine and hemlock, and hardwoods (maple, beech, and birch). This separate and temporary storage of chips permitted the controlled mixing of chips of these three main types into the precise recipe for the grade of paper being produced. Once drawn from the silo into the digesters, there was no stopping the flow of chips into paper.

PULPMAKING

The pulp made at Androscoggin was of two types: Kraft pulp (produced chemically) and groundwood pulp (produced mechanically). Kraft pulp was far more important to the high-quality white papers produced at Androscoggin, accounting for 90 percent of all the pulp used. Kraft pulp makes strong paper. (Kraft is German for strength. A German invented the Kraft pulp process in 1884.) A paper's strength generally comes from the overlap and binding of long fibers of softwood; only chemically was it initially possible to separate long wood fibers for suspension in water. Hardwood fibers are generally smaller and thinner and help smooth the paper and make it less porous.

Aerial view of International Paper Company's Androscoggin Mill. In the foreground are the clarifiers and the wood and chip storage areas; beyond these are the chip silos, power plant, pulp mill, and paper machines. *(Tom Jones Photo, Courtesy of International Paper Company)*

The groundwood pulping process was simpler and less expensive than the Kraft process. It took high-quality spruce and fir logs and pressed them continuously against a revolving stone that broke apart the wood's fibers. The fibers, however, were smaller than those produced by the Kraft process and, although used to make newsprint, were useful at Androscoggin only in providing "fill" for the coated publication gloss papers of machine 3, as will be described later.

The chemical Kraft process worked by dissolving the lignin that bonds wood fibers together. It did this in a tall pressure cooker, called a digester, by "cooking" the chips in a solution of caustic soda (NaOH) and sodium sulfide (Na_2S), which was termed the "white liquor." The two digesters at Androscoggin were continuous digesters; chips and liquor went into the top, were cooked together as they slowly settled down to the bottom, and were

drawn off the bottom after about 3 hours. By this time, the white liquor had changed chemically to "black liquor"; the digested chips were then separated from this black liquor.

Upon leaving the digester, the digested chips entered the blow tank which was maintained at a significantly lower pressure than the pressurized continuous digester. The pressure difference literally exploded the wood fibers apart, since there was no lignin left to bond them together.

The black liquor entered a separate four-step recovery process. About 90 percent of the black liquor could be reconstituted as white liquor, thereby saving on chemical costs and significantly lowering pollution. The four-step process involved (1) washing the black liquor from the cooked fiber to produce weak black liquor, (2) evaporating the weak black liquor to a thicker consistency, (3) combustion of this heavy black liquor with sodium sulfate (Na_2SO_4), and redissolving the smelt, yielding a "green liquor" (sodium carbonate), and (4) adding lime which reacted with the green liquor to produce white liquor. The last step was known as recaust.

Meanwhile, the wood-fiber pulp was purged of impurities like bark and dirt by spinning the mixture in centrifugal cleaners. The pulp was then concentrated by removing water from it so that it could be bleached more economically.

By this time, depending on the type of pulp being made, it had been between 3.5 and 5 hours since the chips had entered the pulp mill. About 85 percent of all the Kraft pulp was bleached; carbonizing tissue was the key product using unbleached pulp. Bleaching took between 7 and 8 hours. It consisted of a five-step process where (1) chlorine (Cl_2) was introduced to the pulp and then washed; (2) sodium hydroxide (NaOH) was then added to the pulp and washed; (3) chlorine dioxide (ClO_2) was introduced, (4) extracted once again with sodium hydroxide, and then (5) chlorine dioxide reintroduced to the pulp. The result was like fluffy cream of wheat. By this time the pulp was nearly ready to be made into paper.

From the bleachery, the stock of pulp was held for a short time in storage so that a string of additives (e.g., filler clay, size, resins, brighteners, alum, dyes) could be mixed into the pulp according to the recipe for the paper grade being produced. Here, too, "broke" (paper wastes from the mill itself) was recycled into the pulp. The pulp was then once again cleaned and blended into even consistency before moving to the papermaking machine itself.

PAPERMAKING

The paper machine was a simply awesome engineering creation, stretching hundreds of feet. At Androscoggin, there were five of varying size. The paper machine had a wet end and a dry end. The pulp entered the machine at the headbox, which released the heavily diluted pulp through a slit onto a moving belt of synthetic fabric. This belt was called the "wire" because originally it was made of bronze mesh. Many paper machines, including the two machines at Androscoggin devoted to the production of carbonizing tissue, still used the bronze "wire."

As the wire with its deposit of pulp stock moved away from the headbox, water drained through it. Suction was also applied. Within 60 feet after the headbox slit, so much water had been removed that it could be said the wire carried paper, rather than a suspension of pulp in water. From the wire, huge woolen felts picked up the paper "web" and started it through a series of rollers and steam-heated drying drums, which pressed and evaporated even more water out of the web. If the paper was to be coated, the coating would be applied first to one side of the paper and then the other and more drying done. If the paper was to be shiny, it would be pressed on smooth, shiny rollers called calenders. Drying and pressing having been done, the paper was essentially finished and was picked up from the machine on winders.

The speeds at which all this happened were incredible. The machine set at the slowest speed (#2, the older of the two machines producing the very thin carbonizing tissue) still produced a mile of paper every 3 minutes. The fastest machine (#3, devoted to publication gloss) produced a mile of paper every 2 minutes. This great speed was made possible by continual improvements made by the machine's builders and by computerized process controls, which constantly adjusted the machine's settings based on the values registered by numerous electronic sensors scattered along the length of the machine.

Once on the winders, the "logs" of paper could be slit directly into widths the customers had ordered, or they could be slit into two logs of equal widths and stored until needed. The unslit logs, called "parent logs," were then placed on rewinders for successive slitting to customer order. Once cut to order, rolls were packaged, labeled, and then shipped.

Continuous digesters at the pulp mill. These work like pressure cookers, dissolving the lignin bonds between wood fibers. *(Courtesy of International Paper Company)*

A slow-moving rake forced the settled sludge to the middle, where it was removed to be burned.

2. In a 37-acre lagoon the clarified effluent was aerated by a collection of churning fountains, and a special collection of microorganisms broke down the effluent over the course of 7 or 8 days.

3. A secondary clarifier (two more large basins) settled more solids from the water.

The entire treatment process took about 10 days.

Since waste water treatment at paper mills was still a relatively new enterprise, it was not as well understood as it would be in the years to come. While the water released to the river met the standard, there were variations in the quality of the discharge that were not completely understood. This was a source of management concern and technological effort.

Air pollution control was another area where great strides had been made since the early 1960s. Gas collection systems to collect and burn noncondensible gases from the digester and evaporators had helped to eliminate the hydrogen sulfide ("rotten egg") smell that had been characteristic of paper mills. Scrubbers on the stacks at Androscoggin had gone even further in removing sulphur and other particulates from the smoke and air at the mill. Also, utilization of black liquor oxidation had helped in odor removal.

MAINTAINING THE ENVIRONMENT

Being a relatively new mill, Androscoggin had environmental control equipment designed into it. Pulp and paper mills were large users of water. Androscoggin took water from the river, filtered it, and then used it in the process. Before being released back to the river, the water was treated in three stages to remove the effluent it had picked up.

1. A primary clarifier (two large cone-shaped basins) allowed particles to settle to the bottom.

THE DESIGN OF THE ANDROSCOGGIN MILL

VERTICAL INTEGRATION

The Androscoggin Mill was vertically integrated; that is, it combined pulpmaking and papermaking at the same site. Not all mills, especially not the older ones, were designed to combine both activities. Several advantages argued strongly for vertical integration:

1. Integration removed the transportation costs that would have been incurred if pulp had to be

transported between a pulp mill and a paper mill. Vertical integration eliminated the double handling of pulp, a cost saving in any event. In addition, because the mill shipped all over the country, transportation costs for finished paper were not affected significantly by the mill's location; and so a location near the supply of pulp was highly desirable.

2. Integration provided for better quality control. Since the quality of the paper produced depended heavily on the quality of the pulp, vertical integration permitted hour-by-hour control over the quality of pulp entering each paper machine. Such control greatly reduced the chances for paper breaks on the machine and eliminated any quality problems caused by old pulp or other deficiencies.

3. The pulpmaking operation generated sawdust, bark, chemicals, and wood chips that could be burned as fuel for the whole plant, thus cutting down on plant-wide energy costs.

While the Androscoggin Mill integrated pulpmaking and papermaking, the extent of the mill's vertical integration could have been even broader. For example, only about 40 percent of the wood used at the mill was cut from land owned by International Paper. The company could have integrated backward even more by raising that 40 percent figure. It chose not to do so, however, since the 40 percent figure, and modest variations around it, (1) permitted good forest management of International Paper's own land and (2) meant that the company could add directly to the area's economy by purchasing from independents. There were no substantial cost differences between independent and company tree harvesting. Only if independent loggers could not supply the mill's needs would the company have harvested more from its own land.

By the same token, the operations at Androscoggin could have been extended by forward integration, so that the plant converted more of its paper into end uses (e.g., sheets of bond paper rather than

rolls of it, carbonizing of the tissue rather than simply its fabrication). The company chose not to do this as well. For one thing, adding converting facilities would have greatly increased Androscoggin's already large size and would have diluted management's attention from the mission of producing quality paper efficiently. Converting operations were also best located closer to markets since the nature of conversion often placed the paper in bulkier and more awkward packages, which were harder to ship and were often shipped in smaller quantities than Androscoggin's full truck and rail carloads. Splitting conversion from papermaking, at least for white papers, meant lower overall transport costs, whereas there were no real economies in the linking of the two operations.

CAPACITY

Over time, the size and capacity of individual paper machines had grown enormously. There were distinct advantages to this large scale of operation, since the largest and latest machines could produce more tons of paper per worker, thus saving costs. At Androscoggin, for example, machines 2 and 5 both manufactured carbonizing tissue. Machine 2, built in 1965, could produce paper 208 inches wide at a speed of 1750 feet per minute. Machine 5, in contrast, built in 1977, could produce paper 230 inches wide at a rate of 1800 feet per minute. In only 12 years, the capacity of the machine per unit of time had increased by nearly 14 percent. A similar comparison between machines 1 and 4 was even more striking—31 percent. This increase in machine size and speed enabled the newer mills to house fewer paper machines and workers than older mills and yet produce more paper at the same time.

The Androscoggin Mill, at its current size, was about as large as it was likely to grow. The output rates of its five paper machines (approximately 410,000 tons per year), its two continuous digesters, its groundwood mill, and its three woodrooms (approximately 442,000 tons per year) were all rea-

Paper machine 5, built in 1977. *(Courtesy of International Paper Company)*

sonably well balanced. As it was, the pulp mill had been deliberately built larger so that another mill down the river and other International Paper mills could be supplied with pulp.

LOCATION

The Androscoggin Mill's general location in central Maine was attributable largely to three factors:

1. The production of strong, quality white office papers demanded long wood fibers. This demand favored a Maine location because cold winter weather favors the production of longer fibers in both the soft and hardwood trees that Maine has in abundance.
2. A paper mill uses so much water that it has to be located on either a lake or a river, and preferably a river because of environmental factors.
3. This part of central Maine enjoyed the availability of a good supply of labor.

TECHNOLOGY

In pulpmaking and papermaking, keeping abreast of the latest changes in process equipment and technology is critical to a company's continued success. At International Paper the main responsibility for keeping up with technology rested with the corporate staff. They were also instrumental in the selection of any new equipment or in process changes. The plant, however, did play an important role by providing managers (e.g., the plant engineer, the paper mill superintendent) who joined the corporate staff in studying any new capacity addition or process technology change. This team was responsible for developing the capital appropriations request and its supporting documents.

LOADING THE FACTORY

PRODUCTION PLANNING

Orders for any of the white papers produced at Androscoggin would be taken by one of International Paper's regional sales offices, which would transmit them to the company's control order department in New York. Orders would gather there awaiting the determination of the next 4-week cycle of production. Four weeks before the start of any 4-week cycle, the manager of operations control and the various product line managers within the White Papers Group would meet to plan the production schedule for the cycle. This production schedule allocated the types and weights of paper to be produced at each plant by each machine for every day of the 4-week cycle. These machine assignments and the orders they represented were then transmitted to each of the company's plants and were acknowledged by them.

The assignment of types and weights of paper to each paper machine was a sophisticated enterprise. Because the company's machines were all slightly different from one another, due primarily to their different vintages, their capabilities differed. That is, they were often relatively more successful and/ or more cost efficient at making certain types and weights of paper than others. In assigning products to machines, therefore, the corporation took care to make the assignments in such a way that the company's total contribution to profits and overhead

was maximized. This assigning required not only information on the mix of papers demanded for the period and on machine capabilities, but on distribution and transportation costs as well. Thus, for some grades, colors, or weights of paper, depending on the situation, Androscoggin might have filled an order that might otherwise have been filled by a mill much closer to the customer.

At present, Androscoggin's five paper machines were likely to be assigned the following "paper machine products":

- Machine 1—various types of bond or offset paper in white or colors
- Machine 2—carbonizing tissue
- Machine 3—coated publication gloss
- Machine 4—various types of bond, ledger, envelope, and tablet paper (all white)
- Machine 5—carbonizing tissue

Since machine 4 was both larger and faster than machine 1, it was devoted to fewer different kinds of paper and thus longer production runs than machine 1. In that way, the mill could produce more total paper than if machine 4 continually had to be stopped and reset for different colors, grades, or weights. Better to stop and start machine 1 for such changes.

Currently, the demand for paper was strong; Androscoggin and other mills were running flat out. In fact, sales were so strong that regions had to be put on allocation; orders had to be turned away. This situation was far different from recessionary times when the mill would take any order and still had to cut back production.

While the company's central order department (operations control) decided what would be produced on what machine on which days, the mill still had its own considerable production planning problems. Customer orders not only specified the type of paper but also the size (width) to be cut, the quantity (the diameter of the roll), and some other features. In planning for any specific run on a paper machine, the mill wanted to group together all

Paper machine 4, for the production of carbonizing paper. *(Courtesy of International Paper Company)*

those orders calling for the same diameter and in such a way that the entire width of the paper machine's output was accounted for. The mill did not like to leave any waste, since even an inch of paper unaccounted for could cost the company forgone revenue of several thousand dollars.

The mill also wanted to schedule the slitting of the rolls to minimize additional handling. This goal meant slitting as much off the winder as possible, observing that small widths should be cut from the center portion to reduce the risk of distortion in slitting.

Three production planners scheduled orders on the mill's five machines. They had to remain flexible enough to allow at least some amendments to customer orders as late as the Wednesday before the start of the next week's production. The mill also had to schedule trucks and railcars for the shipment of orders.

INVENTORIES AND PURCHASING

Most of the wood the Androscoggin Mill used was provided by contract for 10,000 to 100,000 cords per year. International Paper did not cut its own wood, but contracted that task out as well. The company's woodlands division was responsible for purchasing the mill's wood and managing the woodyard at economical inventory levels. In addition, the mill stood ready to purchase, by weight, the wood of small, independent loggers without prior commitments being made. The mill did, however, deliberately seek the building up of wood in inventory in the fall and winter so that the spring thaw and the mud it brought did not disrupt the mill as it disrupted logging. It was not uncommon to have 30 days of production in pulp wood inventory.

All the work-in-process inventories were small and temporary, used mainly to permit the mixing of different types of wood chips or pulp.

The extent of finished goods inventory varied. Comparatively little finished goods were held for the products of machines 2, 3, and 5 (carbonizing tissue and publication gloss). Some was kept to permit the filling of stray orders or order amendments, but most paper production was soon headed out the door, waiting only long enough for all items in the order to be gathered together. The finished goods inventory for machine 1 (bond and offset papers) was very much larger, typically about 25 days of production. Such a large inventory was needed to meet customer needs on any of the 48 paper machine products that machine 1 was qualified to manufacture, with only a small number of machine setups over the course of a year.

At Androscoggin, all responsibilities for production planning, loading machines, product distribution to customers, and finished goods inventories rested with the Planning, Scheduling, and Distribution Department since it was felt that all of these items affected one another at the plant and should be controlled by the same authority.

THE WORKFORCE

The Androscoggin Mill employed about 1300 people, about 200 of whom were salaried. The 1100 or so hourly employees, so called because they were paid according to the hours worked, were represented by three international unions. The United Paper Workers International Union represented the woodyard, woodroom, pulp mill, paper mill, maintenance, finishing, and shipping workers; the International Brotherhood of Firemen and Oilers represented the power house employees and plant electricians; and the Office and Professional Employees International Union represented many of

	Monday Tuesday Wednesday Thursday Friday Saturday Sunday	Monday Tuesday Wednesday Thursday Friday Saturday Sunday	Monday Tuesday Wednesday Thursday Saturaday Sunday	Monday Tuesday Wednesday Thursday Friday Saturday Sunday
7:00 A.M.— 3:00 P.M.	A A A A A D D	D D D D D C C	C C C C C B B	B B B B B A A
3:00 P.M.—11:00 P.M.	(1) D D D D C C C	(2) C C C C B B B	(3) B B B B A A A	(4) A A A A D D D
11:00 P.M.— 7:00 A.M.	C C B B B B B	B B A A A A A	A A D D D D D	D D C C C C C
OFF DAY	B B C C D A A	A A B B C D D	D D A A B C C	C C D D A B B

Notes:
1. Schedule repeats every 4 weeks.
2. Three out of every 4 weeks each shift works 5 days and is off 2.
3. One out of every 4 weeks each shift works 6 days and is off 1.
4. One out of every 4 weeks each shift works 5 days and has a 4-day weekend.
5. Average hours worked, 42.
6. Average hours paid, 48.

FIGURE 1-2　Shift schedule for International Paper Company's Androscoggin Mill. (From Labor Agreement, p. 57)

Few people were needed to man the power plant control room. *(Courtesy of International Paper Company)*

the office and clerical workers at the mill. The agreements were specific to Androscoggin and had been negotiated by the plant's management.

Work was defined as either day work or tour (shift) work. Most work was in fact tour work. The first tour or shift worked from 7 A.M. to 3 P.M., the second from 3 P.M. to 11 P.M., and the third from 11 P.M. to 7 A.M. Each worker remained at his position until relieved by the next shift's worker so that continuity of production was assured. The three shifts were manned by four separate crews; on any given day, one crew would be off. Each crew worked an average of 42 hours each week, scheduled as 3 work weeks of 5 days and 1 work week of 6 days in every 4 weeks. The crews rotated among the shifts; each crew, over the span of 4 weeks, worked 7 consecutive days on each shift separated by breaks of 4 days, 2 days, and 1 day. (See the shift schedule in Figure 1-2.) Sunday work was paid at a rate of time and one-half; second and third shift work was awarded a special "shift differential" in-

crease. In total, these rate increases added 6 hours' worth of regular pay to the average of 42 hours worked.

Even though one crew or another was at the mill 24 hours a day, there were still some occasions that warranted overtime pay. Sometimes, for example, another worker's not showing on time would precipitate an overtime situation. Other times, generally extra work situations, management would request overtime work of some individuals as, for example, to help during a machine changeover.

All of the jobs in the mill were classified and assigned different rates of pay according to the hierarchy of talents and responsibilities required. When job openings came up, usually precipitated by a worker's transferring or terminating for one reason or another, workers in the next lower position were advanced according to seniority, assuming they demonstrated the abilities required of the new job. When a high-level job became vacant, a cascading of open positions was triggered, as workers moved up in the hierarchy. Transfers within the mill were permitted in addition to promotions within the same department. Seniority governed transfers as well. For most hourly workers, the typical career path would entail transfers and promotions up to the highest paying jobs and/or from tour work to day work.

Management's relationships with the unions were harmonious and constructive. Worker complaints were relatively few and, if not adjusted on the job, could be adjusted by a four-step grievance procedure involving successively higher levels of union and management officials. The fourth and final step was arbitration, which was seldom invoked, perhaps once or twice a year. About three-quarters of the complaints involved the procedures for assigning overtime or emergency work. Overtime had to be distributed more or less equally among the workers when and where an overtime situation was created.

Over the years, as papermaking equipment grew in size, speed, and sophistication (particularly with the advent of computerized process controls), papermaking became less and less an art and more and more a science. This change left its imprint on the workforce. Not only could a new paper mill be operated with fewer workers than an old one, but the requisite worker skills were less manual and more cerebral. The latest breed of papermakers were more highly educated, in general, and more analytical. As one would expect, some of the older workers were frightened by the automation and its demands on them. Management had to be understanding of this, and considerable resources were expended on training. Fortunately, any worker anxiety about automation was not evident in labor–management relations.

CONTROLLING THE OPERATION

The entire papermaking process at Androscoggin was designed to manufacture paper with as little downtime as possible. Equipment maintenance could generally be scheduled during the monthly changing of the paper machine's "clothing" (i.e., changing the worn wire and felt). Process control equipment and workforce skills were geared to react instantly to production disruptions, like paper breaks, or to product changes in weight or color. The time it took to correct a disruption like a paper break varied enormously (from, say, 3 minutes to an hour). A color change normally took about 10 minutes, and a careful weight change could be done without any downtime.

Paper was continually being tested for quality, and the feedback to the workforce was swift so that any needed adjustments could be made. In general, however, operations at the mill could be described as quiet and watchful. Because the elements of the process were so interdependent, skilled managers and workers were required in every phase of the mill's operations. Indeed, many of the mill's supervisors had been promoted out of the ranks and were thus intimately familiar with the mill's operations.

Changes in the process, routine capital acquisition, and maintenance were the province of plant engineering. Plant engineering was constantly engaged in projects. Here is a sampling:

- A new, larger storage tank for broke (waste paper) for machine 4.
- A proposal to dry bark using exhaust gases.
- Converting burners from oil to coal fuel.
- Replacing a worn section of a debarking drum.
- Installing steam meters.
- Overseeing the repair of a roof.
- Laying out specifications for a new gas scrubber.

EVALUATING MILL PERFORMANCE

The mill was evaluated as a cost center; it had no control or authority over prices, markets, or revenues. The mill operated to a budget. Given a sales forecast from marketing in New York, prices, and a product mix, the mill developed standard costs for producing the quantity of each paper product forecasted. The budget reflected these standard costs and the mill was held to the budget. However, if the product mix changed, the resulting cost changes were charged to marketing, not the mill. The mill was accountable only for those costs over which it had control.

While the efficient production of paper was an important goal, it was by no means the only aspect of mill operations that was evaluated. Others played an important role: employee safety; management and worker training; commitment to environmental controls (not only meeting present standards, but keeping the environmental control equipment balanced in capacity with the rest of mill operations and advancing in technology); expenditures for new capital appropriations and for maintenance; and industrial relations.

PART TWO

DISCUSSION

The International Paper Company is in no way responsible for the following views and presentation. They remain solely the responsibility of the author.

THE PROCESS FLOW

The process of making paper, while a frightfully complicated endeavor, follows a clear-cut and rigid pattern. All of the paper that the Androscoggin Mill produces—however different in appearance, weight, and feel—proceeds through essentially the same production steps, from logs of wood in the woodyard to "logs" of paper at the shipping dock. This kind of production process can be readily portrayed in a diagram like Figure 1-3, which is commonly called a *process flow diagram*.

The process flow diagram of Figure 1-3 is a fairly

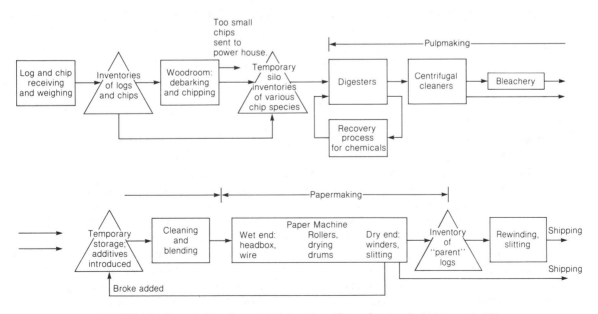

FIGURE 1-3   Process flow diagram for International Paper Company's Androscoggin Mill.

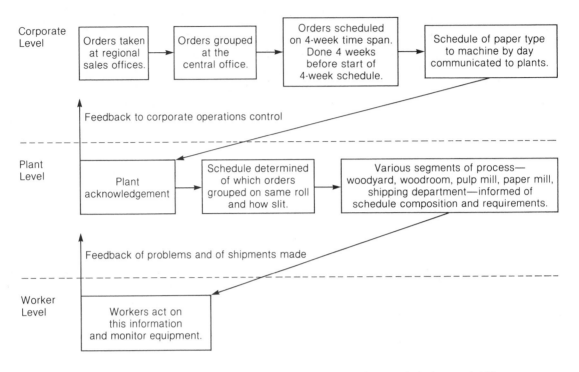

FIGURE 1-4 Information flow diagram for International Paper Company's Androscoggin Mill.

general one and could be made considerably more detailed. Whether more detail is desirable depends, naturally, on the use to which a process portrait like Figure 1-3 is put. Several points about the diagram ought to be noted:

1. Actual processing operations are usually distinguished from storage points in the process. In the diagram, processing operations are indicated by rectangles and inventories by triangles.

2. Several operations could be bypassed and are indicated by two arrows emanating from one operation and pointing to others. For example, all of the woodroom's output need not have gone directly to the silos but could have been placed in the woodyard for storage. Similarly, the bleachery was bypassed by pulp destined to become carbonizing tissue, and the rewinders were superfluous for those orders that could be slit directly from the main winders.

3. The continuous nature of the process is evident by the very few inventories there are and by the designation of the silo chip and pulp additive inventories as temporary ones.

INFORMATION IN THE PROCESS

A production process is more than a series of operations performed on a collection of materials. What a process flow diagram can depict—the sequencing of process steps, the choice of equipment and technology, the capacity of process steps, the tasks required of the workforce—while critical, is only part of the story. Another part of the story involves the procedures that have been put in place to direct the process flow. We can usefully think of a companion to the process flow diagram—namely, an information flow diagram. Figure 1-4 provides one example of what might be placed in such a diagram. Note how the actions of different layers of managers and workers are distinguished in the diagram and how information is fed back up the channels of communication.

Most of the information flow in this continuous flow process is directed from the top down. Feedback is needed only to acknowledge receipt of information and to signal significant problems in the actual workings of the process. The process is designed with such care and the workforce so carefully trained that workers do not have to be in repeated touch with management to do their jobs well. The information needs of the process simply are not great, although the thought and effort standing behind that information (e.g., the scheduling tasks of both the corporate office and the mill itself) are considerable and sophisticated.

CAPACITY

Capacity in this continuous flow process is fairly well defined and can be spoken of in physical terms—namely, tons of pulp and paper manufactured and cords of wood consumed. Likewise, there is a straightforward meaning to the term *capacity utilization*. In fact, all one needs to do is check to see whether the paper machines are running. If they are, capacity (all of it) is being utilized. Simply by compiling the time the paper machines have run over some period of time and dividing that sum by the total available machine-hours gives a splendid indication of capacity utilization. Indeed, only when sales are insufficient or when the machine is broken or down temporarily for a setup or a change of "clothing" would we expect capacity utilization that was less than 100 percent.

Despite the relative ease with which we can talk of capacity and capacity utilization in this continuous flow process, on closer inspection of the concept, a number of disquieting ambiguities surface. The ambiguities surface largely because the capacity of the mill is dependent on a number of factors. Among them:

1. *Product mix.* Some grades and weights of paper are more difficult to produce than others. The Androscoggin Mill's carbonizing tissue, a very thin paper, must run at a slower speed than the stronger, thicker publication gloss. Newer machines, of course, are apt to run at faster speeds than older machines, given the same kind of paper. But, given similar vintage paper machines, thin papers and high-quality finish papers have to run at slower speeds than others. Thus comparing the capacity of the Androscoggin Mill with that of other paper mills or with its own in other years can only be done with some understanding of the product mixes involved.

2. *Run lengths.* Every time a paper machine must be set up for a different grade, weight, or color of paper, capacity is lost. Although some changes are inherently more time-consuming than others, every change implies at least a small reduction in theoretical capacity. The capacity from machine 1 was much lower than that of machine 4 at least in part because machine 1 was scheduled to produce 48 different paper machine products in white and in colors, whereas machine 4 was devoted to white only.

3. *Maintenance.* A paper machine might also lose capacity because it was being repaired or because its "clothing" was being changed. The machines that could be kept running until only regularly scheduled maintenance interrupted production were those that lost the least capacity.

4. *Slitting schedule.* The slitting of paper "logs" from the winders and rewinders was purposefully scheduled so that as little waste as possible resulted. The more successful the schedule, the less waste there was.

For these reasons, the terms *capacity* and *capacity utilization* were not as unambiguous as might have been anticipated. Nevertheless, the process was extraordinarily well balanced and smooth-running, and this made discussion of capacity and capacity utilization easy.

DEMANDS OF THE PROCESS ON WORKERS

Over the years, papermaking, like other continuous flow processes, has become a process where increasingly machinery "does it all." Pulpmakers and papermakers have been systematically removed from playing their traditional direct, "hands-on" roles in the process. Instead, papermakers are more and more "indirect" labor—setters, monitors, and repairers of equipment that makes paper much faster and more reliably than any crew of traditional papermakers could using the older technology and their own skills. Where papermaking was "art," it is now "science." The lengthy apprenticeships from sixth hand on a paper machine to machine tender are no longer so easily justified by the need to learn the art. Despite the change to science, the level of skill required in the process remains high. The workforce may have been removed to gazing at control panels, adjusting knobs, and throwing switches, but the technical demands of the process are even higher in a modern, as compared to traditional, paper mill. Training is therefore an important consideration and an apprenticeship, while different from before, is still required. The lines of worker progression in the mill are clear (in fact, they are diagramed for each department in the labor agreement), and workers are paid accordingly.

What comprises any job in the mill is fairly restricted. That is, the content of most jobs is small although it widens as one approaches the prestige jobs in the mill (e.g., machine tender, pulp mill operator, control room operator). Pay is invariably by the hour worked.

Skilled workers are needed everywhere in the process, largely because the process is so interdependent. If one aspect of the process falls down (e.g., quality of the pulp), another aspect is likely to suffer (e.g., increased risk of a paper break).

DEMANDS OF THE PROCESS ON MANAGEMENT

The interdependence and capital-intensity (i.e., a high ratio of plant and equipment value to labor payroll) of a continuous flow process like papermaking place tremendous demands on management, especially in the realms of coordination and of the choice and care of equipment. Furthermore, these demands are made not only of the mill's own management but of the corporation as a whole. Profitability in such processes largely rests on (1) assuring that the proper technology is selected, (2) balancing the capacities of all segments of the process so that as little capacity goes to waste as possible, (3) scheduling the use of that capacity as completely as possible, and (4) keeping the equipment running up to speed and up to quality standards. Let us review these points in turn.

CHOICE OF TECHNOLOGY

The march of technological change is inexorable. While the output of continuous flow processes seldom changes by much, there can be upheavals in how that output is manufactured. The introduction of process control equipment to papermaking is a case in point. Management must be constantly aware of equipment advances across the industry, and savvy manufacturers engage in regular dialogues with equipment makers so that their own ideas and needs can be tried out in new equipment designs. The impact of technology is so fundamental that the corporate staffs of continuous flow process industries are usually charged with monitoring and selecting new technology for all the plants of the company. Individual plants may have representatives on any plant and equipment choice studies, but corporate level managers are apt to take the lead in the study and decision-making process.

What is true for technology decisions is also true for decisions on how vertically integrated the process should be. This is generally also a corporate decision and one that is the province of corporate staff.

BALANCING CAPACITIES

The papermaking process, as we have seen, can be broken down into distinct segments (as in the process flow diagram); associated with each of these segments are machines and other equipment, often very large. Frequently, these machines and equipment are manufactured by different companies and do not come in just any size. It is management's responsibility to select the equipment for each process segment that represents both the suitable technology and size for the contemplated plant or plant expansion. One segment's capacity should be balanced, as well as possible, against that of other segments, so that as little extra capacity as possible has to be financed. After all, in an integrated, continuous flow process the capacity of the entire process is determined by the lowest capacity segment.

In reality, balancing process segment capacities is a difficult chore, and choices have to be made as to which process segments are to be assigned whatever excess capacity may exist. Often such a choice entails an investigation of equipment costs, with the relatively cheaper equipment being assigned any excess capacity. In papermaking, for example, the big bucks get chewed up in financing paper machines and bleacheries. Woodrooms, digesters, and rewinders are relatively less expensive. Thus, frequently, the spare capacity is to be found at the ends of the process (woodrooms, rewinders) rather than in the middle (bleacheries, paper machines). Having spare capacity at the rewinders increases

the flexibility of the process as well to modifications of the product mix or order specifications. With excess capacity in place, unusual orders can be serviced without undue strain or delay.

SCHEDULING

Continuous flow processes are devoted to the production of large quantities of standard items. Typically, they are low-cost processes, but they often sacrifice the ability to respond quickly to changing customer specifications without introducing a lot of waste and thus destroying their low-cost character. In order then to satisfy customer orders at low cost, continuous flow processes must schedule their capacity well in advance, offering their customers longer lead times than may be common in other types of processes or else filling orders out of a finished goods inventory.

At International Paper, as we saw, the broad "paper machine products" scheduling proceeded 4 weeks in advance of production and the schedule devised was for a 4-week period. Which customer orders were produced in which runs, however, was set at the plant level only 5 days in advance of production. As many customer orders as could be slit right off the winder were scheduled, to eliminate rehandling of paper logs. More exotic orders for special colors, grades, or weights from machine 1 were often filled out of finished goods inventory to avoid having to schedule special production runs. Scheduling at International Paper, as these observations indicate, was a sophisticated enterprise.

The idea, of course, behind such sophisticated scheduling is to keep the process flowing as continuously as possible. Generally, the process could be more responsive to customer order, but to do so would necessarily mean interrupting production to set up equipment. Capacity would be reduced and costs increased. By stretching out deliveries or by keeping finished goods inventories, the continuous flow process can keep its costs down.

EQUIPMENT MAINTENANCE

Most continuous flow process plants are evaluated as cost centers. As with the Androscoggin Mill, such plants are not given authority over revenues (no sales forces are tied to them), and so the plant is judged by how well it can adhere to a budget. The plant has an incentive then to keep its equipment well maintained; if it does not, it risks assuming costs that can be very high (e.g., equipment breakdowns force high repair costs and expensive make-up work). Given such an evaluation scheme, most managers would opt to spend all of their budget for maintenance to avoid the chance, however slim, of suffering a huge cost increase and an instantly bad reputation for plant management.

QUESTIONS

1. Briefly outline the main features of the papermaking process, paying particular attention to the two different types of pulpmaking.

2. Why did the Androscoggin Mill choose vertical integration for its design? What would be some of the advantages and disadvantages of forward integration?

3. What general principles of location choice would you draw from the example of the Androscoggin Mill? What other aspects of location might be considered for other production processes?

4. If you were a production planner at the Androscoggin Mill, what areas might you be most likely to consider important? Why?

5. How is the workforce organized at the mill? What are some of the operational implications of this workforce composition?

6. How would you describe the nature of the information flow, capacity, and demands on the workers in a continuous flow process? As a manager, which aspects of such a process appeal to you? Which aspects might you like less?

SITUATION FOR STUDY
BEACON GLASS WORKS

Beacon Glass Works, located in Marysville, West Virginia, manufactures hollow glass tubing for use in catalytic converters. Beacon is a large division of one of the leading glass manufacturers, and was founded when the Environmental Protection Agency strongly urged the development of anti-pollution devices for trucks and automobiles. The hollow glass tubing manufactured at Beacon comes in around 30 different size combinations. The lengths are from 6 to 12 inches, and the inside diameter ranges from 1/32 inch to 1/16 inch.

These tubes are produced by extrusion. The molten glass is first forced through a die that determines the inside diameter of the tube. The tube then is cooled and cut to the proper length. After the cut edges have been finished so that they are smooth, the product is sent to a holding area where it waits to be packaged. Once the tubing is packaged, it is again stored, this time awaiting shipment to Beacon's customers, the four major domestic motor vehicle manufacturers.

The extrusion process is basically a make-to-stock operation driven by production scheduling. Based upon anticipated stock shortages, Jose Zotts, the production manager, schedules the next week's production, and the necessary dies are readied. Each die is used until about one month's demand has been produced. Then, the dies are changed and another product with a different inside diameter is run. Actually, since several lengths have the same inside diameter, several products can be extruded with one extrusion run.

Once the product cools to the proper cutting temperature, the cutting area cuts the proper lengths, again based upon the stock needs determined by the production manager. The product is then stored in a holding area waiting to be packaged. Packaging is usually done to customer order,

as different customers want different quantities and want them packaged differently.

Sometimes, however, Jose will schedule the packaging department based on what he believes will be the customer orders, so that he can use the packaging machinery efficiently. This scheduling sometimes results in excess inventory for one customer while another customer's order will have to be backordered because of a stockout.

Jose is concerned that his scheduling of the process is not as good as it could be and thinks that possibly the first step he should take is to diagram the production flow and the information flow for the process.

1. Diagram the production flow.
2. Diagram the information flow.
3. Discuss possible problem areas for Beacon's production process.

2

A JOB SHOP

Norcen Industries
Jersey Shore, Pennsylvania

It had been years since Joe Gehret finally gave in to his desire to control his own company and resigned his position as general foreman in the machine shop of the Litton Industries plant in Williamsport, Pennsylvania. In July 1967, Joe and a partner (who had since left the firm) began Norcen Industries by selling stock and taking over an old garage in Jersey Shore, about 15 miles northwest of Williamsport. They initially intended for Norcen to be a plastics distributor and fabricator, but it soon became apparent that both their experience and the demands of industry in north central Pennsylvania dictated a change of course. Norcen quickly became mainly a metal-working machine shop, and now the machine shop accounted for almost 90 percent of gross revenues. Steady growth marked the company's history; total employment now stood at 27 and orders were shipped all over, even abroad. Continued growth would insist that Norcen soon move to a new, larger facility.

PART ONE

PROCESS DESCRIPTION

PRODUCTS, SALES, AND ORDER HANDLING

As a general machine shop, Norcen was capable of producing a seemingly endless succession of small-scale metal parts that a host of companies typically assembled into machines and other products. Almost all of Norcen's customers were manufacturers, but 90 percent of this business Norcen had to win by submitting low bids. The purchasing departments of Norcen's customer firms generally requested Norcen and at least two other machine shops to "quote" the work they wanted done. The request always specified (1) the number of pieces desired, which varied enormously from 10 pieces to over a thousand, (2) the nature of the material required and whether it was supplied by the cus-

INFORMATION:

Material cost 6.46

COMPANY & ITEM: 24937 Roller Chemcut

VARIANCE	PRICE		HOURS	COST				VOL.	COMP. DATE 73	JOB # INVOICE	DATE 72	P.O. NUMBER
	UNIT	TOTAL		MATERIAL	LABOR	SERVICE	TOTAL					
5.09/7.24	12 34	765 08	69.8	136 40	178 87		315 27	62	3/7	6313 3479	12/15	54962
4.85/7.49	12 34	740 40	54.5	132 00	159 01		291 01	60	8/2	7076 3234 73	7/5	57755
2.61/9.73	12 34	1246 34	13.5	222 20	41 38		263 58	101	10/8	7430 3967		
4.31/8.69	13 00	1313 00	627	251 49	183 46		434 95	101	6/5 74	8679 4520	4/18	61556
6.59/9.13	15 72	1100 40	72.2	189 70	271 91		461 61	70	1/6 77	13623 6432	10/8 76	71736
8.06/16.06	22 12	752 08	71.2	73 78	273 93		273 93	34	8/16	14935 7105 77	6/23 78	74628
6.81/13.09	19 90	736 30	342	100 27	151 74		252 01	37	4/20 78	16666 7829	2/17 78	77287
	24 92	523 32		135 66	378 78		514 44	21	1/29 79	18628 8612	11/13	80945
14.69/10.23	24 92	623 00	76	161 50	—		161 50	25	2/2	18674		

Notes:

1. This record card is for a roller for the Chemcut Company. The roller is distinguished at Norcen by its part number, 24937, which corresponds to a blueprint and process sheet.

2. The material to work on is not furnished by Chemcut but costs Norcen Industries $6.46 to procure.

3. The part has been ordered eight times, beginning on December 15, 1972 (shipped on March 7, 1973) and ending with November 13, 1978 (shipped on January 29, 1979 and February 2, 1979).

4. The latest order was split into two batches of 21 and 25 pieces, respectively.

5. The quoted price for the part, in the latest instance, was $24.92 per piece. The total billing to Chemcut was $1146.32 ($523.32 + $623.00) for the 46 pieces shipped.

6. A total of 76 labor-hours were spent on the latest order and the labor cost to Norcen Industries was $378.78. Total materials costs were $297.16 ($135.66 + $161.50). Thus, total costs for materials and labor amounted to $675.94.

7. On a per unit basis, this total cost for materials and labor was $14.69 ($675.94/46 pieces). This cost figure is shown in the first half of the column headed "variance." The difference between $14.69 and the quoted price of $24.92 per piece is $10.23, which is recorded in the second half of the variance column. This figure of $10.23 per piece, the balance between received price and material and labor costs, goes to pay overhead expenses (e.g., worker benefits, building and equipment costs, manager salaries), stock dividends, and the like. What is left after such disbursements is profit.

8. The invoice numbers (18628 and 18674), the job number (8612), and the order number (80945) are shown in the columns labeled as such.

FIGURE 2-1   A sample record card for a particular item manufactured at Norcen Industries.

tomer, (3) the design of the piece (a blueprint would be sent), and (4) the date by which the order had to be received. Norcen bid on about 125 such requests each week, knowing that on a long-run average its quote would be accepted about 14 percent of the time. Roughly half of the manufacturer requests were for pieces that Norcen, at some time, had already produced for that company.

Joe Gehret was responsible for deciding all quotes. Naturally, it was easier for him to quote jobs that Norcen had done before. Not only did he know the hourly charge-out rate (currently $15 per hour), which would cover both direct labor and overhead expenses, but he had a past record of what the piece had actually cost Norcen to make on all previous occasions. (See Figure 2-1 and the discussion on recordkeeping below.) In addition,

Norcen would already have a blueprint of the piece and a "process sheet," which would outline the steps the shop had previously taken to manufacture it and the time standards for each of those steps. Deciding quotes for pieces Norcen had not previously made was more difficult. In such cases, Joe had to ponder the blueprint and develop, at least in his mind, a rough-cut process sheet. Sometimes the request for the quote included a process sheet developed by the company itself, and this was a great aid. Other factors such as delivery dates (rush orders, being more trouble, commanded higher margins), and the prevailing load in the shop (the more slack in the shop, the lower the margin) also influenced the quote.

The acceptance of a Norcen quote typically came by phone and was confirmed later by letter.

Norcen Industries' main machining room as seen from outside the office. *(Courtesy of Norcen Industries)*

Chemcut

ORDER No. 80945   JOB 8612

PART No. 24937   LOT SIZE 40

MATERIAL 6.46 ea

DELIVERY 1/17

Date	Name	Operation		Qty.	Hrs.	Acc. Hrs.
1/7	AT	5	34 75		1	1
	DL	1	3 50		1	2
	R B	15.5	85 25		5	7
	G L	3	13 50		3	10
1/14	LS	28.5	142 50		1.5	11.5
1/21	KK	3.5	11 20		3.5	15
	R B				10.5	25.5
	DD	5	26 50		5	30.5
	D. Lorson	11	37 95		11	41.5
	LS				16.5	58
	AT				4	62
	LS				2	64
1/28	LS				8.5	72.5
	RD	3.5	23 63		3.5	76
		76	378 78			
	chgd	18628				
	Shipped	46				

Notes:

1. This job sheet corresponds to the latest Chemcut roller order, job number 8612 and order number 80945.

2. An initial lot of 40 pieces was ordered for delivery on January 17, 1979. As we know already from the record card (Figure 2-1), 46 pieces were actually shipped; apparently there was less scrapped than expected. This shipment of 46 pieces came in two batches of 21 and 25 each, and both shipments were later than initially desired (January 29, 1979 and February 2, 1979). The tardiness of delivery in this instance was caused chiefly by the late arrival of materials.

3. The order was worked on beginning the week of January 7 and ending the week of January 28. Nine different workers worked on the order at one time or another, as indicated by the nine different sets of initials. The job was set up 14 different times for periods of time ranging from 1 hour to 16½ hours, as indicated by the column headed "hrs."

4. The total hours put in by each worker are summed in the first portion of the column headed "operation." The sum of these hours, 76, agrees with the bottom entry in the accumulated hours column.

5. The actual labor costs incurred by Norcen Industries are reported in the last portion of the operation column and in the quantity column. For example, worker AT spent 5 hours on the job and at his pay rate of $6.95 per hour incurred $34.75 of labor expense. Similarly, DL spent only 1 hour, but his pay rate was much lower, $3.50 per hour. Worker RB had still a different rate of pay, $5.50 per hour, and thus incurred $85.25 in labor expense for his 15½ hours of work on the order. Total labor cost amounted to $378.78.

6. Labor costs were charged on invoice number 18628.

FIGURE 2-2 A sample job sheet used at Norcen Industries.

Upon notification of acceptance, Joe's wife, Lillian, who was responsible for all bookkeeping, wrote up two copies of a job sheet (Figure 2-2). One copy was kept in a record book and the other was attached to a blueprint and placed in a special tray. Joe was then responsible for looking over each job sheet to see whether any materials not provided by the customer needed to be ordered and whether any tooling needed to be done. Job sheets that awaited materials or tooling were kept in a separate tray. When enough materials were on hand to complete the order, the job sheet and blueprint were placed in a special drawer. This action released the order to the shop.

PLANT AND PERSONNEL

The machine shop operated on two shifts: 7 A.M. to
3:30 P.M. and 3:30 P.M. to 12 midnight, with a half-
hour break for lunch or dinner and two 10-minute
break periods. The day shift consisted of 19 hourly
workers while the evening shift presently ran with
only 5 workers. Norcen's hourly wages (the highest paid by any of the machine shops in the area)
started at $3 per hour for unskilled workers and
went to $7 per hour for the most demanding work.
This pay was augmented in two ways:

1. Overtime pay at time and a half
2. A bonus plan, payable at Christmas and in the
   summer

The size of each bonus depended on the fortunes
of the company over the previous 6 months. It was
Joe Gehret's policy to distribute as much to the
workers as Norcen paid out in dividends to its
shareholders; recently this meant an increase of
about 7 percent to each worker. (Gehret himself
owned only 19 percent of the shares outstanding.)
The size of the bonus a particular worker required,
as well as vacation time, depended on seniority.
The workers recognized this system as an incentive for continued good work. In the words of a
lathe and drill press operator: "The better we are to
the company, the better the company is to us."

A rough layout of the plant, showing the general
groupings of machines, is included as Figure 2-3.
An inventory of the most important machines in
the shop, along with their 1976 replacement costs
and their weekly average hours in use, is provided
in Table 2-1.

THE WORKINGS OF THE SHOP

Although Joe Gehret spent a good deal of time on
the shop floor, responsibility for shop operations
rested with Bill Lundy, the shop foreman. Like Joe,

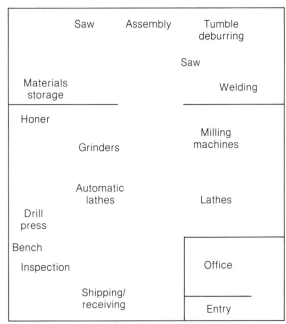

FIGURE 2-3 Plant layout and workforce at Norcen Industries.

Bill had been a shop foreman at Litton Industries.
Bill's duties were varied, but his first concern for
the smooth running of the shop was to see that all
workers were assigned tasks and that they understood these tasks well, both their nature and their
time standards. Moreover, Bill knew that it was
important to the success of the company that tasks
be assigned in a way that saved Norcen money.
Cost reductions could come about in several ways:

1. Before an operator could machine any of the
   myriad jobs Norcen was capable of performing,
   the necessary machine had to be set up. The
   setup varied from about a half-hour for simple

TABLE 2-1   Inventory of Major Machines
(Norcen Industries)

MACHINE AND NUMBER OWNED	1976 REPLACEMENT COST (thousands of $)	HOURS USED PER MACHINE PER WEEK (rough estimate)
Table saw	$ 2.8	2
Small grinder	3.0	30
Jig saw	3.5	10
Second operation lathe	4.5	60
Vertical milling machine (3)	7.0	50
Large grinder (3)	8.5	30
Lathes (5)	10.0	50
Four-spindle drill press	12.0	50
Horizontal milling machine	13.0	50
Automatic grinder	15.0	40
Automatic horizontal hand saw	16.0	12
16-inch engine lathe	20.0	20
Automatic lathe	22.5	80
Small tape mill	30.0	50
Automatic chucking machine	30.0	80
Hand turret lathe	50.0	25
Large tape mill	55.0	80
Inspection equipment (e.g., opticalcomparator, microscopes)		80

jobs to 4 hours for the most complex. An average setup was about 1.5 hours. Since, once set up, the machine could produce any number of pieces with only minor adjustments, it made sense to run full lots whenever possible. In this way, setup costs were spread over all the units in the order.

2. Frequently, especially with automatic equipment, the running time of the machine per piece produced was long enough so that, by staggering operations, a single operator could attend two different machines at the same time. That is, while one piece was being machined, the operator could be working at another machine, typically inserting new material or removing a finished piece. To exploit these possibilities, Joe and Bill had grouped similar kinds of machines together on the shop floor. It was to Norcen's advantage for Bill to identify and to match together those jobs that permitted this kind of labor saving.

3. As might be expected, some operators could perform certain machining tasks relatively better than others and thus held a comparative advantage over other workers in the shop for some jobs. It was worth it for Bill to keep these special capabilities in mind in his assignment of jobs.

4. Cost reductions could also occur through improvements in the process sheets that Bill kept in special binders. Often, changes in the sequence of drilling, cutting, milling, grinding, threading, deburring, and so on, could have profound effects on the total time Norcen had to allocate to a particular job. Bill had to be alert for possible improvements he could make in the process.

5. The probability of successfully reducing costs was naturally greater for more complex operations and for repeat business. Furthermore, cost reductions could lie in more than process sequence changes. For example, Norcen fabri-

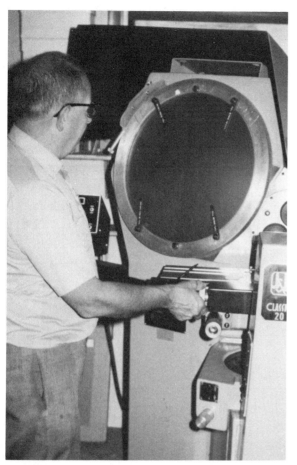

Joe Gehret with some inspection equipment. *(Courtesy of Norcen Industries)*

cated and assembled grid and font drums for the Mergenthaler Linotype Company. Through experience with the product, Norcen had been able to halve its costs by (1) ordering certain parts rather than fabricating them in-house, (2) building special fixtures to increase speed and accuracy, and (3) modifying the process steps, as discussed above. Such dramatic success was not to be found often, but its significance was great enough to demand a good deal of Joe's and Bill's thoughts.

Even more important to Bill than assigning tasks in money-saving ways was seeing to it that the delivery schedule was met. Norcen could not miss deliveries and still expect to receive repeat orders. Bill was constantly aware of the promised delivery dates, and he attached high priorities to imminent deliveries due.

Bill's scheduling of jobs was further influenced by Norcen's cash flow needs. Other things being equal, and particularly at the end of the month, small jobs were given preference so that billing could proceed at once.

As foreman, Bill dealt also with worker morale, training, and development, with materials handling, and with quality control. (As for the latter, workers were responsible for checking their own work; in addition, spot checks were made of all outgoing shipments.) But job scheduling was the most demanding on Bill's energies. He tried to stay one day ahead of his workers, so that he knew precisely which job would go next to every machine, who would work that job, and when they would start on it. As Joe Gehret put it: "Scheduling is the most difficult function we have around here. It's the easiest thing in the world to say no to a customer, that we can't fit his job into the shop. But after a few noes, you may not have a customer."

Frequently, planned schedules were interrupted so that quick, remedial action could be taken. Consider a typical example:

A new, automatic lathe had been set up to thread a rather complex piece when a feed arm broke. The machine could no longer perform any threading, but it could still do some simpler work. After brief consultation, Bill and Joe decided to call in the machine's service people rather than to fix it themselves, since the machine was still on warranty. While waiting for service, they set up the machine for a simpler, rush order job that had not yet been worked on. Since the delivery date for the threading job was also coming up soon, they decided to reroute it through the shop. The piece would now be milled before threading, and Bill ordered that one of the milling machines be set up for the task.

Not all jobs, of course, could be rerouted through the shop, but it was possible with a sizable number, especially those that were neither very simple nor very complex. In general, Bill preferred to have lathe work performed first, then milling, and only then grinding; but he was willing to abandon this order if necessary.

RECORDKEEPING

When an operator completed his assigned task on any job, he completed the job sheet (Figure 2-2) attached to the blueprint. On this sheet he filled in his name, the date, the operation he performed, the quantity he completed, and the length of time it took him to complete the task, including setup time. In addition, at the end of the day, each operator completed a time card (Figure 2-4), listing the time spent on each job during the day.

In this way, Lillian Gehret had two records of the time each operator spent on each of the jobs done in the shop. Knowing the times and the wages of each operator involved in any job permitted Lillian to calculate the labor cost of that job. She made this calculation weekly and took care to see that any discrepancies in the two time records were resolved. Usually, the daily time cards were more accurate than the job sheets.

Knowing this information, at the close of every job Lillian would complete the record card (Figure 2-1), which Joe relied on for making quotes on repeat business, including the posting of any variance in actual cost from the price quoted. As a rule of thumb for calculating the profitability of a job, Lillian multiplied total labor-hours by the charge-out rate of $15 per hour and compared that total against the total price Norcen had quoted. She alerted Joe to any major deviations in that comparison, either positive or negative. Subsequent bids could be based accordingly.

612	Bierly, Seth						1/7/79	
EMP. #	EMPLOYEE SIGNATURE						WORK PERIOD	
START		6.00	600	600	600	600	600	
STOP		3 30	330	3.30	330	3·30	12.00	
CHARGE NO	SUN	MON	TUE	WED	THUR	FRI	SAT	Total Hours
8700		1						1 0
1102		5						5
1103		5						5
8861		2 5						2 5
8734		2 5	5 0	5 0				12 5
8932		2	4 0	2 5	1 5			10 0
919				1 5				1 5
8432					3	5	4 5	8 0
8849					4	4 5		8 5
8693							6 0	6 0
TOTAL		9 0	9 0	9 0	9 0	9 0	6 0	51 0

Notes:

1. This is Seth Bierly's time card for the week of January 7, 1979. Seth worked from 6 A.M. to 3:50 P.M. Monday through Friday and came in on Saturday for 6 hours of overtime.

2. During the week, Seth worked on 10 different jobs, ranging from a low of a half-hour each on jobs 1102 and 1103 on Monday to a high of 6 hours on job 8693 on Saturday.

FIGURE 2-4 A sample operator time card used at Norcen Industries.

Lathe operators at work at Norcen Industries. *(Courtesy of Norcen Industries)*

PART TWO

DISCUSSION

Norcen Industries is in no way responsible for the following views and presentation. They remain solely the responsibility of the author.

THE PROCESS FLOW

Compared with the continuous flow process at International Paper's Androscoggin Mill, the job shop process at Norcen Industries is strikingly loose and ill-defined. A process flow diagram becomes difficult to draw in any precise or meaningful way. For example, we might sketch a process flow diagram such as in Figure 2-5. Although many of the parts made at Norcen Industries would have passed through exactly this sequence of operations, many more would have required a different set of operations and a different order. Some of the differences might be minor, but there are a host of parts for which the differences are major. At best, Figure 2-5's flow diagram can be termed a dominant flow or, perhaps, a preferred, simplified flow. For the most part, the job shop process exhibits great product flux and flexibility. Work-in-process can be routed anywhere within the shop so that even extraordinary machining requirements can be done.

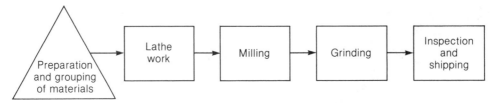

Notes:

1. Other tasks could be sequenced before, in between, or after the three middle tasks.

2. Work-in-process inventories exist between each operation.

FIGURE 2-5   A dominant, or preferred, process flow diagram for Norcen Industries.

THE INFORMATION FLOW

What is not flexible but is almost totally rigid in the job shop is the flow of information through it. In stark contrast to the diversity of paths a machined part can take through the shop, information flows in a prescribed way (see Figure 2-6). Recordkeeping is done in the same manner for every order; the responsibilities of the workers, bookkeeper, and managers toward information in the process never vary. Everyone has fixed information tasks to perform: quoting, job sheet and blueprint preparation, release to the shop, filling out of job sheets and time cards, labor cost calculations, updating of quote record cards, and signaling of any variances.

The reason for all this rigidity, of course, is that the job shop lives and dies by its ability to process information. Significantly, too, the information flows in the job shop are as much from worker to management (job sheets, time cards, process suggestions, machine breakdowns) as from management to worker (job and machine assignments, schedules, quality control checks, troubleshooting, training). Without suitable records, there would be no clear or readily available means of routing an order through the shop or of specifying exactly what should be done to satisfy it. Without suitable records, the job shop's managers would have little idea how to bid for various jobs. Without suitable

records, advances in productivity would be more sporadic and less well retained for future use. Without suitable records, managers would not be able to load the shop effectively. Information and the responsibility of everyone in a job shop to maintain its accuracy and smooth flow constitute the glue by which this type of process is held together.

CAPACITY IN THE JOB SHOP

In the job shop at Norcen Industries, capacity is as ambiguous as the process flow's pattern. No single measure of capacity makes complete sense. While a paper mill can measure its capacity rather straightforwardly in tons per day or some similar measure, a machine shop like Norcen Industries cannot readily do the same thing. The large and constantly changing mix of products in the typical job shop ensures that a simple count of units produced is a meaningless way to gauge what the shop's effective capacity really is. We must avoid that simple measure in favor of one that transcends the product mix problem. The easiest remedy is to measure capacity in dollar terms, but that still leaves us with a variety of options. Dollars of typical output per unit of time? Dollars of output per worker? Dollars of output per machine? Dollars of output per dollar of machine value (at cost? at re-

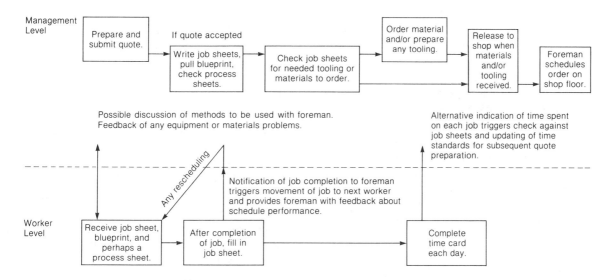

Management Level

Prepare and submit quote.

If quote accepted

Write job sheets, pull blueprint, check process sheets.

Check job sheets for needed tooling or materials to order.

Order material and/or prepare any tooling.

Release to shop when materials and/or tooling received.

Foreman schedules order on shop floor.

Possible discussion of methods to be used with foreman. Feedback of any equipment or materials problems.

Alternative indication of time spent on each job triggers check against job sheets and updating of time standards for subsequent quote preparation.

Any rescheduling

Notification of job completion to foreman triggers movement of job to next worker and provides foreman with feedback about schedule performance.

Worker Level

Receive job sheet, blueprint, and perhaps a process sheet.

After completion of job, fill in job sheet.

Complete time card each day.

FIGURE 2-6 An information flow diagram for Norcen Industries.

placement cost?)? All of these measures grab a piece of what we mean intuitively when we say capacity, and yet no one of them fully describes the concept. Only over the long term, when we can feel comfortable that the mix of products has been representative, can we point at differences in shop output over time or output per worker or output per machine as valid measures of high or low capacity. In the short run, no capacity measure is clearly appropriate. Any measure of the shop's capacity is dependent on a host of factors, such as:

1. *Lot sizes.* The larger the lots ordered, the fewer the setups in any one day and the greater the number of pieces produced, other things being equal.

2. *Complexity of the pieces worked on.* The more complex the piece, the more likely it will require a large succession of operations and thus the more likely its manufacture will demand a succession of time-consuming setups and difficult scheduling decisions. Of course, this factor is relatively more important in accounting for differences in the number of units manufac-

tured than it is in accounting for differences in dollar value measures of capacity.

3. *Mix of jobs already on the shop floor.* The number and nature of orders already released to the shop floor affect the capacity of the shop in at least two ways: shifting bottlenecks and worker-machine interference.

Many of the orders in the shop may require the services of particular machines. We can expect, then, that some orders may back up while awaiting a particular machine or operation. Further, we can expect to see such bottlenecks occurring from time to time all over the shop. That is, we can expect to see work-in-process inventories building up in different places and at different times in the shop. A smooth-running, well-scheduled job shop will have a low number of such "shifting bottlenecks," but given the diversity of output and run lengths within a job shop process, they are absolutely unavoidable.

In a typical job shop, there will be many machines that require the constant attention of a worker when they are in operation. Increasingly, however, automatic equipment is entering the shop with its ability to perform without the constant "hands-on" attention of the workforce. This advance is not without a challenge of its own. While automatic equipment frees up worker time, only the (sometimes fortuitous) scheduling of two or more jobs to the same worker actually leads to greater worker productivity apart from any speed advances built into the automatic equipment itself. If the scheduling cannot mesh two or more jobs together, the machine can be said to "interfere" with the worker, and capacity in the shop drops relative to the situation where the worker can easily operate two or more pieces of equipment at once. For this reason, Joe Gehret and Bill Lundy positioned machinery within the shop to maximize the possibilities for reducing worker-machine interference.

4. *Ability to schedule work well.* As Joe Gehret himself put it, "Scheduling is the most difficult function we have around here." The matching of workers to machines and of workers and machines to jobs often separates a profitable job shop from an unprofitable one. Good scheduling lessens shifting bottlenecks and worker-machine interference. Poor scheduling introduces more work-in-process inventory to the shop than is necessary. In particular, if too many rush orders are permitted in the shop, their scheduling will become difficult, often necessitating the interruption of runs on machines already set up.

5. *Process improvements.* Any advances in the methods employed in producing a part at Norcen Industries permitted the shop to increase its capacity and thus its profitability. With so many orders passing through the shop, there are many opportunities for improving the process: resequencing of operations, different use of machines, quicker setups, special jigs or fixtures for increasing speed and/or accuracy, possible redesign of the piece ordered. Because any of these improvements takes time to work through, it is likely that only the higher volume, repeat business will benefit from such attention.

6. *Number of machines and their condition.* It is obvious that, even without expanding the workforce, the addition of equipment to the shop is likely to increase capacity detectably. For one thing, rush orders will be less likely to necessitate the dismantling of existing machine setups before completion of the run. More machines also increase the probability of finding favorable combinations of orders to lessen worker-machine interference. Fewer bottlenecks, too, are likely to occur with the addition of more equipment. It is evident as well that machines in good condition are less likely to break down and thus demand attention for both themselves and for the rescheduling of operations through the shop.

7. *Quantity and quality of labor input.* Another obvious set of factors affecting the capacity of a job shop is drawn from the labor force itself. Overtime and second shift work is a standard way to augment capacity with the same stock of plant and equipment. Employing inexperienced workers and having to train them is a drain on capacity, however.

   Obvious in identification but subtle in design and application is an incentive system for the workers. At Norcen Industries, the bonus plan that was dependent on company profits was viewed by the workers as a fair and reasonable spur for continued good work. But it is not the only payment system that could be installed; different systems might have different effects on worker effort and thus capacity.

Increasing the capacity of a job shop in the ways outlined above, at little or no cost, is important to the shop because that is how it makes its money.

Of course, the shop must be flexible enough to bid on a tremendous variety of jobs, but the shop's ability to earn any profit once granted the business is linked fundamentally to its capacity and its knowledge of that capacity. As we have discussed, these two items are influenced by a number of factors, many of which require the accurate processing of information around the shop.

THE ROLE OF STANDARDS AND INCENTIVES

Time standards for all of the operations to be performed at Norcen Industries are an integral feature of its cost estimation and bidding responsibilities. Some of the standards are developed internally, mostly through past experience doing the same thing; but others are supplied by the customer when bids are solicited, having been worked out for or by the customer.

The standards are a useful guide for both workers and managers. For the workers, the standards (written on the job sheet) provide continual feedback on how well they are doing the job. For managers, the standards provide information on how long certain jobs should take and thus how they might be scheduled. The standards also provide management with a yardstick for worker performance that is useful not only for advancement/layoff decisions but also for determining which tasks each worker does relatively better.

Other than by furnishing feedback for each worker, the time standards are not tied formally to any incentive system. Incentives for good and/or for speedy work are provided either through knowledge that such work often contributes to better company profits (although such work is not the only determinant of profits, by far) or by the prodding and cajoling of the foreman. In job shops like Norcen Industries, the foreman carries much of the responsibility for pacing work through the shop and for ensuring that the quality is satisfactory.

QUESTIONS

1. Write up a hypothetical job sheet for a Chemcut order and briefly explain each column entry. How do the functions of the job sheet and the record card differ?

2. What are three of the main ways Norcen's shop foreman reduced costs? Can you make any generalizations about cost reduction from this example? Do these generalizations apply to any other process with which you are already familiar?

3. Why might scheduling be "the most difficult function" in a job shop?

4. "The job shop lives and dies by its ability to process information." Discuss this comment and compare the information flow in the job shop with that in another type of process.

5. Discuss three of the factors that influence a job shop's capacity. What might be "the perfect set of circumstances" in a shop foreman's eyes?

6. As a worker, which would you prefer: the calm predictability of the continuous flow process or the frequently frantic unpredictability of the job process? How might your attitude affect the setting of standards and incentives in each process?

SITUATION FOR STUDY

WECAN INC.

Fred and Ralph own and operate a small machine and metal fabrication shop. Most of their business involves small orders from local industry. These orders are usually ones that the larger customer firms farm out because they do not have the excess capacity. In other words, Fred and Ralph provide "slack" capacity to the larger firms. Figure 2-A shows the plant layout.

Fred and Ralph feel that if they can once get an order in their shop, they can learn how to make the part and then underbid on future orders. Moreover, they think they can make most parts more cheaply than the customer can in house.

They are currently considering bidding on part 273. Figure 2-B is an engineering sketch of this part. For the first order the customer will supply a coil of 1 ⅝" cold rolled steel (CRS), but Fred and Ralph are investigating to see whether other processes might use other sizes of raw material more efficiently. The proposed order is for 500 pieces, with possible future orders of 500 per month. The proposed bid must be submitted in two weeks, the bid award determined within one week, and the 500 units delivered one month after that.

Fred has generated the estimates shown in Table 2-A. The cost estimates used for bids are $10.55 per

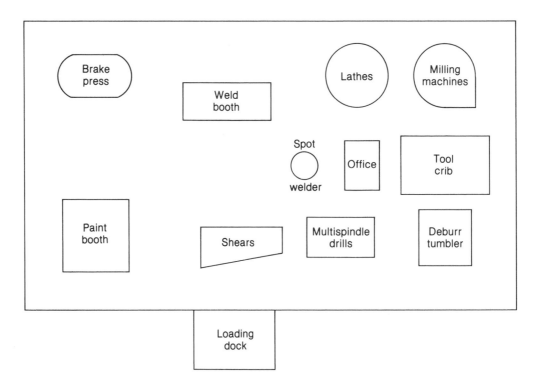

FIGURE 2-A   Plant layout for Wecan, Inc.

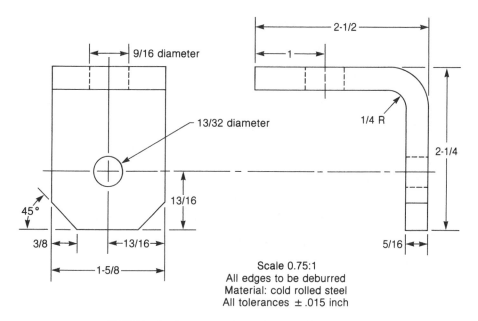

Scale 0.75:1
All edges to be deburred
Material: cold rolled steel
All tolerances ± .015 inch

FIGURE 2-B   Engineering sketch for part 273, a bracket.

hour for labor and $18.50 per hour for machines— or $29.05 per hour for one worker/one machine operations. Any time "sold" at this rate makes Wecan a margin of 25 percent with which to cover indirect costs such as administrative costs.

1. If you were Fred and Ralph, what other aspects of the shop, the market, and the future would you consider regarding the bid for part 273?
2. Analyze the current proposal and generate a bid to the customer and a rough shop schedule.

TABLE 2-A   Process Sheet for Part 273
(Wecan Inc.)

OPERATION SEQUENCE	MACHINE	OPERATION	SETUP TIME (minutes)	OPERATION TIME PER UNIT (minutes)
1	Shear #3	Shear to length	5	.030
2	Shear #3	Shear 45° corners	8	.050
3	Multispindle Drill press #1	Drill both holes and deburr	15	3.000
4	Brake press	Bend 90°	10	.025
5	Tumbler	Deburr	5	*
6		Pack in boxes		30.000

*The deburr operation can be left unattended, and so the only labor required is to load and unload.

3

A BATCH FLOW PROCESS

Jung Products,Inc.
Cincinnati, Ohio

Jung Products was founded in 1917 by George H. Jung, Jr., who pioneered the use of elastic knit fabric for an arch brace and later (1930) for an ankle brace. Under the brand name "Futuro" (1936), Jung became a leading manufacturer of elastic supports of all kinds, selling to the public through drug and shoe stores, and also producing private label goods (e.g., pads, athletic supporters) for the major sporting goods houses. After a hiatus during World War II caused by the shortage of rubber, the company resumed its growth, gradually adding products such as elastic stockings and consolidating its leadership of direct over-the-counter sales of elastic health supports.

In 1948, George Jung, Jr., died and management of the company was assumed by the former advertising manager, H. M. Stuckenberg. Meanwhile, Bob Conway married into the Jung family and joined the company in 1958. When Mr. Stuckenberg retired in 1962, Bob was able to succeed him.

Under Conway, Jung Products continued to expand its health supports (Futuro) and sporting goods (Grid) product lines at the rate of one or two products a year. In 1969, building on its strength in drugstore distribution, the company introduced an entire line of convalescent products (e.g., canes, crutches, bedpans, wheelchairs), which it sold through drugstores under the Futuro Patient-Aids brand name.

Even as Jung Products was broadening its product offerings, it began to integrate backward by acquiring or establishing three companies:

- Rampon Products, Inc. of Asheboro, North Carolina. Rampon was a manufacturer of elastic knitted products and fabric, which Jung Products acquired in 1965. Besides supplying Jung Products with elastic knit fabric, Rampon also produced men's support hose and women's support stockings and pantyhose. About 40 percent of Rampon's dollar output was currently supplied to Jung Products' Cincinnati operations.

- J.R.A. Industries of Asheboro, North Carolina. J.R.A. was established in 1969 as a further step backward in process integration. J.R.A., situated next door to Rampon, manufactured the elastic "thread" used in knitting elastic products. About 20 percent of J.R.A.'s production was used as a raw material by Rampon.

- Theradyne Corporation of Jordan, Minnesota (near Minneapolis). In 1973, Jung Products acquired the Theradyne Corporation, a leading manufacturer of wheelchairs and related products. Theradyne continued to market its products under its own brand name in addition to supplying items for the Patient-Aids product line.

PART ONE

PROCESS DESCRIPTION

THE MARKET FOR JUNG PRODUCTS

Jung marketed about 130 different products in a wide assortment of styles and sizes. This total could be broken down into the three product lines roughly as follows: 30 products in the elastic Health Supports line, 75 products in the Patient-Aids line, and 25 products in the Grid (private label sporting goods) line. (Figure 3-1 lists some of the products sold.)

Other than its sales to the major sporting goods companies (Wilson, Rawlings, Spalding, and MacGregor), Jung Products sold almost exclusively through drugstores. About 70 percent of its sales went through drug wholesalers and about 30 percent through drugstore chains. Jung was the dominant company in over-the-counter sales of elastic health supports and convalescent products in the drugstore.

Jung's sales were international. Sales were broken down by region as follows:

3% Cincinnati metropolitan area
8% Elsewhere in the Ohio-Kentucky-Indiana region
20% Elsewhere in the Midwest
59% Nationally, other than in the Midwest
10% International

Bob Conway could cite a number of reasons for Jung's success. The company took pride in its ability to supply its wholesaler customers quickly and dependably. Such service meant that the wholesalers could provide same-day delivery to their retail accounts without having to keep excessive inventories. Jung's products were also among the most sophisticated and innovative on the market. Many company resources were devoted to advancing product designs. Jung had been innovative in merchandising as well. In the 1950s the company had been the first to introduce a health supports "department" to the drugstore. Jung enjoyed broad distribution through drug wholesalers, most of whom featured Futuro products; the company's sales force made regular calls on retailers nationwide. Jung was not, however, the low-price producer, but then again the market was not too price sensitive.

THE PROCESS FLOW

Jung's Cincinnati operations were located in a 215,000 square foot plant in Mariemont, a suburb just east of Cincinnati. The company had relocated there in 1974 after its former, downtown buildings were bought by the county for a new courthouse complex. This factory produced about 60 of the company's 130 different products; others were either made by Jung's subsidiaries or were subcontracted. The Cincinnati operation produced 20 of 30 items in the Health Supports product line, 25 of 75 items in the Patient-Aids product line, and 15

Futuro Health Supports

BRACES

Wrist wraparound
Rib belt, male
Rib belt, female
Wrist splint, left
Wrist splint, right
Knee, X-Action
Bandage — 2 inches
Bandage — 3 inches
Bandage — 4 inches
Abdominal
Elbow
Wrist, cuff
Knee
Ankle
Posture-Aid
Sacroiliac
Hernia-Aid

STOCKINGS

Over knee, open toe, casual
Under knee, open toe, casual
Under knee, orthopedic
Over knee, full foot, firm lift
Full foot, sheerest, beige
Full foot, sheerest, taupe
Men's super socks

Men's support socks

Pantyhose, beige
Pantyhose, taupe
Men's coolweight socks

SUPPORTERS AND BELTS

Swimmer
V-Gard
Sports-3
Youth size
Cup style, adult
Cup style, youth
Wide band
Van Gard, nondet.
Van Gard, det.
Suspensory, elastic
Suspensory, nonelastic

Futuro Patient-Aids

Cane—walnut, plastic handle, 7/8 inch
Cane—walnut, 7/8 inch
Cane—black, plastic handle, 7/8 inch
Cane—black, 7/8 inch
Cane—"T" style, 5/8 inch
Cane—ebony, 3/4 inch
Cane—rosewood, 1 inch
Cane—"T" style, 3/4 inch
Cane—deluxe, 7/8 inch

Cane—aluminum telescopic
Cane—aluminum, 7/8 inch
Cane—quad—large
Cane—quad—small

Crutch—wood—adult
Crutch—wood—medium
Crutch—wood—youth
Crutch—aluminum—standard
Crutch—forearm—adult

Walker—regular—adjustable
Walker—folding—adjustable

Commode—U.P.S.—adjustable

Wheelchair—easy-roll
Wheelchair—standard
Legrest—elevating—left
Legrest—elevating—right

Bedpan—hospital style
Bedpan—fracture style
Sitz bath
Urinal—female
Urinal—male
Incontinence pants—lined
Liner—Olefin fiber
Incontinence pants—unlined
Liner—cotton flannel

Cervical collar—adjustable
Cervical sleep collar
Cervical traction kit

Invalid ring
Cushion—wheelchair

Crutch tips—"Super Grip"
Crutch handgrips
Crutch pads—underarm

Waterproof sheeting—crib
Waterproof sheeting—hospital
Waterproof sheeting—double

FIGURE 3-1   A partial listing of products manufactured by Jung Products, Inc.

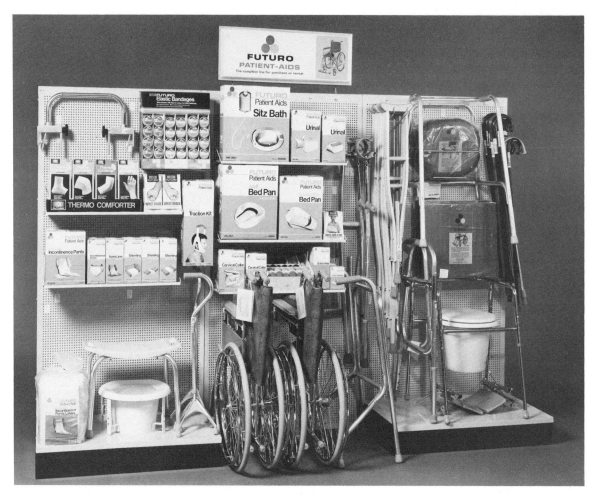

The product line developed by Jung since the 1960s was geared toward convalescents but was still sold primarily though drug-stores. *(Courtesy of Jung Products, Inc.)*

of 25 items in the Grid product line. Considering the variety of styles and sizes, the factory was responsible for a huge assortment of products. Thankfully, the production process was not complex.

All of the products manufactured in the Cincinnati factory could be classified into two groups: brown goods and white goods. Brown goods generally comprised those items that were worn on exposed areas (e.g., knees, elbows, ankles) as braces; the bulk of the Health Supports line and some of the Patient-Aids line were brown goods. White goods, on the other hand, generally consisted of items that were worn under clothing as supporters; all of the Grid line and some of each of the other two product lines were white goods.

The production of these classes of products differed because only brown goods contained latex, which required special treatment. All production was accomplished in batches, generally of 200

The Grid line consisted only of white goods. *(Courtesy of Jung Products, Inc.)*

items each, a convenient number for handling the materials. Brown goods production started with the assembly of raw materials, which in most cases was simply the woven or knit elastic fabric generally supplied by Rampon Products. The fabric was then cut according to various patterns. To secure the severed latex in the cut fabric, the edges of the fabric were painted with liquid latex and then placed on racks to dry. Drying was rapid and the batch of latexed fabric was then put into movable bins (laundry carts) and delivered to the people who sewed the fabric pieces into the designated shape. General purpose industrial sewing machines

were used for this task. For many products, only one work station of sewing was required; others demanded several work stations. After the material was sewn, the seams were pressed using special machines. Sometimes trimming was also required. The then finished goods were packed into boxes and dispatched to the warehouse. The warehouse was an important operation since most orders from drug wholesalers and drug chains called for a mix of products delivered within a matter of days. Products had to be sorted carefully, and all orders filled had to be tracked reliably.

White goods manufacture was very similar to

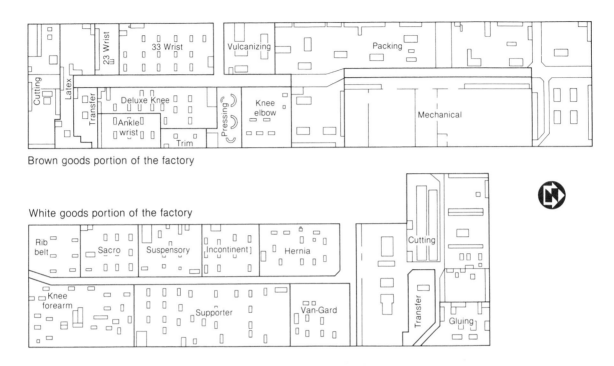

Brown goods portion of the factory

White goods portion of the factory

FIGURE 3-2   Layout of the Jung Products factory.

that of brown goods except that the latex application and materials pressing steps were unnecessary. Despite this simplification of the process, white goods fabrication was in general more complicated than that for brown goods (i.e., more operations were done on each item) and thus demanded more cutting and sewing time.

A schematic layout of the factory is provided in Figure 3-2. On it are indicated the general movements of products of various types through the process. Documenting specific product movements would require almost individual plant layout plots.

THE WORKFORCE AND THE OPERATIONS OF THE PIECE-RATE SYSTEM

Jung Products employed approximately 200 people at its Cincinnati location. This largely female labor force was drawn from all over the Cincinnati metropolitan area, including Northern Kentucky, and did not reside primarily in any one portion of that area. Labor turnover in the plant stood at about 10 percent a year, which was low for the garment industry; many workers had been with the company for years. Absenteeism was also low, averaging about 6 or 7 percent. All of the plant's workers were represented by the Amalgamated Clothing Workers. Management relations with the union were well established, cordial, and constructive.

Factory lead people, warehouse workers, and hand knife cutters were paid on an hourly basis. However, all of the other 150 factory workers (other cutters, latex painters, sewers, pressers, trimmers, and packers) were paid on a piece rate—that is, according to the number of items they completed. Every operation that a factory worker performed (there were 3200 possible operations) had an established rate of so many cents per 100 completed items. These "prices" for work accomplished were designed so that any worker in the factory who worked at the standard rate of speed could earn an agreed-upon "base rate" wage. In fact, the plantwide average for piece-rate earnings ran about 10 percent above the base rate, and some workers earned as much as two-thirds again the base rate.

Operators were assigned not to particular products or even product lines, but to machines (e.g., single needle sewing machine, double needle sewing machine). During a typical day, some workers worked through successive batches of the same product while others changed products two or three times. Most operators' work required the use of only one work station, although some workers had to use as many as three different machines to perform the indicated sequence of operations. Supervisors were responsible for the assignment of batches, and usually batches to be finished were stacked up behind each worker. If any worker ran out of work to do and the supervisor did not have a new batch to assign, the worker would be paid for any idle time in excess of 15 minutes.

Each batch came with a deck of small computer cards (see Figure 3-3) in a plastic envelope. Each card designated a particular task for a particular

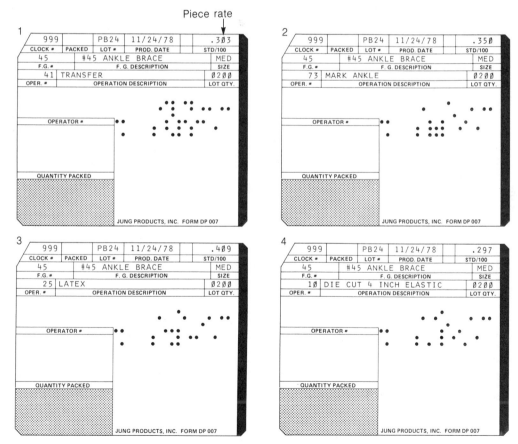

FIGURE 3-3 Sequence of factory operations for a product (ankle brace) manufactured by Jung Products—one card for each operation. (*continues on next page*)

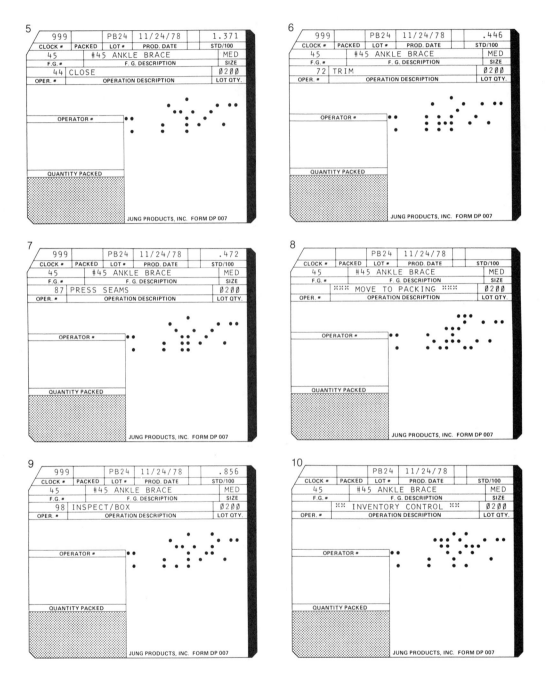

FIGURE 3-3 Sequence of factory operations. (*continued*)

product and quoted the piece rate for it. After completing the batch, the operator would take the card for the task assigned out of the plastic envelope, sign it, and place it in her own pay envelope. At the end of the day, she would turn in this pay envelope and be paid accordingly. In this way, management could keep account of who had completed which tasks. The company's computer kept track of these decks of routing and pay cards and cross-checked completed batches against the cards workers turned in so that double payments for the same job could not be made.

Piece rates could be changed only for changes in materials, methods (e.g., a different type of stitch), or machines. Given a change in one of these three, Jung Products' industrial engineers would establish a new, temporary piece rate incorporating the change. Time study techniques (e.g., stopwatch study) were used to establish new piece rates. It was understood that any worker being studied had to perform at an average pace. Under the union contract, the operator was obliged to try working with the new piece rate for 2 weeks, during which time she would be paid the average of her recent work. After that 2-week period, the piece rate would go into effect. If the worker felt that the new piece rate was too low, she could complain; the fairness of the new rate was a legitimate issue for the company-union grievance procedure. Typically, however, management would restudy suspect piece rates and could exercise the option to reset the piece rate up to 3 months after it was last established. Once that period of time had elapsed, however, the piece rate was inviolate. Between 250 and 300 piece rates were either established or revised each year.

Of the factory workers, only trainees were not paid according to piece rates. Jung Products preferred to hire accomplished operators who could be "up to speed" in a matter of days, since training a completely inexperienced sewer, for example, could take as long as 6 months. Under the union agreement, the probationary period for new workers was 3 months, after which the company could not fire anyone except for just cause.

CONTROLLING THE PROCESS

PRODUCTION CONTROL

Jung Products filled its orders from a finished goods inventory of all its products. In general, the company liked to have 2 to 4 weeks of expected sales on hand as inventory. Since sales were somewhat seasonal, the actual volume of desired inventory would fluctuate during the year. Production was geared to replenish this inventory. The sales that were made in any week triggered production the following week, so that this week's production tried to match last week's demand. This chase strategy frequently necessitated some Saturday work (at time and a half), if demand greatly exceeded the average factory production rate of about 125,000 units per week.

An annual forecast of sales was somewhat helpful in planning aggregate levels of production in any week. However, the vagaries of the marketplace and the quick response expected of Jung Products to wholesaler demands meant constant disruption of this aggregate plan and the derivative master schedule of work, which typically called for 1 week's production needs in cutting, 2 weeks in sewing, and 1 week in packing. This constant disruption, however, was the norm in the factory and the process, because of its organization and relative simplicity, was extraordinarily flexible. The production cycle times for most products, if need be, could be as short as 2 or 3 hours; warehouse stockouts discovered in the morning were filled that afternoon or certainly during the following day.

QUALITY CONTROL

The quality control of finished goods was not a problem. Items were inspected cursorily by the

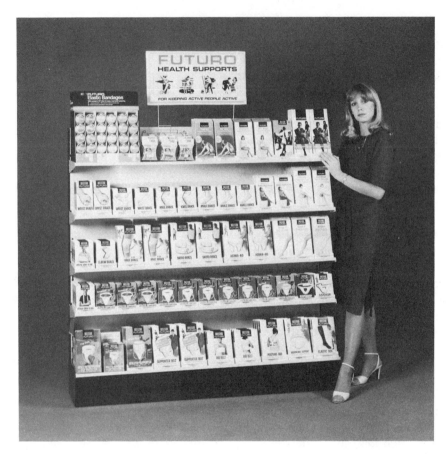

Like the Grid line, the Health Supports line featured the use of elastic knit fabric, but it consisted of both white and brown goods. *(Courtesy of Jung Products, Inc.)*

sewer and by the packer. The supervisors were also charged with random inspections of work-in-process. Raw materials were sampled statistically for quality inspections.

PURCHASING

On the average, materials accounted for 60 percent of a product's sales price, while labor accounted for 15 percent. Jung Products drew its supplies from all over. By value:

10% from the Cincinnati metropolitan area
15% from elsewhere in the Ohio-Kentucky-Indiana region
20% from elsewhere in the Midwest
50% from national sources outside the Midwest, principally the South (Rampon Products) but also from cities like New York and Philadelphia
5% from international sources

About 1.1 percent of new sales was spent on freight charges for incoming raw materials, and about 3.6 percent of net sales was spent on freight charges for outgoing finished goods.

PART TWO

DISCUSSION

Jung Products, Inc. is in no way responsible for the following views and presentation. They remain solely the responsibility of the author.

THE PROCESS AND INFORMATION FLOWS

In comparison with the job shop of Norcen Industries, the flow of production at Jung Products is markedly more well defined. While the production process differs in important ways between brown goods and white goods, within each category we can compose a process flow diagram that adequately represents the process, although it is not totally accurate for all products. Figure 3-4 depicts a plausible process flow diagram for brown goods manufacture at Jung. As noted in the figure,

an operation like trimming may be skipped for particular products, while for other products the extent of sewing or pressing may vary tremendously.

These variations underscore the still very strong need of the batch-flow process for information and control. In its own way, the information flows of this process are inflexible; but, compared to the job shop, the flow of information from workers to management is attenuated (see Figure 3-5). Workers are responsible only for removing and signing the cards that call for their particular operations. In essence, the deck of cards serves as both process sheet and job sheet, to borrow language from the Norcen Industries example; the cards inform the worker of what must be done to the batch and they keep track of who did what to each batch of work.

The increased stability of the process flow also reduces the amount of information that must be

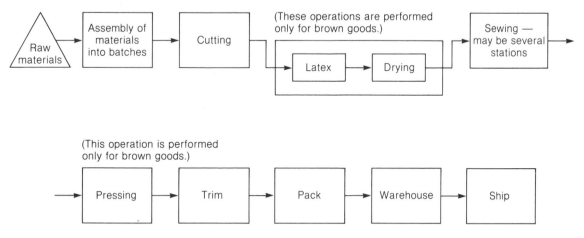

Notes:
1. Not all products are routed through all of these operations or in this sequence.
2. Work-in-process inventories exist between all of the operations indicated.

FIGURE 3-4   A process flow diagram for Jung Products, Inc. showing the dominant flow.

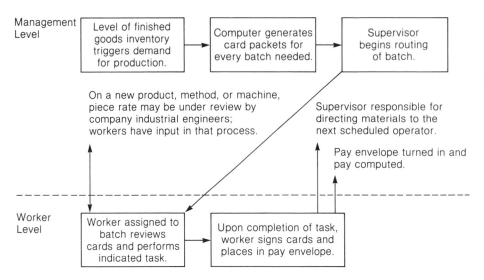

FIGURE 3-5   An information flow diagram for Jung Products, Inc.

communicated from management to workers. The foreman typically has less troubleshooting and expediting to do and fewer scheduling changes to make. Therefore, it is often possible to supervise more people in a batch-flow operation than in a job shop.

The need for a continuous ebb and flow of information is reduced in the batch-flow process primarily because its product selection, while large, is limited and well known in advance. Furthermore, it seldom has to bid for contracts, and so precise, order-specific cost information is not required.

CAPACITY IN THE BATCH-FLOW PROCESS

The notion of capacity is only slightly less ambiguous in the batch-flow operation than in the job shop. The wide arrays of products that can be produced in any one week make it difficult to specify capacity in units of output, without pegging it first to some standard mix of products. Dollar value is

probably a more stable indicator of capacity, although still a considerably vague measure.

The capacity of the batch-flow process is influenced by many of the same factors that determine the capacity of a job shop:

1. *Batch (or lot) sizes.*   Although the setup times for any batch of products are exceedingly low at Jung Products, there are other batch-flow processes for which the setup times can be substantial. In these instances, larger batch sizes are to be preferred, other things being equal.

2. *Complexity of the products run through the operation.*

3. *Nature of the jobs already on the factory floor.*   Batch-flow operations, like job shops, are subject to shifting bottlenecks and worker-machine interference. However, the definite limits to product diversity in the former generally mean that the severity and frequency of these two capacity thieves are reduced.

4. *Scheduling.*   Scheduling is still an important

consideration for the managers of a batch operation, but the task is generally simpler than in the job shop. Again, the reduction in products and capabilities offered accounts for the bulk of this difference. With the batch operation, scheduling begins to shed its critical importance to the success of the operation. With the continuous flow process, scheduling, while important, is more routine and limited in significant ways by the process itself.

5. *Process improvement.*

6. *Number of machines and their condition.*

7. *Quantity and quality of labor input.*

The last three major influences on capacity, like many of the other influences cited, take on less importance for the typical batch operation than for the typical job shop. Because the process itself is more well defined, with workers more apt to be assigned to particular machines and less free to float among machines, the batch operation generally has less to gain from investments in process improvement or more machines (without more workers). In a sense, the transition from job shop to batch operation accounts already for quite a bit of process improvement (e.g., methods, jigs/fixtures, quicker setups), as represented by the routing tickets, assigned machines, and special training. The batch operation is more likely to feel that machines and workers are one producing unit, and thus capacity can be enhanced significantly only by increasing both in similar proportions.

THE ROLE OF STANDARDS AND INCENTIVES

At Jung Products the role of standards takes on a different function than at Norcen Industries. At Norcen, you will recall, standards were used to estimate time and costs for bidding on jobs and also to provide information for scheduling jobs through the shop. While this second function for standards is retained at Jung Products, because there is no bidding for new orders, standards are not used for before-the-job cost estimation. Rather, standards in the form of piece rates are used explicitly for determining worker compensation and for spurring worker effort and output. In a sense, the piece-rate standards act to pace work through the factory.

As the process description made plain, the setting of piece rates at Jung Products is serious business. Great care is taken to see that they are both accurate and fair. Considerable time and expense are spent setting new piece rates, observing workers trying out the piece rates, and testing out modifications. The entire procedure involving piece rates—their setting, their use, the union-company resolution of disputes involving them—is well established and routine, as it should be for a smooth operation of the system.

QUESTIONS

1. What were some of the benefits to Jung Products of integrating backward? How did it bring about this integration?

2. Briefly describe the main features of the operation of Jung Products' piece-rate system. Do the same for its quality control.

3. Compare and contrast the characteristics of the information flow in the batch flow process used by Jung Products with the information flow characteristic of two other processes. Which process requires least in the way of information flow from its managers? from its workers?

4. What is the most stable indicator of capacity in a batch flow process? Describe three of the major influences on capacity in this process.

5. How are the roles of standards and incentives affected by the batch flow process? Compare their roles in this process with their roles in another.

6. How would you describe the market for Jung Products? What relationship, if any, does this market have to the production process chosen by the company?

SITUATION FOR STUDY

BROWN. SMITH & JONES (BS&J)

Paul Alvarez has just been hired by BS&J as superintendent of the Fabricated Tank Division. Paul's previous experience had been with a leading manufacturer of home heating systems where the processes were highly automated. At the previous firm the goods were also processed in a continuous manner, with a product line being set up for a year or more of production.

The products manufactured by the Fabricated Tank Division were typically oil storage tanks made from sheet steel, which were sent to the customer much like a kit and were erected in remote oil fields. Occasionally, the firm sold the tanks in various sizes to other customers for other uses, such as to the military for the storage of diverse liquids like water and jet airplane fuel. Figure 3-A is an example of a tank and some of the parts that must be fabricated. Table 3-A is a partial process sheet for these parts. Figure 3-B is a layout of the relevant processes.

TABLE 3-A Partial Outline of the Process
(Brown, Smith & Jones)

STAVE		ROOF AND FLOOR SECTIONS	
OPERATION	*PROCESS*	*OPERATION*	*PROCESS*
Shear edges true	Sheet shear	Shear edges and split each sheet on diagonal	Sheet shear
Punch bolt holes in both ends	Brake press setup with punches	Punch/shear small end*	Punch press
Punch bolt holes in both sides	Brake press setup with punches	Shear large end	Circle shear
Roll to tank diameter	Pyramid rolls	Clean and paint	Paint line
Flange both ends	Brake press setup with correct flange	Pack and ship	
Clean and paint	Paint line		
Pack and ship			

*For typical tank sizes there were punch press tools for this. Others had to be laid out, circle sheared, and single punched.

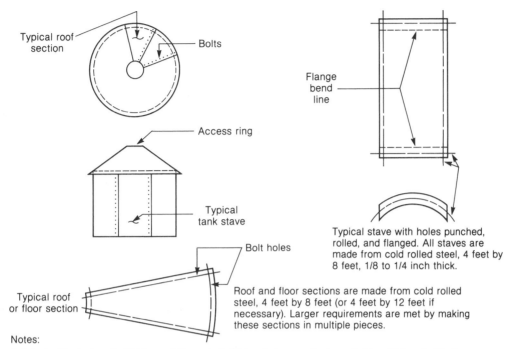

Typical roof section

Bolts

Access ring

Typical tank stave

Bolt holes

Typical roof or floor section

Flange bend line

Typical stave with holes punched, rolled, and flanged. All staves are made from cold rolled steel, 4 feet by 8 feet, 1/8 to 1/4 inch thick.

Roof and floor sections are made from cold rolled steel, 4 feet by 8 feet (or 4 feet by 12 feet if necessary). Larger requirements are met by making these sections in multiple pieces.

Notes:

1. A typical tank stave is (1) trimmed (if needed), (2) has holes punched on all sides, (3) is rolled to the approximate shape (depending on the tank diameter) on the pyramid roll, and (4) flanged on both ends in a large brake press. The press is set up with a flanging that also causes the stave to be formed to the final shape according to the tank diameter. There is a flanging tool for each diameter tank.

2. The roof and floor sections are made from material similar to the tank staves, ranging from 1/8 inch to 1/4 inch, per the engineering design. If necessary, these sections can be made from material 4 feet by 12 feet. BS&J uses standard mill sizes to avoid the extra costs involved in having special sizes available; also, pieces that are too big would create construction problems. Two sections are usually cut from a single sheet:

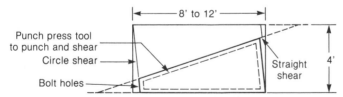

Punch press tool to punch and shear

Circle shear

Bolt holes

8' to 12'

Straight shear

4'

(The view is somewhat exaggerated to demonstrate the method.) If a top or bottom piece were too long, it would be made from two pieces:

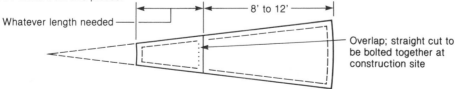

Whatever length needed

8' to 12'

Overlap; straight cut to be bolted together at construction site

FIGURE 3-A   Typical tank and parts.

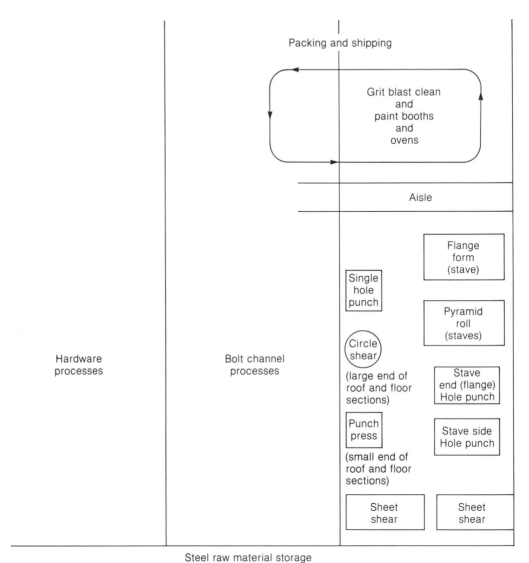

FIGURE 3-B Fabricating process layout for a side stave, roof section, and floor section.

Many of the smaller parts are common to most tanks, and they are made on a continuous basis to inventory requirements. There are three parts that are somewhat unique to each tank size: the tank side parts called staves, the triangular roof, and the bottom sections. The smallest tank, 1500 gallons capacity, requires 5 staves, 5 roof sections, and 5 floor sections. A 55,000 gallon tank, 5 rows high, requires 13 roof sections, 13 floor sections, and 65 staves. The typical order is for three tanks of the same size, but an order can be as small as one tank and has been as large as 15 tanks. The tanks are made to order, but BS&J has a backlog estimated at one and one-half months' production.

Paul was hired because the Fabricated Tank Division has been unable to meet scheduled shipping dates, quality problems are cropping up, and the workers are unhappy about never being able to earn any incentive pay. Paul thought he would focus on the manufacture of the side staves, roof, and floor sections. What information does he need next? What information should be included on parts routing sheets?

1. Draw a process flow diagram for the two major tank parts.
2. What information would you need in order to set up a production schedule for this shop?
3. What approaches would you suggest to Paul to help him with both his quality problems and his incentive pay problems?

4

A HYBRID (BATCH/CONTINUOUS FLOW) PROCESS

Jos. Schlitz Brewing Company
Syracuse, New York

In November 1976, the Jos. Schlitz Company's eighth brewery, situated near Syracuse, New York, began production. The plant manager had been on site during the brewery's construction over the previous three years and had coordinated the plant's staffing and start-up.

The brewery itself was huge, at the time the largest brewery ever built at one time. It occupied 1.3 million square feet of floor space on 193 acres of land and could produce, at capacity, about 6 million barrels of beer per year. (A beer barrel, abbreviated bbl., is equal to 31 gallons.) The brewery's construction, including its nearby waste water treatment plant, cost a total of $150 million.

PART ONE

PROCESS DESCRIPTION

THE BREWING AND PACKAGING OF BEER

Beer is in essence a grain-flavored drink that is fermented and carbonated. It has been popular for thousands of years and, in one form or another, exists in almost every culture on earth. Although known and enjoyed for so long, the chemistry of brewing is very complex and is still not understood in all its particulars. Brewing remains very much an art despite rapid innovation over the past 15 to 20 years; brewing automation and control has reduced the brew house workforce to a quarter of its traditional size and placed much of its control on instrument panels.

The brewing process itself can be divided into two main stages: (1) the production of natural grain sugars, called wort production, and (2) fermentation and finishing. (The process is depicted in Figure 4-1.) At Schlitz, a batch of beer typically took about a month to brew.

WORT PRODUCTION

Wort production starts with the weighing, cleaning, and milling of the grain which gives beer its flavor. The chief grain, malting barley, and an ad-

59

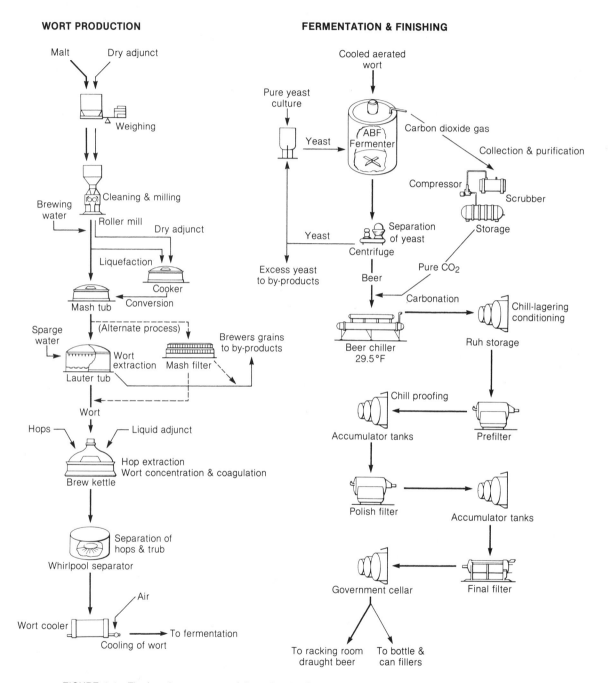

FIGURE 4-1 The brewing process as followed at the Syracuse plant of the Jos. Schlitz Brewing Company.

junct (corn, rice, and/or liquefied corn) are milled separately. The adjunct is used because malting barley can convert more than its own weight of starch to fermentable sugars. The Syracuse brewery was the first in the Western Hemisphere to install wet milling, which has certain cost and quality advantages over the traditional dry milling of barley. To the milled barley and adjunct is added the brewing water, which is specially treated by filtering and pH adjustment to remove impurities. This addition of water to grain is known as mashing and, at Schlitz, was done by the so-called "double mash upward infusion" method. This method demands two separate mashing vessels — an adjunct cooker and a mash tub. These are large, stainless steel vessels in which the milled grain and brewing water can be stirred together and brought to a boil. The double mash upward infusion method ensures that the adjunct is of sufficiently small particle size so that it can best be exposed to the malt and the brewing water for quick and complete breakdown of its starches. The adjunct is therefore mashed separately in the adjunct cooker and then added to the malt mash in the mash tub.

After mashing, the mixture is transferred to a lauter tub, which separates the liquid (the wort) from the undissolved solids of the mash. The lauter tub is a large, circular tub with a false bottom and a rotating set of "rakes" that can be raised or lowered. These rotating rakes smooth out the mash as it enters the lauter tub. Undissolved particles in the mash settle to the false floor of the lauter tub. Once settled, the liquid wort can be drawn off with the aid of hot, "sparging" water, which helps the wort to flow out of the lauter tub. The undissolved mash is then collected and sent to the nearby Murphy Products Company (a Schlitz subsidiary), where it is processed into a highly nutritious livestock feed.

The drawn-off wort then enters the brew kettle where it boils for 2 hours. This boiling stabilizes the wort by killing off bacteria, deactivating enzymes, and coagulating any still undissolved particles. During this boiling, hops are introduced to the wort to enhance its flavor. Boiling also increases the concentration of the wort through evaporation. Once boiled, the hops and trub (coagulated sediment) are separated out by whirlpool action in a special vessel. The hot wort is then cooled and aerated.

FERMENTATION AND FINISHING

Only after yeast has been introduced to the cooled wort and fermentation is complete can the product be called beer. The yeast that is introduced to the 50-foot high fermentation tanks transforms glucose and other sugars in the wort to alcohol and carbon dioxide. Schlitz's fermentation is accomplished by a patented process called "accurate balanced fermentation." During fermentation, carbon dioxide gas is collected and purified. After fermenting has finished and the yeast has been separated from the beer by centrifuge, the carbon dioxide is reintroduced to the beer (carbonation) and the beer is chilled.

Once fermentation is complete and the yeast separated, the remaining finishing consists of a string of storage and filtering steps. The chief aging occurs in the ruh cellar, where the beer is held for between 7 and 12 days. Once properly aged, the beer is filtered several times through diatomaceous earth. Final storage occurs in what is called the government cellar, where the next day's production is inventoried and where the quantity of beer subject to federal tax is monitored.

Out of the government cellar, the beer flows in through pipes in a wall and out to the keg, canning, and bottling lines. From here on, the beer is no longer under the control of the brewmaster.

CANNING, BOTTLING, AND KEGGING

The Syracuse brewery operated two canning lines, four bottling lines, and a keg line. Each line per-

The 500-gallon brew kettles can hold the equivalent of 5300 12-ounce bottles of beer or 900 six-packs. *(Courtesy of Jos. Schlitz Brewing Company)*

formed essentially the same functions: (1) filling and capping and (2) pasteurizing; cans and bottles were also boxed into six-packs and cases, and cases were placed on pallets for shipping by truck or rail. The process from filling to palletizing ran continuously, with no buildup of inventories in-process unless a piece of equipment in the line broke down. The key piece of equipment on the line was the filler (an investment of $400,000)—the limiting element for capacity. All of the machines that followed had rated capacities in excess of the filler; so any equipment breakdown after the filler did not necessitate shutting down the entire line.

The can lines could run at 1500 cans per minute, the bottling lines at 900 bottles per minute, and the keg line at 400 half-barrels per hour. At present, only 12-ounce cans could be run on the can line. With two canning lines, however, two of the three brands brewed at the plant could be canned at the same time. Alternatively, cans with two different types of pop-top lid could also be run at the same time. Four bottling lines were needed not only to match the demand for bottles but also to permit bottles of different shapes and sizes to be run at the same time. In addition, returnable bottles were separated from new bottles for filling and packaging. A canning line shift required 8 workers, while a bottling line shift required 15.

WAREHOUSING

The Syracuse plant preferred to load the beer directly from the line into railcars or trucks rather than warehouse it. (See the plant layout in Figure

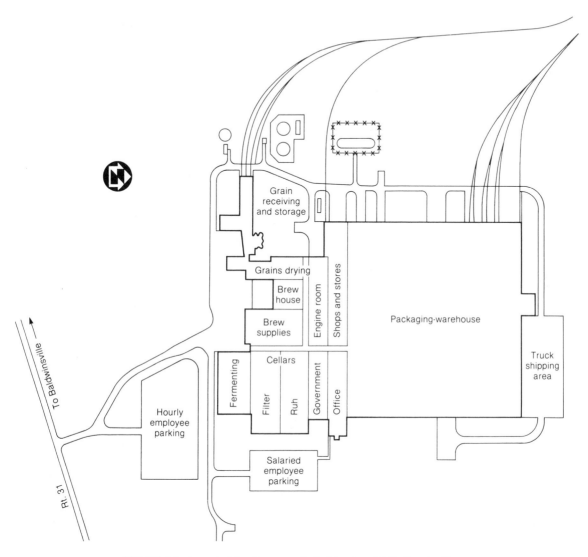

FIGURE 4-2 Layout of the Syracuse plant of the Jos. Schlitz Brewing Company.

4–2.) In fact, about half of the plant's output was shipped without any intermediate storage in the warehouse. The warehouse itself averaged only about a day's output in storage, and few items failed to turn over within a week.

The warehouse's fully enclosed railroad docks could store 28 60-foot-long freight cars. In addition, 21 truck loading docks were available. The warehouse was designed so that up to 70 percent of capacity output could be shipped by either rail or truck; it did not matter which.

The warehouse stored some items that were not produced at the plant. For example, Schlitz Malt Liquor was not brewed at Syracuse, nor were 16-ounce cans filled. These items had to be supplied by other Schlitz plants.

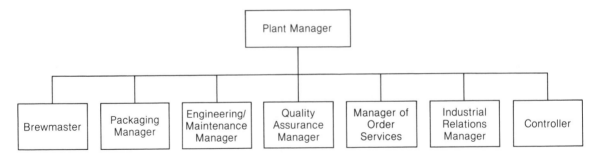

FIGURE 4-3   Organization chart for the Syracuse plant of the Jos. Schlitz Brewing Company.

LOADING THE PLANT

ORDER TAKING

Schlitz's Syracuse brewery served 122 wholesalers in nine northeastern states including New England, New York, New Jersey, and Pennsylvania. A wholesaler would generally handle one of the major national brands and perhaps a smaller, regional brand. Each wholesaler would service a range of retail accounts (e.g., liquor stores, bars, grocery stores) within a specified geographic area.

At the middle of each month, every wholesaler would place an order for delivery next month. This procedure meant that the brewery had lead times of 2 to 6 weeks for each order. The order, entered either directly by computer or mailed in, would specify item, quantity, and date (sometimes hour) for delivery of the beer ordered. The brewery offered a remarkable diversity of items: three types of beer (Schlitz, Old Milwaukee, and Schlitz Light) in cans, bottles, or kegs of various sizes, with different lids and in different kinds of cardboard cartons. In all, there were about 100 beer and packaging variations that a wholesaler could order. Wholesalers could pick up their order by truck, paying the expenses themselves, or they could have the plant load a special Schlitz-assigned rail freight car and direct it to the wholesaler's own rail siding. The truck option offered greater speed and reliability of delivery than rail, thereby cutting down on the inventory the wholesaler had to carry, but it cost considerably more. About 60 percent of the plant's volume was shipped by rail and 40 percent by truck.

The Syracuse plant monitored the inventory positions of each of its wholesalers, and it followed trends in the marketplace as well (e.g., promotional campaigns and their effect). The plant sometimes made suggestions to its wholesalers on what and how much to order, especially if it felt strongly that a wholesaler might not have ordered correctly.

PRODUCTION PLANNING

Production planning was intimately related to order taking and was performed in the same department. (See the organization chart in Figure 4-3.) The role of the production planners was to figure out how the brewery could best fill the orders placed by its wholesalers. A good production plan was one that satisfied all of the wholesalers' demands with (1) little repositioning of the requested delivery dates, (2) few layoffs or new hires of the workforce, and (3) full usage of the existing equipment.

Planning and scheduling production for each month meant determining (1) how much beer of which type was required and the timing of its delivery and packaging and (2) the precise sequencing of lines and beer/packaging combinations on each line.

Because it took a month to brew beer, the brewmaster had to produce to a forecast of sales rather than to customer order. This production to forecast was a key reason why the plant kept close tabs on retail activity and made buying suggestions to its wholesalers. It also helped greatly that beer could be stored in the ruh cellar for a variable time (7 to 12 days) and that other such slack existed in the brewing cycle. The packaging of beer, on the other hand, could be, and was in fact, done to customer order.

In planning packaging for any given month, it was advantageous to:

1. Group runs of the same beers together, such as packaging Old Milwaukee on several lines at the same time.

2. Group similar packaging sizes and types together, such as running all quart bottles at the same time rather than interspersing them among other production runs.

3. Run similar lines at the same time, such as running the two can lines in tandem. To run a second line, given the first was running, required only four more workers rather than the eight it took to run the line by itself.

4. Run a canning line together with the keg line, since the joint workforce for such a combination could then be shifted en masse to a bottling line if need be. In that way, the groups working on any line would not have to be split up and reassembled as often.

Once the next month's wholesaler orders were received, the production planners went to work to schedule the production to fulfill that demand. This scheduling was accomplished manually using trial and error but with reference to decision rules like the four mentioned above. After the production plan became "final," the wholesalers' delivery dates and order quantities were acknowledged on a week-by-week basis, giving the wholesalers two weeks' notice. About 70 percent of the wholesalers'

original orders were acknowledged without any changes in dates or quantities. For the other 30 percent, all quantities were filled with timing dislocations that were always less than two weeks. Fully 96 percent of all the acknowledged orders were shipped on time.

Wholesalers could request changes in the schedule after their initial orders had been placed. This meant calling a production coordinator who could change the production plan or arrange swaps between wholesalers (since the brewery was aware of all wholesaler inventory positions). Major modifications of the production plan rarely had to be made. Minor adjustments were made about twice a week, but these occurred normally for production problems such as a machine breakdown. The production plan was declared fixed as to labor content one week in advance of production. It was declared fixed as to packaging variations only one day in advance of production. About one shift's production was kept as a safety stock so that snafus in demand, production, or logistics would not necessarily affect delivery.

The production plan had another role somewhat different from the weekly scheduling of machines to match orders exactly. This role had to do with anticipating the seasonality of beer drinking. There was a definite seasonal trend to beer sales. Demand peaked from May through September, with the height of the peak accounting for sales roughly double those of the winter trough.

Since Schlitz's pasteurized beer averaged only two living organisms per 12 ounces (milk had 100,000 per milliliter), the beer did not spoil. The brewery could therefore cushion itself somewhat for the peak season demand by building up inventories, both in its own warehouse and in the warehouses of its wholesalers. In this way, the brewery did not have to hire or lay off as many workers during the periods when demand was changing abruptly. The brewery and its wholesalers built up inventories during the late spring and ran them down as summer progressed.

Purchasing

The purchasing function for the plant was housed in the same department that handled order taking and production planning. This arrangement made sense since the production plan implied, in a straightforward way, the materials needs for the entire process.

All of the brewery's major materials inputs (malt, adjuncts, cans, bottles, cardboard) were purchased on long-term contracts from major suppliers. These contracts were all negotiated by Schlitz's headquarters staff in Milwaukee. The Syracuse plant negotiated on its own only those contracts for materials and services that went into the maintenance of the brewery itself and were not an integral part of the final product. Still, there were plant-specific negotiations for 2500 contracts each year. Also, even though Milwaukee headquarters may have negotiated for a specific material, there was often a direct supplier–brewery relationship. For example, American Can Company built a plant close by specifically to supply the brewery. The same was true for the nearby Owens-Illinois glass bottle factory.

The brewery placed orders for these major materials in much the same way that Schlitz's wholesalers placed orders with the brewery. For example, the July order for cans or bottles would be placed on June 10. At that time, the brewery would place a firm 4-week order and an estimate of the succeeding 4 weeks' demand.

The inventory levels for any one of these major materials depended crucially on the dependability of the supplier. If the supplier had proven reliable and no special circumstances intervened, the brewery would want to hold only enough of the material to last until the next delivery. As it was, special circumstances were continually intervening, and so the brewery often adjusted the amount it ordered to take advantage of volume discounts in price or seasonal differences in sales or expectations about a strike in the supplier's plant. Some typical inventory levels for major materials were:

Cans	1–2 hours of production
Bottles	less than 8 hours of production
Malt	5–7 days
Cardboard cases	2 weeks
Bottle labels	4 months

THE WORKFORCE

The brewery currently employed 350 people, producing on two shifts a day, 5 days a week. Of these, 120 were salaried (managers, chemists, clerical staff) and 230 were paid hourly. The hourly workers were represented by a union, the International Brotherhood of Teamsters.

Since the plant had only recently started up, most of the workforce was new, hired from within a 50-mile radius. Sixty-five of the 120 salaried workers were drawn from other Schlitz breweries, but only 7 of the hourly workers came from other Schlitz breweries, mainly because they had to be volunteers and had to pay for their own move. A couple of dozen other production workers had worked before at breweries that were now defunct. During plant start-up a strong effort was made to hire persons so that there was a representative mix of ages, races, and sexes.

The hourly workers were divided into two main groups: the production workers who actually brewed and packaged the beer, and the engineering and maintenance workers who cared for and fixed the plant's equipment. The maintenance workers were paid about 5 percent more than the production workers, since their jobs required greater expertise and wider skills.

Once in a department (brewing, packaging, engineering/maintenance), workers tended to stay, often doing the same job. This status quo was frequently by choice, since workers who complained of boredom were generally shifted to more complex jobs or made relief workers (spelling other workers who were taking breaks). Advancement through the ranks and into management was al-

A packaging employee used a mallet to seal a keg, much in the way kegs and barrels have been closed for centuries. *(Courtesy of Jos. Schlitz Brewing Company)*

ways possible, especially in brewing and packaging, although the odds were short. Most movement among the hourly employees was from second- to first-shift work; such moves were based on seniority.

Labor relations between management and the union were particularly cordial, especially for a period of plant start-up. Only 25 grievances had been initiated in the first year of operation and all of these had been resolved quickly.

CONTROL AND EVALUATION OF THE OPERATION

QUALITY ASSURANCE

Quality assurance (Q.A.) at the brewery was an important activity, employing 26 people in four separate labs: microbiology, brewing, packaging, and incoming materials. The staff at those labs performed 1100 separate tests on each batch of beer brewed at the plant. Q.A. staff worked round the clock, 7 days a week. Quality assurance had the authority to stop operations at any point in the process. The Q.A. manager was responsible for dealing with and rectifying any customer complaints.

Here are two examples of the specifications that the Q.A. staff tested for, one set by the corporation's brewing staff and the other set by the corporation's packaging staff:

1. The brewing staff had set a standard of 16 million yeast cells (±2 million) per milliliter of beer during fermentation. Quality assurance tested for this standard twice for every fermentation tank's batch. The test had to be completed within the first 4 hours of fermentation so that any necessary corrective measures could be taken. The test was accomplished by taking a 4-ounce sample from the tank, diluting it in three steps, and then counting yeast cells by microscope.

2. The packaging staff had established a standard that the air content in a 12-ounce can of beer be no more than 1 cubic centimeter, since too much air in a can can make the beer taste tinny. The Q.A. staff tested for this standard by checking six times each canning shift, taking three cans from each line each time. If the cans were off specification, the Q.A. staff would quarantine all the line's beer up to the last good check and then systematically inspect the quarantined lot until the beginning of the off-specification beer was encountered. The beer that passed inspection was released and the beer that failed inspection was discarded. As it turned out, about 90 percent of any quarantined beer was eventually released as good product.

Rarely did any of the batches of beer fail to satisfy standards, but the quality assurance department prided itself on its vigilance. It viewed itself as the early warning station for detecting any encroaching degradations of the process's integrity.

Information Flows within the Process

Most of the information flows within the process were directed in only one way, from the top down. If the process was working smoothly, workers needed to be informed of only routine things, such as the changeover in a line from one beer to another or the shifting from one line to another. Most jobs did not vary that much anyway, and so the information that was transmitted could be sparse without any detrimental effect.

The only information that flowed to higher management from the workforce was that signaling breakdowns in the process. After such signals the engineering and maintenance force would be called in. These troubleshooting jobs were generally regarded as the most complex at the brewery and the most pressure filled. A good engineering/maintenance department was a real asset and a chief way to keep costs low by maintaining high speed and high yields.

Evaluating Plant Performance

Each week management at the brewery developed an operations summary that listed goals and actual results for an entire list of performance measures such as productivity (barrels per worker), cost per barrel, packaging line efficiencies, material losses, beer losses, beer rejected by Q.A., deliveries made on time, shipment errors, wholesaler complaints, and worker absenteeism. Each week, too, the plant's beer was evaluated by a taste test in Milwaukee. More than any other test, this was the one the plant always wanted to pass.

In many respects, the plant's performance could only be fine-tuned from week to week. The major elements of plant performance were either already decided (plant design) or beyond the scope of plant management (the plant's sales volume). As the plant manager admitted: "The heaviest decision in our industry is capital equipment investment."

A packaging employee inspects a bottle of beer as it comes out of the pasturizer. While brewing beer remains an art, its packaging is an exact science, requiring continual attention as the bottles flow quickly from operation to operation. *(Courtesy of Jos. Schlitz Brewing Company)*

Major cost and quality advances were very much a function of the equipment the company's design people in Milwaukee decided to incorporate into the plant.

Over the past 10 to 15 years, breweries had also been built larger than before. There were real cost savings implied by larger brewery size: vats and tanks could be larger and still make quality beer at lower cost per barrel, and packaging line speed and capacity could be fully utilized. The size for the Syracuse brewery was decided upon as a sort of "lowest common denominator" for different "lumpy" capital investments. Specifically, the largest lauter tub can process 3 million barrels of beer a year, and the mandatory assortment of packaging lines (one line each for kegs, cans, one-way bottles, and returnable bottles) can process 4 to 4 ½ million barrels a year. With the addition of another canning line and another bottling line, packaging capacity then precisely matches the output of two lauter tubs—hence a brewery capacity of 6 million barrels a year.

What the plant manager worried about depended a lot on volume. As he noted, "Volume solves everything." When volume was high, all the manager had to worry about was whether the workers would accept the necessary overtime and whether maintenance could hold everything together. At capacity, quality and meeting shipments were chief concerns, with product cost lower in priority. When sales volume dropped, however, meeting cost targets became relatively more important and that meant tightening up on staff and laying off workers. The plant was operated as a cost center, since it had no responsibilities for revenue raising (e.g., no marketing at the plant) and its geographic market area was fixed. Plant management was concerned chiefly for the maintenance of the plant and the motivation of the workforce; with them came high yields, quality beer, and on-time shipments.

PART TWO

DISCUSSION

The Jos. Schlitz Brewing Company is in no way responsible for the following views and presentation. They remain solely the responsibility of the author.

THE PROCESS FLOW

Much of the Schlitz brewery's operation is reminiscent of the continuous flow process at International Paper's Androscoggin Mill. Even though there are about a hundred beer and packaging variations, most of these modifications require setup times that are tiny in comparison with the run length. The process flow is well defined, and every product goes through the same steps in the process. (See Figure 4-1 for a process flow chart.) Over time, equipment advances have speeded up the process and have driven labor out of the product's value.

The job contents of the direct labor in the process are of two kinds, polar extremes. Most workers have well-delineated tasks, most of which are repeated time and again as the product is manufactured. These jobs, typically, are not very demanding. At the other extreme lies the brewmaster.

Despite great strides in automation and control, the brewmaster's duties still lie within the realm of art. Brewing is still imperfectly known enough to require great experience to produce a quality product.

Requiring nearly comparable levels of skill and experience are the plant engineers. Plant engineering and maintenance are crucial to an operation, such as a brewery, where the capital investment is enormous and the success of the process so dependent on meeting quality standards and delivery schedules, and on maintaining high yields of output. All of these goals are influenced importantly by the design and upkeep of the equipment in the plant. Moreover, *all* of the equipment must be functioning smoothly for *any* of the product to meet its specifications. Breakdowns or below-specification performance of any of the equipment is likely to lead to poor quality, poor shipment performance, or excessively high costs (e.g., low packaging speeds).

Despite these important similarities to the continuous flow process at the Androscoggin Mill, the Schlitz brewery is not strictly a continuous flow

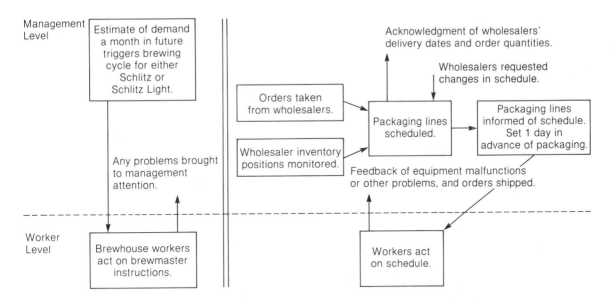

FIGURE 4-4   An information flow diagram for the Syracuse plant of the Jos. Schlitz Brewing Company.

operation. This is true primarily because the brewing phase of the process is done on a batch basis. True, these batches are large, but it is only because of their sequencing and the accumulation of a work-in-process inventory just before packaging that the batch operation in brewing can supply a steady flow of beer to the continuous flow that is packaging. The work-in-process inventories in the ruh and government cellars separate the two different types of processes. Without such an inventory, even though the daily or weekly capacities of the two processes (brewing and packaging) may be matched perfectly, the lumpiness of the batch flow operation's output cycle would cause severe problems for the smooth-running continuous flow operation.

THE INFORMATION FLOW

The inventory between brewing and packaging does more than even out production. It also separates the information needs of the two processes. The brewmaster need only know how much beer of which kind to brew, and the packaging department need only know what, when, and how much it is to package. Moreover, the timing of the information flows is much different. The precise packaging department schedule is set as final only one day prior to packaging. Up to that time, adjustments to the schedule can be accepted. Needless to say, the brewmaster cannot react so quickly. Since it takes about a month to brew a batch of beer, the brewmaster can only work to an estimate of demand, not from firm wholesale orders. The work-in-process inventory between brewing and packaging, then, acts as a safety stock of beer as well, so that last-minute changes in demand can be accommodated. It also serves as the dividing line between production triggered by estimate (brewing) and production triggered by firm orders (packaging). This difference in information requirements, as much as anything else, sets aside the Schlitz brewery as a hybrid (batch/continuous flow) process.

The separation of information needs and flows at the brewery is depicted in an information flow diagram (Figure 4-4). Note that the information basically flows in only one direction (top down) except for the usual signaling of equipment breakdowns and acknowledgments of orders shipped. In this way, the information flows are reminiscent of the Androscoggin Mill.

CAPACITY MEASURES

The capacity of the brewery is a firm and easily understood number, 6 million barrels of beer a year. Barring a major breakdown of equipment, the capacity figure is simply what the existing plant and equipment permit. Neither product mix nor scheduling has much impact on capacity. Other than to maintain the equipment and keep quality up, there is little the plant itself can do to improve the quantity of good product brewed and packaged.

By the same token, capacity utilization is a well-defined concept. The capacity of any piece of equipment is known because it was engineered that way, and the current capacity is also easily measured. Moreover, because the plant's designers want to leave as little waste or spare capacity unused as possible, the capacity utilization for any single piece of equipment is often very close to the capacity utilization figure for the process itself. Since the process's capacity utilization is determined by the bottleneck operation, one can say that all equipment capacities are likely to lie close to the bottleneck capacity.

STANDARDS AND INCENTIVES

The standards that matter at the Schlitz brewery are not the type of standards that managers of batch or job shop operations get concerned about. Labor standards (output per worker per unit of time) do not exist at the brewery. Rather, it is machine standards (units processed per hour) and quality standards that capture management's attention and influence their behavior. These are the standards management strives to meet.

Similarly, labor incentives are absent from the brewery. The plant's output is so overwhelmingly

related to machine rather than worker performance that worker incentive schemes make little sense.

DEMANDS OF THE PROCESS ON THE WORKERS

The process at this Schlitz brewery places a variety of demands on a variety of different work groups within the brewery. Art, science, and routine are all found. For the brewhouse workers, even with the panels of controls that now abound, the brewing process still requires art, a "feel" and a "taste" for what makes quality beer. In many breweries, it still is true that the brewmaster's skills have been handed down from generation to generation.

While science may not have overtaken all aspects of the brewing art, it rules the quality control operations of the brewery itself (although the Milwaukee taste test is still the single most important check on the brewery's quality performance). Science is evident everywhere in quality control, from the chemistry involved to the statistical sampling. The training for the quality assurance department can thus be long and rigorous.

Science and art are mixed in the plant's maintenance activities, which are an important and prestigious activity. The capital intensity of the process dictates heavy reliance on maintenance and the ability to troubleshoot problems quickly so as not to waste time and output needlessly. Only with the line jobs in packaging does routine best characterize the process. Still, switching from canning to bottling to kegging provides a measure of diversity in the job from day to day.

DEMANDS OF THE PROCESS ON MANAGEMENT

Schlitz's Syracuse brewery and International Paper's Androscoggin Mill place many of the same kinds of demands on management. The high degree of capital intensity they both share dictate concern for (1) selection of the proper technology and (2) the balancing of capacities in all segments of the process. Over time, technological advance has dictated numerous advances in the process itself (centrifuges, stainless steel tanks, panels of process controls) and in the scale of the process (larger tanks than ever before). The design, choice, and matching of equipment are critical decisions for a brewer like Schlitz.

Scheduling production, while a nontrivial matter, is not as critical to a brewery's success as it is to a job shop. As important, or even more so, as the positioning of orders within any work shift or within any week's production is the accurate forecasting of demand. A Schlitz wholesaler who is out of a particular beer or package risks that the consumer will merely choose a different brand. It is up to the brewery to track sales reliably and to forecast sales, especially seasonal sales, accurately.

Good forecasting also plays a significant role in managing suppliers' deliveries and inventories (e.g., cans, bottles) well. Since individual breweries do not negotiate price, delivery becomes the key aspect of brewery-supplier contact.

QUESTIONS

1. Describe briefly the two main processes involved in a brewery. What are some of the implications of these processes for quality control?

2. What did Schlitz consider to be the elements of the satisfactory production plan and the requirements for good package planning? What particular elements of Schlitz's hybrid process planning might be applicable to the hybrid process in general? Why?

3. The Schlitz brewery in Syracuse shipped 90 percent of all acknowledged orders on time. In your opinion and from the information supplied, what were the main factors contributing to this record?

4. How does the composition of the brewery workforce differ from the composition of the Jung Products workforce? In what ways are they similar?

5. What similarities are there between the Schlitz brewery operation and the Androscoggin Mill operation? What dissimilarities?

6. Compare and contrast the demands of the process on Schlitz workers and management with the demands on the same groups in two other processes you have studied.

SITUATION FOR STUDY

COUHYDE GELATIN COMPANY

Thomas Brewer is the plant manager for Couhyde Gelatin Company, maker of powdered gelatins for human consumption. The main component of gelatin is collagen, a fibrous substance that is mostly protein. Steerhide, a major source of collagen, is the main ingredient in the gelatin powder produced at Couhyde's Kansas City, Kansas, plant.

Figure 4-A shows the process that Couhyde uses to produce its gelatin. First, the steerhides are treated (acid is added to remove the hair, then neutralized), weighed, and put into storage. Enough steerhide is treated at one time to provide two days' worth of production. The hides are then stored for about two weeks so that they begin to "break

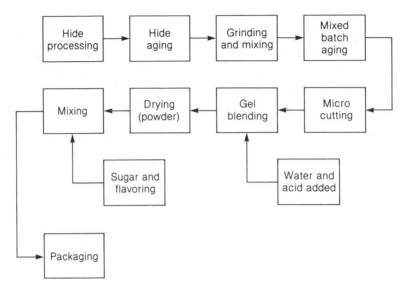

FIGURE 4-A   The production process at Couhyde Gelatin Company.

down" and can be blended with the other ingredients. This storage is called "aging."

Once several batches of steerhides (1500 kilograms each) have aged properly, enough batches are ground (to about the consistency of hamburger) to run one week's production. These mixed batches (5500 kilograms each) are then aged again for a few days before they are mixed into a gel blend (8000 kilograms, of which about half is water). One gel blend is enough for one day's production of gelatin.

Once mixed and aged, the mixed batch undergoes micro cutting, which cuts the material into very small pieces. It then is mixed with water and an acid to form the gel blend. Next the gel blend is forced through a dryer to make it a powder. Under proper conditions, the powder can be stored almost indefinitely, until needed for final production.

Final production consists of two stages. First, the powder is mixed with sugar and a powdered flavoring (unless the final product is to be an unflavored gelatin); second, the product is measured and packaged. Final production, although continuous, is done to customer order. All stages in the process

are highly mechanized and workers are needed only to monitor it.

Tom feels that quality control at Couhyde can be adequately handled by three types of highly trained process control workers: solutions technicians, powder technicians, and line technicians. The solutions technician is responsible for the proper acid balance, salts, density, percent of solids, and the like of the gel blend. The powder technician's main responsibility is proper mixing of the final product—i.e., the proper proportion of powder, sugar, and flavoring. The line technician is responsible for packaging.

Tom is wondering how he should schedule production at the various stages in the process, including the scheduling of labor and machines. In addition, he is uncertain how much inventory should be carried, and in what form. He feels he could begin to answer his concerns about scheduling and inventory control by (1) analyzing the characteristics of the process and (2) asking himself what aspects of the process would help him in scheduling production and controlling inventories and which ones would hinder him.

5

A MACHINE-PACED LINE FLOW PROCESS

General Motors Corporation, GM Assembly Division
Tarrytown, New York

The Tarrytown plant of the GM Assembly Division (GMAD), situated on the Hudson River just north of New York City, was one of the oldest of the 18 domestic assembly plants operated by the GM Assembly Division. The plant was huge, stretching over 97 acres with 2,250,000 square feet of space under roof. About 3700 production workers and 500 salaried workers were employed on two production shifts. The plants assembled cars with Body Type X—Chevrolet Nova, Pontiac Phoe-

nix, and Buick Skylark—and delivered truckloads of these cars to over 5000 auto dealers in the United States.

The Tarrytown plant was not the only one to assemble cars with Body Type X; a sister plant in Willow Run, Michigan, also assembled the Nova, Phoenix, and Omega. Either plant, however, could deliver cars to any dealer in the country. There was no specific geographic territory to which each plant was assigned.

PART ONE

PROCESS DESCRIPTION

HOW A CAR WAS ASSEMBLED: A SIMPLIFIED DESCRIPTION

The production process at GMAD-Tarrytown was a classic but modern example of the moving assembly line so closely associated with Henry Ford and the Model T. The essence of the process was to build up the car bit by bit by having workers perform the same tasks on each car as it moved through their work stations on a conveyor system. Any automobile could be viewed as the marriage

of two large subassemblies: one for the body (everything from the windshield on back) and one for the chassis (everything in front of the windshield) and the undercarriage. The assembly plant was organized to build up the body and the chassis separately, to "marry" them at the "body drop," and then to finish the car's assembly and inspection. Each of the body and chassis lines was fed by

Power trains move along the assembly line to meet the chassis frame. *(Courtesy of General Motors Corporation)*

smaller subassembly lines, so that pictorially the process resembled a tree with two main branches and smaller branches shooting off from them. Figure 5-1 provides just such a rough picture of the entire process. (A more detailed version would require more space and explanation than is merited.)

The entire line was composed of about 1050 work stations, and automobiles passed through each work station at an average rate of one per minute. A work station consisted of (1) a worker or maybe two, one on either side of the line, (2) some space in which to work, (3) equipment specific to the job, and (4) in many stations, some racks or bins stocked with parts to be assembled onto the car. Naturally, a great deal of variety existed from one work station to another. For example, a work station in the paint shop might be enclosed in a spray booth so that paint could be applied through hoses. An inspection station would have intense lights and raised platforms so that the inspectors could easily identify any flaws and mark them for

correction. In the chassis area there were pits where workers could secure the body to the frame and make other adjustments to the cars moving along above them. About the only thing that was consistent across work stations was that the work averaged about a minute per car.

For some models and options, however, a worker might have to take somewhat over a minute. This deviation was termed being "overcycled." Naturally, a worker could not be continually overcycled without falling behind the pace of the line. To keep up, overcycled jobs had to be quickly balanced off by undercycled jobs for the workers affected. Given the existence of overcycled jobs, then, the sequencing of cars along the line so as to provide a balance of overcycled and undercycled work was an important endeavor.

Much of the overcycled work occurred along the hard and soft trim lines (see Figure 5-1), where many of the multitude of options were added to the car. Workers were advised what options to in-

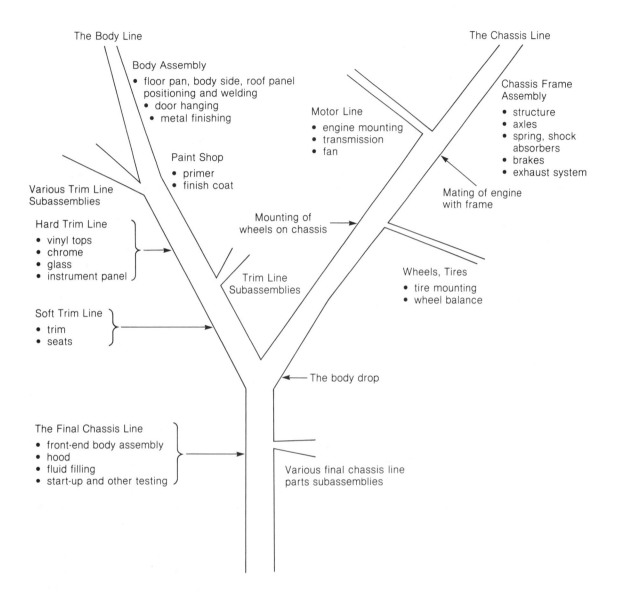

FIGURE 5-1 A rough diagram of automobile assembly.

clude on any car by reading the "broadcast," an instruction sheet attached to the right front door of the car. The broadcast was the primary information by which the worker could determine what part or component was to be placed on that particular vehicle.

LOADING THE PLANT

PLANNING PRODUCTION

Because cars and the parts to make them were both expensive and bulky, considerable resources were spent to limit inventories at the plant. No finished goods inventories were kept; all of the cars assembled were trucked to individual dealers within a short time after coming off the production line. Therefore, all the cars destined for a particular dealer had to be scheduled for completion at roughly the same time to avoid significant delays of truck trailers and finished cars.

Furthermore, all of the cars produced were to dealer order as to make, model, color, and options. GMAD-Tarrytown, on its own, was not permitted to ship any dealer a car that the dealer had not ordered. Roughly 30 to 50 percent of a dealer's order represented cars that were already sold to particular customers. The remainder represented the dealer's speculation as to what the dealership would be able to sell. Such production to order, given the wide range of options permitted in any car, placed tremendous demands on the plant's materials function to schedule the proper mix of cars through the line and to secure enough of the proper parts to fill the order.

The scheduling and materials procurement functions were characterized by successive tiers of orders and due dates representing ever more precise refinement. At the broadest level, the corporate office in Detroit would determine a rough production schedule for the year. This schedule would serve as a target for the company's outside suppliers and for its own internal supply groups (e.g., Fisher Body plants, engine plants, transmission plants). As dealer orders came in, the schedule would become increasingly firm. Two major order systems regulated the supplies coming to the plant:

1. *Fisher Body system.* This system applied to parts with long lead times, such as metal body parts determining make and model and trim items for the numerous options. In this system, orders for assembly 5 weeks away were given to the supplier, with the latest 3 weeks being frozen. That is, starting with only 3 weeks to go before assembly, no changes to the prevailing order were accepted.

2. *GMAD Central Office system.* This system ap-

plied mainly to chassis items (e.g., engines, transmissions), many mechanical parts, and standard features such as air conditioning, radios, and cruise controls. These items were standard enough that only 5 days of frozen orders were necessary, although orders were typically placed long before that time.

For GMAD-Tarrytown's own scheduling, on any day it was known what cars would be assembled over the next 10 days, although the firm schedule of which cars would be assembled on which specific days was known with certainty only 5 days in advance. The freedom to schedule precisely only 5 days out of 10 days of orders was an important one, since the plant could not assemble just any assortment of Novas, Phoenixes, or Skylarks. The line was flexible in handling many make/model and option variations, but there were certain limitations. Only so many vinyl tops or air conditioning units, for example, could be produced in an hour without causing imbalance in the system. Thus, restrictions were imposed on what would be assembled during any shift.

The need for a congenial mix of makes, models, and options also applied to the car-by-car assembly schedule during any shift. Vinyl tops, air conditioning units, and other options were typically spread out as evenly as possible along the line so that no worker experienced a string of overcycle conditions. For similar reasons, the line generally alternated four-door and two-door models. However, paint colors were bunched as much as possible since color did not affect worker cycle times adversely. In fact, the bunching facilitated worker effort and quality control.

The car-by-car assembly schedule—the "manifest"—was known about 7 to 8 hours in advance of any shift. The trim and chassis lines operated in exact synchronization to this manifest. The body shop schedule could be slightly different in sequence from the manifest, but it matched the model/make/color composition of the shift's manifest.

High up on the body line, spot welding continues forming the body. *(Courtesy of General Motors Corporation)*

PURCHASING AND RAW MATERIALS INVENTORY AND CONTROL

There were about 5500 active parts and components to be assembled into the automobiles at the Tarrytown plant. Most of these parts and components, except for some tires and batteries, were purchased by GMAD's Central Office. These purchases were generally on long-term contract; some, of course, came from GM divisions that acted as suppliers to the assembly plants.

To avoid massive raw materials inventories, the Tarrytown plant scheduled the delivery of raw materials very tightly. It was essential that suppliers be reliable in their deliveries. For most parts, only between 2 and 5 days of production were kept in inventory at the plant, with 3 days being typical. For some large parts, like car roofs, only 1 day's production was inventoried. Even small items like screws were stocked for only 15 days. How many days of inventory were held depended on (1) volume (the more regular its use, the tighter it was

scheduled), (2) dollar value (the higher the value, the tighter the schedule), (3) physical size (the larger the part, the tighter the schedule), and (4) transportation reliability (the less reliable the service or the worse the weather (e.g., winter), the greater the days of inventory held). GMAD-Tarrytown unloaded 75 railroad cars and 55 truck trailers a day.

With raw materials deliveries scheduled so tightly, it was necessary to monitor the entire supplier network constantly. Failure to have on hand a key part (e.g., a side or roof panel) could shut down the plant. A constant vigil was kept on the number and whereabouts of all supplies coming to the plant. Every day a "critical list" of parts that might turn up short (out of stock) over the next 2 days was developed. The GMAD Central Office was notified, and ways to expedite the parts were sought. Usually, expediting involved securing the part from either the supplier or the GMAD sister plant in Willow Run, Michigan, and switching delivery to a faster (and generally more expensive) form of transportation. But even a chartered plane was cheap if the alternative was shutting down the plant. It was typical for the plant to run out of only three or fewer kinds of parts in a week; except at the very end of the model year, the plant was never short a part for more than a day. Any cars short a part were not shipped but waited for the expedited part and were then completed.

The monitoring of materials involved not only the materials department at Tarrytown (i.e., staff tracking shipments, materials unloading and handling people) but the line workers and their supervisors as well.

CONTROLLING THE OPERATION

While the plant did not have much leeway in the purchase of materials or the mix of makes, models, and options it was to assemble, it did have considerable leeway in the design and management of the assembly line itself. Key roles in this effort were played by the industrial engineering staff, the plant engineering staff, and the quality control group.

INDUSTRIAL ENGINEERING

The industrial engineering department was charged with (1) translating the engineering design of the automobile into a step-by-step procedure for assembling it; (2) laying out the line, work stations along the line, and any production assists (e.g., equipment, fixtures) for the work station; (3) assigning work to each worker on the line and measuring that work so that it was appropriate; (4) establishing the authorized level of the workforce and monitoring that level; and (5) devising methods improvements or other ways to lower costs and/or increase productivity.

The department was continually involved in assessing the functioning of the line. This was a routine commitment, however.

As mentioned earlier, the line was designed in such a way that all workers averaged about a minute's worth of work on each car. Given any major model changes, the line would have to be thoroughly redesigned so that workers, assigned possibly very different work tasks from what they were used to, still had only about a minute's work each on every car. This was what line rebalance was about.

In greater detail, the rebalance of the line followed a number of stages:

1. Given the car's engineering and design, the industrial engineer described what had to be done to assemble the car. This description involved painstaking detail. For example, one could not simply specify "mount headlight" since that task may take either shorter or longer than the desired cycle time. Mounting the headlight would involve a number of separate actions, which might include walking 5 feet to supply bins, reaching for headlight and screws, walking back to the line, positioning headlight in socket, and using a power screwdriver to screw in four mounting screws.

2. Each of these separate actions (job elements) was assigned a time. These times were primarily determined by reference to standard time data established by GMAD, although some times were determined by special stopwatch studies where an engineer would time a worker performing the task. The standard time data typically were derived from numerous stopwatch studies, films of workers, and other sampling studies of specific worker tasks.

3. Once times were assigned to specific elements, an industrial engineer would review them with the relevant supervisor on the production line to determine whether they were reasonable. Changes would then be made.

Body surface is sanded and prepared for paint finish before the trim line subassemblies. *(Courtesy of General Motors Corporation)*

4. Once some agreement was reached, the task, its elements, element time estimates, and whether the task was performed on all cars or only a few were placed in computer-readable form. A computer program then planned the production schedule. It tried to balance workloads among the workers such as by taking job elements from one worker and placing them with another or otherwise shifting assignments to distribute the work properly.

5. Generally, the initial computer schedule left some workers with either too much or too little to do. What was to be avoided was putting workers in an overcycled condition where they would consistently have too much work to perform for the time cycle decided on. If an imbalance in the line was serious and could not be remedied easily, the task could sometimes be taken off the main line and performed as a separate activity. This course of action was considered a last resort, however.

On the basis of the computer run, tasks and times were adjusted and a subsequent computer run made. This run was then studied for reasonableness and again adjustments were made. Numerous iterations of this adjustment/rerun process were generally performed before the line was satisfactorily balanced, at least on paper.

6. The "paper" balance of the line was then ready for trial on the factory floor. The danger was that the predicted and actual times would not mesh. If this in fact occurred, the first thought was to help the worker improve the time, either by changing the layout of the work station, adding fixtures or other equipment, or changing methods. Such action was usually sufficient, but if need be another operator could be added or a modest rebalance of the line effected.

PLANT ENGINEERING

The plant engineering department directed all the construction, maintenance, and repair of the Tarrytown site's land, buildings, and equipment (except tooling, which was dealt with separately). All of the plant's requests for capital appropriations originated with plant engineering.

Plant engineering was constantly on the alert for technological improvement, such as the recent introduction of minicomputers to the paint line and to wheel assembly. The department also sought to anticipate process changes that might be developed over the next 5 years or that might be forced on the company by competition or by the government. Keeping the process as flexible as possible was a strived-for goal. Maintaining this technological momentum was a continual management concern and called for many seminars both outside and inside the plant and many personnel development and apprentice programs.

QUALITY CONTROL

At GMAD-Tarrytown quality was religion. Everywhere, banners and signs (many worker-initiated) exhorted the workforce to maintain the plant's enviable reputation within the corporation for product quality (i.e., the best warranty record in the country). While workers and supervisors could almost take for granted that materials would always be available, quality was the one feature of the product that no one could take for granted.

The quality control department coordinated three distinct functions: inspection, reliability, and audit.

1. Inspection referred to those work stations spaced throughout the line where inspectors checked features of every car produced. Often, these inspectors would mark on both car and paper what corrective work ought to be done further down the line. Although situated in the paint shop or the chassis line or wherever, the inspectors were not under the same supervision as the production personnel but rather reported to their own supervisor. Some of the inspection stations were mandated by Detroit, but the plant always added other inspections to the minimum.

   Checking incoming materials was still another aspect of the plant's inspection procedures.

2. The reliability group inspected the work of the inspectors as well as the work of the production workforce to determine whether both were actually doing what they said they were doing. The group was also responsible for implementing any engineering changes that Detroit specified for the car.

3. Five cars every shift (1 percent of production), selected at random, were subjected to a thoroughgoing audit that graded all aspects of the car's assembly and performance (body shop,

paint, chassis frame, motor line, chassis pit, computer torque, hard trim, soft trim, final chassis, electrical, water test, and road test). A 145-point scoring system was used, with various demerits knocking from 1 to 20 points off the perfect score. A 135-point score characterized a quality car and this was the sought for, and at Tarrytown, the achieved goal. Every so often, unannounced, a quality team from Detroit would perform their own audit of 15 cars. This procedure served as a check on the plant's daily audit.

GMAD-Tarrytown's goal, of course, was to build in quality rather than to inspect it in.

THE WORKFORCE AND THE PERSONNEL DEPARTMENT

The plant's nonsupervisory personnel were paid by the hour worked, hence the appellation hourly employees. The plant was currently operating two shifts of production with an hour of scheduled overtime each shift, a total of 18 hours of production a day. The first shift began at 6 A.M. and lasted until 3:30 P.M. with a half-hour for lunch. The second shift began at 4:30 P.M. and ended at 2 A.M. In addition, production was being scheduled for about every other Saturday.

The hourly employees were represented by the United Auto Workers. The bulk of the agreement between GM management and the plant's workers was spelled out in a nearly 400-page national agreement covering a wide range of topics including wage payments, fringe benefits, seniority, grievance procedures, overtime, layoffs, health and safety, production standard procedures, and numerous other topics. There was also a smaller (less than 100 pages), additional agreement between the local UAW organization and GMAD-Tarrytown's management. This separate agreement provided detailed information on wages, layoff procedures, health and safety measures, and the like.

Plant relations with the union were extremely cordial and constructive, fostered by daily dialogue between the parties and a great deal of mutual respect. Almost all worker complaints (e.g., leaky roof, safety problem, worker discharge) were resolved verbally without recourse to the grievance procedure. Only 10 to 15 grievances were formally filed in any week for the plant's 3700 hourly employees; 95 percent of these were resolved at the first of the four steps of the grievance procedure. Only three or four grievances in an entire year would reach the final (arbitration) level.

The plant's personnel department was an essential aspect of plant management. Not only did the personnel department oversee labor relations with the UAW, but it was also charged with training responsibilities (e.g., new models, new safety regulations and programs) and with seeking improvements in the "quality of work life," as it has come to be known. Personnel managers were constantly exploring new ways for the hourly employee to become more involved in the process itself even if it meant changes in managerial style at the plant. In addition, the personnel department supervised plant safety and security and hiring practices.

GMAD-Tarrytown offered the hourly employee a number of possibilities for advancement and work preference, from the simple movement from one shift to another to transfers between departments and promotions to higher pay classifications. Hourly employees could also move up to management by becoming supervisors.

SUPERVISION

Work on the line was directly overseen by first line supervisors. Typically, the supervisor was directly responsible for about 25 workers on a shift. He was thoroughly familiar with all aspects of work

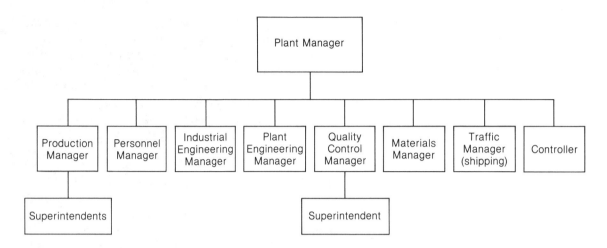

FIGURE 5-2 Organization chart for the GM Assembly Division, Tarrytown.

within his section of the line and with what workers could or could not be expected to do, largely because he had in many instances once been one of them. At the start of the shift, the supervisor's immediate concern was manning the production line, making a count of absentees and being sure that the line was fully manned. So-called relief workers were always present and were available during the first hour of shift start-up to fill in along the line. After that, the relief workers would spell others on the line, the relief worker being trained for a variety of jobs. All workers received 23 minutes personal relief in each of the first and second halves of their 8-hour shift.

Once the manning of the line was assured, the supervisor spent much of the remainder of the shift in two activities: (1) troubleshooting any problems on the line (e.g., equipment malfunctions, impending part shortages, defective materials) and (2) checking quality. Very little of the supervisor's time was spent in his office. For most of the shift, the supervisor would walk the line, talking with the line's workers, trying to solve any problems they might have, and maintaining quality in production.

Four or five supervisors would in turn report to a general supervisor, and the general supervisors would report to one of five superintendents for either the body shop, the paint shop, the soft trim line, the hard trim line, or the chassis line. In addition, the quality control department had its own superintendent. In most cases the superintendent reported to the production manager (see the organization chart in Figure 5-2).

The superintendent's job included many aspects of the first line supervisor's plus other responsibilities. The superintendent was concerned primarily with quality and safety but also spent considerable time and effort on cost control, human relations, and housekeeping chores. Some of his tasks were everyday (e.g., meeting with union committeemen, checking absenteeism, conferring with other superintendents), but there were always special plans or meetings and unexpected problems on the line to overcome.

For most supervisors, actually putting the car together posed no headaches. Most of the challenge of the job centered on people: recognizing their achievements and integrity and trying to solve their problems, both on and off the job.

PART TWO

DISCUSSION

The GM Assembly Division is in no way responsible for the following views and presentation. They remain solely the responsibility of the author.

THE FLOW OF THE PROCESS AND OF INFORMATION

The process flow in a factory such as GMAD-Tarrytown is among the most complex one can run across. A blizzard of different tasks, equipment, and skills are required to assemble an automobile. Yet the process flow can be diagramed in a very straightforward way. Figure 5-1 represents a rough-cut process flow diagram. A more detailed version would consist of a recounting of the 1050 work stations along the production line; it is these work stations through which every car passes. Thus, compared to a job shop or a batch flow process, the classic assembly line has a very well-defined process flow.

With a process as complex and as closely scheduled as an automobile assembly plant, it is not surprising that the information flow is complex as well. Figure 5-3 portrays an information flow diagram for GMAD-Tarrytown. While the information flow is essentially one-way, from the top down, the need to track materials both inside and outside the plant implies a great deal of communication between workers and management in the

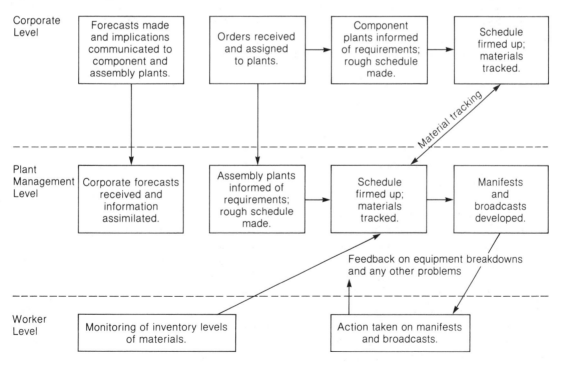

FIGURE 5-3   An information flow diagram for the GM Assembly Division, Tarrytown.

plant and between the plant, corporate level managers, and outside suppliers.

CAPACITY

The notion of what capacity is in a machine-paced line flow process like GMAD-Tarrytown is as clear as it ever gets. At GMAD-Tarrytown, one car rolls off the end of the production line every minute. Everything in the process is geared to making that happen. It is as though the process were a huge on-off switch: when it is on, one car a minute is produced; otherwise, nothing is produced.

Likewise, the notion of capacity utilization is relatively unambiguous. When the plant is open, capacity utilization is 100 percent. Otherwise, it is zero. Simply by tallying the hours the plant actually runs and dividing it by a count of hours the plant could be open gives an idea of what capacity utilization is. How many hours the plant could be open is subject to some debate, however. For example, it may be contrary to corporate policy to schedule a third shift of production, and so a capacity utilization measure should be based on two shifts only. Another problem may lie in the determination of how much overtime is the maximum the plant could schedule without antagonizing workers. Is it an hour a day? Two hours a day? Every Saturday? Questions like these make a capacity utilization calculation fuzzy, but it is clear how much the process is capable of producing when it is up and running.

In a machine-paced line flow process, capacity in the short run is severely constrained; it can be modified only by scheduling more or fewer hours. In the medium run, however, capacity can be substantially modified (without huge, new additions of plant and equipment) by adjusting the balance of the production line. Thus, while the machine-paced line flow process cannot modulate its capacity smoothly, as can occur in job shops and batch flow processes, capacity can be adjusted in abrupt steps and by varying amounts. This concept of line balance is worth exploring.

❋ ASIDE ❋

LINE BALANCE

As this description of the line flow process has indicated, the balance of tasks along the line is an important consideration. When products and/or desired rates of production change, the line must be rebalanced. The strength of a line flow process lies in the specialization of labor: a complex manufacturing assignment is split into small pieces, and a worker (any worker) is more adept at doing a few tasks repeatedly than many tasks intermittently. The observation that the total labor content of a product can be reduced by dividing up the process rather than having workers responsible for manufacturing the entire product was made famous by Adam Smith, the father of modern economics. In his *Inquiry into the Nature and Causes of the Wealth of Nations* (1776), Smith cites the fabrication of pins, noting that pin production was greatly increased by specializing labor.

The keys then to line balance are (1) breaking down a complex product and process into its component pieces and tasks and (2) juggling the coordination of those pieces and tasks so that the process is smooth and no bottlenecks are built into it.

The first of these keys to line balance is greatly aided by a precedence diagram, which portrays the individual elements that make up the fabrication and/or assembly of a product and the order they must logically or technologically follow. Figure 5-4

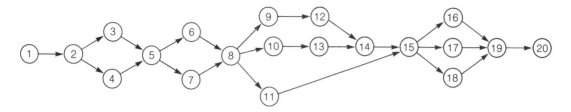

FIGURE 5-4   A sample precedence diagram for a line flow process.

is an example of a precedence diagram; Table 5-1 lists the time estimates for accomplishing each task (job element). These job elements are merely an example (they are not derived from General Motors data), but they are indicative of many different kinds of line flow activities.

Our assignment is to use the information in Figure 5-4 and Table 5-1 to develop a line flow process capable of turning out 300 units of the product in an 8-hour day. Here is one possible means of developing the process.

1. By adding up the job element times in Table 5-1, we know that 14.99 minutes are required to assemble the product.

2. The desired number of units per day is 300, and so 4497 (14.99 × 300) minutes of production are needed in any one day to produce the desired daily output.

3. Assuming that a worker puts in an 8-hour day with two 15-minute breaks, 450 minutes of production are available from each worker. Dividing the total production time (4497 minutes) by the available minutes per day per worker (450 minutes per worker) suggests that 10 workers are needed to produce 300 units each day.

4. With 10 workers, the 14.99 minutes needed to assemble the product can be divided into 10 segments of 1.5 minutes each. That is, the assembly process can be viewed roughly as a 10 station assembly line with each worker putting in 1.5 minutes per unit. Every 1.5 minutes another unit of the product can be expected to come off the line. This figure (1.5 minutes) is sometimes termed the "control cycle."

5. With the length of the control cycle established, developing the line involves picking 10

TABLE 5-1   Job Elements and Estimated Times for the Process Diagramed in Figure 5-4

JOB ELEMENT	ESTIMATED TIME (minutes)	JOB ELEMENT	ESTIMATED TIME (minutes)
1	0.65	11	1.10
2	0.11	12	1.75
3	0.37	13	0.94
4	0.75	14	0.62
5	0.10	15	0.45
6	0.58	16	0.81
7	0.25	17	0.87
8	1.01	18	1.60
9	1.17	19	0.60
10	0.43	20	0.83

TABLE 5-2   A Suggested Grouping of Job Elements into Work Stations

WORK STATION	JOB ELEMENTS	TOTAL TIME/UNIT (minutes)	BALANCE DELAY (minutes)
1	1,2,4	1.51	−0.01
2	3,5,6,7	1.30	0.20
3	8,10	1.44	0.06
4	9,12	1.46	0.04
5	9,12	1.46	0.04
6	13,14	1.56	−0.06
7	11	1.10	0.40
8	15,17	1.32	0.18
9	16,18	1.21	0.29
10	16,18	1.21	0.29
11	19,20	1.43	0.07

sets of job elements from Table 5-1 so that each of their sums totals 1.5 minutes. In this picking process, the precedence relationships portrayed in Figure 5-4 must also be adhered to.

Table 5-2 gives a suggested grouping of job elements into work stations. It prompts several observations:

1. One more work station than the initial determination of 10 had to be assigned. Because the estimated times for the various job elements differed widely from the control cycle time, they could not be easily grouped together to sum to it.

   Naturally, then, some inefficiency is introduced to the line. It was hoped that 10 stations, each with a cycle time of 1.5 minutes, could be assigned—a near-perfect match of 15 minutes of worker time allocated to assemble a product estimated at 14.99 minutes of labor input. Instead, 16.50 minutes of worker time (11 stations × 1.5 minutes per station) have to be allocated. With every unit produced, about 1.5 minutes are extraneous—a loss of about 10 percent relative to a perfect grouping of job elements to match the control cycle.

2. Some work stations are more out-of-kilter than others. The "balance delay" column in Table

5-2 is the measure of how the total estimated time for the elements comprising each work station differs from the control cycle. As is readily seen, two work stations (1 and 6) have estimated times in excess of the control cycle. Several other work stations, notably 7, 9, and 10, have slight rest periods built into their work cycles; that is, workers at these stations ought to be able to complete their tasks well before 1.5 minutes go by.

What can be done about such bottlenecks and slack stations? In practice, companies often try to devise work aids or other assistance to lessen the impact of any bottleneck. Both bottlenecks or significant balance delays may trigger a review of the steps in manufacture and/or the product design itself. This review may lead to a new set of job elements and/or times with advantages for the balance of the line.

3. This particular assignment of work stations deliberately places four workers "overcycle." Stations 4, 5, 9, and 10 have people working on every other unit instead of every unit that passes down the line. Had not two workers been placed on job elements 12 and 18, significant bottlenecks would have been encountered.

This example of assembly line balance is obviously simpler and more mechanical than that faced by a company like General Motors. A number of refinements and caveats to line balancing will be noted here.

ACCURACY OF TIME ESTIMATES*

Proper line balance depends on accurate estimates of the time it will take to perform each of the job elements that the entire assembly process can be broken into. The time estimates themselves are usually derived from actual observation of the task itself or something very similar. The observation, commonly called a time-and-motion study, can occur in any of a variety of ways; often industrial engineers will use more than one to establish a time standard:

- *Stopwatch studies.* A traditional but less and less popular means of estimating time standards is to stand by a worker who is performing a task and take stopwatch readings of how long it takes him or her to accomplish the task. As one might expect, the presence of the industrial engineer may cause the worker to slack off somewhat, casting doubts on the estimate. Sometimes this inaccuracy is avoided by having the industrial engineer stand near one worker but actually monitor another worker at a distance. Even this bit of sneakery has not remedied all the problems associated with stopwatch studies, which remain a costly way of setting time standards.

- *Films and video tapes.* A less obtrusive way of estimating time standards is to film workers in action over an extended period of time and then take time measurements from the film itself. This has become an increasingly popular way to estimate time standards; it reduces the cost and worker-influence problems of stopwatch studies.

- *Work sampling.* Another, and less expensive, way to determine at least the relative times

spent performing various tasks is to take a series of random "snapshots" of a task rather than a "full-length film." If, for example, in every 100 random looks at a particular task, 40 observe a particular action, then we can infer that 40 percent of the cycle time is spent performing that task. This technique is generally termed "work sampling."

- *Task decomposition.* Since so much information has been accumulated on the time it takes to perform so many bodily movements, sometimes time estimates can be pieced together strictly by breaking the task into its component movements and using stock time estimates for each movement. Summing these individual times is one way to estimate the time standard for a radically new job element, which can then be checked by any of the previous three observational methods.

No matter how individual job element time standards are developed, it is dangerous to expect that adding more than a few together will generate accurate time totals. Table 5-1's list of 20 job elements totals 14.99 minutes. It is foolish to expect that a single worker could actually work through all 20 steps in 15 minutes, let alone maintain that pace throughout a workday. The strength of a line flow process, as mentioned above, lies in the specialization of labor to a limited number of tasks; the corresponding time standards can be considered accurate only when relatively few job elements are strung together. The rebalance of any line flow process always entails reevaluations of new tasks and/or regroupings of elements, since so many time variations can be introduced to combinations of job elements and the materials handling and positioning requirements that accompany them.

NON–TIME-RELATED ASPECTS OF LINE FLOW PROCESS LAYOUT

The 20-element example of line balancing introduced above does not assign any special characteris-

---

*More on this topic can be found in Chapter 9.

tics to any of the job elements listed. In that sense the exercise was mechanical. Often, however, in many line balance situations attention has to be focused on some special features of the process that may constrain the composition of work stations in particular ways. Among these special features can be included:

- Materials handling requirements
- Space constraints within the factory that may force the line into a particular shape
- Special equipment needs
- Product bulkiness or weight, requiring two or more workers to work together
- Segregation of worker skill levels

Any of these features can in themselves define a work station, quite apart from the simple grouping of job elements according to time estimates alone.

PROCEDURES FOR GROUPING JOB ELEMENTS

The 20-element example above was simple enough that we can trust a little trial-and-error in selecting the composition of the line's work stations. In more complex situations, however, more formal rules can sometimes be helpful in assigning job elements to specific work stations. Unfortunately, no one means of assigning elements to stations—not even very sophisticated computer techniques—can guarantee a minimum degree of balance delay and inefficiency. It seems that there will always be a role for common sense in line balancing.

At any rate, some procedures have proved helpful in developing candidate line balances:

- Assigning the longest time estimates first
- Assigning first the elements that have the most other elements following them

In addition, there are both heuristic and com-puter-based methods of generating candidate assembly line balances.[1] It bears repeating that none of the methods is certain to generate an optimum line balance by themselves.

CYCLE TIME ALLOWANCES

Some procedures for line balancing, though by no means all, factor in special allowances for fatigue. These allowances lengthen the cycle time. The time standards for individual tasks, under this system, have no slack of any kind built into them, and so it would be inappropriate to expect that they could apply for a full day's work load. Special allowances for fatigue then have to be added to make the computed cycle time realistic. Other line balance procedures try to establish sustainable time standards from the beginning, and so allowances need not be introduced.

SPEED VERSUS BALANCE DELAY

As has been mentioned repeatedly, the appeal of a line flow process lies in its ability to reduce the labor time in a product's manufacture by breaking down the fabrication/assembly process into pieces that can be done rapidly and repeatedly by operators along the line. Generally speaking, the smaller the job content of a work station, the more efficient labor can be. What prevents us from breaking tasks into single job elements? Apart from concern for the mind-numbing character of such jobs, the problem of balance delay militates against such an atomistic approach to line balance. Individual job elements will vary greatly; the greater the variance, the more apt that some combination of job elements will have to occur to prevent high levels of balance delay all down the line. Thus line flow processes with cycle times that are combinations of job elements are typically more efficient than ones with minimum cycle times.

*

A RETURN TO THE PROCESS DISCUSSION: DEMANDS ON THE WORKFORCE

A machine-paced assembly line places special demands on a worker. In a sense, the worker is a "slave to the iron monster," which is the moving assembly line. He cannot simply decide to take a break from his work and wander about chatting with co-workers. (But then neither can the second-grade teacher.) Moreover, the assembly line worker must perform the same, fairly routine task repeatedly throughout the workday. Many people view that as monotonous or degrading or worse.

But not all people hold to that view and therein lies a fundamental point about assembly lines and assembly line workers. Happily, people are very different from one another in tolerances for certain activities (e.g., enduring long car trips) and in expectations about their jobs. One class of personality savors proximity to power and influence and will forgo higher salaries to do so (e.g., many staff workers on Capitol Hill), while another will sacrifice salary for considerable freedom of schedule and the chance to be "their own boss" (e.g., many college professors). If the assembly line worker can be typed in this way at all, it is that he has forgone diversity in his job for relatively high wages and freedom from the anxiety many people suffer when they are confronted with decision making. For many people, that is not a bad trade to make.

Nevertheless, despite the sorting out of personalities to job types that goes on continuously in our economy, progressive companies like General Motors are constantly searching for ways to improve the quality of work life for their workers. In fact, GMAD-Tarrytown is a classic example of how management concern for the quality of work life turned around a worsening factory situation. Robert H. Guest, writing in the *Harvard Business Review*, tells the story of how GMAD-Tarrytown, in the space of 7 years (1970–77), moved from "one

of the poorest labor relations and production records in GM" to its current, enviable position as one of the better run sites in the company.

In the late 1960s and early 1970s, the Tarrytown plant suffered from much absenteeism and labor turnover. Operating costs were high. Frustration, fear, and mistrust characterized the relationship between management and labor. At certain times, as many as 2000 labor grievances were on the docket. As one manager puts it, "Management was always in a defensive posture. We were instructed to go by the book, and we played by the book. The way we solved problems was to use our authority and impose discipline." The plant general superintendent acknowledges in retrospect, "For reasons we thought valid, we were very secretive in letting the union and the workers know about changes to be introduced or new programs coming down the pike."

Union officers and committeemen battled constantly with management. As one union officer describes it, "We were always trying to solve yesterday's problems. There was no trust and everybody was putting out fires. The company's attitude was to employ a stupid robot with hands and no face." The union committee chairman describes the situation the way he saw it: "When I walked in each morning I was out to get the personnel director, the committeeman was shooting for the foreman, and the zone committeeman was shooting for the general foreman. Every time a foreman notified a worker that there would be a job change, it resulted in an instant '78 (work standards grievance). It was not unusual to have a hundred '78s hanging fire, more than 300 discipline cases, and many others."[2]

How was the situation at GMAD-Tarrytown turned around? The process was long and complex, and indeed is still going on. Guest refers, however, to several events and changes of heart:

1. In 1971 a plant manager decided to work with rather than against the union on what he recognized as important joint concerns.

2. Shortly after that products in the plant changed, and management was willing to entertain ideas from the workforce in relocating the hard and soft trim lines within the factory and in redesigning their layouts and methods. The workers made hundreds of worthwhile suggestions, many of which management adopted.

3. In 1973 the plant endorsed a United Auto Workers–General Motors agreement that explicitly addressed ideas and procedures for upgrading the quality of work life as a goal for both the union and the corporation.

4. In 1974 an outside consultant was hired to establish a joint worker-supervisor training program. Two coordinators were selected, one each by management and the union; a small group of workers and supervisors from the Soft Trim Department were brought together on Saturdays to learn about each other and to work on solutions for problems of joint concern.

5. In 1977 this training program was expanded plantwide, with 11 pairs of worker/supervisor trainers to lead small groups of workers and supervisors in 3 full days of paid training sessions.

The trainers used printed materials, diagrams, charts, and slides to describe products and model changes, how the plant was laid out, how the production system worked, and what the organizational structures of management and the union are. Time was spent covering safety matters, methods used to measure quality performance, efficiency, and so forth. The work groups were shown how and where they could get any information they wanted about their plant. Special films showed all parts of the plant with a particular worker "conducting the tour" for his part of the operation.

To develop effective problem-solving skills, the trainers presented simulated problems and then asked employees to go through a variety of some experiential exercises. The training content enabled the workers to diagnose themselves, their own behavior, how they appeared in competitive situations, how they handled two-way communications, and how they solved problems. By the final day "the groups themselves are carrying the ball," as the trainers put it, "with a minimum of guidance and direction from the two trainers."[3]

It is worth noting that GM's commitment to this program, at a cost of $1.6 million, was not tied to immediate measurable results. In Guest's words, "getting the process of worker involvement going was a primary goal with its own intrinsic rewards. The organizational benefits followed." Nevertheless, there are some perceptible benefits.

The production manager says, for example, "From a strictly production point of view—efficiency and costs—this entire experience has been absolutely positive, and we can't begin to measure the savings that have taken place because of the hundreds of small problems that were solved on the shop floor before they accumulated into big problems."

Although not confirmed by management, the union claims that Tarrytown went from one of the poorest plants in its quality performance (inspection counts or dealer complaints) to one of the best among the 18 plants in the division. It reports that absenteeism went from 7.25 percent to between 2 and 3 percent. In December 1978, at the end of the training sessions, there were only 32 grievances on the docket. Seven years earlier there had been upward of 2000 grievances filed. Such substantial changes can hardly be explained by chance.[4]

We will talk more about quality of work life in Chapter 9. Suffice it here to observe further from the process description (1) the importance that the personnel department at GMAD-Tarrytown enjoyed and the mandate it bore for worker training, safety, and promoting worker involvement in the process; (2) the challenge supervisors felt for recognizing worker achievement and integrity and for assisting their workers in solving problems both on and off the job; and (3) the care with which the industrial and plant engineers studied the tasks that make up automobile assembly and devised ways to eliminate or simplify more difficult or dis-agreeable ones.

Within most machine-paced line flow processes, the career path of the worker is much less well de-fined than it is in many continuous flow processes or in the batch flow process. Lines of progression are not spelled out as directly, and most workers earn about the same pay. Most job changes involve transfers from evening or night work to day work, or from one department to another with what may be perceived as easier or more exciting work. Some promotions in job categories are frequently possible as well.

DEMANDS OF THE PROCESS ON MANAGEMENT

The machine-paced line flow process places a num-ber of taxing demands on management. The products it produces are typically consumed in high volumes; therefore they are likely to compete on price as well as on product performance, work-manship, and perhaps even the reliability of deliv-ery. This is a broad front on which to compete and it means that line flow managers must devote their attention to cost reduction measures (items 1 through 4 below) and to product performance and workmanship measures (items 5 and 6 below):

1. *Balance.* The definition and balance of the line, as discussed above, is a critical aspect in assuring that as little labor as necessary is placed on the line.

2. *Materials management.* Like the continuous flow process, the line flow process places very regular and steady demands on its suppliers. Be-cause of this regularity, the line flow process can often avoid drawing on large raw materials inventories and paying the necessary finance charges, but only by carefully managing the purchase and logistics of supplies. Such mate-rials management involves the establishment of

superb information and control systems so that (1) parts in imminent danger of falling short are identified and noted and (2) parts from suppliers are tracked thoroughly and delivered on time.

3. *Technological change.* In processes as complex as most line flow ones there are always ways to improve their workings. Most such changes are incremental in nature, but periodically more significant steps can be taken either to speed up the process or to eliminate some stations through the introduction of new equipment. The minicomputer and more versatile machine tools have often made significant contributions to process improvement.

4. *Capacity planning.* The managers of a process as rigid in capacity as the machine-paced line flow process must be very careful to plan dili-gently for its future capacity needs. Line re-balance may be called for or more drastic modifications to the design of the line. These must be thought through carefully from the be-ginning of any planning cycle.

5. *Product design.* The high volume products of the typical line flow process must be designed to be manufactured; the more exotic the demands the product places on the design of the line and the tasks workers perform, the more likely the competition will bury the product on price. Yet, some of the best assembly line products give the impression that they were custom-made, there being so many options for the customer to choose from. Automobiles are often this way. The trick, of course, is to design flexibility into the product so that the same general worker task results in a different appearance or per-formance in the product.

6. *Workforce management.* In so many line flow processes, quality is fundamentally dependent on the workforce. Fostering pride in workman-ship when the tasks performed are as repetitious as they are is a challenge, but an essential one.

QUESTIONS

1. Why is the production process at GMAD described as "classic but modern"? Mention specifically the assignment of tasks to workers and the function of personnel management.

2. Compare and contrast the methods used at GMAD with those used at Schlitz for planning production, purchasing, and raw materials inventory and control. In general, how does the hybrid process differ from the machine-paced line flow process?

3. It has frequently been said that the industrial engineering department is the most important control of operation in a machine-paced line flow process. Do you agree? Why or why not?

4. What are the connections between the workforce and its supervision and quality control at GMAD-Tarrytown?

5. "Relative to a job shop or a batch flow process, the classic assembly line has a very well defined process flow." Do you agree or disagree with this statement? Mention specific elements of the flow in each to support your position.

6. Discuss in detail the relationship between the notion of capacity in a machine-paced line flow and the theory of line balance.

7. What are some of the main methods used to perform a time and motion study? Which is most successful? Why?

8. Based on the five different operations you have so far studied, which operation would you rather work in? In which would you rather be a manager? In which would you like least to be a worker? a manager? Support your answers with specific references to the processes.

GREAT WESTERN TIME INC.

Adele Welch is a senior at Western Theoretical University, majoring in operations management. The university has a cooperative student-work study arrangement with the local plant of Great Western Time Inc. The students are hired for six months, from June to December of their senior year, as full-time first line supervisors or the equivalent.

Adele has just started at Great Western as a supervisor over an assembly line for electronic watches. The watch assembly line is a moving belt 25 feet long at which 28 workers assemble, solder, and test watches through the complete assembly process.

Initially, an assembly line balancing is developed from the order of operations, the time required for each operation, and the number of units desired. This information is also used to determine the crew size. In order to achieve the required production volume, this line balancing design usually calls for several work stations for some operations. The work stations are simple and require simple tools, and so idle work stations do not represent major losses in terms of equipment.

In the actual operation the watch case is placed on the conveyor belt, and the other subassemblies are added by workers by taking the case off the line, putting it in a fixture, performing their assigned operation, and placing the watch back on the conveyor. If there are five identical work stations, each of the five workers is expected to perform that operation on every fifth watch. Since the product is so small and light, there is little difficulty in returning an unfinished watch to the beginning of the line, if necessary. However, a large number of returns indicates an imbalance in the work arrangement.

Adele has 23 people assigned to her; when one or more does not report for work, she has no labor pool from which to draw. Moreover, if a worker does not feel well and leaves at noon, Adele has to rebalance the assembly line quickly and adjust the belt speed to the rebalanced line. Table 5-A shows the sequence of operations and the times involved in the manufacture of the Slinky Slim watch.

Although Great Western would like all assembly operations to go like clockwork, upper management has factored in a value for determining the "average" output requirement. The performance measure used to evaluate Adele and her colleagues is the labor content of each assembled watch compared to an engineered standard. Adele feels that her primary job is to generate a new line balance at any time. In particular, she wants to generate, ahead of time (in case absenteeism forces her to re-

TABLE 5-A Sequence of Operations and Times for Producing the Slinky Slim Watch (Great Western Time Inc.)

OPERATION	PRECEDING OPERATION(S)	TIME REQUIRED (minutes/unit)
1	—	.2
2	1	.3
3	1	.3
4	1	.5
5	4	.2
6	3	.2
7	4	.4
8	2	.5
9	3, 5, 7	.6
10	8	.6
11	9, 10	.3
12	10, 11	.1
13	9	.2
14	11	.5
15	12, 14	.3
16	15	.2

balance the line), a set of line balances and work assignments for the following numbers of workers on the Slinky Slim assembly line: 23, 22, 21, 20, 19, 18.

REFERENCE NOTES

1. For heuristic methods of generating candidate assembly line balances see, for example, M. D. Kilbridge and L. Wester, "A Heuristic Method of Assembly Line Balancing," *Journal of Industrial Engineering* 12, no. 4 (July–August 1961). For computer-based methods of generating candidate assembly line balances see, for example, A. L. Arms, "Comsoal: A Computer Method of Sequencing Operations for Assembly Lines," *International Journal of Production Research* 4, no. 4 (1966).

2. Robert H. Guest, "Quality of Work Life—Learning from Tarrytown," *Harvard Business Review* 57, no. 4 (July–August 1979): 77.

3. Ibid., p. 84.

4. Ibid., p. 85.

CHAPTER

6

A WORKER-PACED LINE FLOW PROCESS

Burger King® Restaurant
Malden, Massachusetts

The Burger King Restaurant in Malden, Massachusetts was one of over 2200 fast food restaurants operated nationwide by Burger King Corporation, a wholly owned subsidiary of The Pillsbury Company, and its franchisees. The restaurant offered a wide selection of hamburger sandwiches, as well as a ham and cheese sandwich, a fish sandwich, french fries, onion rings, soft drinks, shakes, apple pie, and a frozen dessert. The restaurant was open from 10 A.M. to 11 P.M. Monday through Thursday, from 10 A.M. to midnight Friday and Saturday, and from 11 A.M. to 11 P.M. on Sunday.

The Malden Burger King was located on Broadway near the Everett–Malden town line. The area was a busy one, very diverse in land use. A shopping center was directly across the street, small businesses and a bank lined the street on both sides, an apartment house and a school flanked the shopping center, and a residential neighborhood lay to the rear and one side of the restaurant. Two other restaurants were within 200 yards: a local Chinese restaurant and a Kentucky Fried Chicken fast food store.

The restaurant itself was square in design, free-standing on about an acre of land, and constructed largely of brick and glass. The building occupied the front of the lot, freeing the rear for 58 parking places. Within the restaurant were 106 seats, arranged mainly as picnic-style tables with benches of two seats facing one another. Seating accounted for about half of the interior space; the other half of the space was dominated by the kitchen and counter areas.

PART ONE

PROCESS DESCRIPTION

KITCHEN OPERATIONS

ORDER TAKING (THE FRONT COUNTER)

After entering the restaurant, the customer walked up to a counter above which was displayed the menu and prices. At the counter were three registers. Behind each stood a counter hostess, who greeted the customer and took the order. The hostess read the order into a microphone, keyed the contents of the order on the register (e.g., punched the key for the Whopper®—a large hamburger with lettuce, tomato, onions, pickles, ketchup, and mayonnaise), read the printed total for the order, took the customer's payment, gave change, and then assembled the order. Assembling the order meant going to the pick-up counter between the kitchen and the front counter to gather the sandwiches, fries, shakes, and other items ordered and, frequently, to go to the ice tray and soft drink machine to draw any soft drinks ordered. The assembled order was then brought to the customer and the next customer greeted.

This system was called the "hospitality lineup" and differed from the system that Burger King had originally used. The old system had customers wait in one line for a single register. The hostess there took the order, but others assembled it. The new system, while somewhat more labor-intensive, could handle peak hour demand more efficiently and was thus preferred.

ORDER FILLING (THE BACK ROOM)

Burger King differed from McDonald's and some other fast food restaurants in that comparatively little finished goods inventory was kept. Sandwiches were assembled continuously. While an order might not have been assembled as quickly as when larger inventories were kept, this approach offered the distinct advantage of producing to order. As a Burger King slogan had it, you could "Have it your way,"® say, by ordering a Whopper® with double cheese, no pickle, and mustard, or a hamburger with extra onions.

Providing this kind of customer order variation with minimum customer waiting demanded a production system that was extraordinarily flexible. In fact, two kinds of flexibility were required: flexibility to meet special customer orders and flexibility to match large surges in customer demand during the lunch or dinner hours. Numerous aspects of the production system contributed to this flexibility.

The "Line": Layout and Job Descriptions

Making sandwiches and filling orders at Burger King was explicitly viewed as an assembly line. All the hamburger sandwiches (burgers, for short) followed a straight path from the back of the kitchen to the front counter; along this path were a series of work stations.

Any of the various burgers were begun by placing the appropriate meat pattie (Whopper® size or regular) and bun onto the chain drag at the feed end of the specially constructed infrared broiler. The broiler cooked the meat and toasted the bun. After leaving the broiler, the meat and buns could be kept warm in a work-in-process inventory that was used primarily during peak demand periods.

Next in the line came the "board," where buns and meat were transformed into Whopper® sandwiches, hamburgers, Whopper Jr.® sandwiches with cheese, double cheeseburgers, and the like. This was the key portion of the line where the burger was assembled "your way" (e.g., hold the pickle, double cheese). The "board" itself was a long table on which pickles, onions, cheese slices, plastic squeeze bottles of ketchup and mustard, sliced tomatoes, shredded lettuce, mayonnaise, and tartar sauce were kept. Above the table were two microwave ovens, one facing each side of the board. Beyond the board, on the pick-up counter, were two tiers of chutes that held completed sandwiches.

On either side of this main burger assembly line were the frying vats and the drink machines. There were three frying vats, which were flanked by inventories of thawed french fries, and frozen and blanched (i.e., half cooked) onion rings and fish portions. Two of the three vats were designated expressly for french fries, while the other was used for fish portions (for the Whaler® sandwich) or onion rings or for cooking the apple pie dessert.

The drink machines were found on the other side of the burger line. The ice bin and the soft

A customer could read the menu over the front counter. *(Courtesy of Burger King Corporation)*

drink machine (Coke®, root beer, Sprite®) could be accessed from either the front counter or the back room. The shake machine (chocolate, vanilla, strawberry) could be operated only from the back room.

These work stations were manned differently depending on the pace of demand at the restaurant. When demand was very slow, a skeleton crew operated the restaurant: one hostess at the front counter, someone to operate the broiler (feeding and "catching" at the drop) and the shake machine, and someone to prepare sandwiches at the board and to operate the frying vats. As demand picked up, more workers were added to the operation and job assignments became much more specialized. At any time the preferred ratio of front counter hostesses to back room production workers was about 1 to 1.5. During a peak period the crew would increase to 12. In addition to the kitchen and counter crew, there was one hostess in the dining room, charged mainly with keeping that area clean.

During the peak, five hostesses were positioned at the front counter—calling in orders, taking money, and assembling orders. They did not have to draw their own soft drinks; that task was now assigned to the drinks station. The drinks station operator also drew all the shakes.

During this peak period, broiler operations were

Here a meat pattie is placed on the chain drag leading to the infrared broiler. *(Courtesy of Burger King Corporation)*

divided in two parts: feeding and catching. The catcher also had responsibility for monitoring the work-in-process inventory of broiled meat patties and toasted buns. The size of this inventory during any hour of the day was dictated by the restaurant manager, who indicated it on a sheet of paper for ready reference. Feeding the broiler, then, could be initiated either by the feeder hearing a call for a double cheeseburger or two Whopper® sandwiches or by reference to the manager's instructions for the work-in-process inventory.

During the peak demand period, work on the board was also split in two. The product mix commonly sold at the restaurant influenced the nature

of this division of the board work, be it Whopper®-size sandwiches on one side and small sandwiches on the other, cheese on one side and noncheese on the other, or some other system.

The fry position worker was responsible for all french fries, fish sandwiches, onion rings, and apple pies. This meant raising and lowering bins into heated shortening, salting the fries, and bagging them with a special scoop.

During the peak demand hours, there was also a worker designated as the production leader. The production leader acted as a floater in the back room, helping with the multitude of tasks that needed doing at a moment's notice: replenishing a

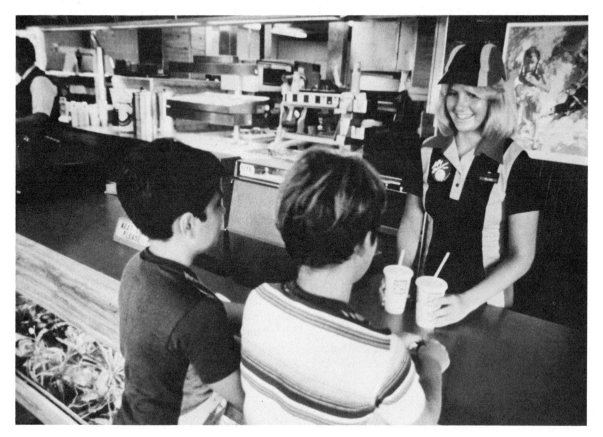

During nonpeak hours a hostess could draw soft drinks for customers rather than passing on the order to a special operator of the drink station. *(Courtesy of Burger King Corporation)*

spent bin of mayonnaise with a fresh one from one of the walk-in refrigerators, or mopping up a drink spilled by a counter hostess, or helping the fry position during a big run on french fries.

Triggering Production

During any very slow period of demand, much of the sandwich and drink production was triggered by the counter hostess calling in the order to the kitchen. The burger given to the customer might be the one actually placed on the broiler chain in response to the call-in of that order. For sure the order's drink was drawn in direct response to the call-in. Orders for french fries were treated a bit

differently, however. Fries took about 4 minutes to cook, too long a time to have the customer wait for an order to be cooked. Instead, fries had to be awaiting the customer in finished goods inventory.

As demand picked up, it became more and more likely that finished goods inventories of the major burgers (hamburger, cheeseburger, Whopper® sandwiches, Whopper® sandwiches with cheese) would be kept and that the broiler feeder would be loading the broiler more and more in response to the inventory situation and less and less in response to the call-in of orders. The board workers as well began keeping a close eye on the finished burger inventory at the pick-up counter, in an effort to maintain that inventory. Typically, a board worker would keep assembling burgers to replenish the inventory to a given level, until she heard the call-in of a special order that would affect her. Upon hearing the special order, she would note it on the sheet of paper that wrapped the burger and would then proceed immediately to fill it. Time was saved by drawing the proper bun and meat from the work-in-process inventory.

Coping with Bottlenecks

Surges in demand, large numbers of special orders, or runs on particular items could strain the production system and cause it to miss its established service standards. Two service standards were tracked every lunch and dinner: (1) door-to-door time—the elapsed time between a customer's walking into line and the person's walking away from the counter with his or her order—and (2) transaction time—the elapsed time between the hostess's call-in of the order and its presentation to the customer. The Malden Burger King restaurant's own goals for these times were 2.5 minutes and 45 seconds, respectively.

To reach these goals consistently required that bottlenecks in production be avoided. Responsibility for heading off any potential bottleneck rested chiefly with the manager and the production leader. By providing both guidance to the crew and two sets of spare hands, the manager and production leader could assure a smooth operation. During peak hours especially, it was not uncommon to see the production leader stepping up to the board to assemble a sandwich or drawing a shake from the machine or bagging fries or replenishing materials. One could also see workers with some slack time helping those who were overloaded—for example, a Whopper® sandwich board worker assembling some small burgers.

This mandate to keep production smooth and efficient placed special demands on the manager and the production leader. First of all, both had to be thoroughly familiar with all aspects of the operation so that they could step into any work station

to provide instant emergency assistance. Moreover, only they had to be aware of all the orders that were called into the back room from the counter. The Whopper® sandwich board worker could ignore anything that did not begin with the word "Whopper,"® but the manager or production leader had to listen to all orders to be able to assess where strains in the operation might appear. Not only ears but eyes, too, had to be searching for potential bottlenecks. Clues such as too many counter hostesses waiting for food (a back room bottleneck) or a low fries inventory had to be sought constantly.

Adequate prepeak period preparation also meant a great deal in coping with bottlenecks. If the shake machine was not completely filled with ingredients or if a cash register tape was close to running out, the operation was in danger of some bottlenecks that might affect service adversely. The restaurant manager had to check the status of items like these to be assured that incomplete preparation did not detract from the success of the operation.

PURCHASING AND MATERIALS MANAGEMENT

The restaurant was responsible for placing orders for all supplies. Ordering was done on a weekly basis. Order quantities were determined by taking the usage for the previous week and adjusting it for special trends or conditions such as holidays or school vacations. A small buffer stock was ordered to ensure that the entire menu would always be available. Usage was so high that the restaurant never needed to worry about spoilage even for produce or dairy products.

Materials were generally received in the early morning or in the evening. Fresh buns were delivered four times a week. Other materials were delivered three times a week.

Most supplies used at the Malden restaurant were purchased from Distron®, a Burger King Cor-

Salting the fries was one of the jobs of the fry position worker. *(Courtesy of Burger King Corporation)*

poration subsidiary. The individual restaurant need not necessarily deal with Distron, though; other suppliers were also approved by the corporation, and the restaurant could lobby at the regional level for a change in supplier.

Most equipment repairs in the restaurant were covered by service contracts negotiated at the regional level.

THE WORKFORCE

All of the workforce was part-time, and nearly all were high school students, most of them female. Wages were paid for hours worked. The days and hours to be worked were scheduled in advance. The schedule tried to reflect worker preferences as to amount and timing of work. The daily rise and fall of peak and off-peak demand, as mentioned above, required continual changes in crew size so that neither too few nor too many workers were at work at any one time. Flexibility in the schedule was needed; it was achieved by using part-time high school labor and scheduling their arrivals and departures at different times—some, for example, just 15 minutes prior to the noon rush hour. The only restriction was the federal government's regulation that the workers work at least 3 hours in any day. The use of high school labor permitted even day-to-day adjustments in the schedule, such as when hot weather struck and customers forsook Malden for the beach. Since many high schoolers would as soon be on the beach as working, adjustments to such daily weather patterns were possible by permitting some workers to go home early.

Work assignments were frequently shuffled. A prime reason for shuffling assignments was to promote worker cross-training and thus increase the operation's flexibility. A manager might also be forced to shuffle assignments because of worker scheduling or absentee problems. For these reasons, the front counter hostesses knew how the back room operated and the back room knew how to take orders. This cross-training also had the welcome benefit of heightening the tolerance any one worker had for the momentary troubles of other workers.

MANAGEMENT

The Malden Burger King had a manager and two assistant managers. Since the week contained 14 shifts and each manager worked five shifts a week, one of the three was always there. In fact, for one shift each week, an overlap of managers would occur.

Any manager's primary responsibility was to ensure that a quality product was promptly served in a clean environment. While a manager's abilities to control costs were valued, meeting the corporation's service goals came first. Meeting service goals fundamentally meant developing the capabilities of the production crew and maintaining its morale. Thus, the manager was first and foremost a crew foreman, teaching new hires, guiding work assignments, checking quality, and providing an example for the crew.

Layered on these responsibilities came others: ordering materials, receiving deliveries, checking and posting standards of performance (e.g., the door-to-door and transaction times, by stopwatch), checking on the preparations for the day or for the peak period, and scheduling the part-time workforce.

While the manager's role as foreman was the most important, scheduling the workforce was often seen as the most difficult. Labor was the chief controllable cost, and the corporation's primary means of cost control lay in limiting the labor-hours any restaurant scheduled. The number of hours that could be scheduled was determined by a formula. This formula permitted more hours for restaurants with (1) higher sales, (2) longer hours of operation, and (3) more service features such as a drive-through lane. In addition, a fixed block of hours was allocated for cleanup and maintenance. It was sometimes taxing to meet anticipated service needs and still stay within the formula's allotted number of labor-hours.

To guide the manager's decisions, including the scheduling of worker hours, the restaurant's computerized cash register network could print out sales reports. From these the manager could learn how well his scheduling decisions worked, since he could match sales against crew size for any time of day. Trends in products purchased could also be identified and measures taken to assure their continued and timely supply.

Managers entered the corporation as trainees and spent 6 weeks at the nearest branch campus of Whopper College. Selected restaurants in the area served as training centers where the trainees could observe and participate in restaurant operations.

Individual restaurant managers were supervised by district managers. The management organization, geographical in structure, is depicted in Figure 6-1.

FACILITIES AND TECHNOLOGY

Decisions on locating new stores were taken up at the area and regional levels. Usually the region general manager, area manager, and regional real estate director (on the regional staff) made the deci-

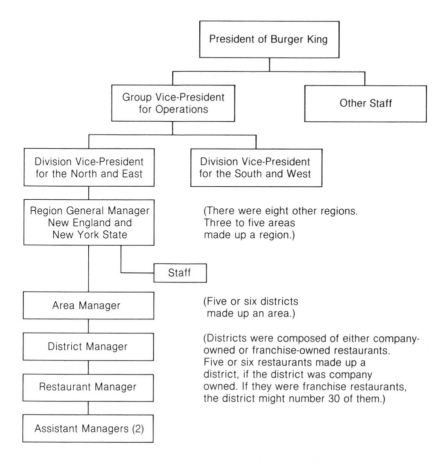

FIGURE 6-1   Organization chart showing the relationship of a Burger King Restaurant to the Burger King Corporation.

sion on site, size, and features. The region's staff architects would then design the restaurant to fit the site and offer the range of features and space decided upon. Most new restaurants seated 105 to 110 and had between 65 and 80 parking spaces. Most of the equipment was provided by Davmor®, a division of Burger King Corporation, but other suppliers could be chosen if their equipment met company specifications.

Burger King was constantly seeking improved technology. Recently the frying vats had been modified so that the temperature of the shortening in them was adjusted automatically. This modification freed the fry position operator from having to adjust temperature depending on the number of bins lowered into the heated shortening.

A more fundamental operations change was just being introduced and would eliminate the need to call in orders over the microphone. Instead, new registers would be tied to printers at each work station. Rather than having to listen for a particular special, the worker need only look at the latest printout at her station. The microphone system would be kept only as backup.

PART TWO

DISCUSSION

The Burger King® Corporation is in no way responsible for the following views and presentation. They remain solely the responsibility of the author.

THE FLOW OF THE PROCESS AND OF INFORMATION

In most service industries, the time delay between service provision and service consumption is necessarily very short. Put another way, one can rarely inventory a service, at least not for very long. Hotel room-nights cannot be inventoried nor can timely tips on the stock market nor can tasty hamburgers. Hence, a whole degree of freedom is removed from the service manager, which heightens the importance of capacity choice in most service industries.

It is also frequently the case that services must be particularly flexible so that they can be customized to individual consumer needs. Think of the travel agent, the salesperson, the cab driver, and, yes, the fast food restaurant.

These two basic features of many service businesses place substantial demands on the process design and information systems of an enterprise like Burger King. Flexibility in both product and volume is paramount, and Burger King has adopted some classic policies for yielding such flexibility.

Figure 6-2 is a process flow diagram for assembling an order. It is simple, and that is one of its advantages. Responsibilities are clearly demarcated, and yet all of the key tasks for customizing the hamburger rest with the worker who actually assembles the sandwich at the board. This fact, in turn, simplifies the information flow so that only

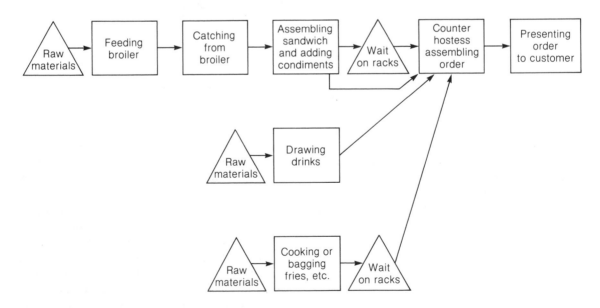

FIGURE 6-2 A process flow diagram (nonpeak period) for the Burger King Restaurant, Malden, Massachusetts.

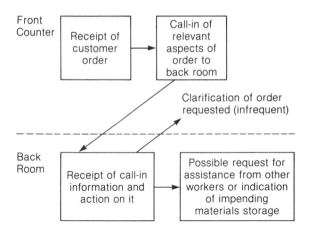

FIGURE 6-3   An information flow diagram (nonpeak period) for the Burger King Restaurant, Malden, Massachusetts.

one worker need pay strict attention to the call-in of a special order. (An information flow diagram is found in Figure 6-3.) In this way, with a clear delineation of tasks and direct information flows, rapid product changes can be facilitated.

Flexibility in changing production volumes is achieved by a continual rebalancing of the sandwich production line. The time pattern of demand is well known from past experience, and this knowledge has permitted the staggering of work hours for the part-time workforce so that varying numbers can be on hand at any one time. The workforce ebbs and flows from three during slack periods to 12 during peak periods. As more workers are added, the job contents narrow and, importantly, the flow of information changes. No longer is production keyed completely to the call-in of the order. More and more, production is keyed by the levels of the finished goods inventory and of the work-in-process inventory of broiled burgers and toasted buns. Instead of reacting to the order call-in, the broiler feeder reacts to the manager's posted list of burgers to be held as work-in-process, feeding the broiler so as to maintain the desired inventory level. Similarly, the board workers respond

to the level of finished goods inventory, although these board workers must also respond to any special orders that are called in. Special orders, of course, must take precedence over the maintenance of the finished goods inventory. The peak period changes in the process and information flow diagrams are pictured in Figure 6-4.

DEMANDS OF THE PROCESS ON THE WORKFORCE

The flexibility of the Burger King fast food operation demands flexibility from its workers. The job contents and the production pace vary markedly throughout any worker's shift during the day, requiring a special tolerance. Workers on a machine-paced assembly line get used to the rhythm of the conveyor. But, on a worker-paced line, and particularly one in a service industry, any rhythm may soon dissolve.

What is especially true of worker-paced lines is that the crew on the line views itself as a team, largely because they are so dependent on one another. This fact often permits worker-paced lines where the demand is steady (unlike at a fast food restaurant) to be paid according to a group incentive scheme. Some standard of production—X units per time period—is established and the crew on the line, if it can better the standard, is paid extra for doing so. This kind of group incentive pay scheme can tie a crew together as a team even more thoroughly than usual.

DEMANDS OF THE PROCESS ON MANAGEMENT

An operation like a Burger King restaurant places specific demands on management for dual reasons: status as a service operation and status as a worker-paced line flow process. As a line flow process,

Process Flow Diagram for Burgers

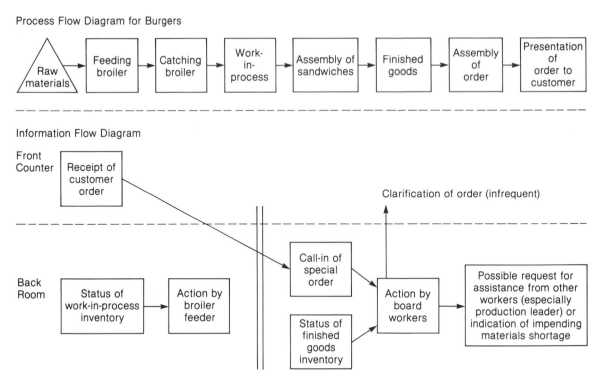

Information Flow Diagram

FIGURE 6-4   Process and information flow diagrams (peak period) for the
Burger King Restaurant, Malden, Massachusetts.

many of the issues discussed above with respect to GMAD-Tarrytown surface:

- Balance of the line
- Materials management
- Technological advance
- Capacity planning
- Product design
- Workforce management

Managers of worker-paced lines should be sensitive to all these issues, since to fall down on any one could seriously jeopardize the entire operation.

The issue of technological advance is particularly acute, since such an advance may enable a smoother, more regular flow of the product. After all, a worker-paced line flow usually remains worker- rather than machine-paced because there is as yet no easy way to guard against a succession of overcycle conditions striking a worker all at once (e.g., a run on "Whoppers, hold the pickles"). If the mix of product options can somehow be smoothed out or if particular advances can be made in product or work station design, a worker-paced line can easily be transformed into a machine-paced line. In other words, the worker-paced line is somewhat more vulnerable to radical, rather than incremental, change than is a machine-paced one.

A Burger King's status as a service operation only heightens the importance of capacity planning, since service firms cannot ordinarily inventory their product. The importance of work-force management is also heightened, because the worker-customer interaction is part of the service. Ordinarily, one cannot hide the service process as readily as one can hide the manufacturing process. Keeping the workforce productive and interested in their jobs is a key challenge for managers in service operations.

QUESTIONS

1. Visit a fast food restaurant with a friend to perform an experiment. While one of you times the other's entry and exit and the time from the placing of the order to its receipt, the other observes how many workers are actually involved with the order. Visit the fast food restaurant at a slack time and at a peak time, and compare the differences in time and number of workers.

2. Would you prefer to work on a machine-paced assembly line or a worker-paced one? (Remember that you're likely to earn more doing the first type of work.) What particular elements influenced your decision?

3. Watch for bottlenecks the next time you are in a fast food restaurant (or any worker-paced service operation). Where do they arise and why? How might they be remedied?

4. Compare the importance of technological innovations and the importance of worker cohesiveness in a worker-paced service operation.

5. Why is flexibility one of the key features for success in a worker-paced assembly line operation such as Burger King's?

LEGACY HOMES

Tom Wurkard had been employed part-time as a "rough carpenter" by Legacy Homes while he completed his degree at Interstate Tech University. After his graduation, Legacy hired Tom as a construction superintendent; this job combined the duties of foreman, scheduler, and expediter.

By building only to order, Legacy took a conservative approach to the ups and downs typical of the home construction industry. Legacy offered a limited number of home designs; Tables 6-A and 6-B show the work involved on most of them — usually about 90 days' worth. When a buyer arranged a home loan from a lending institution, the local practice was to allow the construction company to receive the money in partial payments (cash draws) depending on the degree of completion of the home. Thus, for Legacy to receive the money, Tom needed to finish a home as fast as possible.

Legacy had a nucleus crew of highly skilled workers that it wanted to keep working most of the time. Other workers could be hired to supplement this crew when necessary. Table 6-C shows this crew and the various tasks they are capable of performing. Each crew member knew well a primary function such as plumbing but could be counted on to help with other functions such as

TABLE 6-A Crew Size and Times for Various Tasks
(Legacy Homes)

TASK #	DESCRIPTION	TYPE OF WORK*	MINIMUM/MAXIMUM CREW SIZE	DAYS TO COMPLETE (with minimum crew)
1	Concrete footer	A	2–4	1.00
2	Foundation	F	Subcontract	1.00
3	Grading	A	2–4	0.50
4	Framing	B	5–8	2.60
5	Roofing	F	Subcontract	1.00
6	Concrete	A/B	3–5	1.50
7	Wiring	C	2–4	1.00
8	Furnace and ducts	C	2–4	2.25
9	Plumbing	C	2–3	2.50
10	Insulation	B	1–3	2.25
11	Dry wall	F	Subcontract	1.00
12	Siding	F	Subcontract	5.50
13	Sewer line	A	2–3	2.00
14	Painting	F	Subcontract	1.50
15	Finish carpentry	D	2–4	2.50
16	Tile	D	1–2	5.00
17	Electrical trim	C	1–2	1.50
18	Finish plumbing	C	1–2	3.50
19	Heating trim	C	1–3	2.50
20	Carpeting	F	Subcontract	2.00
21	Cleanup	E	1–3	2.00

*A = excavate; B = rough carpentry; C = plumbing, heating, electrical; D = finish carpentry; E = part-time cleanup; F = subcontract

rough carpentry. The crew who installed the plumbing, for example, also installed the heating and electricity. This overlap of skills was possible for two reasons: (1) most of the work on a Legacy house was rather straightforward and did not entail the total skill requirements of journeymen in any of the trades, and (2) Legacy hired nonunion workers.

Table 6-A shows the minimum and maximum crew sizes for completing each task. For example, task #8 requires a minimum of two workers because one person working alone cannot position the furnace or handle the duct work; two people working on separate houses would take much longer to complete their work on both houses than if they worked together on one house at a time. At the maximum crew size, of course, it can happen that workers interfere with each other's work. Tom assumed that additional workers could work at the same rate as workers already on the job; he therefore scaled the number of workers up or down proportionately. For example, in task #1 if two workers can do the job in one day (i.e., two labor days are required), three workers can do the job in two-thirds day (two labor days divided by three workers available), and four workers can do it in half a day.

All operations have been designed so as to require a low level of skill; thus any worker can shift to another operation with only a negligible loss of

TABLE 6-B Precedence Relationship
(Legacy Homes)

JOB #	PRECEDING OPERATION(S)
1	
2	1
3	2
4	3
5	4
6	2
7	4
8	5
9	5
10	7, 8, 9
11	10
12	10
13	9
14	11
15	14
16	14
17	14
18	15
19	14
20	6, 12, 13, 16, 17, 18, 19
21	20

TABLE 6-C Labor Force
(Legacy Homes)

TYPE OF WORK	CURRENT LABOR AVAILABLE	TASKS PERFORMED*
A Excavate	3	1, 3, 6, 13
B Rough carpentry	5	4, 6, 10
C Plumbing, heating, electrical	4	7, 8, 9, 17, 18, 19
D Finish carpentry	2	15, 16
E Part-time cleanup	1	21
F Subcontract		2, 5, 11, 12, 14, 20

*See Table 6-A for an explanation of these numbers.

efficiency. Usually one worker is used as parts chaser and relief. The supervisor can help with the parts chasing but is not expected to take part in operations except as a troubleshooter.

Although the products (houses) do not move, Tom feels that the principles of worker-paced lines can be applied with beneficial results.

1. Design a process flow for Tom.

2. What is the minimum time requirement to build a house? How many houses should be being built to keep the permanent crew busy? What is the maximum number of houses that should be under construction at one time?

3. Is the workforce balanced? If not, which crew sizes should be changed?

4. What type of information flow should Tom set up?

5. Set up a sequence for raw material flow for Tom.

7

A COMPARISON OF
PRODUCTION PROCESSES

In the preceding chapters, six different production processes were introduced and their key features described. There were threads in common among some of them as well as some sharp differences. The purpose of this chapter is to tie together the common threads and expose the sharp differences by comparing the processes described.

TRENDS

First we should recognize that there are some clearly discernible trends among the six processes introduced. The trends become evident when the processes are arrayed in the following order, a sort of "spectrum" of production processes:

- Job shop (example: Norcen Industries)
- Batch flow (example: Jung Products, Inc.)
- Worker-paced line flow (example: Burger King Restaurant — Malden, Massachusetts)
- Machine-paced line flow (example: GM Assembly Division — Tarrytown, New York)
- Continuous flow (example: International Paper Company, Androscoggin Mill)

The hybrid process represented by the Schlitz brewery at Syracuse, New York, which displayed aspects of both a batch flow and a continuous flow process is somewhat more difficult to place since it is not as pure an example as the other five. Many of its features, however, resemble the continuous flow process more than the batch flow process; also, a hybrid process generally has some distinct features all its own. For the purpose of analyzing trends, I would position a batch/continuous flow hybrid like the Schlitz brewery in between the line flow processes and the continuous flow one. The revised alignment would be:

- Job shop
- Batch flow
- Worker-paced line flow
- Machine-paced line flow
- Batch/continuous flow hybrid
- Continuous flow

ANALYZING THE TRENDS

In order to provide some cohesion and organization, this discussion of process trends is divided into six parts, each part devoted to a comparison and analysis of some specific features: (1) product features, (2) general process features, (3) materials-oriented features, (4) information-oriented features, (5) labor-oriented features, and (6) management features. These six features will be addressed in turn.

Product Features

Arrayed as they are above, the different processes introduced demonstrate some distinct trends involving the types of products manufactured and how those products compete against others. Specifically, the more one goes from a job shop toward a continuous flow process, the more it is generally the case that:

1. The number of different kinds of products made declines.
2. Product volumes increase to the point where the continuous flow process is essentially producing a commodity for the mass market.
3. Product customization declines and product standardization increases.
4. New product introductions become less frequent, and are more costly to bring about once decided upon.
5. Competition is more likely to be on price.
6. Competition, at least in the middle ranges of the array, is more likely to emphasize quality aspects like workmanship, product performance, and product reliability; but as the process becomes more and more a continuous flow, the quality differences between rival products become narrower and narrower.

General Process Features

There are complementary trends in some general process features as well. For example, as one progresses down the array of processes from job shop to continuous flow, it is generally true that:

1. The pattern of the process becomes more rigid, and the routing of products through their various process steps becomes less individual and unprescribed and more well defined.
2. Equipment becomes more specialized.
3. The operation becomes huge, and economies of scale are possible.

4. More, and generally larger, equipment is part of the process.
5. Equipment is less likely to be idle. Pieces of equipment become better balanced in size and speed to one another.
6. Equipment setups are fewer in number and run lengths longer.
7. The pace of the process is determined largely by machine capabilities or regulated by machines or conveyors.
8. The pace of production keeps increasing.
9. The notion of capacity becomes less ambiguous and more measurable in physical, rather than dollar, units.
10. Additions to capacity come in large chunks, and incremental additions to capacity become less viable.
11. Bottlenecks become less and less movable and thus better understood.
12. Incremental change to the nature of the process itself becomes relatively more frequent and routine, but the impact of radical change to the process is likely to be more sweeping and thus scarier to contemplate.

Materials-Oriented Features

Again, keeping the array of different processes ordered from job shop through continuous flow process, some general trends in materials-oriented features can be observed. For example, as the process becomes more and more a continuous flow one, it becomes more and more the case that:

1. The span of the process (i.e., vertical integration) becomes broader. A plant is more and more likely to start with "very raw" raw materials and transform them into products that may need little or no "finishing" before consumers purchase them.
2. As time draws closer to actual production, materials requirements are generally known with more certainty.

3. Raw materials requirements are large, but their purchase and delivery can be made steady.
4. Supplier ties are long term.
5. Because of large production volumes and steady purchases, control over suppliers for price, delivery, quality, design, and the like is great.
6. Control over the delivery time of the finished product becomes greater.
7. Work-in-process inventories, because of process design, become scant.
8. Finished goods inventories are larger (relative to other inventories).
9. Finished goods are sold through formal distribution channels and can sometimes be forced down those channels for the sake of keeping production running smoothly.

Importantly, however, the batch/continuous flow hybrid process does not follow all of these trends. There is a definite work-in-process inventory situated between the batch flow portion of the process and the continuous flow portion. At least some of the raw materials are inventoried as a buffer stock to be drawn down in perhaps unexpected or haphazard fashion, while others are purchased to coincide with the production plan.

INFORMATION-ORIENTED FEATURES

A number of trends are evident as well for many information-oriented features of the various production processes. As the process changes from job shop to continuous flow, generally it is more and more likely that:

1. Production has not been instigated by a bidding procedure.
2. Longer term sales forecasts are used and orders are "frozen" well ahead of time.
3. The corporation outside the plant is an integral part of the plant's scheduling and materials movement tracking.

4. Order scheduling is done on a very sophisticated basis.
5. A finished goods inventory is managed.
6. Little information flow from workers to management is required.
7. Quality control measures become formal.
8. Inventory adjustments become important in responding to seasonal or business cycle changes in demand.
9. The process is less flexible in making swift adjustments to demand changes and so production must be carefully planned in advance.

LABOR-ORIENTED FEATURES

Again, trends are evident across the spectrum of production processes explored, this time concerning labor issues. Progressing from job shop to continuous flow process, it is more likely that:

1. The labor content of the product, relative to the product's value, becomes smaller and smaller.
2. Job contents diminish, although "art" is more likely to be found at either end of the process spectrum.
3. Labor is paid by the hour rather than by some incentive system. In fact, the progression of wage payment schemes tends to go from hourly or individual incentive rates for the job shop, through individual and then group incentive schemes, and then on to hourly rates.
4. The importance of setting standards for labor remains high. The mechanization of the continuous flow process, however, means that such standards are useful less to define the process and its capacity than to assign the workforce to the equipment.
5. As production moves more and more to mechanical or technological pacing, the scramble to complete a lot of production to meet monthly goals or billings becomes less and less prevalent.
6. The path of worker advancement becomes more well-defined and even formal.

TABLE 7-1   Ratio of Management Staff to Hourly Employees

COMPANY	PROCESS	MANAGEMENT STAFF/ TOTAL EMPLOYMENT
Norcen Industries	Job shop	3/27 = 0.111
Jung Products, Inc.	Batch flow	about 25/225 = about 0.111
GMAD-Tarrytown	Mechine-paced line flow	500/4200 = 0.119
Schlitz-Syracuse	Batch/continuous flow hybrid	120/350 = 0.343*
International Paper, Androscoggin Mill	Continuous flow	200/1300 = 0.154

*Reflects many quality control workers.

MANAGEMENT FEATURES

Lastly, some trends can be identified as well for several aspects of the management of these diverse production processes. Progressing from job shop to continuous flow process, it is more and more the case that:

1. Staff operations concerning such topics as materials movement, scheduling, capacity planning, new technology planning, and quality control become more important relative to line operations.
2. The size of the plant's management (line and staff) is larger relative to the size of the workforce both because the capital intensity of the operation is greater and because staff operations are more important. Table 7-1 uses statistics from the processes we have discussed to show the ratio of management staff to total employees; you can see this trend in these ratios.
3. Given that the plant involved is part of a multiplant company, the involvement of managers situated at the corporate offices (rather than at the plant itself) becomes greater. The corporation's influence may extend to operations as well as to capital planning and spending.
4. The operation is controlled more as a cost center, as opposed to a profit center.
5. The major challenges that management faces are significantly altered, largely shifting from day-to-day operational considerations to very long-term, high expense items.

THE PROCESS SPECTRUM

By comparing these trends it is fairly plain that entire lists of characteristics hang together to describe particular processes. Table 7-2 is an effort to compile just such lists for the range of production processes that have been introduced. Note that the batch/continuous flow hybrid, exemplified by the Schlitz brewery, has been segregated from the others so that the process spectrum stretching from job shop through to continuous flow process remains as pure as we can reasonably expect.

Table 7-2 offers some generalizations about particular types of production processes, drawing mainly from the processes discussed in Chapters 1 through 6. Not all of the generalizations may ring true for all of the production processes one may conceivably classify in each category from job shop to continuous flow process. Most of the generalizations, however, are representative of a typical production process in each category.

THE PRODUCT-PROCESS MATRIX

Another useful way to visualize some of the similarities and differences among different types of production processes is to array the processes within what has been called the product-process matrix.[1] This matrix is nothing fancier than a box, one side of which describes the varieties of product mixes that are possible and another side of which describes the process patterns (i.e., the ease of flow

TABLE 7-2 Comparing Processes of Different Types

FEATURES	(1) JOB SHOP (example: Norcen Industries)	(2) BATCH FLOW (example: Jung Products, Inc.)	(3) WORKER-PACED ASSEMBLY LINE (example: Burger King® Restaurant, Malden)	(4) MACHINE-PACED ASSEMBLY LINE (example: GMAD, Tarrytown)	(5) CONTINUOUS FLOW (example: International Paper, Androscoggin Mill)	BATCH/CONTINUOUS FLOW HYBRID (example: Schlitz Brewery, Syracuse)
Product Features						
Product mix	Generally custom products	Lots of generally own designed products	Mostly standard products; some opportunities for selected options	Same as for 3	Standard products with little or no customization possible	Same as for 3 and 4
Products compete largely on:	Speed of delivery, product customization, new product introduction	Product performance, product reliability and workmanship, delivery reliability, new product introduction, flexibility to produce either low or high volumes	Product performance, price, product reliability and workmanship, delivery reliability	Product performance, price, product reliability and workmanship, delivery reliability	Price	Product reliability and workmanship, price
Products unlikely to compete on:	Price				New product introduction, product customization	
New product introduction	All the time; easy	Frequent; routine	Sometimes	Sometimes; generally expensive	Hardly at all; very costly	Infrequent; expensive
Process Features						
Process pattern	No rigid pattern; product can be routed anywhere; sometimes a dominant flow	Not all procedures performed on all products; product can be routed many ways; often a dominant flow	Clear pattern, though special treatment of some products sometimes permitted	Clear, rigid pattern, though some off-line work possible	Clear, very rigid pattern	Same as for 5
Type of equipment	General purpose	Mostly general purpose	Specialized	Same as for 3	Same as for 3	Same as for 3, 4, and 5
Balance of equipment	Balance of speed and time done in only the grossest, long-run terms. At any one time, an imbalance is likely to exist	Balance likely to be imperfect between segments of process but better coordinated than typical job shop	Machinery speed and size in good balance with peak needs	Speed and size of equipment very well balanced. Capable of being adjusted together over small changes in line speed	Good balance of speed and size. Any excess capacity often placed in latter portion of process to provide insurance against breakdowns or unusual order requests	Same as for 5
Capital utilization	Labor intensive; machines frequently idle	Labor intensive, although less machine idleness	Although equipment is specialized, it is fairly cheap; labor still a big item	Capital intensive	Very capital intensive; machines nearly always utilized	Same as for 5
Typical size of operation	Generally small	Generally medium-size	Variable	Large	Mammoth	Same as for 4
Economies of scale	None	Few, if any	Same as for 2	Some, perhaps	Yes	Same as for 5
Notion of capacity	Very fuzzy; definable vaguely in dollar terms; useful only in long run	Fuzzy; product mix implies a dollar definition only	Increasingly clear; some physical unit measures possible	Clear; physical unit measures	Same as for 4	Same as for 4 and 5

(continues on next page)

TABLE 7-2 Comparing Processes of Different Types (*continued*)

FEATURES	(1) JOB SHOP (example: Norcen Industries)	(2) BATCH FLOW (example: Jung Products, Inc.)	(3) WORKER-PACED ASSEMBLY LINE (example: Burger King® Restaurant, Malden)	(4) MACHINE-PACED ASSEMBLY LINE (example: GMAD, Tarrytown)	(5) CONTINUOUS FLOW (example: International Paper, Androscoggin Mill)	BATCH/CONTINUOUS FLOW HYBRID (example: Schlitz Brewery, Syracuse)
Process Features (continued)						
Additions to capacity	Incremental over full range of possible capacity	Larger increments possible, but over full range of possible capacity	Same as for 2	Changes can be made, but costly to do so because capacity comes in large chunks; otherwise, mild fluctuations possible within relatively narrow limits (e.g., line rebalance)	Only modest range for incremental change; otherwise, huge chunks of capacity required	Comparatively modest range for incremental change; then huge chunks of capacity required
Speed of process (dollars of output/ unit of time or dollars of output/dollars of input/unit of time)	Slow	Reasonably slow	Increasingly fast	Fast	Fast, sometimes astounding	Same as for 5
Pacing	Worker discretion key	Worker-paced	Worker-paced but set within some bounds by management action (e.g., line balance)	Machine-paced, but can be a management goal as well (e.g., line balancing)	Determined technologically; built into equipment	Generally determined technologically but some leeway available
Bottlenecks	Movable; frequent	Movable, but often predictable	Movable, but often predictable	Generally known and stationary	Known, stationary	Same as for 5
Nature of process change	Incremental	Mostly incremental; some significant radical changes possible	Mostly routine (rebalance); sometimes radical (equipment)	Same as for 3	Most change incremental but radical change possible: means big bucks and sweeping conversions	Sometimes radical; sometimes incremental
Place of technological change in process itself	Little impact; unlikely to be revolutionary	Important once in a while, usually incremental though	Increasingly important; embodied in equipment	Important; embodied in equipment	Far-reaching; surprisingly regular	Same as for 4
Setups	Many; varied expense	Some setups needed, but generally easy to do	Same as for 2	No setup required; line already set up	Few and expensive, if any; process organized to simplify most kinds of setups	Little or no setup required; process simplifies need for most kinds of setups
Run lengths	Short	Medium	Some long, some short	Long	Very long	Same as for 5
Materials-Oriented Features						
Materials requirements	Uncertain	Can often be placed statistically within reasonably narrow bounds	Known statistically within fairly close limits	Certain once production plan established	Same as for 4	Some aspects certain, others known statistically

TABLE 7-2 Comparing Processes of Different Types *(continued)*

FEATURES	(1) JOB SHOP (example: Norcen Industries)	(2) BATCH FLOW (example: Jung Products, Inc.)	(3) WORKER-PACED ASSEMBLY LINE (example: Burger King® Restaurant, Malden)	(4) MACHINE-PACED ASSEMBLY LINE (example: GMAD, Tarrytown)	(5) CONTINUOUS FLOW (example: International Paper, Androscoggin Mill)	BATCH/CONTINUOUS FLOW HYBRID (example: Schlitz Brewery, Syracuse)
Vertical integration	None	Sometimes backward, sometimes forward	Same as for 2	Sometimes backward, often forward	Often backward and forward	Same as for 2 and 3
Inventories						
Raw materials	Small; most raw materials purchased to coincide with orders	Moderate; some purchased to coincide with orders and some purchased to provide buffer stock	Varies; often steadily purchased since material needs are generally known within reasonably narrow bounds	Varies; often steadily purchased to coincide with production plan	Often large, but can vary and be steadily purchased to coincide with production plan	Varies; some purchased for buffer stock and some purchased to coincide with production plan
Work-in-process	Large	Moderate	Little	Same as for 3	Very little	Inventory placed between batch and continuous flow segments of process; moderate batch WIP, little continuous flow WIP
Finished goods	Low, if any	Varies	Same as for 2	Can vary; often thrust down distribution channels	Varies; often thrust down distribution channels	Same as for 5
Control over suppliers	Low	Moderate	Great	Same as for 3	Same as for 3	Same as for 3, 4, and 5
Control over customers	Little or none	Same as for 1	Same as for 1	Some, as to delivery	Same as for 4	Same as for 4 and 5
Supplier ties	Informal; spot buys	Some spot buys, some longer term contracts	Contracts increasingly long term	Formal; long term	Formal; generally long term	Same as for 5
Customer ties	Informal; repeat business encouraged, however	Some informal, some formal distribution	Can be informal or formal	Formal distribution channels	Same as for 4	Same as for 4 and 5
Information-Oriented Features						
Order handling and sales	Often bid for; sales are to order	Varies; some to order, and some from stock with lagged adjustments to that stock	Same as for 2	Sales well established ahead of time or from finished goods inventory; lagged adjustments to stock	Sales well established ahead of time or from finished goods inventory	Same as for 5
Degree of information coordination outside factory	Needed only for bids, receipt of any supplied materials, and to initiate supplies	Needed only to monitor sales and to initiate supplies	Needed to monitor sales and to place orders for supplies; sometimes for order scheduling	Elaborate order scheduling, materials tracking; various levels of forecasts; great deal of corporate communication	Elaborate order scheduling, materials tracking, forecasting; great deal of corporate communication	Monitoring sales, placing supply order; little corporate communication on day-to-day operations

(continues on next page)

TABLE 7-2 Comparing Processes of Different Types (continued)

FEATURES	(1) JOB SHOP (example: Norcen Industries)	(2) BATCH FLOW (example: Jung Products, Inc.)	(3) WORKER-PACED ASSEMBLY LINE (example: Burger King® Restaurant, Malden)	(4) MACHINE-PACED ASSEMBLY LINE (example: GMAD, Tarrytown)	(5) CONTINUOUS FLOW (example: International Paper, Androscoggin Mill)	BATCH/CONTINUOUS FLOW HYBRID (example: Schlitz Brewery, Syracuse)
Information-Oriented Features (continued)						
Information systems within factory	Elaborate, viewed as central; lots of flow between factory and workers and management	Less elaborate, but still considerable; less feedback required	Little information needed, basically just to communicate order; flow from management to workers. Opposite flow used primarily to signal breakdowns; more informal	Same as for 3	Little information needed, basically just to communicate product change; flow from management to workers. Opposite flow used primarily to signal breakdowns; generally more informal	Same as for 5
Trigger for production	Order itself	Could be order or level of finished goods inventory	Level of finished goods inventory, longer term forecasts, or "frozen" orders	Same as for 3	Same as for 3	First portion of process triggered by forecasts; second portion triggered by "frozen" orders
Scheduling	Uncertain, flexible; always subject to change	Flexible but not as uncertain; less subject to change	Process designed around fixed schedule	Same as for 3	Easy to group similar jobs or orders; fixed schedule often set in advance	Similar jobs or orders grouped together; fixed schedule set in advance, at least for second portion of process
Quality control	Informal, by each worker; spot checks	Can be more formal, though often is not	Some on-line checks, some postassembly checks; blame traceable	Same as for 3	Essentially done by process control people; designed into process; periodic sampling often done	Much of quality designed into process; periodic sampling often done
Response to cyclicality in demand	Overtime, shift work, some subcontract, hire/fire	Overtime; adjustments can be made by building and depleting inventory, shift work, and hire/fire	Overtime work or closing line early; some adjustments can be made by building and depleting inventory, rebalance, and close down shift or plant	Same as for 3	Inventory adjustments; otherwise, shift or plant is shut down	Same as for 5
Labor-Oriented Features						
Labor content per $1 of product value	Very high	High	Medium	Low	Very low	Same as for 4
Job content	Large	Medium	Small	Same as for 3	Often small "push button" staff; but can be "art" as well	Same as for 5
Importance and development of standards for labor	Key for scheduling and planning growth; big purpose of information system; sometimes key for wage payment	Often key for wage payment; needed also for scheduling product mix	Crucial for process design	Same as for 3	Important largely for assigning workforce to equipment	Same as for 5

TABLE 7-2 Comparing Processes of Different Types *(continued)*

FEATURES	(1) JOB SHOP (example: Norcen Industries)	(2) BATCH FLOW (example: Jung Products, Inc.)	(3) WORKER-PACED ASSEMBLY LINE (example: Burger King® Restaurant, Malden)	(4) MACHINE-PACED ASSEMBLY LINE (example: GMAD, Tarrytown)	(5) CONTINUOUS FLOW (example: International Paper, Androscoggin Mill)	BATCH/CONTINUOUS FLOW HYBRID (example: Schlitz Brewery, Syracuse)
Worker payment	Hourly; piece rate or other incentive wage	Often piece rate or other incentive wage	Hourly base; sometimes also tied to percentage of standard that crew achieves	Hourly	Same as for 4	Same as for 4 and 5
Advancement for worker	Knowledge of more and more machinery and machine capabilities. With more skills and/or seniority acquired, greater pay and responsibilities given, such as "lead worker." Seniority can lead to change in shift assignment	Knowledge of more and more machinery and machine capabilities. With more skills and/or seniority acquired, greater responsibilities given, such as "lead worker." Seniority can lead to change in shift assignment or department	With more skills and/or seniority acquired, greater responsibilities given, such as "lead worker" or "group leader." Seniority can lead to change in department or shift assignment	Seniority can lead to change in department or shift assignment	Seniority can lead to change in shift or, sometimes, department assignment	Same as for 5
End-of-month syndrome (i.e., more produced at end of month for billing than at beginning)	Inevitable	Often happens	Close to nonexistent	Same as for 3	Nonexistent	Same as for 5
Management Features						
Staff-line needs	Small staff (information, quotes, and new product development). Great line supervision needed	Small staff (generally methods related). Line supervision more critical	Large staff for process redesign, methods, forecasting, capacity planning, and scheduling. Line supervision and troubleshooting still critical	Same as for 3	Large staff for technology and capacity planning, and scheduling. Line supervision less crucial	Same as for 5
Degree of corporate influence on operations, if plant within a multiplant company	Modest	Same as for 1	Same as for 1	Great, for both operations and capital expenditures	Same as for 4	Variable; more likely that corporate influence is with capital expenditures than with day-to-day operations
Means of control	Usually a profit center	Can be either a profit center or a cost center	Same as for 2	Usually a cost center	Same as for 4	Same as for 4 and 5
Challenges to management	Scheduling, bidding, information flows, expediting, product innovation, shifting bottlenecks	Order processing, labor issues and pay, handling cyclicality	Balance (process design), product design, managing workforce, technological advances, capacity planning, materials management	Same as for 3	Capital needs, site, technological change, materials management, vertical integration	Same as for 5

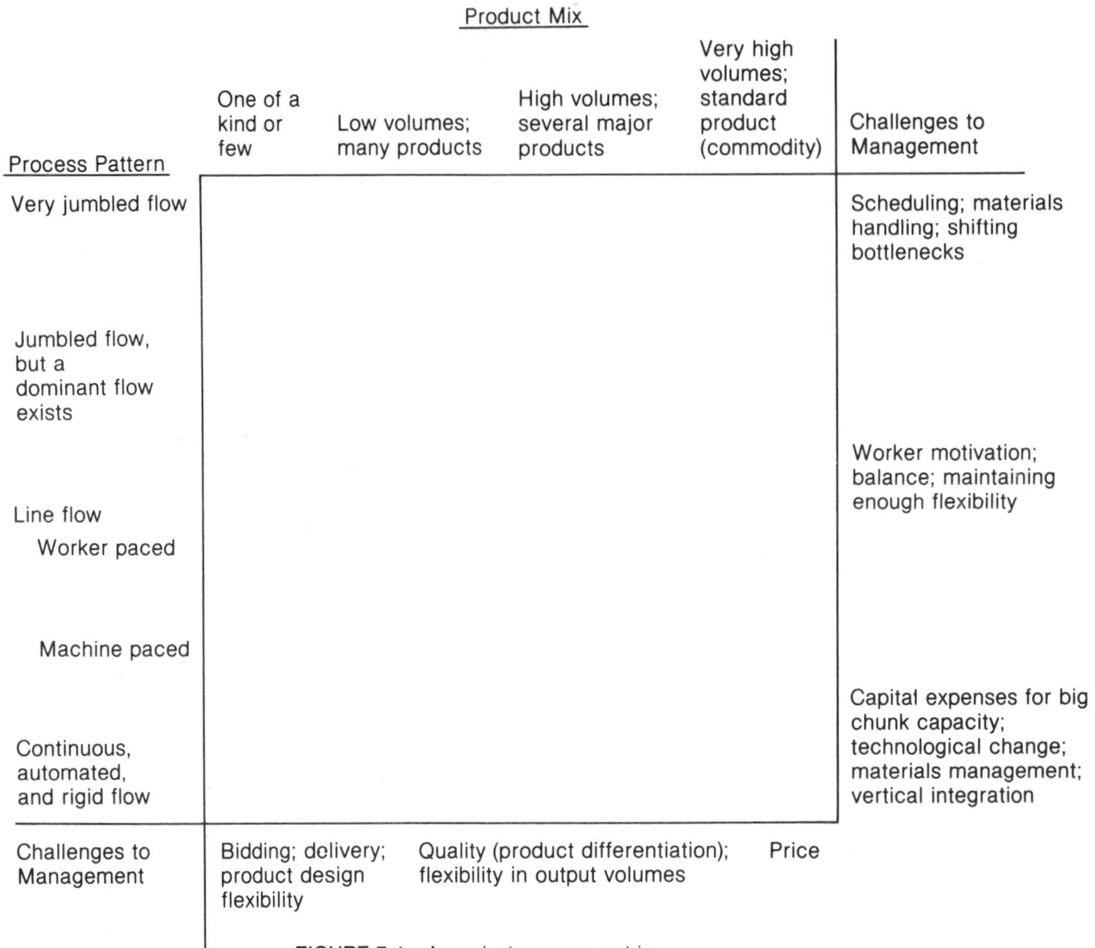

Product Mix

Process Pattern	One of a kind or few	Low volumes; many products	High volumes; several major products	Very high volumes; standard product (commodity)	Challenges to Management
Very jumbled flow					Scheduling; materials handling; shifting bottlenecks
Jumbled flow, but a dominant flow exists					
Line flow Worker paced					Worker motivation; balance; maintaining enough flexibility
Machine paced					
Continuous, automated, and rigid flow					Capital expenses for big chunk capacity; technological change; materials management; vertical integration
Challenges to Management	Bidding; delivery; product design flexibility	Quality (product differentiation); flexibility in output volumes		Price	

FIGURE 7-1   A product-process matrix.

of product through the process) that are possible. Figure 7-1 portrays this.

As we can see in Figure 7-1, the mix of products handled by the plant may range from a one-of-a-kind item (e.g., a work of art or a custom-designed house) to a very standard product that is produced and consumed in high volumes (e.g., sugar). In between, a company can produce many different products, each at relatively low volumes, or it can cut down on the number of different products offered but produce higher volumes for each.

As we might expect, management faces different sets of challenges in bringing each of these different product mixes to market. For example, a commodity item undoubtedly has to compete on price. While there may be a limited number of grades of the commodity, the ability to offer the item at low cost is absolutely critical to company success, whether the company produces paper clips or paper.

At the other end of this product mix spectrum, the one-of-a-kind item is frequently purchased with scarcely a thought about price. Since it is a custom item, the buyer is likely to have contracted for it beforehand. Once contracted for, the buyer typically becomes concerned for whether the product meets specifications and whether it can be delivered on time. This places a different set of demands on the manufacturer. Instead of paying near-exclusive attention to product cost, the manufacturer must pay particular attention to product design flexibility and delivery, since the manufacturer's success depends more on these features of the production system. Because most work is contracted for, management must be accomplished at developing bids for each, which entails thorough knowledge of costs within the factory.

In between these two extremes, management confronts somewhat different challenges. When many different products—each with low production volumes—are made or when fewer products—each with substantial production volumes—are made, product features such as quality or the ability to gear up (or down) rapidly in production become relatively more important than before. Product quality is a key element in differentiating one's product from others available, and is a chief reason why some products command price premiums. Flexibility in production volumes, while less evident to the marketplace than quality, is often a reason why some companies have been so successful—either beating their competitors to the market with seasonal, cyclical, or faddish products (e.g., building supplies, fashions) or turning off production when the market for a product appears to have dried up. Depending on the situation, product design flexibility, price, and delivery can still be very important to the manufacturer; but it is likely that as product design flexibility or quality rises in importance, price falls in importance.

These then are the chief challenges that various product mixes pose for their managers. A corresponding set of management challenges derive from the process patterns depicted in Figure 7-1. As the matrix reveals, the process pattern varies from a very jumbled flow to a continuous, automated, and rigid production flow. The process patterns in between exhibit varying degrees of rigidity and pacing.

For the jumbled process pattern, the challenges to management include scheduling, routing materials efficiently, and coping with shifting production bottlenecks. At the other end of the process pattern spectrum, the continuous, automated, and rigid process flow demands increased attention to such items as capital expenses for large-scale capacity increases, technological change in the process, materials management, and vertical integration. Between the process poles, factors like worker motivation, balance of capacities for different process segments, and process flexibility become relatively more important.

The arrays of product mix, process patterns, and their respective challenges to management line the outside of the product-process matrix. Now to fill in the inside. As our survey of production processes has revealed, different process types follow different process patterns and are also better suited to particular product mixes. It is easy then to match process types to the appropriate position within the matrix, as Figure 7-2 does.

As is readily apparent from the chart, process types should fill out the diagonal of the product-process matrix, from projects and job shops in the upper left corner down to continuous flow processes in the lower right corner. Only by being on the diagonal do processes match properly the process pattern to the prevailing product mix. Consider what it means to be off the diagonal. Suppose, for example, that a company tries to manufacture low volumes of many different products using a continuous, automated, and rigid flow process that is typically capital-intensive and vertically integrated. The match is clearly inappropriate since the process would have to be interrupted constantly and retooled often to permit the kind of product flexibility needed to produce low numbers of lots of products. Not only is the match inap-

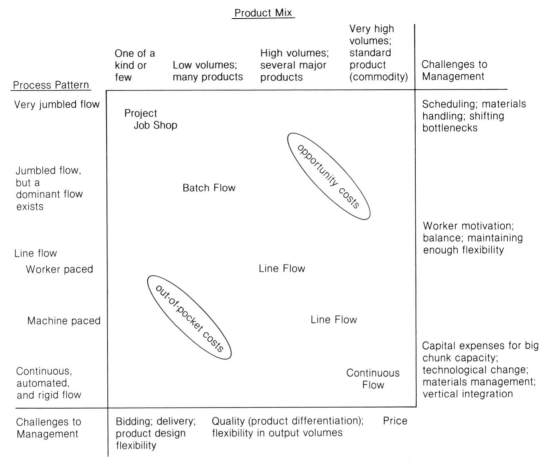

Product Mix

Process Pattern	One of a kind or few	Low volumes; many products	High volumes; several major products	Very high volumes; standard product (commodity)	Challenges to Management
Very jumbled flow	Project Job Shop				Scheduling; materials handling; shifting bottlenecks
Jumbled flow, but a dominant flow exists		Batch Flow	*opportunity costs*		
Line flow Worker paced			Line Flow		Worker motivation; balance; maintaining enough flexibility
Machine paced		*out-of-pocket costs*	Line Flow		
Continuous, automated, and rigid flow				Continuous Flow	Capital expenses for big chunk capacity; technological change; materials management; vertical integration
Challenges to Management	Bidding; delivery; product design flexibility	Quality (product differentiation); flexibility in output volumes	Price		

FIGURE 7-2   The product-process matrix filled in.

propriate, but it is expensive to boot. The purchase prices of the automated machines and the cost of product changeovers would be staggering, involving a great deal of out-of-pocket expenses.

Being above the diagonal brings on costs of a different kind. In this case, suppose a very standard product consumed in great quantity were manufactured in a jumbled flow process pattern. Here again the match is clearly inappropriate, though not because too many dollars go out-of-pocket to buy expensive machinery. Rather, operating costs (mainly, labor costs) are much higher than they

could be, which means that the profit margin on each unit of the product made is much lower than it should be. By not substituting specific, special purpose machinery for high labor input and general purpose equipment, the company forgoes profits that it would otherwise earn.

OPPORTUNITY COST

This phenomenon goes by the name of "opportunity cost," since by not investing in more equipment and a more rigid production flow, the company is forgoing the *opportunity* to earn increased profits. These costs are every bit as real as the payment of dollars out-of-pocket.

This notion of opportunity cost can be reinforced by a famous saying of Benjamin Franklin, no slouch himself at operations management. To make the point, however, we must make a brief excursion into logic. One truth of logic is the validity of the so-called contrapositive, which says simply that if the statement "If A, then B" is true, then it is also true that "If not B, then not A." That is to say, if every time A occurs B follows, then we can be sure that if B does not occur, then A did not occur as well.

Enough of logic then, and back to Ben Franklin. One of his Poor Richard sayings is that "A penny saved is a penny earned." We have all recognized the truth of that since childhood, but I assert that by this saying Ben showed us he knows everything about opportunity cost. After all, what is the contrapositive of "A penny saved is a penny earned"? A penny *not* earned is a penny *not* saved (i.e., a penny spent). All we are saying by this notion of opportunity cost is that "a penny not earned (an opportunity forgone) is a penny spent." We shall often have occasion to consider opportunity costs, as well as out-of-pocket costs, in analyzing and deciding various operations issues.

QUESTIONS

1. What are the main changes in product features in each of the six processes? Why should these particular features change as they do?

2. Compare and contrast the process features and information-oriented features of the job shop and the continuous flow processes.

3. In what ways does the hybrid flow process vary from the continuous flow process?

4. Discuss some of the main challenges management faces in bringing different product mixes to market. What other management challenges can you think of with regard to product mix that have not been included in the product-process matrix?

5. Examine some of the implications of the concept of opportunity cost for a company and its attitude toward profit. Give some examples from your own experience that exemplify the notion of opportunity cost.

SITUATION FOR STUDY

HALL RUNNERS

Robert Hall was a marathon runner. Earlier in his running career, Bob had some problems with his feet due to the running. Dr. Baines, an orthopedist, diagnosed Bob's problem as one requiring special running shoes. Consequently, Bob became interested in this problem and, while in graduate school, started "building" running shoes for himself, and later for a few friends. These shoes were designed by Bob in consultation with Dr. Baines. Figure 7-A is a rough sketch of the "Hall Runner." During the first few years, Bob made the shoes in the garage of his parents' home using their sewing

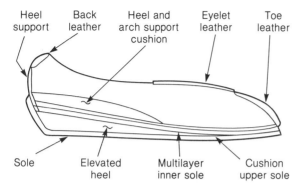

Heel support   Back leather   Heel and arch support cushion   Eyelet leather   Toe leather

Sole   Elevated heel   Multilayer inner sole   Cushion upper sole

Body material is cushioned nylon.
Tongue has extra cushion sewn on.

FIGURE 7-A Sketch of a typical "Hall Runner."

machine. For other processing equipment he invented methods and processes to get the job done cheaply.

Bob's method of manufacture was to purchase what he could and make what he could not. At the beginning, he purchased all of his material in flat sheets or in rolls and cut out the various patterns with scissors much as he had seen his mother do with dress patterns. He made some wooden shoe lasts on which he "built" the shoe after he had all the necessary parts. He converted an old clothes dryer into a drying oven by removing the drum drive. This process was necessary to dry the glues and solvents that held most of the shoe together.

Bob had started this business just before the "jogging for health" fad started sweeping the country. He was now selling some of his shoes through independent shoe stores in three large cities within 200 miles of his home. He had developed master patterns for all of the shoes that he made, and he now employed seven part-time workers to help in his "shop."

The current manufacturing process differs little from that which Bob started in his parents' garage, except for larger batches, some heavier duty equipment (including two industrial sewing machines), and the rental of a larger building. Figure 7-B shows the layout of the current shop. Bob has been considering future expansion, and he has some ideas—some practical in the near future and some probably impractical, even for the distant future. He has jotted these ideas down in trying to assess their worth (Table 7-A).

TABLE 7-A   Ideas for Improving the Process for Making Hall Runners

CURRENT TASKS	CURRENT METHOD	PROPOSED METHOD	POSSIBLE FUTURE METHOD(S)
Cut material to shape	Scissors to pattern	Punch press ("steel rule" die)	"Hard" punch press tool; laser cutter using numerical control
Sew upper portions together	Sewing machine (hand control)	Sewing machine (numerical control)	"Super" glues
Shape and fit material to last	Hand fit; glue in tubes	Pneumatic fixtures on lasts; hose application of glues from large containers	Robot assembly
Dry solvents and glue	Converted clothes dryer	Conveyor belt through ovens	Microwave ovens, conveyor fed
Packaging	By hand	Automatic packaging machine	

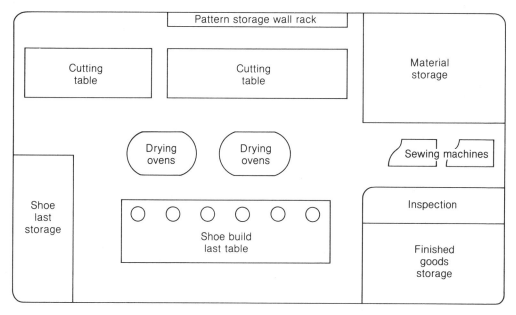

FIGURE 7-B Shop layout for producing Hall's running shoes.

All the "Hall Runners" are currently made in the same basic style except for the tread design. There are three of these—one for street, one for cross-country, and one for track. The only other variation is in size. Bob has also noted that more and more people are wearing running shoes as casual attire or as everyday shoes. This trend may warrant developing different styles and colors.

Both Bob and Dr. Baines feel that the market potential is great for quality running shoes, and they intend to enlarge their production capacity. Bob realizes that they started as a custom job shop and have grown slightly to almost a batch process.

1. At this point in the development of the market, the product, and the process, what would you suggest that Bob, Dr. Baines, and their financial backers consider?

2. In the continuum from job shop to continuous flow where is the "Hall Runner" and what should the next step be?

REFERENCE NOTE

1. The concept of the product-process matrix owes much to Robert H. Hayes and Steven C. Wheelwright. See the two articles by Hayes and Wheelwright in the January–February and March–April 1979 *Harvard Business Review* entitled "Link Manufacturing Process and Product Life Cycles" and "The Dynamics of Process-Product Life Cycles," respectively.

II

IMPROVING EXISTING OPERATIONS

This segment of the text discusses the problems and concerns that surface repeatedly in the day-to-day operations of a business. As the previous segment has demonstrated, production processes can differ markedly and, as a consequence, so too can the problems and concerns of the managers who run them. Throughout this segment, the relationship between problem and process should be clear.

Four areas of day-to-day management concern are the foci for the chapters in this segment:

1. *Bottlenecks.* Having enough capacity in the short run is a constant headache, especially in job shop and batch flow production processes. Identifying where bottlenecks are or might occur and taking measures to overcome them are always on an operation manager's agenda. They are the subject of Chapter 8.

2. *Workforce.* A good workforce is a company's most prized asset. Building up a team of skilled workers who truly care about what they are doing takes a lot of care from a company's managers. Workforce management is a rich topic and can be as diverse as individual company situations. Chapter 9 concentrates on the important and universal concerns of worker motivation, wage schemes, and the forces and issues

behind worker representation by industrial
unions.

3. *Materials.* The movement of materials from a
"raw" to a "finished" state is what a production
process is all about. Managers justly worry
about having either not enough or too much
material at various times during the production
cycle, since it often costs significant amounts of
money to purchase and to hold materials. Managing materials and inventories of all types
takes thought and is the topic of Chapter 10.

4. *Planning and controlling production.* Even as
most operations managers are wrestling with today's problems, they must keep an eye out for
the problems sneaking up over the horizon.
Trying to meet future sales demands in a timely
and inexpensive way is both a worthy goal and
one that requires much planning. Keeping the
process functioning smoothly and producing to
the desired quality standard requires a good deal
of control. The planning, and control, and
scheduling of production are the concerns of
Chapter 11.

CHAPTER

8

BREAKING BOTTLENECKS

Production bottlenecks are generally considered to be temporary blockades to increased output; they can be thrown up anywhere along the course of a production process. Some are easy to identify and to remedy, while others are devilish.

The bottleneck that is easy to cope with is stationary. Work-in-process inventory piles up quickly behind it; clearly, little is getting through. Its cause is usually also clear—a machine has broken down or key workers are absent or demand has simply outstripped the clear, rated capacity of a machine—and the remedy follows easily.

More subtle are bottlenecks that shift from one part of the process to another or that have no clear cause. Inventories build up in different places and at different times. Such bottlenecks creep up on management and demand more thorough investigation. Perhaps they were detected as flaws in a product's quality caused inadvertently by one or more workers trying to keep pace with production demands that should not have been placed on them. Or, they are caused by missing parts. Or, they may be caused by new product start-up or changes in the mix of products through the factory. In such cases the remedies are less clear-cut, and some analysis is called for.

ANALYZING BOTTLENECKS

In analyzing bottlenecks it is always helpful to trace the production process by using a process flow diagram and to assign what capacity numbers are available to each stage of the process. Simply being systematic in this way and being as precise as possible with capacity measures can uncover primary and secondary bottlenecks straightaway. Such an analysis is naturally easier with well-delineated processes and ones where capacity is unambiguous. The process flow diagram, in that case, becomes a planning aid for breaking significant, stationary bottlenecks.

As an example, consider the steel industry. The process is a continuous flow one and capacity, in tons, is well known and dependent primarily on equipment capabilities. A process flow diagram for a steel mill, with associated capacity measures, might well look like the one shown in Figure 8-1. The diagram makes it clear that the bottleneck at this steel mill is the blast furnace; in order to increase the mill's capacity, blast furnace capacity must be enlarged. The secondary bottleneck resides in the casting and semifinishing operation; that is, once the blast furnace is expanded past 4.7

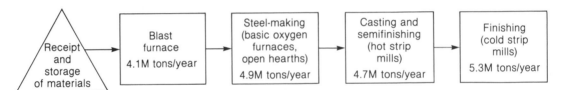

FIGURE 8-1   A process flow diagram for a steel mill.

million tons per year, casting and semifinishing will be the bottleneck.

The most slack element of the process flow shown in Figure 8-1 appears to be the finishing mills. In most steel mills, however, the nominal capacity of the finishing mills is purposefully greater than the other elements of the process to ensure capacity under all kinds of product mixes. Thus, even in steel mills the notion of capacity becomes somewhat blurred and ambiguous. A process flow diagram must be modified somewhat and interpreted if it is to be useful for analyzing bottlenecks.

Even more modification and interpretation of process flow diagrams is needed when less rigid production processes (e.g., batch flow, job shop) are involved. In such processes, not only are capacity figures potentially very volatile, but the process flow itself may be indeterminate. Identifying bottlenecks in these processes becomes a formidable task. Typically, ranges of capacity must be used and different arrangements of the process flow must be tried. Still, judicious and systematic use of a process flow diagram can be a valuable tool in identifying the process elements *and conditions* that account for bottlenecks.

Another useful tool in analyzing bottlenecks is an inventory buildup graph, a pictorial way of accounting for the rates at which inventories are either piled up or depleted. These graphs are particularly useful when the demand on an element of the process is especially erratic, such as occurs routinely in the processing of many raw agricultural commodities but can occur in other industries as well. To illustrate the use of an inventory buildup graph, consider Situation 8-1.

SITUATION 8-1

DEVINE NUTS, INC.

It was autumn and the peanut harvesting season was winding to a close. Frank Coyne, the proprietor of Devine Nuts, was reflecting on the past season and speculating whether he would have enough peanut drying capacity for next year, especially if the local crop increased by 10 percent, as many of the peanut farmers were saying.

Frank Coyne was a peanut broker. Devine Nuts purchased peanuts from farmers in the area (Devine, Texas is situated about 30 miles southwest of San Antonio) and sold them to peanut processing companies and cooperatives, which used them for making peanut

oil, peanut butter, candy, and a host of other items.

Devine Nuts' principal operating functions were straightforward. During the peanut harvesting season, farmers delivered loads of so-called "green" peanuts to Devine Nuts. The trucks, with their loads, were weighed and records kept by the issuance of scale tickets. After weighing, a moisture sample was taken. This inspection step was critical since the peanut processing companies would not accept any peanuts without the government's grading certificate on them, and a grading certificate would not be issued unless the moisture content of the peanuts was 10.5 percent by weight or lower. If a delivered load of peanuts met this moisture standard and was thereby granted a certificate, another sample of peanuts would be drawn, weighed, and shelled so that the kernels could be classified into four size categories (large, regular, medium, and small). Kernel weight and size determined the price the farmer would be paid, typically about 25¢ per pound. Once the price was determined, the peanuts were loaded into railcars or trucks and shipped to a shelling plant. Sometimes immediate transportation could not be arranged, and the graded peanuts would have to be stored in Devine Nuts' bulk warehouse, which had room for 5500 tons.

More often than not, the delivered loads of peanuts would not meet the moisture standard and would have to be dried and then reweighed and graded. Devine Nuts owned a number of dryers of various sizes: 38 6-ton capacity dryers, 10 11-ton capacity dryers, and 14 14-ton capacity dryers. How long a load of peanuts would have to remain in a dryer depended on its moisture content. Peanuts with a moisture content of only 10 to 15 percent could be dried in about 12 hours, but peanuts with a moisture content of 15 to 25 percent could take anywhere from 24 to 36 hours to dry. Devine Nuts did not have any storage for wet green peanuts; they were dumped directly from the farmers' trucks into the dryers. If dryer space was not available, trucks had no recourse but to wait until it became available.

The drying operation was critical because harvested peanuts that were wet began growing a fungus about 12 hours after harvesting. To avoid spoilage, it was essential that drying start within 12 hours after harvesting. A day's harvesting began after the morning dew had dried and continued until dusk. Deliveries to Devine Nuts began about noon and lasted until about 10 P.M. in a more or less steady stream.

Frank Coyne's success as a broker rested on his ability to meet the needs of the farmers who brought their crops to him each year. If Frank could not dry a farmer's peanuts on time, he stood an excellent chance of losing that customer forever to another broker. In addition, if Frank left too many trucks waiting too long for available dryer space, he risked souring his customer relations, since the farmers needed those trucks out in the field for the next day's harvest.

On most days, Devine Nuts' drying capacity was more than enough to handle the demand. A typical day's delivery would be about 120 tons; roughly half would have a moisture content between 10 and 15 percent, and half between 15 and 25 percent. What grayed Frank Coyne's hair were the peak days that would occur right after a rainstorm. Storms usually kept the farmers from harvesting, and so loads that ordinarily might be stretched over several days would be bunched together in just a few. On such days, 300 tons of green peanuts might be delivered. What made matters much worse was that the peanuts were soaking wet from the rain and had moisture contents that required 36-hour drying.

Devine Nuts had been able to handle the past season's peak days without turning away a customer, although some trucks had to wait at times to unload. Frank Coyne's immediate concern was calculating whether a 10 percent increase in the local crop (which he translated into a 10 percent increase in peak day activity) would overload his drying capacity and (1) force trucks away, (2) cause them to wait longer than dawn (6 A.M.) of the day following their delivery, or (3) cause them to wait longer than 12 hours to unload.

DISCUSSION OF DEVINE NUTS

In analyzing the situation Frank Coyne finds himself in at Devine Nuts, it is helpful to picture what is going on—how peanuts build up in inventory after delivery and how the inventories are drawn down by completed drying. What is of concern to Frank are the peak days, when 300 tons of soggy peanuts arrive during a 10-hour period and have to be dried for 36 hours. Figure 8-2 pictures how inventories build up at Devine Nuts during a succession of peak days, assuming an even distribution of truck arrivals.

Figure 8-2 assumes that at noon on day 1 all the dryers are empty. As loads of peanuts arrive from

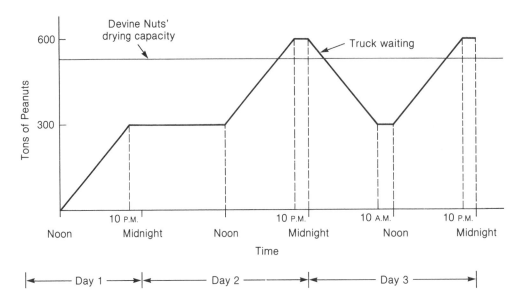

FIGURE 8-2 *Inventory buildup at Devine Nuts after several peak days.*

then on, at an average rate of 30 tons per hour, dryers are successively filled up. By 10 P.M. when the farmers' shipments cease for the day, 300 tons of peanuts are in the dryers. Because they are so wet, these peanuts will not be removed from the dryers until after midnight ending day 2. In the meantime, another day's worth of soggy peanuts will have arrived. Most of these can be transferred directly to waiting dryers, but some will have to wait until day 1's peanuts are removed.

How many tons of peanuts will have to wait for dryers and how many hours will they have to wait in their trucks? Devine Nuts' total drying capacity is 534 tons, figured as [(38 · 6) + (10 · 11) + (14 · 14)]. Thus, 66 tons of peanuts (600 − 534) cannot be transferred immediately from trucks to dryers. Since peanuts are arriving at a rate of 30 tons per hour, dryer capacity can be expected to run out at 2.2 hours (66/30) before 10 P.M. on day 2. The dryers will not be available until midnight, but at that time dryer space will be released at the rate of 30 tons per hour, the same rate that peanuts entered the dryers. The first truck that cannot dump its load immediately into a dryer will have to wait un-

til midnight to be unloaded, a wait of 4.2 hours. Because the withdrawal rate of peanuts from the dryers exactly matches the arrival rate of peanuts to Devine Nuts, all of the trucks will wait an average of 4.2 hours. The last truck will be free to return to its farm at 2.2 hours after midnight. Thus, Figure 8-2 confirms Devine Nuts' record over the past season: trucks did have to wait, but none had to be turned away or came close to spoiling the peanuts or not getting back to the fields on time.

How does a 10 percent increase in peak day deliveries affect operations? Figure 8-3 deals with that situation. The slightly steeper slopes pictured in this inventory buildup graph reflect the increased average arrival rate of 33 tons per hour. Since drying still must take 36 hours, Devine Nuts runs out of capacity sooner than in Figure 8-2. Specifically, Devine Nuts' capacity falls 126 tons short (660 − 534) and the dryers begin overflowing at 3.82 hours (126/33) before 10 P.M. Since the dryers will not be available until midnight, each truck will have to wait an average of 5.82 hours before unloading. The latest arriving truck will still be free to return to service at 3.82 hours past midnight,

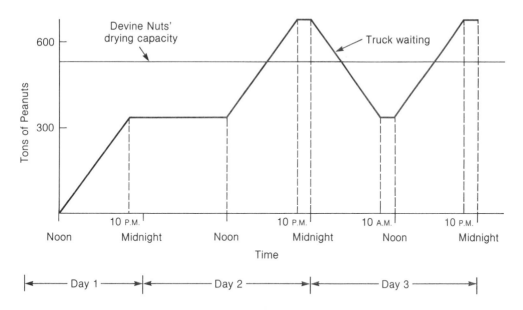

FIGURE 8-3 Inventory buildup at Devine Nuts when peak day tonnage has increased by 10 percent.

well before dawn. Thus, even with an increase of 10 percent in peak day tonnage, Devine Nuts can expect not to have to turn away customers for lack of capacity.

Frank Coyne may also be interested in knowing how much peak day demand would have to grow before Devine Nuts' present capacity would be insufficient to free up the delivery trucks by dawn. To find the answer to this question, we need to calculate how short of the peak Devine Nuts' capacity would have to be before 6 hours (midnight to dawn) would be too little time to work down the excess.

Let x represent the factor by which we would have to multiply present demand to yield the peak day demand that strains capacity. Thus, the total tonnage of peanuts accumulating in dryers and in trucks at 10 P.M. on day 2 would be the present 600 times x. In the 6 hours after midnight, x times the present rate of 30 tons per hour would be freed from the dryers each hour. Thus, we can write out the following relationship:

$$6 \cdot 30x = 600x - 534$$

$$\left(\begin{array}{c}\text{drying capacity}\\\text{freed up in 6 hours}\end{array}\right) = \left(\begin{array}{c}\text{wet peanuts}\\\text{waiting for dryers}\end{array}\right)$$

Solving for x, we get

$$180x = 600x - 534$$

$$534 = 420x$$

$$1.27 = x$$

Thus, peak demand will have to rise by 27 percent over the present level before Devine Nuts' present capacity will be insufficient. Frank Coyne should be reassured.

This type of calculation, where the general question is asked "At which point does one alternative begin to dominate another?" is often called a *break-even* calculation. Here we asked "At what level of demand would Devine Nuts' capacity begin to be insufficient?" and the break-even point was a demand 27 percent greater than the present. As one might expect, the break-even calculation can be exceedingly useful and flexible, and we shall be using it in different guises throughout this text. It is particularly useful in gauging the sensitivity of a decision to variations in a particular variable. In fact, the break-even computed above is a form of sensitivity analysis: How sensitive is Devine Nuts' capacity needs to an increase in peak demand?

With the background of these tools of analysis — the process flow diagram, the inventory buildup graph, and break-even calculations — we turn now to remedying some bottlenecks of various types.

DEALING WITH BOTTLENECKS

Consider Situation 8-2.

SITUATION 8-2

WYOMING VALLEY FURNITURE COMPANY

It was the first part of July, time for another monthly planning meeting on the production schedule for the upcoming 16-week period. George Sowerby, owner and president of Wyoming Valley Furniture, normally relished this opportunity to grapple with what he viewed as the most important management activity in the furniture business. Today, however, he was a bit apprehensive because the newly arrived order from Pennsylvania House threatened another bottleneck in the lathe department, just like the one the company had suffered through only last month.

The Wyoming Valley Furniture Company was a small manufacturer of casegoods furniture (i.e., all wood furniture as opposed to upholstered furniture), situated in the Wyoming Valley of Pennsylvania, near Wilkes-Barre. It was one of thousands of small firms in the furniture industry. The company did not produce its own brand; it was a subcontractor to several of the large furniture retailers such as Pennsylvania House and Ethan Allen. A retailer like Pennsylvania House authorized Wyoming Valley Furniture to manufacture a variety of pieces (e.g., hutches, tables, bureaus) and each month ordered so many thousand dollars of furniture, specifying a particular mix of the items authorized. It was up to a company like Wyoming Valley Furniture to deliver the ordered pieces within its 16-week planning period and to have them pass the retailer's quality standards.

The Threatened Bottleneck

About 4 months ago, Pennsylvania House placed an order for 150 of a newly authorized piece, a rather elaborate dining room buffet table. Last month was the first time Wyoming Valley Furniture manufactured the buffet; the time and trouble it took to make it were greater than expected. The buffet's legs, in particular, demanded more time and care in lathe work than Wyoming Valley Furniture had allocated. (Machine setups, for example, took 15 minutes for each lot rather than the planned 8 minutes, and run times per leg were 20 minutes rather than the planned 15 minutes. In addition, considerably more rework was required than expected.) As this became evident, the company began scheduling overtime in the lathe department. Still, the buffets were delivered late. What is more, the slowdown the order caused in the lathe department spilled over into the finish mill, and 10 workers in the finish mill were without work for about 8 percent of their time over the 2-week period the buffet order was scheduled through their shop. Management had been caught with no work suitable to give those workers, as orders got bottled up in the lathe department. This failure in production scheduling was not only embarrassing but also expensive. (Wages averaged $6 per hour, and workers generally worked 40 hours per week.)

The Furniture Making Process and Coping with Bottlenecks

Wyoming Valley Furniture's production process was similar to that employed by most other casegoods manufacturers. It started with the purchase and storage of rough-cut lumber of various species and grades. This lumber was then dried on racks for 2 weeks in the predrying shed (a large enclosure in which moderately heated air was circulated) and for 2 weeks in the kiln, where higher heat was applied. From the kiln the lumber was sent to the rough mill, as it was called, where an assortment of power saws (for lengthwise ripping, mitering, and end cutting), planers, tenoners, lathes, gluing machines and presses, and other tools formed the basic parts out of which the piece of furniture was assembled. Typically an order spent 3 weeks in the rough mill.

From the rough mill the order traveled to the finish mill, which was responsible for boring, routing, and sanding the rough milled parts and for a modest amount of subassembly. Three weeks in the finish mill was standard for an order. All of the parts needed for the assembly of a piece of casegoods furniture were gathered at the finish mill before being sent to the assembly and finishing departments. The assembly department put together each piece of furniture, and the finishing department applied the stain and lacquer to each. Inspection and packing for shipment completed the process. The typical order spent 2 weeks in assembly and finishing. Thus, the entire process took about 12 weeks. By adding a month, the planning period of 16 weeks was determined.

Ordinarily, Wyoming Valley Furniture was thoroughly familiar with the particular demands that the various authorized pieces of furniture it manufactured placed on machines and workers. These demands could be accommodated in the development of the production schedule so that the entire factory ran as close to perfect balance as possible. Of course, perfect balance was an ever-elusive and only momentarily achieved goal. In striving for this balance, however, the company employed a variety of rules of thumb that helped determine which orders would be grouped together in the same week and which ones shifted into other weeks. For example, only one model of dining room suite would be scheduled in one week, and only one model of hutch. In essence, bottlenecks were coped with by scheduling around them whenever possible.

Most of the bottlenecks that struck the factory could not be anticipated. New products and their start-ups (e.g., the buffet) were a persistent cause of bottlenecks. New wood species also caused occasional problems (for example, a recent switch to oak in a particular model had caused problems). Machine breakdowns, especially of one-of-a-kind machines, always created a stir in the factory. If demand was particularly high, bottlenecks might occur simply because more orders were released to the factory than the factory could realistically be expected to work through.

Most bottlenecks were overcome by throwing more labor-hours at them—usually through calling for overtime, but sometimes by hiring or transferring workers to the bottleneck task. Other bottlenecks, usually the chronic ones, were broken by buying new equipment.

Dealing with the Threatened Bottleneck

What was particularly disheartening to George Sowerby and his production scheduler, Vic Baiz, was that there seemed to be no way that the current order of 300 buffets could be scheduled through the lathe department without incurring overtime; the demand on the lathe department was unavoidably constant. Of the 400 labor-hours estimated now for the entire order (300 pieces • 4 legs per piece • 20 minutes per leg), only 250 could safely be scheduled during regular hours. The remaining 150 hours appeared headed for overtime and a pay rate of 1.5 times the regular rate.

George and Vic were eager to avoid the problem that occurred last month, when overtime in the lathe department created scheduling problems in the finish mill that could not be resolved easily by working on orders further back in the queue. To some extent, they would rely on better scheduling now to permit smoother functioning of the finish mill, but exactly how much smoother operations would be was unknown.

An alternative to this strategy of running lots of overtime during the order and hoping for the best was a strategy of working a modest amount of overtime beginning immediately and inventorying quantities of the troublesome buffet leg. This, of course, meant incurring some inventory carrying expenses. Vic Baiz estimated the inventory expense at an average of 25¢ for every buffet leg that had to be produced in overtime.

Here were two ways of coping with the upcoming bottleneck, and George Sowerby wondered which he ought to authorize. One involved some certain extra costs (i.e., inventory expense); the other involved an uncertain, but possibly lower, cost—the disruption that significant amounts of overtime in the lathe department might have on the finish department. George wondered how little the disruption would have to be before the latter option dominated the inventory one.

Discussion of Wyoming Valley Furniture Company

Wyoming Valley Furniture knows that a bottleneck is coming, a definite advantage, but it is disadvantaged because its normal means of dealing with bottlenecks (namely, to schedule around them) appears inadequate. If the company could routinely expect such heavy demands on the lathe department, George Sowerby might feel free to expand its equipment and workforce. However, the lathe demands made by this particular piece of furniture are unusual and, as yet, it is not a steady order. Only three or four orders for the buffet are likely in any year. Wyoming Valley Furniture seems to occupy some no-man's land between capacity expansion and the status quo.

As it stands, the company can plan for lots of overtime when the entire order is scheduled for production and hope that no disruption will occur to the finish mill. Or, the company can try to stock up early on the problem buffet leg. In this case, the same number of overtime hours will have to be scheduled, although they would be stretched over a longer period of time. In fact, stretching out production will almost surely increase the setup times involved on the lathe, implying even more overtime.

How costly would a disruption be if it occurred again in the finish mill? The previous order of 150 pieces, half the current order, disrupted 10 workers for 8 percent of their time over 2 weeks. Thus, 64 worker hours (10 workers · .08 · 2 weeks · 40 hours/week) were lost at a cost of $6 each, for a total cost of $384. If twice the number of pieces causes twice the level of disruption, $768 would be sacrificed. Unfortunately, we do not know whether this level of disruption in the finish mill will be maintained or whether better production planning will leave enough slack so that the finish mill workers can work around any stalled buffet legs. This uncertainty suggests some of the same sort of sensitivity analysis that we did in the Devine Nuts situation.

How costly is the inventory building alternative? The estimated overtime is 150 hours, implying that 450 legs (150/400 · 1200 legs) will be completed using overtime. At an average inventory expense of 25¢ per leg, $112.50 would be spent for the inventory itself.

This $112.50 inventory expense is considerably below the $768 estimate for the "grin and bear it" alternative. Yet both figures are "soft" and require some interpreting. The inventory expense figure, for example, is almost surely too low because it does not include the extra time it would take to set up the lathes for the numerous small lots that would have to be run. We can make some estimate of how much setup time and expense would be required. Suppose the overtime on the legs takes 10 hours per week for 15 weeks, and that the 10 hours each week consists of one lathe operator working 1 hour longer on each weekday and 5 hours on Saturday. Thus, 6 setups of 15 minutes each would be required each week, for a total of 90 setups (6 · 15) over the next 15 weeks. At 15 minutes per setup and $6 per hour, the 90 setups would cost an additional $135. A better estimate of the cost of the inventory building alternative would be $247.50 ($112.50 + $135).

The cost is still considerably below the $768 estimate for the "grin and bear it" alternative. This $768 figure, too, may need to be revised. If, for example, the order does not create any of the disruptions in the finish mill that prevailed last time, the $768 figure vanishes to nothing. The $768 figure assumes the same kind of 8 percent disruption that occurred with the previous order. With the company on the alert now, it is likely that something less than an 8 percent disruption in the finish mill will actually occur. How much less of a disruption would be needed before the "grin and bear it" option dominates the inventory buildup one? The same kind of sensitivity analysis that we introduced with Devine Nuts can be employed here.

Let x be the fraction of the 8 percent disruption needed to equalize the costs of the two options.

Then,

$$x \cdot \$768 = \$247.50$$

$$x = .32$$

This calculation suggests that if Wyoming Valley Furniture feels that it can lower the finish mill disruption to less than a third of its previous level, it should treat the order like any other. If, on the other hand, the company feels that more than that level of disruption would occur, the inventory buildup option should be followed. While these calculations do not make George Sowerby's decision for him, they serve to focus the issue.

LESSONS FROM WYOMING VALLEY FURNITURE COMPANY

Wyoming Valley Furniture was unfortunately caught in a very uncomfortable position. The company did not have sufficient capacity so that the rescheduling of the order could alleviate the impending bottleneck, nor was the extra demand on the lathe department steady enough to warrant an expansion of its equipment and workforce. The company was limited in its options: it could try to

head off its problems by building up an inventory of parts or it could try to "gut" it out. The assessment of such nebulous bottleneck situations is one of the chronic management dilemmas of job shops and batch flow processes. In this case, a new product introduction, which changed the product mix considerably, placed excessive demands on a single department and threatened to clog up the flexibility in scheduling that keeps a job shop or batch flow process from grinding to a halt every time a problem like this is encountered. The threat to the factory's flexibility could just as easily have come from engineering changes or quality problems demanding rework or missing parts from a supplier or something similar.

Coming to a decision on how to remedy the bottleneck called for an analysis of the costs associated with each of the options. Specifically, the analysis involved comparing the *extra* costs incurred by each alternative, since those were the only costs that differed between the options being considered.

The importance of this type of analysis and the role of demand as well as supply considerations in confronting bottlenecks is pursued in Situation 8-3.

SITUATION 8-3

CITRUS AIRLINES

Larry Klock had to confess that he hadn't thought of it, but his operations manager, Dave Dove, had proposed an intriguing, possible solution to Citrus Airlines' present shortage of seats. Larry was the president of Citrus Airlines, a small intrastate carrier operating between Miami, Jacksonville, Orlando, Fort Lauderdale, Tampa, Tallahassee, and a host of smaller Florida cities. Recently, business had been booming, largely, Larry thought, because of an upturn in the economy. Citrus Airlines was using much of its equipment to the hilt and faced the prospect of having to purchase more in order to provide more seats. Larry

was leery of this option because of both the tenuousness of the current economic recovery and the comparatively recent financial good health of the airline. Dave Dove's proposal struck an imaginative middle ground.

Dove had proposed that Citrus abolish first-class seating on all of the Boeing 727s that Citrus owned. (The 727s operated primarily between the major Florida cities, averaging 91 flights each day.) By abolishing first class, space would be provided for more seats. According to the cabin configuration of seats that Citrus had always maintained, 20 of the plane's total of

125 seats were provided for first-class passengers. If the first-class cabin were reconfigured to conform to the coach cabin, an additional eight seats could be provided. These seats could be added because coach sat five across in each row of the airplane as against four across in each first-class row and because the distance between rows in coach was slightly less (less legroom) than in first class. Dave Dove estimated that it would cost $15,000 to alter each of the 15 727s in Citrus' fleet.

Of course, abolishing first class meant abolishing first-class fares as well. At present, the average first-class fare in the Citrus system was $71 as opposed to the average coach fare of $56. On the other hand, first class was a little more costly to serve, an average of $3.28 versus $1.77, because first-class food and beverage service was more elaborate.

Larry was concerned that the abolition of first-class service would adversely affect the patronage of Citrus' first-class travelers, even though Larry knew that the availability of more seats could mean substantially more revenue. To investigate these matters, Larry had called upon Sarah Hammans, the airline's marketing manager. Hammans' report is shown in Figure 8-4.

Dave Dove's suggestion about eliminating first-class service would surely help cut down on the number of flights that leave standbys behind, but Larry Klock couldn't help but wonder whether that benefit would offset the costs of reconfiguring the first-class cabins and of losing loyal first-class passengers.

Memorandum

To: Larry Klock
From: Sarah Hammans
Subject: Abolition of First-Class Seating on 727s

You asked for analysis of two points related to the abolition of our "sun-kissed" (first-class) service. Let me address them in turn.

1. Retention of "sun-kissed" travelers. Although our retention rates will vary by city-pair depending on our competition and the prevailing flight schedules, I think we would be hard-pressed to retain more than 60 percent after abolition, if these travelers can go with another airline. If the loads continue high or if other airlines abolish first class as well, we may retain them all. It's a tough call.

2. Current loads in first class and coach. Over the past two months (61 days) on our 727s, we have averaged a first-class load factor of 61.2 percent and a coach load factor of 82.9 percent. The distribution of flights by load factor over the same period is shown in the table below:

Range in Load Factors (Percent of 727 Flights)

	Less than 50%	50-60%	60-70%	70-80%	80-90%	90-100%	1-5 Standbys Left	More than 5 Standbys Left
Sun-kissed Service	42.3	11.6	12.7	13.8	10.9	7.7	1.0	---
Coach	16.4	10.4	10.7	11.3	20.9	18.3	7.4	4.6

FIGURE 8-4   The report on abolishing first class on Citrus Airlines' 727s.

DISCUSSION OF CITRUS AIRLINES

Citrus Airlines is experiencing a bottleneck. Given the heavy loads it has been carrying recently, an increasing number of standbys have been left at the airport. The heavy loads and the high number of completely booked flights have no doubt caused a number of customers to switch flight times or even airlines. If such a strong demand continues, Citrus may be well advised to add equipment and offer more flights.

As a way around the current bottleneck, Dave Dove has suggested that Citrus can fly eight more seats on every flight if first-class service is abolished. This change has some real appeal. Not only does it solve the present oversubscription of some flights, but Citrus could conceivably make more money by flying an all-coach airplane.

How is this true? For every first-class passenger under the present scheme, the airline receives $71, on the average, and expends only $3.28 on services. The company thus stands to gain $67.72 for every first-class passenger. This is money it can use to pay back its debt on the planes and other facilities and the overhead it buys. This money is also the source of its profits. The figure ($67.72) is an important one; it is known as the *contribution* per first-class passenger.

�֍ ASIDE �֍

Contribution and Variable Cost

Technically, *contribution* is the difference between a company's revenue and its so-called variable costs. *Variable costs*, as the name suggests, are the costs that vary directly with production activity. Drinks and dinners served on airlines are variable costs since they are only expenses to the airline when passengers are in their seats to drink and eat them. The lumber used in making furniture and the labor used to transform it are variable costs; they vary directly with the quantity of furniture produced. Similarly, the natural gas for drying peanuts and the casual labor used to run Devine Nuts are examples of variable costs.

These variable costs are easy to see, largely because they can be readily assigned to the units of output that people pay for—airplane tickets, pieces of furniture, tons of dry graded peanuts. The "variableness" of other costs may not be quite so neat. For example, are flight attendants' salaries a variable cost? Salaries are certainly variable when it comes to devising the schedule of flights; more flights mean more flight crews. But once the flight schedule is set, the salaries paid flight attendants do not vary with the number of passengers. In terms of our situation at Citrus Airlines, the revamping of airplanes to eliminate the first-class cabin does not alter the flight schedule or the number of flight crews. Crew salaries then are fixed and only materials expenses are variable in this instance. This example serves to illustrate that one must be careful to think through which costs are fixed and which are variable with the particular production activity under consideration.

The $67.72 contribution per first-class passenger goes to pay crew salaries as well as to pay off airplane costs, ticketing, and a host of other costs which, for this decision, are fixed. Every additional passenger to first class who can be accommodated will contribute $67.72 to pay off these fixed charges and to secure a profit for Citrus Airlines.

Note that we can speak of contribution in a variety of forms. Total contribution is measured in dollars, as revenues less all variable costs. Contribution per unit is total contribution per unit of output and is measured in dollars per unit. In using this notion of contribution, both total contribution and contribution per unit supply the same information, but it is sometimes easier to think in terms of one rather than the other. What is essential,

however, is that the costs that are considered variable be consistent with the nature of the decision for which the contribution figures are being used.

✳

BACK TO CITRUS AIRLINES

At present, the contribution per first-class passenger is $67.72. The similarly calculated contribution per coach passenger is $54.23 ($56 − $1.77). Given both an empty first-class seat and an empty coach one, Citrus Airlines would naturally prefer to have a first-class passenger saunter up to the ticket counter. The issue, however, is not which type of passenger the airline prefers, but whether Citrus Airlines should abolish its first-class seating.

At present, a full cabin of 20 "sun-kissed" travelers contributes $1354.40 (20 seats • $67.72 contribution per passenger). If these 20 seats were eliminated and replaced by 28 coach seats, the total contribution would be $1518.44 (28 seats • $54.23 contribution per passenger). Thus, if Citrus Airlines can be assured of filling its converted first-class cabin with coach travelers, the company will make more money than it currently does—$164.04 ($1518.44 − $1354.40) per flight more.

By performing the same kind of sensitivity analysis that was introduced with Devine Nuts and Wyoming Valley Furniture, we can easily see that the $15,000 cost of cabin conversion can be paid off

in just 92 flights. To wit:

$$\$15,000 \text{ cost } = \$164.04 \text{ contribution/flight} \cdot x \text{ flights}$$
$$x = 92 \text{ flights}$$

If each Citrus Airline plane flies one completely booked flight every 4 days, the cabin conversion cost would be paid off in a year.

This analysis suggests that Dave Dove's recommendation to convert the first-class cabin should be followed. Yet, on closer examination, this entire analysis hinges on the assumption that the *additional* eight seats placed in the converted first-class cabin will be occupied. It is not enough to state that the *average* load factor for coach is higher than the average load factor for first class or that, if the plane were full, more contribution would ensue if all seats were coach. The decision rests with what Citrus Airlines can expect will actually happen with the additional seats in the former first-class cabin. This mode of thinking about decisions concentrates on the incremental (often called marginal) change involved; the use of such marginal analysis is absolutely fundamental to management decision making.

───── ✳ ASIDE ✳ ─────

Marginal Analysis and Sunk Costs

The concept of marginal (incremental) analysis for decision making is not fancy. It's just common sense that finds application in one business situation after another. In basic terms, marginal analysis states that the decision to do something should depend only on how that decision would change the situation and on nothing else. The question to

ask is not whether a company will be profitable after some investment or policy change has been implemented, but whether the company will be *more* profitable for having made the choice than it would otherwise have been. Everything that has gone on before is irrelevant to the decision at hand.

This kind of situation is all too common: a project is almost finished when it is recognized as a turkey. Because the finish is so close, someone argues that "for just a little more money the project could be completed and the investment outlays to date will not be wasted." Marginal analysis says that what has gone before is irrelevant; the costs incurred are "sunk" and have no bearing on the decision. If the *additional* investment it takes to complete the project does not return *additional* revenues that are greater, the investment should be junked. As the old saying goes, "Don't throw good money after bad." The saying is absolutely right;

the "bad" money represents sunk costs and they have no bearing on the decision.

We shall have occasion many times to employ the concept of marginal analysis in this text. In fact, the analysis already completed on Wyoming Valley Furniture was couched implicitly in marginal (incremental) terms. The decision there rested on whether the *additional* costs from one option (build an inventory of legs) were likely to be lower than the *additional* costs from the other option (grin and bear it). In both cases, the *additional* revenues to be earned from the order were the same.

✳

BACK AGAIN TO CITRUS AIRLINES

Can Citrus Airlines fill enough of the additional eight seats so that the total contribution of an all-coach plane exceeds that of the present airplane configuration? We have some information from the marketing report memorandum.

In the first place, we know about the standbys that have been left behind. Assuming an average of 2 left behind in the "1 to 5" category and 6 left behind in the "more than 5" category, we can calculate the number of passengers that we could have been sure to seat on the 91 daily flights over the past 61 days. To wit:

$$\frac{61 \text{ days} \cdot 91 \text{ flights}}{\cdot 1\% \cdot 2 \text{ standbys/flight}} = 111.02$$

$$\frac{61 \text{ days} \cdot 91 \text{ flights}}{\cdot 7.4\% \cdot 2 \text{ standbys/flight}} = 821.55$$

$$\frac{61 \text{ days} \cdot 91 \text{ flights}}{\cdot 4.6\% \cdot 6 \text{ standbys/flight}} = \underline{1532.08}$$

$$2464.65 \text{ people}$$

At a contribution per coach passenger of $54.23, these stranded passengers could have provided a total contribution of $133,660 in those 2 months if the first-class cabin had been remodeled.

This is not the full story, of course, since the previous first-class passengers must be accounted for. At best, Citrus Airlines will forgo the in-

creased contribution that the first-class passengers made on all of the 727 flights. This "opportunity cost" is every bit as real a cost as the $15,000 per plane conversion change. The difference in contribution is $13.49 ($67.72 − $54.23) per first-class passenger. Over the past 2 months the total added contribution forgone (the opportunity cost of remodeling the cabin) would have been $916,568 (61 days • 91 flights • 20 seats • 61.2% load factor • $13.49).

This figure is naturally much larger than the gain in contribution from seating standbys in the eight additional seats provided by remodeling. The vast contribution gained by having first-class passengers on the flights that are not completely booked far outweighs the opportunity costs represented by standbys who could not get on existing flights. This comparison is all the more unfavorable to remodeling the first-class cabin if in fact customers begin deserting the airline.

Given these considerations, Dave Dove's ingenious plan for increasing capacity and breaking a bottleneck does not appear to be attractive enough to implement.

LESSONS FROM CITRUS AIRLINES

The Citrus Airlines situation brings together three of the basic concepts that guide good decision making at all levels of a company:

1. Opportunity cost (revenue forgone)
2. Contribution, and its companion concept, variable cost
3. Marginal analysis, and its companion concept, sunk cost

A useful analysis of Citrus Airlines' decision on "sun-kissed" service demands that these concepts be melded together. By the conclusion of this text these concepts should be second nature to every reader.

Let us review how each concept fits into the analysis of Citrus Airlines' situation:

1. *Opportunity cost.* By eliminating first class the airline was forgoing the difference in contribution between sun-kissed service and coach service. This loss would be every bit as much a cost to the airline as the cabin conversion expense of $15,000 per plane.
2. *Contribution.* For an already scheduled flight, the cost of adding more passengers is small since all the expenses of flying are fixed except for the drinks and food the airline serves. Thus, variable costs are very low, and the contribution each passenger makes to pay off the fixed investment in equipment and salaries is high. Contribution (revenue less variable costs) is the key statistic used in deciding the issue in this situation.
3. *Marginal analysis.* The decision about eliminating first-class service rested on the use of the additional eight seats put into the first-class cabin. Could the change they represented, including the opportunity cost incurred, be expected to generate enough contribution to pay off the added expense of converting that cabin?

From this discussion of the basic tools for analyzing and remedying the pervasive capacity bottleneck we turn to the critical issue of managing the workforce.

SOME COMMENTS ON STOCHASTIC EVENTS

In analyzing the situation faced by Frank Coyne at Devine Nuts, we assumed that the truckloads of soggy peanuts arrived for drying at the even pace of 30 tons per hour. In reality, of course, truck arrival is likely to be a much more random occurrence (sometimes referred to as a "stochastic event"). For example, there might be an early rush on the dryers that would put 300 tons of peanuts before the dryers within 2 or 3 hours after noon. In

that case, Figure 8-2 might be altered to look like Figure 8A-1. Here, on day 2, 300 tons of peanuts arrive for drying by 2 P.M. We already know that, once all Devine Nuts' dryers are filled, it will be midnight before any of the first dryers to be used will be free again. In fact, our calculations showed that it would be 2.2 hours after midnight before the last truck could unload into the dryers and head home. If we have trucks waiting from near 2

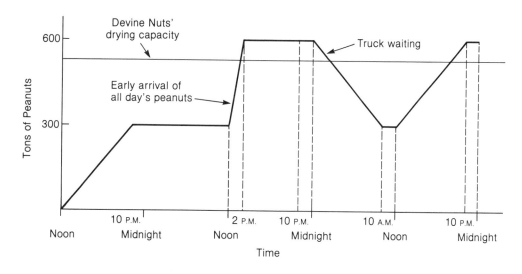

FIGURE 8A-1 Inventory buildup at Devine Nuts when day's supply of peanuts arrives early.

P.M. in the afternoon until after 2 A.M. the following morning, those trucks will have been waiting over 12 hours and their peanuts may be ruined. Such a situation is exactly what Frank Coyne wishes to avoid.

How likely is such an occurrence? Should Frank be worried? A good bit of research has been devoted to problems of this type, commonly referred to as queuing, or waiting line, problems and a sophisticated body of theory has grown up to deal with them.

ANALYZING THE RUSH ON THE DRYERS—THE POISSON AND GAMMA DISTRIBUTIONS

It has been discovered that many ordinarily occurring phenomena—radioactive decay, calls coming into a telephone switchboard, as well as people or trucks entering lines—come close to obeying a particular kind of probability distribution called the Poisson distribution, named for the French mathematician who first studied it in 1837.

According to a Poisson distribution, the probability that exactly k events occur in a time period of length t is equal to

$$(1) \qquad \frac{e^{-\mu t}(\mu t)k}{k!}$$

where e is the base of the natural logarithms ($e \approx 2.71828$) and $k!$ (k factorial) means $k \cdot (k - 1) \cdot (k - 2) \cdot \cdots \cdot 1$. As it turns out, this distribution has a mean (arithmetic average) of (μt) and a variance of (μt) as well.* We can think of μ, then, as indicating the number of events that occur per unit of time t.

Moreover, it can be shown that if events occur in accordance with a Poisson probability distribution like expression 1, the time spent waiting for the rth event (say, the tenth truckload of peanuts) follows a probability distribution of

$$(2) \qquad f(t) = \frac{\mu}{(r - 1)!}(\mu t)^{r-1}e^{-\mu t}$$

when $f(t)$ is the probability that the rth event occurs in time period t. This expression is called a gamma distribution with parameters r and μ.

This gamma distribution implies in turn that the probability that the number of events occurring in the time from 0 to t is at least r is equal to

$$(3) \qquad 1 - \sum_{k=0}^{r-1} \frac{1}{k!}(\mu t)^k e^{-\mu t}$$

---

*The variance of a distribution, $f(\ )$, of a random variable, x, is a measure of how dispersed the distribution is. It is obtained by squaring each deviation of x from the mean, $\bar{x}$, and weighting the squared deviations by their corresponding probabilities. Symbolically for a discrete distribution of N values, the variance (var x) can be written as

$$\text{var } x = \sum_{i=1}^{N} P_i(x_i - \bar{x})^2$$

where P_i is the probability that x_i occurs. Alternatively, it may be written as

$$\text{var } x = \sum_{i=1}^{N} P_i(x_i^2) - \bar{x}^2$$

The standard deviation is another way to express the dispersion of a distribution. It is merely

$$\text{standard deviation, } s_x = \sqrt{\text{var } x}$$

The standard deviation has the advantage that it is measured in the same units as the random variable x itself.

where Σ indicates a summation of different terms where k takes on integer values from 0 to $r-1$ in successive terms.

While awkward, expression 3 is a tool we can use to soothe a potentially worried Frank Coyne. How so? Well, first we can assume that the arrival of truckloads of peanuts follows a Poisson distribution. The next step is to come up with a plausible value for μ, the rate at which arrivals occur per unit of time. On a peak day we know that 300 tons of peanuts arrive in 10 hours, and so it is fairly natural to assign the value of 30 tons per hour to μ.

We are ready now to define our problem in terms of expression 3. What we want to find out is the probability that 300 tons of peanuts arrive in the space of 2 hours. The values to plug into expression 3 are

$$\mu = 30 \text{ tons per hour}$$
$$t = 2 \text{ hours}$$
$$r = 300 \text{ tons}$$

Expression 3 can be rewritten as

(4) $$1 - \sum_{k=0}^{300-1} \frac{1}{k!}(30 \cdot 2)^k e^{-30 \cdot 2}$$

The first term of the summation is thus

(5) $$\frac{1}{0!}(60)^0 e^{-60} = 1 \cdot 1 \cdot e^{-60} = 8.75 \cdot 10^{-27}$$

and the last term is

(6) $$\frac{1}{299!}(60)^{299} e^{-60}$$

which, unfortunately, is very tedious to evaluate since 60^{299} and 299! are such huge numbers that they blow up even the most sophisticated calculators.

Fortunately, we can scale down our problem to manageable size and lose little in the process. Instead of setting μ at 30 tons per hour, let us set it at one truckload per hour, implicitly assuming that

one gargantuan truck arrives, on the average, each hour with 30 tons of peanuts. Thus, r becomes 10 truckloads instead of 300 tons. Expression 3 can be rewritten as

(7) $$1 - \sum_{k=0}^{10-1} \frac{1}{k!}(1 \cdot 2)^k e^{-1 \cdot 2}$$

Table 8A-1 evaluates expression 7 to determine the probability that 10 30-ton truckloads of peanuts will descend on Devine Nuts in the space of 2 hours. Using these data, then

$$\text{value of } 1 - \sum_{k=0}^{9} \frac{1}{k!}(2)^k e^{-2} = 1 - .9999 = .0001$$

The result, of course, is that Frank Coyne need not fret at all, if indeed peanuts arrive at Devine Nuts in the way we have assumed. There is next to no chance that Devine Nuts would be inundated with peanuts so quickly. Even if the time were extended to 3 hours, the probability would rise to only .0012.

We can use the Poisson distribution to answer still another question surrounding the situation at Devine Nuts. Recall that a crop increase of 10 percent was expected in the next year and that Frank

TABLE 8A-1   Evaluating Expression 7

k	Value of $\frac{1}{k!}(2)^k e^{-2}$
0	.1353
1	.2707
2	.2707
3	.1804
4	.0902
5	.0361
6	.0120
7	.0034
8	.0009
9	.0002
Total	.9999

Coyne had translated that figure into a corresponding rise of 10 percent in his expected peak day. Was Frank justified in doing that? Will the peak day's harvest increase in direct proportion to the increase in the total year's harvest?

Let us assume again that the Poisson distribution does an adequate job of describing the arrival of peanuts at Devine Nuts. An increase in the year's harvest will raise the daily mean harvest, since the days of harvesting cannot be expected to change. A 10 percent increase in the year's harvest can thus be expected to raise the daily mean harvest by 10 percent as well. But what about the peak day?

Suppose we class a peak day as any day that is at least two standard deviations (2σ) greater than the mean (μ). What we want to know is what happens to the positioning of the peak day ($\mu + 2\sigma$) when μ is increased. Remember that in a Poisson distribution the mean and the variance are the same. Thus, one standard deviation is equal to $\sqrt{\mu}$. An increase of 10 percent in the mean, say, from 1.00 to 1.10 will only increase the peak day's harvest, as we have defined it, from

$$1.00 + 2(1.00) = 3.00$$

to

$$1.10 + 2(\sqrt{1.10}) = 3.20$$

which is an increase of only 6.6 percent. Under a Poisson distribution, the size of the peak day's harvest rises at a rate that is less than proportional to the increase in the average daily harvest.

This result should be even more comforting to Frank Coyne. Not only is it unlikely that he will be swamped by a too rapid delivery of soggy peanuts on a peak day, but his estimate of how much greater the peak day's arrivals will be as a consequence of the farmers' increased planting is high.

THE GENERAL ANATOMY OF WAITING LINE PROBLEMS

The situation at Devine Nuts is but one variant of an entire family of waiting line problems. The tremendous variety of waiting line problems is due to the many combinations of the following types of characteristics they can exhibit:

1. The arrival (or input) process
   - Do the arrivals follow a Poisson distribution such as assumed for Devine Nuts' truckloads, or is some other distribution more applicable?
   - Do the arrivals come singly, or do they sometimes also come in bulk (think of customers waiting to be seated at a restaurant in parties of one, two, three, four, and more)?
   - Does the length of any line serve as a deterrent to arrivals, or will the arrivals all simply take their chances?

2. Queue discipline (the order in which arrivals are served)
   - First come, first served? Last come, first served? Random? Or just what?
   - Are arrivals permitted to leave the waiting line? If so, what characterizes their leaving ("reneging")?

3. The service process
   - What type of probability distribution describes how arrivals are served by the process? In analyzing the situation at Devine Nuts we implicitly assumed that each dryer ran for exactly 36 hours before being freed up to dry another load of soggy peanuts. While perhaps a good enough approximation to what happens, we might also have characterized the freeing up of dryers as a stochastic event that follows a Poisson-like distribution. Clearly, in many types of service situations the amount of time a service employee must spend with a customer can vary markedly; we have all kicked ourselves for choosing the wrong line at the bank, or ticket counter, or supermarket.

- Is there more than one line? How many?

- Must arrivals go from service person/station to service person/station, or can one handle all of an arrival's needs?

- What kinds of paths through any mixed system—i.e., more than one line (sometimes called channel) and more than one person/station (sometimes called phase)—are there?

With so many possibilities for the arrival and service processes and the queue discipline, it is easy to appreciate that most queuing problems are tackled either by (1) simplifying the problem so that mathematically tractable means can be applied to the problem, such as was done above for Devine Nuts, or by (2) using computer simulation techniques to ape what we think the true behavior is and draw out its implications.

❋ ASIDE ❋

Simulation

The ever-increasing size and speed of computers has made simulation a more and more attractive means of obtaining some acceptable solutions to large-scale and/or complex problems, such as many queuing problems. In many ways simulation substitutes brute force (i.e., raw computer power) for the elegance (but lack of realism) of the mathematical model. Although often more realistic, simulation is much more art than science; mathematical models can often be characterized as right or wrong, whereas simulation models tend to be either good or bad. The typical simulation model is a kind of mathematical "black box" that takes some initial inputs, processes them, usually over a number of periods of time, and spits out some outputs.

The first step in constructing such a model is to identify the variables of interest. Variables, quite naturally, refer to those values within the simulation that are permitted to vary over time. The choice of variables for a simulation takes judgment, since only variables that are important to the result should be included and they should be defined in units of measure that are appropriate. A simulation of truck arrivals at Devine Nuts, for example, would surely define arriving peanuts (measured in, say, tons per hour), truck wait (hours), and peanuts processed as variables. One might also include the moisture content of the peanuts as a variable as well, freeing the analysis from the assumption that all the arriving peanuts are uniformly soggy and thus need a full 36 hours in the dryer. On the other hand, the unloading time per truck may not matter much and thus not be worth including. Once identified, the variable should be set with some initial values (subject to change, of course) in different model runs.

Initial conditions apply not only to variables but also to some of the parameters of the simulation. Parameters, in contrast to variables, are those simulation values that remain fixed during any single run of a simulation. Often, successive runs of a simulation will modify one or more parameters intentionally, but during any one run all parameter values remain fixed. For example, the *mean* rate of arrival of peanuts to Devine Nuts and the company's total drying capacity are likely parameters for a simulation of Devine Nuts' operations.

A crucial stage in developing any simulation model is detailing the relationships among the variables and parameters and how they will vary, if at all, with the march of time. A number of these relationships will almost always be of an accounting nature, but many will serve to "drive" the model. The kinds of relationships that alter variable values in important and often systematic ways are frequently termed *decision rules*. They specify under which conditions variables of all kinds will be changed and how. In a simulation of Devine Nuts' situation, for example, one decision rule might check to see whether the drying capacity has been reached and then allocate arriving peanuts either to dryers or to the truck wait. Accounting relationships would then keep track of the peanuts dried and drying, and the trucks waiting.

Simulation models can be either deterministic or probabilistic. That is, the simulation can be built to yield exactly the same outputs, given the same sets of initial conditions and parameters (a deterministic model); or some elements of chance can be introduced so that the same initial conditions and parameters would yield different, although probably similar, outputs (a probabilistic model). The most useful simulation of Devine Nuts' situation would be a probabilistic one (also called a Monte Carlo simulation after the casino in Monaco, along the French Riviera), which would draw at random a value for the arriving peanuts variable

from a probability distribution like the Poisson. The choice of probability distribution for such purposes is thus another important feature of building a simulation model.

Once a simulation model has been constructed—variables, parameters, initial conditions, accounting relationships, decision rules, probability distributions—it is put through its paces. Usually a lot of tinkering goes on—more or fewer periods are run, parameters changed, initial conditions revised, relationships altered, variables added. All of this tinkering occurs to check on the simulation model's behavior. Are the results plausible? Do changes in parameters, initial conditions, or relationships yield the expected results?

After the model has been debugged and is functioning smoothly, its outputs can either be used directly for some decision making or (as is common for probabilistic models) be accumulated in a data bank and then investigated with statistical tools and hypothesis testing.

QUEUING THEORY AND DECISION MAKING

The raison d'être for both the mathematical and simulation techniques for analyzing queuing problems, of course, is to provide insights for management action on the queues themselves. Typically, queues can be managed in a host of ways. Earlier, in discussing the anatomy of waiting line problems, elements of the arrival process, queue discipline, and the service process were noted. Many of these elements can be affected by particular management actions. Indeed, in service industries, where customer happiness while waiting in line is crucial, significant management attention is focused on managing the queue properly and in various ways.

To illustrate the importance of waiting line management to a company and the types of management actions available to it, consider the Burger King restaurant in Malden, Massachusetts (Chapter 6). In the description of that restaurant's operations, it was noted that a major shift had occurred in the way Burger King managed customer wait. The company had switched from a single-line system that was multistation (a single channel, multiphase system in the jargon) to the so-called hospitality lineup, which is multiple line but single station (a multichannel, single-phase system in the jargon). No longer did people place their orders with one hostess and receive their order from another; one hostess took care of all tasks. Furthermore a single, sometimes long line was replaced by shorter, multiple lines.

While somewhat more labor-intensive, the hospitality lineup apparently could serve more people, cutting down on customer wait. The hospitality lineup may also have trimmed the number of potential customers who might have balked at the length of the single line, especially during peak hours. We can be sure that this switch to the hospitality lineup was something that commanded considerable management attention at Burger King. It certainly is the type of waiting line problem that would lend itself to analysis by computer simulation. A simulation could have estimated potential labor costs (i.e., number of checkout counters and hostesses), given the maintenance of selected service standards (i.e., door-to-door time, and transaction time) and various levels and distributions of demand, both peak and nonpeak hour.

In an operation like Burger King's, the operations of the kitchen and the mix of duties between kitchen and counter are also important to managing customer wait, since they influence the speed with which each customer can be served. For example, it was noted in Chapter 6 that during off-peak hours counter hostesses were responsible for drawing their own soft drinks from a dispenser mounted between kitchen and counter. However, during peak hours, a kitchen worker was responsible for drawing drinks, thus freeing the counter hostess to devote more time to direct customer contact and whittling away at the time that a customer must wait.

In fact, attention to customer wait stands behind the careful modulation of capacity (line rebalancing) that occurs both in the kitchen and at the front counter. The decision on when during the day to add another checkout stand and hostess is another important one and a direct application of waiting line analysis.

QUESTIONS

1. What do you understand by the term *bottleneck?* Describe one method of analyzing bottlenecks.

2. What is a break-even calculation and why is it used? Formulate your own example to show how the break-even calculation is used.

3. What was the fundamental decision faced by Wyoming Valley Furniture? Why was the company's initial problem characterized as a bottleneck problem? Could the company have arrived at the same decision by any other management method?

4. Define the three important decision-making concepts embodied in the problem-solving process undertaken by Citrus Airlines. Taking an example of your own, show how these concepts can be applied.

5. What is meant by the terms *stochastic event, Poisson probability distribution,* and *gamma distribution?* Of what value is the application of these concepts to bottleneck problems?

6. Waiting line problems have similar general characteristics. What are these? Give an example of each from the situations presented in this chapter.

7. Devise a simulation model of a queuing problem which you have observed on campus or at your work. Make sure you include all relevant variables, parameters, initial conditions, and probability distributions.

PROBLEMS

1. How can bottlenecks arise in a multistage production system?

2. How can bottlenecks be remedied? Be specific.

3. What is contribution?

4. Explain opportunity cost.

5. Explain marginal analysis.

6. Hope Hospital currently has 80 rooms and is able to charge $75 per day for occupancy of each room. Because Hope has had to turn away patients several times during the last two months, the administrator is considering expansion of the facilities to 100 rooms at a cost of $500,000. Assuming that variable costs per day average $60 per room and that all rooms will be filled, how long will it take the expansion to pay for itself?

7. If Hope Hospital expands to 120 rooms, it can do so by spending $600,000 rather than the $500,000 in problem 6. In addition, however, variable costs will increase to $65 per room per day, and it is expected that the average occupancy rate will be only about 90 percent.

a. How does this change your analysis from problem 6?

b. Which alternative is better?

c. If revenue per day could be changed for the second alternative, at what revenue per day would the two alternatives break even?

SITUATION FOR STUDY
BEACON GLASS WORKS REVISITED

Jose Zotts, production manager at Beacon Glass Works, Marysville, West Virginia (see Chapter 1 situation for study), recently decided that the packaging department of his plant should package all finished goods and place the goods in stock rather than wait for customer orders.

The packaging department had four sections: finished goods storage, package breakdown, breakdown storage, and final packaging. Figure 8-A is a diagram of the packaging area. The finished goods storage consisted of a circular conveyor that held trays of 1000 pieces of each product. This conveyor could hold up to 5000 trays of products, depending upon the mix of lengths and diameters of the products. The production process could feed up to 3000 trays of tubing per day into the storage area. The package breakdown area was necessary because different customers wanted different numbers of pieces for each order—normally, anywhere from 100 to 500 pieces per container. The breakdown area consisted of four long conveyors, each of which could handle a maximum of 400 trays per day. The foreman in charge of the breakdown area, Jesse Brown, normally scheduled breakdown by looking in the storage area to see what product had the largest quantity in storage.

Once the trays were broken down into individual containers, they were passed to a breakdown storage area with 10 gravity-feed conveyors that could store the equivalent of 5000 trays at any one time. The final packaging area had five packaging stations, fed by a conveyor belt that went from the breakdown storage into the packaging area. Here packaging could be done at a rate of 500 trays per day per station. Final packaging originally had been done to customer order, but because of storage

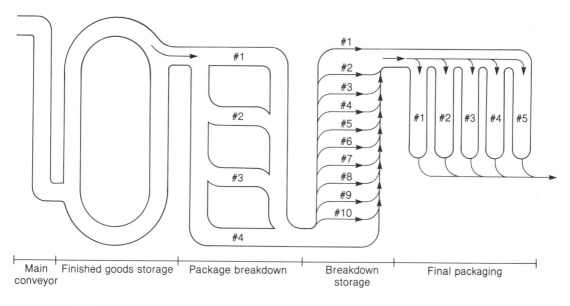

FIGURE 8-A   The flow of goods through the packaging department at Beacon Glass Works.

problems at the finished goods storage area, Jose had decided to package to stock.

After three months of trying the new packaging procedure, Jose noticed that (1) finished goods storage was continuing to pile up, (2) package breakdown was almost always running at full capacity, (3) breakdown storage was full, and (4) final packaging was still being done basically to customer order, with "expeditors" running around the packaging area looking for products to fill customer orders.

1. What is the information flow in the packaging area? How should information be processed in this area? Why?

2. What suggestions do you have for Jose to "break the bottlenecks" in the packaging area? How would your suggestions help?

3. What other information would you like to have to make the "best" economic decision about how to break the bottlenecks? Explain how you would use this information.

CHAPTER

9

MANAGING THE WORKFORCE

What makes a truly effective workforce supervisor is a topic that will be studied as long as there are workers and supervisors. No text can pretend to teach people all the subtleties involved in successfully managing workers. This text certainly does not. It can only aspire to introducing some of the issues involved in understanding worker performance and behavior in the workplace. To this limited end, this chapter is divided into two parts, the first of which deals with the motivation and direction of workers and the second of which is a primer on labor relations.

PART ONE
ISSUES IN WORKER MOTIVATION AND DIRECTION

JOB DESIGN AND STANDARDS

From taking our various plant tours we already know that a great deal of time and effort is spent piecing together the specific tasks that any worker will spend hours doing. Standards of one sort or another are usually established to document those tasks and to provide time estimates for their completion. This mesh of standards and job design is an exceedingly important endeavor in all of the types of processes we have studied, but for somewhat different, although allied, reasons.

For example, time standards are essential to a job shop like Norcen Industries, for only through realistic time standards can the shop place reasonable bids for the jobs submitted to it. Time standards also play a key role in the scheduling decisions of the job shop foreman, since they provide him with target job start and stop times for each worker. It is these scheduling decisions, along with the job and process sheets, that are responsible for job design in a job shop.

In the line flow process, such as at an automotive assembly plant or a fast food restaurant, the design of individual jobs is the critical task in designing the entire process. As we saw, great care is taken in balancing "the line"; time standards for individually identified and detailed operations (job

154

elements) determine how the line will be balanced.

In the continuous flow process, by contrast, it is likely to be equipment time standards, not worker ones, that help design a worker's job. Equipment capabilities will often determine as well how many workers should be assigned to a particular portion of the process.

TIME STANDARDS[1]

As was mentioned in the Chapter 5 discussion of line balance, time standards are arrived at in a variety of ways: stopwatch studies, films/video tapes, work sampling, and task decomposition. All have their faults.

Stopwatch studies and, to a lesser extent, filming or taping disrupt operations. An industrial engineer must be physically present to do a stopwatch study, and filming or taping may require special lights or equipment. Aware of being watched, workers may slow down operations deliberately so that any time standards that are established can be beat at will. This kind of very natural behavior has stimulated several corrective measures: (1) less obtrusive stopwatch studies or filming/taping, e.g., standing by someone while measuring someone else or investing in low light and highly portable filming or taping equipment, (2) a judgmental (and too often arbitrary) "rating of the pace" of the job so that any time estimates are factored up by a figure that reflects the industrial engineer's judgment of how much dogging it on the job persisted while the stopwatch study was underway, and (3) study of managers or engineers performing the worker's tasks to avoid having to rate the pace. The most promise rests with the first corrective measure.

Work sampling is the random observation of a person at work and the ensuing calculation of the relative amounts of time spent performing specific tasks. While less disruptive and thus less likely to introduce deliberately slow work, this technique can be as time-consuming as stopwatch study and is usually less accurate and detailed. It entails a surprising degree of travel throughout the factory and a long time before a sufficient sample of observations can be made to calculate relative times on specific tasks. In its favor, work sampling enjoys some advantages over stopwatch or film/tape studies. For example, a single industrial engineer can study a number of tasks simultaneously. If the tasks involve a considerable degree of machine time, as opposed to operator time, work sampling can be more efficient. For nonstandard jobs, notably in support functions (e.g., engineering) or in service industries, work sampling is often the preferred means of studying the job and suggesting revisions to the responsibilities assigned.

Translating relative time calculations into time standards, if that is desired, requires knowledge as well of the typical day's output of the studied worker. To make the translation, relative times are applied to the daily output figures to yield the relevant absolute time standards. For most operations such translation is possible, but there are some operations for which an individual operation's output cannot be easily counted (e.g., many service operations); the resulting failure to develop absolute standards is a weakness of work sampling. On the other hand, many operations falling into this category do not require time standards.

Task decomposition is most useful when new jobs are being developed and it is not possible to study anyone. This method suffers for the understandable reason that it often cannot hope to be as accurate as actual, experimental data.

There are several commercially available task decomposition schemes, the most widely used being methods time measurement (MTM). In many companies, however, data for task decomposition come not from outside sources but from a backlog of the company's own previous stopwatch and film/tape studies. Since many new worker tasks are but modest changes from existing (or former) tasks, an internally generated data base is often helpful in the first stages of new job design. Once task decomposition methods suggest a first cut at the appropriate design, many companies then resort to stopwatch or film/tape studies, and the intimate knowledge of supervisory personnel to refine the job design further.

METHODS IMPROVEMENT[2]

The use of time standards is an important aspect of job design, but it is only one aspect. Another whole realm involves the establishment and improvement of methods. Methods engineering is too little appreciated in many companies. It is detailed, nitty-gritty work, but it can pay handsome and repeated rewards.

Methods improvement basically requires an open inquisitive mind, an eye for detail, and a passion for keeping things simple. There are no pat solutions to apply in most instances; thus, methods improvement usually involves a systematic study of the current methods, an appreciation of what the job really calls for, and a disdain for any explanation that is not thoroughly persuasive.

Process flow diagrams of the form introduced in Segment I (but vastly more detailed) are often helpful in tracking materials movement and in documenting how long it takes to perform particular operations. They can even involve a floor plan such as was included in the Jung Products process description. Process flow diagrams typically focus on what happens to products as they progress—where they get caught in bottlenecks, how materials are handled, what has to come together before a product can proceed.

Another way of thinking about methods is to track what individual workers and individual machines do. This tracking can be in general terms or it can be as specific as the hand, feet, and body movements necessary to perform a given task. One popular such analysis is to chart a machine's cycle time against the cycle time of the machine operator and what he or she is supposed to do, so that

any conflicts between the two can be isolated and resolved. Figure 9-1 is an example.

Over time, a whole series of do's and don'ts have evolved about good methods practice, especially as regards the actions of individual workers. These do's and don'ts are only common sense. Here is a sampling:

- Separate materials handling work from operator work. An operator should not have to perform much materials handling. Materials handling itself should be as simple and as easy as possible, with gravity feeds or mechanical conveyances rather than human effort.

- A worker's hands should be used as a unit, complementing rather than fighting one another.

- Work should be secured and processed in fixed and comfortable positions whenever possible. Many worker aids are jigs and fixtures that readily position materials, keep those positions fixed, and guide tools easily. Tools should also be fixed whenever possible.

- Avoid unnecessary movement of materials or unnecessary movements by workers.

- Look hard at automating everything possible in the process.

- Encourage a natural rhythm to an operation where possible. Sharp, irregular movements should be avoided.

Good methods engineering is seldom accomplished by appealing to stock solutions or guidelines. Most methods improvements have to be tailored specifically to the job at hand. Such tailoring of methods requires an understanding of the mission underlying the job and a willingness to think deeply about details.

Frequently, especially in service industries, a more efficient way of accomplishing a task must be balanced against the maintenance of a particular standard, even though other standards may be greatly improved. Consider Situation 9-1.

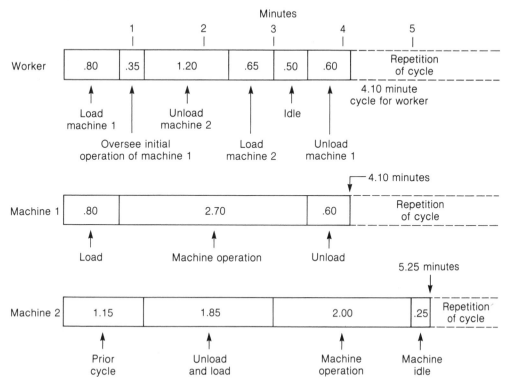

FIGURE 9-1   A simplified example of a worker-machine chart.

SITUATION 9-1

EASTERN BELL TELEPHONE COMPANY

The more Charlie Harris thought about it, the more attractive it became, but it still meant a significant change in the telephone company's repair practices. Charlie was a young district manager with responsibility for installation and repair of telephone equipment in a 200-square-mile area north of the city. In response to some higher level pronouncements about the importance of measured installation and repair productivity, Charlie conceived the idea of changing the way telephone repair technicians were assigned to residence repair jobs.

In the prevailing system, each repair technician reporting to the garage in the morning would be as-

signed to the repair of a subscriber's telephone that had been reported and checked out at the central office as out-of-service. After repairing that phone, the repair technician would call in to the dispatcher, who would assign the next repair task. Over three-quarters of the repair tasks involved telephones out-of-service, but the rest involved trouble not severe enough to cut off service (e.g., an extension phone out of order, a worn cord, a sagging wire from the telephone pole to the house). The repair technician would not know, starting the day, how many jobs he or she would have to do or where any of them would be. The person was at the mercy of the dispatcher.

Because the Bell System's standards for responding to trouble calls were so demanding (i.e., respond to out-of-service calls within 24 hours), a considerable portion of the repair technician's day was spent in transit, chasing the urgent calls for service by the telephone company's customers. If the repair technician could be routed better, less time would be spent in transit, and more service calls could be made. Better routing, however, meant bunching up more service calls geographically, which could be done only by waiting longer and collecting more trouble calls. Charlie recognized that improving work productivity almost always implied a lowering of existing service standards. Charlie knew that he could never wait to accumulate out-of-service trouble calls; they would always require immediate action. However, the less severe trouble, involving calls where the home still had telephone service on at least one phone, was a candidate for delayed service with better routing of the repair technicians.

Charlie wondered how best such a delayed response system could be implemented. Several questions still plagued him:

1. How much delay would the customer accept? Should the customer be granted the right to insist upon immediate service like before?
2. How could a program of bunched orders and better routing be designed to promote worker productivity in the best way? Should the dispatching system remain the same as before, with the repair technicians calling in for their next assignment, or should they be given a full day's load from the start? Should the same person be assigned to this bunched order work, or should the work be rotated among all repair technicians? If rotated, how long should a person be assigned to such work?
3. Would the benefits in increased productivity outweigh the diminishing level of service that the proposed system necessarily implied?

Discussion of Eastern Bell Telephone Company

It is clear that Charlie Harris's idea to accumulate the noncritical repair calls and bunch them up to provide better routing and thus higher productivity will reduce the company's ability to meet its established service standard on repairs. The issue is whether the service standard itself is worth keeping. The notion of having customers indicate how perturbed they are without service is probably a good one. Particularly irate customers can then be put in with the out-of-service trouble calls for immediate attention. A simple question asked of customers (such as "We can fix it the day after tomorrow. Is that all right with you?") when they phone in their complaints may placate them and yet accumulate enough calls to ease the routing problem.

Bunching orders in this way to facilitate routing may not only improve productivity in the repair of noncritical service calls, but also provide some demonstration effects if in fact productivity rises markedly, say from 8 calls to 12 calls per day. This improvement could make the entire repair fleet more conscious of productivity. This argument for a demonstration effect suggests that the noncritical calls be rotated among the repair technicians so that the productivity gains are experienced firsthand by everyone. The duration of the assignment should be long enough to make an impact but short enough so that everyone can get into the act during the year. Perhaps 2 weeks to a month on this assignment would do. The demonstration effect suggests further that the repair technician be given a full day's load in the morning. Counting orders then will probably have more impact than counting up the day's accomplishments on the way home from work.

JOB DESIGN AND QUALITY OF WORK LIFE

Job design as discussed to this point could be characterized as a "dissection" of jobs — simplifying them by breaking them apart, "deskilling" them, and adding more equipment to them. Most of the efforts in job design since the industrial revolution itself have been along these lines, with increased productivity as an explicit goal.

Recently, however, more and more questions have been raised about the effects of such an approach to job design. Many job design projects have deskilled and simplified operations but in the process have made workers feel that the job is not worth doing. Quality declines; waste, absenteeism, and labor turnover increase.

In response to this worker disaffection but with increased worker productivity still the explicit goal, a growing list of companies has begun seeking ways by which work can be restructured so that it is more meaningful to workers and thus more likely to receive their full attention and care. Such action may be just in time. There is some evidence that worker discontent is on the rise. According to a recent survey of worker attitudes, 36 percent of American workers believe their skills are underutilized and over 50 percent complain about a lack of control over days worked and jobs assigned.[3] In just the time period 1973–77, the proportion of workers surveyed who thought their jobs contained "interesting work with opportunity to develop abilities and freedom to decide how to do the job" dropped from 51.3 percent to 41.5 percent.

One reason for the growing disaffection of workers may lie in the fact that real incomes are much higher now than ever before and workers, generally speaking, feel more secure about their jobs. Certainly workers' compensation and unemployment compensation have helped to take much of the sting out of recessionary times and the prospect of work layoffs. Thus, with respectable levels of wages and job security, present-day workers can take wages and job security more for granted than at any time to date. In fact, several surveys in the United States and abroad have documented the increased importance of such items as "more information on what is happening and why" and "full appreciation of work done" relative to wage and job security matters.[4] Worker concerns can then be expected to pass on to other issues. With the increases in people's real earnings over time has also come an increase in education, and this rise is likely to have induced at least some more concern for broadening, rather than narrowing, the bounds of a job. A number of factors have emerged as important dimensions of satisfaction with one's job and workplace, and each demands some attention from managers concerned about workforce well-being and productivity. In no particular order:[5]

- *Adequate and fair compensation*—still an important consideration for all workers. Is the pay sufficient, and is it in line with expectations and demands of other, perhaps similar, jobs?

- *Safe and healthy working conditions.* Is the plant structurally sound and is the machinery safe to operate? Is the workplace attractive and comfortable? Are the hours long? Is there flexibility in the time workers can start or stop work?

- *Immediate opportunity to use and develop human capacities.* Does the job give the worker a sense of identity? Does it call for substantial autonomy? Is the job self-contained or merely a small piece of a task with no real identity itself? Does the job call for planning as well as execution? Does it call for multiple skills? Is the job tied into the larger flow of information about the process and the control of that process?

- *Future opportunity for continued growth and security.* What opportunities exist for advancement on the job? How secure is the employment? Will the job provide the training and development needed to tackle still larger jobs?

- *Social integration into the workplace.* To what degree is the workplace open and supportive of each worker? To what degree is the workplace free of prejudice and status symbols? How upwardly mobile are workers?

- *Rights in the workplace.* To what extent does the rule of law and due process characterize an individual's rights in the workplace? Are privacy, free speech, and equity fully respected?

- *Work in perspective.* Are the demands of the job in balance with family and leisure dimensions of the worker's life?

- *Company vis-a-vis society.* Is the company perceived as socially responsible and socially accepted?

With these kinds of considerations in mind to deal with worker dissatisfaction, a host of work restructure policies have been tested by companies like General Foods, Procter and Gamble, General Motors, TRW, Scott Paper, General Electric, Cummins Engine, Eaton Corporation, and Mars, Inc.,

among others. The work restructuring that has been tested in these and other companies tends to be very idiosyncratic; no two programs are alike. Goals are held to only loosely and timetables are extraordinarily flexible. The goals are dual; the intended benefits are to be reaped by both management and the workforce. The adopted programs work by altering the "culture" of the workplace. Walton summarizes the process in a diagram (see Figure 9-2).[6]

More specifically, work restructuring has included, in roughly ascending order of complexity:[7]

1. Job rotation on a periodic basis.

2. Cross-training of workers (i.e., training workers for jobs other than their main one).

3. The combining of simple tasks into more demanding ones that are allegedly less monotonous to perform.

Level I **Design techniques** ———▶	Level II **Work culture ideals** ———▶	Level III **Intended results**
Job design	High skill levels and flexibility in using them	*For business:*
Pay	Identification with product, process, and total business viewpoint	Low cost
Supervisor's role		Quick delivery
Training	Problem solving instead of finger pointing	High-quality products
Performance feedback	Influence by information and expertise instead of by position	Low turnover
Goal setting		Low absenteeism
Communication	Mutual influence	Equipment utilization
Employment stability policies	Openness	*For quality of work life:*
Status symbols	Responsiveness	Self-esteem
Leadership patterns	Trust	Economic well-being
	Egalitarian climate	Security
	Equity	

Note: The design techniques, culture ideals, and intended results listed above are presented as illustrative, not as comprehensive nor even as universally applicable. Also, the items in the three columns are not horizontally lined up to relate to each other. The arrows indicate influence.

FIGURE 9-2   Three-level conception of work improvement. (From Walton, "Work Innovations in the United States," p. 90)

4. The creation of an egalitarian factory with, for example, a salaried workforce and no time clocks to punch, no probationary periods for workers, fewer disciplinary rules, more integration between production and maintenance workers, "round table" meetings with management to discuss problems or topics of interest, no assigned parking spaces for management, a single cafeteria and locker room, offices that are not separate or "closed door" enclosures, and glass walls between factory and offices. Some companies now invite workers to production planning meetings and the like.

5. Production teams that are responsible for a complete portion of the production process or the manufacture of a well-defined segment of the product itself. Such production teams are charged with activities like maintenance, quality control, materials, industrial engineering, and personnel matters like hiring, all in addition to their production duties. These teams must decide, often under the direction of a team leader, how each of these activities should be manned and managed. Different management groups (e.g., quality control, industrial engineering) may be called in for training and/or consultation. The teams, in essence, take on many decisions that were previously the domain of the first line supervisors. Sometimes pay is determined by the different jobs a worker knows how to perform, rather than by an hourly wage or some incentive pay scheme. Sometimes the team has a mandate to determine wage increases itself.

   The creation of such teams is new and is still evolving; but many results are encouraging, and the list of committed companies is growing, particularly in continuous flow processes where team (i.e., department) watchfulness and coordination are important in the success of the process.

Such efforts at work restructuring, particularly the last type, involve changing much or all of the "culture" of the workplace—worker attitudes toward the job itself, toward the product, toward fellow workers, toward management. As one might expect, new social systems sometimes step on toes; there has been some low-level management backlash to work restructuring, as well as upper-level management indifference, since work restructuring can be viewed as a "deskilling" of supervisory roles that, in addition, demands a lot of work and communication. Pressures on the new plant social system have had to be overcome, such as demands for high-volume production or new production introduction, which tend to lengthen hours, reduce time for team meetings, introduce rivalries into the system, and slow personnel development. Decisions about pay and worker advancement have sometimes been sidestepped because of the touchiness of peer evaluation. On balance, work restructuring has proved to be a modest success and much more experimentation and development of the concept can be expected in the years ahead.

Work restructuring must be carefully evaluated since it has not been, nor is it likely to be, embraced wholeheartedly by all company workforces. There are still many instances where workforces resist change and do not want to assume managerial roles. Often, workers would rather have more time off than more responsibility. Any work restructuring must be carefully tuned to the situation at hand.

STANDARDS, INCENTIVES, AND WAGE PAYMENTS

Time and service standards have been discussed so far as the means for shaping job design or for estimating costs and capacity. These are important goals and the most frequent use of standards. In fact, almost all companies use standards for these purposes. In somewhat less than half of all manufacturing companies, time standards are used as well in the development of incentive wage schemes.[8]

We have already become acquainted with one type of incentive wage, namely the piece rate system, which was described in Chapter 3 on Jung Products, Inc. It is widely used in the apparel industry. The appeal of incentive wages is readily understandable: the worker is paid according to how much he or she produces, not by how long he or she works. It is generally accepted that workers on some set of incentive wages work harder than those who are paid by the hour, other things being equal.

What kind of incentive wage schemes exist? There are many. Here is a brief description of the major ones:[9]

- *Piece rate system.* In a piece rate system every unit of output has its own wage reward. Workers are paid strictly according to how much they produce. There are no wage floors or ceilings. About a third of those companies employing wage incentives use a piece rate system.

- *Standard hour.* In a standard hour system, there are no wage "price tags" on every unit. Rather, a certain rate of output per hour is set as a standard and pay is geared according to what percentage of the standard is actually achieved.

  There are many variations of this system. Some pay proportionally (e.g., a 115 percent average performance for the week will earn 115 percent of the standard wage); others use a different formula, perhaps based on a tally of "points" earned. Many variations place a floor on earnings (a "base rate") with the standard set so that the typical worker can expect to better the standard consistently (e.g., 110 or 120 percent of the standard). Others have no wage floor. These standard hour systems are the most popular of all wage incentive schemes, prevailing in about three-fifths of the company wage incentive programs.

- *Group incentives.* There are a variety of group incentive programs, but all encourage cooperation among workers by rewarding each according to how the group, rather than how an individual, performs. Many group incentives are initiated because figuring out what one individual produces depends on what others before him or her do, as in an assembly line. Group incentives can vary in their operation much as the standard hour schemes do.

  A particularly interesting example of a group incentive plan is the so-called Scanlon plan, which apportions among workers and management any savings in total costs in the plant, no matter what the cause. Such a system unifies labor and management interests and typically spawns a steady stream of suggestions on how to improve operations. A Scanlon plan requires a rather complete system of cost control (so that cost savings information can be generated) and a thorough evaluation system to judge proposed suggestions. Running a Scanlon plan is a lot of work, but many companies are pleased with its performance.

  Group incentives of all types are found in about a fifth of all companies adopting wage incentives.

- *Bonus and profit-sharing plans.* While bonus and profit-sharing plans might be formally classified as a type of group incentive, such plans typically depend on company revenues as well as costs and are thus fairly far removed from individual worker effort and imagination. They are found in about a seventh of all companies with wage incentive schemes.

The attractiveness of wage incentives is, of course, their spur to worker effort. But are there unattractive features as well? Consider Situation 9-2.

SITUATION 9-2

TOWER MANUFACTURING COMPANY

"Boy, did I just get ambushed. I haven't been dressed down like that since I forgot my wife's birthday a few years back. Those guys are steaming and we better do something about it." Bruce Hillman, foreman of the machine shop, was addressing his supervisor, Clint Oster, the manager of machining operations at Tower Manufacturing Company. Tower Manufacturing, a supplier of chassis components for heavy, customized, off-highway trucks and construction equipment, had recently added a second computer-controlled milling machine to the machine shop. It was the worker response to this second machine and its implications for worker compensation that had Bruce Hillman agitated.

Bruce continued. "I don't know how we're going to fix things. All I know is that this current arrangement simply has to go. We can't continue to pay Bestmann for piecework on both machines. His pay is way out of line. The others in the shop like him all right but pulling in almost half again the pay of the others is plain ridiculous. Everyone is clamoring for an increase in the rates or an override in the standard pay."

Clint Oster was kicking himself for not anticipating this confrontation. The machine shop at Tower Manufacturing had traditionally been a high-skilled shop, stocked with general purpose machine tools, with workers compensated through a piece-rate incentive wage system. Times had been changing, though, and the increasing stability of Tower's major contracts had made possible the introduction of complex numerically controlled (N/C) machines into the shop. Management had agonized over the decision, since even one such machine was an investment of hundreds of thousands of dollars. But Clint was convinced that Tower had to purchase such equipment if it was going to stay competitive. Compared to what even a first-class machinist could do with conventional equipment, the computer-controlled machine was far superior. It took much longer to set up for a job, but once set up, its speed and quality of output were extraordinary. All the operator had to do was feed the machine with material and remove the completed, machined output. For longer production runs, which was the situation now at Tower,

the new machine was ideal.

When Tower purchased its first computer-controlled machine, Clint and Bruce assigned one of the shop's best workers, Jay Bestmann, to it. It had taken quite a while for Tower's industrial engineers and Bestmann to get the bugs out of the new machine, but, once accomplished, everyone was satisfied with the machine's capabilities. During this start-up period, Bestmann had agreed to be taken off incentive pay. Instead he was paid an hourly rate equivalent to his last two months' average pay. When the new machine was proven out, Bestmann agreed to a piece rate that was two-thirds of the rate for equivalent output from conventional machines. This rate worked out to be slightly higher than the rate of pay he was earning just prior to the introduction of the new machine, but Clint Oster had agreed to it since none of the shop's machinists wanted to work on this less-skilled job. Setups for both the new computer-controlled machine and conventional machines were paid at the same rate.

It had been planned from the beginning that one operator would be responsible for two of the new machines, since otherwise the operator would be idle much of the time, watching the machine do the job. Therefore, when the second computer-controlled machine was installed, Bestmann was assigned to it. Once again, the piece rate had to be adjusted. The engineers felt it was unlikely that both machines would always be perfectly syncopated (so that Bestmann never had to be at both machines at once); the piece rate therefore was not cut in half (to one-third from two-thirds of the rate applicable to conventional machines), but rather was set at 40 percent of the rate other workers were given—also as sort of a bribe to get Bestmann to accept the assignment to the two machines.

Since this rate was agreed on, however, two things had happened to increase Bestmann's pay considerably. One was that Bestmann began setting up one machine while the other was working. This procedure entailed a lot of movement between machines so that the working one was always fed with material, but it meant that Bestmann was carrying piece rate pay even when setting up one of the machines, something the company's industrial engineers had not planned for. The other occurrence was an increase in the lot size with which the N/C machine was loaded. This increase meant fewer setups and a lengthened time for the fast output rate of the machine. Both of these factors combined to push Bestmann's pay to levels far in excess of the pay levels for other workers.

This fact, of course, was not wasted on the other workers—hence their confrontation with Bruce Hillman. If Bestmann was going to be paid so much more, they wanted a more equitable arrangement for everybody in the shop.

Clint Oster was in a quandary. He could reset the already agreed-to piece rate for the new machine and risk antagonizing Bestmann or anyone else who might be assigned to the machine. Or, he could take the machine off incentive pay and put it on hourly pay, risking not only Bestmann's displeasure but the suspicion of the other workers in the shop about the future abandonment of piece work, a wage scheme that had widespread approval among them. Or, he could place a much lower-skilled worker on each of the new machines, put Bestmann back on conventional machines, and risk even more suspicion from the workforce about trends in the shop and their jobs in it.

LESSONS FROM TOWER MANUFACTURING COMPANY

This situation uncovers a number of the problems associated with incentive wage schemes, the most important of which is the gradual erosion of the time standards on which the incentive wage is based. The erosion of standards is to be expected in many cases because workers are clever and knowledgeable about what they do and can often find ways to beat the standard. At Tower Manufacturing, for example, Bestmann found a way to beat the standards set for the new N/C machines and his pay jumped appreciably. The resulting inequities in the factory have to be dealt with.

Dealing with these inequities, however, is no easy task. Tightening up on the standards can sometimes be done, but naturally does not make management popular with the workforce. In most union contracts involving incentive pay, after a given period of time the standards cannot be changed without first changing the product, materials, methods, or machinery; any such change is subject to the union-management established grievance procedure.

Of course, changing a standard is far from a costless endeavor. The task must be studied, often by stopwatch, and that takes time. This fact tends to

make wage incentives less popular in companies that undertake a lot of product or product mix changes or that are subject to repeated innovation in the production process itself. Wage incentives, and piece rates in particular, are more likely to flourish in processes where (1) the output of every worker is easily measured; (2) the jobs are standard, clear-cut, and unlikely to be altered much through technological changes; (3) the flow of the process is regular and thus every worker has a backlog of work to do; and (4) workmanship is either easy to judge or not critical to the product. It is no accident then that piece rates predominate in the needle trades.

The situation at Tower Manufacturing is delicate because it would be difficult, if not impossible, to change the standard now that it has been established. If the job were switched to an hourly paid one, suspicion would likely grow in the factory that all jobs in the department would be switched to hourly pay or that N/C equipment would gradually take over. These changes might mean a switch in pay schemes and a deskilling of the operation, both fearsome developments for the workforce. Some reassurances about pay policy and the direction the department is taking are definitely called for. Perhaps even the formation of a distinct new department for the N/C equipment would help allay some fears and still enable the company to continue with a program of modernization.

This predicament at Tower Manufacturing brings up another aspect of wage incentives — their effect on supervisors. Often supervisors let the wage incentives themselves manage the workforce. That is, given wages as an effective prod for production, some supervisors step back from taking an active role in discovering productivity gains or in monitoring the pace of production. Under an hourly pay scheme, the supervisor is much more directly responsible for the pace and quality of the work.

A different kind of problem with wage incentives and productivity is illustrated in Situation 9-3.

SITUATION 9-3

BALDRIDGE CHAIN SAW

The numbers on the page he was staring at said so, but Dave MacDonald still couldn't believe it. Productivity on the new lightweight chain saw assembly line had declined for the second consecutive week. There was no way now that the company could meet its commitment to a large national retailing organization. That entire account, not to mention MacDonald's own job, appeared to him to be in serious jeopardy.

Dave, a recent M.B.A., was in his first year at Baldridge Chain Saw. The company was a small, family-owned manufacturer of chain saws used primarily by professional loggers. Baldridge marketed these professional chain saws under its own name. Recently, however, the growing demand for small, lightweight chain saws by what the company regulars termed "weekend woodsmen" had triggered the current project to design and manufacture a lightweight chain saw to compete with McCulloch, Homelite, and others. On the basis of its reputation, Baldridge had won a substantial trial contract from a large mass merchandiser. If quality and delivery expectations were met, Baldridge could anticipate regular orders. Dave MacDonald was the so-called project manager, responsible for shepherding the project through the company. The job was a mix of marketing, engineering, production, sales, and finance.

The new lightweight chain saw that Baldridge's engineers had developed was not very complex, at least not as complex as the company's other models. The saw had fewer parts and used many standardized parts that were readily procured either from other operations at Baldridge or from outside suppliers.

The company's industrial engineers had designed a 14-station assembly line for the new saw. This line was staffed half with assemblers pulled from other models' assembly lines and half with new employees. The new employees were paid at a fixed hourly rate for the first month (the start-up) and then they went on incentive pay. During the same start-up period, the experienced workers were paid at the average of their last month's wages; then they too went on incentive. The incentive, similar to that which prevailed in Baldridge's other assembly lines, depended on the output of the entire line. If the line operated at 110 percent of standard, all of its assemblers would receive a given percentage increase in their base pay. Production at 120 percent of standard would yield a higher pay increase. The engineer-rated speed of the line was such that the average expected wage for all assembly workers was set at 110 percent of standard. Production below 100 percent of standard was paid at the start-up wages. The trial contract could just be met, if the workers averaged 110 percent of standard for the 12-week life of the trial contract.

Because the workers could be expected to continue learning how to assemble more efficiently, the standard inched up higher each week after week 4 and then leveled off after week 8. The company's industrial engineers had developed this new, ever-tightening standard based on the company's past performance with other chain saws.

It was now six weeks into the contract's life. Productivity, relative to standard, had traced this pattern (with standards higher in weeks 5 and 6):

Week	% of Standard
1	70%
2	90
3	101
4	111
5	107
6	98

When production slipped in the fifth week, Dave MacDonald had called in the industrial engineers to check whether the line had been properly set up. Dave was concerned lest the line be unbalanced. In that situation, one or more workers might be constituting a bottleneck for the whole line. Dave's concern was heightened by a report from Vic Elgin, the line's foreman, that several of the experienced workers had been complaining about the standards. After studying the matter, however, the industrial engineers reported back that they saw no reason to alter any of the stations along the line. Dave had to wonder then what was holding up production.

LESSONS FROM BALDRIDGE CHAIN SAW

The situation at Baldridge Chain Saw is suspicious, but probably not as perplexing as Dave MacDonald senses it to be. After all, the productivity drop coincides with the tightening of the group incentive wage scheme. The complaints about the standards registered by the older workers to Vic Elgin are other indications that the fall-off in productivity results from a deliberate slowdown in worker pace, as a veiled protest against what the workers would insist are too tight standards. This slowdown may also be a protest against MacDonald himself or the new lightweight saw product line. In any event, the probabilities are that the workers are "pegging their production."

What to do about it? It may already be too late to save the trial order for the mass merchandiser. If it is, the company may want to maintain the standards as they are, deliver late, accept its fate, but make a point about the company's resolve in establishing production standards. If, on the other hand, it is not too late to save the order, the tightening of the standards may have to be postponed and perhaps some overtime scheduled in order to catch up. This approach, of course, would increase costs. Neither of these alternatives is very attractive, but then the situation the company finds itself in does not leave much room for maneuvering.

With this discussion of job design, standards, quality of work life, and wage schemes as background, we turn now to an introduction to labor organization in the United States and what it can mean to operations.

PART TWO

A PRIMER ON LABOR RELATIONS

The trade union movement in the United States is about a hundred years old, spawned as a reaction against some sorrowful management exploitation of labor that must stand as one of the lowest points in business history. Seen against this backdrop, the accomplishments of the union movement are dramatic and heart-warming, won as they were against fierce opposition, although with too much violence from both sides.

Since World War II, however, while the union membership rolls have generally continued to increase (22.8 million in 1974),[10] the percentage of the employment of nonagricultural establishments which is unionized has steadily dropped. In 1974, only 25.8 percent of the employees of nonagricultural establishments were union members, down from 33.2 percent in 1958 and from a high of about 35 percent in 1945.[11]

The unionization of production workers in manufacturing is considerably higher than this, as

TABLE 9-1   Comparison of Estimates of the Extent of Unionization
of Production Workers in the U.S. Manufacturing Industries

| INDUSTRY GROUP | EXTENT OF COLLECTIVE BARGAINING COVERAGE | | EXTENT OF UNION MEMBERSHIP |
	BLS SURVEY OF ESTABLISHMENT (1958)[1]	ESTABLISHMENT SURVEY (1968–72)[2]	HOUSEHOLD SURVEY (1973–75)[2]
Primary metal industries	89%	88%	73%
Transportation equipment	87	87	71
Paper and allied products	76	72	67
Ordnance and accessories	84	79	64
Stone, clay, and glass products	78	78	62
Products of petroleum and coal	89	74	59
Food and kindred products	68	65	52
Rubber products	81	56	51
Fabricated metal industries	71	56	51
Electrical machinery	73	58	46
Machinery, except electrical	68	57	46
Tobacco manufacturers	63	76	42
Chemicals and allied products	65	68	46
Printing, publishing, and allied industries	65	49	38
Apparel and other finished textile products	60	53	36
Miscellaneous manufacturing industries	54	52	34
Leather and leather products	49	57	34
Instruments and related products	52	44	33
Lumber and wood products	44	35	30
Furniture and fixtures	50	49	29
Textile mill products	30	26	17
All industries (U.S.)	67	61	49

1. H. M. Douty, "Collective Bargaining Coverage in Factory Employment, 1958," *Monthly Labor Review* 83, no. 4 (April 1960).
2. Richard B. Freeman and James L. Medoff, "New Estimates of Private Sector Unionism in the United States," *Industrial and Labor Relations Review* 32, no. 2 (January 1979): 143–74.

might be expected. Still, the extent of unionism in manufacturing has declined somewhat over the last generation. Table 9-1 presents some data on the extent of unionization for major industry groups and its change over time. Nevertheless, unions remain an important influence on managers. Wage rates in many companies are set to be comparable with union-bargained rates in other companies in the same industry or in the same geographic area. The same can be said of benefits packages. Business decisions (plant locations, for example) are often made with unions, or their avoidance, in mind.

The apoplexy with which unionism is greeted by many companies, however, is caused less by the additional wages or benefits that companies must pay because of unions. Most managers would agree that keeping unions out of a company is as expensive or even more so than having them in, at least in terms of wages and benefits. The major management complaint rests more with the inflexibility that can creep into a plant as a result of unionism. This complaint is mainly against so-called "work rules," which are largely rules and procedures governing the manning of a plant. Frequently, the work rule agreed to years ago and insignificant then comes back to haunt a manager who for a reason like technological change wants to alter the way things are done. It often takes great management foresight to avoid future pitfalls with work rules; with a union, bad management decisions, many think, are more difficult to remedy. Moreover, the importance of work rules has gradually increased as more and more issues are bargained over by labor and management at contract time.

TABLE 9-2   Two Views of Trade Unionism

	UNION EFFECTS ON ECONOMIC EFFICIENCY	UNION EFFECTS ON DISTRIBUTION OF INCOME	SOCIAL NATURE OF UNION ORGANIZATION
Anti-Union Arguments	Unions raise wages above competitive levels; hence there is too little labor relative to capital in unionized firms. Union work rules decrease productivity. Unions lower society's output through frequent strikes.	Unions increase income inequality by raising the wages of highly skilled workers. Unions create horizontal inequalities by creating differentials among comparable workers.	Unions discriminate in rationing positions. Unions (individually or collectively) fight for their own interests in the political arena. Union monopoly power breeds corrupt and nondemocratic elements.
Pro-Union Arguments	Unions reduce quit rates, induce management to alter methods of production and adopt more efficient policies, and improve morale and cooperation among workers. Unions collect information about the preferences of all workers; hence the firm can choose a "better" mix of employee compensation and a "better" set of personnel policies. Unions improve the communication between workers and management, leading to better decision making.	Unions' standard-rate policies reduce inequality among organized workers in a given company or a given industry. Union rules limit the scope for arbitrary actions concerning the promotion, layoff, recall, and the like of individuals. Unionism fundamentally alters the distribution of power between marginal (typically junior) and inframarginal (generally senior) employees, causing union firms to select different compensation packages and personnel practices than nonunion firms.	Unions are political institutions that represent the will of their members. Unions represent the political interests of lower-income and disadvantaged persons.

Source: Richard B. Freeman and James L. Medoff, "The Two Faces of Unionism," *The Public Interest*, no. 57 (Fall 1979), p. 75.

Despite these arguments against unionism, there are still some strong arguments in its favor. Table 9-2 summarizes the major arguments for and against unionism.

The remainder of this section examines what it means to unionize, focusing on a situation faced by the fictitious Volpe Metals Company. Many of the elements of current labor law are discussed in the next pages. After this examination of union organizing comes the publication of the key sections of an actual labor contract between the Savage Arms division of Emhart Corporation and the International Association of Machinists and Aerospace Workers, AFL-CIO and Hassett Lodge No. 1420. This contract was selected because it was neither too long and complex, nor too short and simple, and because it discusses both hourly and incentive pay schemes.

VOLPE METAL PRODUCTS*

After graduation with a degree in metallurgical engineering from one of the country's leading

---

*Copyright © 1975 by the President and Fellows of Harvard College. All rights reserved.

engineering schools 15 years ago, Peter Volpe took a job as a customer service representative in the research department of a major steel company. Peter progressed very rapidly and came to be highly regarded by the steel company and many of its customers to whom he proved very helpful in solving difficult material and production problems. However, Peter was eager to have his own company and after 10 years, when the owner of a small machine company (50 employees) he had been servicing became seriously ill and had to retire, Peter saw his opportunity. His father-in-law, a successful general contractor, arranged the necessary bank financing and thus was born Volpe Metal Products.

Peter decided to spend most of his time and effort on the research and development area of the business. Eric Berg, who had been superintendent of production under the previous owner, was highly regarded by Peter and eventually promoted to vice-president of manufacturing. The two made an excellent team. The company became known as a dependable supplier of special metal parts. In 10 years it grew from 50 to over 500 employees, including 40 in research and development.

One morning when Peter was driving to work he noticed several men and a woman at the plant gate passing out mimeographed flyers. Peter took one as he drove in. He was surprised to find that it was an invitation to his employees to join a union, the International Metal Workers Union (IMWU). When he got to his office Eric was waiting for him.

* * *

VOLPE: Eric, what do you make of this?

BERG: First thing I knew about it was 15 minutes ago when I drove in. I've talked to the foremen. Bill Evans says he thinks it's the work of the men in the forge room. You know they haven't been happy about the new incentive rates. Bill thinks a new man, Paul Berry, whom we hired down there may actually be an inside organizer.

VOLPE: Isn't this the same union that organized Paul Brown's company a couple of years ago?

BERG: Yes, I think it is and they've had a lot of trouble.

VOLPE: Well, I guess we're babes in the woods when it comes to this business, Eric. Why don't I call Paul and see if he has any advice for us.

* * *

In a few minutes Peter Volpe was talking with Paul Brown.

* * *

BROWN: Pete, I'm glad you called. You know we're having a hell of a lot of trouble with that X-42 part you make for us. It just won't take it.

VOLPE: Oh, I'm sure we got that licked, Paul. We're putting more alloy in it. It's really tough now. Jerry will bring you some samples in a few days. But I've got my own problem here, Paul. I need your advice. The IMWU is trying to organize us. Isn't that the outfit that organized your plant?

BROWN: Yeah, that's our union. I've been wondering how long before they'd hit you guys.

VOLPE: Well, Eric and I don't know anything about this union business. They're out there now handing out literature and talking to our people as they come in. What can we do about it?

BROWN: The most important advice I can give you, Pete, is to get a damn good labor lawyer. The biggest mistake we made here was relying on our regular law firm for advice and help in the beginning. You need a guy who specializes in labor law. We use John Gould now, and if we had used him from the beginning we'd be a lot better off today. I'd recommend John, but there are several other good labor lawyers in town. The best thing you can do is hire one of them and follow his advice. This labor law is a complicated and changing business. You can get burned plenty if you don't have good advice. The IMWU has expert lawyers and you'd better have one too. Why don't you call John Gould?

CALLING IN A SPECIALIST IN LABOR LAW

Peter took Brown's advice and called John Gould. They talked briefly on the phone and Gould agreed to meet with Peter and Eric at the plant the following morning.

* * *

VOLPE: Well, I guess you got one of their invitations to join on the way in. Some of the men told Eric they've also received letters at their homes and that the union is trying to get them to sign membership cards. We think they have an inside organizer by the name of Berry down in the forge room. Eric and I think we should get rid of him right away, just to be sure. Can we do that under our New Jersey laws or do they have everything stacked against us? But we're here to listen, so why don't you talk.

GOULD: Actually the state law isn't involved here. There is a New Jersey Labor Relations Act, but that applies only to small companies involved only in intrastate business. I assume you do business with companies in other states and have gross sales of over $50,000.

VOLPE: Oh yes, we do a lot more than $50,000 and we sell all over the country and in a number of foreign countries.

GOULD: Then your labor relations come under a federal law, the National Labor Relations Act (NLRA), which was passed in 1935 and was modified by the Taft-Hartley Act in 1947 and by the Landrum-Griffin Act in 1959 plus a number of minor modifications.*

The NLRA is administered by the National Labor Relations Board (NLRB), which is an independent agency of the federal government. The agency actually consists of two separate parts—the Board and the General Counsel. The Board consists of five members who are appointed by the President with the consent of the Senate for staggered five-year terms. The Board functions like a court and hears unfair labor practice charges against employers and unions. The General Counsel, who is also appointed by the President with the consent of the Senate, carries on all the investigatory and prosecutory activities of the agency and also supervises the 31 regional offices, each of which is headed by a regional director.

The agency's main functions are to deal with unfair labor practices (ULP) and hold elections to determine whether employees desire to be represented by unions. Any person or group can file an unfair labor practice charge at any one of the regional offices.† A field examiner then investigates the charge and recommends either dismissal of the charge or issuance of a ULP complaint. The regional director reviews the recommendation and either dismisses the charge or issues a complaint. If a complaint is issued, a formal hearing is held before an administrative law judge. A lawyer who represents the General Counsel presents the case against the respondent. The administrative law judge renders a written decision including a remedy. Either side may appeal the decision to the Board in Washington; if either party is not satisfied with the Board's decision, it can appeal to a federal court of appeals. In election cases the Board in Washington has delegated its authority to the regional director, whose decisions on such matters are usually final.

---

*The National Labor Relations Act applies only to businesses whose labor problems may "affect" *interstate* commerce, but the term "interstate commerce" has been so broadly interpreted by the federal courts that many enterprises which think of themselves as "local business" are covered by the act. However, the NLRB has set certain minimum size limitations below which it will not assert jurisdiction:

1. Nonretail enterprises—$50,000 per year gross inflow or outflow of revenue.
2. Retail establishments—$500,000 per year gross business volume. (There are special limitations for office buildings, shipping centers, public utilities, newspapers, radio and t.v. stations, telephone companies, hotels and motels, transit systems and educational institutions.)

Since the passage of the NLRA in 1935 at least 16 states have passed state labor relations acts patterned after the NLRA, but applicable to enterprises that "affect" only intrastate commerce. Since 1959 the state labor relations boards may assume jurisdiction also over any labor dispute that the NLRB refuses to take under its minimum size rules.

†In fiscal 1974 a total of 17,978 unfair labor practice charges were filed against employers and 9654 were filed against unions.

In general conversation we tend to use the terms "NLRB" to indicate the entire agency and not just the five-person board in Washington. When I use that term, I'll be referring to the agency and not just to the board.

The original NLRA (1935) stated that it is the policy of the United States to help interstate commerce by *"encouraging collective bargaining."* Thus, as a businessman you may feel that the act is one-sided. The NLRA gives employees the right to join or not to join unions and also to engage in union activities, including organizing other employees even on company property so long as it is not done on company time. Employers are not permitted to discriminate or discharge employees for such activities.

VOLPE: You mean this guy Berry can try to get our people to sign up here in the plant even when we're paying him?

GOULD: Not when he's supposed to be working. But when he's coming to and from work, during coffee breaks, and at lunchtime he's free to do so without interference from you. Of course, you can discharge him for legitimate reasons that would be cause to discharge any employee, but you'd have to have a good case against him. If the NLRB should determine that your real reason for firing him was his union activity, then it could be very costly to you. In general the penalties under the act are very mild for first offenses. The NLRB usually just issues a cease and desist order. However, in case you discriminate against or discharge an employee for joining or being active on behalf of a union, the NLRB will order you to reinstate him with full seniority and benefit rights and make him whole— that is, provide him with all the pay he may have lost (minus what he may have earned elsewhere during the period) plus 6 percent annual interest.*

VOLPE: Well, Eric, I guess we'd better forget about firing Berry. Evans, his foreman, said he hasn't done anything wrong on the job. But, John, what about those people who are passing out literature? They don't work here. Yesterday they even came into our parking lot.

GOULD: Well, they have a right to pass out literature outside the gates, to talk to people, and try to get them to join so long as they don't threaten anyone or use force. Coming into the parking lot is another matter. It depends on your policy and practice. If you haven't allowed other groups to solicit on company property, you can keep them out too. What's been your practice?

VOLPE: We've never allowed anyone else to do it.

GOULD: OK, then you can insist that the union organizers stay outside the gates. Why don't you just have one of the guards inform them that it's against company policy to allow any strangers inside the gates.

VOLPE: What kind of a counterattack do you think we should make?

GOULD: I don't think we should do anything except get more information now and do some educational work with the supervisors and management groups. From what I have heard, you have treated your employees very well and have a lot of loyalty among them. The union may not get much response and give up very quickly. In the meantime, you should tell your foremen and supervisors not to make any threats or promises regarding unionization. That applies to you and Eric, too. If anyone asks you, you can tell them you think they are better off without a union here, but don't go any further than that without checking with me. Let's wait a couple of days and see what happens. If anything turns up, call me at any time. I gave your secretary my home number.

WAIT-AND SEE-STRATEGY

The next two workdays, Thursday and Friday, the organizers continued to pass out literature at the gate. As Volpe watched from his office window,

---

*During the fiscal year 1974 the NLRB awarded backpay totaling $8.4 million to 7041 workers.

however, it seemed to him that most of the workers weren't very interested. Eric reported that the foremen were of the opinion that only a small group of forge room employees wanted a union. Some of the older men had told Eric they were definitely against it.

On Monday morning when Volpe drove up to the plant gate, he was surprised and pleased to see that the organizers were no longer there. He waited until about 10:00 and then called Gould to tell him the good news.

* * *

VOLPE: They're not out there this morning. I guess you were right. Maybe we got excited over nothing.

GOULD: Well, it's a good sign, but maybe they're just taking a day off or have decided to use other tactics. Let's wait and see. Give me a call if anything happens.

* * *

As each day passed and nothing happened, Peter and Eric became more and more convinced that the union had given up. By Friday evening they were quite confident. The next Monday morning, however, Volpe received a registered letter from the IMWU which read in part:

> We represent a majority of the maintenance and production employees in your manufacturing plant. We would be happy to have you check our signed membership cards. Would you please suggest a time and place where we can meet to bargain with you on their behalf.

Volpe immediately called Gould and read the letter to him.

* * *

VOLPE: What do we do now?

GOULD: Well, this is an entirely new ball game. Evidently they have more support then we suspected, but it doesn't mean we have to bargain. They may not have a majority signed up, and even

if they do, they might not win an election. However, if you think they represent a majority of your employees and you want to bargain with them, you are legally free to do so.

VOLPE: Well, I don't want to bargain with them unless I have to.

GOULD: OK, then I'll prepare a letter for you to send to them in which you will say that you sincerely doubt they represent a majority. If the union believes it does represent a majority, it can then ask for an election. We'll have at least 30 days to carry on a campaign to convince the employees to vote for "no union." In the meantime if one of the union men should bring the cards to you, don't look at them. If you check them over and find they do have a majority, you may be required to bargain without an election.

The next day Volpe signed the letter that Gould had prepared and sent it to the union. Four days later he received a letter from the district director of the NLRB informing him that the IMWU had filed a petition for representation accompanied by signed membership cards for what it claimed to be more than 30 percent of the company's employees. He said the union had requested an election for the purpose of certification as the bargaining agent for all of the production and maintenance employees, including the assistant foremen.

The next day Gould met again with Volpe and Berg.

ESTABLISHING THE BARGAINING UNIT

GOULD: The Board requires a union to show that it has cards signed by at least 30 percent of the employees in a bargaining unit before it will consider an election. The purpose of this 30 percent rule is to prevent elections that the unions have no chance of winning. They must convince the Board that there is a sizable group, at least 30 percent, that want an election. Actually I know of no union that would ask for an election unless it had well over 50 percent of the employees signed up. One of the IMWU representatives once told me that they never ask unless they have at least 70 percent. But don't let that scare you. Despite the signups, unions lose about half of the elections.* A worker often signs a card to get the union off his back, but votes against it in the secret election.

VOLPE: Well, Eric and I are not convinced that a majority of our people want a union.

GOULD: I'm not either.

VOLPE: Well, what do we do about it?

GOULD: Now you must be even more careful than before that none of your management or supervisory people promises or threatens the employees or takes any other action that the NLRB could interpret as preventing a fair and free election. The filing of an election petition marks the beginning of what the NLRB considers to be the election process, during which it insists that "*laboratory conditions*" (that is, "conditions as nearly ideal as possible to determine the uninhibited desires of the employees") be maintained. One of the first things we'll have to do is to see if we can reach agreement with the union on the *bargaining unit*.

VOLPE: What's a bargaining unit?

GOULD: It's a distinguishable group of employees that have the legal right as a group to determine in an election whether they wish to be represented by a union. Usually it consists of all the maintenance and production workers in a plant, in other words an *industrial unit*. But it can consist of a smaller *craft group*, such as your forge room employees or your electricians. There can also be multiplant units, but we needn't be concerned about that, because you have only one plant.

VOLPE: From what Eric tells me, we'd probably lose an election in the forge room. Does that mean we'd have to bargain with the union for the forge workers even though the rest of the employees don't want a union?

GOULD: It could, if the forge room employees were set up as a separate unit, but I don't think we'll have to worry about that. The IMWU is an industrial union, and they are likely to seek a *plant-wide* unit.

VOLPE: Who determines the bargaining unit?

GOULD: If we can reach an agreement with the union, the Board will usually accept our wishes. However, if we can't agree with the union, then the Board will make the decision.

VOLPE: Do they have some kind of a formula?

GOULD: No, it's done on a case-by-case basis. The Board has found it to be an elusive concept, but it has stated that in determining the appropriate bargaining unit, it will be guided by such things as history, organization, interest of employees, and interchangeability of employees. A term frequently used by the Board in this respect is "community of interest." However, as I said before, I don't think we'll have any trouble agreeing on an industrial unit, that is, one that will include all the production and maintenance workers. That's what the union asked for in their letter to you and their petition to the Board. So I suggest that I call up Ed Grannery, their business representative, and tell him we're agreed on that.

VOLPE: What about the chemists and other professionals out in the lab? My guess is they'd all vote against the union. Can we get them in the unit?

GOULD: If the union would agree, we could include the professionals in the unit. However, if the union objected to having them in and the NLRB had to make the decision, then under Section 9(b)(1) of the NLRA there would have to be an election among the professionals to determine whether they wanted to be in the same unit as the other employees or have a separate unit. But, before we take action to try to get them in the unit, I think you'd better be sure you want them in. It's true that their votes might be enough to swing the election against the union. On the other hand, if we

---

*In fiscal year 1974 the NLRB conducted 8368 collective bargaining elections in cases closed that year. 461,145 employees or 89 percent of those eligible voted. The average number of voters in an election was 55. Unions won 4273 or 51 percent of the elections.

were successful in getting them in the unit and the union won anyhow, would you be happy to have to bargain about wages, hours, and conditions for your chemists and engineers?

VOLPE: I guess we'd better think that one over. Maybe we should not try to get the lab in the unit.

GOULD: We'll probably have some difficulties agreeing with the union regarding whether some of your foremen or assistant foremen should be in the unit, and also your guards.

VOLPE: You'd better explain that to us. I just assumed the guards and foremen would *not* be in the union. Who is going to represent our interests around here if they all belong to the union? I want you to keep all of them out, Gould.

GOULD: It isn't that simple. If the guards meet the NLRB's definition of a guard, they won't be allowed to vote in the election. But if they're really just watchmen and the union wants them in, the NLRB will put them in.*

VOLPE: I think you'll find our guards are not just watchmen. They are all sworn in as deputy sheriffs and they all carry guns.

GOULD: With respect to the foremen, the NLRA draws a distinction between employees and supervisors. Employees are protected from discrimination for union activities and have the right to vote in an election. Supervisors are *not* protected and do not have the right to vote. However, just because you call a person a supervisor or a foreman doesn't make him or her one under the NLRA. Section 2 (11) of the law contains the following definition of a supervisor. Reading from the act:

> The term "supervisor" means any individual having authority, in the interest of the employer, to hire, transfer, suspend, lay off, recall, promote; discharge, assign, reward, or discipline other employees, or responsible to direct them, or to adjust their grievances,

or effectively to recommend such action, if in connection with the foregoing the exercise of such authority is not of a merely routine or clerical nature, but requires the use of independent judgment.

You notice that it says *or*. He doesn't have to have all those authorities, but he must have one of them. How about your supervisors and foremen?

VOLPE: I think there's no doubt about our supervisors and foremen. They have the authority. I have some doubts about the assistant foremen.

GOULD: Do you think we should try to keep them all out of the unit?

VOLPE: I'd like to have the assistant foremen vote but not have them represented if the union wins the election.

GOULD: You can't have it both ways.

VOLPE: Then I guess we'd better play it safe and try to keep them out.

GOULD: With your authority then I'd like to call Granary and see what he wants in the way of a unit. We'll probably be able to agree on most of it. If we can't agree, the district director of the NLRB will decide for us. I'll give Granary a call tomorrow. I guess that's about as far as we can go today. Give me a call if you have any questions.

*   *   *

The next day Gould called Volpe to tell him that he had talked with Granary and that they had been able to agree that the unit would consist of all production and maintenance employees in the manufacturing plant and would not include the lab employees. They agreed also that the supervisors and foremen would not be in the unit. However, Granary had insisted that the assistant foremen had no real authority and, therefore, should be in the unit.

*   *   *

---

*The 1947 Taft-Hartley amendments to the NLRA provided that "the Board shall not . . . decide that any unit is appropriate . . . if it includes, together with other employees, any individual employed as a guard to enforce against employees and other persons rules to protect property of the employer or to protect the safety of persons on the employer's premises." However, unionization of guards is permitted and protected under the act, but a union will not be certified for guards by the NLRB if it admits other employees into membership or is affiliated with a union that admits other employees.

GOULD: We'll have to let the NLRB decide on the assistant foremen. If we could have reached an agreement on that and could have agreed on the time and place of the election, we could have had a consent election. However, since we are in disagreement on the assistant foremen issue, we'll have to have what is called a formal hearing. The union and the company will be given a chance to argue the assistant foremen matter before a hearing officer and we can present a written brief later if we want to.* This will all take more time, but that may well be to our advantage.

VOLPE: OK, John, we'll be guided by your advice. We do have another question. What about part-time employees, temporary employees, and employees on layoff?

GOULD: Regular part-time employees and employees on layoff who have a reasonable expectation of being recalled can vote. Temporary employees cannot.

* * *

Several days later Volpe received a notice of a formal hearing from the NLRB. The date and time of the hearing had been arranged to suit the calendars of the two parties and the hearing officer. Volpe was asked to bring an alphabetical list of all his employees.

At the hearing Gould argued that the assistant foremen did possess authority to make decisions and, therefore, should not be permitted to vote. The lawyer for the IMWU took the opposite position. It was agreed that the parties could file written briefs within two weeks following the hearing. One week after the briefs had been filed, Volpe received a decision from the regional director of the NLRB. It supported the union's position that the assistant foremen were not "supervisors" as defined by the act and therefore were eligible to vote. The decision stated also that the election would be held in the plant cafeteria 30 days later.

That afternoon Gould met again with Volpe and Berg.

* * *

GOULD: I was afraid the regional director would decide against us on the assistant foremen. They really don't have much authority. The decision of the regional director on an issue like this is practically final. The Board in Washington would probably not accept an appeal on it.† Anyhow there may be an advantage to us in having them in the unit. They may vote against the union.

VOLPE: Eric, how do you think the assistant foremen will vote?

BERG: My guess is they're all strongly opposed to the union.

GOULD: From now on until the election date the IMWU will probably carry on a very active campaign to convince the employees to vote for them. They'll promise to try to negotiate a big increase in wages and benefits. You may disagree strongly with some of the things they say.

VOLPE: What can we do about it? Are they allowed to lie to the employees? Can we correct any false statements?

GOULD: The Board doesn't try to edit the statements made by either side. However, you can reply and correct any statements made by the union. But remember what I said earlier. You can't prom-

---

*The hearing is a nonadversary procedure conducted by either a regional field officer or a regional attorney of the NLRB. At the close of the hearing all the evidence is turned over to a regional attorney for preparation of a decision, which is never written by the same person who conducted the hearing. The decision is then reviewed by and sent out over the signature of the regional director. Essentially there is no appeal of the unit determination. Although the regional director may decide to permit a review, he does so in less than 0.5 percent of all cases.

†It is possible for a company to circumvent the apparent bar to review of a unit determination by refusing to bargain with the newly designated union. Then if the union files an unfair labor practice charge, the employer can raise the question of the appropriateness of the bargaining unit as a defense.

ise the employees anything for not voting for the union or threaten them with anything if they do. And that applies not just to you two, but to all the foremen and supervisors or anyone else who is your agent.

BERG: We know that the boys down in the forge room are sore about the rates down there. Some of them have told Evans that if they got 10 percent, we could forget about the union.

GOULD: Would you have raised the forge room rates at this time if the union hadn't come along?

BERG: Oh, no. Those rates will be OK as soon as the bugs are out of the new equipment.

GOULD: Then you can't change them now just to try to influence some votes. That would be an unfair labor practice.

VOLPE: What about our hospital and life insurance plans? We usually review them this time of the year and make new benefits, if any, effective July 1. That might help us a lot coming just before the election, especially if we give a sizable boost. On the other hand, maybe we ought to hold back and see whether the union wins. If they do, we'd be in a better bargaining position if we hadn't made the changes.

GOULD: The law is that you should act exactly the same as you would have acted if we had no election pending. You can't raise the forge room rates, but you should increase the hospital and life insurance plans on July 1 by whatever amounts you intended to increase them before you knew about the union. Otherwise, you could be guilty of an unfair labor practice.

VOLPE: You mentioned unfair labor practices. What's the penalty if we are found guilty?

GOULD: The usual penalty for a first offense is that the Board will issue a cease and desist order, which you would have to post in the plant.

VOLPE: That doesn't sound like much.

GOULD: It isn't. However, if you should violate the cease and desist order, the Board would secure a court order, and if you should violate that, you would be in contempt of court, which can carry very heavy penalties. Another penalty, even for a first offense, can be a reelection if the union loses or, in extreme cases, an order to recognize and bargain with the union without another election. As a lawyer, I am sworn to uphold the law and I would not advise you to knowingly break it even though the penalty may be pretty light.

VOLPE: I agree with that, John. How do you suggest we beat the union and stay within the law? Some of the things the union has been saying and writing are just not right. Can we tell the people the truth?

GOULD: Yes, you can call the employees together all at once or in small groups and talk with them. You can even talk to them individually, but it would probably be better to have a management witness present. What you can't do is go to their homes or call them up to your office and talk to them there. And remember, you can't promise or threaten. But before you talk to the employees, I think we ought to get all the supervisors and foremen together. They ought to know your position and be ready to answer any questions that the employees raise. You should emphasize with the foremen that if the union gets in, the foremen's authority in the plant and their flexibility to accomplish things may be greatly curtailed.

VOLPE: If I speak to the workers in the cafeteria, do I have to give the union the same opportunity?

GOULD: No, the Board doesn't require you to do so.

THE ELECTION

A meeting was arranged for the supervisors and foremen. Gould briefed them on the NLRA with special reference to what they could and could not say to the employees. He emphasized that they should not threaten or promise but were free to point out the disadvantages of a union as they saw them. He encouraged them to report to Eric any information that they received, but warned them against spying. Volpe gave them data to answer charges made by the union that the company's wages and benefits were below those of unionized firms.

It was decided also that Volpe would write a letter to the home of each of the employees in which he would answer the union's charges. In the letter Volpe pointed out that the company's wages and benefits were as good as those in union plants, using specific examples. He also encouraged any employee who had a grievance to take it up with his foreman and, if he didn't get satisfaction, to bring it directly to Berg or to Volpe himself. The following week meetings of all the employees in groups of 20 to 25 employees were arranged in the cafeteria during working hours.

The next week Volpe received a notice from the NLRB stating that a second union, the Amalgamated Electrical Workers, had filed a petition to be included on the ballot. Volpe called Gould.

* * *

VOLPE: I got a letter from the NLRB saying another union, the AEW, will also be on the ballot.
GOULD: That's not unusual. Once one union has shown that 30 percent or more of the employees want an election, the Board will allow another union on the ballot even if less than 10 percent of the employees have signed cards or a petition for it. Actually that may help us. The AEW may take some votes away from the IMWU.

* * *

The two unions carried on vigorous campaigns during the days remaining before the election. The organizers appeared at the gate each day passing out literature and urging employees to vote for their unions. Every week the employees received letters from the unions. Volpe replied to the charges in each of these. The unions also held a number of meetings of Volpe employees at their headquarters. Volpe received information about what happened in these meetings from foremen who were told by their employees.

During the last week in June the company announced an increase in hospital-medical benefits and a $2000 boost in life insurance. In letters to the employees the unions branded these changes as an unfair labor practice, but took credit for them. A flier from the IMWU read:

> If we can get these kinds of increases for you while we're on the outside, just imagine what we can do for you when we're in. Vote IMWU and get what's really coming to you!

As the time of the election approached, Gould called Volpe to advise him that all meetings and letters had to cease 24 hours before the election.

* * *

VOLPE: How about getting out the vote? Can we send a car out for someone who is sick?
GOULD: Yes, that's OK so long as you don't discriminate. You've got to offer the same service to all employees. You should indeed make every effort to have all the employees vote. The election is won by a *majority* who vote. There are 329 in the unit, but if only 50 vote and 26 vote for the union it becomes the *bargaining agent* for the entire 329. You can be sure the union will get out those who favor it, so you should encourage everyone to vote.

* * *

The election was held in the plant cafeteria on July 10 from 9:00 to 12:00 and from 1:00 to 4:00. A table was placed in the front of the cafeteria with the ballot box on it. The NLRB election officer, two representatives of the company, and one representative from each of the unions sat at the table. As each employee entered, his name was checked off the eligibility list. The union or the company representatives or the NLRB election officer could challenge any employee's right to vote. The union representatives did challenge two employees whom they claimed were really foremen rather than assistant foremen. Their votes were placed in special sealed envelopes and placed in the ballot box. A decision would be made on them later if the outcome depended on them.

Each employee was given a ballot which had a place to vote for:

IMWU	_____
AEW	_____
No Union	_____

Each employee took his ballot to one of the secret voting booths and marked his preference. He then folded it, brought it back to the table and placed it in the ballot box in front of the NLRB election officer, the company representatives, and the union representatives.

At 4:00 P.M. the polls were closed. The NLRB officer then opened the ballot box and counted the votes in front of the four representatives. Of the 329 employees on the list 312 voted. The results were:

For the IMWU	177
For the AEW	53
For no union	77
Spoiled ballots	3
Challenged ballots	2
Total	312*

The next day Gould met with Volpe and Berg.

* * *

VOLPE: The election results were a shocker to me. I never thought our people would vote for a union. What do we do now?

GOULD: Unless we file an objection to the election or an unfair labor practice charge against the union, the NLRB will now certify the IMWU as the bargaining agent for all the employees in the bargaining unit.

VOLPE: What about the two voters whom the union challenged? Will they be in the unit?

GOULD: We'll try to work that out with the union, and if we can't agree the Board will decide. What's your preference?

VOLPE: Now that the election's over, we'd rather have them out of the unit. They are really foremen, but we knew they'd vote against the union so we told them to try to vote.

GOULD: Since the union challenged them, I imagine Grannery will agree they should be out. I'll call him about it.

VOLPE: Are we stuck with the union forever?

GOULD: Probably, but not necessarily. Once an election is held, the Board won't hold another election for a year. If the union had lost, you would have been free from dealing with any union for a full year. But the IMWU won and they will be certified by the Board as the representative of the employees and that can't be changed for a year. You'll have to recognize the IMWU as the representative of your employees for a full year, even though during the year a majority of the employees could decide they no longer want IMWU to represent them. It's known as an *election bar*, and it lasts, as I said, for one year. There's also what is known as a *contract bar*. If you sign a labor contract with the IMWU, it will serve as a bar to another election for up to 3 years, depending on the length of the contract. If the contract is 2 years long, it will bar another election for 2 years; if 3 years, for 3 years; but if over 3 years, an election could still be held at the end of 3 years.

VOLPE: So there is a possibility we can get rid of the union sometime?

GOULD: Yes, the employees could vote it out just as they have voted it in. It's called a *decertification election*. If 30 percent of the employees sign a peti-

---

*In this election IMWU received a majority of the votes. However, if no entrant on the ballot had received a majority of all the votes cast, the NLRB would have conducted a runoff election between the two with the highest number of votes. For example, if the result had been IMWU—142, AEW—53, and no union—116, a runoff election would have been held with only "IMWU" and "no union" on the ballot.

tion asking for a decertification election, the Board will hold one, assuming there is no election bar or contract bar in effect. If a majority of those voting were to vote for no union or for another union, then the IMWU would be decertified and you no longer would have to bargain with it.*

VOLPE: What happens to the AEW? It got 53 votes. Do I have to bargain with it, too?

GOULD: No. Under our law we have *exclusive representation*. Management has to bargain and must bargain only with the union that wins the election, in this case the IMWU. Even though 53 of your employees voted for the AEW, you do not have to bargain with that union and indeed you must not do so. At the same time the IMWU must represent in good faith not just its own members and those who voted for it, but also those who opposed it, including some who may have joined and may still be members of the AEW.

VOLPE: Will everyone have to join the IMWU now?

GOULD: Oh, no. No one has to join the IMWU or pay dues at this point even though the IMWU has to represent them. Membership is a matter for bargaining between the company and the union. If you and the IMWU should negotiate a union shop, then everyone in the union would have to pay dues to the IMWU, but that's something we'll bargain with them about later. None of your employees will have to join a union unless you agree to it.

CONTRACT NEGOTIATIONS

One week after the election Volpe received a notice from the NLRB certifying the IMWU as the bargaining agent for the employees in the bargaining unit. Later that week he received a letter from Grannery requesting a time and place for begin-

ning contract negotiations, together with a copy of the union's proposed contract.† Volpe called Gould and they met that afternoon.

* * *

VOLPE: We can't agree to that contract. It would put us right out of business!

GOULD: Grannery doesn't expect you to agree to it as it is. He'd be very much surprised and upset if you did. Those just represent his demands. We'll give him some counteroffers that are lower than we expect to settle for and then we can begin to bargain. Don't take these original demands too seriously. But we do have to meet and bargain with him. The NLRA in Section 8(a) (5) makes it an unfair labor practice for an employer to refuse to bargain with the certified representative of his employees. We have to meet with him and make a serious effort to reach an agreement and he does too. If either one of us fails to do so, we would be guilty of an unfair labor practice. We both are required to *bargain in good faith*.

VOLPE: What does bargaining in good faith mean? There are some things in the union's list of proposals that are unacceptable. Does bargaining in good faith mean I've got to give in on them?

GOULD: No. Just because you or the union engage in tough bargaining doesn't mean you are not bargaining in good faith. I don't foresee any problem because I assume you honestly want to reach a fair and reasonable agreement with the union. The Board considers what it calls the "totality of conduct" of the parties, and I'm sure we'll be well within the boundaries.

VOLPE: Do we have to bargain about any issue that the union raises? For example, they are asking for a 20 percent increase for employees who are already retired.

---

*In the fiscal year 1974 the NLRB conducted 490 decertification elections. Unions won in 152 elections involving representation of 13,227 employees and lost in 338 elections involving representation of 11,470 employees.

†Frequently the negotiation of the contract is done by a union official who has not been in charge of the organization drive. In this case, however, Grannery assumed both roles.

GOULD: Section 8(d) of the NLRA provides that the parties must bargain with respect to *"wages, hours, and other terms and conditions of employment."* "Conditions of employment" is a broad phrase, but there are a lot of things it doesn't cover and payments to employees already retired is one of them. The Board has divided issues into three types with respect to bargaining: prohibited items, permissive items, and mandatory items. There are some things, such as a closed shop or a secondary boycott, that you and the union are not permitted to negotiate even though you both may agree to do so.* Then there are items that you can bargain about if both of you agree to do so, but not if one of you objects. Pensions for already retired employees is one of the permissive items. You can bargain about it if you want to, but you don't have to, and it is illegal for the union to strike over the company's refusal to bargain on a prohibited or a permissive item. Finally, there are those items that you must bargain about if the other side so desires. These are the mandatory items and are those that the Board and courts have decided are included in the phrase "wages, hours, and other terms and conditions of employment." It's a long list, which over the years has grown and grown.†

VOLPE: One of their demands is that every employee must join the union 30 days after he is hired. Is that legal?

GOULD: Yes, it's legal and a mandatory bargaining item in this state. Remember, I told you right after the election that no one has to join the union because it won the election, but that that is a matter about which the union and you can bargain. There are a number of different union security or compulsory membership clauses that you can bargain about and one, the closed shop, that is prohibited. A *closed shop* is one in which all employees must join the union before they can be hired. A closed shop is illegal. You couldn't bargain that even if you wanted to. However, Section 8(a) (3) of the NLRA provides that an employer and a union may bargain a union shop. A *union shop* is where the employer is free to hire union or nonunion employees, but they must join the union after they are hired. The law provides that they cannot be required to join until 30 days after being hired. Many contracts extend that to 60 or 90 days. Other compulsory membership clauses such as *maintenance of membership, modified union shop,* or *agency shop,* are also legal in this state.‡ I emphasize this state because Section 14(b) of the NLRA

---

*See next column for a definition of closed shop. A secondary boycott contract clause is one in which the employer agrees not to do business with unorganized employers or with organized employers with whom the union has a strike in process.

†Included among the growing list of mandatory bargaining items are hours of work, overtime, hourly pay rates, piece rates, incentives, merit pay, overtime rates, shift differential bonuses, profit sharing, stock purchase plans, vacations, holidays, sick leaves, pensions, health and welfare plans, life insurance, severance pay, rest periods, lunch breaks, safety, work environment, work loads, seniority, promotions, demotions, transfers, layoffs, discipline and discharge, subcontracting, plant rules, grievance procedures, arbitration, no-strike clause, management rights, checkoff, and union security.

‡In addition to the *closed shop,* which requires the employer to hire only union members and is illegal, there are a number of different types of union security clauses that are permitted by the NLRA. Among these are *union shops,* in which as a condition of employment an employee must join the union, but not until after he has been employed for at least 30 days; *modified union shop,* in which all new employees must join the union, but workers who were employees of the company before unionization do not have to join; *maintenance of membership,* in which no employee has to join the union, but if he does join must maintain membership in good standing for the duration of the contract; (under all of the above clauses the employee may not be discharged for not being a union member if he has been denied membership for any reason other than failure to pay the dues and initiation fees uniformly required by the union); *agency shop,* in which an employee does not have to join the union, but must contribute to the support of the union, usually an amount equal to the regular dues. Section 9(e) of the NLRA provides that if 30 percent of the employees in a bargaining unit petition for an election to eliminate a union security clause, the Board will hold such an election and if the majority vote against the clause, it shall no longer be enforced by the employer. In 1974 the NLRB held 118 of these *deauthorization elections.* The unions lost in 58 percent of the elections (covering 6261 employees) and won in 42 percent (covering 3084 employees).

provides that a state may adopt legislation that prohibits any type of compulsory union membership, and 20 states have such laws, which are known as right-to-work laws.

VOLPE: I notice the union is demanding that we collect their dues for them. Is that legal?

GOULD: Yes, it's called a *checkoff* and is a mandatory bargaining item. You don't have to agree to a checkoff, but many companies do so to avoid collection of dues in the plant. Before you can check off the dues from any worker's paycheck, you must get his written consent to do so.

VOLPE: Who will do the bargaining for the union and the company?

GOULD: The union has the right to choose its negotiators. IMWU usually follows the pattern of having one of its international representatives, in this case Grannery, do the bargaining aided by the president of the local union and half a dozen or so representatives from the bargaining unit. I imagine that's what they will do here, but they could decide to have some others do it and we'd have to bargain with them. The same is true on your side of the table. You can do the bargaining aided by whomever you wish, or you can have someone else do it for you.

VOLPE: I don't think I should do the bargaining. I'm afraid I'd blow my top. I think it would be better to have someone with more patience and a lot more knowledge about labor relations. What about you, could you take care of it?

GOULD: I think it would be wise for you not to be at the bargaining table, but for another reason. You can make final decisions for the company. It's better to keep you in reserve. I do the bargaining for a number of companies and I'd be happy to do it for you. Of course, I'd like Eric and some of the other company men to sit in with me. If I'm to be your negotiator, you have to give me the free authority to negotiate effectively. Of course, you can set the ranges within which I can operate, but I must have authority to reach an agreement that can be subject to your ratification if you want to reserve that right.

VOLPE: I want you to do the negotiating and you'll have authority to reach an agreement.*

GOULD: OK. Then we should develop our counteroffers and also get together a lot of data prior to the first meeting. We'll need to know what our wage rates and benefits are and how they compare with the wage rates and benefits at other plants in the industry and in the area. We'll need to know also what each cent per hour increase will cost the company and many, many other things if we are to be able to bargain effectively. Do you have someone who can work with me to develop such material?

VOLPE: Yes, Art Brown in payroll would probably be the best.

GOULD: OK. I'll start working with him later this week. In the meantime the union will probably be asking you for wage and other information. Under the law you must supply them with wage and employee benefit information. Any other information they ask for check with me. Unless we decide to plead "inability to pay," we don't have to give them financial data.

AN IMPASSE AND A STRIKE THREAT

A few weeks later the company and union representatives opened negotiations. Gould kept Volpe informed after each meeting and also held a number of meetings with the foremen and supervisors to get their opinions on various items. At the end of three weeks everything except the general wage increase had been agreed upon. Gould had insisted that the wage issue be kept open until everything

---

*Many employers prefer not to have a lawyer as negotiator. If the company uses a lawyer as negotiator, the union may feel that it should have a lawyer, too. Frequently, the negotiator for the company is the director of industrial relations and does not have a law degree.

else was settled. After several days of bargaining on the wage issue an impasse was reached. The union refused to come down below 18¢ per hour the first year, 12¢ per hour the second year, and 10¢ per hour the third year plus a cost-of-living adjustment every three months. The company refused to increase its offer beyond 12¢, 10¢, and 10¢ with no cost-of-living adjustment. The union then informed Gould that unless a contract was achieved by a certain day, it intended to strike. That night Gould met with Volpe.

* * *

GOULD: I think the union is serious about striking unless we up the wage offer.

VOLPE: Then I guess we'll have to take a strike. I don't see how we can offer more. Isn't there some way the government can make them settle for a reasonable amount?

GOULD: No. Under the NLRA the union is free to strike a private employer if it isn't satisfied with the wage offer or other mandatory bargaining items. Incidentally, you are also free to lock out, that is, close down the plant when an impasse is reached until the union agrees to a settlement satisfactory to you even if the union would prefer to continue to work at the old rates.*

VOLPE: What about our people who don't want to strike?

GOULD: Section 8(b) (1) (A) outlaws violence or coercion on the picket line. Moreover, after the strike you can refuse to reinstate any employee who engages in violence.

VOLPE: Can I hire new employees to replace them?

GOULD: Yes, you can hire new employees, and when the strike is over, you don't have to replace them with striking employees. You have to take the striking employees back only if their jobs are unfilled after the strike is over.

VOLPE: What about violence?

GOULD: Section 8(b) (1) (A) outlaws violence or coercion on the picket line. Moreover, after the strike you can refuse to reinstate any employee who engages in violence.

VOLPE: Isn't there anything we can do to head off this strike?

GOULD: Yes, we can ask the Federal Mediation and Conciliation Service to help us by sending in a mediator. I haven't called them because I imagine Grannery has done so and we'll be getting a call from them. The FMCS is an independent agency of the government. The mediators who work for it try to help the parties resolve impasses such as we have here. They have no power to force an agreement, but many times they are successful in breaking a deadlock.

* * *

The following day Joseph Sweeney, a federal mediator, arranged a meeting with the bargaining group. Both Grannery and Gould had worked with Sweeney in other negotiations and had confidence in him. After several days of bargaining under Sweeney's supervision and with his help, the parties reached agreement on a new 3-year agreement.

LIVING UNDER AN AGREEMENT

The day after the agreement was signed, Volpe

---

*Under the NLRA a union is free to strike the employer when there is no contract in effect except where:

1. The purpose of the strike is to force bargaining on a nonmandatory issue.
2. There has been a contract in effect and the union has not given the employer 60 days notice of its intent to terminate it.
3. The President has determined that the strike would imperil national health or safety, in which case he can secure a court injunction postponing the strike for 80 days. (At the end of the 80 days, however, the union is then free to strike.)

With respect to lockouts by an employer it is necessary to distinguish between a lockout that is used to avoid collective bargaining entirely and one that is used as an economic weapon after an impasse has been reached. The former is illegal, but not the latter.

asked Gould to come to his office.

VOLPE: Now that we have an agreement, what does it mean?

GOULD: First, since it's a 3-year contract, there can't be another certification election here for 3 years, so the IMWU is in for that long at least. Second, the union can't strike until the end of the agreement and then only after giving 60 days notice before the termination date. Third, under Section 301 of the NLRA the union or the company can be sued in a federal court for violating the agreement. Moreover, under the Boys Markets doctrine the federal courts will quickly issue an injunction ordering the employees back to work if they strike in violation of the no-strike clause and the arbitration provision of the agreement.*

VOLPE: Speaking of arbitration, I notice that the grievance procedure ends in the words "final and binding arbitration." What if I strongly disagree with an arbitrator's award? Can I get a court to change it?

GOULD: Generally speaking, no. The courts will enforce an arbitrator's award even though they may disagree with it. Only if you can prove that the arbitrator had a conflict of interest, was bribed, exceeded his jurisdiction, was insane, or rendered a decision that violates the law will the court alter an award.

VOLPE: Some time back you said the union had to represent all the employees in good faith. Does that mean it has to carry a nonmember's grievance to arbitration? Suppose one of our old nonunion employees brings a grievance directly to me or

Eric, as he has in the past. Can we still work it out with him?

GOULD: The union has to represent every employee in good faith, but that doesn't mean it has to take up a grievance if it honestly believes it doesn't have merit. Any employee can bring a grievance directly to management rather than through the union grievance procedure. However, the IMWU has a right to have a representative present and any settlement you make with an individual employee cannot violate the agreement.

VOLPE: It's nice to have everything settled for 3 years.

GOULD: That's not completely true. There are some mandatory items we didn't bargain about during these negotiations. Under the Jacobs Manufacturing Company doctrine, the union (or the company) can insist on bargaining during the life of the agreement on any mandatory bargaining item that is not covered in the agreement and was not bargained to an impasse.†

VOLPE: Then we don't really have a closed contract. Couldn't you have bargained a clause that would have closed it up?

GOULD: We could have tried to get a so-called "zipper clause," in which the parties agree that they have considered all possible mandatory items and the contract represents a complete expression of agreement. However, in the *New York Mirror* case in 1965 the Board ruled that such a clause does not by itself constitute a sufficiently clear waiver of a specific mandatory bargaining item. However, I don't think you have to worry too much about the

---

*The Norris-LaGuardia Act passed by Congress in 1932 (3 years prior to the passage of the NLRA) placed severe limitations on the issuance of court injunctions in labor disputes. Prior to 1970 the Supreme Court interpreted the Norris-LaGuardia provisions as preventing it from enforcing the no-strike provisions of labor contracts. (See *Sinclair Refining* v. *Atkinson* 50 LRRM 2420 issued in 1962.) However, in 1970 in *Boys Markets, Inc.* v. *Retail Clerks, Local 770* (77 LRRM 2257) the Supreme Court reversed its position and ruled that a federal court can issue an injunction to halt a strike where "a collective bargaining contract contains a mandatory grievance adjustment or arbitration procedure."

†In 1951 in *NLRB* v. *Jacobs Manufacturing Company* (30 LRRM 2098) a federal court ruled that an employer has a continuing duty to bargain during the term of a labor agreement "as to subjects which were neither discussed nor embodied in any of the terms and conditions of the contract."

fact that the contract isn't completely closed. The union isn't likely to insist on bargaining again until the contract terminates 3 years from now. Even if it does, it can't strike to force us to give in on anything. Our no-strike clause protects us from such action.

VOLPE: It's a relief to have it all over. Now Eric and I can forget about this union stuff and put our minds to running the business again.

GOULD: Well, the contract negotiations are finished, but that's only one part of dealing with a union. Now you'll have the problem of living with it. I think we negotiated a good contract, but during the next 3 years there probably will be many grievances and perhaps a few arbitrations as you and the union try to interpret and apply it to specific situations. If I can be of help anytime, give me a call.

DISCUSSION OF VOLPE METAL PRODUCTS

The surprise that Peter Volpe expressed on finding out that most of his workers supported a union is typical. Most plant managers whose plants become organized cannot believe that it has actually happened; this disbelief is an indication that those managers have not been as close to their workers as they thought. So-called "open door" policies—where employees with gripes are told that they can walk into the plant manager's (or president's) office with them—are generally ineffective since such a confrontation can be terribly intimidating to a worker. In the absence of good communications between workforce and management, the workforce's disaffection with management policies is likely to show up in a variety of places: high worker turnover, high absenteeism, declining productivity, quality problems with output, and grievances not dealt with. These are telltale signs that can sometimes telegraph the birth of an organizing effort at the plant.

The appeal of a union is strong: an effective communication channel from workers to management is established, grievances can be handled speedily and fairly, workers are guaranteed more consistency of treatment, management's fringe benefit programs are more likely to match up with worker-felt needs, and higher levels of wages and job security are in many cases forthcoming. It has even been claimed that some companies are better run with unions present than without.

Over the years, corporate managements have become increasingly better attuned to worker needs. The place of the worker has been elevated, wage and benefit packages have improved, and in many subtle ways companies have cut into the labor union movement's appeal. Whether such a trend will continue to weaken the union movement in manufacturing companies, however, remains to be seen. At this writing, unionism remains a powerful force in the thinking of operations managers.

A LABOR AGREEMENT

Following are excerpts from an agreement reached between Savage Arms and the International Association of Machinists and Aerospace Workers. This contract is included as an example of the types of issues that are addressed in labor-management bargaining and how some of them are resolved.

AGREEMENT BETWEEN
SAVAGE ARMS, DIVISION OF EMHART CORPORATION
AND
INTERNATIONAL ASSOCIATION OF MACHINISTS
AND AEROSPACE WORKERS, AFL-CIO
AND HASSETT LODGE NO. 1420
NOVEMBER 1, 1978 THROUGH OCTOBER 31, 1981

This agreement, effective the first day of November, nineteen hundred and seventy-eight, by and between *Savage Arms, Division of Emhart Corporation*, Westfield, Massachusetts, hereinafter referred to as "Company," and the *International Associa-*

tion of *Machinists and Aerospace Workers, A.F.L.-C.I.O.* and *Hassett Lodge No. 1420,* hereinafter referred to as *"Union,"* to cover wages, hours of labor, and working conditions in the plant of the *Company* in Westfield, Massachusetts.

WITNESSETH:

WHEREAS, the parties desire to conclude a mutually satisfactory agreement concerning rates of pay, hours of work, and other conditions of employment, to the end that understanding and cooperation will be promoted and efficient production insured.

It is now hereby mutually agreed as follows:

Article 1
Union Recognition

1.1 The *Company* recognizes and will bargain with the *Union* as the sole and exclusive bargaining agent for the purposes of collective bargaining in respect to rates of pay, hours, and working conditions for all employees of the unit comprising all production, maintenance and factory clerical employees at the plant of the *Company* in Westfield, Massachusetts, but excluding salesmen, supervisory employees, salaried employees, office and clerical employees, employees in the engineering department, the research and development department, the experimental department and guards.

1.2 In the event that the *Company* should relocate within Hampden County, Massachusetts, or expand on adjoining premises, the *Company* will recognize the *Union* in such new or expanded plant as the exclusive bargaining agency for the employees in the categories included in the unit referred to in Article 1, Section 1.

1.3 Present employees shall be given first choice of jobs if the *Savage Arms Division* should move its operations as set forth in Article 1, Section 2.

Article 2
Management Rights

2.1 It is mutually agreed that the management of the *Company* and the direction of the working force is vested exclusively in the *Company*. This shall include, but shall not be limited to, the right to hire, suspend, discharge for cause, promote, demote, transfer, discipline for cause, and maintain discipline and efficiency of employees; to transfer or lay off because of lack of work or for other legitimate reasons; to determine the extent to which the *Company's* interest shall be operated, production or employment increased or decreased, including the right to plan, direct and control its operations; to introduce new or improved methods or facilities, de-skill or break down operations; to determine the products to be manufactured, the scheduling of production, and the methods, processes, and means of manufacturing.

Article 3
Union Security

3.1 As a condition of continued employment, all employees covered by this agreement shall not later than the thirty-first day after the effective date hereof, or, in the case of new employees, not later than the thirty-first working day after their hiring date, become and remain members in good standing in the *Union* for the duration of this agreement.

3.2 Membership in good standing in the *Union* is hereby defined to mean the tendering of the initiation fee at the time the employee first becomes a member of the *Union,* and periodic membership dues, both uniformly required as a condition of acquiring and retaining membership, provided, however, that any *Union* member who authorized deduction of initiation fees and dues, pursuant to Article 3, Section 6, and directs that such deductions commence with his first pay following the date of his employment, shall be deemed to have paid the aforementioned initiation fee and weekly dues. The *Company's* Personnel Department will distribute to new employees at the time of their hire a payroll deduction authorization card for the deduction of initiation fees and dues as aforesaid.

3.3 In the event the *Union* claims that an employee, who has not authorized the deduction of his dues, has failed to maintain his membership in good standing as defined herein, or, in the case of a new employee or nonmember, that he has refused to become a member in good standing as herein provided, such claim shall be certified to the *Company* in writing directing the *Company* to discharge such employee, and the *Company* will discharge such employee. If it thereafter is determined that said discharge was unjust, the *Union* will hold the *Company* harmless in respect to any payments ordered to be made by the *Company* in respect thereto. In consideration for this "save harmless" clause, the *Company* agrees that if the *Company* unilaterally determines that it desires attorneys to represent it in defense of such actions, it shall do so at its own cost and not at the cost of the *Union*.

Article 4
Shop Committees

4.1 (a)   The *Company* agrees to recognize and work with all the accredited members of the *Union* Negotiating Committee, the *Union* Shop Committee, and Department Stewards, who must be employees of the *Company*, in all matters relating to the present agreement between the *Company* and the *Union*. The *Company* agrees to meet with the *Union* from time to time, during the life of this agreement, to discuss problems which may arise affecting employees and which may not be specifically provided for herein.

4.3 There shall be a *Union* Negotiating Committee and a *Union* Shop Committee. Both Committees shall total not more than seven (7) employees, and shall function in accordance with the provisions of this agreement.

4.6 The *Union* agrees that there shall be no *Union* activity during working hours except that which is herein provided.

Article 5
Seniority

5.1 Definition

Seniority is defined as the aggregate of the time during which a person has been on the *Company's* active payroll as an employee within the bargaining unit. This definition is subject to the following provisions of this Article and shall apply wherever the term "seniority" is used in this agreement.

5.2 Loss of Seniority

Seniority shall be lost for the following reasons:

(1)   Voluntary quitting or retirement.
(2)   Discharge for good and sufficient cause.
(3)   Layoff for lack of work for a period equal to the employee's length of service, but in no cases shall the period exceed four (4) years.
(4)   Failure to report back to work when recalled within five (5) calendar days after receipt of certified return receipt letter notifying the employee to return, sent to the last known address as shown in the *Company* records.
(5)   Failure to notify the *Company* of the reason for absence within four (4) working days after start of absence, except when failure to notify is for a reasonable excuse.
(6)   Failure to report back to work at the expiration of a leave of absence or an extension thereof, unless there is a reasonable excuse for not reporting.
(7)   Giving a false reason for obtaining a leave of absence.

5.3 New Employees

New employees shall be considered probationary employees for a period of thirty (30) working days from date of hire. Upon successful completion of such probationary period they shall become regular employees. All contract benefits shall be enjoyed, by new employees, during their probationary period, except recourse through the grievance and arbitration procedure for discharge.

5.4 Top Seniority and Shift Preference

Union Shop Committee members, Local Lodge President, Vice-President, Secretary-Treasurer and Recording Secretary shall have top seniority for layoff, recall, temporary transfer and shift preference, and Stewards shall have top departmental seniority on their shift during their term of office for layoff, transfer, and recall.

5.5 Seniority Roster and Records

(a) The *Company* shall prepare and maintain a seniority roster to record the status of each employee in the bargaining unit. The seniority roster shall indicate each employee by name, classification, rate of pay, shift, and seniority date.

(d) Employees on a temporary transfer shall not be denied opportunity for overtime on their regular job assignments.

5.7 Transfers

(a) The *Company* and the *Union* endorse the principle of advancing employees to better positions, including management positions. An employee who is promoted to a management position from date of this contract, shall retain his or her seniority accumulated prior to the promotion for six (6) months; thereupon he or she shall have the option to return to the bargaining unit or sever all rights to return to the bargaining unit. The employee(s) so promoted may, during the six (6) month period, have the option to return to the bargaining unit; the *Company*, likewise, during such period may return the employee(s) to the bargaining unit. But in no case will the employee(s) so returned displace another bargaining unit employee.

5.8 Layoffs and Reductions in Classifications

(a) Layoffs

When a layoff is to occur, the following procedure will be followed by the *Company* and the *Union*:

(1) The *Company* will meet with the Chairman of the Shop Committee to advise him of an impending layoff(s), number of employees involved, and the shifts involved.

(2) The Chairman of the Shop Committee and the Personnel Manager or his designee will review the seniority roster of the job classification(s) affected and determine the status of employees affected as to the extent that they can exercise their contract rights.

(3) After the above meeting has been held, the *Company* and the *Union* will (A) notify employees affected and (B) post notice showing the number of employees, job classifications, and shift(s) affected.

(4) The least senior employees in the job classification(s) affected shall be laid off from their job classification(s) based on seniority except where special skills or training are essential to the job. Any dispute regarding the exception referred to, shall be resolved between the *Company* and the *Union*.

(5) Any employee affected by such layoff shall be allowed to bump any less senior of any bargaining unit classification, provided the employee is capable of performing the work satisfactorily within a period not to exceed five (5) days, and also provided the least senior employee in the classification shall be the one displaced. In the event the employee does not satisfactorily perform the work within the five (5) day period, he shall be placed on an open job, as may be available and which he is capable of performing or considered on layoff, without further bumping rights, and the displaced employee shall be recalled.

(6) The *Company* shall give five (5) days' notice in advance of any layoff, in writing, to the employees affected or five (5) days' pay in lieu of such notice, and copies of such notice shall be simultaneously given to the *Union*. If the five (5) days' pay is given in lieu of notice, it shall be at the employee's regular hourly rate or A.S.T.H.E.,

as provided in this agreement.*

(7)   Employees who may accept an open job offered to them at the time of layoff shall be considered eligible for recall rights just as though they had, in fact, exercised their bumping rights.

(8)   The *Union* President or his designee shall be present at any meeting or interview with any employee affected by layoff.

(b) Reductions in Classifications

(1) An employee affected due to a reduction in his job classification shall be allowed to bump a less senior employee in the bargaining unit, on his shift, or at his option another shift, provided the employee is capable of performing the work satisfactorily, and further provided that the employee bumped shall be the least senior employee in the job classification bumped into.

5.9 Recall

A. The right of seniority in recall shall be accorded any displaced employee before any additions to the workforce in his former job classification are made. If an employee elects not to return to his former job classification, when offered, he thereby loses his right to do so in the future except by subsequent bidding.

B. Employees shall be recalled to work in the order of seniority and capability before new employees are hired for any job classification.

Article 6
Posting and Bidding

6.1 (a) Vacancies and new job classifications created shall be posted on the *Company* bulletin boards for two (2) working days. Such postings will state the number of jobs to be filled, shift, depart-

ment and the labor level and rate range for each job to be filled. The *Company* may fill such jobs by temporary transfer during the posting and bidding procedure. The *Company* and *Union* shall not be obligated to notify absent employees of such vacancies.

(1) Vacancies in the case of incentive classifications will first be filled by the highest seniority man in the job classification involved, who requests such opportunity. The vacancy thus created shall be posted.

(2) When there is an opening in a job classification family, as listed under Appendix A, the most senior employee in the next lower job classification shall be promoted prior to posting, provided he has the ability to fulfill the requirements of the job classification involved.

(3) When there is an opening in the job classification families designated in the trades (Appendix B), the most senior employee in the next lower job classification shall be promoted prior to posting, provided he has the ability to do the job. Employees shall not be awarded such job classifications unless qualified by vocational education, training, and/or experience in the work of such classification. (Exceptions to these qualifications may be made by mutual agreement of the parties.)

(b) Applicants for posted vacancies will be selected on the basis of seniority and qualifications and possessing the basic skills of the job classification involved, requiring only a short period to become familiar with specific methods and procedures for applying such ability or skill in the particular job classification concerned, while under adequate instruction and supervision. Successful applicants will be permitted to bid on open job classifications only once in any four (4) month period. A new employee as defined herein shall not be eli-

------

*Average straight-time hourly earnings computed as the average amount per hour earned, including incentive and shift bonus but excluding overtime premiums, pay for hours not worked, pay for time worked on the taking of inventory during the regular inventory period, and pay for time worked during vacation shutdown.

gible to bid on posted job classifications for a period of ninety (90) days from the completion of the employee's thirty (30) day probationary period.

(c) All bids shall be made within two (2) working days of the date of original posting on forms supplied by the *Company* and such bids shall be in writing, signed by the employee bidding; one copy to the *Union* Steward and one copy to the *Union* office or Shop Chairman.

(d) The *Company* shall post its selection, or the fact that no one has been selected on the *Company* bulletin boards within five (5) days after the original posting. If a successful bidder has been determined, the *Company* will fill the job as soon as the successful bidder has been replaced in his former job, which shall take place no later than thirty (30) days from the date of selection, except in cases where a replacement cannot be made because of special skill requirements, or due to the difficulty filling the opening by hiring, or as agreed by the parties. Upon the date of assignment the successful bidder shall be given the classification and paid the base rate on the job for standard hourly workers. Dayworkers, upon assignment, shall be given the classification and paid in accordance with Article 12, Section 12.3C.

(e) If at any time within a thirty (30) working day trial period (actual days worked), it becomes evident that the employee selected cannot fulfill the requirements of the job classification involved, he shall be returned to his former job if it has not been permanently filled or eliminated. Accordingly, if his former job is not available, he shall be given any other open job which may be available and which he is able to perform satisfactorily. The employee may reserve the right to return to his former job within the first five (5) days of such trial period.

(f) It is not the intent of the parties to fill temporary vacancies (such as those caused by accident, illness, or leave) by this system.

(g) No classification will be posted until any displaced employee of such classification has been recalled.

Article 7
Job Descriptions

7.1 All current and active jobs have been classified into three (3) categories as follows:

1. Daywork jobs
2. Incentive jobs
3. Trades

In each category the jobs have been graded into appropriate labor levels, on the basis of their relationship to each other, as determined by the job description agreed to, and initialed, by the parties.

7.2 The job descriptions describe the activities required to perform the job.

7.3 Employees shall not be required to perform work outside their job classification except as permitted by this contract, such as 5-6(a) (Temporary Transfers), or by agreement with the *Union*.

7.4 An employee shall be paid the rate of pay assigned to the labor level containing the job classification.

7.5 When a new job is created, or when a job changes sufficiently so that a revision of descriptions becomes necessary, the *Company* shall prepare a suitable job description of each job.

Article 8
Grievance Procedure

8.1 For the purpose of this agreement, the term "grievance" means any dispute between the *Company* and the *Union* or between the *Company* and any employee concerning the effect, interpretation, application, claim of breach or violation of this agreement.

8.2 (a) The *Company* agrees to meet duly accredited *Union* representatives concerning all grievances, disputes, and differences pertaining to wages, hours of work, and working conditions arising between the *Company* and the *Union*, for the purposes of adjusting of said grievances, disputes, and differences and any such grievance shall be settled in accordance with the following grievance procedure:

Step 1. Any employee having a complaint or grievance shall take the matter up with his steward. The steward shall discuss the matter with the Foreman with a view toward resolving the issue. In the event the matter is not satisfactorily resolved, the steward shall reduce the grievance to writing with a brief explanatory statement citing the violation and the Foreman shall give his written answer with a reason for denial; both shall date the grievance. The time for processing a grievance in the first step shall not exceed two (2) working days from the time the grievance is brought to the Foreman.

Step 2. Any grievance not satisfactorily resolved in Step 1 shall be referred in writing to the *Union* Area Committeeman who shall investigate and attempt to resolve the grievance. The Area Committeeman shall present the grievance to the Personnel Manager and the Production Superintendent, or Manager of area concerned and the parties shall meet with the individual(s) involved to discuss and resolve the grievance within two (2) days from date of written answer from the first step. The Personnel Manager and the Production Superintendent, or Manager of area concerned shall have one (1) working day from date of meeting to give their written answer.

Step 3. Any grievance not satisfactorily settled in Step 2 shall be referred to the *Union* Shop Committee and they shall present, discuss, and attempt to resolve such grievance with the Vice-President of Industrial Relations and Plant Manager at a meeting to be held within four (4) days from date of written answer to the grievance at second step. The Vice-President of Industrial Relations and Plant Manager shall give their written answer to all matters reviewed at such meetings within four (4) working days from date of such meeting.

(a) Grievances affecting a group, or groups, of employees may be initiated directly at Step 2 by either party if it is deemed necessary.

(b) In the event a grievance is settled in Step 2 or 3 of the above listed grievance procedure, the written settlement shall be distributed to all persons directly involved in the grievance procedure.

(c) The time elements of this procedure exclude Saturdays, Sunday, Holidays and Vacations and may be extended by mutual agreement of the parties.

(d) In the event the grievance is not satisfactorily settled in Step 3, either party (*Union* or *Company*) may submit such grievance to arbitration in the manner hereafter provided. If such grievance is not submitted to arbitration within ten (10) working days, the grievance will be considered settled.

8.3 All grievances and other disputes arising out of the terms of this agreement, which have not been satisfactorily adjusted as heretofore provided, may be submitted to arbitration at the election of either party. The matter to be arbitrated shall be submitted to the arbitrator as follows:

Within ten (10) calendar days after written notification to arbitrate is given, a meeting shall be held to select an arbitrator. If the parties cannot agree upon an arbitrator at this meeting, a request for a list of seven (7) arbitrators shall be made to the Federal Mediation and Conciliation Service by the party desiring arbitration. Beginning with the party desiring arbitration, the parties shall alternately strike a name from the list until only one (1) name remains, which shall be the arbitrator. The arbitrator shall have no authority to amend, modify, alter, subtract from, or add to this agreement unless the parties agree to give him specific authorization to do so; and he shall render his award within thirty (30) days. The decision of the arbitrator shall be binding on both parties and shall be complied with within ten (10) calendar days from the date of decision. The fee of the arbitrator and his expenses, if there are such expenses, shall be shared equally by the parties concerned.

8.4 Either party to this agreement shall be permitted to call employee witnesses at any step of the grievance procedure. The *Company* will make any records pertaining to employee status, job content, or rate data available upon request well in advance of formal proceeding of any step in the grievance procedure.

8.5 Either party shall have the right to designate an alternate, from time to time, to act for him at the various steps of the grievance procedure.

8.6 The grievance procedure and arbitration provided for herein shall constitute the sole and exclusive method of decision, adjustment, or settlement between the parties of any and all grievances as herein defined. The above mentioned time limits may be changed, or extended, by mutual consent of both parties of this agreement.

Article 9
Discharges

9.1 No employee shall be discharged or disciplined without good and sufficient cause. Any employee who has been discharged shall, if he so requests, be granted an interview with his shop steward before he is required to leave the plant. A written notification of discharge stating the reason for such action will be sent to the *Union* within five (5) working days after date of discharge.

9.2 Should there be any dispute between the *Company* and the *Union* concerning the existence of good and sufficient cause for a discharge, such dispute may be processed as a grievance in accordance with the terms of this agreement, provided that any such grievance must be filed within five (5) working days immediately following receipt, by the *Union*, of written notification of discharge.

9.3 Whenever possible the *Company* shall give advance notice to the *Union* of any contemplated discharge or disciplinary action.

Article 10
Hours of Work

10.1 The normal pay week shall run from Monday through Sunday inclusive. The normal workweek shall be forty (40) hours, eight (8) hours per day, five (5) days per week, Monday through Friday inclusive.

10.2 The starting and quitting times of the normal shifts shall be as follows:

First shift: 7:00 A.M. to 3:30 P.M.
Second shift: 3:45 P.M. to 12:15 A.M.
Third shift: May be scheduled by mutual agreement of the parties hereto.

The foregoing hours include a one-half (1/2) hour lunch period to be established by mutual agreement of the *Company* and the *Union* and posted in each department.

10.3 The *Company* will not schedule a regular workweek of less than forty (40) hours per week, except that it may do so in the following situations:

(a) weeks in which holidays occur, vacation and inventory periods,

(b) temporary shutdowns due to interruption in the flow of materials or work in process,

(c) change in standard workweek by Federal or State authority,

(d) conditions beyond the control of the *Company*, such as fire, flood, loss of power, unusually severe weather, strikes or shutdowns in plants or suppliers, acts of God and the like,

(e) agreement with the *Union*.

Article 11
Overtime

11.1 Time and one-half shall be paid in each or any of the following instances and each instance shall not be dependent on any other instance:

(a) All time worked in excess of eight (8) hours in any one working day.

(b) All time worked in excess of forty (40) hours in any one workweek.

(c) All time worked on Saturday, as such, except when the regular scheduled Friday shift runs into Saturday.

(d)   Call-in-time as defined in Article 16 whenever falling on Saturday.

(e)   All work performed during the lunch period, except in the case of maintenance employees.

11.2 Double time shall be paid in each or any of the following instances and each instance shall not be dependent on any other instance.

(a)   All time worked on Sunday, as such, except when the regular scheduled Monday shift starts on Sunday.

(b)   All work performed in excess of eleven (11) hours in any twenty-four (24) hour period.

(c)   All work performed on any of the holidays listed in Article 14, Section 2. For the purpose of second and third shift operations, the twenty-four (24) hour period beginning with the regular starting time of such shift on the holiday shall be considered the holiday, it being understood that no holiday premium shall be paid for work during any other hours.

11.3 (a) The *Company* will make every reasonable effort to distribute overtime equally among the employees in respect to their classifications and departments.

(b) If a sufficient number of employees do not volunteer for overtime work, assignment of overtime will be made on the basis of reverse seniority of employees in the job classifications who are qualified to do the work.

(c) The Foreman shall maintain current overtime records which shall record overtime worked and overtime refused. Employees who refuse overtime and have been given notice per Section 11.5 shall be recorded as having worked for overtime distribution purposes. Employees who do not work overtime when requested but have not been notified per Section 11.5 will not be charged for such overtime for distribution purposes.

11.4 Any employee who has worked overtime at any time during the week shall be permitted to work out the balance of a normal workweek as defined in Article 10.2.

11.5 Employees requested to work shall receive advance notice by noontime for daily overtime, and by the end of the shift on Thursday for weekend overtime.

11.6 It is understood and agreed that there shall be no pyramiding of overtime under this agreement, nor shall the *Company* pay overtime on overtime for the same hours worked.

Article 12
Wages

12.1 Rates for all job classifications within the plant have been established by agreement between the parties and shall remain in effect during the continuance of this collective bargaining agreement. Said rates are set forth in Schedule A, B, C attached.

12.2 (a) New employees on daywork or trades job classifications shall start at a guaranteed minimum of not less than the minimum rate of the job classification for which they are hired as shown in the wage schedules attached. Such daywork or trades employees may receive the first step of their automatic steps at the end of their probationary period, or depending on prior job experience, may receive a rate up to and including the top of the automatic progression increments.

(b) New employees on incentive shall receive the base rate of the job classification for which they are hired as shown in the wage schedules attached, and will be paid in accordance with the prescribed procedures for incentive work through equitable and proper time standards as outlined in Article 13.

12.3 A. All employees in daywork or trades job classifications shall progress from the minimum rate to the top of the automatic increments of their labor level in accordance with the attached schedule (Schedule D).

(a) All employees starting at the minimum of the rate range will be reviewed on an automatic basis at three (3) month intervals from date of job assignment for the first six (6) increments of the rate range, but in no event to exceed the first six (6) steps of the rate range.

B. All employees in daywork or trades job classifications shall progress from the top of the automatic progression increments to the maximum of their labor level in accordance with Schedule D attached on the basis of their performance. The procedure shall be as follows:

(a) Employees in the rate range beyond the first six (6) automatic increments shall have their performance reviewed from date of job assignment each three (3) month period for the seventh (7th) step and each six (6) month period for the eighth (8th) step of the range, and shall be informed of the results of the review within five (5) working days.

(b) Satisfactory performance, as determined by the review, shall result in a wage increase, provided that the increase will not bring the resulting rate above the maximum rate of the labor level involved.

(c) The *Company* may grant a wage increase based on performance, within shorter periods of time, if so justified.

12.4 The minimum weekly pay for an employee shall be his base rate multiplied by the total number of hours which he worked during the week; however, in the case of a piecework employee transferred to another piecework job with which he is not familiar, said transfer being necessitated by a cut-back for lack of work, or in the case of an employee recalled after a layoff for lack of work and placed on a piecework job with which he is not familiar, he shall receive his incentive earnings on the job, but in no case less than his base rate, whichever is higher.

12.5 (a) A premium of fifteen cents (15¢) per hour will be added to the base rate of incentive employees working on the second shift, and a premium of twenty cents (20¢) per hour will be added to the base rate of incentive employees working on the third shift.

(b) A premium of thirty cents (30¢) per hour will be added to each clock hour worked for daywork and trades employees working on the second shift, and a premium of thirty-five cents (35¢) will be added to each clock hour worked for daywork and trades employees working on third shift.

(c) A premium of thirty-five cents (35¢) will be added to each clock hour worked for employees involved in the start-up operations when they report to work prior to 5:00 A.M. for their eight (8) hour shift.

12.6 An employee who works on the taking of inventory during the annual inventory period shall be paid $4.46 per clock hour worked for each year of this agreement.

12.8 (a) In the event an employee reports for work on his regular shift without having been previously notified not to report, he shall be given at least four (4) hours' work within his classification or four (4) hours of other work which he can perform. If such employee is assigned to other work, he shall be paid his base rate, or the base rate on the job, whichever is higher.

(b) If, after reporting to his foreman, no other work is available, he shall be given four (4) hours pay at his average straight-time hourly earned rate, as defined in Article 13, Section 11 (a), or his base rate, whichever is higher.

Article 13
Incentive Plan

13.1 Objective

The *Company* shall continue the standard one hundred percent (100%) allowed hour incentive plan, and shall establish correct and equitable time standards where this is feasible and practical. The standard time values thus established will indicate the time allowed to perform specific job tasks.

13.2 Time Standards

(a) Time standards are based on the performance of normal individuals. Average qualified operators working under normal job conditions shall be able to earn twenty-five percent (25%) above the evaluated rate while performing the work as specified in the standards and working at a proportionate incentive pace. The *Company* agrees to continue its basic policy if not limiting the earnings of any worker whereby an average qualified operator may exceed earnings of twenty-five percent (25%) in direct proportion to the effort and skill expended.

(b) All time standards shall be based on a careful analysis of the work to be done, the operation sequence of elements within the cycle, the material, equipment, methods, speeds, feeds, setups, and specifications that are to be used and followed, including the surrounding work conditions, and a proper record kept of the relative influence of such factors in any specific time standard.

(c) Time standards shall include the actual time for each and every function required of the operator with the time element for each and every function set forth in elements leveled to normal and including all allowances as required by this agreement.

(d) Elemental studies of each job or operation shall be made by the *Company* with the aid of a stopwatch graduated decimally, using either the continuous reading method, snap-back method when needed, or by the use of appropriate standard reference data.

(e) Time standards are generally expressed in hours per one hundred (100) pieces. Where this is not practical, the standards are expressed in other units which are both controllable and measurable.

13.3 Permanent Time Standards

(a) Time standards presently in effect shall remain unaltered, regardless of earnings, except (1) as provided otherwise in Article 13, Section 13.9 hereof, (2) for clerical errors, or (3) where changes have occurred in the job content, methods, tooling, equipment, or materials used in the manufacture of the product.

(b) Only such elements or allowances that have been changed or directly affected by such change

shall be revised, but they shall not be revised in order to limit or curtail an employee's potential earnings. The employee shall continue to be paid in proportion to the effort and skill expended.

13.4 Temporary Time Standards

(a) Where circumstances and conditions are such that it is impractical to set permanent time standards for productive work, temporary time standards may be established and applied.

(b) An adequate compensation factor will be allowed where necessary because of nonstandard conditions that may exist in order to conform with principles of this plan.

(c) Temporary standards will generally be applied on a job lot basis and shall be automatically voided with the completion of the lot.

13.5 Leveling

(a) The actual observed time shall be leveled, or "normalized" to one hundred percent (100%) by multiplying the actual time by the rated performance.

(b) Studies shall be made using normal operators whenever possible; however, there shall be no ceilings placed on the rating of the speed and efficiency of operators giving better than a normal performance.

(c) If any study shows an operator to be below normal, the time study observer will notify the foreman who will in turn notify the operator of this fact before such standard is placed in effect.

13.6 Allowances

(a) All time standards will be supplemented by a minimum allowance of fifteen percent (15%) for personal time, rest for overcoming job fatigue, and unavoidable delays with additional allowances where warranted by unusual or abnormal conditions.

(b) Allowance factors over fifteen percent (15%) will be determined by studies and surveys for each specific job task.

13.7 Machine Controlled Incentive

Downtime will be paid only in instances in

which the workload has been decreased in a machine assignment to the extent that causes an operator to wait for equipment, thus curtailing incentive opportunity. The machine assignment through time study observation can be made flexible to compensate for machine cycle variations and other activity requirements within a group of operations. A job is machine cycle controlled only when the cycle is basis of payment. When downtime occurs, the employee (unless assigned to other work) will be paid base rate, provided that the employee notifies his supervisor or foreman as soon as possible after the downtime starts.

13.8 Instructions

(a) The operator shall be informed of the standard, rate, and other necessary instructions in order to properly perform the operation prior to being assigned any incentive job. Final responsibility for instructions and assignment of work is that of supervision.

(b) Incentive workers shall perform the operations as instructed.

13.9 Grievances

(a) If after working under a new piece rate for five (5) days with reasonable application of skill and effort, an employee feels that the time standard for his operation is incorrect, he shall immediately notify his department representative, who shall then process the grievance in conformity with the regular grievance procedure, provided in Article 8 starting with Step 1.

(b) Whenever a dispute occurs with respect to a rate, the *Company* will restudy such rate as soon as possible, but not later than five (5) working days, except in case of emergency. Whenever a restudy becomes necessary as a result of an alleged inadequate time standard or rate, the aggrieved employee shall be studied whenever possible.

(c) When a standard has been processed through the grievance procedure and a disposition has been made, such standard may not be again processed as a grievance for the same reasons as long as no

changes have taken place in conformity with Section 13.3, Paragraphs (a) and (b).

(d) Records of time standards showing the detailed sequence of operation will be available in the Foreman's office. The rate for each operation will continue to be available in the centralized rate book.

(e) If the time standard is found to be incorrect, any adjustment which may be developed as a result of the grievance will be made retroactive to the date of submission.

(f) If a grievance involving a time standard is submitted to arbitration, the determination of the correctness of the standard shall be limited to and based on the principles provided herein.

13.10 General

(a) In the event that the *Company* places on incentive any job not now covered by some form of incentive, it will observe the foregoing statement of principles in establishing incentive standards.

(b) Any question dealing with the incentive plan not specifically contained or covered herein shall be discussed by the *Company* and the *Union*. When such questions arise, and if no agreement can be reached, they shall be resolved through the grievance procedure.

(c) The *Company* agrees that the incentive plan provisions, described herein, will not be altered during the term of this agreement, without prior negotiations and agreement with the *Union*.

13.11 Average Straight-Time Hourly Earnings

(a) For the purposes of this article, average straight-time hourly earned rate shall mean an employee's average straight-time hourly earnings computed on the basis of the average amount per hour earned, including incentive and shift bonus, but excluding overtime premium, pay for hours not worked, pay for time worked on the taking of inventory during the regular inventory period, and pay for time worked during vacation shutdown, which the employee earned during the payroll quarter preceding the application of such payment.

(b) The average straight-time hourly earned rate, as defined in the preceding paragraph, will be paid for time spent by incentive employees who are temporarily assigned to other than their regular job assignments for any of the following reasons:

(1) Attendance at meetings called by the *Company* during their regularly scheduled working hours, unless otherwise provided herein.

(2) For time spent by an employee assigned to instruct another employee where such instruction will result in an interference with his incentive earnings.

(3) For time spent by an employee temporarily assigned to try out new equipment or a new process, or to work on an experimental or development job.

(4) For time spent by an incentive operator placed on work on which no standard has been established until such time as a standard for the operation is issued.

(5) For time spent by an incentive operator assigned to a regular daywork job, when the employee could have continued doing incentive work and earned incentive wages. It is agreed that such employee is expected to perform at an incentive pace.

Article 16
Call-In Pay

16.1 An employee recalled to work after the termination of his regular shift, to do any production work, shall receive no less than two (2) hours' work or two (2) hours' pay at double his average straight-time hourly earned rate, as defined in Article 13, Section 11 (a).

16.2 If an employee is called in for emergency maintenance work at a time not within his regularly scheduled hours of work and such work neither continues into nor is directly in addition to his regularly scheduled hours, the *Company* will provide not less than four (4) hours' work, or four (4) hours' pay in lieu thereof, at his base rate.

Article 23
Safety

23.1 The *Company* agrees to establish and maintain conditions of health and sanitation in the plant as required by all applicable State and Federal laws.

23.2 The *Union* agrees that there shall be a rigid observance of factory safety regulations. It agrees to undertake to promote in every way possible the education of its members in accident prevention, and to recommend to the *Company*, from time to time, ways and means for the prevention of accidents.

23.3 The *Company* and *Union* shall form a joint Safety Committee, consisting of two (2) *Union* representatives and two (2) *Company* representatives. This committee will meet once a month for the purpose of discussing and recommending safety improvements in the plant to the *Company* Safety Director, who will be the Chairman of this committee. The *Union* representatives assigned to this committee will be paid at their personal rate, or A.S.T.H.E. rate for any time spent at such meetings.

Article 24
Visitations

24.1 Accredited representatives of the International *Union* shall have the right to visit the factory premises of the *Company* during working hours to assist in handling of grievances and to observe whether the terms of this agreement are being properly administered. Such representative shall first notify the Personnel Manager or his designee to announce his presence and state the purpose of his visit.

Article 27
Supervisory Employees

27.1 Supervisory employees and all persons outside the bargaining unit shall not be permitted to perform work normally performed by any bargaining unit employee on any job covered by any job classification of this agreement except under the following conditions:

(a) In the instruction or training of employees.

(b) In extreme emergencies when the performance of such work would be necessary to prevent damage to machinery, equipment, or *Company* property.

(c) In cases where technical knowledge, experience, and engineering type requirements necessitate participation together with properly classified employees of the unit.

(d) In emergencies when employees within the unit who are qualified to do the work are not immediately available, but not exceeding the remainder of the workday.

(e) In the performance of necessary work when production difficulties or troubles are encountered.

Article 28
Outside Work

28.1 The *Company* will not normally subcontract work to outside contractors not owned or controlled by or affiliated with the *Company*, in situations where such subcontracting would result in a layoff of employees or in a reduction of scheduled hours, without first giving consideration to such factors as available equipment, manpower, production requirements, and cost of manufacture and distribution.

Article 31
No Lock-Out, No Strike

31.1 The *Company* agrees that it will not lock out its employees during the life of this agreement.

31.2 The *Union* and the employees expressly agree that during the life of this agreement there will be no strikes, slowdowns, picketing, work stoppages, mass absenteeism, or other interference with the production or the operations of the business.

31.3 The *Union* will not authorize, ratify, or condone any strike or other activity described in Section 31.2.

31.4 Any or all employees participating in such strike or other activity described in Section 31.2 shall be subject to disciplinary action by the *Company* up to and including discharge; but any such measures imposed on an employee by the *Company* shall be subject to the grievance and arbitration procedures of this agreement.

QUESTIONS

1. What are two important elements of worker motivation and direction? How are these achieved? Mention specific operations.

2. If you ran a plumbing business and had three plumbers on call, what might you consider when you were assigning tasks to these service people?

3. "Quality of work life" is a relatively new concept in industry. What does it mean? What are some of the ways it can be enhanced?

4. What are some of the advantages and disadvantages of incentive wage schemes? What are some of the main kinds of schemes?

5. Tower Manufacturing Company and Baldridge Chain Saw have problems. In what ways are their problems similar? In what ways are they different?

6. List the main steps in the unionization of Volpe Metal Products.

7. From the Volpe case study, make a list of the

rules of procedure by which management must abide during the unionization process and afterward. List the corresponding rules of procedure that must be obeyed by the union and its potential members.

8. Would you classify the situation at Volpe as a crisis situation or a natural one? Why?

9. Define the following terms: *bargaining unit, collective bargaining, election bar, exclusive representation, closed shop,* and *checkoff.*

10. Summarize the main issues covered in the agreement between Savage Arms and the Machinists. What have you learned about union agreements from studying this agreement?

PROBLEMS

1. What is job design and how can it affect production/operations management?

2. How can time standards be used?

3. Compare work sampling to direct time study.

4. Discuss how job design and quality of work life are related.

5. Talk to a personnel manager of a local firm. If that firm is unionized, find out how the union has affected productivity. If the firm is not unionized, find out what might be the effects of unionization.

6. Refer to Article 13 of the agreement between Savage Arms and the Machinists. What implications does the incentive plan have for productivity at Savage Arms?

COUHYDE GELATIN COMPANY REVISITED

Thomas Brewer, plant manager for Couhyde Gelatin Company (see Chapter 4 situation for study), noticed that every time he went into the break room, at least one of the process control technicians was drinking a cup of coffee, reading a book, or generally being nonproductive. He concluded that the technicians did not have enough work to fill their 8-hour shifts, and he asked Connie Darvin, the personnel manager, to look into the situation. Connie proceeded as follows:

1. A preliminary work sampling study was done to find out what the technicians were doing.
2. Some changes were implemented based upon the preliminary study.
3. A second work sampling study was done to determine the effects of the study.

The preliminary work sampling study was done over a 10-week period; of the 1200 working hours for the three types of technicians, about 15 percent (or 180 hours) were observed. The results of the study are shown in Table 9-A for the three technician types. The figures represent the average percentage of an 8-hour shift that was spent performing the duties listed. The technicians spent approximately 20 to 25 percent of the time preparing for testing (such as cleaning glassware) and doing paperwork and calculations; 25 to 34 percent of the time, the technicians were idle.

Several points need to be raised about Couhyde at the time of the study: (1) the plant was running at about three-fourths of capacity, (2) the job procedures were not clearly defined, (3) technicians were performing menial tasks and, therefore, had a

TABLE 9-A   Results of Preliminary Work Sampling
(Couhyde Gelatin Company)

	PERCENTAGE OF SHIFT		
DUTIES	SOLUTIONS TECHNICIANS	POWDER TECHNICIANS	LINE TECHNICIANS
Prepare	10%	6%	0%
Check floor samples	18	22	26
Run tests (in lab)	17	18	15
Do paperwork and calculations	11	17	29
Consult with supervisors	2	4	2
Run extra tests and retests	8	7	3
Idle time	34	26	25

low concept of job worth, and (4) technicians had serious communication problems with production foremen and others who should be using their information.

As a result of the preliminary study, the powder technician's duties were consolidated into the duties of the line technician and solutions technician; the powder technician's job was eliminated.

After these changes, Connie observed the work of the line technicians on four different dates. The percentage of 8-hour shifts was recorded, and these results are shown in Table 9-B. Connie noticed that some changes had occurred other than just the change in work duties. For example, before the changes, the technicians would complete whatever work they were doing before taking breaks (albeit long ones); however, after the changes, the technicians took their breaks by the clock regardless of whether the particular test they were working on was completed. Also, several technicians were observed to be making the data "fit" rather than completing long tests.

These results led Connie to question (1) whether the work sampling studies were done properly and (2) whether the changes in job were proper. What suggestions do you have for Connie?

TABLE 9-B   Line Technicians' Duties after Changes
(Couhyde Gelatin Company)

	PERCENTAGE OF SHIFT			
DUTIES	4/10	4/11	4/16	4/17
Retrain*	7%	4%	0%	0%
Take measurements and readings†	19	27	21	31
Obtain samples†	9	12	15	13
Run tests (in lab)	6	2	10	4
Do paperwork and calculations	29	38	31	36
Consult with supervisors	4	1	4	1
Run extra tests and retests	11	6	6	5
Idle time	15	10	13	10

*The line technicians had to be retrained when they took over some of the duties of the powder technicians. Preparation became a duty of the solutions technicians only.
†These two categories are very much the same as the category "check floor samples" in Table 9-A.

REFERENCE NOTES

1. For additional information on time standards, see Ralph M. Barnes, *Motion and Time Study: Design and Measurement of Work*, 6th ed. (New York: John Wiley & Sons, 1968) and Benjamin W. Niebel, *Motion and Time Study*, 6th ed. (Homewood, Ill.: Richard D. Irwin, 1976).

2. Additional information on methods improvement can also be found in Barnes, *Motion and Time Study* and in Niebel, *Motion and Time Study*.

3. "Quality of Employment Survey, 1977," University of Michigan Survey Research Center, 1979.

4. See, for example, "What about the Workers?" a survey by the Opinion Research Centre, Great Britain, 1974; and Michael R. Cooper et al., "Changing Employee Values: Deepening Discontent?" *Harvard Business Review* 57, no. 1 (January–February 1979): 117–25.

5. The following list is drawn from Richard E. Walton, "QWL Indicators — Prospects and Problems," *Studies in Personnel Psychology* 6, no. 1 (Spring 1974), pp. 7–18.

6. See Richard E. Walton, "Work Innovations in the United States," *Harvard Business Review* 57, no. 4 (July–August 1979), pp. 88–98.

7. The literature on job design and work structuring is large and growing. For some additional information, see:

Davis, L. E., and A. B. Cherns. *Quality of Working Life: Problems, Prospects, and State of the Art.* Glencoe, Ill.: Free Press, 1975.
Dickson, Paul. *The Future of the Workplace.* New York: Weybright and Talley, 1975.
Foy, Nancy, and Herman Gadon. "Worker Participation: Contrasts in Three Countries." *Harvard Business Review* 54, no. 3 (May–June 1976): 71–83.
Gyllenhammar, Pehr G. "How Volvo Adapts Work to People." *Harvard Business Review* 55, no. 4 (July–August 1977).
Hackman, J. Richard. "Is Job Enrichment Just a Fad?" *Harvard Business Review* 53, no. 5 (September–October 1975).
Hulin, C. C., and M. R. Blood. "Job Enlargement, Individual Differences, and Worker Responses." *Psychological Bulletin* 69 (1968): 41–55.
Rosow, Jerome, ed. *The Worker and the Job.* Englewood Cliffs, N.J.: Prentice-Hall, 1974.
Scobel, Donald N. "Doing away with the Factory Blues." *Harvard Business Review* 53, no. 6 (November–December 1975).
Upjohn Institute for Employment Research. *Work in America.* Cambridge, Mass.: MIT Press, 1973.
Walton, Richard E. "How to Counter Alienation in the Plant." *Harvard Business Review* 50, no. 6 (November–December 1972).
Walton, Richard E. "Improving the Quality of Work Life." *Harvard Business Review* 52, no. 3 (May–June 1974).
Walton, Richard E. "Successful Strategies for Diffusing Work Innovations." *Journal of Contemporary Business* (Spring 1977).
Walton, Richard E. "Work Innovations in the United States." *Harvard Business Review* 57, no. 4 (July–August 1979): 88–98.

8. See Robert S. Rice, "Survey of Work Measurement and Wage Incentives," *Industrial Engineering* (July 1977), pp. 18–31.

9. For additional information on incentives and wage schemes, see:

Dearden, John. "How to Make Incentive Plans Work." *Harvard Business Review* 50, no. 4 (July–August 1972): 117–24.
Dunn, J. D., and F. M. Rachel. *Wage and Salary Administration.* New York: McGraw-Hill, 1971.
Moore, Brian E., and Timothy L. Ross. *The Scanlon Way to Improved Productivity.* New York: John Wiley & Sons, 1978.
National Commission on Productivity and Work Quality. *A Plant-Wide Productivity Plan in Action: Three Years of Experience with the Scanlon Plan.* May 1975.

10. *Directory of National Unions and Employee Associations*, 1975, Bulletin 1937, U.S. Department of Labor, Bureau of Labor Statistics, 1977, p. 60.

11. Ibid., pp. 62–63.

10

MANAGING MATERIALS

As was clearly evident from the six plant tours, a great deal of management attention is devoted to ensuring that the proper materials get directed to the right workers in timely fashion and at low cost. Managing materials well is not easy. To aid in a discussion of materials management, it is useful to break the topic into three broad and interrelated areas:

- Procurement

- Materials control (including inventory control and production planning and control)
- Logistics (including the transportation and distribution of plant inputs and outputs)

This chapter will discuss each of these topics, except production planning and control, which is the subject of the next chapter. Let us consider procurement first.

PART ONE

PROCUREMENT

The procurement function of any plant is involved with the purchase and delivery of the plant's raw materials and with so-called "make-buy" decisions (that is, what is to be made on the inside and what is to be purchased on the outside). Many of the tasks of procurement fall to the purchasing department, although commonly the make-buy decision will not be the exclusive province of the purchasing department, since it involves factory operations as well.

The common duties of a purchasing department include:

1. *The selection and evaluation of suppliers* (commonly termed, vendors), which is usually a continuing function. Many companies like to have at least two vendors supplying each raw material, because they feel that the competition for the business encourages lower vendor prices and better deliveries and because re-

liance on a single source may be risky if something adverse happens to the vendor.

2. *The negotiation of price, delivery, and quality.* Purchasing typically must decide whether it wants a long-term (e.g., multiyear) contract with a vendor or short-term or spot (i.e., single transaction) contracts. Frequently, a long-term contract is required even to interest a vendor in providing a specific item, particularly if it is nonstandard. Otherwise, price expectations and views of supply risks usually play a major role in choosing between long- and short-term contracts. On many long-term contracts the specific price may not be settled ahead of time but may instead be negotiated at regular intervals.

The degree to which vendor delivery can be closely controlled is usually a function of the size and importance of the contract. As we saw in the plant tours, the huge demands of operations like GMAD-Tarrytown and Schlitz-Syracuse permit those companies to seek—and be accorded—regular deliveries, thereby cutting down on inventory storage and carrying charges. In any case, the purchasing department must give each vendor adequate warning about the plant's actual or estimated materials needs. As regards estimated needs, the department must provide vendors with forecasts of various types well in advance.

Quality checking is also something that varies from contract to contract. Most plants inspect incoming supplies, either all or a sampling, and the vendor contract often specifies acceptable quality levels for supplies. Some large contracts even specify the posting of inspection teams within the vendor's plant to monitor both quality and delivery.

3. *The placing of actual purchase orders with the vendors.*

4. *Working out problems with vendors and tracing and expediting orders.* Here is where a purchasing department wins its reputation, for good or for ill. Rarely does all go smoothly in the order and delivery of materials. The typical purchasing department must chew up a substantial chunk of its time dealing with vendor quality or delivery problems—tracing and expediting orders that, for one reason or another, are needed prior to a vendor's quoted lead time or for which shipment has been delayed. The purchasing department can thus act as an early warning radar for materials shortages that could affect the factory's own schedule.

In large, multiplant companies, purchasing can proceed at different levels. The corporate staff, for example, may negotiate and monitor the large supply contracts that feed a number of plants. By centralizing this activity the company may be able to exert more clout over price and delivery terms than could individual plants acting on their own. In addition, centralizing such purchasing may aid plant-to-plant coordination of materials. Smaller supply contracts may then be left to individual plants to negotiate.

THE MAKE-VS.-BUY DECISION

Although typically not the responsibility of the purchasing department, the decision as to what the factory should make for itself and what it should purchase on the outside is one for which the purchasing department is a key source of information. The make-buy decision is a common one, especially in companies that have purposefully split their supply needs between in-house operations and outside vendors.

What does a make-buy decision entail? Consider Situation 10-1.

DISCUSSION OF DULANEY TOY COMPANY

The decision Rick Jerauld faces, that of pulling in some subcontracted parts, is one that companies in cyclical industries face regularly. The five criteria that Jerauld considers appropriate are all issues that a manager should consider for a make-buy decision. A part should not be pulled back to the injection molding department unless (1) it would make a significant dent in the excess labor the company is experiencing, (2) it costs less to do it inside (more comment on this below), (3) the vendor would not be so adversely affected that it could not be counted on for future contracts, (4) the part is not in danger of becoming obsolete in the near future, and (5) the part could be fitted into the shop fairly smoothly.

SITUATION 10-1

DULANEY TOY COMPANY

He knew that the business was sometimes boom or bust, but that still didn't mean he liked the "bust" part. Rick Jerauld, the manager of the injection molding department at the Dulaney Toy Company, was on the horns of a dilemma. After several years of record sales and growth, Dulaney Toy appeared to be in for a slow year. Sales for Dulaney's two latest entries in the fickle toy market—the Incredible Smiling Monster and the Cynical Santa—simply did not appear to be taking off as the company's marketing people had claimed. Given the sales declines of some of Dulaney's older toys, which was characteristic of product life cycles in the industry, many of Dulaney's manufacturing departments had spare capacity. The injection molding department, which was responsible for all the plastic injection-molded parts of Dulaney's toys, was among them.

Rick was loath to lay off any of the workers in his department, particularly given the company's often stated goal of lifetime employment for its loyal and productive workforce. What this left was for Rick to start pulling back to his department the manufacture of plastic parts that Dulaney had subcontracted to other firms. Fortunately, Dulaney had a battery of such plastic injection-molded parts, but this abundance did not lessen Rick Jerauld's concern about which of the parts now produced by vendors (suppliers) he should pull back to his own department.

As Jerauld thought about it, several criteria appeared to be appropriate to deciding the issue:

1. Whether the part demanded many labor-hours because of its complexity or because it was produced in large quantities.

2. Whether the part could be manufactured as cheaply at Dulaney Toy as at the vendor's. At present, Dulaney Toy's formula for such cost comparisons called for comparing the vendor's price for the part (adjusted upward for the expected costs Dulaney Toy would incur in purchasing the part and in having it transported and inspected) against the calculated, internal factory cost for the part, which included all materials, labor, and overhead.

3. What effect pulling the part back would have on the vendor and on Dulaney Toy's expected future use of the vendor in boom times when Dulaney Toy was short of capacity. Rick was naturally leery of doing anything to antagonize his vendor base to the point where many vendors would be reluctant to bid for Dulaney Toy's business in the future.

4. What risk the part carried for becoming obsolescent in the near future.

5. What impact the part would make on shop operations, given the prevailing conditions in the shop. That is, would the part need special tooling or require setup times that would make its coordination with other parts running through the shop difficult?

One of Rick's assistants had developed a sheet of candidate parts for pulling back to the factory (Table

10-1). Some were made exclusively by vendors, while others were made both by the injection molding department and by vendors. The candidate parts identified to date derived from two of the company's more successful toys, Walter the Caboose and the Little Monkey Crib Gym.

Rick needed to decide which of the parts should be pulled back inside his department and which should be left with the vendors. Also, Rick wanted to develop a system whereby he could put priorities on those which should be brought back first and those which could be allowed to wait.

TABLE 10-1 Candidate Parts for Pulling Back to the Factory
(Dulaney Toy Company)

PART	AVERAGE VOLUME PER MONTH	CURRENT STATUS	VENDOR PRICE (includes adjustment)	INTERNAL COST—ACTUAL OR ESTIMATE				COMMENTS
				MATERIALS	*LABOR*	*OVERHEAD*	*TOTAL*	
Caboose under-carriage	6000	Long-term contract; made in shop before	11.97¢	3.20¢	1.37¢	5.20¢	9.77¢	Vendor problems with quality and delivery
Caboose roof	6000	Long-term contract	9.60	2.77	3.93	12.57	19.27	
Caboose railings	12,000	Short-term contract	3.79	0.88	3.03	5.75	9.66	Same vendor as caboose roof
Crib gym bar	2000	Long-term contract; made in shop before	22.39	5.91	6.70	9.53	22.14	
Crib gym flower	8000	Long-term contract; always made outside	18.26	3.58	4.43	11.66	19.67	$1500 in tooling needed

Judgment is required in assessing many of these. The cost comparison is more mechanical, but it should be noted that Dulaney Toy's present method for comparing costs is plainly incorrect. The present cost comparison ignores the fact that the make-buy decision is a marginal one, just like the Citrus Airlines situation examined in Chapter 8. That is to say, while the vendor's price, as adjusted, is a variable cost to Dulaney Toy, not all of the internal factory costs vary with the factory's level of production. Overhead expenses, for example, would have to be covered no matter what the level of factory output. And, if Dulaney Toy is really serious about lifetime employment for its workers, it can be argued that, for the short run at least, the factory's labor costs are fixed as well.

TABLE 10-2 Contribution Figures for Candidate Parts
(Dulaney Toy Company)

PART	VENDOR PRICE PER UNIT (includes adjustment)	INTERNAL VARIABLE COST (materials and labor)	CONTRIBUTION PER UNIT (if pulled back to factory)	CONTRIBUTION PER MONTH
Caboose undercarriage	11.97¢	4.57¢	7.40¢	$444.00
Caboose roof	9.60	6.70	2.90	174.00
Caboose railings	3.79	3.91	− 0.12	− 14.40
Crib gym bar	22.39	12.61	9.78	195.60
Crib gym flower	18.26	8.01	10.25	820.00

Thus, by bringing in-house any product for which the materials-plus-labor factory cost is less than the vendor quote-plus-adjustment, Dulaney Toy's contribution (see Chapter 8) would be enhanced. Table 10-2 computes the contribution for each of the candidate parts listed in Table 10-1.

Table 10-2 suggests that under no circumstances should the caboose railings be pulled back to the factory. In fact, the vendor producing both the caboose railings and the caboose roof looks like it should be encouraged to produce even more than it is, since its prices look very good indeed. Perhaps, the short-term contract for railings should be extended to long-term. The possibility remains, however, that the vendor price is not low, but that the factory's estimated cost is high. This should be investigated.

Dulaney Toy would earn additional contribution by pulling in any of the parts except the caboose railings. Even the $1500 tooling expense for the crib gym flower would be paid for out of added contribution within 2 months. The issue remains, however, in what order the various parts should be pulled back to the factory, at least according to the prevailing economics. In a sense, what we are looking for is to pull back the parts with the most "bang for the buck." In this case, the most "bang for the buck" translates into the most contribution per some unit of scarce resource, which might be something like factory time or labor cost. In fact, time and labor costs are likely to be highly correlated. This means that an index constructed as contribution per unit/labor cost per unit should give us a fair picture of which parts can add the most contribution quickly. Table 10-3 displays the values for this index of contribution per penny of labor cost.

It is clear from Table 10-3 that the company is best served by pulling in-house the caboose undercarriage first, then the crib gym flower, followed

TABLE 10-3 Index of Contribution per Penny of Labor Cost
(Dulaney Toy Company)

PART	CONTRIBUTION PER UNIT (if pulled back to factory)	LABOR COST PER UNIT	CONTRIBUTION PER PENNY OF LABOR COST
Caboose undercarriage	7.40¢	1.37¢	5.40¢
Caboose roof	2.90	3.93	0.74
Caboose railings	− 0.12	3.03	− 0.04
Crib gym bar	9.78	6.70	1.46
Crib gym flower	10.25	4.43	2.31

by the crib gym bar, and the caboose roof. From the comments in Table 10-1 this priority appears consistent with some of the other criteria mentioned for the make-buy decision. We must be sure, however, to include in the evaluation whether the crib gym flower, with the tooling required, will be pulled back for a long enough time to justify pulling it back.

A break-even calculation can help here. Let x be months. We want to calculate the number of months it would take before the crib gym flower would contribute as much as the crib gym bar, knowing that we would rather pull in the flower because its contribution per penny of labor cost is higher. Drawing from the contribution per month figures in Table 10-2,

$$contribution\ from\ bar\ =\ contribution\ from\ flower$$
$$\$195.60x\ =\ \$820.00x\ -\ \$1500$$
$$x\ =\ 2.40\ months$$

Thus, if we plan to produce crib gym flowers for 2.4 months or more, we can expect to gain more contribution than by producing the crib gym bar, in addition to enjoying a higher rate of contribution per penny of labor cost.

PART TWO

MANAGING INVENTORIES

Our investigation of the six different production processes of Segment I has already uncovered a number of places within the typical process where inventories come in handy. In broad terms, we saw inventories of raw materials, work-in-process, and finished goods.

Other things being equal, of course, a company would like not to hold any inventories since they mean tying up its cash in goods that cannot improve the company's earnings like a new piece of machinery can, or even like putting cash in the bank. In other words, inventories represent some very real opportunity costs to the company since, by financing inventories, the company forgoes the opportunity to earn a better return by using its cash in some other, income-generating way.

As we also saw in Segment I, some processes are organized in certain ways expressly for the purpose of reducing inventories of one kind or another. The job shop, for example, typically produces only to order—eliminating any concern for managing a finished goods inventory. Because many orders require very specialized raw materials either supplied by the customer or placed on special order, the job shop's need to manage raw materials inventories is very modest. It is in the realm of work-in-process inventories that the job shop is truly challenged with the control of inventories.

The inventory concerns of the continuous flow process are almost exactly the reverse of those of the job shop. The entire design of the continuous flow process revolves around speeding the manufacture of a very standard product, which implies a rock-bottom level of work-in-process inventory. Because the process's appetite for raw materials is so steady and predictable, raw materials inventories can usually be held down by insisting on long-term supply contracts with a steady flow of materials. It is only at the finished goods end where inventories can mushroom and where their control presents real management challenges.

Process types in between the poles of job shop

and continuous flow generally strike some middle ground in the importance of raw materials, work-in-process, and finished goods inventory control.

THE OBJECTIVES OF INVENTORY MANAGEMENT

The tools that production managers can wield in dealing with work-in-process inventories are frequently very different from the tools they can use to control raw materials or finished goods. As we shall soon see, the available techniques for controlling either raw materials inventories or finished goods inventories are relatively well developed and widely known. Because of this, it is often taken for granted that these inventories are managed adequately; when many production managers think about managing inventories, they think about work-in-process inventories. Here the management tools are more ill-defined, since reducing work-in-process inventory generally means grappling with the production process itself and/or with the flow of information through it.

To control work-in-process inventory levels, the manager might contemplate ways to shorten production cycle times (e.g., more special-purpose equipment to drive labor out of the process, a more closely coupled operation) or ways to break existing production bottlenecks or ways to improve the flow of information around the process. Often, such policies mean controlling inventory by "yelling" it down. Some situations already discussed (8-1 and 8-2) have dealt with such means of managing work-in-process inventories and more situations to come will deal with it, since this kind of inventory management is intimately involved with the planning of production, with capacity changes, and with the organization of operations. For the time being, we will be concerned solely with managing stocks of goods such as are found in either raw materials inventories or finished goods

inventories in manufacturing and in service companies alike.

MANAGING INVENTORY STOCKS

It is not too far off the mark to visualize the problem of managing either raw materials inventory or finished goods inventory as one of managing piles of "stuff" that either the process itself or consumers in the marketplace draw down. The objective of good inventory management in this case is to offer good service to either the process or the market at reasonably low cost. This objective, in turn, means deciding how much "stuff" should be in each pile, when orders to replenish the piles ought to be placed, and how much each of those orders should contain. Managing inventory stocks (as opposed to managing work-in-process) essentially means deciding these three questions of pile size, order time, and order size.

DIFFERENT PHILOSOPHIES ABOUT INVENTORY STOCK MANAGEMENT

AN ANTICIPATORY APPROACH

One way for a company to manage its inventory stocks, particularly raw materials in a manufacturing situation, is to anticipate their use and to plan the order size and timing accordingly so as to keep the stocks at some desired, low level. One ideal for such an anticipatory approach to inventory is to have no finished goods inventory over and above that expressly planned for, and little or no raw materials inventory. Work-in-process inventories then would account for by far the greatest chunk of total inventory costs. What is needed to accomplish this anticipatory approach to inventory is a firm fix on exactly what products are to be produced and when, what materials go into making each product, when in the production cycle each part or material is used, and how long it takes suppliers to deliver these parts or materials. This is a lot of information, but every bit is needed if in fact inventories are going to be matched to a company's output. In more formal phrasing, such an approach to inventory managment demands the following pieces of information:

1. Master production schedule — when each product is scheduled to be manufactured. Usually the master production schedule is developed for a month, but longer or shorter (e.g., weekly) schedules are found as well. The firmness by which the schedule is held to can vary markedly from company to company and from time to time.

2. Bills of materials for each product — exactly which parts or materials are required to make each product.

3. Production cycle times and materials needs at each stage of the production cycle — how long it takes to manufacture each product and at what points along the way different parts and materials are needed. For many products the production cycle time is so short that all of the product's "ingredients" must arrive at essentially the same time. For more complex products, the manufacturing time is considerable; if all parts were delivered at the same time, a portion of them would be lying around for months before being incorporated into the product. Here, then, the staggering of parts delivery makes good sense.

4. Supplier lead times — how long it takes each supplier to deliver each part purchased from it.

These four pieces of information work together to determine what should be ordered and when. The master production schedule, together with the bill of materials, determines what should be ordered; the master production schedule, the production cycle times, and the supplier lead times jointly determine when the order should be placed.

These elements form an anticipatory approach to inventory management, which lies at the heart of a concept called *material requirements planning* (MRP). MRP can become quite a bit more involved than this in actual practice (as we shall see later in the chapter), but at its roots lies this relatively simple notion of managing raw materials stocks by anticipating their use.

Nonanticipatory Approaches[1]

Some techniques for managing inventory stocks do not try to match those stocks exactly to anticipated use. These techniques are sometimes called non-time-phased inventory systems, meaning simply that they do not attempt to be so precise about timing orders to expected use. Their purpose is the same, however: to replenish a pile of "stuff" in timely fashion and at reasonably low cost.

The two major non–time-phased techniques have these differing philosophies:

1. Replenish the pile of stuff on a regular basis (e.g., daily, weekly, monthly) and bring it back up to the size you want (we will talk shortly about the desired size of the pile). The amount by which you replenish the pile may vary from one time to another, but you always replenish the pile. This basic strategy is often called a *periodic reorder system*.

2. Keep a constant watch over the pile. When its size dips to a predetermined level (we will talk shortly about this level), replenish the pile with enough stuff to bring it back up to the size you desire. Under this philosophy, the amount by which you replenish the pile stays the same, but the time spans between replenishments may vary. This basic strategy is frequently termed a *reorder point system*, the "reorder point" being the predetermined level that, once reached, triggers the replenishment of the pile by the same amount.

Before continuing the discussion of each of these inventory management philosophies — material re-

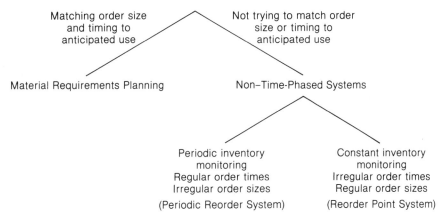

FIGURE 10-1   Different philosophies of inventory management.

quirements planning, periodic reorder systems, and reorder point systems—a glance at Figure 10-1 may help to summarize the fundamental differences in their approaches to inventory management.

THE WORKINGS OF NON–TIME-PHASED INVENTORY SYSTEMS

THE PERIODIC REORDER SYSTEM

The periodic reorder inventory system is governed by the simple decision rule of "order enough each period (day, week, month, or whatever) to bring the pile of stuff inventoried back up to its desired size." But what is the desired size?

If we know in advance exactly how much will be needed during any period, the answer is easy: order the amount that will be used and no more. So, as the truck pulls in with the supply for next period, the last unit of this period's supply is being drawn off. This technique is similar to the basic philosophy of material requirements planning—to order just what is needed.

Unfortunately, not all companies can know in advance how much will be needed. Some adjustments must be made to determine the desired size of the inventory when demand is uncertain.

———————————— ✳ ASIDE ✳ ————————————

Demand Uncertainty

Numerous companies produce only to firm orders and thus have no uncertainty about the quantities of each input they require to manufacture their products. Many other companies, however, must cope with uncertainty, not knowing as they manufacture a product how many will be purchased. This uncertainty poses a dilemma for inventory management: how much to hold so that the vagaries of demand in the marketplace do not catch the company too much off guard. We know that the company must hold more than it would if the average demand placed on it were known for sure in advance, but the issue is how much more it ought to hold.

One way we can get a handle on the solution is first to ask ourselves how often we would tolerate a

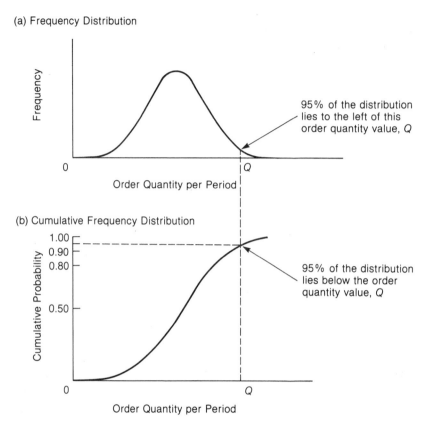

(a) Frequency Distribution

Frequency

95% of the distribution
lies to the left of this
order quantity value, Q

0

Order Quantity per Period

(b) Cumulative Frequency Distribution

Cumulative Probability

1.00
0.90
0.80

0.50

95% of the distribution
lies below the order
quantity value, Q

0   Q

Order Quantity per Period

FIGURE 10-2   The pattern of demand.

situation where the company could not fill the demand: 5 percent of the time? 10 percent of the time? 1 percent of the time? never? If we had some feel for a suitable percentage (we shall discuss below a way to calculate a suitable percentage), then we could use some of the product's past history (if it has one, that is) to inform us how much to stock.

The sales of many products follow a fairly well-defined distribution pattern. A typical distribution pattern would have relatively few high values during a particular time period (say, a month), few low values, and most values right around the average or expected value. A bell-shaped curve (a so-called normal curve) such as that in Figure 10-2a is often a good characterization of the pattern of demand. If

the product's sales have fallen into some distribution like this, and if you are reasonably confident that the distribution will prevail for the current period, then Figure 10-2a can be used to determine how much stock to carry. All you want to be sure to do to cover the company for all but, say, 5 percent of the time is to carry at least the level of stock that is greater than all but 5 percent of the distribution. That level of stock can be found either by counting the actual historical figures or by computing the area under the curve in Figure 10-2a. Figure 10-2b is merely a graph of the area under the curve in Figure 10-2a, which is an easy way to pick out the stock levels corresponding to various degrees of coverage of the demand. If the normal curve does a reasonable job of describing the pattern of demand, then the level of stock, relative to the average, can be calculated easily using some tables found in all elementary statistics books or embedded into some of the more elaborate electronic calculators.

So we see that we can use statistical distributions of past demand to determine how much stock to inventory so that an enterprise is covered against stocking out any more than a given percentage of the time. To reinforce this use of statistical distributions, consider Situation 10-2.

SITUATION 10-2

DIMARZO COSTUME COMPANY

The DiMarzo Costume Company rented theatrical costumes of all sorts to theater groups, colleges, schools, churches, and the like. During the Christmas season, one of the most popular costumes (aside from Santa Claus) was Frosty the Snowman. (Data on orders placed for Frosty the Snowman costumes over all 20 years of the company's history are given in Table 10-4). The company could not detect a trend in orders over the years; orders seemed to be fairly random. The company, however, wanted to be able to fill about 95 percent of all its orders for Frosty and wondered how many costumes it should stock at Christmas.

TABLE 10-4   Past Demand for Frosty the Snowman (DiMarzo Costume Company)

YEARS AGO	DEMANDED	YEARS AGO	DEMANDED
1	411	11	296
2	347	12	382
3	412	13	473
4	385	14	320
5	441	15	423
6	402	16	354
7	395	17	512
8	370	18	389
9	480	19	378
10	416	20	392

Discussion of the DiMarzo Costume Company

Given no discernible trend in the demand over the years for Frosty the Snowman costumes, the DiMarzo Costume Company can let the past 20 years be its guide in selecting the number of Frosty costumes it should stock.

A Historical Count Approach. The easiest, if not the most scientific, way to select an appropriate stock level so that the company can expect to cover 95 percent of the orders placed on it is to make a count of the data. The company could expect that a stock level at or above the highest number demanded over the past 20 years would be too high.

Company history shows that in 95 percent of the years (19 of 20) demand was less than 512 but more than 480. It would seem reasonable, then, to select a stock level between 480 and 512.

A Statistical Approach. A more formal way of selecting an appropriate stock level is to apply some statistics to the data. Two so-called "summary statistics" are particularly useful in this regard:

1. The *sample mean*—the arithmetic average of the sampled observations. Formally,

$$\overline{X} = \left(\sum_{i=1}^{n} X_i \right) \Big/ n$$

where

$\overline{X}$ is the calculated mean
n is the number of observations
X_i is the ith observation

$\sum_{i=1}^{n} X_i$ represents the sum of all n observations

In this case, the mean of the distribution of demand for Frosty the Snowman costumes over the past 20 years is 398.90.

2. The *sample standard deviation*—a measure of how dispersed the distribution is around the mean. The lower the standard deviation, the more tightly bunched are the observations; the higher the standard deviation, the more spread out are the observations. Formally,

$$S = \sqrt{\frac{\sum_{i=1}^{n} X_i^2}{n} - \overline{X}^2} = \sqrt{\frac{\sum_{i=1}^{n} X_i^2}{n} - \left(\frac{\sum_{i=1}^{n} X_i}{n}\right)^2}$$

where

S is the computed sample standard deviation
X_i is the ith observation of the random variable X
n is the number of observations

In this case, the sample standard deviation of this distribution of demand for Frosty the Snowman costumes is 50.63.

These summary statistics (sample mean and sample standard deviation) are *estimates* of the unknown true population mean, μ, and the unknown true population standard deviation, σ, which underlie the demand for costumes at DiMarzo Costume Company. Often, we do not know how the full population of observations is distributed and we must depend on samples from that full population to draw inferences about the population itself. Such is the case at the DiMarzo Costume Company. The summary statistics, $\overline{X}$ and S, can help us condense the Table 10-4 data into a more easily digested bar graph of the frequencies with which the data fall into various classes. Figure 10-3 displays such a bar graph. For intelligibility, the classes are set at 25, about half of the standard deviation, and the figure is centered on 400, which is just above the true mean of 398.90.

Figure 10-3's bar graph can be approximated by a bell-shaped curve known as the "normal" distribution, which is the most important distribution in statistics. Figure 10-4 gives a better idea of some of the properties of the normal distribution. We know that the Table 10-4 data fall roughly into a normal distribution pattern since (1) 70 percent of the 20 observations fall within one standard deviation of the mean (i.e., 14 of the 20 observations fall between 350 and 450) versus 68.2 percent in a true normal distribution, (2) 20 percent of the 20 observations fall between one and two standard devia-

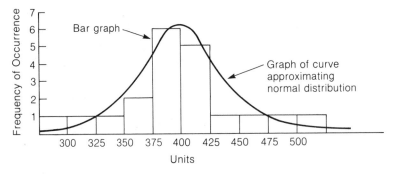

FIGURE 10-3 Frequency distribution of monthly sales for DiMarzo Costume Company.

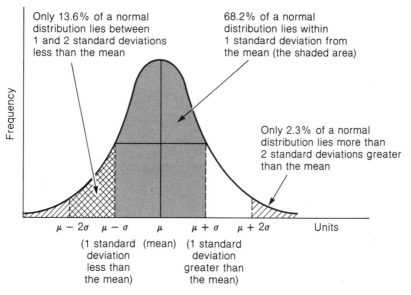

Only 13.6% of a normal distribution lies between 1 and 2 standard deviations less than the mean

68.2% of a normal distribution lies within 1 standard deviation from the mean (the shaded area)

Only 2.3% of a normal distribution lies more than 2 standard deviations greater than the mean

$\mu - 2\sigma$ $\mu - \sigma$ μ $\mu + \sigma$ $\mu + 2\sigma$ Units

(1 standard deviation less than the mean)   (mean)   (1 standard deviation greater than the mean)

FIGURE 10-4   The normal distribution.

tions from the mean versus 27.2 percent in a true normal distribution, and (3) 10 percent of the 20 observations fall beyond two standard deviations from the mean versus 4.6 percent in a true normal distribution. It seems reasonable then to presume that the demand for Frosty the Snowman costumes is normally distributed with a mean of 398.90 and a standard deviation of 50.63.

In a normal frequency pattern, the top 5 percent of the distribution falls above the value of +1.645 standard deviations from the mean. In this case, we can presume then that 95 percent of the demand for Frosty costumes will fall below

$$398.90 + 1.645(50.63) = 482.19$$

We can thus take this figure, 482 or 483, as a suitable stock level to assure ourselves that 95 percent of our expected orders can be serviced.

Many frequency distributions can be approximated by a normal distribution. Moreover, under some very reasonable assumptions, the means of a number of random samples drawn from *any* distribution tend themselves to be distributed normally. That is, by drawing a number of samples of data at random we do not have to know what the underlying distribution is to work with it. All we have to do is transform the sample means in the following way:

$$y_i = \frac{x_i - \bar{x}}{\frac{s}{\sqrt{n}}}$$

where

x_i is the ith sample mean
$\bar{x}$ is the mean of the sample means
s is the standard deviation of the sample means
n is the sample size

(Note that $\bar{x}$ and s are analogous to, but not the same as, $\bar{X}$ and S defined above.)

Given this transformation, especially as n becomes large, we can be increasingly confident that the random variable y follows a normal distribution with a 0 mean and a standard deviation of 1.

This useful result is due to the central limit theorem of mathematical statistics.

Returning to Coping with Demand Uncertainty

We are now a good way through solving our problem of how to manage inventory when demand is uncertain, but we are not yet all the way there. We know how to find the stock level given a suitable percentage coverage for demand, but we have yet to discover a way to choose that suitable percentage intelligently.

Common sense insists that the level of coverage be higher if the cost of carrying too little inventory and thus stocking out greatly exceeds the cost of carrying too much inventory. The former cost is commonly called the "cost of being under" or the cost of underage (C_u) and the latter is commonly called the "cost of being over" or the cost of overage (C_o).

The suitable percentage coverage that a company ought to seek for its inventories subject to uncertain demand is approximated by the following formula:*

$$\text{Suitable percentage coverage for stock} = \frac{C_u}{C_o + C_u}$$

---

*The ratio of $C_u/(C_o + C_u)$ is called the critical fractile (or percentile). While technically it applies only to single-period holding of inventories and linear costs of underage and overage, it is a useful enough approximation to be applied more generally.

The basic argument underlying the derivation of the critical fractile is, once again, incremental in origin. Suppose we arbitrarily select q^* as the best level of inventory there could be. It must be true then that we receive an incremental gain by inventorying q^* as opposed to one unit more or less (that is, either $q^* + 1$ or $q^* - 1$). This being the case, we can write formally the following inequality:

$$(1) \qquad C_u[P(d > q^*)] \leq C_o[P(d \leq q^*)]$$

By stocking q^*, the expected expense of being under when demand is greater than q^* (the cost of underage times the probability that demand is greater than q^*) must be less than or equal to the expected expense of being over (the cost of overage times the probability that demand is less than or equal to q^*); otherwise, it would make sense to stock another unit so that one is not caught being under. Similarly, we can write the following inequality:

$$(2) \qquad C_u\{P[d > (q^* - 1)]\} \geq C_o\{P[d \leq (q^* - 1)]\}$$

By stocking q^*, the expected expense of being under when demand is greater than $q^* - 1$ must be greater than or equal to the expected expense of being over; otherwise, it would make sense to stock one unit less in order to save some money.

Using the fact that $P(d > q^*)$ is equal to $[1 - P(d \leq q^*)]$ we can rewrite inequality 1 as

$$(3) \qquad C_u[1 - P(d \leq q^*)] \leq C_o[P(d \leq q^*)]$$

or

$$C_u \leq (C_u + C_o)[P(d \leq q^*)]$$

or

$$(4) \qquad \frac{C_u}{(C_u + C_o)} \leq [P(d \leq q^*)]$$

In similar fashion we can rewrite inequality 2 as

$$(5) \qquad \frac{C_u}{(C_u + C_o)} \geq \{P[d \leq (q^* - 1)]\}$$

Inequalities 4 and 5 suggest that $C_u/C_u + C_o$ is the relevant ratio for picking off the point in the cumulative probability distribution that corresponds to the optimal level of inventories, q^*.

A more thorough explanation of the critical fractile, and that on which this explanation is based, can be found in Barbara B. Jackson, *The Critical Fractile Model*, Note 4-175-058 of the Intercollegiate Case Clearing House, 1974.

This formula meets the test of common sense in that if the cost of carrying too little and stocking out is high relative to the cost of carrying too much, then the suitable percentage coverage will be high. The formula also makes sense in that it cannot reach 1 in value nor can it fall to zero; it must range in between, just like the range for cumulative probability.

What are costs of underage and costs of overage? Let us consider the costs of overage first since they are a bit easier to think about. The costs of overage are all the costs that would be incurred by carrying one extra unit of inventory. There are basically three types of these costs:

1. Finance charges
2. Physical costs
3. Obsolescence charges

The finance charges we assign against inventory items are incurred because we tie up money purchasing them and perhaps adding value to them.

This money could have gone to another, income-generating purpose, even if it were only sitting in the bank drawing interest. This is simply the opportunity cost argument, but opportunity costs (those financing charges) are typically a large portion of inventory carrying costs. Another key portion of carrying costs represents the actual physical costs incurred in storing, handling, and accounting for inventory. Still another portion of carrying costs is often composed of an allocation against obsolescence. That is, many times a company risks having whatever it keeps in inventory lose value because of obsolescence. Since the greater the risk of obsolescence, the less valuable large stocks in inventory are, the company can create the proper incentives to shy away from such large inventories by adding to its carrying costs.

The cost of underage is the penalty incurred by failing to have a unit of inventory on hand when demand calls for it. At worst, the cost of underage is the lost contribution to profit and overhead incurred because the unit was unavailable for sale.

TABLE 10-5   Deciding the Inventory Level under Demand Uncertainty

PROCEDURE	INFORMATION REQUIRED
1. Choose the suitable percentage cover for the stock.	
A. Determine cost of overage (C_o).	Inventory carrying cost per unit
B. Determine cost of underage (C_u).	Contribution per unit; probability that a full sale would be lost by a stockout
C. Use data in formula ($C_u/[C_o + C_u]$) to approximate the suitable percentage coverage.	
2. Use the percentage cover calculated to choose the appropriate inventory level.	
A. Plot the distribution of past demand by period.	Records of sales or use by period
B. Gauge the reasonableness of the past distribution of demand for the current period and make any adjustments.	Any trends in sales or use over time
C. Sum up the frequencies of each level of demand. (It may be useful to characterize the distribution as "normal" or as some other well-known shape.)	
D. From actual count or from knowledge of the distribution of that type, find the level of inventory needed to match a demand which falls at or below that level X percent of the time, where X percent is the calculated suitable percentage coverage (from step 1C above).	Suitable percentage coverage; cumulated frequency distribution of demand

Again, the concept of opportunity cost intrudes into our thinking—here, in the form of contribution forgone. Forgoing all of a unit's contribution is the worst that can happen since that assumes that the buyer goes away empty-handed and will never again return to purchase the item. Frequently, however, stocking out of an item does not mean *all* of a lost sale, especially if the purchaser is willing to substitute another item for the one out of stock (e.g., another color, another model, another size) or if he or she agrees to come back when the item is received again in stock. Market research can frequently determine a reasonable expectation for this cost of underage.

Having then introduced the costs of overage and underage and how the relation between the two can guide the setting of a stock level for inventory, our brief excursion into coping with demand uncertainty is complete. Table 10-5 reviews the procedures and information for choosing the level of inventory stock needed to service demand at reasonable cost, when that demand is uncertain.

*

RETURN TO THE WORKINGS OF THE PERIODIC REORDER SYSTEM

With this excursion into the determination of the desired order size under demand uncertainty, the workings of the periodic reorder system become fairly clear and straightforward:

1. If demand for the period is known with certainty, order just enough to last until the end of the period, when the next order takes effect.

2. If demand is not known with certainty, order more than the expected average of demand. Calculate how much is needed by using the procedures outlined in Table 10-5.

We can add one more level of sophistication to this discussion of the periodic reorder system. If placing an order requires the outlay of some funds, it is conceivable that the company may not want to place an order in every period. This situation may occur because the cost of ordering exceeds the expected losses to the company if it stocked out. The company may want to let things ride until the inventory level falls below a certain point and then order enough to bring the inventory up to its desired level, as determined by decision rule 1 or 2 above.

What is the "certain point" below which an order is triggered? Figure 10-5 graphs the expected loss from stocking out versus the inventory level. The quantity OX represents the desired inventory level for the period as determined by the procedures outlined in Table 10-5. It corresponds to a definite expected dollar loss because not all potential demands are covered with sufficient inventories. Inventory levels lower than OX correspond to higher expected losses because they risk even more frequent potential stockouts.

If the inventory level falls between OX and OY, as the figure shows, it does not make sense for the company to place an order, since the cost of ordering exceeds the expected loss in contribution from stocking out. Only at inventory levels lower than

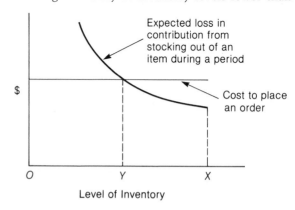

FIGURE 10-5 The expected loss from stocking out versus the inventory level.

OY should orders be initiated since at those levels, the expected loss in contribution exceeds the cost of ordering.

With this added wrinkle, our discussion of the periodic reorder system, one of the two basic non–time-phased inventory systems, is complete. We turn now to a discussion of the other basic system, the reorder point system.

THE REORDER POINT SYSTEM

The reorder point inventory system follows the decision rule of "watch withdrawals from the pile of inventory until the designated reorder point is struck and then order the fixed amount needed to build the pile back up to its desired size." But, again, the question is what the desired size is.

The desired size in this case is not determined, as in the periodic reorder system, by the expected usage over the period, since there is no regular period following which inventory needs are checked. The pile is monitored continually, not every so often. Instead, the size of the pile depends fundamentally on a quantity called the "economic order quantity" or EOQ, which we soon shall examine.

The choice of reorder point depends on how soon a shipment of the EOQ can arrive. If the shipment can, once ordered, arrive instantaneously, then the reorder point is zero. If shipment takes a while, the choice of reorder point depends on an estimate of the present pace of demand. The reorder point must leave enough so that a stockout does not occur while waiting for delivery of the EOQ. Computing this reorder point is much like computing a buffer inventory for uncertain demand in a periodic reorder system. Thus, even a reorder point system often requires some knowledge of time and of the time pattern of demand on the inventory. No matter what the reorder point, however, the decision rule stays the same: when the reorder point is struck, order the EOQ.

How does the company determine how much the EOQ should be? The key to this order quantity and the reason it can be claimed as economic is the process by which it is found. The EOQ is chosen as the order quantity that minimizes the "total variable costs associated with changing order quantities." Every word of this phrase is meaningful. There are a variety of EOQ formulas, but what is important is the *process* by which the EOQ is found, not any formula that might seem to apply.

Let us consider a very simple, conventional, but suggestive case where we can discover a minimum for the "total variable costs associated with changing order quantities" or TVCAWCOQ for short. In this case, there are only two variable costs that are in any way associated with any changing of order quantities:

1. *Inventory carrying costs.* These carrying costs vary directly with the order quantity since the larger the order quantity, the larger is the average inventory held and thus the larger the carrying costs incurred. To illustrate this point in greater detail, let us make the common—and convenient—assumption that the demand on the inventory is absolutely steady, as is represented in Figure 10-6. Given this constant rate of draw upon the inventory, the average number of units in inventory is half of the order size. So, if Q is the order size (see Figure 10-6),

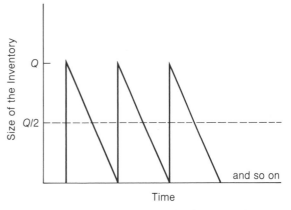

FIGURE 10-6 Graph depicting the assumption of steady demand on an inventory.

the average inventory is Q/2. As we shall discuss later, this is an important simplification in this computation of minimum TVCAWCOQ.

2. *Order costs.* The costs of actually placing the orders for the inventory vary inversely with the order quantity. The larger the size of the order (for a fixed annual demand), the fewer the orders that have to be placed, and thus the lower the order costs are.

It is important to note what is not included as a variable cost associated with changing order quantities. For example, the cost of the inventory itself is not included because, for a fixed annual demand and a fixed price per unit, the cost of the inventory does not vary with changes in the order quantity. However, if a supplier were willing to give discounts on orders above a certain size, for example, the cost of the items in inventory would become a cost that varies with different order quantities and should be included in the TVCAWCOQ calculation. Transportation costs are also assumed not to vary with changes in the order size, nor are any production or other related costs.

With the knowledge that the only variable costs we can associate with different order quantities in this case are carrying costs and order costs, we can define TVCAWCOQ in symbols as:

$$\text{TVCAWCOQ} = \text{order costs} + \text{carrying costs}$$

$$= (\text{cost per order})(\text{number of orders}) + (\text{period carrying cost as a percentage}) (\text{value of average inventory})$$

$$= (S)\left(\frac{D}{Q}\right) + [i]\left[C\left(\frac{Q}{2}\right)\right]$$

where

S = cost per order

D = period demand, usually annual demand

Q = order quantity

i = period carrying cost as a percentage (includes opportunity cost, physical costs of handling and storage, obsolescence)

C = *variable* cost per unit inventory

$\frac{Q}{2}$ = average number of units in inventory, assuming a steady and constant demand

We want to solve for the order quantity (Q) for which TVCAWCOQ is a minimum. Given the particular expressions for carrying cost and order cost, one way to solve for this minimum is to set the order cost equal to the carrying cost, since the intersection of these two lines falls directly below the low point of the graph of TVCAWCOQ (see Figure 10-7).*

Setting order cost equal to carrying cost and solving for Q yields

$$S\left(\frac{D}{Q}\right) = iC\frac{Q}{2}$$

$$2SD = iCQ^2$$

---

*In general, of course, one cannot rely on friendly mathematical functions to solve for the minimum of an expression like that for TVCAWCOQ. One must rely on calculus to develop an expression for the slope and solve for Q, the order quantity, at the lowest point, where the slope is zero. Differentiating TVCAWCOQ with respect to Q and setting the resultant expression equal to zero yields

$$\text{TVCAWCOQ} = S\left(\frac{D}{Q}\right) + iC\left(\frac{Q}{2}\right)$$

$$\frac{\partial \text{TVCAWCOQ}}{\partial Q} = -\frac{SD}{Q^2} + \frac{iC}{2} = 0$$

$$Q = \sqrt{\frac{2SD}{iC}}$$

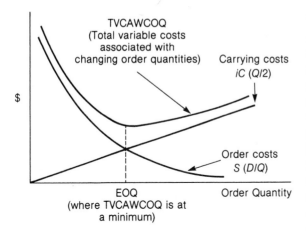

TVCAWCOQ
(Total variable costs
associated with
changing order quantities)

Carrying costs
$iC\ (Q/2)$

$

Order costs
$S\ (D/Q)$

EOQ
(where TVCAWCOQ is at
a minimum)

Order Quantity

FIGURE 10-7 Costs versus order quantities for the simple case of carrying costs and order costs only.

$$\frac{2SD}{iC} = Q^2$$

$$\sqrt{\frac{2SD}{iC}} = Q$$

What does this solution mean for this simple example? It has the intuitively appealing properties that the cost-minimizing order quantity, the EOQ, rises with increases in period demand and cost per order and declines with increases in the inventory carrying-cost rate and in the variable cost of the inventoried item. Importantly, the EOQ varies by the square root in this simple case. That is, an increase in company sales does not require a proportional increase in inventory to service it, but merely an increase according to the square root. In other terms, a doubling of demand does not require a doubling of inventories, but merely an increase of 41 percent, all other things held constant.

To reiterate, the key thing about the determination of an EOQ within a reorder point inventory system is not the formulas themselves, but the method by which an EOQ is found—namely, by use of the framework of "total variable costs associated with changing order quantities." To see this point more clearly, consider Situation 10-3.

SITUATION 10-3

GONDER-ODELL MANUFACTURING COMPANY

The Gonder-Odell Manufacturing Company placed a number of orders each year with local job shops. A typical order was for some machining of small castings provided by the company. In assembling its own products, Gonder-Odell drew upon an inventory of these parts at a more or less steady rate. At issue was how large an order the company should place each time and thus how much inventory to hold. Some relevant information is as follows:

- Usage expected: 5000 units per year
- Order cost: $10. This figure constituted only costs that the company viewed as varying with each order, such as mailing and phone fees, transporting the castings to the job shops, and some necessary computer time. It did not include any clerical time, as that was regarded as a fixed cost.

- Inventory carrying cost percentage: 20%
- Volume discounts on machining:

    $25 per unit if less than 100 ordered each time
    $22.50 per unit if 100 to 499 ordered each time
    $22 per unit if 500 or more ordered each time

- Transport costs: $20 for each pallet of 100 units; 30¢ for any unit not part of a 100-unit pallet. (The castings could be packed and shipped on standard pallets in quantities of 100. This factor greatly helped transportation and unloading.)
- Handling cost: $5 for each pallet of 100 units; 10¢ for any unit not handled in 100-unit pallets.

TABLE 10-6 Order Size Cost Calculations
(Gonder-Odell Manufacturing Company)

ORDER SIZE	ORDERS PER YEAR (given 5000 unit usage)	PURCHASE COST	ORDER COST	TRANSPORT COST	HANDLING COST	CARRYING COST	TOTAL COST (TVCAWCOQ)
50	100.00	$125,000	$1000.00	$1500	$500	$ 125	$128,125.00
100	50.00	112,500	500.00	1000	250	225	114,475.00
500	10.00	110,000	100.00	1000	250	1100	112,450.00
1000	5.00	110,000	50.00	1000	250	2200	113,500.00
400	12.50	112,500	125.00	1000	250	900	114,775.00
600	8.33	110,000	83.30	1000	250	1320	112,653.30

Discussion of Gonder-Odell Manufacturing Company

We have observed that deciding how much inventory is optimal involves balancing the costs that increase with order size against the costs that decline with increases in order size. In the simple case we first considered, only carrying costs and order costs varied with changes in the order size. Deciding upon the optimal inventory in that case involved merely finding the order size that minimized the sum of carrying and order costs. The basic EOQ formula was derived in just this spirit.

The situation facing the Gonder-Odell Manufacturing Company is not nearly so simple. In particular, carrying costs and order costs are not the only ones that vary with changes in the order size; purchase costs, transport costs, and handling costs also depend on the order size. The total of all the "variable costs associated with changes in the order quantity" would thus involve summing up all of these costs. They are displayed and totaled in Table 10-6 for a variety of order sizes. Note that the carrying costs reflect the actual purchase price of the units and not some generalized or average figure, and that they assume a steady draw upon the inventory so that the average inventory is half the order size.

An examination of Table 10-6 reveals that an order size of 500 and average inventory holdings of 250 minimize the total variable costs associated with changes in the order quantity (TVCAWCOQ). This result is not so surprising since (1) the lowest price starts with the 500 order quantity, and (2) the carrying costs rise more rapidly than order costs fall, suggesting that the company should carry as little inventory as it can. These two factors combine to yield 500, the lowest end of the lowest price category, as the optimal order quantity.

The table, except for the order size of 50, looks only at order sizes ending in even hundreds. We need not look at 501 or 499 as possible optimums because of the structure of the transport and handling costs. Non–even-hundred orders involve special transport and handling cost rates for the odd pieces, and these cost increases wipe out any carrying cost or order cost savings such quantities could bring. Put another way, the graph of total variable costs against various order sizes is a discontinuous one that follows the general pattern of Figure 10-8.

This discontinuity, coupled with the inclusion of so many variables in the calculation, makes the determination of an optimal order size something of a trial-and-error process. No neat formulas as we derived before can lead us easily to an answer. All we can do is converge on an answer in much the same manner as the table does.

CHOOSING BETWEEN PERIODIC REORDER AND REORDER POINT INVENTORY SYSTEMS

These then are the major elements of both the periodic reorder and the reorder point inventory systems. Both, remember, are non–time-phased systems. Situation 10-4 will help us consider why one might institute one system over another.

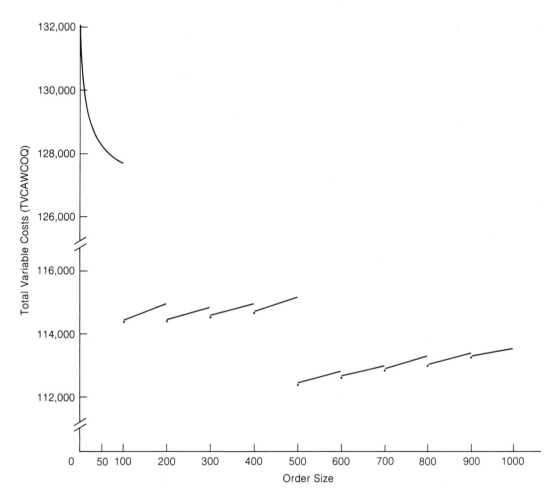

FIGURE 10-8   Total variable costs graphed against order size.

SITUATION 10-4

DRISCOLL LUMBER COMPANY

Spurred by some informal conversation at a recent Lions Club luncheon, Aubrey Driscoll was reflecting on the way in which he stocked items for his lumber company. Together with his brother, Burney, Aubrey owned and operated the Driscoll Lumber Company in Devine, Texas. Devine, a small town southwest of San Antonio, depended largely on cattle ranching and peanut farming for its livelihood. The Driscoll Lumber

Company was a major retailer of lumber, hardware, construction materials, and ranching supplies (e.g., corral gates, posts, barbed wire, fencing) for the area surrounding the town.

The Lions Club discussion caused Aubrey to think of dividing his inventory of goods into distinct classes, some of which might be ordered better through a periodic reorder system rather than the standard "order when low" system that prevailed in the lumberyard now. As Aubrey saw it, his stock could be classified into several major categories:

1. *Seasonal vs. nonseasonal demand.* The lumber and hardware that the Driscoll Lumber Company sold followed no seasonal pattern. Housing construction and repair in South Texas could be maintained in winter, due to the region's mild climate. Sales of barbed wire and steel fencing, however, were more likely in the late fall and winter, as ranchers and farmers shifted their attention from the raising of peanuts, hay, and other crops to the repair and construction of fields, pastures, and corrals.

2. *Items easily counted for inventory and items more difficult to count.* Most of the items the lumber company stocked were easily counted for inventory. Lumber, plywood, roofing material, cement, and the like were kept in open bins in the company's shed; low levels of any of these items were immediately obvious from just a quick glance around the shed. Some items, however, were more time-consuming to count, particularly those that came in many different sizes, shapes, or grades. Some hardware items such as pipes and fittings were among these as well as special bolts stored in small compartments. Glass was another such item

because it often had to be cut to order, and keeping track of the usable remains was difficult.

3. *Ordered lumber vs. rolling lumber.* Most of the lumber Aubrey Driscoll sold had been ordered about 30 days in advance. What was shipped to the Driscoll Lumber Company was exactly what had been ordered, usually in packaged bundles of standard lengths and a fixed count of pieces. Frequently, however, West Coast sawmills specializing in Douglas fir, spruce, hemlock, and other softwoods dispensed with filling specific orders. Instead, the mill would fill railroad boxcars with just what it was sawing at the time, set the boxcars rolling on the rails toward various regions of the country, and rely on lumber brokers to sell off the boxcars before they reached the end of the line. Retail lumber companies could often enjoy significant purchasing discounts by buying lumber in this way, although it frequently meant that some lengths or grades would be overstocked for a time.

To Aubrey Driscoll's way of thinking, these were the major categories of items that he inventoried. He wondered whether he should continue to order all of them only when they were low (a reorder point system) or whether he should make periodic checks of at least some items and order variable quantities (a periodic reorder system). Which items seemed more suitable to one system or the other?

Discussion of Driscoll Lumber Company

Aubrey Driscoll's three categories of items serve as a useful starting point for a discussion of the pros and cons of either a periodic reorder system or a reorder point system.

1. *Demand seasonality.* The calculation of an order quantity for a reorder point inventory system implicitly assumes that demand is steady. That is, the minimization of TVCAWCOQ generally assumes that over the relevant time period the draw on the inventory is constant. Thus, if an order quantity is calculated with an annual demand figure, it is inappropriate to use if marked demand seasonality exists. While one

could calculate different EOQs for different seasons, it is often simpler to use a periodic reorder system for those items whose demand is seasonal. Other things being equal, the Driscoll Lumber Company would be better advised to use a reorder point system for its lumber and hardware (nonseasonal) and a periodic reorder system for barbed wire and steel fencing (seasonal). If the lumber company placed barbed wire and steel fencing on a reorder point system, it might risk carrying too little inventory in fall and winter and too much the rest of the year.

2. *Ease of taking inventory.* A reorder point system requires that the inventory be monitored

constantly. If inventory is difficult or expensive to take, a reorder point system is less desirable. At the Driscoll Lumber Company, lumber and other open-bin items are easily inventoried and thus can be maintained under a reorder point system. Glass and certain hardware items, however, are tough to inventory and thus argue for a periodic reorder system.

3. *Price discounts.* The possibility of price discounts on West Coast "rolling lumber" and their irregular timing disrupts both periodic reorder and reorder point inventory systems. Deciding whether or not to buy such lumber, once offered, demands a quick inventory of existing stocks and a computation of how much of the purchased lumber will be used during the ensuing time frame. In a sense, this computation lies outside the routine workings of either inventory system. The fact that an inventory of the existing stocks is required suggests that such price discounts are perhaps more compatible with a reorder point system, but they are still compatible with a periodic reorder system.

Considering all of these features then suggests that the Driscoll Lumber Company may be best off using a reorder point system for its lumber and larger hardware supplies and a periodic reorder system for its small, hard-to-inventory hardware items, its glass, its barbed wire and fencing, and similar items.

In more general terms, a periodic reorder system has a relative advantage over a reorder point system when the costs of taking a physical inventory are high or when there are savings in regard to information (e.g., seasonal data), production scheduling, price discounts, or transport costs from ordering items on a regular basis. If these cost savings are not significant, however, a reorder point system has the striking advantage of being able to minimize the total variable costs associated with changing order quantities. Broadly speaking, the economics of inventory control favor the reorder point system but only when the important, practi-

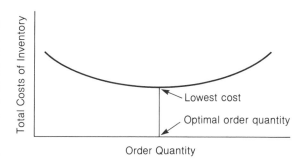

FIGURE 10-9   Inventory costs graphed against order quantities.

cal costs of inventory control and administration are not significant.

The saving grace in all of this is that failing to calculate the precisely optimal order quantity under any inventory system is not likely to be devastating. The costs of various order quantities are, in most instances, fairly near one another. In other words, a graph of inventory costs against various order quantities is likely to be shallow (saucer-shaped, as in Figure 10-9), rather than steep (bowl- or cup-shaped). Making some sensible decisions about inventories so as to get oneself "into the ball-park" is thus more important than landing on precisely the best order quantity.

While prevalent in both manufacturing and nonmanufacturing businesses, non–time-phased inventory systems, like the periodic reorder and reorder point systems described above, are perhaps best suited to retail and wholesale situations (e.g., Driscoll Lumber Company), where the source and precise timing of demand is seldom known with much certainty. These conditions often apply to manufacturing as well, but there are many manufacturing businesses that know far more about the source and timing of demand for their products, and hence for the parts that make up their products. It is in these instances of known or easily provided demand that the time-phased inventory system, such as material requirements planning, makes good sense. We turn now to a discussion of the workings of an MRP system.

RETURNING TO MATERIAL REQUIREMENTS PLANNING: A DESCRIPTION OF ITS OPERATION[2]

Earlier, material requirements planning (MPR) was introduced as a way to manage inventories by anticipating their use. As it was explained there, the basic philosophy of an MRP system is to time the procurement and/or fabrication of the specific items comprising a particular product to synchronize with that product's master production schedule. Given a firm schedule of when and how many of particular finished goods are desired, an MRP system details which component parts ought to be purchased/fabricated in what quantities and at what times.

In order to meet this desirable goal, a material requirements planning system must continually keep track of:

1. *Master production schedule* of end products. These data "drive" the entire system.
2. *Bills of materials* for each product and, indeed, each product variation, so that the demands for individual component parts can be detailed.
3. *Inventory status* of each component part.
4. *Lead time status* of all parts to be purchased or fabricated so that their availability is timed exactly to meet anticipated needs.
5. *Product construction schedule*. This schedule indicates when specific parts or subassemblies will be needed in order to meet the established master schedule for the end product.

To illustrate how this information gets used by and processed through an MRP system let us ponder a very simplified example, a toy tractor-trailer. This toy tractor-trailer consists of (1) a yellow plastic tractor cab to which is attached two yellow plastic axles and four black plastic wheels (the wheels must first be mounted on the axles and then the axles snapped into place underneath the cab), and (2) a blue plastic, flatbed trailer (which also has a yellow axle on which two black plastic wheels, identical to those under the tractor cab, are mounted). A "product structure" diagram of the tractor-trailer and its component parts might look like Figure 10-10.

Figure 10-10 serves as the *bill of materials* for the product. Notice that it can be depicted in a series of levels. These levels structure the product into various subassemblies and detail the components of each subassembly. Such a breakdown and structur-

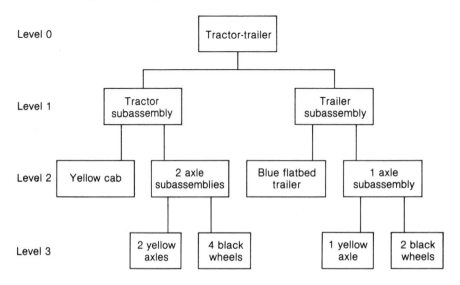

FIGURE 10-10 Composition of a toy tractor-trailer.

	Week					
	1	2	3	4	5	6
Toy Tractor-Trailers	6	10	3	12	15	8

FIGURE 10-11   Master production schedule
for the toy tractor-trailers.

ing enables us to keep separate track of inventories of tractor, trailer, or axle subassemblies and their components. We will see the usefulness of this.

Figure 10-11 is a *master production schedule* for tractor-trailers over the next 6 weeks. The 6-week production horizon is generally somewhat arbitrary and could be extended or shortened as a matter of company policy. In any event, it represents a *firm* commitment to make so many tractor-trailer units by such-and-such a time. Exactly when during the course of the week the tractor-trailer units are desired depends upon the convention used. For example, the call for 10 units in week 2 can mean that 10 units should be shipped the first day of the week or the last day of the week or even the midpoint day of the week. The choice is entirely the company's. For our example, let us adopt the convention that the week's master scheduled output is to be shipped on the final day of the week. The time period of a week is used here since it is the most popular for scheduling purposes; but time periods of a month, a day, or something else could be used. The same MRP logic applies in any case.

An inventory record for axle subassemblies is provided in Figure 10-12. Note that there are 18 axle subassemblies (i.e., black plastic wheels mounted on yellow axles) on hand that can be used to meet any immediate needs. Any other axles will take at least a week to assemble as the lead time statement in the record indicates. Similar inventory records and lead times exist for all component items and subassemblies for the product.

The value of an MRP system is its ability to determine quickly how many more axle subassemblies (or whatever) to order and when those orders ought to be placed. To do this, the material requirements planning system ties the various inventory records to both the bill of materials and the master production schedule. Such a tie is depicted in Figure 10-13, which shows the level-by-level link be-

		Week					
Lead Time = 1 Week		1	2	3	4	5	6
Gross Requirements							
Scheduled Receipts							
On Hand	18						
Planned Order Releases							

FIGURE 10-12   Inventory record for axle subassemblies
of toy tractor-trailer.

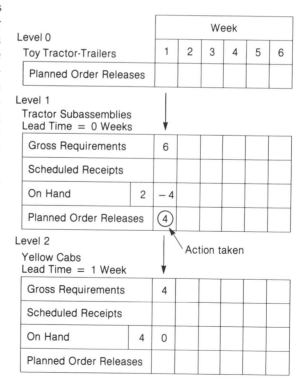

FIGURE 10-13   Linked inventory records in an MRP system
and a partial explosion of requirements.

tween tractor-trailers, tractor subassemblies, and yellow cabs.

It is worth devoting some attention to Figure 10-13 and what underlies it. Level 0 simply reproduces the master production schedule found in Figure 10-11. The "planned order releases" for the tractor-trailer units constitute "gross requirements" for the tractor subassemblies of level 1. That is, the need to ship, say, six toy tractor-trailers at the end of week 1 (the current week) places a demand for six tractor subassemblies for week 1. Two of the required six tractor subassemblies can be supplied out of existing inventories on hand (which we know because the bill of materials has been structured into subassemblies and thus we can keep track of them), but that leaves us four tractor subassemblies short, as indicated by the "−4" in the "on-hand" row. This shortage in turn

leads us to take action—namely, to order the four yellow cabs that we will need to manufacture that subassembly. This planned order release at level 1 is translated into a gross requirement at level 2, which keeps track of the yellow cabs. Thankfully, four yellow cabs are on hand and this order can be met out of existing inventories.

At every level, the net requirement for a part or subassembly in any period is calculated in the same way:

$$\begin{aligned}\text{Net requirements} &= \text{Inventory on hand from}\\\text{for a given period} & \quad \text{the previous period}\\ &+ \text{quantity on order}\\ & \quad \text{for delivery in the}\\ & \quad \text{given period}\\ &- \text{gross requirements}\\ & \quad \text{for the given period}\end{aligned}$$

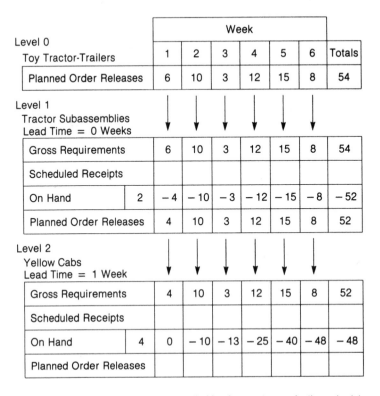

FIGURE 10-14   Net requirements implied by the master production schedule.

In our diagrams, the net requirement is written in the row labeled "on-hand." If this net requirement is negative, then some action must be taken (e.g., an order placed) if production is not to fall behind schedule. If it is zero or positive, all is well, at least for the time being.

A material requirements planning system can trace out in advance the net requirements for subassemblies or component parts at all levels. Figure 10-14 does such a tracing of requirements for both level 1 (tractor subassemblies) and level 2 (yellow cabs) under the assumption that all shortages of tractor subassemblies trigger planned order releases in the same way as traced out in Figure 10-13. On level 2 the on-hand balances (net requirements) accumulate since no orders have yet been released.

Calculating the planned order releases for the yellow cabs is not as straightforward as calculating the planned order releases for the tractor subassemblies since the yellow cabs can only be fabricated with a lead time of 1 week. Thus, for example, if the need for 10 yellow cabs in week 2 is to be met, an order for 10 cabs must be placed in week 1. Figure 10-15 follows through with this logic, depicting the required planned order releases for level 2.

As yet, no entries have been made in the row labeled "scheduled receipts." These receipts, however, are linked directly to planned order releases. As soon as an order is "released" it becomes a scheduled receipt. Its position in the time phasing diagram is determined by its expected lead time.

Thus, the net requirements implied by the master production schedule, as indicated in Figure 10-14, can be rewritten in terms of scheduled receipts, assuming no complications with the indicated lead times. Figure 10-16 displays this. Note that each of the planned order releases has been transferred to the scheduled receipt square for the appropriate week. The on-hand inventories also reflect the emergence of a series of scheduled receipts.

In practice, of course, planned order releases can be expected to "mature" and be released one at a time, as in Figure 10-13, rather than in entire batteries, as Figure 10-15 may lead one to believe.

Before going on to introduce some "wrinkles" to this basic MRP logic, let us step back a moment and review its fundamental steps:

1. The master production schedule is the data introduced to the MRP system that "drive" it. All the entries and actions taken must be in agreement with the master production schedule. This schedule is assumed by the MRP logic to be correct and "frozen" over some time period.

2. A detailed bill of materials for all products and product variations must also exist, and should be structured in successive tiers to reveal subassemblies as well as individual component parts. Given the master production schedule and the relevant bills of materials, an MRP system "explodes" the bills of materials through successive tiers to calculate how many parts or

Level 2 Yellow Cabs Lead Time = 1 Week		1	2	3	4	5	6	Totals
Gross Requirements		4	10	3	12	15	8	52
Scheduled Receipts								
On Hand	4	0	−10	−3	−12	−15	−8	−48
Planned Order Releases		10	3	12	15	8		48

FIGURE 10-15 Planned order releases when lead time must be accounted for.

Level 0 Toy Tractor-Trailers	Week						Totals
	1	2	3	4	5	6	
Planned Order Releases	6	10	3	12	15	8	54

Level 1
Tractor Subassemblies
Lead Time = 0 Weeks

Gross Requirements		6	10	3	12	15	8	54
Scheduled Receipts		4	10	3	12	15	8	52
On Hand	2	0	0	0	0	0	0	
Planned Order Releases		4	10	3	12	15	8	52

Level 2
Yellow Cabs
Lead Time = 1 Week

Gross Requirements		4	10	3	12	15	8	52
Scheduled Receipts			10	3	12	15	8	48
On Hand	4	0	0	0	0	0	0	
Planned Order Releases		10	3	12	15	8		

FIGURE 10-16   Scheduled receipts implied by the master production schedule and by the planned order releases.

subassemblies of a particular type are required to satisfy the master production schedule.

MRP logic permits the computation of net requirements by adjusting the gross requirements for a particular subassembly or part by the number of units already on hand and those that are expected to be received.

3. The timing for planned order releases depends on the expected lead times for procuring/fabricating/assembling component parts or subassemblies. Orders are actually placed in anticipation of their need, as dictated by the master production schedule and the derivative explosion of the bills of materials.

The data requirements for the computer files that handle the processing for an MRP system are voluminous and include:

- Master production schedules for the weeks indicated

- Bills of materials for all products and product variations

- Existing inventory levels for all parts and subassemblies

- Lead times for all parts and subassemblies

- Orders placed but not yet received (so-called open orders)

The processing of an MRP system—the explosion of the bills of materials, the updating of the inventory file records, and the releasing of orders and spotting of scheduled receipts—can be an irregular event (say, once a week) or can proceed all the time. If an MRP system is run at distinctly spaced intervals, the system is said to be regenerative since the computer file records on master schedules, bills of materials, inventory levels, lead times, and open orders are updated ("regenerated") in their entirety all at once. Such a regeneration conserves computer resources, but it also runs the risk of letting the information on which the entire MRP system depends deteriorate over time.

A net change MRP system, on the other hand, permits the information in any computer file on the system to be updated. More importantly, it also permits the consequences of that updating to be followed through, be they changes in planned order release dates or changed quantitites of an item on hand or something else. A net change MRP system chews up more computer resources, but it maintains the timeliness of the system for all its uses. Of course, for a net change system to operate effectively, all the consequences of any transaction in any computer file must be traced to their ultimate conclusion. Records must be tied or "chained" to one another both upward and downward by special "pointers." By following these pointers, a net change MRP system is updated by a series of partial "explosions" rather than by calling for the large, infrequent, full explosion of a regenerative MRP system.

"Wrinkles" to Add to the Basic MRP Logic

Common Parts

In our example of the toy tractor-trailer, the black plastic wheels and the yellow plastic axles are used in both the tractor and the trailer subassemblies. When it is time to review the net requirements for wheels and axles, we must be sure that the gross requirements from both tractor and trailer subassemblies are added together. The explosions of the bill of materials must be careful to keep track of all the instances where a certain part or subassembly is called for. Figure 10-17 shows the demand for black plastic wheels in various weeks emerging from both tractor and trailer assembly. Note that two wheels are needed for each axle assembly and that a tractor uses two axles and a trailer just one.

Same Parts Used at Different Levels

Although it does not happen in our toy tractor-trailer example, it is easily possible for a part to be

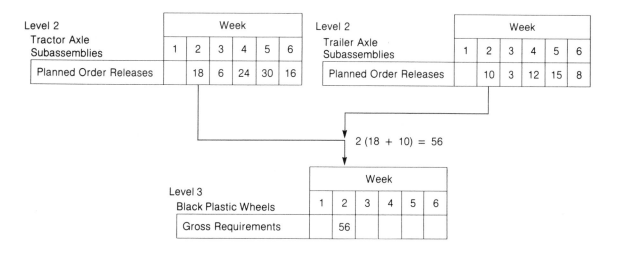

FIGURE 10-17 Dealing with common parts in an MRP system.

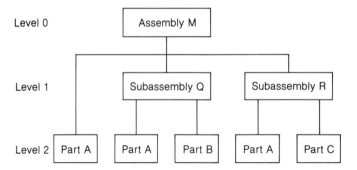

FIGURE 10-18 Bill of materials' product structure dealing with the same part on potentially different levels.

used at both level 2 and level 3, say, of a product structure for a bill of materials. Trying to keep track of all the demands for such a part is awkward (and expensive for the computer) if some simplifying convention is not adopted. In most instances, this problem is solved by structuring the bills of materials in a way that places all of the same parts or subassemblies at the same level. In Figure 10-18, for example, part A, which could have been placed in two different levels of the bill of materials' product structure, is depicted as occurring all at the lowest level possible. In this way, the MRP computer program need only encounter it at one level and sum up its requirements there.

Lot Sizing

Up to this point, material requirements planning has been used to place orders that represent pre-cisely the number of units of anticipated use, no more and no less. As we have seen elsewhere in the discussion of materials management, price discounts or some other feature may make it advisable to purchase more than the anticipated need. This possibility makes it desirable to use some economic order quantity reasoning along with the batch-for-batch, anticipatory philosophy of MRP.

The MRP logic also makes it explicit that TVCAWCOQ should be minimized on a period-by-period basis, as more information is revealed about future needs, costs, and item availabilities. In practice, being so precise about minimizing a changing TVCAWCOQ may not be worth all the effort, but some lot sizing approximations can be built into an MRP system. Figure 10-19 displays how planned order releases would look given a specific lot size to order rather than a batch-for-batch order scheme.

Level 2 Yellow Cabs Lead Time = 1 Week Lot Size = 15		Week						
		1	2	3	4	5	6	Totals
Gross Requirements		4	10	3	12	15	8	52
Scheduled Receipts								
On Hand	4	0	5	2	5	5	12	
Planned Order Releases		15		15	15	15		60

FIGURE 10-19 Lot sizing in an MRP system.

Safety Stocks

An MRP system can also accommodate safety stocks of items. In general, it is best to think of safety stocks of finished goods—"kits" of component parts—rather than individualized safety stocks for all of the component parts themselves. The accounting is easier if the safety stocks are thought of, and even actually held, in that way. The existence of safety stocks, however, goes somewhat against the grain of the material requirements planning philosophy, since safety stocks cannot be thought of in terms of time phasing for anticipated use. Companies also run the constant risk that their managers, once discovering the presence of safety stocks, will adapt their own decisions to use up the safety stock early and for purposes for which they were not intended.

MATERIAL REQUIREMENTS PLANNING AS A MANAGEMENT TOOL

A main function of an MRP system, of course, is to control inventories so that they can adequately meet projected production requirements at low carrying cost. When all is working smoothly, an MRP system can do just that. However, the test of any materials management system lies not with fair weather but with foul. Events in a materials manager's life invariably go awry. It is in coping with the unexpected and in planning the future that an MRP system can often earn its own way.

A material requirements planning system can serve as a useful management tool in a variety of ways:

1. *As a scheduling and schedule-revising device.* Not only can an MRP system detail what should be ordered when but it can indicate how and when late items will affect other aspects of production. It can signal which orders now awaiting delivery ought to be expedited and how any tardiness will alter the existing production schedule (e.g., how much final delivery will be delayed, which demands will

now be placed in subsequent weeks). Similarly, if advance supply delivery or higher yields or some other positive development occurs, an MRP system can signal which orders to de-expedite or even cancel.

When such positive or negative developments strike, an MRP system can automatically reschedule orders (or, more often, indicate to the materials manager the necessity for rescheduling orders), either moving them forward or backward. For example, the spoilage of some inventory or the breakdown of machinery (both of which may reduce the number available in the future) can trigger the rescheduling of an order in the proper week to avoid a stockout. Unexpected developments could even lead to a change in the master production schedule or in the lot size permitted. Typically, an MRP system identifies a range of possible actions to be taken by the materials manager.

2. *As a marketing and capacity need estimating device.* An MRP system can be used for some "what-if" thinking by management. For example, information on how quickly a specific order can be handled may help land a sale. An MRP system can be used to fit in such a "trial run" and the information relayed to marketing.

In a similar vein, an MRP system can help determine how much of a load on the factory will be implied by an increase in sales or a change of product mix. This information can be used to plan capacity expansion over the short to medium term.

3. *As a costing and performance measuring device.* By adding standard cost data to the data in an inventory file, an MRP system can be transformed into a device for estimating product costs for new bill of materials' product structures. These standard cost data can be used as well to calculate the level of inventory investment being carried.

At its best, then, a material requirements planning system can be a real boon for a manufacturing operation. MRP has been made feasible by the advent of computers, and no doubt the future holds even more promise for the expansion of MRP systems in numbers and in abilities.

CHOOSING MRP OR THE TWO NON–TIME-PHASED INVENTORY SYSTEMS

Although an MRP system radiates many desirable qualities, it does so at a cost. The question still persists as to when a company should adopt an MRP system and when it should stay with a less versatile but less expensive non–time-phased system. Consider Situation 10-5.

DISCUSSION OF HEWITT-EVERETT DIVISION

The lobbying effort directed at Mike Hewitt is well intentioned. An MRP system stretching across division lines at Winchester International does promise to reduce the production cycle time of the release mechanisms that have been at the root of management's present concern. It could well reduce that cycle time by the 2 to 3 weeks its proponents claim could be shaved off. There would probably be other benefits as well, such as better control over other components of the automatic weighing and measuring systems the division sold.

Installing a material requirements planning system, however, is not the only way by which the division's production cycle time could be reduced.

SITUATION 10-5

HEWITT-EVERETT DIVISION

The Hewitt-Everett Division of Winchester International, Inc. manufactured automatic weighing and measuring equipment, which was used primarily by agricultural cooperatives for mixing feeds and fertilizers. The equipment released selected quantities of grain, nutrients, or fertilizer into a hopper for either bulk or bag loading. The heart of the product—and the toughest part to make—was the release mechanism, for it had to be both sturdy and exact. Much of the rest of the equipment was sheet metal; forming it presented no particular difficulties.

Over the past year, Hewitt-Everett had modified the release mechanism to include a new electronic sensor and control system. This electronic system was more rugged, more versatile, and quicker than the mechanical system it replaced. Its introduction had strengthened the product in the market, and sales were running strong.

Hewitt-Everett offered its weighing and measuring equipment in over 70 varieties of sizes and configurations. Since this equipment was bulky and rather expensive, no finished goods inventories were kept. Rather, production proceeded on an order-by-order basis. For the 70-odd different equipment offerings, however, there were only eight different release mechanisms required, which simplified matters considerably. A like number of electronic sensor and control systems were needed as well.

The sole supplier of the electronic sensors and controls was another division of Winchester International, which specialized in the original equipment electronics market. Hewitt-Everett was delighted with the product's quality; but recently, as sales continued their steady upward climb, deliveries from this other Winchester International division had lagged. The late deliveries were causing increasing concern among Hewitt-Everett's management because they were stretching out Hewitt-Everett's own cycle time in fabricating its weighing and measuring equipment. If the company's cycle time were stretched much further, the company would lose its ability to compete for many of the late fall orders, a prime order-taking period. That is, if the company could not deliver its equipment by late winter in time for spring planting, it was in danger of losing any order placed after the first of November.

As a remedy for this disturbing situation, a group of managers within the company had been lobbying Mike Hewitt, the company's founder and still its president, for the introduction of a material requirements planning system that might even cross division lines within Winchester International. The essence of their argument was that Hewitt-Everett needed to give its sister division more time to react to the order for sensors and controls. At present, when Hewitt-Everett received an order, only the assembly department was notified of model and quantity. That department was then responsible for placing a subsequent, derivative order with its suppliers, including the department making the release mechanism. The release mechanism department, in turn, was responsible for placing an order with the sister division. The managers lobbying Mike Hewitt thought that 2 to 3 weeks could be saved by notifying the sister division directly of the equipment orders as they were received, instead of waiting for the domino effect of department-by-department ordering. They

reasoned that a material requirement planning (MRP) system could coordinate this materials ordering procedure much more quickly and efficiently than the present set of procedures could. They estimated that establishing an MRP system would cost Hewitt-Everett about $100,000 and that maintaining it would cost about $25,000 per year.

To Mike Hewitt, this sounded like a lot of money, but he also recognized that something clearly had to be done to shorten the cycle time in manufacturing. (Some figures on product cost and quantities are given below for the latest year.)

Units sold	420
Present growth rate of unit sales	9%
Average unit cost	$13,500
Average standard cost of release mechanisms	$ 3,100
Average transfer price of electronic sensors and control systems	$ 1,250

An alternative worthy of consideration is a simple one—namely, providing a buffer stock of the sensors and controls that have been delivered tardily. The Hewitt-Everett Division could then draw immediately on this "decoupling" inventory and at the same time place an order with the sister division that would result in the restocking of the buffer inventory. Since only eight different sensor and control systems are required anyway, the inventory would not have to be that large and diverse to be effective.

Either the MRP system or the buffer inventory plan would succeed in eliminating the waiting associated with the present system of one department or division placing orders on other departments or divisions. Choosing between the two rests largely on the costs of each. The expected MRP system expenses are already provided. What must be estimated are the carrying costs of the buffer inventory.

Calculating the Carrying Cost
of the Buffer Inventory

Although the particular quantities of each of the eight sensor and control systems needed would depend on the expected pattern of demand, for a back-of-the-envelope calculation we might expect to have to inventory 4 weeks of production, on the average. The company's inventory carrying cost percentage is not quoted in the situation, but 25 percent is not likely to be far off the mark. The expected annual inventory carrying cost would then be:

$$420 \text{ units/year} \cdot 4 \text{ weeks/52 weeks} \cdot$$
$$\$1250 \text{ cost per system} \cdot .25 \text{ carrying cost percentage}$$
$$= \$10,100 \text{ per year in carrying costs}$$

This cost is only slightly more than a third of the annual expense of maintaining an MRP system. The required weeks of inventory could be doubled and the buffer inventory costs would still be less than the MRP system's. Thus, the side benefits of the MRP system would likely have to be significant for an MRP system to be preferred.

In addition, it is likely that the time needed to install a formal, computerized material requirements planning system could be significantly longer than the time it would take the sister division to build up an inventory of sensor and control systems. MRP systems typically take many months to install and debug. While a buildup of a buffer inventory would not be quick, especially considering the recent pattern of late deliveries, at least some inventory could be built up with the next order placed on the sister division.

All things considered then, the simpler, less sophisticated, buffer inventory approach to cutting down on the division's production cycle time appears to be the preferred solution to Hewitt-Everett's present concerns.

When Implementing an MRP System Is Less Desirable[3]

As the workings of a material requirements planning system were described above, a tremendous amount of data must be accumulated and updated continually—master production schedules, bills of materials, inventory status, production cycle times, materials needs at each stage of the production cycle, and supplier lead times. The more easily a company can check off the data in its master schedule, bills of materials, and the like, the more likely that it has its production well under control. Simply going through the exercise of assembling such data in preparation for the implementation of an MRP system is a tremendous learning experience for most companies and suggests a host of useful changes in operations. There is no denying that the MRP philosophy can pay huge dividends to plant management.

On the other hand, there are some circumstances under which implementing an MRP system taxes company resources too much to be

worth the effort. The Hewitt-Everett Division situation is one where the benefits of an MRP system do not mesh well enough with the problem to justify its use in preference to a decoupling inventory. In other instances, an MRP system is not justified because of data accumulation and updating difficulties and costs.

For example, in situations where the master production schedule is not stable (i.e., not known with certainty well in advance) an MRP system is harder to justify. An MRP system works best when products are made to stock and not to order, when large buffer stocks of finished goods exist, and when sales are not very sensitive to abrupt seasonal or cyclical swings.

A material requirements planning system is likewise tougher to implement when bills of materials for products are not stable. An MRP system is best off when the number of new product introductions over time is modest, when there are few engineering changes released, and when there is little or no tinkering on the shop floor by engineers or others.

In a similar vein, an MRP system is likely to run more smoothly and be more effective when the process itself is stable. That is, when the process is not new or state-of-the-art itself, and when it is not likely to exhibit significant variances in product yields and quality, an MRP system stands a better chance. Also, if the time periods when various inputs are used in the process are well established, implementing an MRP system is easier. Lastly, an MRP system is best off when supplier lead times are known and dependable.

In sum, the material requirements planning approach to materials control has many attractive features and can be a significant unifying force for all of a company's manufacturing. Yet, it has to be embraced with some caution; other means may lead a company to the same ends at less expense in time, money, and headaches.

This concludes the discussion of both anticipatory (MRP) and non–time-phased inventory systems (periodic reorder and reorder point) for managing stocks of items in either raw materials or finished goods inventories. We push on now to a discussion of managing work-in-process inventories.

MANAGING THE WORK-IN-PROCESS

As should be abundantly evident from the situation at the Hewitt-Everett Division, inventory systems (especially those of an anticipatory nature) are inextricably interwoven with planning and controlling production itself. This is nowhere more evident than in managing work-in-process inventories, for it is here that managers must keep alert to the interactions of the process and inventory.

How can work-in-process inventories build up? The process descriptions of Segment I help to isolate some general reasons. Among them are production bottlenecks, line changeovers, parts shortage, and uncoordinated production control.

PRODUCTION BOTTLENECKS

As we have already observed, the production bottleneck is a classic explanation for the buildup of work-in-process inventories and the bane of the job shop in particular. When bottlenecks occur, good inventory management means taking a close look at the balance of capacities in the process. In particular, if demand has increased or if the mix of products going through the shop or the production methods or equipment has changed, a careful process flow diagram-type analysis can work wonders for diagnosing the problem and suggesting possible solutions.

LINE CHANGEOVERS

Again, as noted in Segment I, the typical line flow process is a rather inflexible agent for producing a broad mix of products. Often, different products must be run separately and serially on the line. Thus, if the company is to offer a complete product mix, inventories must be built up for each product in turn. Naturally, the more inflexible the line flow and the more dependent the company is on a small number of lines, the greater the inventory buildup is apt to be. In this case, the impact of the process on inventories can be dramatic. Frequently, a company's flexibility is enhanced by establishing production lines that are smaller but more numerous rather than production lines that are fewer in number and larger in size.

PARTS SHORTAGE

A classic and all-too-common explanation for the buildup of work-in-process inventories is the lack of one or more parts for completing a unit. In many continuous and line flow processes, the lack of a part would shut down operations altogether; but in other processes parts shortages can frequently be worked around, and are, especially when pressure for delivery is exerted. Unfortunately, although working around a parts shortage may be the quickest way to manufacture a given unit, an entire operation that works in this way reduces productivity considerably. Invariably, extra time is spent figuring what to work around, how to do it, placing work-in-process in limbo somewhere on the factory floor, fetching it for rework, figuring out how to proceed again, actually reworking the unit, and interrupting ongoing operations all along the way. Often, by having to cope with parts shortages and the factory floor difficulties they pose, the company pays the consequences for poor raw materials inventory management in the first place. For many operations, the stockout penalty for a part in raw materials inventory does not include the many petty but cumulatively significant problems that a parts shortage can introduce to the factory floor.

More frequently still than a faulty raw materials safety stock decision, a parts shortage develops because of delivery problems with a supplier. The purchasing department may have ordered enough and may have given the supplier sufficient notice considering past delivery performance, but the supplier simply falls down on the job. There may not be a lot the manufacturer can do in such a situation. We have already discussed (1) the make vs. buy option, which is sometimes a way out of chronic delivery problems, and (2) the multiple supplier option, which can help to assure deliveries as well as reasonable prices.

A third means of coping better with such a situation may be the division of attention within the purchasing department to supplies of various kinds. One popular way of dividing up the responsibilities for ordering, monitoring, and expediting supply deliveries is the so-called ABC system. The A items are typically those which are few in number but high in value; the C items are generally the reverse, numerous but low in value; the B items fall somewhere in between. Different people can be assigned to each group. The A group people, for example, might keep close check on the delivery status of their items, mainly the ones where delivery is likely to be a problem. The C group people are probably dealing with commodity items where their concerns are less with delivery and more with price differences by vendor, price discounts for large volumes, and EOQ-type calculations. (With an MRP system in effect, however, an ABC system is usually redundant; the speed and comprehensiveness of an MRP system makes it fairly easy to treat a C item like an A item.)

UNCOORDINATED PRODUCTION CONTROL

As we have seen from the latest situation, there can be a mismatch in the product mix processed in different segments of the operation, especially when broad, changeable, and/or variably demanded product mixes are involved. This mismatch in production signals can be purposefully sought (the "decoupling" inventory in the Hewitt-

Everett situation) or it can be inadvertent. In either case, a work-in-process inventory builds up. Note that this reason for an expansion of work-in-process results not from a production bottleneck per se, since the aggregate capacities of different segments may match up very well. Rather, this work-in-process inventory develops because one segment's output, on a specific product-by-product basis, does not match in the short run a succeeding segment's output needs. In the longer run, of course, unless there is obsolescence, the two segments will produce matching product mixes. The challenge here lies in understanding when production and inventory control is better served and more effective with a work-in-process inventory that buffers segments of the full production process and their information needs from one another, and when such an inventory is merely taking up space, swallowing financing dollars, and confusing and disrupting operations.

One common way that inadvertent work-in-process accumulates in this way is when one portion of the process demands a substantially different setup expenditure than another portion. The typical reaction to a high setup cost is to make the run long. While such a strategy often makes good sense, it is not always the best course of action. Long runs may build up too much inventory for too long a period and risk stockouts of items with more pressing demands. The balance of setup costs against inventory expenses and stockout penalties ought to be done in every case.

Another common way that uncoordinated production control can stack up undesired work-in-process inventory is when expediting within the factory rages out of control. As more and more rush orders are placed on the factory floor, the regular flow of the process becomes increasingly disrupted. This raises work-in-process inventory and lowers productivity (labor time per unit increases). Existing machine setups are likely to be broken repeatedly, necessitating time-consuming rework of the setups themselves. As Segment I's process descriptions revealed, rush orders are incompatible with line flow and continuous flow operations. In job shop and batch-flow operations, production control policies become critical. This is not to imply that rush orders should not be permitted. Rather, it is an admonition that a company whose work-in-process inventories seem to be ballooning ought to look carefully at the extent of rush orders within the process and whether a restructuring or expansion of the process or a segregation of rush orders might be a more effective way to maintain both productivity and service levels.

PART THREE

ISSUES IN LOGISTICS[4]

Logistics is chiefly concerned with the movement of products to markets and of materials to manufacturing facilities. It is a frequently neglected aspect of operations, but one whose potential impact on costs and profits is greater than most realize, as evidenced by the figures in Table 10-7. Total distribution costs, as shown there, are roughly as high a percentage of sales as direct labor costs.

In managing logistics, two issues dominate much of the thinking:

1. Which modes of transportation should be used?

2. Where should various inventories, especially finished goods inventories, be held and how much should be held at each location? (This is often regarded as warehousing or distribution strategy.)

MODE CHOICE

Transportation mode choice tends to be a very specialized field of inquiry. Mode choice decisions require reams of very detailed information on

TABLE 10-7   Distribution Costs as a Percentage of Sales Dollar

	OUTBOUND TRANSPOR-TATION	INVENTORY CARRYING	WARE-HOUSING	ADMINIS-TRATION	RECEIVING AND SHIPPING	PACK-AGING	ORDER PROCESSING	TOTAL
All manufacturing companies	6.2%	1.3%	3.6%	0.5%	0.8%	0.7%	0.5%	13.6%
Chemicals and plastics	6.3	1.6	3.3	0.3	0.6	1.4	0.6	14.1
Food manufacturing	8.1	0.3	3.5	0.4	0.9	—	0.2	13.4
Electronics	3.2	2.5	3.2	1.2	0.9	1.1	1.2	13.3
Paper	5.8	0.1	4.6	0.2	0.3	—	0.2	11.2
Machinery and tools	4.5	1.0	2.0	0.5	0.5	1.0	0.5	10.0
Pharmaceutical	1.4	—	1.2	0.7	0.5	0.1	0.5	4.4
All other	6.8	1.0	2.9	1.2	1.4	0.4	0.4	14.1
All merchandising companies	7.4%	10.3%	4.2%	1.2%	0.6%	1.2%	0.7%	25.6%
Industrial goods	5.9	13.7	2.9	0.7	0.2	2.0	1.0	26.4
Consumer goods	8.1	8.5	4.0	1.3	0.9	0.9	0.5	24.2

SOURCE: Data from B. J. LaLonde and P. H. Zinszer, *Customer Service: Meaning and Measurement* (Chicago: National Council of Physical Distribution Management, 1976).

transport costs and delivery times by mode for different classes of shipments characterized by weight, volume, and specialized shipping requirements (e.g., refrigerated or not, open flatcar or enclosed, under pressure or not). Less than truckload or less than carload rates tend to be very different from full truckload or full carload rates. Mode choice is further complicated by a proliferation of rates. A company's traffic department cannot merely think of truck, rail, water, or air but must think in terms of common truck carrier, owner-operator trucks, own fleet trucking; regular rail service, piggyback (truck-rail) service; ocean, lake, or river barges; commercial jet shipping or private jet shipping; and a number of other variations. Rates and deliveries vary, as does the impact of federal and state regulation, which can for no good reason dictate substantially different shipping rates from seemingly equivalent shipping points or different rates between two points depending on which direction shipment is made.

Other than to note some of the many peculiarities that afflict the nation's transportation system and thus the mode choice decisions of companies, this text will leave to more specialized and detailed treatments this issue of transport mode choice.[5]

DISTRIBUTION STRATEGY

Should a company keep its inventory of finished goods centralized, or should it disperse its finished goods into a number of regional or metropolitan warehouses and service centers? This question can be a subtle one and an answer to it depends on the resolution of a traditional conflict between the merits of centralized distribution for keeping inventory in control and the merits of decentralized distribution for the speedy servicing of field accounts.

THE ARGUMENT FOR DECENTRALIZATION

The argument in favor of dispersing finished goods inventories in a number of locations is clear and compelling. The time it takes to fill an order can be cut markedly if sales and service people can call on a nearby facility. Fewer errors are likely to be made as well since field people can be in close, informal touch with the warehouse or service center. Sales may even be stimulated if customers react favorably to knowledge of a facility nearby dedicated to serving them.

THE ARGUMENT AGAINST DECENTRALIZATION

Despite all the aid decentralized distribution can promise field sales and service people, it can also lead to an expansion of inventory to be carried and a loss of control over that inventory. Four major points argue against decentralized inventories, as will be covered next.

Administering Decentralized Distribution

Inventory spread among a number of facilities is more difficult to keep track of than when it is in one or just a few facilities. Record-keeping is more voluminous and thus subject to error. Swaps between facilities may be so informal that records are not even entered. Moreover, the sales and service people may become so possessive of "their" facility that a hoarding mentality takes over, especially with items that are scarce and that a central authority may want to call in for allocation somewhere else. Such items may purposefully become "lost" in the distribution system.

Irregular Demand and Buffer Stocks: The Law of Large Numbers

The demand in any one region of a company's market area is likely to follow a more irregular pattern than the company's overall demand. Greater-than-average demand for a particular product in

TABLE 10-8   Total Demand for Two Geographic Areas

COMBINED DEMAND DURING PERIOD	DEMAND PROBABILITY	COMPUTED AS
0	.04	$Pr(0) \cdot Pr(0) = (.2)(.2)$
1	.24	$2[Pr(1) \cdot P(0)] = 2(.6)(.2)$
2	.44	$Pr(1) \cdot Pr(1) + 2[Pr(0) \cdot Pr(2)] = (.6)(.6) + 2(.2)(.2)$
3	.24	$2[Pr(1) \cdot Pr(2)] = 2(.6)(.2)$
4	.04	$Pr(2) \cdot Pr(2) = (.2)(.2)$

one region may well be balanced by below-average demand for the same product in another region. Thus, the buffer stock that a centralized facility would have to carry is likely to be considerably less than the sum of the buffer stocks of decentralized facilities, for the same level of protection against stockouts. This result is a variation of the so-called "law of large numbers." The variance of demand for a single, large service center will almost always be less than the variance of demand faced by smaller, dispersed service centers offering the same coverage against stockouts.

An example is helpful in understanding this point. Assume that the demand in two distinct geographic areas is independent and can be described according to the following probability distribution:

Units Demanded during Period	Demand Probability
0	.2
1	.6
2	.2

Expected sales during the period in each area are thus 1 unit. By combining these probability distributions we can describe the total demand for both geographic areas, as shown in Table 10-8. If only 2 units are held in inventory at a centralized warehouse, the expected loss in sales would be

.32 units = .24 units if demand is 3
            + 2(.04) units if demand is 4

If, on the other hand, two decentralized ware-

houses are kept, the expected loss in sales would be 0.2 from each warehouse, for a total of 0.4. Thus, by centralizing the warehousing, the expected loss in sales due to stocking out of the product is reduced from 0.4 to 0.32, a not insignificant amount. If the company is to offer the same protection against stockouts, more inventory would have to be held in a decentralized warehouse system, given that our assumption of independent demand holds, than in a centralized warehouse system.

Scattered Warehousing and the Optimal Inventory Calculation

The logic of our EOQ calculation can be applied to the case of many, scattered warehouses versus a single, large warehouse. Much as we derived earlier, let

D = expected period demand over the entire company
i = inventory carrying cost percentage
S = cost per order
C = variable cost per unit of inventory
N = number of scattered warehouses, all of the same size

From our calculations before for the simple case where carrying cost and order cost were the only costs that varied with changes in the order quantity, the optimal order quantity, Q, was found to be

$$(1) \qquad Q = \sqrt{\frac{2SD}{iC}}$$

Now let's consider a small warehouse, one of N identical warehouses that the company operates. The demand that each small warehouse will face during the period is D/N. We can substitute this into our formula to find the optimal order quantity, Q^*, for the small warehouse.

$$(2) \qquad Q^* = \sqrt{\frac{2S(D/N)}{iC}}$$

But there are N small warehouses and so the total of all the order quantities would be

$$(3) \qquad N \cdot Q^* = N\sqrt{\frac{2S(D/N)}{iC}} = \sqrt{N}\sqrt{\frac{2SD}{iC}}$$

We can substitute equation 1 in to find a relationship between Q^* and Q, namely,

$$(4) \qquad N \cdot Q^* = \sqrt{N}\sqrt{\frac{2SD}{iC}} = \sqrt{N}\,Q$$

Thus, merely by dispersing inventory in N facilities and allowing each to optimize its order quantities under a reorder point inventory system, we find that the order quantities demanded of the factory—and by implication inventories since in this case average inventory is $Q/2$ or $Q^*/2$—increase by the square root of the number of warehouses. If we establish four small, identical warehouses instead of one, and if we follow a reorder point system for each one, then inventories will be double what they would be if we established a single warehouse.

This argument is meant to be more suggestive than exact. The regional warehouses of most companies are not organized so that individual reorder point systems prevail. But they are organized differently in many cases precisely to avoid the heavy inventory burden that the line of reasoning sketched above leads to.

Tiered Inventories and Pipeline Momentum

Many distribution systems are tiered. They have a centralized inventory that sits above a number of regional inventories; these, in turn, sit above local, metropolitan inventories. In some of these systems, the central inventory feeds products to the regional

TABLE 10-9   Tiered Inventory System and Disjointed Decision Rules—The Steady State

TIER	ITEM	AMOUNT
A (Local)	Beginning inventory	40
	Sales in week	20
	Ending inventory	20
	Desired inventory	40*
	Order on the next tier	20
B (Regional)	Beginning inventory	40
	Sales in week	20
	Ending inventory	20
	Desired inventory	40*
	Order on the next tier	20
C (Companywide)	Beginning inventory	40
	Sales in week	20
	Ending inventory	20
	Desired inventory	40*
	Order on factory or to be absorbed by buffer stocks	20

NOTE: Weekly sales demand at level of tier A is 20.
* Twice the demand of 20.

inventories, and the regional inventories feed the local ones. This kind of division can work quite well. However, if the decision rules for holding inventory are disjointed rather than coordinated, such a tiered system can lead to substantial swings in demand and somewhat higher levels of inventories than a completely coordinated system.

To illustrate what is meant, think of an inventory system of three tiers and each tier is mandated to hold 2 weeks' worth of demand. For a weekly demand of 20, then, the corresponding levels of inventory and orders on the next tier would look like Table 10-9. Note that in each tier the desired inventory is twice the weekly sales, and orders on the next tier proceed accordingly. Observe, however, what happens when demand falls by a single unit (5 percent) at the level of tier A (the local level) and stabilizes there (at 19). The period-by-period adjustments implied by the myopic decision rule of "hold 2 weeks' worth of sales in inventory" are traced in Table 10-10.

As the table shows, this tiered inventory system with its myopic replenishment rule takes four peri-

TABLE 10-10   Tiered Inventory System and Disjointed Decision Rules—
Reaction over Time to 5 Percent Demand Reduction

TIER	ITEM	PERIOD 0	PERIOD 1	PERIOD 2	PERIOD 3	PERIOD 4
A	Beginning inventory	40	40	38	38	38
	Sales	20	19	19	19	19
	Ending inventory	20	21	19	19	19
	Desired inventory	40	38	38	38	38
	Order on the next tier	20	17	19	19	19
B	Beginning inventory	40	40	34	38	38
	Sales	20	17	19	19	19
	Ending inventory	20	23	15	19	19
	Desired inventory	40	34	38	38	38
	Order on the next tier	20	11	23	19	19
C	Beginning inventory	40	40	29	46	38
	Sales	20	11	23	19	19
	Ending inventory	20	29	6	27	19
	Desired inventory	40	22	46	38	38
	Order on factory or to be absorbed by buffer stocks	20	0	40	11	19

ods to settle into a steady state. What is more, the orders placed on successive tiers become more and more erratic and vary wildly from period to period. When the initial demand reduction occurs, it is covered by the inventory already in the pipeline and no orders are placed on the factory. However, the pipeline's inventory is soon depleted and the next period's factory order is huge. This is an example of the "pipeline momentum" that can afflict a tiered inventory system or tiers of suppliers in a multilevel supply network. Not only does it cause great variability in period-by-period demands on each tier, but it can sometimes cause more inventory to be held, over time, than necessary.

Avoiding the whiplash of this pipeline momentum effect calls either for more coordination among the tiers (so that tier C can adjust immediately to the problems tier A is experiencing) or more foresight in the lower tiers (so that these tiers can anticipate the erratic demands that will be placed on them). In either case, avoiding the pipeline momentum effect means junking the myopia that is implied by a seemingly innocuous decision rule like "hold 2 weeks' worth of sales in inventory."

In any event, this pipeline momentum effect can be one more argument against a decentralization of warehousing or service centers.

PART FOUR
ORGANIZING THE MATERIALS FUNCTION

This chapter began by calling attention to the three major divisions of materials management: procurement, materials control (which includes both inventory control and production planning and control), and logistics. In traditionally organized companies, these three functions often report to three different department heads—procurement to a general manager, materials control to a manufacturing manager, and logistics to a marketing manager. In the last decade, however, con-

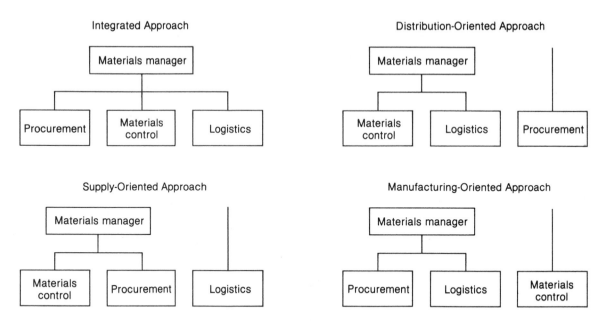

FIGURE 10-20   Four possible organization charts for materials management.

siderable organizational restructuring of the materials function has occurred, elevating the importance and visibility of the "materials manager" within the corporate organization.

Four organizational variants have emerged in many companies, and they seem to be about equally popular. Borrowing from Miller and Gilmour, these variants follow the organization charts depicted in Figure 10-20 and are labeled, respectively:[6]

- *Integrated approach.* All materials functions report to a single materials manager.
- *Supply-oriented approach.* The materials manager assumes authority over procurement and materials control, leaving logistics to report elsewhere.
- *Distribution-oriented approach.* The materials manager assumes authority over materials control and logistics, leaving procurement to report elsewhere.

- *Manufacturing-oriented approach.* The materials manager assumes authority over procurement and logistics, leaving materials control to report directly to a manufacturing manager.

The choice of organization appears very much to depend on the types of materials problems that the company is experiencing. If the problems straddle the traditional boundaries of procurement, materials control, and logistics, then it is much more likely that a materials manager will be assigned to oversee the functions in question. For example, if the company is having difficulty deciding how to balance inventory carrying costs against volume discounts from purchasing in quantity, a materials manager who oversees both procurement and materials control may help to resolve the issue. Similar types of problem overlaps across the traditional functional lines explain many of the recent materials management reorganizations that have been sweeping across the industrial landscape.

QUESTIONS

1. How does the situation at Dulaney Toy Company illustrate the main principles of procurement and the principles of a make-vs.-buy decision?

2. Outline clearly how the inventory needs of the job shop vary from those of the continuous flow process.

3. Compare and contrast the purpose and natures of the anticipatory and nonanticipatory approaches to inventory management.

4. What benefits may be derived from using a statistical approach to stock levels rather than a historical count approach? Outline the key concepts that are used in the statistical approach.

5. Of what value is the concept and application of the critical fractile model to a situation of demand uncertainty? What else is involved in deciding inventory level under demand uncertainty?

6. In what ways do the periodic reorder system and the reorder point system differ from each other? Be specific and use graphs where relevant.

7. "The key thing about the determination of an economic order quantity within a reorder point inventory system is not the formulas themselves." What, then, is the key determinant, and how is this determinant manifested in the example of the Gonder-Odell Manufacturing Company?

8. There are numerous elements that a material requirements planning system must continually keep track of. What are these, and how are they exemplified in the toy tractor-trailer inventory?

9. Review and summarize the fundamental steps in material requirements planning. Make sure you include the data requirements for computer files for such a system. What are some of the most common complications that can arise in such a system?

10. What are some of the factors that influence the decision whether to go with an MRP or a non–time-phased system? Give an example.

11. How can work-in-process inventories build up?

12. What are some of the advantages and disadvantages of a decentralized distribution strategy?

13. What are the most popular variants of organizing the materials function?

PROBLEMS

1. Joe Little has been assigned the task of designing and acquiring 12 engine oil containers for the Major Motors Corporation. The containers are to have a capacity of 110 gallons plus; they must be able to be moved by forklift trucks and to be stored on existing racks. The containers are needed to make the handling of the oil easier and the engine oil-fill operation more efficient. A preliminary analysis has indicated that the estimated cost savings will generate a payback within 6 months at most.

Joe's design requires only basic "metal bending" and welding processes, and these processes are part of the plant capacity of Major Motors. Joe has received bids from three external shops and has summarized them as follows:

Vendor	Cost per container	Delivery
1	$565	In 6 months
2	$578	Maybe in 2 months, but in 4 months for sure
3	$535	In 1 month, but this vendor has a reputation of not meeting delivery dates and of taking shortcuts

Joe's next step was to make an analysis of having the maintenance and machine shop departments fabricate the containers in-house. The following figures are the result:

Material	$294
Labor @ $7 per hour wages + $7 per hour fringes = $14 per hour to shear, bend, assemble, and weld; 3.5 hours for maintenance; and 6.5 hours for machine shop	140
Factory overhead @ 2.5 × direct labor = $17.50 per hour	175
Total per container	$609

His analysis also indicates that the maintenance workers can only be allowed to work on the containers in their spare time because their primary function is to keep the plant operating. The machine shop has a backlog of orders, but the necessary work can be squeezed in within the next month.

Analyze the various alternatives for Joe and discuss the various implications of the nonquantified information.

2. The Digital Watch Company has demand for the year of 1200 units. It has found that its average order cost is $9 per order and its carrying cost is $0.10 per unit per year. What is its economic order quantity?

3. Digital has found that it can order watchbands from an outside vendor on the following price schedule:

Order quantity	Price
500 or less	0.50
50l or more	0.45

With demand and cost information from problem 2, what is Digital's economic order quantity?

4. Digital's inventory manager has taken an introductory course in production/operations manage-ment and, given a recent increase in the banks' prime lending rate, now feels she can more accurately estimate carrying cost at 30 percent of the purchase price. From the information in problems 2 and 3, what is Digital's economic order quantity for watchbands?

5. Digital Watch has found that it can produce watchbands at a rate of 40 per week, and that demand is 24 per week (assuming 50 weeks). Digital's setup cost is $9 per run, and its carrying cost remains $0.10 per unit per year.
a. What is Digital's economic production quantity?
b. For how many weeks will Digital produce at a time?
c. How many production runs will be made in a year?
d. What is Digital's maximum inventory?
e. What is Digital's average inventory?

6. Given the following information on watches, derive the planned orders for watchbands, using lot-for-lot order sizing.

Watches

Period: 1 2 3 4 5 6 7 8 9 10
Demand: 10 20 40 0 50 30 30 40 50 30
On-hand inventory: 50 units at the beginning of period 1
Outstanding orders: 30 units to arrive at the beginning of period 3
Lead time: one period

Watchbands

Usage: one per watch
On-hand inventory: 0
Outstanding order: 0
Lead time: two periods

7. Information on product A is shown in Figure 10-A and Tables 10-A and 10-B. Using this information and lot for lot as the order sizing rule, derive the planned orders for part F.

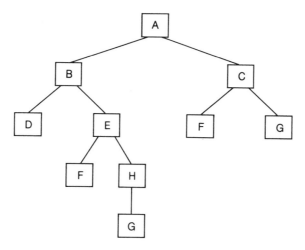

FIGURE 10-A Components of product A.

TABLE 10-A Factors in the Production of Product A (Problem 7)

ITEM	LEAD TIME (weeks)	HOW MANY USED	ON-HAND INVENTORY
A			40
B	2	1	30
C	3	2	60
D	2	1	80
E	3	1	50
F	2	2 (1 in E, 1 in C)	30
G	1	2 (1 in C, 1 in H)	20
H	1	1	10

TABLE 10-B Master Schedule for Product A (Problem 7)

WEEK	REQUIREMENT	WEEK	REQUIREMENT
1	20	11	20
2	40	12	50
3	10	13	40
4	30	14	0
5	25	15	10
6	30	16	20
7	15	17	15
8	0	18	45
9	80	19	0
10	30	20	30

SITUATION FOR STUDY

TIFFANY TIRE COMPANY

George Blimpo has recognized that his distribution operation is consistently carrying too much inventory. He wonders whether he can reduce that inventory by implementing some sort of inventory system.

Tiffany Tire Company is a small midwestern distributor of radial tires. It is composed of three retail outlets and one warehouse. The warehouse buys its supply of tires directly from the factory and supplies only the three retail outlets. Also, the

TABLE 10-C   Demand for Tires
(Tiffany Tire Company)

MONTH	DEALER 1	DEALER 2	DEALER 3
January	400	600	500
February	300	800	400
March	200	400	900
April	600	300	600
May	800	500	200
June	600	300	600
July	300	400	800
August	200	500	800
September	400	600	500
October	350	650	500
November	250	350	900
December	600	600	300

TABLE 10-D   Inventory Costs
(Tiffany Tire Company)

DEALER	ORDER COST	CARRYING COST (per tire per year)	LEAD TIME (months)
1	$90	$1.60	1
2	45	2.20	1
3	60	0.90	1
Warehouse	150	0.75	2

three dealers buy only from Tiffany's warehouse.

Table 10-C shows last year's demand for tires, by month, for the three dealers. As you can see, demand has remained fairly constant over the last three years. The variations in demand are random rather than seasonal or part of a trend.

Table 10-D shows the results of a study done last year to determine inventory costs for the dealers and the warehouse. The differences in cost are due to the locations of the dealers and the warehouse.

For example, Dealer 2 is located in downtown Detroit and the cost of renting storage space is much higher than it is in Mt. Vernon, Illinois, where Dealer 3 is located. Also, the dealers have higher carrying costs than the warehouse because of the transfer pricing policies of Tiffany; the dealers are paying a higher price per tire than the warehouse. A similar explanation could be given for the differences in order cost.

George expects that the demand and cost estimates shown in these two tables are representative of what will happen in the future.

What would you recommend that George do to develop a new inventory system for the dealers and the warehouse, given that the existing system is just an educated guess?

REFERENCE NOTES

1. Good sources of additional information on nonanticipatory approaches include Elwood S. Buffa and Jeffrey G. Miller, *Production-Inventory Systems: Planning and Control*, 3rd ed. (Homewood, Ill.: Richard D. Irwin, 1979), particularly Chapter 4; George W. Plossl and Oliver W. Wight, *Production and Inventory Control: Principles and Techniques* (Englewood Cliffs, N.J.: Prentice-Hall, 1967), particularly Chapters 3–5.

2. The current bible on MRP is Joseph Orlicky, *Material Requirements Planning* (New York: McGraw-Hill, 1975).

3. A good discussion of many of the points about implementing an MRP system is found in Robert W. Hall and Thomas E. Vollman, "Planning Your Material Requirements," *Harvard Business Review* 56, no. 5 (September–October 1978), pp. 105–12.

4. For additional information on logistics, see James L. Heskett, Nicholas A. Glaskowesky, Jr., and Robert M. Ivie, *Business Logistics: Physical Distribution and Materials Management*, 2d ed. (New York: Ronald Press, 1973).

5. An issue related to mode choice is the determination of when deliveries ought to be expedited, perhaps by using a faster, more expensive mode of transportation. See D. P. Herron, "Managing Physical Distribution for Profit," *Harvard Business Review* 57, no. 3 (May–June 1979), pp. 121–32.

6. Jeffrey G. Miller and Peter Gilmour, "The Emerging Materials Manager," working paper 79-17 of the Graduate School of Business Administration, Harvard University (January 1979).

11

PLANNING AND CONTROLLING PRODUCTION

The six plant tours of the first segment of this text have already provided some insight into how the issue of what to produce and when is resolved in different kinds of processes and how production is monitored and controlled. There are wide variations in the means by which such decisions are made and transmitted. A quick review of key planning and control features of our selected production processes is in order.

1. Job shop (Norcen Industries). Mix of products and due dates is in perpetual flux. Production to order is done without firm knowledge of what future orders will be. What is on the shop floor at any one time is a function of which orders are released to the shop and how the foreman schedules them. The schedule is heavily influenced by due dates. At best, the foreman decides on a firm schedule only about a day in advance. Complications and bottlenecks are encountered continually, demanding rescheduling. Reaction can be immediate. Overtime is frequent; there is a skeleton second shift. The foreman is responsible for following up production and for overseeing quality. The workforce is also relied on heavily for monitoring quality. Formal quality checks are done typically at the end of the process and on a sample of production only.

2. Batch flow (Jung Products). Production is geared to the replenishment of the finished goods inventory; in effect, one week's production is largely determined by the previous week's demand. Although there is some idea of longer term demands, the planned production schedule is repeatedly interrupted. The production system can respond in a matter of hours. There is occasional overtime, but no second shift work. Quality control is largely the responsibility of supervisory personnel and the workers themselves.

3. Worker-paced line flow (Burger King). This service type of production process has remarkable flexibility. Production is done to order, but the general pattern of demand is known statistically in advance and preparation is geared to that forecast. Routing of the product through the process is fixed. The restaurant is staffed to match expected variations in the time pattern of demand. Quality control is largely the responsibility of supervisory personnel and the workers themselves.

4. Machine-paced line flow (GM Assembly Division). Production is done to order, but the pro-

cess is only somewhat elastic and cannot stretch to fill all orders with the same lead time. Long-term demand can be estimated and used to set the speed of the line and to guide suppliers. There are two production shifts each weekday. Variations in demand are usually dealt with through overtime; longer term change can argue for extra shifts or line rebalance. Lead times vary from 1 week to 5, with the assembly schedule frozen 5 days ahead of time. A complex and sophisticated materials function tracks the flow of materials to plant in order to assure meeting the schedule. Quality is a constant concern for workers and supervisory personnel. Random samples are taken daily and analyzed by a separate quality control group.

5. Continuous flow (International Paper's Androscoggin Mill). Rigid 4-week planning cycle. Great care is taken in matching specific products to machines. Long runs are sought. The mill runs round the clock, every day. Scheduling is done to leave little or no waste and to avoid additional handling of rolls of paper. The schedule is frozen at least 5 days prior to the run. Quality is greatly influenced by machine operation and is constantly monitored.

6. Hybrid (batch/continuous flow) process (Schlitz-Syracuse). The brewing portion of the process is planned to a forecast, while canning and bottling are done to specific wholesaler order. Modest adjustments are made to some wholesalers' initial timing requests. Lead time is generally 2 to 6 weeks. The schedule is fixed as to labor 1 week in advance, but as to packaging only 1 day in advance. The extent of shift work varies with the level of demand and its seasonality, but the brewery is designed for a three-shift operation. A multitude of quality checks are made, largely by sample taking; sophisticated procedures and specially trained personnel are involved.

As this brief review clearly reveals, these six examples share several common features in production planning and control, but they differ on several as well. The remainder of this chapter is devoted to a more detailed discussion of the aspects of planning and control that these six process examples have introduced.

The material in this chapter is divided into two major topics of interest: planning and monitoring a production schedule, and controlling the process and quality. Each will be addressed in turn.

PART ONE

PLANNING AND MONITORING A PRODUCTION SCHEDULE

FACTORS IN THE DESIGN OF PRODUCTION PLANS

For all of these different kinds of processes the planning goals are much the same: match the workforce and materials to the available equipment and technology so as to meet deliveries of the entire range of the product mix offered at low cost. Where the processes differ is in how this broad goal is translated into more specific policies.

MEETING DELIVERY

In all six of the processes described in Segment I, there was a sincere desire to produce to exact customer specifications and to ship precisely when the customer indicated. This goal was not fully achievable in all of the processes because of some inherent constraints. In those that did achieve this goal, various policies were adopted.

Production to customer order and timely delivery were best achieved at Burger King, Jung Products, and Norcen Industries. It is not surprising that these processes were the best performers on this criterion, since they all lie toward the job shop end of the process spectrum and are more apt to view their strengths as lying in customer service. Yet, their customer service was outstanding because of three different policies of production planning:

- *Modulating capacity.* At the Malden Burger King, timely delivery of the customer's precise order is assured by continually modulating the restaurant's capacity so that it is not swamped by the lunch and dinner peak hours. Capacity is adjusted by altering the size of the workforce and by continually rebalancing the restaurant's "assembly line." Modulated capacity is a common production planning policy in service industries since many services cannot be inventoried and so demands must be met primarily by adjusting capacity.

  Jung Products and Norcen Industries also employed this policy of modulating capacity to meet their delivery demands although in the more prosaic form of scheduling overtime for their workers.

- *Inventory buffers.* Jung Products filled its orders out of the finished goods inventory it held in its warehouse. Individual products were not customized, but the orders that the company handled could be vastly different. Jung Products maintained its high level of customer service by adopting a production planning policy that geared production to the maintenance of a finished goods inventory large enough to buffer the company against erratic demand patterns.

- *Managing demand.* In trying to assure the timely delivery of its customized products,

Norcen Industries could act both directly and indirectly. Scheduling overtime was a direct action it could take to expand its capacity. Alternatively, by adjusting the level of its bid on any order, Norcen Industries could indirectly, and more imperfectly, control the load on the shop and thus the shop's ability to deliver on time. In effect, Norcen Industries could manage demand. In times of high demand on capacity, its bids for business could be on the high side to help choke off the business it would have trouble delivering on time; similarly, in times of excess capacity, it could lower its bids and hope to draw in more business.

The other processes described — International Paper's Androscoggin Mill, GM Assembly Division-Tarrytown, and Schlitz's Syracuse brewery — all did a superb job of meeting their customer orders, but their inflexibilities sometimes constrained delivery. For example, Schlitz and GMAD-Tarrytown sometimes had to defer production for a particular order until room appeared in the schedule. The time deferred was never particularly long, usually a week or two; but these delivery dislocations were an inevitable consequence of the rigidity within the process itself.

To cite another example, if the demand for paper were particularly strong, delivery simply could not be made. Carrying spare pulp and paper capacity is an increasingly expensive undertaking, and so the capacity utilization of pulp and paper mills is generally high to begin with. A peak demand situation, such as described in Chapter 1, is likely, then, to imply a rationing of paper to customers.

IDENTIFYING THE SCARCE RESOURCE

In almost all cases, the match of the workforce and materials to the available equipment and technology (discussed above as part of the goal of production planning) cannot be perfect. Either the workforce will be the scarce resource and idle equipment will exist, or equipment will be the scarce resource and idle workers will exist. What the scarce resource is has a critical impact on how production is planned. Is the production plan designed to keep the equipment loaded (long production runs), or is it designed to keep the workforce busy (perhaps through many setups and shorter production runs)?

Since more workers can generally be added to any process, production plan design is essentially concerned with the economics of the process. Is equipment relatively cheaper to hold idle than labor, or is the reverse true? The question is easy to state, but in practice it may be very difficult to answer. On the one hand, it is easy to see why a company like International Paper devotes its talent to a careful scheduling of all the paper machines it owns; an unnecessarily idle paper machine costs the company a bundle in forgone revenues (the opportunity cost is high). On the other hand, it stands to reason that a job shop like Norcen Industries would house a number of machine tools that would lie idle a good deal of the time. Some machines have specialized uses and remain idle for that reason, while others can pay for themselves by being used strictly for sporadic in-tandem jobs with another machine or for breaking chronic bottlenecks. At Norcen Industries at least, holding equipment idle is cheaper than holding labor idle; production planning could call for a schedule of short runs if they would lead to on-time delivery and fewer bottlenecks.

These two examples are polar cases. In between is a sea of gray. For many largely batch and line flow processes it is not always clear whether it is cheaper to hold idle some equipment or some labor, and thus whether the long production run is to be valued above a series of smaller runs. The decision depends on factors such as the costs of equipment, labor, inventory carrying, and inventory stockouts, and on production speeds and prices. We shall return to this point later.

IDENTIFYING THE VALUED ASPECT OF THE PRODUCT OR SERVICE

If the full range of a company's product mix cannot be produced on time, which of the product mix ought to be produced? The production plan should be sensitive to those products or services that earn more contibution per unit of time or per unit of some other scarce resource. Production plans, particularly at the end of a month, quarter, or year, are often weighted heavily toward high contribution items or toward those that can easily be completed and billed. In many companies, the great end-of-month scramble to push product out the door is a scramble to push out the "winners," leaving poorer selling or poorer earning products until the next month. This kind of scheduling, of course, is more prevalent in job shop and batch flow processes; the more inflexible processes follow more rigid production plans.

An important management task is identifying how planning and scheduling can help gain or sustain high levels of contribution. Recent planning and scheduling in the airline industry is a good case in point. Prior to the deregulation of the airlines in the late 1970s and the subsequent boom in air traffic, airline load factors were not as high. The schedule of flights was used as a weapon to attract travelers; the prevailing wisdom was to schedule flights to be as convenient as possible, even if it meant cutting back on the time airplanes were scheduled to be in the air. Given the prevailing modes of competition, the valued aspect of the service was convenient time slots in the major city markets each airline served. The airlines that could provide the most convenient departure and arrival times were seen as high earning ones.

With deregulation and the significant price declines that ensued, the mode of competition shifted from convenience to price. Load factors shot up, and the valued aspect of the service became airplane seats at low prices, not convenient times. There were travelers who demanded plane travel at every hour of the day, not merely at convenient hours. Airline planning and scheduling adjusted. Schedules were revised to lengthen the time airplanes were in the air, even if it meant some modestly inconvenient departure or arrival times for passengers. With the scheduling adjustments, airline profits (contribution per unit of scarce resource) shot up dramatically.

MATERIALS

All processes require that the necessary materials be available for use in the product at the right time. What differs among processes is how materials are meshed with various steps in each process. In continuous flow and machine-paced line flow processes, the product cycle times are fixed and materials can be tightly scheduled, to mesh with the production plan, if in fact their delivery is reliable. The automobile assembly plant is the classic example of the tight coupling of materials and the production plan. With less rigid job shop and batch flow processes, the coordination of production plan and materials to within days of one another is less feasible and also less desirable. Such processes should exploit their flexibility; lock-step synchronization of materials to the production plan would only rob these processes of their ability successfully to alter the production plan on extremely short notice.

We have already discussed material requirements planning systems that are designed expressly to couple materials movements with a frozen production plan. Other, statistical inventory systems could be employed as well, but generally they function best when close coordination of materials with the production plan is not required, such as at Jung Products, Inc.

Decoupling Inventories

The Schlitz brewery, which has been identified as a hybrid batch/continuous flow process, is intriguing precisely because it mixes materials and production planning systems. The brewing portion of the process is triggered by a sales forecast; raw materials inventories are not managed by strict material requirements planning but rather by more traditional, statistical means. The packaging portion of the process, on the other hand, is triggered by actual orders; the major materials used are managed by what is essentially an MRP system.

What permits the brewery the luxury of being able to plan production and manage materials in two different ways is the existence of an inventory of beer that separates the brewing process from the packaging process. This inventory "decouples" one from the other. Without an inventory that functions in this manner, the packaging portion of the process would have to be geared to the sales forecast and not actual orders, and the brewery would probably have to store more beer in finished goods inventory, at higher cost, than it does now. Incentives would also be introduced to lock wholesalers into longer lead time orders than is now the case.

The key advantage of such a decoupling inventory is that it breaks up the information and materials management needs of the entire process into pieces that can be managed more easily on their own. There is a cost, of course, since the inventory must be financed, but the cost can often be substantially less than the introduction of process-wide MRP systems or financing increased finished goods inventories.

The peak demand period at the Malden Burger King offers another example of a decoupling inventory. There, as demand builds up, the information that triggers the meat patty broiling operation shifts from the call-in of orders to the maintenance of a work-in-process inventory of broiled meat and toasted buns. This intermediate inventory is a decoupling one that is very effective in speeding up service and in keeping all of Burger King's sandwiches freshly made.

Materials Handling

There are two common philosophies of controlling the handling of materials through a process. One is to supply fixed work stations with parts and other materials. This philosophy prevails in line flow and continuous flow processes. The other philosophy "picks" the appropriate parts from inventory at the beginning and places them into "kits," which then are assembled into products. Under the former philosophy, the management challenge is to keep abreast of the materials' inventory status at each work station. Under the latter philosophy, the challenge is to avoid the pilfering of completed kits for parts that have shown up "short" in products being worked on elsewhere in the process. Procedures for identifying short parts and for expediting their acquisition under either of these philosophies are needed; systems for detection and for coordination with purchasing and inventory control must be developed.

ESTABLISHING A PRODUCTION SCHEDULE[1]

The production schedule must reflect orders actually booked or those expected, as determined by a forecast.* Some day-to-day or week-to-week leeway is permitted in the schedule; it is the job of the production scheduler to use this leeway in devising a production schedule that places as balanced a demand on the process as possible. This means that the scheduler must be thoroughly aware of the capacities of each segment of the process and where any bottlenecks are likely to show up. This kind of knowledge often leads a scheduler to concoct rules of thumb that help develop a schedule that is feasible, balanced, and reasonably low cost. In some of the processes described earlier, several such rules of thumb were mentioned:

- Schedule autos of the same color together.
- Space out along the line those autos with special features requiring overcycle production.

---

*Forecasting will be addressed in Chapter 12.

- Do not schedule more than one dining room set per week through the furniture factory.

The production schedule must also reflect materials availabilities. In the interest of clarity and order on the factory floor itself, it is generally unwise to release an order whose component parts have not yet arrived or to release an order just to "get it moving" through the process. In both of these situations, work-in-process inventories build up; as discussed in the previous chapter, excessive work-in-process is too often disruptive and time-consuming to manage. Often companies are better off risking that some of their workers may be temporarily idled by a lack of work on the floor than they would be purposefully littering the floor with work-in-process. The hidden costs of work-in-process–induced inefficiencies are often greater than the highly visible costs of idle labor.

In some processes (notably continuous flow ones), the payoff from proper scheduling is so great that much care is taken in devising the schedule. Often this means using sophisticated mathematical techniques, such as mathematical programming and simulation, to establish the schedule rather than the more common trial-and-error procedures that guide most production schedules. As we saw, these kinds of advanced (and expensive) techniques were used by International Paper's operations control scheduling staff.

At least with such continuous flow processes, mathematical techniques have proved successful in establishing a desirable schedule. But, by all accounts the most difficult scheduling task is to schedule a job shop. Fine minds have spun their wheels for years trying to devise decision rules and scheduling procedures that job shops could successfully adopt. A number of such decision rules— work on the shortest time jobs first, work on the oldest job first, work first on the job with the closest due date, work first on the job with the most successor operations, and others—have been tested. What is apparent from all the testing is simply the intuitively appealing notion that there is an inherent conflict in a job shop between getting all the orders done on time and spending the least amount of shop time actually working on those orders. It is tough for a shop to be both smooth and timely. No one rule stands out as clearly optimal although some simulation techniques have helped load particularly large job shops. Job shop scheduling will continue to attract considerable operations research, although the smart money is still betting that the problem will continue to elude solution.

While we may be forced to acknowledge that good job shop scheduling is a gradually acquired skill, the production schedules of a good many other processes are amenable to more deliberate, and mathematical, analysis. Since so much of the planning and control of operations begins with and revolves around the production schedule, it is worthwhile discussing how it can be created in many processes and what criteria separate good schedules from bad. To focus this discussion, consider Situation 11-1.

SITUATION 11-1

RIDGELY SPORTING GOODS COMPANY, LEATHER GOODS DEPARTMENT

The Leather Goods Department of the Ridgely Sporting Goods Company manufactured two major products: baseball gloves and hockey gloves. By far the larger selling item was baseball gloves. The market for them was fairly stable, tending to follow population growth trends. Recently, the modest drop in the birth rate had been compensated for by a rise in sales to girls. Sales of hockey gloves were localized predominantly in the Northeast, the upper Midwest, and Canada. The market for these gloves was only about a fifth the size of the baseball market but was growing at about 5 percent a year.

Sales of each type of glove naturally paralleled the sport's season, although sales were greater just before and just after the start of each season. For baseball gloves in particular, the Christmas season was

also a strong sales period. The forecast for the 9 months beginning in July is given in Table 11-1. The factory had to be sure that the company's distributors were fully stocked with gloves about 2 months before the season's official start in April for baseball and in November for hockey. Operationally, this timetable meant that a third of the department's forecast sales for this 9-month period had to be produced by the first week in February (baseball) and September (hockey).

The baseball gloves were easier to manufacture, requiring roughly 45 minutes of labor per glove. The hockey gloves took about 2 hours per pair. The average factory variable costs of the gloves were $17 (baseball) and $40 (hockey).

The department liked to keep the production rate steady over the course of the year since hiring and

TABLE 11-1   Forecast of Sales by Product Line, July–March
(Ridgely Sporting Goods Company, Leather Goods Department)

PRODUCT LINE	JULY	AUG.	SEPT.	OCT.	NOV.	DEC.	JAN.	FEB.	MARCH	TOTAL
Baseball gloves (units)	4000	3000	2500	1000	500	5000	2000	4000	7000	29,000
Hockey gloves (pairs)	100	100	700	1600	2000	1900	1450	1200	1400	10,450

NOTE: Each month has four weeks of production.

then laying off workers was disturbing and expensive. Layoffs cost the company $400 per worker in severance pay and hiring cost, $50 per worker in out-of-pocket expenses, and 2 weeks of inefficient productivity (an average of 50 percent of standard) while the new hire was trained. Recalls of previously laid-off workers cost only half of the new hire expense. Worker pay plus fringes averaged $8 per hour. Adding a second shift to the factory was possible, but it meant an additional 15 percent wage hike per worker to institute, in addition to the new hires such an action would generate.

There were no readily identifiable costs in changing over from the production of one type of glove to another. However, given the many variations in the basic styles of each type of glove, it was considered too confusing to make both baseball and hockey gloves at the same time. Thus, separate days were generally allotted to each kind of glove. A finished goods inventory was used to smooth out the demand on the factory. The inventory carrying cost rate was determined to be 20 percent.

The Leather Goods Department was in the process of planning production for the next 9 months to meet forecasted demand. Maintaining at all times an inventory equal to 100 percent of current monthly demand was considered prudent. To facilitate planning, the work weeks were grouped into fours and labeled with the months in which most of the production occurred. The inventories of gloves were 6500 (baseball) and 700 (hockey). At present, also, there were 26 workers in the department.

RIDGELY SPORTING GOODS — GENERAL DISCUSSION

As we can tell from the situation at Ridgely Sporting Goods, developing the master production schedule means deciding how much capacity the factory should gear up for over the short term and how that capacity should be realized. At some point, the factory must commit itself to meeting the sales forecast or some other agreed-to pattern of shipments. But, generally speaking, it can accomplish this task in several ways:

1. *Chasing demand.* The factory can raise and lower its production rate so that it produces only as much of each item as it expects to ship that month. If forecasted sales vary greatly, such a "demand chase" strategy will generally entail a good deal of (a) overtime and/or (b) layoffs and recalls or new hiring.

2. *Leveling production.* Under this alternative, no changes in the workforce size or overtime policy are planned over the planning period. All variations in shipments are absorbed by a finished goods inventory. Thus, over the planning period, inventory is built up and depleted on a regular, planned basis.

3. *A combination approach.* A pure "chase" strategy and a pure "level" strategy are extreme, polar cases. In between lies a whole range of cases where some chasing of demand and some leveling of production occur.

No matter what the strategy, developing a master schedule involves decisions on a number of important issues and data from a variety of sources. Among them:

- Decisions
  a. Desired inventory levels by production period (e.g., a month)
  b. Desired workforce levels by production period
  c. Desired levels of overtime by production period
  d. Desired mix and pattern of production, by product and by production period
- Data
  a. Reliability of the short-term forecast of sales in each product line
  b. Current capacity of the operation, by product line
  c. Cost and productivity of overtime
  d. Cost and productivity of second or third shift operation

e. Cost of layoff, hiring, and recall of the workforce

f. Cost of carrying finished goods inventory

g. A sense of how rapidly adjustments can be made in the product mix produced, which has an impact on the size of any buffer stocks

h. Costs and difficulties of shifting work among different products

The process of developing the production schedules which the factory follows and by which it tries to control operations takes several stages. The transition through these stages occurs as sales become more and more certain and as details are learned about the quantities to be manufactured of product lines, products, models, and variations like color and extras. The scheduling process begins with rough approximations; generally, months later firmer and firmer numbers take hold. The initial approximation is termed the "aggregate plan" since the plant, at that stage, deals only in aggregates of workers, product models, and even products themselves. Over time, as sales forecasts become firmer, the aggregate plan can be refined and detail added to yield a "master schedule." The master schedule is an important document since it triggers actions such as workforce assignments, personnel actions, and more detailed materials flows. Even more detailed production schedules, which can sequence and synchronize the work of the factory, are derived (again with even firmer information) from the master schedule.

ATTACKING THE MASTER SCHEDULE AT
RIDGELY SPORTING GOODS

What we need to do is to determine how many baseball and hockey gloves the company ought to produce each month and the corresponding size of the workforce, inventory levels, and overtime levels, given that the forecast of Table 11-1 must be met. A more detailed schedule would indicate the precise mix of catcher's mitts, first base gloves, and fielding gloves in which style, model (e.g., Rod Carew autograph), and variation (right- or left-handed) to be produced, and on which days. Our present task, of course, is not so detailed, but it involves the same type of thinking.

The first task is to decide whether a chase or a level strategy should guide our thinking. If holding inventory is cheap relative to the costs of overtime, laying off, recalling, and/or hiring, then a level production strategy is recommended. If, on the other hand, inventory cannot be held or is costly relative to such personnel actions, a chase demand strategy becomes attractive. How costly then is inventory holding and the various personnel actions?

- Holding inventory
  1. At a carrying cost rate of 20 percent, a baseball glove costs $3.40 per year, on the average, to hold in inventory (0.20 · $17 variable cost), or about 28¢ per month.
  2. Carrying a hockey glove is more expensive— $8 per glove per year or about 67¢ per month.
- Personnel actions
  1. Layoffs cost $400.
  2. New hires cost $50 out-of-pocket plus the equivalent of one week's wages, which amounts to $320. The total new hire cost is $370. Recalls cost only $185.
  3. A second shift's labor bill would cost 115 percent of the first shift.
  4. Overtime costs are 150 percent of first shift labor costs.

With these data as background, it is useful to ask questions like the following in gauging the extent to which a chase or a level strategy should be followed:

- How long would you be willing to keep a worker on the job (thus producing units of output that have to be carried for some time) rather than lay off the worker now and recall him or her later?
- At what point would the cost of having the existing workers work overtime give way to hir-

TABLE 11-2   Inventory Accumulation over Time
(Ridgely Sporting Goods Company, Leather Goods Department)

	MONTH 1	MONTH 2	MONTH 3	MONTH 4
Worker production	80	80	80	80
Inventory built up	80	160	240	320
Accumulated inventory— months to finance	80	240	480	800
Inventory costs at 67¢/month/unit	$53.60	$160.80	$321.60	$536.00

ing another worker, or indeed, hiring an entire second shift?

Questions such as these are difficult to answer definitively since they often involve many hidden contingencies. For example, the perceived need for 300 more units of output 6 months from now may be met by having one worker work for 6 months, by having two workers work for 3 months each, by having three workers work for 2 months each, or some similar choice. It is difficult to analyze all of the situations conceivable, and each has its own cost.

Nevertheless, some reasonably straightforward calculations can provide some insight into the relative attractiveness of chase and level strategies. In trying to answer the first question alone, we can calculate a break-even point where the inventory carrying costs incurred by keeping a worker on the job just equal the hire and recall costs. Suppose a worker can produce 80 hockey gloves in a month. Over time the inventory grows as Table 11-2 indicates. Inventory is built up according to an arithmetic progression whereby 80 gloves are added each month. The accumulated inventory is simply the sum of this arithmetic progression, which fortunately has an easy formula:

$$\text{Sum} = \frac{n}{2}(a + l) = \frac{n}{2}[80 + n(80)]$$

where n is the number of months, a is the first inventory value, and l is the last inventory value.

We can use this formula to solve for the break-even value of n that equates inventory carrying costs with the layoff and recall costs involving a single worker.

$$(.67) \quad \cdot \left\{ \frac{n}{2}[80 + n(80)] \right\} \quad = \quad 400 \quad + \quad 185$$

(inventory · (sum of inventory = (layoff + (recall
carrying   months to finance)   expense)   expense)
cost per
month)

Working out this break-even value involves solving a quadratic equation for a positive root using the quadratic formula,

$$\frac{-b \pm \sqrt{b^2 - 4ac}}{2a}$$

In this instance, the solution yields a break-even value of n of 4.2 months. Thus, it takes 4.2 months of inventory accumulation before the costs of carrying that inventory outweigh the expenses of laying off and then recalling a worker. This calculation is helpful in that it confirms the view that the company should not lay off workers at the first seasonal downturn in hockey glove sales. Only if the sales drop is persistent would it be less costly to lay off some workers. What is more, if demand is high once it turns up, having accumulated so much inventory would be advantageous since many workers would have to be hired to produce a lot in a short time.

TABLE 11-3   Trial Master Production Schedule
(Ridgely Sporting Goods Company, Leather Goods Department)

PRODUCT LINE	JULY	AUG.	SEPT.	OCT.	NOV.	DEC.	JAN.	FEB.	MARCH	APRIL
Baseball Gloves										
Sales target	4000	3000	2500	1000	500	5000	2000	4000	7000	
Production	4800	0	3200	3200	0	6400	4800	3200	4800	
Starting inventory	6500	7300	4300	5000	7200	6700	8100	10,900	10,100	7900
Hockey Gloves										
Sales target	100	100	700	1600	2000	1900	1450	1200	1400	
Production	600	2400	1200	1200	2400	0	640	1280	680	
Starting inventory	700	1200	3500	4000	3600	4000	2100	1290	1370	650
Workforce	30	30	30	30	30	30	30.5	31	31	

Total cost of this schedule = $383,737

Production rates:	Baseball gloves—Given 30 workers, 6400 per month
	Hockey gloves—Given 30 workers, 2400 per month
	These rates, as well as the trial schedule, ignore the start-up inefficiencies of the four newly hired workers. However, these amount only to a total of 213.33 baseball gloves or 80 pairs of hockey gloves.
Inventory goals:	Baseball gloves—9667 in February
	Hockey gloves—3483 in September

It should be emphasized that this break-even calculation is meant only to suggest the relative advantages of a chase versus a level production strategy. The calculation ignores the costs of carrying inventory past the break-even point as well as the extra costs involved in hiring many new workers to build up production in a hurry to the level of the inventory being carried.

With similar logic, however, some crude trade-offs between various other personnel actions (e.g., overtime, second shift) and inventory holding can be evaluated as well.

THE TRIAL AND ERROR OF MASTER SCHEDULE DEVELOPMENT

Having established, in rough fashion, the relative attractiveness of a level production strategy for Ridgely Sporting Goods, we need to develop a master production schedule that satisfies the sales forecast and the other suggested constraints such as (1) inventories a third of the total 9-month sales in the relevant months (September for hockey, February for baseball), and (2) inventories at the beginning of the month large enough to cover all of that month's demand.

Table 11-3 is a first trial at matching production to these requirements. It is based in part on the workforce needs implied by the sales forecast of Table 11-1 (as depicted in Table 11-4). The trial master schedule begins by hiring four more workers immediately to bring the workforce to 30 workers; one more hockey glove worker is hired midway through January to bring ending inventory for hockey gloves to within 50 of July's starting level. In most months, both baseball and hockey gloves are produced and no overtime is employed. The inventory goals—9667 baseball gloves by February 1 and 3483 pairs of hockey gloves by September 1—are met easily, as is the goal of having starting inventory greater than the month's expected sales.

The cost of this master production schedule is $383,737, broken down as follows:

TABLE 11-4 Workforce Levels Implied by the Sales Forecast
(Ridgely Sporting Goods Company, Leather Goods Department)

PRODUCT LINE	JULY	AUG.	SEPT.	OCT.	NOV.	DEC.	JAN.	FEB.	MARCH	TOTAL
Baseball gloves (units)	18.75	14.06	11.72	4.69	2.34	23.44	9.38	18.75	32.81	135.94
Hockey gloves (pairs)	1.25	1.25	8.75	20.00	25.00	23.75	18.13	15.00	17.50	130.63
Total	20.00	15.31	20.47	24.69	27.34	47.19	27.51	33.75	50.31	266.57
Average workforce level implied for all previous months	20.00	17.66	18.59	20.12	21.56	25.83	26.07	27.03	29.62	

Worker wages:	30 workers • 9 months • $1280/month + 1 worker • 2.5 months • $1280/month	= $348,800
Hiring costs:	5 workers • $370	= 1,850
Inventory carrying:	$.28 • 66,100 inventory unit-months (baseball)	= 18,508
	$.67 • 21,760 inventory unit-months (hockey)	= 14,579
		$383,737

No doubt some dollars can be whittled off this cost figure by investigating alternative hiring patterns and production patterns by product and by month. Successive trial-and-error schedules would consider such alternatives and compare them against this first trial effort. Many actual master production schedules are derived by just such trial-and-error means. Stability of the product mix and/or sales levels over time is naturally helpful in this search for better and better master schedules.

"OPTIMAL" AND "NEAR-OPTIMAL" AGGREGATE PLANS AND MASTER SCHEDULES

To this point, we have used common sense and trial-and-error to devise aggregate plans and more detailed master schedules. As with almost any trial-and-error approach to problem solving, one always suspects that "a better way" must exist, or a way that guarantees some "optimal" solution. In the case of the Ridgely Sporting Goods Company,

we cannot help but think that a lower cost means of meeting all the shipping and inventory requirements exists.

In the schedule development for Ridgely Sporting Goods, what costs should be minimized and what constraints must be satisfied? We have already talked about them, but it is helpful to state them more formally. In essence the costs of the plan that we want to minimize include wage costs, inventory carrying costs, and costs of hiring and laying off workers; the constraints that we want to satisfy include the inventory targets for each month, some reasonable expectations on how much overtime can be worked, and some more prosaic requirements such as how many units of which product line can be produced in any month and how inventory and the workforce can be added to or subtracted from. To be even more formal about the Ridgely Sporting Goods situation, we seek to minimize

$(1280W_1 + 1280W_2 + \cdots + 1280W_9$ (Regular shift wage costs since W_t is the level of the month's workforce and $1280 is monthly pay per worker)

$+ 1920OT_1 + 1920OT_2 + \cdots + 1920OT_9$ (Overtime wage costs since OT_t is the level of overtime worked on a monthly basis and $1920 is the cost of a month's worth of overtime)

$+ .28BI_1 + .28BI_2$
$+ \cdots + .28BI_9$

(Inventory carrying costs for baseball gloves since 28¢ is the carrying cost per month for baseball gloves and BI_t is the stock of baseball gloves carried each month)

$+ .67HI_1 + .67HI_2$
$+ \cdots + .67HI_9$

(Inventory carrying costs for hockey gloves since 67¢ is the monthly carrying cost and HI_t is the stock of hockey gloves carried each month)

$+ 370WFI_1 + 370WFI_2$
$+ \cdots + 370WFI_9$

(Costs of increasing the workforce since it costs $370 for each new hire. WFI_t is the size of the workforce increase in each month.)

$+ 400WFD_1 + 400WFD_2$
$+ \cdots + 400WFD_9)$

(Costs of laying off workers since each layoff costs $400. WFD_t is the size of the workforce decrease in each month.)

subject to the following constraints:

1. The following variables must all be greater than or equal to zero for all months t where t can range from 1 to 9

$$W_t, OT_t, BI_t, HI_t, WFI_t, WFD_t, BP_t, \text{ and } HP_t \geq 0$$

where

W_t = workforce in month t
OT_t = overtime in month t
BI_t = baseball glove inventory in month t
HI_t = hockey glove inventory in month t
WFI_t = workforce increase in month t
WFD_t = workforce decrease in month t
BP_t = baseball glove production in month t
HP_t = hockey glove production in month t

2. Regular workforce hours and overtime hours are composed of those devoted to baseball glove production and those devoted to hockey glove production:

$$W_t = WB_t + WH_t$$
$$OT_t = OTB_t + OTH_t$$

where

WB_t is regular workforce hours devoted to baseball glove production in month t

WH_t is regular workforce hours devoted to hockey glove production in month t

OTB_t is overtime hours devoted to baseball glove production in month t

OTH_t is overtime hours devoted to hockey glove production in month t

3. Production is governed by the following relationships:

$$PB_t = 213.33WB_t + 213.33OTB_t$$
$$PH_t = 80WH_t + 80OTH_t$$

The figure 213.33 is derived by noting that, in 4 weeks of 40 hours per week, 213.33 baseball gloves can be produced at an average of 45 minutes per glove; the figure 80 is derived by noting that during the same 160-hour period only 80 pairs of hockey gloves can be produced since an average of 2 hours are required for each pair.

4. Overtime, however, has a practical ceiling, which we might peg at a quarter of the hours spent on regular shift work. Thus,

$$OTB_t \leq .25WB_t$$
$$OTH_t \leq .25WH_t$$

5. Inventory for the period must be accounted for by the following:

$$BI_t = BI_{t-1} + BP_t - BS_t$$
$$HI_t = HI_{t-1} + HP_t - HS_t$$

where BP_t and HP_t represent production of baseball and hockey gloves, respectively, and BS_t and HS_t represent sales or shipments of baseball gloves and hockey gloves, respectively. BI_{t-1} and HI_{t-1}, of course, refer to inventories in the prior period.

6. The size of the workforce in any period must also be accounted for by the following:

$$W_t = W_{t-1} + WFI_t - WFD_t$$

Remember, both WFI_t (workforce increase) and WFD_t (workforce decrease) are defined to be nonnegative numbers.

7. Shipments must be equal to the forecasted figures of Table 11-1; inventory levels in any month must be greater than or equal to the forecasted sales in the next month; and the special inventory goals of $BI_7 \geq 9667$ and $HI_2 \geq 3483$ must also be met.

8. To be compatible with the trial master schedule of Table 11-3, some initial and closing conditions must be specified:

(Initial conditions) $BI_0 = 6500, HI_0 = 700, W_0 = 26$

(Closing conditions) $BI_9 = 7900, HI_9 = 650$

Fortunately, there exists a mathematical technique that can solve this minimization problem subject to the constraints we have specified, largely because all of the relationships specified are linear ones. That is, the relationships are those of variables multiplied by constants and added together (geometrically, straight lines or planes) with no squared terms, trigonometric functions, inverse terms, logarithmic functions, or anything even fancier. In still other words, variable values rise and fall in proportion to one another. This optimization technique is called linear programming and it merits further discussion.

❋ ASIDE ❋

BASIC CONCEPTS OF LINEAR PROGRAMMING

The statement of our problem above can be broken down into pieces. First, there is the mathematical expression for schedule cost, which we wish to minimize; this expression is often termed the "objective function" since minimizing that function is our objective. Second, there are the numerous constraints or restrictions that we have placed on the solution. These constraints, in turn, can be broken down into "structural constraints" (2 through 8 above) and "nonnegativity conditions" (1 above). Together, the structural constraints and the nonnegativity conditions define the so-called "feasible region."

The notion of a feasible region is important since it is only within the feasible region that all of the constraints are met. Thus, our cost minimum, given the constraints, must also be found within the feasible region. Our example of the Ridgely Sporting Goods Company is too complex to represent in two-dimensional graphic terms; let us scale down the problem to consider only two structural constraints and two nonnegativity conditions. Arbitrarily, let us choose the following:

Structural constraints: $1.5X + Y \leq 12$
$-X + Y \leq 5$

Nonnegativity conditions: $X \geq 0, Y \geq 0$

What is the feasible region defined by these constraints? Figure 11-1 offers a picture of the implied feasible region. Note that the feasible region is bounded by straight lines. That is what is meant by a *linear* program; lines (in two dimensions) or planes (in three or more dimensions) always serve as boundaries of the feasible region. In turn, this linearity means that the feasible region has very definite corners, the importance of which we will soon explore. Only in the feasible region are all of

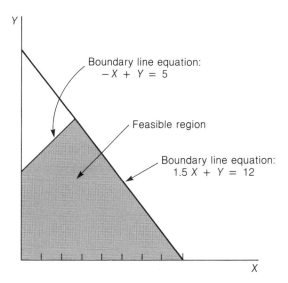

FIGURE 11-1 The feasible region defined by structural constraints and nonnegativity conditions.

in solving a linear problem we need only evaluate the corners of the feasible region to determine those values of the variables that either maximize or minimize the given objective function. This statement is one form of the basic theorem of linear programming.

We may be able to see this result geometrically, but what does this really mean in terms of our cost minimizing example? The logic is this. If by pursuing an activity (X or Y) we can cut costs, we should pursue that activity as long as we can. Because of the linearities involved, costs always remain proportional to changes in X or Y. No economies or diseconomies of scale are encountered; production is always at constant returns to scale. If pursuing an activity like X or Y cuts costs, then we should use up as much X or Y as we can. We cannot be penalized for using too much. In our example, using Y always adds to costs; thus we should use as

the inequalities of the constraints met, and it is in this region that our solution will be found.

Let us turn now to consider the objective function to be minimized (or to be maximized, since linear programming can do either). Arbitrarily again, let us define the following as the objective function to be minimized: $-X + 2Y$. We can interpret this objective function as a cost function that we want to minimize. If we introduce cost, then, as a third dimension, we see that the objective function is a plane that cuts through our feasible region, as demonstrated in Figure 11-2. Again, the *linear* nature of our problem assures us that the objective function will be a plane, and not some curved shape.

Solving our minimization problem then becomes a matter of choosing the point in the feasible region over which the objective function plane is lowest. Although this task may sound difficult, the linearity of the geometry involved assures us that the minimum cost point will occur *not only on the feasible region's boundary but at a corner as well!* This is an extraordinarily convenient result:

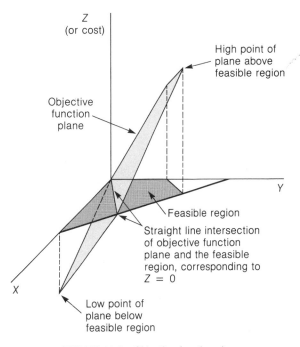

FIGURE 11-2 Objective function plane depicted with feasible region.

little Y as possible — in fact we can get away with using none. Using X, on the other hand, always cuts costs; so we should use up as much X as we can — namely, 8 units, as determined by our feasible region. This logic forces us to the corner solution of $X = 8$, $Y = 0$, and a cost minimum of -8.

This fundamental result that objective function minimums or maximums always occur at corners can be seen another way, by using isocost lines. We can think of cutting the objective function plane with another plane that is parallel to the feasible region's XY plane but that takes on different values of Z (cost). The intersection of these two planes is a straight line such as is shown in Figure 11-2. Such lines are isocost lines: any combination of X and Y that lies along such lines shares the same cost. The projection of these isocost lines onto the XY plane (the feasible region's plane) is a family of parallel lines. In our particular example, the isocost lines all have a slope of $-\frac{1}{2}$. Figure 11-3 depicts this family of isocost lines superimposed on the feasible region.

As a study of Figure 11-3 should make clear, the lowest valued (or the highest valued) isocost line that intersects the feasible region will always intersect that region at a corner.* Thus, solving for the

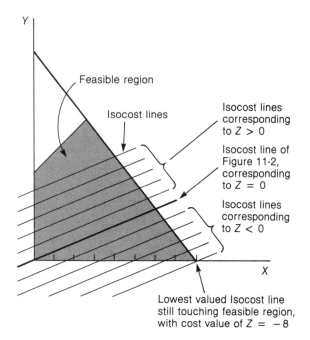

FIGURE 11-3 Isocost lines and the feasible region.

optimum value of the objective function of a linear program need only entail an evaluation of the corners of the feasible region.

Linear Programming in Practice

That linear programs can be solved by evaluating just the corners of the feasible region is comforting, but the fact that there were only four corners to the feasible region in our small example should not fool anybody into believing that solving linear programs is necessarily easy. In our situation with the Ridgely Sporting Goods Company and the 99 variables and 153 constraints we must define in order to state its linear program for schedule cost minimization, the number of corners to the feasi-

ble region is well over 10^{24}. Hardly a reassuring number.

It is of some importance then to note that several techniques can be programmed on computers to search systematically through the astronomical numbers of possible corner positions for the optimal solutions to linear programs. The most notable of these techniques is called the *simplex method*. It does not evaluate all the corners of the feasible region but rather selects, in a very systematic way, those areas of the feasible region that best improve upon the value of the objective function. With

---

*Unless, of course, the slope of the isocost lines is the same as that of a boundary line, in which case the entire boundary as well as its two corner end points will be optimal.

each selection, the method gets closer and closer to the optimum; after so many of them we are guaranteed a solution, if in fact one exists.

Since it is highly unlikely that future business managers will be called on to solve linear programs by hand using the simplex method—after all, that is what computers are for—this book does not attempt to describe the workings of the simplex method.[2] However, it is important to know how to set up a problem like an aggregate plan or master schedule development so that a "canned" computer program can solve it.

The Leather Goods Department of the Ridgely Sporting Goods Company provides an appropriate example and one that has effectively been stated in a form suitable for entry on a computer. We can restate the linear program for it here, using the symbol Σ (sigma) to indicate the summation of terms.

Objective function

minimize

$$\sum_{t=1}^{9}(1280W_t + 1920OTB_t + 1920OTH_t + .28BI_t$$

$$+ .67HI_t + 370WFI_t + 400WFD_t)$$

subject to

Nonnegativity conditions

$$W_t, WB_t, WH_t, OT_t, OTB_t, OTH_t, BI_t, HI_t,$$
$$WFI_t, WFD_t, BP_t, \text{ and } HP_t \geq 0$$

and structural constraints

$$W_t - WB_t - WH_t = 0$$

$$OT_t - OTB_t - OTH_t = 0$$

$$PB_t - 213.33WB_t - 213.33OTB_t = 0$$

$$PH_t - 80WH_t - 80OTH_t = 0$$

$$.25WB_t - OTB_t \geq 0$$

$$.25WH_t - OTH_t \geq 0$$

$$BI_t - BI_{t-1} - BP_t + BS_t = 0$$

$$HI_t - HI_{t-1} - HP_t + HS_t = 0$$

$$W_t - W_{t-1} - WFI_t + WFD_t = 0$$

$BS_1 = 4000$	$HS_1 = 100$
$BS_2 = 3000$	$HS_2 = 100$
$BS_3 = 2500$	$HS_3 = 700$
$BS_4 = 1000$	$HS_4 = 1600$
$BS_5 = 500$	$HS_5 = 2000$
$BS_6 = 5000$	$HS_6 = 1900$
$BS_7 = 2000$	$HS_7 = 1450$
$BS_8 = 4000$	$HS_8 = 1200$
$BS_9 = 7000$	$HS_9 = 1400$
$BI_0 = 6500$	$HI_0 = 700$
$BI_1 \geq 3000$	$HI_1 \geq 100$
$BI_2 \geq 2500$	$HI_2 \geq 3483$
$BI_3 \geq 1000$	$HI_3 \geq 1600$
$BI_4 \geq 500$	$HI_4 \geq 2000$
$BI_5 \geq 5000$	$HI_5 \geq 1900$
$BI_6 \geq 2000$	$HI_6 \geq 1450$
$BI_7 \geq 9667$	$HI_7 \geq 1200$
$BI_8 \geq 7000$	$HI_8 \geq 1400$
$BI_9 \geq 7900$	$HI_9 \geq 650$

$$W_0 = 26$$

When this formulation of the linear program to minimize the cost of the master schedule at Ridgely Sporting Goods is entered on a computer and run, a solution like that found in Table 11-5 results. (The entries in this table are to the nearest integer.) Several things about the optimal master schedule are worth noting:

1. The workforce is not increased right away but later on and to necessarily higher levels than the level strategy adopted in Table 11-3.

2. Inventory levels are lower than in Table 11-3. Lower inventory carrying expenses are incurred in this schedule, more than balancing off the higher hiring costs incurred.

3. Somewhat remarkably, though, the cost of the linear program's optimal solution is only a few thousand dollars less than the trial-and-error schedule developed earlier.

TABLE 11-5 Optimal Master Production Schedule as Determined by Linear Programming
(Ridgely Sporting Goods Company, Leather Goods Department)

PRODUCT LINE	JULY	AUG.	SEPT.	OCT.	NOV.	DEC.	JAN.	FEB.	MARCH	APRIL
Baseball Gloves										
Sales target	4000	3000	2500	1000	500	5000	2000	4000	7000	
Starting inventory	6500	3000	2500	1000	500	5000	4317	9667	7550	7900
Production	500	2500	1000	500	5000	4317	7350	1883	7350	
Hockey Gloves										
Sales target	100	100	700	1600	2000	1900	1450	1200	1400	
Starting inventory	700	2493	3535	4540	4832	3413	2650	1200	2050	650
Production	1893	1142	1705	1892	581	1137	0	2050	0	
Workforce	26.0	26.0	26.0	26.0	30.7	34.5	34.5	34.5	34.5	

Total cost of this schedule = $380,525

The last observation is important. While linear programming is immensely attractive for developing optimal solutions to sophisticated problems, there is no guarantee that the optimal solution will be much different from a solution arrived at through common sense and trial and error. In this case, going through the pain, suffering, and expense of developing a linear program to capture Ridgely Sporting Goods' needs and of solving it seems scarcely worth the effort. Nevertheless, in other instances, such linear programming would more than pay for itself.

Cautions about the Use of Linear Programming

In addition to this concern for the cost effectiveness of applying linear programming techniques to situations like master schedule development, there are several fundamental cautions that any manager contemplating the use of linear programming should be aware of. Among them:

1. *Meeting the linearity assumptions.* As we have observed above, the objective function and the structural constraints must all be linear for a programming problem to be capable of solu-

tion by a technique like the simplex method. In particular, the production relations defined in the constraints must exhibit constant returns to scale, and all prices and costs must be fixed and invariant with quantity (i.e., no price discounts allowed). In many cases, of course, constant returns to scale production, especially in the short term, is a very reasonable assumption, as is the absence of any significant price or cost discounts. In fact, the applicability of these assumptions has largely facilitated the already existing use of linear programming techniques in production planning. Yet, companies should be acutely sensitive to those times when such linearity assumptions stretch reality too much to be useful.

2. *The time horizon.* The solution to most linear programming problems is sensitive to the time horizon chosen. In the case above, a time horizon of 9 months was chosen and ending inventories of certain sizes were specified. If the time horizon were extended to, say, 12 months or shortened to, say, 6 months, the specifics of the solution might vary significantly. This is, of course, a general caution about planning hori-

zons, but it is especially relevant to techniques like linear programming since their solutions tend to be very volatile, with nary a presentiment that a future beyond the problem's time horizon even exists.

3. *Problem size.* Our problem at Ridgely Sporting Goods spanned only two products and 9 months. Yet, the size of the linear program developed was substantial. For more products and more months to be included, even larger computers must be called on. At some point, applying linear programming, however attractive it appears, simply becomes infeasible and not merely cost prohibitive.

Other Applications of Linear Programming

As we have seen, linear programming has a natural application in the development of aggregate production plans and schedules. There are other operations problems, however, for which linear programming has been used with success.

Product Mix Decisions. Companies are constantly bumping up against capacity constraints and must make decisions about which of their products they should produce during any span of time. Some products, of course, are relatively more profitable than others. All products are likely to make different demands on a company's scarce resources. Given these scarcities, then, and the profitability of each product, what mix of products should be produced? This question is somewhat different from the one we faced in aggregate production planning. There we asked for the lowest cost way of meeting a particular schedule, given some constraints. Here we ask for the most profitable mix of products, given other constraints. This formulation of linear programming has found application in many continuous flow operations (e.g., oil refineries) when there is little question that all of their output can be sold on the open market with no modification to price. It is a feature of linear programming solutions that the number of products that ought to be produced will not exceed the number of structural constraints in the problem. This fact implies often that the breadth of a product line to be run at a refinery should be reduced if maximum profits are to be earned.

Product Specification Decisions. A variant of the foregoing application of linear programming is to use the technique to determine the lowest cost mix of inputs for a given product, given that certain requirements (e.g., product performance) must be met. Animal feeds, paints, gasolines, and similar products are classic examples where certain inputs can be substituted for others and where cost and performance characteristics can be balanced off against one another. Linear programming can thus be used as a purchasing tool, or even as a make-vs.-buy decision tool.

Transportation and Distribution Decisions. How should a company supply its warehouses from its plants so that its transportation costs are as low as possible? This problem is so well known that it has been termed "the transportation problem" and there are special solution algorithms that can cut down on the expense of solving problems of this type. The mathematical description of the transportation problem is as follows:

minimize:

$$\sum_{i=1}^{m} \sum_{j=1}^{n} c_{ij} X_{ij}$$

subject to:

$$\sum_{j=1}^{n} X_{ij} \leq S_i \text{ for } i = 1, 2, \ldots, m \text{ (a supply constraint)}$$

$$\sum_{i=1}^{m} X_{ij} \geq D_j \text{ for } j = 1, 2, \ldots, n \text{ (a demand constraint)}$$

$$X_{ij} \geq 0 \text{ for all } i \text{ and } j \text{ (the nonnegativity condition)}$$

The X_{ij}'s are quantities shipped from plant i to warehouse j during a given time period. The cost of shipping between i and j is represented by c_{ij}. Each plant i is limited to shipping S_i of the good, and each warehouse must have at least D_j of it. There are m plants and n warehouses.

Plant Location Decisions. Some companies, particularly those in the food industry, that incur significant transportation expenses in taking their products to market use linear programming as an aid in their new plant location decisions. This application is an extension of the transportation problem. Proposed new plants are added to the existing network of plants, and the minimum costs of transport for the expected levels of sales to each geographic market are calculated. Various location trials are made and the lowest cost locations for fulfilling the expected level and pattern of demand are seriously scrutinized for new plant start-ups.

✳ ASIDE ✳

DUALITY AND THE ECONOMIC INTERPRETATION OF LINEAR PROGRAMMING

Linear programming can be used either to minimize or to maximize an objective function. As it happens, however, any linear program designed to minimize an objective function can be restated as a completely equivalent linear program to maximize a different, although related, objective function. This complementary linear program is termed the *dual*. All linear programs, therefore, come in pairs—a primal program and its dual. It does not matter which is designated the primal program and which the dual, since the dual of the dual is the original primal program.

How are the dual and primal programs related? Suppose the primal program, like the production schedule development at Ridgely Sporting Goods, involves cost minimization and can be characterized abstractly as follows:

minimize

$$C_1N_1 + \cdots + C_mN_m$$

subject to

$$a_{11}N_1 + \cdots + a_{1m}N_m \geq P_1$$
$$\vdots \qquad \qquad \vdots$$
$$a_{n1}N_1 + \cdots + a_{nm}N_m \geq P_n$$

and

$$N_1 \geq 0, \cdots, N_m \geq 0$$

Then the dual program can be written as:

maximize

$$P_1Q_1 + \cdots + P_nQ_n$$

subject to

$$a_{11}Q_1 + \cdots + a_{n1}Q_n \leq C_1$$
$$\vdots \qquad \qquad \vdots$$
$$a_{1m}Q_1 + \cdots + a_{nm}Q_n \leq C_m$$

and

$$Q_1 \geq 0, \cdots, Q_n \geq 0$$

It is worth noting some of the transpositions and changes involved in setting up the dual:

1. The goal of minimizing the primal's objective function becomes the maximization of the dual's own objective function.

2. The coefficients on the primal program's objective function variables become the right-hand-side constraints in the dual program, and the right-hand-side constraints in the primal be-

come the objective function variable coefficients in the dual.

3. The m variables of the primal's objective function and the n constraints of that program are rearranged into n variables of the dual's objective function and m constraints in the dual.

4. The matrix of coefficients of the constraints in the primal program are transposed around the main diagonal to yield the corresponding dual matrix. Thus, if there are n constraints involving m variables in the primal program, there will be m constraints involving n variables in the dual program. The a_{ij}th coefficient in the primal program is transposed to be the a_{ji}th coefficient in the dual.

5. Inequalities reading "$\geq$" in the primal program read "$\leq$" in the dual.

6. The variables denoted by N in the primal program are replaced by variables denoted by Q. Further, if the N variables could be interpreted as physical quantities in the primal program, the Q variables of the dual can be interpreted as dollar values.

What does all this mean? Let us consider once again our problem of developing a master schedule for the Ridgely Sporting Goods Company. In that problem we wanted to minimize schedule costs and the variables we were interested in were physical quantities like inventories, production rates, and workforce levels. The dual of this problem, al-though yielding the same solution, carries with it a different interpretation. The dual, rather than seeking to minimize costs, seeks instead to maximize profit. The variables we are interested in are the dollar-valued portions of the profit we can impute to each item such as inventories, workforce, and production level. In purely economic terms, these contrasts between primal and dual programs make sense. Minimizing costs is likely also to lead to maximizing profits, and the optimal quantities of several variables are likely also to lead to an optimal apportionment of the profit among the rival variables.

Let us push this evaluation of the meaning of the dual and its solution even further. In seeking to maximize profits, the dual program's solution for the Q's tells us what would be added to the company's profits if somehow any input Q_i could be increased past its constraint of C_i. But what is this telling us? Merely what the *marginal* value of Q_i is to us in increasing company profits. When profits are maximized, any other imputation of the profits among the variables will not yield higher profits. That is, the *opportunity costs* of a different apportionment are negative or zero. Thus, lurking in the background (the dual) of all programming problems are these fundamental concepts of marginal value and opportunity cost. Solutions to the basic problems facing businesses, those involving the allocation of their scarce resources, simply cannot avoid the fundamental concepts of marginal value and opportunity cost.

✱

Alternatives and Refinements to the Linear Programming Approach

It is worth mentioning, if only in passing, that there exist some alternatives and refinements to the linear programming approach to aggregate plan and master schedule development.[3] Some (like dynamic programming and the linear decision rule approach of Holt, Modigliani, and Simon) yield op-timal results although at the expense of some restrictive assumptions.[4] Often, too, these techniques, for computational reasons, are simply unworkable for problems of any more than a very small size.

A refinement to the linear programming approach, the hierarchical system concept, shows some promise. This approach tries to enlarge the size of problem that linear programming can tackle by breaking it up into separate but manageable pieces (hierarchies). Naturally, something is lost by such disaggregation; but if the problem is broken apart cleverly, that "something" may be small. Different products placing demands on different equipment, for example, might be broken apart for separate analysis. Or, different levels of decisions might be separated from one another (e.g., assignment of products to plants, aggregate plans within plants for broad product lines, specific items within a product line) and analyzed separately, given the results of the next highest step in the hierarchy.

MONITORING A PRODUCTION SCHEDULE

Monitoring the production schedule is least required in flow processes where the pace of production is either mechanical or technological; typically, only a few formalities are required for monitoring output in such processes. However, when the pace of production is not mechanical, monitoring the schedule is an important cog in controlling all of production. Usually, the monitoring of schedules is greatly facilitated by the use of some visual aids depicting the status of various jobs or batches as they progress through distinct process steps or days of production. The use of such visual aids was popularized by Henry Gantt in the early 1900s, and they are often called Gantt charts, after him.

Schedule-monitoring visual aids can be laid out in many ways. Two common ways can be described as follows:

1. *Diagonal tracking schedule monitors.* Figure 11-4 is an example of a schedule monitoring device that tracks progress down a diagonal. Jobs or batches that are on schedule form a diagonal running from the upper right to the lower left. Those that are behind schedule show up as the lines ending above and to the left of the diago-

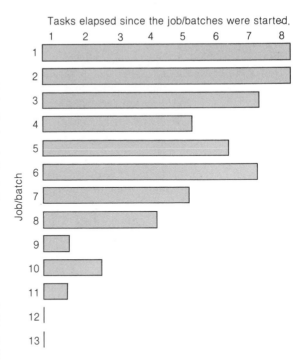

FIGURE 11-4   A diagonal tracking schedule monitor.

nal formed by the jobs that are on schedule. Jobs or batches that are ahead of schedule show up as the lines below and to the right of the diagonal. A device like Figure 11-4 is best able to indicate which jobs are relatively ahead or behind schedule. By a quick glance at a visual aid like Figure 11-4 managers can readily identify those jobs that need their attention. Perhaps the job is short a part, or a piece of equipment has failed, or some other bottleneck has arisen. Whatever the reason, such an aid plays an important role in alerting management to the major problems needing attention. In Figure 11-4, for example, job/batches 4 and 9 are behind schedule.

Figure 11-4 is a relatively simple chart; it is laid out for a process where all the same tasks must be accomplished for each job/batch. Also, no desired completion dates are indicated on the chart. This kind of information is indicated more readily on a column tracking scheduling chart.

2. *Column tracking schedule monitors.* Figure 11-5 is an example of a schedule monitoring device that tracks progress down a column indicating the present day or week of production. The figure illustrates job/batches that were scheduled to begin on different production days and whose expected durations varied. Expected durations are indicated by the box outline itself while completed production is indicated by the shaded portion of the box outline. Those job/batches whose shaded-in portions fall left of the panel indicating the present production day are behind schedule; those whose shaded-in portions are right of the panel are ahead of schedule.

A device such as Figure 11-5 offers somewhat more information than the simpler diagonal tracking chart of Figure 11-4. For example, tasks with scheduled starts and stops that differ can be readily portrayed. Also, job/batches that take up unscheduled time can be depicted (e.g., job/batch 2 and the lighter shaded portion of the line). Because the chart is laid out for production days rather than tasks, different tasks can be represented by the same production day. Of course, the capacities and capacity utilizations of various tasks or machines must be accounted for separately so that too much is not asked of any task or machine.

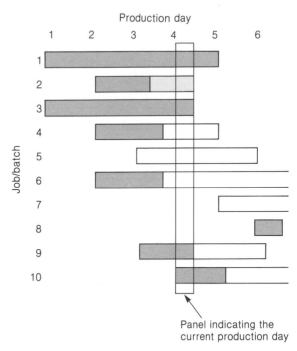

FIGURE 11-5   A column tracking schedule monitor.

Such visual aids lend themselves to a variety of graphic conventions. For example, different symbols or colors can distinguish wait time or maintenance time from actual production. Different symbols or colors can indicate the task or factory department in which the job/batch is, was, or will be. This choice of convention depends solely on what information is useful and what is available.

PART TWO

CONTROLLING THE PROCESS AND QUALITY

SOME GENERAL COMMENTS ON PRODUCTION CONTROL

Controlling production effectively means assembling up-to-date information on the status of orders, materials, and the process itself and being able to communicate that information to higher levels of management in a clear and timely fashion, with priorities spelled out, so that management can take corrective action. In large measure, production control is inseparably intertwined with

TABLE 11-6   Worker Information Requirements in Different Processes

PROCESS	WHAT SHOULD BE WORKED ON	HOW IT SHOULD BE DONE	HOW LONG IT SHOULD TAKE	WHERE PRODUCT IS TO BE DIRECTED NEXT
Job shop	Told by foreman	Written on process sheet attached to order	Written on job sheet attached to order	Written on a routing slip attached to order
Batch flow	Told by foreman or implied by a priority numbering scheme for batch	Either known from training or written on process sheet attached to batch	Implied by piece rate or written on process sheet accompanying batch	Written on a routing slip
Line flow	Determined by sequencing of line	Basically known from training, though options may be indicated on a process sheet	Implied by known worker standards or mechanical pacing of line	Known from the layout of the line
Continuous flow	Determined by process layout	Known from training; few options available indicated by independent information from management	Determined by process layout	Determined by process layout

materials management (purchasing, inventory control) and with production planning and scheduling. In order to supply the information it takes to correct a problem like behind-schedule delivery, the production controller must be aware of the schedule, the status of inventories, the status of parts orders, the location of the order on the factory floor, and the remaining steps to completion. Thus, all of the discussion on materials management and production planning that has preceded this section has a direct bearing on the topic of production control.

What is sometimes forgotten in the rush to satisfy orders and bird-dog materials is that some of the wealth of information that can help guide and control the process relates to the workforce. Workers need to know several things before they can plunge comfortably into doing their work: what they should work on, how they should do it, how long it should take, and where their output ought to be directed next. As should be clear from the various plant tours, sometimes this information must be transmitted to the workers repeatedly; other times they already know what is required of them. Table 11-6 summarizes the worker information requirements that are typical of various processes.

Naturally, some production control systems for routing jobs, determining their priorities, and detailing the tasks required of each worker are better than others. When a job shop or batch flow shop becomes cluttered with work-in-process, it is a good bet that the routing, priority determining, or process detailing systems are breaking down under the stress and are in need of modification. A shop, for example, with every other job lot flagged red for immediate work needs to sort out its time priorities so that the chaos prevailing there can be reduced.

Good production control is more than timely expediting; it involves anticipating problems before they happen and taking corrective action early. A necessary part of production control involves generating and digesting "out-of-stock" lists, "parts shortage" lists, and lists of orders past due or behind schedule. Effective production control must do this and more, however, if an operation is to become (or remain) low cost, with adequate customer service and an inventory investment that is not extravagant. As we have already observed, one of the attractions of a material requirements planning system is that it is a far-seeing, anticipatory approach to managing materials and one that ties materials and orders together. This kind of thinking fosters good production control, as does attention to the information that workers receive from, and give back to, management. Good production control even becomes involved with keeping the process running in good order.

The production process that never breaks down has yet to be invented. In every process there are procedures for dealing with breakdowns or other foul-ups. Some are informal (e.g., walking over to the foreman) and some are very formal (e.g., activating a special alarm or pulling out a checklist). Naturally, the penalties that companies have to pay for errors differ widely. Incorrectly drilling 20 or 30 metal pieces in a company like Norcen Industries, while vexing, is not nearly the calamity that a paper break on a paper machine may be when a highway of paper shoots out in all directions. Thus, especially in high volume production processes, huge amounts of time and expense are devoted to assuring that production proceeds at as rapid a pace as possible, consistent with the established quality standards. Maintenance, especially preventive maintenance, becomes an important endeavor in such processes and worthy of considerable care in scheduling.

QUALITY CONTROL[5]

The term "established quality standard" is important to an understanding of quality control because quality control refers not only to what everyone would recognize as "top quality" (e.g., Rolls Royce cars or Maytag appliances) but to every level of quality. At each stage in a product's development, producers typically must balance a product's price against its level of quality. But even low-price, low-quality level producers must be concerned with maintaining their production to the standard of quality that they have established as consistent with the price they charge.

Product quality can be improved upon and gauged in several ways:

- *Automation.* Automation can promise a company many things: faster speed, lower costs, and standardized, reliable quality. The more that manual tasks are replaced by machines, the greater are the opportunities for "designing away" process and quality problems. This is not to say that machines cannot do a lousy job on something. They can, but their rate of quality failure tends to be lower than for more labor-intensive methods, and the reason for any failure tends to be easier to detect and often to correct.

  The great strides that have been made over the last 20 years in computer and sensing device technology have yielded high returns in the control of processes. As mentioned in Chapter 1, papermaking is now faster and more reliable, with less concern for calamitous paper breaks because process controls have been added. The same can be said for canning and bottling (Chapter 4) and for a host of other high volume process industries like steel, oil refining, and printing.

- *Maintenance.* Particularly for high volume processes, the maintenance of equipment and the quick repair of any equipment failures are critical. Often, many of a factory's most coveted, and highest paying, jobs lie in the maintenance and repair department.

- *Product design.* After a new product has been introduced to the factory, it is frequently discovered that a particular component or aspect of it is difficult to manufacture and leads either to a bottleneck or to a high level of rejections. Sometimes the root of this difficulty can be eliminated by redesigning the product or by substituting materials in it.

- *Testing for quality.* While it is true that quality cannot be inspected into a product but, rather, must be built into it, it is nevertheless advantageous for an operation to check quality in a systematic way. What managers learn from such systematic analysis can guide their actions in improving the process or product so that quality is enhanced. Quality checks often serve as early warning stations for impending process breakdowns. Installing quality checks throughout a process can not only help isolate problem areas, but also save costs; no company wants to squander its time and resources completing products that are already so screwed up that they are not worth repairing.

QUALITY CONTROL TESTING

There are a variety of issues in quality control that bear discussion:

- How many quality checks should a process have?
- Where in the process should quality checks be placed?
- Should every product be checked or only a sample?
- What kind of clout should the quality control department have?

As one might expect, the most common places for quality checks are at the beginning and end of a process. Almost all companies have some sort of final inspection station, even if it is more or less a token gesture. Nearly as many devote at least some resources to inspecting incoming materials. Some go so far as to station inspectors in their suppliers' plants to monitor both quality and delivery.

How many more quality checks there should be and where in the process they ought to be located depends largely on a comparison of the expected cost of adding a quality check and the expected benefit accruing to the company by avoiding the shipment of below-standard output. This calculation, like so many others, is a marginal calculation: we can expect that the more quality checks we already have in the process, the less likely that an additional check will be cost effective.

While conceptually this marginal calculation is clear, actually determining the additional costs and benefits of another quality check is often a dilemma. What constitutes the impact of shipping below-standard output is a foggy notion at best. On the one hand, there are product liability considerations associated with many products and the damage awards can be very high. On the other hand, below-standard quality may cost the company little or nothing in customer ill will and lost sales. To compound the ambiguity of such a benefit calculation, it is seldom known with certainty just how effective a particular quality check will be in weeding out below-standard products. Not only is the check itself likely to be new and untried, but relatively few quality checks can be made so mechanical that either a machine or low-skilled labor could be entrusted to make it. For most quality checks, some judgment is often required; despite efforts to make the quality check criterion clear and unswerving, "bad" units of output can be expected to be approved. Inspectors are human and tests are seldom foolproof. In addition, there are the understandable lapses in the criteria when demand is high and supplies are tight. In that case, suppliers can often ship below-standard parts, some previously rejected, and have them pass inspection. Quality standards, like other aspects of production, are likely to slip when the pressures for delivery become too great.

The expected costs of a quality check are likewise fuzzy. The fact that a check is new makes cost estimation difficult, largely because the check may have to be redesigned to perform as expected. It is frequently tough to design a quality check that is at once effective and does not damage the product. However, more and more quality control checks have been mechanized. These cost-reducing checks incorporate such advances as minicomputers and robot-like machines but also some simple tools like gauges that at a glance can indicate whether a dimension is too large or too small.

The benefit/cost calculation on a quality check may argue against its introduction, particularly for job shop and batch flow processes. These processes typically deal with many different kinds of products and considerable customization and new product introduction, characteristics that hinder establishing sophisticated quality checks. Inspectors may have to roam around the factory, since all products are not likely to be routed the same way; this can be costly. Moreover, the workers in these processes are generally highly skilled and capable of checking quality as they work. However, the more the process resembles line and continuous flow processes (with their standardized products, long production runs, and fixed routing of products), the greater the probability that any quality check's benefits will exceed its costs.

Harking back to the six plant tours of Segment I, we can see that quality control was much more formalized at GMAD-Tarrytown, the Schlitz brewery, and at International Paper's Androscoggin Mill. At Norcen Industries, Jung Products, and the Malden Burger King, quality checks were less numerous and more informal. Of course, this is not to say that the quality of these companies' products is any less than that of the former group of companies. Rather, it is merely a statement about the means by which that quality is controlled.

The marginal benefit/cost calculation introduced above is helpful also in outlining where in any process a quality check ought to be placed. The benefit/cost ratio is likely to be high (i.e., more defects caught and/or more additional future costs avoided relative to the cost of the test) at some

of the following kinds of places within the process:

- Before operations that add a lot of value to the product. Thus, already defective products get weeded out before additional costs are incurred.
- After operations with demonstrated low yields—again so that significant value is not added to already defective products.
- Before operations that render product repair very difficult or impossible (e.g., before beer is canned or before the body drop at an auto assembly plant or before an automobile is painted).
- At points in the process where testing is relatively cheap.

Quality checks can be made following a variety of patterns. Representative examples of these quality control patterns have already been introduced in the six plant tours.

1. *100 percent inspection.* All of the on-line inspection at GMAD-Tarrytown is inspection of every car that passes by. Similarly, all of the batches of beer brewed at the Schlitz brewery were tested. One hundred percent inspections are generally made when inspection costs are low relative to the costs avoided by identifying, and possibly remedying, faulty products. Since much of General Motors' and Schlitz's reputations hang on their quality images, it is not surprising that much of their quality control involves 100 percent inspections.

2. *Start-up inspections.* Inspections are sometimes concentrated at the start of a production run and then reduced in number and intensity as the run proceeds. For example, many of the machine setups at Norcen Industries were checked before production began. The start of any new run of paper at a paper mill can be expected to trigger an increased level of quality testing. In general, start-up inspections prevail

when equipment, once set properly, can be relied on to produce a uniform product.

3. *Random sampling.* When the costs of quality checking are high relative to the benefits, 100 percent inspection becomes less and less desirable. If, in addition, the process itself can be counted on for reasonably steady operation and quality, inspecting only a sample of production becomes attractive. The best way to test quality in such an instance is to draw a sample, at random, from the entire production run; the size of the sample is determined by the degree of precision desired in extrapolating the sample's results to the entire run and by the costs of the testing. The daily audit of cars at GMAD-Tarrytown is an example of a random sample quality check.

4. *Sequential sampling.* The larger the sample taken from any population, the more precise we can be about its implications for all of the population, but also, as mentioned above, the more costly testing becomes. Often it is economical to take first a small sample to make some crude inferences about the total population, throwing out production that clearly looks defective, accepting what clearly looks good, and subjecting any production whose sample yields in-between results to additional testing. In essence, the idea behind sequential sampling is to use a small sample as a screen to separate out production that is clearly bad or good and to sample more intensively any production with ambiguous results. Some of the quality checks at the Schlitz brewery involve sequential sampling. For example, the test for air content in a filled can can be viewed as a sequential sampling test. The quality assurance staff tested for air content six times each shift, taking three cans at a time. If the three-can average missed the specification, a 100 percent inspection of the cans between the current and the previous checkpoint was triggered.

The construction of random samples and sequential sampling patterns depends heavily on statistics and can quickly become rather involved. A taste for the application of statistics to quality control is provided in the next section.

Some Statistics Related to Quality Control

When inspection or testing of all products or parts is impractical or too costly, sampling becomes a desirable alternative. With sampling come some complications, however, since we simply cannot discard only those products or parts that show up bad. We do not know where all the bad items are and so we cannot be as selective as we might like. Actions we might take will typically involve entire batches of items and the workings of the process itself. We thus want to be very careful in deciding what to do.

Few industrial processes are so precise that every item produced is exactly identical to every other item. Most processes produce items whose discernible characteristics fall into distributions such as displayed in Figure 11-6. Of course some distributions may be tighter than others (i.e., bunched more closely around the center), but in most there is a distinct possibility that some wild, outlying

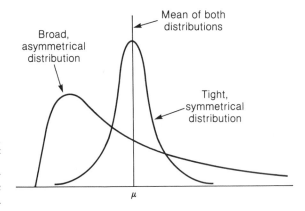

FIGURE 11-6 Samples of distributions.

value will be observed even though the distribution itself is fairly tight. Doing something drastic like junking an entire production batch on the basis of a single outlying observation is to be avoided.

To get around this problem, many samples taken are of a number of items each, and the mean (i.e., arithmetic average) value of the metric in question is recorded. In this way, the effects of outlying observations are muted. Still, the means of the small samples taken will tend to fluctuate some.

Control Charts

One important issue in this vein is determining whether something in the process is "sick" and thus creating a distribution of output that is fundamentally different from what it is supposed to produce. To continue with the medical analogy, a sample mean recording is like taking a "temperature reading" of the process. Before corrective action is taken, however, it is desirable to have some "patient history" so that nothing rash is done. A "temperature chart" is a type of patient history, a convenient, easily read visual aid, useful in spotting trends over time and in judging when the patient slipped out of the range of "good health."

In operations, visual aids called "control charts" are used like temperature charts to spot and to determine when the process "patient" is sick and in need of corrective action. A control chart can be constructed to record a variety of metrics: physical measurement of the product (e.g., how much air is in a can of beer), proportions of items rejected by inspectors, or proportions of defects in a given volume or mass of the product. No matter what the metric, the control chart is constructed in the same way. The key ingredient in its construction is determining the bounds of "good health."

In general, past history and current observations are needed to determine the bounds of "good health" for a process since it is by these data that we know what the distribution of results is when all is going well. As we observed before in talking about inventory control, the normal distribution describes many phenomena. Moreover, by standardizing the sample means taken by the formula

$$\frac{X - \overline{X}}{\frac{S}{\sqrt{N}}}$$

where X is the sample mean, $\overline{X}$ the mean of the distribution, S the distribution's standard deviation, and N the number of observations in the sample, an approximate normal distribution is traced out. Once it is known that the sample means taken as observations can be expected to fall into a normal distribution, the control boundaries can easily be set because we know what fraction of the distribution falls outside any given multiple of the standard deviation. For example, only slightly less than 5 percent of the distribution lies outside ±2 standard deviations from the mean.

This information about the distribution provides us with all we need for constructing a control chart. That is, if we know the mean of the normal distribution of expected sample means and the standard error of that distribution, we can devise a chart to indicate when an observed mean lies inside or outside a given interval. Such a chart might look like Figure 11-7, where the bounds are set at ±3 standard deviations, wide enough to contain all but 0.3 percent of the distribution of sample

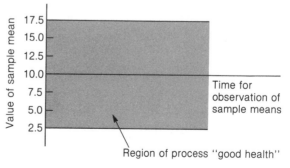

FIGURE 11-7   A control chart of an expected normal distribution where mean = 10 and standard deviation = 2.5.

means. Control charts such as this are useful visual aids for indicating when machines need to be reset or methods revised to bring the process back to its expected quality level of operation.

Sampling Inspection

A control chart gives a useful history of the process's quality performance, but is not intended to be a decision tool for accepting or rejecting a given batch of output. For this task, a variety of sampling inspection plans have been developed. These plans look at one or more samples drawn from the lot in question and, depending on the number of defective items in the sample, either accept or reject the lot.

Using sampling in this way as a decision tool leaves open the possibility of committing two different kinds of errors:

- Type I error: Rejecting a lot when it in fact meets specifications.
- Type II error: Accepting a lot when it in fact does not meet specifications.

While a type I error may cost the company money, it is the type II error that is more likely to cause ill will with customers. For this reason most sampling plans try especially hard to limit type II errors even at the expense of committing more type I errors.

The performance of a sampling inspection plan is often portrayed by an "operating characteristic" curve, which is a graph of the probability of accepting a lot versus the true proportion of defectives in the lot. Figure 11-8 is an example of an operating characteristic curve where the true proportion of defectives is 5 percent of the lot. Ideally one would like to have an operating characteristic curve that looks like the dashed line rectangle in Figure 11-8. This is an unattainable goal, barring 100 percent inspection, and this reality forces us into balancing type II errors against type I errors.

Determining the sampling plan that implies a particular operating characteristic curve can be a

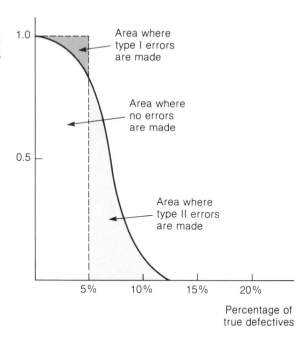

FIGURE 11-8 An operating characteristic curve.

hairy endeavor, and is best left to some applied statistics texts. We can say in general, however, that the more critical one wishes to make the inspection — that is, the smaller the areas for type I or type II errors — the more sampling that will have to be done. Since sampling can become expensive, it is no mean feat to decide on a sampling inspection plan that limits errors sufficiently and is reasonably economical.

The Variety of Sampling Plans

In order to cut down on expense, several different sampling plans have been devised so that the same levels of error avoidance can be maintained at lower cost. The base case sampling plan is termed "single sampling." In single sampling a single, reasonably large sample is taken of each lot to be approved, and the lot is either accepted or rejected depending on the sample's findings.

Generally, a more economical means of passing judgment on the lot is first to take a small sample that can be used straightaway to accept some lots and reject others. With such a small sample, however, there will be times when the sample finding will be inconclusive, just too borderline to base an accept/reject decision on it. In these cases, another sample is taken and added to the first. With this now larger sample, the accept/reject decision is made. This sampling plan is called "double sampling."

This notion of double sampling can be extended to include repeated sampling, embracing more than two draws of even smaller size from the lot. The procedure remains the same: accept or reject what you can, given the initial small sample size,

and draw again to enlarge the sample to be able to accept or reject the lot when the initial sample or samples prove inconclusive. This sampling plan is termed "sequential sampling."

For more continuous flow operations (e.g., the bottling and canning lines at the Schlitz brewery), continuous sampling makes sense. Under such schemes periodic inspections are made. If the test turns negative, a more intensive sampling (or even 100 percent inspection) is triggered to see how widespread the drop in quality is. Once acceptable quality levels return, the initial, less-intensive sampling scheme is reinstituted.

APPENDIX

PROJECT MANAGEMENT AND SCHEDULING

A project—constructing the World Trade Center or sending a man to the moon—shares many characteristics with other types of production processes. We can picture a project with the same kind of precedence relationship with which we pictured the line flow process in Chapter 5. Certain activities must be completed before others begin, and each activity can be expected to take a given period of time, just as in other process types. But our concern for balance in the factory, so prominent in our thinking about production processes, does not trouble us in thinking about a project since a project is, by definition, a one-time endeavor and workers can generally expect to work only so long on it and then move on to something else. It is typical for a project to employ wildly fluctuating numbers of people, many with different skills. We do not worry about idleness—construction workers move on to the next project as do space scientists and engineers.

What does trouble us in a project is getting it done on time, for projects often have important deadlines to meet. Scheduling is thus absolutely critical to the management of a project. Several techniques have been developed to highlight the project activities that must be accomplished on time (or else risk delaying the entire project) and the activities that can be delayed somewhat. One such scheduling technique is called the critical path method; what follows is a brief description of its rationale and workings.

THE CRITICAL PATH CONCEPT

The critical path concept begins with a layout of the project as a precedence diagram, such as that introduced in Chapter 5 (Figure 5-3). On it are indicated the expected times for completing each activity. Figure 11A-1 is a simplified illustration of a

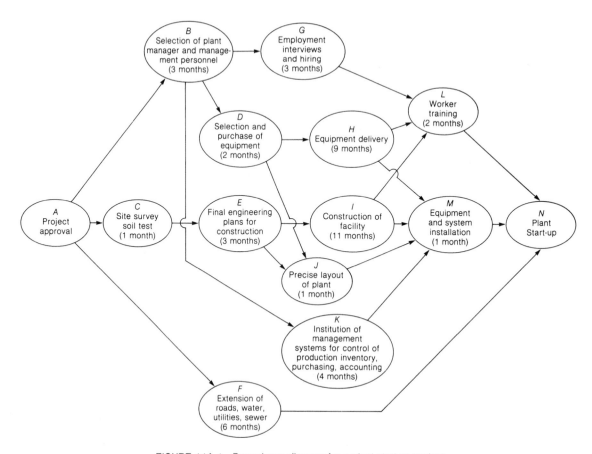

FIGURE 11A-1   Precedence diagram for a plant start-up project.

project many companies face—the start-up of a new plant. The precedence diagram indicates that some activities must precede others but also that many activities can proceed at the same time.

The key principle of the critical path concept is that a project cannot be completed any faster than the longest time path between the project's start and its finish. In Figure 11A-1 the longest path from A (project approval) to N (plant start-up) involves the following activities—A, C, E, I, L, and N; they take a total of 17 months. The longest path between project approval and plant start-up is termed the "critical path," primarily because any delay along this path of activities sets back the en-

tire project. It is this critical path that merits the most management attention.

All the other paths from start to finish enjoy at least a month's slack time, and so they can experience delays of varying lengths and still not harm the 17-month completion schedule. For example, the next two longest paths after the critical path involve the following activities:

1. A-C-E-I-M-N   16 months
2. A-B-D-H-L-N   16 months

There can be delays of up to a month on these two paths without setting back the entire project.

However, note that the first path is very much like the critical path itself; it differs only in that activity M is substituted for activity L. The slack in this path then can be taken only on activity M (equipment and system installation). If a delay occurred on any other activity, say I (construction of the facility), the critical path would also be affected and the entire project would be delayed.

The second path is much more flexible about where its slack can be used up. Only one of its activities, L (worker training), is shared with the critical path. Thus, its month of slack can be used up on activities B, D, or H without affecting the critical path in any way.

Other paths, of course, have considerably more slack and can be accomplished at a more leisurely pace, if need be. For example, the uppermost path in the diagram (A-B-G-L-N) is expected to take 8 months, with only activity L on the critical path. Activity G could be delayed as much as 9 months without making the project late. However, activity B could not be delayed that long, since it is on one of the second longest paths and can be delayed only a month before it would affect the project's completion time.

This example brings up an important point about critical paths and the scheduling of projects. As time wears on in a project's life, delays and even some speed-ups can be expected. What may look like the critical path at a project's start (e.g., A-C-E-I-L-N) may not remain the critical path if many delays (or speed-ups) strike the project. This means that the project manager should periodically recalculate the critical path to check that he or she is focusing on the activities that really matter to finishing a project in the least time.

THE CRITICAL PATH METHOD

To this point we have calculated the critical path solely by inspecting all the paths and choosing the one with the longest duration. In simple cases, such as this generalized plant start-up, inspection is a perfectly feasible and reasonable way of selecting the critical path. When projects get more complicated, with many more activities, inspection as a means of computing the critical path bogs down. Happily there is an alternative procedure, the critical path method, which can cut down the speed of solution markedly.

In essence, the critical path method is just an accounting procedure to identify the activities that have some slack time and those that do not. Those with no slack time, of course, make up the critical path or paths. This accounting procedure has three phases:

1. A pass through all the activities from start to finish, noting the earliest possible times each activity could be started and concluded, given that everything that precedes an activity must be done already. These "early start" and "early finish" times for our plant start-up example are noted in Figure 11A-2.

2. A pass through all the activities but in reverse order, from the finish back to the start, this time noting the latest possible times each activity could be started and concluded, given that everything that follows an activity must be done after it. These "late start" and "late finish" times for our example are noted separately in Figure 11A-3.

3. The final phase is a comparison of the "early start, early finish" and "late start, late finish" times. Activities where the "early start, early finish" or "late start, late finish" times differ have some slack to them. Those that are equal to one another have no slack and thus make up the critical path. Figure 11A-4 combines all the times in one diagram and displays the critical path.

For very large projects, of course, and ones that go into significant detail, even following the critical path method can become tedious. To aid in the

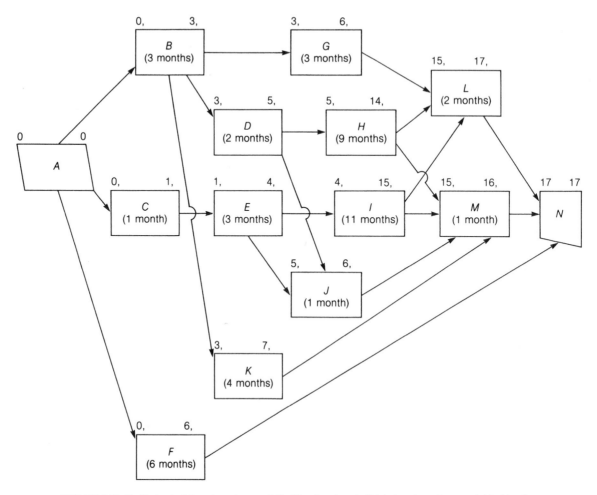

FIGURE 11A-2   Early start (number at upper left of box) and early finish (number at upper right of box) months for the plant start-up project depicted in Figure 11A-1.

analysis, there are computer programs that calculate the critical path. These can be used with ease to determine how differences in expected completion times for various activities (and even the introduction of variations in the network of activities itself) affect the critical path(s).

PROJECT COSTS AND TIMING AND THE CRITICAL PATH METHOD

Frequently, actual projects (such as the new plant start-up outlined in Figure 11A-1) need not be finished in the least time possible but, rather, can be finished during any portion of a "window" of time. When during the acceptable window of time the project's finish ought to be targeted depends largely on the project's managers. Often they are influenced by cost considerations, since it is not uncommon for a project's contract to stipulate rewards for an early finish and penalties for a late finish. These rewards and penalties must be weighed against the costs that hurrying up any of the project's activities could impose on the project's

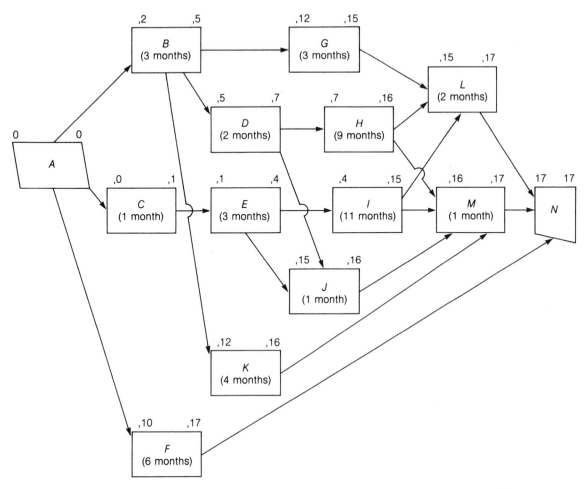

FIGURE 11A-3 Late start (number at upper left of box) and late finish (number at upper right of box) months for the plant start-up project depicted in Figure 11A-1.

budget. The critical path method can help evaluate these decisions on project timing and cost.

WINDOWS OF TIME AND THE CRITICAL PATH METHOD

Windows of time can be easily incorporated into the critical path method; in fact, the terminology is already in place to handle them. The acceptable window of time can be denoted as the difference between the early finish and the late finish (or between the early start and the late start). To return to our example, if the plant start-up could be completed between 17 and 21 months from the start, the values for Figure 11A-4 would be recast as in Figure 11A-5.

Building a window of time in the critical path method makes it important to distinguish between two different kinds of slack time during the project: total slack and free slack. *Total slack* is the length of the time window for the entire project, in this case 4 months. It is the difference between the early and late finishes (or early and late starts)

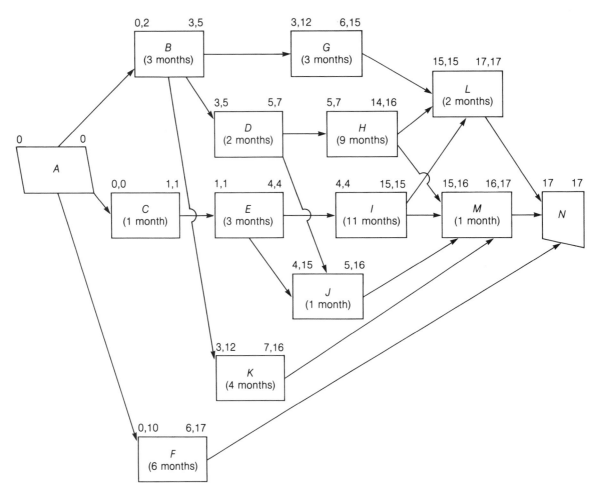

FIGURE 11A-4 Composite of starting and finishing months given in Figures 11A-2 and 11A-3 for the plant start-up project.

along the critical path. The critical path is thus redefined as the path with the lowest value differences between early and late starts (or finishes).

Free slack, on the other hand, is what was initially identified as slack time, the time by which an activity can be delayed without delaying the entire project. *Free slack* is defined as the difference between an activity's early finish time and the earliest of the early start times for *all* its immediate successor activities. Consider the path A-B-K-M-N

in Figure 11A-5. Activity M can be delayed at most a month without risking the delay of the entire project; as it is, its early finish time (16 months) is but 1 month shy of the project completion's (N) early start month (17 months). Activity K has more free slack since its early finish time of 7 months is 8 months shy of its only successor activity's (M's) early start time of 15 months. Its free slack is 8 months. Activity B, the predecessor to activity K, has no free slack since its early finish

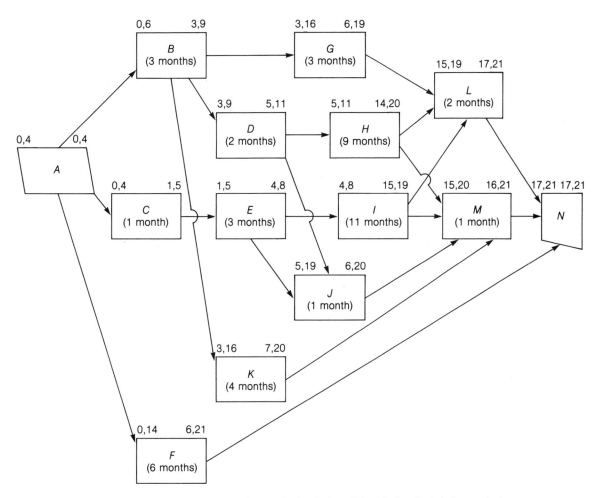

FIGURE 11A-5   The addition of 4 months (a window of time) to the plant start-up project.

time (3 months) is equal to the early start times of both activities G and K.

This lack of any free slack does not mean, however, that if activity B were inadvertently delayed the entire project would be delayed. Activity B, after all, does not lie on the critical path. In fact, activity B could be delayed by a month without necessarily delaying the project since there is at least 1 month of free slack in all the noncritical paths leading away from activity B:

- Path B-G-L-N has 9 months of free slack since activity G's early finish is 9 months less than activity L's early start.

- Path B-K-M-N has 8 months of free slack, as calculated above.

- Path B-D-J-M-N has 9 months of free slack since activity J's early finish is 9 months less than activity M's early start.

- Path B-D-H-L or M-N has 1 month of free slack

since activity H's early finish is 1 month less than either activity L's or activity M's early start.

Free slack can thus be identified with strings of activities off the critical path rather than solely with individual activities.

TRADING OFF TIME AGAINST COST

Suppose up to 2 months of time could be shaved off both the time it took to construct the new plant and the time it took to deliver the necessary equipment, although at a cost. The costs that would have to be incurred to "crash" each of these activities are shown in Table 11A-1. Suppose also that having the new plant on stream a month or two early was estimated to be worth $70,000 per month, since the new plant promised capacity that was unobtainable any other way. Should these activities be "crashed" by 1 or 2 months? How can the critical path method aid in the analysis?

As should be increasingly evident by this point in the text, this decision is one for which marginal analysis is appropriate. That is, it pays to speed up the project if the additional benefits enjoyed are greater than the additional costs incurred. Otherwise, it is best to keep the project on its original schedule.

The critical path method helps, for it indicates, for any project length chosen, exactly which activities have to be speeded up and which can be left on the original schedule. Ideally, of course, we would like to leave slack all that can be left slack and speed up only what must be speeded up (and, if a choice exists, to speed up the least costly activities). Put another way, to the extent possible, we would like every path to be a critical path because in so doing the least expenditure for project speed-up will be incurred.

What does this mean for our example? To complete the plant start-up in 16 months rather than 17, activity I (plant construction) must be crashed since it (not activity H, equipment delivery) lies on the critical path. Activity H can be left as originally scheduled. The costs incurred for speeding up the project to 16 months are thus only $50,000 and the expected benefit from the early completion is $70,000. It is clear that the project ought to be speeded up by at least 1 month. Note that there are now two critical paths: A-C-E-I-L-N and A-B-D-H-L-N.

What about speeding up the project to 15 months rather than 17 or 16 months? To complete the plant start-up in only 15 months would require that plant construction (activity I) be speeded up 2 months and that either equipment delivery (activity H) or personnel selection (activity B) be speeded up by 1 month. The additional costs incurred would be $125,000 ($50,000 + $75,000) for crashing activity I for 2 months and either $20,000 for crashing activity H or $5000 for crashing activity B. Naturally, crashing activity B is the preferred action, and so the total cost of speed-up is $130,000. The benefits, however, are $70,000 for each month for a total of $140,000. Here again, the additional benefits expected outweigh the addi-

TABLE 11A-1 Costs to "Crash" Three Activities in the Plant Start-Up Project

ACTIVITY	COST TO CRASH FIRST MONTH	COST TO CRASH SECOND MONTH
Construction of facility (I)	$50,000	$75,000
Equipment delivery (H)	20,000	40,000
Selection of plant manager and management personnel (B)	5,000	Impossible

tional costs expected, arguing for a 2-month speed-up in the plant's start-up. Note that the critical path method and marginal analysis are both called for in analyzing trade-offs of time and cost in project scheduling.

AN ALTERNATIVE:
PROGRAM EVALUATION
AND REVIEW TECHNIQUE (PERT)

At about the same time as the critical path method (CPM) was developed in the late 1950s, a similar technique called PERT (program evaluation and review technique) was also developed. Both CPM and PERT require the construction of a precedence diagram, such as Figure 11A-1; they both share the concept of the critical path as determining the least time for project completion. In contrast to CPM, PERT offers a different graphical technique and an added wrinkle.

Graphing PERT

Where CPM places activities to be performed at the nodes of the network diagram and uses arrows only to indicate which activities follow others, PERT uses a different convention. Activities are placed on arrows and the nodes of the network serve as events—the starts and completions of various activities. In order to preserve the proper precedence relationships using this graphical convention, dummy activities and events must sometimes be introduced. Figure 11A-6 illustrates this with a portion of the precedence relationships from the plant start-up example. As Figure 11A-6 implies, PERT is more cumbersome to graph than CPM.

Time Estimate Variations

PERT can be used to provide some insight into likely variations in the completion time of the project. Individual estimates of the variance in per-

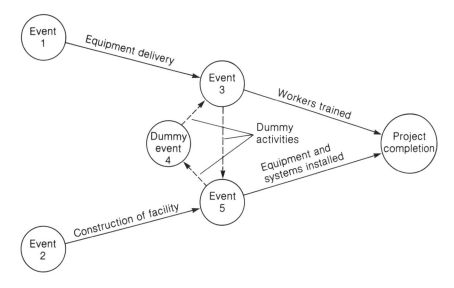

FIGURE 11A-6 A sample PERT network using a portion of the plant start-up example.
(The dummy event and activities are used only to clarify that equipment delivery and facility construction must both precede worker training and equipment and systems installation.)

forming each activity are made. By assuming a certain distribution for these variances and by insisting on the independence of each activity from others, an estimate of the time variance in accomplishing the entire project (and thus the probability of completing it by various dates) can be made by summing up the variances along the critical paths. The assumptions ensure that the distribution of the summed variances will be normal.

As may be surmised, using PERT in this way to calculate a project completion time variance and probabilities of completion by specified dates is a bit concocted. The variance for the entire project can be only as good as the variance estimates for individual activities, and often there is little information on which to base such variance estimates. Using PERT in this way can be more trouble than it is worth.

QUESTIONS

1. What are the main differences in the key planning and control features of each of the following pairs of production processes?
   a. Job shop and continuous flow
   b. Worker-paced line flow and machine-paced line flow
   c. Job shop and a hybrid process

2. The planning goals for the different processes are very similar. However, the factors that affect the attainment of these goals differ in four main areas: meeting delivery, identifying the scarce resource, identifying the valued aspect of the product or service, and materials. Discuss each of these areas briefly, paying particular attention to the policies and/or approaches available within each area.

3. What is the purpose of establishing a production schedule?

4. The development of a master production schedule requires serious decision making, certain types of data, and a strategy for meeting the production goals set. List the main elements in each of these that must be considered. How do these elements influence the preparation of a master schedule at Ridgely Sporting Goods?

5. "Maintenance should be viewed as a machine that must be scheduled like any other." Comment on this statement.

6. Compare optimization and nonoptimization techniques for deriving production schedules.

7. Define and/or give the mathematical expression for the following:
   a. objective function
   b. structural constraints
   c. nonnegativity conditions
   d. feasible region
   e. boundary line
   f. isocost lines

8. The linear programming method has numerous applications in operations problems; it also has several limitations. Discuss each of these in turn.

9. What is the concept of duality as it relates to linear programming? How is it useful in understanding production planning?

10. Describe two ways of monitoring a production schedule. Illustrate your description and discuss the advantages and disadvantages of each monitoring technique.

11. Compare and contrast the worker information requirements in the batch flow and line flow processes.

12. What are some of the main ways in which quality can be controlled and improved? Does adding another quality check always benefit an op-

eration? What are some different kinds of quality checks?

13. Define the following terms and discuss their significance for and application to quality control:

   a. mean

   b. variance

   c. normal distribution

   d. Type I error and type II error

   e. double sampling

14. Briefly describe the critical path method and discuss its relation to project costs and timing. How does PERT differ from CPM?

PROBLEMS

1. Can a material requirements planning system be implemented successfully in a process that operates with a decoupling inventory? Support your answer.

2. As the demand on a factory falls, should its managers adopt different decision rules concerning the number of setups and/or the run lengths desired? Why or why not?

3. It has been observed that large-tract builders do *more* subcontracting than do smaller builders. This runs against the typical view that large size fosters more vertical integration. How can you explain this phenomenon?

4. Wecan, Inc., has been awarded a blanket one-year contract for the requirements for the bracket in Chapter 2. Fred wants to start and end the year with 500 units in inventory for safety stock. The contract is for 6000 brackets (average usage 500 per month) with the following estimated demand:

July	500
August	500
September	350
October	400
November	450
December	450
January	650
February	700
March	500
April	550
May	400
June	550

Fred has made the following estimates of production and inventory carrying costs information: startup costs to produce 1–500 on a single shift are $200; to run a second shift, startup costs are $250; to shut down either shift is $150. Storage will cost approximately 50¢ per unit per month, with maximum storage space for 1500 units.

a. What is Fred's best production schedule for the year?

b. Could you set up this problem for the linear programming simplex problem solving technique? Support your answer.

c. Fred has just learned that the second shift operator will return to college in January, and Fred does not want to replace him. How will this affect your production plan?

5. The Pork & Rind firm manufactures "Tater Chips" and "Cheezy Crackers." The firm has combined some old and some new techniques that have caused these two products to have a high sales volume. They can run 9000 ounces of chips or 16,000 ounces of crackers through the oil spray unit per day; 15,000 ounces of chips or 13,000 ounces of crackers can be baked in the oven daily. What's more, the basic dough is the same for both products, and the firm can mix enough for 12,000 ounces of crackers or 15,000 ounces of chips per day. Pork & Rind can purchase enough potato extract for 6000 ounces of chips and enough cheese for 14,000 ounces of crackers. Pork and Rind anticipates a profit of 14¢ per ounce of crackers and 11¢ per ounce of chips.

a. Prepare a linear program solution for their daily production schedule that will generate the most profit.

b. If Pork and Rind were to try to generate more capacity, on which constraint should they exert the most effort?

c. The firm develops a new product, "Puphy Cheezies," which requires the same inputs as the crackers plus a gun from which to "shoot" them. This gun can produce 8000 ounces per day. The Puphy Cheezies would generate a profit of 8¢ per ounce. Generate a new production schedule that will maximize profit.

6. The Pork & Rind firm decided to go ahead with the production of the Puphy Cheezies, and they need to set up quality control inspection stations. The process flow is from mixer to gun to oil spray to oven and finally to packaging. The cost to put each ounce through each process (i.e., the value added for each process), the expected percentage rejected, and the costs to inspect are in Table 11-A. The tests after the mixer and the oiler require the use of the lab. The other tests are visual only. Where would you suggest that inspectors be stationed?

7. Turnum and Down (T&D) have an automatic screw machine set up to run small brass shafts for a customer. The shaft diameters are supposed to be .375 ± .0025 inches. T&D have determined that the machine is capable of generating the shafts to size normally distributed with a standard deviation of .0005 inches.

a. A sample mean has been taken with a value of .377 inches. What action should be taken?

b. Three sample means of .3755, .376, and .3765 inches have been measured. What action should be taken?

c. Three samples of .376, .3745, and .377 inches were taken immediately after a new load of brass raw material was started. What action should be taken?

d. Three samples were taken of .3755, .3744, and .364 inches. What action should be taken?

e. One sample of .3766 inches was measured. What action should be taken?

8. Kitchener Karson has investigated a future project and has determined the sequence of activities, their duration (both normal and if speeded up), and the cost of overtime (Table 11-B). Mr. Karson has found that for each week over 25 that it takes to finish the project, his firm will have to pay a penalty cost of $325.

a. What is the critical path, and how long is it?

b. Where should Mr. Karson use the overtime, if at all?

c. After the project had been started, Mr. Karson found that a vital piece of equipment had broken down, causing activity F to be delayed an extra two weeks. What, if any, action should he take?

9. The Wyoming Valley Furniture Company (see Situation 8-2) periodically had significant pulses in demand that were difficult to meet without delays in the delivery schedule. In particular, the finish shop would often be pinpointed as the production bottleneck. It was alleged that too much time there was being spent on rush orders and short runs and not enough time on long runs of finished parts.

TABLE 11-A   Quality Control Considerations
(Problem 6)

PROCESS	VALUE ADDED [*]	EXPECTED PERCENTAGE REJECTED [*]	COST TO INSPECT ALL ITEMS [*]
Mixer	$.04	10%	$.02
Gun	.005	3	.01
Oiler	.015	2	.04
Oven	.005	8	.01
Package	.01	4	.005

[*] Per ounce of Puphy Cheezies.

TABLE 11-B   Time and Money Considerations
(Problem 8)

ACTIVITY	FOLLOWS	TIME TO COMPLETE (weeks)	LENGTH ACTIVITY CAN BE SHORTENED (weeks)	EXTRA COST FOR OVERTIME (per week)
A		2⅓	1	$300
B		4	1	$250
C	A	1⅙	none	
D	A	4⅚	1	$275
E	B	1⅙	none	
F	C	10	3	$250
G	D	7	1	$400
H	F,G	4⅚	1	$300
I	E	6⅚	2	$325
J	H	3⅔	none	
K	I	3⅙	none	
L	J,K	6	2	$350

A number of potential solutions had been tossed out for consideration, among them (1) the introduction of a computerized material requirements planning system and (2) a decoupling inventory.

How would you expect each recommendation to work in solving the bottleneck in the finishing department? What kinds of considerations would argue for one solution over the other?

SITUATION FOR STUDY

STAINLESS TANK COMPANY, INC.

Jack Black, the president and chief salesman of the Stainless Tank Company, Inc., has been having difficulty keeping his company "in the black." For several months, Stainless Tank had been showing a loss, even though Mr. Black and the other two salespeople were working hard on generating new sales. Mr. Black had some ideas he wanted to use to increase sales volume and thus offset this loss; but being a cautious person, he thought he would first ask an outside expert to look at his operation. Mr. Black asked Dr. Hanna Hendricks, professor of operations management at the local university, to visit Stainless Tank and, perhaps, provide some insight into the problem.

Mr. Black had purchased the Stainless Tank Company and moved it to its present location. At that time the firm manufactured stainless steel tanks and mounted the tanks and ancillary equipment on modified truck and trailer chassis. These tank trucks were used to transport milk for the dairy industry. This portion of the business had remained stable, both in product design and demand, for the last several years. In addition, the firm contracted with insurance companies for the repair of tanks that had been damaged in accidents.

In recent years the government environmental agency had decided that sewage plants could no longer dump their effluent into the local water-

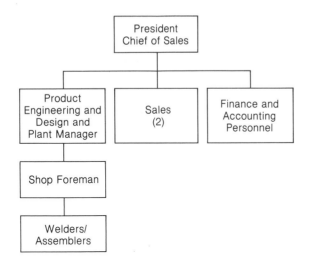

FIGURE 11-A   Partial organization chart for Stainless Tank Company.

Job #		Name
	in	Time clock punch
	out	

FIGURE 11-B   Time card used by Stainless Tank Company.

ways. This regulation opened up a new market for Stainless Tank. Among the current methods of disposing of the liquid and semiliquid output from sewage plants was to haul it to a farmer's field and spread it over or plow it under the field. The sewage tank trucks used the same basic manufacturing technology as the milk tank trucks, with only moderate differences.

The manufacturing process started with the delivery of the truck or trailer from a local dealer. First the truck was modified, as with extra wide fenders and tires that could be fitted before the tank was mounted. The tank fabrication entailed shearing, rolling, and welding. The rounded tank ends, the pumps, and various other parts were purchased. The tank support brackets were fabricated and mounted, after which the tank was mounted. After tank mounting, the piping was done. Some difficulty was usually encountered in getting all the components to fit as they had been designed; thus, that portion of the assembly needed some "cut-to-fit" work.

The workers in the shop were all welders; however, they were expected to do any of the other work necessary to "build" a unit. The shop foreman was the official "expert" on dealing with problems encountered in the construction of a unit. Although Mr. Black knew that this informal delegation of duties and responsibilities would not work well in a large organization, he thought it had worked well for Stainless Tank. See Figure 11-A for a partial organization chart of the company.

After careful scrutiny of the firm and its records, Dr. Hendricks concluded that the major problem was caused by the larger volume of sales. The larger volume had created information needs that could not be handled in an informal manner. The time card for a job (Figure 11-B) recorded that Tom, Dick, or Harry had worked on a particular job for a particular length of time. These cards were the basis for calculating the cost of production both for each unit and for the plant. The total cost of production for each tank was compared to its contracted sales price to determine its profit or loss.

Dr. Hendricks thought the first thing Mr. Black should do to get Stainless Tank back on the road to profitability was to establish a method of scheduling the production of tanks. She thought that this scheduling method would not only provide the shop foreman with the proper sequence of operations and estimated times but also provide management with a comparison of actual progress and planned progress. The analysis of the information and the reconstruction of events from this proposed method should provide insight into where and why the firm is losing money.

1. If you were Dr. Hendricks, what part of the process would you start with to establish a scheduling method? Set up a plan for your proposed investigation.

2. What information or data would you search out? What data would you want the shop to collect and to whom should this information go?

3. How should the materials be controlled in this situation?

4. What do you think of Mr. Black's desire for more volume? How would you discuss this aspect with him?

5. What method of master production scheduling would you use in this case? Support your answer.

6. Do you think linear programming would help Mr. Black? If you do, how would you set it up?

7. Mr. Black particularly likes the critical path method of scheduling and thinks he understands it. How would you counsel him on its use in his tank shop?

REFERENCE NOTES

1. For additional information on production scheduling, see Elwood S. Buffa and Jeffrey G. Miller, *Production-Inventory Systems: Planning and Control*, 3rd ed. (Homewood, Ill.: Richard D. Irwin, 1979) and George W. Plossl and Oliver W. Wight, *Production and Inventory Control: Principles and Techniques* (Englewood Cliffs, N.J.: Prentice-Hall, 1967).

2. For the intellectually curious, a good description of the simplex method is found in W. J. Baumol, *Economic Theory and Operations Analysis*, 4th ed. (Englewood Cliffs, N.J.: Prentice-Hall, 1977). Harvey Wagner, *Principles of Operations Research: With Applications to Managerial Decisions*, 2d ed. (Englewood Cliffs, N.J.: Prentice-Hall, 1975) is also a useful source.

3. For information on alternatives and refinements to the linear programming approach, see Buffa and Miller, *Production-Inventory Systems*, Chapter 6.

4. C. C. Holt, F. Modigliani, and H. A. Simon, *Planning Production, Inventories, and Work Force* (Englewood Cliffs, N.J.: Prentice-Hall, 1960). Also, Holt, Modigliani, and Simon, "A Linear Decision Rule for Production and Employment Scheduling," *Management Science* 2, no. 2 (October 1955), pp. 10–30.

5. For additional information on quality control, see Acheson J. Duncan, *Quality Control and Industrial Statistics*, 4th ed. (Homewood, Ill.: Richard D. Irwin, 1974); Eugene L. Grant and Richard S. Leavenworth, *Statistical Quality Control*, 4th ed. (New York: McGraw-Hill, 1972).

III

DECIDING FUTURE OPERATIONS

The policies and decisions discussed so far in this text have dealt mainly with short-term time horizons and with only modest alterations in the size, design, or scope of operations. In this segment of the text, some costly and fundamental longer-term decisions affecting operations are confronted.

The segment consists of Chapters 12 through 14, each dealing with a different kind of major change:

- *Capacity change.* Managers must periodically consider whether production capacity is sufficient and how any new capacity should be planned, developed, and started up.

- *Technological change.* Technology is always marching forward; this march forward often has implications for a company's products and/ or production processes. This chapter introduces issues in the management of technological change and outlines some of technology's promises and pitfalls.

- *Opportunities for vertical integration.* Companies are repeatedly confronted with opportunities to broaden the scope of their operations by becoming their own suppliers or by taking their products closer to the consumer. They are faced as well with opportunities to narrow this scope. These are make-vs.-buy issues writ large, and this chapter discusses the considerations relevant to decisions about vertical integration.

CHAPTER

12

DEALING WITH CAPACITY CHANGE

In Segment II of this text, which dealt with improving an existing operation, a number of short-term measures to increase an operation's capacity were discussed. Among such measures were:

1. Overtime.
2. Second or third shifts.
3. A more level production rate over time for the purpose of building up finished goods inventory for peak periods of demand.
4. Altering the product mix or the production schedule to reduce setups of machines or work groups and thereby to coax more production out of the operation.
5. Adding more labor to an existing stock of capital—for example, by rebalancing a line flow process.
6. Improving information or materials movement within a process—for example, by introducing material requirements planning systems or decoupling inventories.
7. Modest investments, product redesigns, process modifications, or management innovations that decrease manufacturing cycle times, freeing resources for additional capacity. Many of these measures, with possible long-term implications as well, will be discussed more thoroughly in the subsequent chapter on technological change.

8. Subcontracting products or pieces of the production process. This measure is frequently not an immediately implemented change; it can remain a long-term policy of the company as well as a short-term one.

These measures, either separately or in combination, can have dramatic effects on a plant's capacity. Most of them, however, are short-term substitutes for securing additional space and equipment for production. Overtime, shift-work, revamped production scheduling, and some others can often meet peaks in demand, but they usually cannot be sustained over a long period of time. Improvements to the process, product design, information, or materials handling systems, while desirable long-term policies in themselves, are often incapable of boosting production enough to eliminate a plant's need for more space in the face of sustained increases in demand. While a company normally looks first to such a list of short-term means of adding capacity, more substantial space additions are generally considered at the same time.

This chapter will concentrate on the three "bricks and mortar" choices for adding capacity: (1) on-site expansion of an existing facility, (2) the establishment of a new branch, and (3) the relocation of an existing operation to larger quarters.

Among the issues that surround these choices are:

- How much should any capacity expansion be?
- When should it be timed?
- Where should it be located?

The discussion of these issues and choices comprises the agenda for this chapter. After discussing the basic elements behind the size and timing of capacity expansion in a manufacturing enterprise, we will examine similar issues in a service industry. Finally, we will consider, in more depth, the decision whether to add capacity on site or to establish a new branch or to relocate to larger quarters, and the decision of where to place a new facility.

The decision about contracting capacity is every bit as involved as the decision about increasing capacity—and markedly more difficult for most managers to make. While most of the chapter will deal, implicitly if not explicitly, with capacity expansion, some portions will treat plant closing and contraction as well.

AN OVERVIEW
OF CAPACITY PLANNING

In most companies, most short-term measures to increase capacity (1) can be planned for in a matter of weeks, (2) involve only limited sums of corporate capital, (3) are studied at the plant (rather than the corporate) level, and (4) originate and are carried through in an informal way. While they are the concerns of top management, such short-term capacity measures seldom absorb much of the energies of the top rank of company managers. These short-term measures are apt to be too routine and too devoid of strategic importance to demand the careful study of the layers of management that sit above the particular concerns of individual plants.

Longer-term, bricks-and-mortar capacity expansions occupy top management time to a much greater degree. This is because they involve consid-erable expense, far above the spending authority of even the chief executive officer, and they often have strategic and competitive implications for the company. Moreover, the initiation of capacity expansions is apt to be the result of a formal companywide planning and review procedure rather than the result of a plant's reaction to day-to-day demands.

A typical planning and review procedure is an annual exercise that looks 5 years into the future. (Five years is the typical number. Highly capital-intensive companies like those in the chemical and steel industries may choose 10 years; more consumer-sensitive industries like apparel or fast growing industries like electronics may choose 3 years.) This exercise is driven by a marketing forecast for each year (and quarter, perhaps) of the planning horizon and for each product produced. Available production capacities are estimated as well and the two are meshed together to determine to what extent capacity is in surplus or in deficit. Naturally, both marketing and production estimates are much more nebulous the further into the future the company looks.

More than simply identifying capacity shortfalls and their likely timing over a multiyear horizon, the planning exercise concentrates on alternatives for dealing with such shortfalls. The on-site expansion of certain plants, the character, size, and region for possible new branch plants, or the relocation of some plants may be considered as viable alternatives for coping with capacity shortfalls. The review of the submitted plans normally comes to some tentative decisions about which avenues for remedying capacity shortfalls ought to be explored in more depth and which ought to be shelved, at least for the time being. It is unlikely that firm commitments will be made on any specific proposal but the waters will be tested on many.

The planning and review procedure generally works from the bottom up. (See the organization chart in Figure 12-1.) While the particular indi-

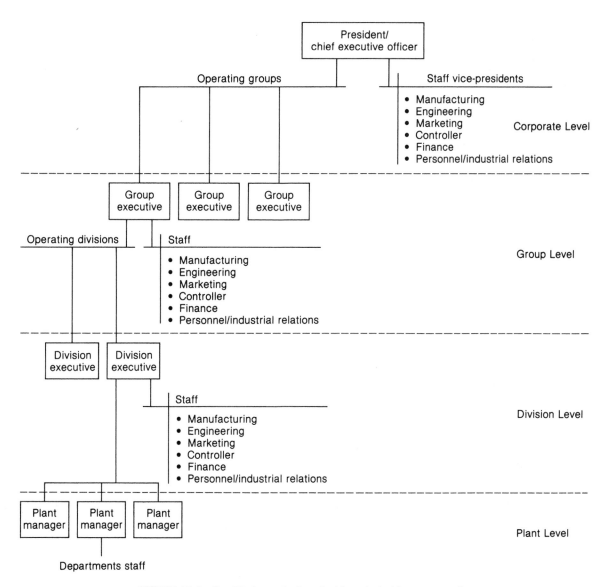

FIGURE 12-1 Simplified organization chart for a typical large corporation.

viduals involved vary from one organization to another, generally plant managers and their staffs work out the lowest tier of corporate needs and priorities. The divisions under which the plants operate review and expand on the plant proposals and needs and address more far-reaching issues. The same kind of review and expansion occurs at the group level (groupings of divisions), if such a level exists, before the corporate level operations committee (or some similar body) reviews the refined proposals. For our purposes, on-site expansion is probably initiated at the plant level and approved at successively higher levels in the corporation, although it could also be initiated at the division or group level. New branch plants and relocations, on the other hand, usually originate not at the plant level (understandably, since the plant itself is not responsible for such an action) but at the division, group, or corporate levels.

As a result of the planning and review procedure, the divisions (and groups) are given a mandate to develop in-depth analyses of the on-site expansion, new branch plant, or plant relocation proposals that surfaced during the planning process. These in-depth analyses include engineering specifications and cost/timing estimates; specific size, product, worker and manager requirements, and location decisions; and an economic analysis (sometimes called a capital budgeting analysis). The analyses, after they have been completed and approved at the group and division levels, make

their way to the company's board of directors for final approval and the authorization to spend the necessary funds.

In broad outline, this planning and review procedure is fairly typical for capacity expansion or contraction.[1] It may sound straightforward, and in many cases it is, but there are many other cases where the choices and issues are complex and require clear and systematic analysis.

DECIDING HOW MUCH CAPACITY TO ADD AND WHEN

How can managers decide how much capacity to add and when to have that capacity in place? To ground a discussion of these uncertainty-riddled decisions, consider Situation 12-1.

SITUATION 12-1

KEMPER GAMES, INC.

The latest sales figures were very encouraging. Laura Kemper, President and Chief Executive Officer of Kemper Games, Inc., could not help but smile. After 4 essentially static years, Kemper Games looked like it was headed for an absolutely fantastic sales year that would carry the small company into the top ranks of the growing game industry. The reason behind this success was Kemper's latest entry in the market, "Bungle, The Game of Life Styles." Laura, an inveterate games player herself, had developed the game over the past 2 years with her husband, Peter, who headed the company's product development department. The company had introduced it about 6 months ago.

Bungle was an adult board game for two to six players. The game produced no winners—everybody lost. This outcome apparently struck a responsive chord in adults of every age and income group. The game's early success had set Peter Kemper to the task of de-

veloping a successor game, Deluxe Bungle, which would soon be ready for production. Deluxe Bungle was played by two-person partnerships (e.g., couples). In playing Deluxe Bungle, not only did everyone lose, but partners were encouraged to turn against one another. Peter had high hopes for the game, although no marketing study had been made as yet.

Bungle's success, however, was soon going to create capacity problems at Kemper Games. The factory could reliably produce about 900 sets per day in two shifts and inventory stood at 3000 sets. The magnitude of the problems anticipated depended in large measure on the particular forecasts for the game's sales (see Table 12-1). The range in the forecasts was due mainly to variations in the assumptions used. Low estimates derived from regarding Bungle as a fad that would soon pass. Higher estimates regarded Bungle as a long-running staple, like Monopoly.

The forecasts influenced not only the size of any ad-

TABLE 12-1   Forecast of Bungle's Sales
by Upcoming Quarters
(Kemper Games, Inc.)

QUARTER UPCOMING*	FORECAST 1† (sets/day)	FORECAST 2‡ (sets/day)
1	600	600
2	750	750
3	1050	1050
4	1500	1500
5	1200	1500
6	900	1500
7	750	1500
8	500	1500

SOURCE: Marketing Department.

* The company plans for 62 days of production each quarter.

† Forecast 1 assumes that Bungle's sales are merely a fad that will peak in quarter 4 and gradually taper off.

‡ Forecast 2 assumes that Bungle's sales will parallel those of Mastermind and Boggle. After rising like a fad, they will sustain themselves at a high level.

ditions to capacity but also the nature of those additions. Laura Kemper confronted a menu of choices concerning capacity:

1. Kemper Games could expand on-site (enough space and lead time were available to do so), or it could lease nearby space to satisfy forecasted requirements. Table 12-2 includes some cost estimates for the various space additions correspond-

ing to the forecasted sales figures. The space could be used for any of Kemper Games' products since nearly all of them required printing, plastic fabrication, gluing, and assembly. Costs for the additional equipment and working capital needed to reach various output levels are also included.

2. The company was going to operate two production shifts in the upcoming first quarter, doubling production from its current rate of 450 sets per day. A third shift was a definite alternative. Wage premiums would have to be paid, though, to attract a suitable workforce and supervisory personnel. In addition, productivity was expected to be less in the third shift, because the workforce quality would probably be lower than that prevailing in the first two shifts and because only a skeletal staff would supervise production. A 25 percent wage premium over first-shift operations was expected as well as an effective output rate of 90 percent of the first shift. Labor constituted 40 percent of a set's variable cost of $2.40.

3. Kemper Games had so far manufactured all its games in its own facilities. However, the company could subcontract the manufacture of the entire game or of certain components (e.g., the printing of the board, the cards drawn as part of the game, the plastic pieces). The convenience of subcontracting was costly. According to one estimate, the 40 percent contribution margin that Kemper

TABLE 12-2   Cost Estimates for On-Site Expansion and Leasing Options
(Kemper Games, Inc.)

A. Costs of on-site expansion (Present space allocated to Bungle production is 40,000 square feet. Current two-shift production capability is 900 sets per day.)

ADDITIONAL PRODUCTION RATE PER DAY OVER TWO SHIFTS	SQUARE FEET REQUIRED	ESTIMATED COST (PLANT)	ESTIMATED COST (EQUIPMENT) AND WORKING CAPITAL
300	15,000	$225,000	$ 75,000
450	20,000	300,000	100,000
600	24,000	360,000	120,000
750	27,000	405,000	175,000

B. Costs of leasing the only nearby existing facility:

20,000 square feet or less—$7.00 per square foot per year
More than 20,000 square feet—$6.50 per square foot per year

Games enjoyed on the $4 factory price of Bungle (the retail price was $7.95, just about a 100 percent markup) would be eroded to 20 percent through subcontracting the entire game.

It was also possible for Kemper Games to reduce or even to eliminate its need for additional capacity by pricing the game higher. However, Laura had decided to accept a lower margin than was the norm in the industry, and thus a lower retail price, in order to spur sales of Bungle and to spread the Kemper Games brand name. The initial marketing report for Bungle with estimated sales at different retail prices is reproduced as Table 12-3. Presently, sales for quarter 1 were running about 60 percent ahead of that market forecast.

Laura felt if Kemper Games was to have enough time to act on the on-site expansion option, she would

TABLE 12-3   Marketing Report on Sales by Price Category (Kemper Games, Inc.)

RETAIL PRICE	CORRESPONDING FACTORY PRICE	SET SALES PER DAY*
$ 7.00	$3.50	420
8.00	4.00	360
9.00	4.50	315
10.00	5.00	285
11.00	5.50	260
12.00	6.00	240

*Set sales per day are estimated at 6 months after introduction.

have to act within the week. Any new on-site construction, begun now, was not likely to be available until the start of quarter 4. Inventory would have to be built up in the interim, which Kemper Games would be able to carry at a rate of 10¢ per unit per quarter.

DISCUSSION OF KEMPER GAMES

Kemper Games finds itself in the joyous predicament of having invented a successful game that now threatens to overtake the company's ability to produce it. What sales will be is rather uncertain, and the marketing department has spun out two scenarios. Both foresee a dramatic increase in sales in the short run. After the first year, however, the two forecasts steadily diverge; one assumes that the game peaks as a fad while the other sees it as a long-lasting success. The marketing people have underestimated sales to date; one might well wonder whether the sales forecasts are still on the low side. It would be reasonable to expect any capacity plan for the future to be robust enough to cope with another sizable increase in forecasted sales.

The first order of business is to assess whether all three courses of action being considered (expansion, third shift, and subcontracting) are feasible, given the prevailing market forecast. Subcontracting seems feasible since no mention was made of any constraints impeding potential subcontractors. In gauging feasibility, then, it is largely a matter of testing the third shift and expansion alternatives.

Let us test the expansion alternative first. Any expansion on site begun now would not be ready for production until the fourth quarter. In the meantime, two shifts would have to suffice. Fortunately, two shifts begun now will be enough to carry Kemper Games until the fourth quarter, with some to spare. Inventory would be built up in the first two periods and depleted in the third. If the on-site expansion involves 24,000 square feet, the corresponding production rate is 600—just enough to combine with the two-shift rate of 900 per day to meet a continued demand for 1500 units per day. Table 12-4 summarizes how demand would be satisfied under the on-site expansion alternative. As the table makes clear, immediate implementation of the second shift leaves the first quarter buildup as an inventory cushion of 18,000 units (calculated as 300 units extra per day times 62 days)—12.5 percent of expected demand over the first three quarters. Such a cushion is welcome and by no means too large, given the possibly explosive sales for the game.

Let us turn our attention now to the feasibility of a three shift operation. The third shift is expected to be more costly and less efficient than ei-

TABLE 12-4   Inventory Buildup under the On-Site Expansion Alternative
(Kemper Games, Inc.)

QUARTER	DAILY DEMAND	DAILY PRODUCTION	DAILY INVENTORY BUILDUP OR DEPLETION	CUMULATIVE INVENTORY ON DAILY BASIS FOR QUARTER
1	600	900	+300	+300
2	750	900	+150	+450
3	1050	900	−150	+300
4	1500	1500	0	+300

ther of the first two shifts, chiefly because of the quality of the labor and the skeletal staffing of supervisory positions. Specifically, only 405 units (calculated as 450 times 0.9) are expected during each third shift. With this in mind, we can construct an inventory buildup table like Table 12-4, using the larger forecast estimates. As is plain from Table 12-5, the third shift can produce enough inventory early on, if implemented in quarter 1, to tide the corporation over until quarter 11. For the short term, then, a third shift is clearly feasible, although over the long term, if the second forecast prevails, a third shift would come up short of capacity. In that case, only on-site expansion would serve.

On the other hand, if forecast 1 prevailed, on-site expansion just for the Bungle game would be overkill since it would be necessary only for quarters 4 and 5. What seems to be suggesting itself is a wait-and-see approach to on-site expansion. A third shift appears to be the best way to meet short-term demand; a decision on on-site expansion can be deferred until the popularity and longevity of Bungle in the marketplace can be ascertained more precisely, perhaps even as late as quarter 7.

While just this analysis of the feasibility of each of the options may be persuasive to many, a carefully documented decision is still far off. The economics of the decision have yet to be discussed.

Compared with the expansion alternative, both the subcontracting and third shift alternatives leave the corporation with less contribution (i.e., dollars allocable to profit and to pay for overhead) per unit produced. By subcontracting, Kemper Games loses half of its 40 percent contribution margin on the $4 factory price of Bungle. Thus,

TABLE 12-5   Inventory Buildup under the Third Shift Alternative and Forecast 2
(Kemper Games, Inc.)

QUARTER	DAILY DEMAND	DAILY PRODUCTION	DAILY INVENTORY BUILDUP OR DEPLETION	CUMULATIVE INVENTORY ON DAILY BASIS FOR QUARTER
1	600	1305	+705	+705
2	750	1305	+555	+1260
3	1050	1305	+255	+1515
4	1500	1305	−195	+1320
5	1500	1305	−195	+1125
6	1500	1305	−195	+930
7	1500	1305	−195	+735
8	1500	1305	−195	+540
9	1500	1305	−195	+345
10	1500	1305	−195	+150
11	1500	1305	−195	−45

the contribution per unit from subcontracting declines to

$$\$4.00 \cdot \frac{.40}{2} = \$ .80 \text{ per unit}$$

from the present $1.60 per unit.

By going to a third shift, the 25 percent labor premium Kemper Games has to pay will also cut into the contribution per unit produced. In this case, we need to calculate the third shift increase in labor costs (composed of variable costs, labor content, and the shift premium) and subtract this amount, along with the variable costs for the first and second shifts, from the factory price:

$$\$4.00 - \$2.40 - (\$2.40 \cdot .40 \cdot .25) = \$1.36 \text{ per unit}$$

Given that the third shift is feasible for the short term and that its contribution per unit produced is much higher than the subcontracting option, it is clear that the subcontracting option should be dropped from further consideration. Of course, the subcontracting of just a part of the Bungle game is a possibility, but that option has not been developed sufficiently within the corporation to address it here.

It remains to investigate the economics of expansion versus third shift operation. After all, if adding capacity is cheap, Kemper Games may be better off holding excess space for a while, until Deluxe Bungle or some other game can fill up the space, no matter which Bungle forecast prevails. As noted, expansion can come either by building an addition to Kemper Games' original structure or by leasing some space very close-by. Let us resolve the build-vs.-lease issue before examining the economics of the expansion/third shift decision.

Since a build-or-lease decision would possibly prevail only for a demand pattern like forecast 2, let us assume forecast 2 for the purposes of the analysis. In order to meet that forecast, an additional 600 units per day will be needed, implying a space requirement of an additional 24,000 square feet. The estimated cost to build and equip this area of plant comes to $480,000—$360,000 for the plant and $120,000 for the equipment. In return for this investment comes the ability to earn a stream of contribution from the manufacture of Bungle. At a contribution of $1.60 per unit and production of 600 units per day, the investment pays itself back in 500 working days.

While it is nice to see a payback so short, the most persuasive way to analyze the economics of capacity choice is to use net present value (NPV) analysis, sometimes referred to as discounted cash flow analysis. Almost all of the largest and most sophisticated companies employ the net present value technique in their capacity planning decisions.

❋ ASIDE ❋

Net Present Value (NPV)

The technique of net present value grows out of that pervasive concept of opportunity cost. For an investment of such and such a size, a corporation expects to generate a stream of earnings that extends into the future. But, by investing so many dollars in that particular investment project, the company forgoes the opportunity of earning a return on those same dollars by depositing them in the bank to earn interest or by using them to finance another income-generating project. In order to decide, then, whether to undertake an investment, a corporation needs to ascertain whether that investment will likely generate a stream of income whose value over time would be greater than bank interest earnings or the return from other investment projects not undertaken.

Put in other words, because income-generating investment opportunities exist, there is a time value to money. That is, having a dollar today is worth more than having a dollar tomorrow because today's dollar enjoys the opportunity of being put to work to finance an investment that will generate a stream of dollars into the future. How much more is today's dollar worth than tomorrow's dollar (apart, of course, from inflation, which is another matter altogether)? It depends, as we might expect, on the return that can be earned from investments.

This rate of return, usually called the discount rate, typically varies from company to company and industry to industry, since some industries and companies are generally more profitable than others. In any case, the discount rate is at least as high as the interest rate quoted by the banks, since all companies have the opportunity of placing their cash in a savings account.

How can the discount rate be used to value the worth of a dollar tomorrow? Suppose r is the discount rate. A dollar (the principal) invested today at the day-to-day rate of return r would be worth

$$\$1 + (r \cdot \$1) = \$1(1 + r)$$

tomorrow. Put another way, tomorrow's dollar is worth only $1/(1 + r)$ of today's dollar; it has a "present value" of

$$\$1\left(\frac{1}{1 + r}\right)$$

How much is a dollar worth 2 days from now? Even more than today's dollar is worth tomorrow because it has the opportunity of earning interest on tomorrow's interest as well. More formally, a dollar invested today at the day-to-day rate of return r would, in 2 days' time, be worth

$\$1$	+	$(r \cdot \$1)$	+	$r[\$1 + (r \cdot \$1)]$
(principal)	+	(tomorrow's return on today's dollar)	+	(the return 2 days from now on tomorrow's total)

$$= \$1 + 2r + r^2 = \$1(1 + r)^2$$

Put another way, a dollar received 2 days from now is worth only $1/(1 + r)^2$ of today's dollar. Its "present value" is

$$\$1\left(\frac{1}{(1 + r)^2}\right)$$

As we should expect, a dollar received 3 days from now is worth $1/(1 + r)^3$ of today's dollar, and so on for successive days.

How can we use the discount rate to value a stream of income, such as would be generated by an investment? Suppose the investment returned a dollar tomorrow and a dollar the next day. How much should we value the investment? Essentially we have already solved for this value. It is merely the sum of the present value of a dollar received tomorrow and the present value of a dollar received 2 days from now. Hence, the value of the stream of dollars received tomorrow and 2 days from now equals

$$\$1\left(\frac{1}{1 + r}\right) + \$1\left(\frac{1}{(1 + r)^2}\right)$$

It is easy to see then that the value today (i.e., the present value) of a dollar received in each of n days is simply

$$(1) \quad \$1\left(\frac{1}{1 + r} + \frac{1}{(1 + r)^2} + \frac{1}{(1 + r)^3} + \cdots + \frac{1}{(1 + r)^n}\right)$$

What would be the value of a dollar received beginning on day 3 and extending to day n? Obviously, it is

$$\$1\left(\frac{1}{(1 + r)^3} + \cdots + \frac{1}{(1 + r)^n}\right)$$

but the ability to add and subtract present values implies that this figure can be computed as the present value of a dollar received from tomorrow through day n less the present value of a dollar received tomorrow and the next day. This ability to add or subtract present values comes in handy when computing them.

It is important to understand how the present value calculation is affected by changes in the discount rate and the time horizon chosen:

1. The higher the discount rate, the lower the present value of any stream of income. Income received in distant periods is particularly hard-hit by high values of r, since $(1 + r)$ is raised to successively higher powers.

2. The longer the time horizon over which income is to be received, the higher the present value of any income stream. As the horizon stretches on, however, less and less is added to the present value, other things being equal.

We have discussed net present value and the discount rate in terms of days. Of course, usually the discount rate is quoted on an annual basis, and the cash flows associated with the investment are grouped into yearly accounts. The cash flows should be adjusted upward each year for the expected rate of inflation when the discount rate is in nominal terms.

The actual calculation of net present values is accomplished by evaluating the expression

$$\text{cash flow}_0 + \frac{\text{cash flow}_1}{1 + r} + \frac{\text{cash flow}_2}{(1 + r)^2} + \cdots + \frac{\text{cash flow}_n}{(1 + r)^n}$$

where the subscripts refer to the year (or period) of interest. This calculation can be done term by term (the only option when the cash flows are all dissimilar) or many terms at a time if a cash flow remains the same over a number of periods and can be factored out. Many calculators are programmed to calculate present values, and tables exist with (1) the present value of a dollar received in a certain period given such and such a discount rate and (2) the present value of a dollar received each period for so many periods at such and such a discount rate.

In investment decisions, if the calculated net present value is positive, the corporation can expect to increase its worth by undertaking the investment. If the net present value is negative, the investment should not be undertaken, at least on economic grounds. (There may be other factors to consider in making such a decision.)

---

*

USING NPV TO ASSESS THE BUILD/LEASE CHOICE AT KEMPER GAMES, INC.

To build an on-site expansion of 24,000 square feet requires an initial outlay of $480,000. For this investment, the company expects a contribution four quarters out of

$1.60 contribution/unit • 600 units/day
• 62 workdays/quarter = $59,520 contribution/quarter

and a stream of annual contributions after that of $238,080 (4 • $59,520) per year. While different assumptions can be made about the relevant discount rate on the investment and the proper time horizon, the choice of a 15 percent rate and a short time horizon of 5 years for the toy and game industry is as defensible as any other. The cash flows involved in this investment, excluding taxes from consideration, are shown in Table 12-6.

TABLE 12-6   A Comparison of Cash Flows (Kemper Games, Inc.)

YEAR	CASH OUTLAY (−) OR RECEIPT (+)	
	ON-SITE EXPANSION	*LEASING*
0	− $480,000	− $120,000
1	+ $ 59,520	+ $ 82,080
2	+ $238,080	.
3	.	.
4	.	
5	+ $238,080	+ $ 82,080

The net present value of this stream at 15 percent is $162,800. Kemper Games can thus expect to make money on this investment. But, we still must compare it against the leasing option to see which would bring the higher expected increase in the company's worth.

Leasing 24,000 square feet of space at $6.50 per square foot per year comes to an annual expense of $156,000. This cost cuts into the $238,080 annual contribution, although leasing eliminates the plant expense of $360,000. Thus, the cash flows involved with leasing (again excluding taxes from the calculation) are also shown in Table 12-6.

The net present value of this stream of cost and contribution at a discount rate of 15 percent is $155,150. Since this figure is less than the $162,800 present value of the build on-site option, the economics say build rather than lease, although there is not much difference between the two.

THIRD SHIFT OPERATION VERSUS BUILDING ON SITE

We can now turn to the economics of third shift operation versus building on site. Suppose forecast 1 prevails. A three-shift operation can meet the sales demand for the five quarters Kemper Games will need in order to determine whether forecast 1 or forecast 2 correctly gauges the market. Thus, for the first year and for the first quarter of the second year, there will be a stream of contribution from the units sold. There will also be a stream of inventory carrying charges (given as 10¢/unit/quarter) for the units actually produced. It is the sum of the net present values of these streams that we are interested in.

Note that because forecasted needs in excess of 900 units per day, which is the two shift capacity, occur only in quarters 3, 4, and 5 of forecast 1, the contribution to be reaped from the third shift occurs only in those quarters. Nevertheless, since third shift production should begin in quarter 1

and last through quarter 5 before being dismantled, inventory will accumulate all through that period. Accumulated inventory must be financed and this is a charge to be considered. This reasoning suggests that both the second and third shifts should be discontinued in quarter 6 so that the excess inventory can be drawn down. This may well be an optimistic action, especially if demand continues at a somewhat higher rate than anticipated by forecast 1. More than likely, only the third shift would have to be discontinued, but for purposes of the calculation, let us stick strictly to forecast 1. We can summarize these flows of contribution and costs as shown in Table 12-7.

The net present value of this stream of cash flows at a 15 percent discount rate is $25,900. This figure confirms that even with the high inventories that are maintained under the option of instituting a third shift, the decision is a profitable one for Kemper Games. It is not hard to see that if forecast 1 prevails, building a plant just to get over the peak demands of quarters 3, 4, and 5 is not advisable. Contribution is raised from $1.36 to $1.60 per unit, but the volumes demanded are so low that total contribution, undiscounted, comes to barely over $100,000 and the total investment required is almost half a million. Thus, if forecast 1 prevails, a third shift operation is preferred.

Suppose forecast 2 prevails, however. How different are the results? We already know that

TABLE 12-7   Contribution and Cost Flows (Kemper Games, Inc.)

| | CASH OUTLAY (−) OR RECEIPT (+) | | |
YEAR	CONTRIBUTION	INVENTORY CARRYING CHARGES	TOTAL
0	$0		
1	+ $63,240	− $29,760	+ $33,480
2	+ $25,296	− $22,630	+ $ 2,666
3	$0	− $ 7,965	− $ 7,965

TABLE 12-8   Contribution Attributable to Sales from Third Shift Operation
(Kemper Games, Inc.)

YEAR	QUARTER	CONTRIBUTION FROM UNITS SOLD FROM THIRD SHIFT	CUMULATIVE INVENTORY ON DAILY BASIS FOR QUARTER, FORECAST 1	INVENTORY CARRYING CHARGES ON THIRD SHIFT PRODUCTION
1	1	0	+705	$4371
	2	0	+1260	7812*
	3	$12,648†	+1515	9393
	4	50,592	+1320	8184
2	5	25,296	+1425	8835
	6	0	+975	6045
	7	0	+675	4185
	8	0	+575	3565
3	9	0	+475	2850
	10	0	+375	2325
	11	0	+275	1705
	12	0	+175	1085

*Calculated as (1260 cumulative inventory held per day of that quarter, from Table 12-5) · (62 days/quarter) · ($.10 inventory carrying charge per unit per quarter)

†Calculated as [(1050 − 900) = 150 units/day of third shift production sold] · (62 days/quarter) · ($1.36 contribution/unit)

three shifts can provide only enough inventory to last through quarter 10 and that, with a lead time of three quarters necessary for the build option, a decision on building a plant expansion can be delayed only until quarter 7. Since Kemper Games must build at some point if forecast 2 prevails, the question then can be rephrased as "If forecast 2 prevails, should Kemper Games build now or later?"

If the corporation builds now, it faces an immediate outlay of $480,000, contribution of $59,520 in quarter 4, and a stream of $238,080 per year in contribution thereafter, as we saw in Table 12-6. The net present value of this stream of cash flows is $162,800.

If the corporation builds later, say beginning in quarter 7, three shifts would be maintained through quarter 10 and inventory carried throughout that period. The extent of the required inventory buildup is already documented in Table 12-5 and the inventory carrying expense for any quarter is simply the quarter's cumulative inventory on a daily basis multiplied by 62 days per quarter and the 10¢/unit/quarter inventory charge. Table 12-8 develops the contribution attributable to sales from third shift operation in the first year, namely $12,648 in quarter 3 and $50,592 in quarter 4. Since demand remains constant at 1500 units per day in forecast 2, the $50,592 figure is maintained in all subsequent quarters. In summary form, these flows of contribution and cost, including the cash outlay for the plant expansion in year 2 and the resulting cash flow from it, are shown in Table 12-9.

The net present value of this stream of cash flows at a discount rate of 15 percent is $200,850. Since this figure is higher than the NPV for the build-now option, the economics argue for deferring the on-site expansion and filling the gap in the meantime with a third shift operation.

Under both forecasts, a strategy of using three shifts until at least quarter 10 is preferred. Not only is it feasible but the economics, under the assumptions made, are superior.

TABLE 12-9 Contribution and Cost Flows from Build Later Option
(Kemper Games, Inc.)

| | | CASH OUTLAY (−) OR RECEIPT (+) | |
YEAR	CONTRIBUTION	INVENTORY CARRYING COSTS AND INVESTMENT COST	TOTAL
0	$0		
1	+ $ 63,240	− $ 29,760	+ $ 33,480
2	+ $202,368	− $500,646	− $298,278
3	+ $220,224	− $ 3,069	+ $217,155
4	+ $238,080	$0	+ $238,080
5	+ $238,080	$0	+ $238,080

Are there any arguments for a build-now strategy? While none of the noneconomic arguments may be strong enough to cause the abandonment of immediate three-shift operation, there are several reasons why on-site expansion may have to be undertaken sooner than quarter 7:

1. If Deluxe Bungle is introduced to the market, and if its sales parallel those of Bungle, Kemper Games may need considerably more capacity than three shifts could ever hope to provide.

2. The marketing department seriously underestimated Bungle's appeal, and there is no assurance that its sales estimates now are correct. Of course, this is a difficult task, at best. If sales are understated again, however, Kemper Games could quickly fall short of capacity.

3. The economics advise establishing a third shift at the same time as a second shift is being established. The addition of so many new workers so quickly is bound to have a serious impact on productivity. The company's managers simply cannot be expected to train two new shifts of workers without considerable start-up difficulties and monumental exhaustion. The capacity plan should allow for the especially low productivity both the second and third shift can be expected to suffer for two or three quarters.

These three considerations ought to temper our enthusiasm for the third shift alternative. While they may not deter the establishment of a third shift in the near term, they should keep us alert to the need for additional production space.

LESSONS FROM KEMPER GAMES, INC.

It should be clear from this discussion that even a relatively simple capacity situation, such as that faced by Laura Kemper, can be surprisingly complex in its analysis. No wonder then that most corporations take months developing and reviewing capacity plan proposals.

As we have seen, there are some critical features to the typical capacity plan and its analysis: the forecast, gauging capacity, the transition to increased space, economic analysis with net present value, dealing with risk, and noneconomic considerations.

The Forecast

The driving force behind the typical capacity planning exercise is a forecast or group of forecasts of sales in the upcoming quarters and years. In most companies, the forecast itself is not the particular responsibility of the production or operations managers, although they might have a hand in it. More often, the marketing department for a particular product or product line is charged with forecasting sales.

Forecasting the long term is frequently a real crap-shoot, especially if the market is not well defined or the product is new or highly dependent on the fortunes of a hard-to-predict national economy.* Over the years, forecasting techniques have become increasingly sophisticated, although one must admit that an entire arsenal of mathematical hocus-pocus may fall short of a single person's "gut feel" or refined intuition.[2]

A production/operations management text is not the proper place for an extended discussion of forecasting methods. Suffice it to point out that forecasts are usually based on (1) the recent history of sales and any trends in that history, and/or (2) polls, samples, trials, and the like, which are designed to indicate the attitudes, preferences, or actual buying patterns of consumers (people or companies). Table 12-10 provides a brief summary of the most popular forecasting techniques.

Forecasting, like market research in general, has become increasingly statistical. In analyzing history and trends, for example, a variety of techniques are available to purge the randomness out of the data, leaving just the trend and any cyclical or seasonal variations around that trend. The available techniques often massage actual data so that they are compatible with prior expectations about how the short-term future will differ from the past. For instance, there are techniques to ensure that future estimates will not differ too wildly from present, past, or other future estimates; these are called smoothing techniques and averaging techniques. One might also expect that the future will depend more on the present and recent past than on the more distant past, and there are weighting techniques of various kinds to ensure this result. These techniques—moving averages, exponential smoothing, and their ilk—rely solely on past values of the item being forecast to predict the future. They are best used for short-run forecasts.

Regression analysis takes a different tack; it permits the inclusion of factors other than past values of the forecasted item in the determination of the new forecast. With regression analysis the impact of one variable thought to influence future sales (say, gross national product) can be isolated from another variable of potentially very different behavior (say, minutes per week of national television advertising) and/or isolated from past periods' sales. In regression analysis, past data on sales, GNP, and TV advertising are used to estimate the so-called forecasting model, and estimates of future GNP and TV advertising can then be used by the model to generate estimates of future sales. If sales really do depend on the variables isolated and in the ways postulated, such regression models can be quite accurate, even in regard to the extended future.

A word of caution about the use of these statistical techniques. As one might expect, the actual forecast depends heavily on the choice of statistical technique; it pays to think through one's expectations about how sales will behave and to choose the statistical technique that is in harmony with those behavioral expectations.

The use of sampling and trials is a more expensive, but often more reliable, way to gauge future sales than reliance on past data. A different kind of statistics is called for here, for these forecasting methods are akin to the design of scientific experiments. How many people to sample and with what

---

*One should be careful to distinguish short-term forecasting, such as we could apply to the aggregate planning and scheduling of Chapter 11, and longer term forecasting, such as usually applies to capacity decisions. In the former case, the forecast need only "project" recent trends into the immediate future, possibly taking into account seasonalities. Such "projections" seldom involve an in-depth analysis of the forces at work in the marketplace. Analysis of the underlying forces behind sales, on the other hand, is an important component of longer term forecasting.

characteristics? How to set up a test market—where, how large an area, how long a period of time? How to advertise and market the product? These are important considerations, but beyond the province of this book.

Production/operations managers ought to be sensitive to the assumptions and methods built into any forecast they must act on, although rarely will they be intimately involved with the forecasting itself. This is not to say that many managers trust the forecasts that marketing concocts; in many circles marketers are notorious for their optimism and resented when manufacturing gets stuck with unsold inventory. A second-guessed forecast that is actually used by manufacturing instead of the "official" forecast is not unknown, and often a sore point between marketing and manufacturing. All this goes to demonstrate that one of the most important interfaces between marketing and operations centers around forecasting and capacity planning and that it often helps for operations managers to be well versed in the forecasting process that must guide many of their decisions.

Gauging Capacity

As we found earlier in this text, production capacity can be very ambiguous, subject to a host of influences. Nevertheless, capacity planning requires some appraisal of present capacity and what can be done to increase capacity by a given amount.

The Transition to Increased Space

As Kemper Games' situation makes clear, it is one thing to recognize the need for increased space in the long term, and quite another to manage the transition from the present to that long-term goal. Capacity increases often come in lumps and in such circumstances managers must devise short-term policies to ease the operation into that capacity increase. At Kemper Games that meant a third

shift but in other situations it may mean subcontracting, an inventory buildup, price adjustments to modify demand, overtime, line rebalance, or something similar.

The nature of this transition, coupled with the needs of the forecast, often determines the timing of a capacity increase. As we saw in Kemper Games, the ability of a third shift to meet demand in the short run enabled the corporation to delay the construction of an on-site expansion until the sales pattern for the admittedly difficult-to-predict Bungle game was known with considerably more certainty.

Economic Analysis with NPV

Finding an economic justification for a particular capacity proposal is an important step in advancing that proposal through approval and implementation. Since capacity plans are almost always multiyear in outlook, the time value of money becomes an important consideration in any economic analysis of a project. With Kemper Games, the technique used to analyze the multiyear economics was net present value, sometimes called discounted cash flow.

The use of present value calculations is clearly superior to the simple, and still widely used, payback calculation. Payback is simply the break-even computation of when a project's income exceeds the investment. Unfortunately, the payback calculation ignores (1) the time value of money (i.e., the fact that income earned in later years is not equivalent, dollar for dollar, to income or expenditures incurred beforehand) and (2) the pattern of expenses and income over time. Thus, wherever the pattern of income and expenses becomes at all irregular, the payback calculation is apt to yield wacky results.

For more subtle reasons, net present value is also preferable to a sophisticated technique called internal rate of return (IRR). The IRR method solves for a rate of discount that yields a net present value of

TABLE 12-10 Popular Forecasting Techniques

TECHNIQUE	HOW IT IS DONE	USES	ADVANTAGES	DISADVANTAGES
Nonmathematical				
Composite of executive opinion (Delphi method)	Simple combination (e.g., averaging) of senior management views on item being forecast	May be used together with mathematical techniques, perhaps to evaluate the latter	Different functional areas of corporation may be represented—sales, marketing, production, materials management, finance.	Can reflect biases of functional areas represented
Composite of sales force	Combination of sales force views, usually in regard to products and/or market areas with which they are familiar	Can be useful in new or nonstandard situations	Builds on experience of sales force	Can reflect the biases (usually optimistic) of the sales force
Composite of customer expectations	Polling of customers about their purchasing desires	Best used when customers can be readily identified	Can capture shifts in customer desires and expectations	Can be expensive
Mathematical—Simple, Requiring Limited Data				
Use of indices	Indices are applied to base data. The indices may come from published sources (e.g., the federal Index of Industrial Production) or may be developed from corporate or industry-specific historical data.	To anticipate shorter term variations in a forecast, especially seasonal or cyclical ones	Cheap, easy to gather data	May be too general for specific use contemplated
Moving averages	Sales are averaged over the previous x periods. Trends identified in these averages can be extrapolated into the short-term future.	To smooth out the randomness of weekly or monthly sales figures (or whatever); work best when little or no seasonality is expected and when explosive growth or rapid decline is not anticipated	Averages may be simple (giving as much weight to distant periods as to recent ones) or weighted (emphasizing a segment of past data, usually the most recent).	Inertia is built in—a handicap when abrupt changes occur
Exponential smoothing	Previous forecast is adjusted by an amount which depends on the difference between that forecast and what actually happened in that period. The formula used is: forecast in period t = forecast in period $t-1$ + α(actual in period $t-1$ less forecast in period $t-1$) The parameter α, usually ranging between 0 and 1, determines how quickly the forecast is modified to reflect actual developments. The higher α is, the more rapid the adjustment. How high to set α is usually determined by an analysis of historical data.	To smooth out the randomness of data from individual time periods	Requires little data and is easy to calculate; works best in shorter time frames	A somewhat arbitrary approach

TABLE 12-10 Popular Forecasting Techniques *(continued)*

TECHNIQUE	HOW IT IS DONE	USES	ADVANTAGES	DISADVANTAGES
Mathematical—More Sophisticated				
Regression analysis	The item forecast (called the dependent variable in the terminology) is postulated to vary systematically with one or more "independent variables." These independent variables can be constructed in a variety of ways, including the use of indices (GNP, industrial production), past values of the dependent variable, and dummy variables (e.g., 1 if the month is May and 0 otherwise). The mathematical aspects of regression analysis fit the specified dependent variable using historical data; this is termed "estimating" the coefficients of the model's specified independent variables. Predictions can then be made by assigning expected values to the independent variables and solving for the dependent variable's values.	Often useful for longer term forecasting	Goes beyond time series extrapolations to ground a forecast on postulated causal relationships. The goodness of the fit of historical data to the specified variables can be judged statistically and can thus lend either credibility or skepticism to the results. The accuracy of regression analysis depends heavily upon the choice of independent variables and the mathematical relationships they are expected to bear to one another.	Can be expensive and time-consuming; requires considerable expertise and judgment to do well
Econometric models	Econometric modeling is a step up from regression analysis. Regression analysis looks at a single dependent variable and one or more independent variables. Econometric models are simply collections of estimated regression equations, where some of the dependent variables in one equation turn up as independent variables in other equations.	Generally reserved for analyzing major "what if" and longer term questions for the corporation	Ideal for determining systematic interrelationships among variables	Developing econometric models is expensive and time-consuming since their data demands are voracious and their estimation tricky.

precisely zero. As might be expected, for most purposes the NPV and IRR methods yield identical results, but there are some offbeat cases where the IRR method can lead to erroneous conclusions and where NPV is considered superior. I leave it to the finance texts to describe the particular cases where the two methods diverge. All that the operations manager has to know is that the net present value technique will always yield a proper figure by which investment projects can be compared. That figure is the gain in the corporation's worth that is likely to result by undertaking the investment.

In any analysis of the economics of a project, assumptions have to be made. It is usually worth exploring how the economics vary under different assumptions. This kind of sensitivity analysis can be applied to (1) the time horizon of the project, (2) the cash flows expected in any year, and (3) the rate of discount to be applied to the cash flows. The sensitivity of a project's net present value to such factors is important because the risks involved with a project may be great; whether it should be chosen may rest on how "robust" its economic value is, given a host of different assumptions. Sensitivity analyses help to identify the projects that entail high risks as well as high returns.

Dealing with Risk

A corporation's capacity decisions are among the more uncertain it faces. While there is no sure-fire way to handle riskiness, it usually is helpful to know whether adding capacity is cheap or expensive and what penalties the corporation faces by having either too much or too little of it. If, for example, capacity is rather cheap to add and falling short of it would forgo substantial contribution, the corporation is probably better off to carry an excess. Many job shops and batch flow processes involve relatively little capital investment and considerable labor-intensity. In such processes, it is often the case that some excess capacity can usefully be kept for peak periods of demand and

left idle the rest of the time. Its use during the peak periods generates more than enough contribution to finance it for the remainder of the year.

Noneconomic Considerations

While the economics of a capacity project are important, it is a narrow-minded manager who bases his or her decision solely on the economics. Three nonquantifiable (or at least difficult to quantify) factors deserve special mention:

1. *The impact of particular choices of capacity and facilities on existing operations.* The transition to enlarged capacity or to a new facility can be time-consuming and troublesome; it is seldom as smooth as either hoped for or planned. It often pays, however, to make some allowance for the impact of a new project on the existing operation. For example, in the Kemper Games situation, the introduction of the second and third shifts simultaneously is bound to involve an extra amount of chaos. How much is problematic, but its presence should be considered in the decision.

   The nature of these impacts on existing operations is varied. Frequently, a capacity or facilities change will alter the character and extent of materials handling and movement within the company. Marketing and/or sales may have to adjust to such a change as well. Often, too, the start-up of the new capacity saps engineering and management attention from the existing operation. Other impacts abound as well, many peculiar to the company or the investment itself.

2. *The competitive reaction of others in the industry to the capacity change.* Many capacity projects cannot be investigated in a vacuum, since their desirability rests in part on how competitors meet a company's particular decision on new capacity. This is particularly true of oligopolistic industries and those that are sen-

sitive to transportation costs. Steel is a prime example. How a competitor reacts may greatly affect the market in a geographic product line area and alter sales or costs.

3. *Flexibility and new capacity.* In fast-paced industries, where new products, markets, and marketing approaches are routine, production must stay flexible. The choice of a capacity project in one form or another may hinder or help the company's ability to keep abreast of the latest developments. Flexibility is very difficult to quantify, but its importance to a firm's continued success can be immense.

CAPACITY IN A SERVICE INDUSTRY

Most services are provided (1) on demand, (2) with interaction between the customer and someone who conveys, and often provides, the service, and (3) without any inventories to help smooth out the supply task. Under such circumstances it is not difficult to understand why capacity planning and choice are a critical element in the management of service industries. As background for a discussion of capacity management of services, consider Situation 12-2.

SITUATION 12-2

QUAKER CITY SQUASH, INC.

So far it had seemed easy, but now Dick Murnane, president of Quaker City Squash, Inc., faced the first tough decision of his young business career: should he expand operations and, if so, how? For the past 2 years, Quaker City Squash, located in the business district of Philadelphia, had been selling half-hour blocks of time on its six squash courts to anyone willing to pay the $8 fee. Squash is a racquet sport generally played indoors by two people and similar in style to handball. It had been enjoying growing popularity, especially at universities. Once out of college, however, players typically had to join downtown clubs to gain access to squash courts. The club fees were invariably high and covered more than just squash.

Sensing this latent demand, Dick (a former college varsity player himself) used some of an inheritance to purchase a building downtown and convert it into six air-conditioned squash courts, locker and shower rooms, several offices, and a bar and grill area where a bartender/short-order cook served drinks and a limited selection of sandwiches. Business boomed. Soon after opening, Dick extended the hours of operation so that now play began at 7 A.M. and continued to 10 P.M.

every day but Sunday. Further, Dick hired a teaching pro who was now drawing a fine salary from teaching and from restringing squash racquets. The squash pro was regarded as a definite asset to the operation. Even the bar and grill was making money by doing a brisk luncheon and cocktail business.

From all Dick could tell, Quaker City Squash attracted mainly young (under 40) professionals who worked in Philadelphia's business district. Most had been introduced to squash while in college or in graduate school and were looking for a way to stay in shape. Over 90 percent of the clientele was male. The peak hours lasted from 11:30 A.M. to 2 P.M. and from 4:30 P.M. to 7 P.M.; it was rare when a court was open during those times. Average usage outside these hours ran about 50 percent. The same 50 percent usage prevailed all of Saturday as well. Standard practice was to reserve a court at least a day in advance, although no reservations except permanent ones (a year's worth of time at a particular hour and day of the week) were accepted for any more than a week in advance. There were no assigned or permanent lockers; players brought their clothes and racquets with them.

With business going so well, Dick naturally pondered the opening of another Quaker City Squash Center. Two different options presented themselves:

1. Open another center in the business district, much like the one presently in operation. A building suitable for the necessary remodeling was available in another portion of the downtown area. It could be purchased for $300,000 and the remodeling for six courts could be done for $275,000. Operating expenses (salaries, utilities, necessary maintenance, taxes) could be expected to run about $115,000 per year, the same rate as at the existing squash center.

   This new squash center would cater to the same market as the old one, but since it would be located in a different part of the business district it would appeal to a different group of young professionals.

   The available building was somewhat larger than the existing center, and that posed some special problems. Dick could add another court, but that would mean paring some space away from the locker rooms and the bar and grill. Or, Dick could expand the locker room space (some of the permanent reservation holders had been clamoring for their own lockers at the existing facility and would gladly pay for them) and/or expand the space of the bar and grill, making it fancier, perhaps adding a waiter, and permitting the kitchen to expand its limited menu in hopes of attracting more players after their games or of catering to a small band of squash "addicts" who might use the squash center as their own "club." The costs seemed roughly comparable; that is, $40,000 more would pay for either the additional court, or the expanded locker room ($10,000) and an expanded bar and grill (between $20,000 and $35,000 depending on decor and modifications to the kitchen).

2. Alternatively, Dick could open a squash center in one of Philadelphia's suburbs. Demand in the suburbs was more spread out and so only a smaller center, say three courts, could be supported at any one location. Building in the suburbs was likely to be considerably cheaper than remodeling a downtown building. For a suburb along the fashionable Main Line, construction estimates, including land, averaged about $200,000 for a three-court squash center. Operating expenses were also likely to be proportionately lower, the best estimate being $48,000 per year.

   Much less predictable was suburban demand for the courts. Dick had no good feel for how strong any one of several trends would be and what each would mean for the operation:

   • Would a suburban location shift demand to more women players than was true of downtown? Was that demand strong enough so that Quaker City Squash should offer nursery services?

   • Would the peak demand period shift from lunch to, say, the early evening, as was true for many indoor tennis clubs?

   • Would the time pattern of play support opening up later than 7 A.M. and extending play to 11 P.M. or even midnight?

   • Three courts would not support a bar and grill, as in the downtown squash center, but Dick wondered whether some vending machines ought to be substituted.

   • Three courts would not support a full-time teaching pro. Dick wondered whether a part-time pro would be necessary, say in the morning, teaching mainly women.

A further concern of Dick's, no matter which alternative was finally chosen, was how competition would affect all of his operations. Not only was there the threat of new squash centers opening up in either the business district or the suburbs, but there was also the threat of the downtown clubs introducing "squash only" privileges at special rates. Dick wondered whether adhering to the same strategy and being first in the market was sufficient, or whether he should try to "lock in" his clientele by offering memberships like the clubs.

TABLE 12-11   A Comparison of Cash Flows
(Quaker City Squash)

YEAR	NEW DOWNTOWN LOCATION			SUBURBAN LOCATION		
	CASH OUTLAY (−)	RECEIPT (+)	TOTAL	CASH OUTLAY (−)	RECEIPT (+)	TOTAL
0	− $575,000			− $200,000		
1	− $115,000	+ $287,040	+ $172,040	− $ 48,000	+ $143,520	+ $95,520
2	.	.	.	.	.	.
.	.	.	.	.	.	.
.	.	.	.	.	.	.
10	− $115,000	+ $287,040	+ $172,040	− $ 48,000	− $143,520	+ $95,520

DISCUSSION OF QUAKER CITY SQUASH

The situation Dick Murnane finds himself in illustrates many of the unique problems with which service firms have to wrestle, most of which are doggedly difficult to quantify.

The first-cut economics of this situation are actually quite straightforward. For each court, Quaker City Squash now receives $8 per half-hour or $16 per hour of use. There are 5 hours of each weekday when all the courts are occupied; for the remaining 10 hours per day and for all of Saturday only half of the courts are occupied. These figures imply a weekly revenue of $5520 ($920/court), and a yearly revenue of $287,040. We can use this revenue figure together with the investment sum required ($575,000) and the expected operating costs of $115,000 per year to analyze the economics of another downtown location. The cash flows for that investment over, say, 10 years are shown in Table 12-11.

The net present value of the investment (10 years at 15 percent) is a handsome $288,430. We can also calculate the average usage level that must be sustained if the investment is to have a net present value of at least zero. The annual revenues would have to be $229,570 per year to have an NPV of zero and this in turn implies an average usage rate of 51 percent. Any rate higher than that and the NPV turns positive.

In similar fashion, the economics of the suburban location can be calculated. The investment comes to $200,000 with expected annual operating costs of $48,000. If the revenue per court remains the same as downtown with 5 hours of peak play and 10 hours of 50 percent usage, weekly revenues will total $2760 and the yearly revenues will come to $143,520. The cash flow pattern is shown in Table 12-11.

The net present value of this suburban investment (10 years at 15 percent) is $279,390, which is almost as high as for the new downtown location. In fact, shortening the time horizon or raising the discount rate makes the suburban location relatively more attractive. The economics, then, do not argue much for one location over the other.

What must guide the decision are a number of other considerations, most of which are exceedingly difficult to quantify. They are what make the capacity decisions of service industries, in many cases, relatively more troublesome than those of manufacturing enterprises. Among these considerations are the mesh of marketing with operations, competitive reactions, demand modification, and nonspace capacity adjustments.[3] These four considerations can all shape thinking about the need for and the design of capacity in service industries. Although their economic impact is frequently difficult to assess, their importance to the success of any service firm's operation can be crucial. At the same time, deciding what should be done about each is quite a burden. As we shall see, the course Dick Murnane should follow with Quaker City Squash is far from evident.

The Mesh of Marketing and Operations in Planning Capacity

Should Quaker City Squash's courts be centrally located in the business district or should it decentralize its capacity? The juxtaposition of marketing and operations is critical in this regard. Is growth to be found in the suburbs? Which is more convenient: squash near home or squash near work? How much a part of the game is camaraderie, and is camaraderie more likely to flourish at a downtown location? Will significant numbers of women be attracted to the game if courts are situated in the suburbs?

Since capacity is often the "product" in a service business, or at least intimately linked to the service provided, knowledge of why a customer purchases the service is a critical item in the plan for and design of new capacity. This is something Dick Murnane must ponder; the answers are by no means obvious.

Related to the issue of increasing the right kind of capacity is the concern about whether new capacity will undercut the service provided by already existing capacity. At Quaker City Squash, will a new downtown location divert players away from the existing downtown site, or will players refrain from downtown play during the day to play at the suburban location in the evening? To answer these questions, one needs knowledge of the customers, where they come from, and why.

Another aspect of the close marketing/operations bond in a service firm's capacity planning is the need for keeping balance in the mix of elements which make up that capacity. For example, at Quaker City Squash there is the opportunity to build a seventh court, although at the expense of the locker rooms and grill. Alternatively, a private locker room could be installed and the bar and grill expanded.

If one assumes that the new court will attract use just like any of the other courts, the economics

are much more likely to support a squash court than to support private lockers or added space in the grill room. What must be questioned is whether a new court, coupled with smaller locker and grill room space, would actually add enough revenue to warrant its construction. It is conceivable that usage would adjust itself not to the number of courts provided but rather to the locker room and/or grill room space. In that case, adding a seventh court would be a disastrous move since total patronage would actually fall.

Competitive Reactions

We have already discussed the importance of gauging competitive reaction for capacity planning in manufacturing companies. Because capacity decisions (i.e., how much, of what type, and where) are so critical to a service firm's competitive stance, the reactions of competitors are usually even more significant in service industries. At Quaker City Squash, for instance, competitive reactions may take the form of other squash centers being opened in downtown Philadelphia or they may be policy changes at some of the existing clubs (say, the inauguration of separate squash memberships for special fees). In any event, competition can quickly change the earnings potential of all of Quaker City Squash's operations.

Modifying Demand

When a bottleneck is reached in the provision of a service (for example, during the noon hour at Quaker City Squash), often that bottleneck can be relieved, at least temporarily, by manipulating demand in various ways through pricing policies and service policies.

Pricing can be used as both carrot and stick to shift the extent and the timing of demand. High prices can shut off demand or shift it into other time periods. Low prices can stimulate demand. Whether a price cut will actually lead to more revenue as well as greater patronage depends on how sensitive the demand by patrons is to price changes. If price changes of X percent lead to changes in the quantity demanded of more than X percent, the demand is said to be *price elastic* and revenues can be increased by cutting price. If an X percent change in price leads to a less than X percent change in the quantity demanded, the demand is termed *price inelastic* and revenues can actually be increased by raising price. Ascertaining whether demand is in fact price elastic or price inelastic is often hit or miss, however, and it is usually under pressure—severe lack of capacity or embarrassingly excess capacity—that prices are altered significantly.

The extension of existing services and/or the provision of ancillary or complementary services can also have a substantial impact on demand. In terms of the Quaker City Squash situation, the teaching pro, the bar and grill, the private lockers, nursery care, the reservation system, and other extras may all have important implications for demand. One or more of them may be instrumental in attracting demand or in shifting demand from peak times to off-peak times. The reservation system is clearly a tool to apportion demand among peak and off-peak periods, and the timing of the teaching pro and nursery services could also have a bearing on broadening demand away from the peak periods.

Adjusting Capacity without Altering Space Requirements

At Quaker City Squash, space means capacity, but there are a variety of other service industries in which capacity can be increased modestly by employing several techniques:

- Using part-time workers for peak times
- Increasing efficiency via methods improvements, labor specialization, labor cross-training, and the like
- Inducing consumers to provide some of the service themselves (e.g., salad bars at restaurants)
- Sharing equipment or other resources with firms or organizations in the same or a related industry

ON-SITE EXPANSION, BRANCH ESTABLISHMENT, AND RELOCATION

Once a company's managers agree that new capacity ought to be erected to satisfy expected future demand, they still face deciding how that new capacity ought to be implemented. Should on-site expansion, the opening of a new plant, or the relocation of an existing one prevail? This decision lies at the heart of Situation 12-3.

SITUATION 12-3

TIGHE PRINTING COMPANY

"Maybe sometimes you can be too successful," Ruth Tighe mused to herself. The Tighe Printing Company, of which Ruth was president, had enjoyed substantial growth. Ruth was increasingly concerned, however, that continued sales increases simply could not be accommodated without increased space.

The Tighe Printing Company specialized in high volume printing of magazines, catalogs, and business forms. The regional sales of magazines like *Newsweek* and *McCall's* were run on Tighe presses and constituted the bulk of company sales. Timeliness, as could be expected, was essential to the company's

success. The company was located in downtown New Haven, Connecticut, in a six-story structure built in 1923. Founded by Ruth's grandfather 10 years before then, Tighe Printing was the building's first tenant. The company bought the structure in 1935.

As the company grew after World War II and thus required more space, it started kicking out other tenants. By the late 1960s, the company had taken over the entire building, all 75,000 square feet (11,500 square feet on each of the six floors and 6000 square feet in the basement). In 1972, again pressured by space needs, the company leased 15,000 square feet of space in the building next door and knocked out a wall in between. Now even this space was fully utilized.

Ruth Tighe was convinced that she would have to decide soon how she was going to structure the company's growth. The possibility of starting fresh with either a new branch facility or a relocation was appealing, albeit more expensive. Ruth would have to weigh these relative benefits and costs.

Ruth Tighe confronted a choice from among three alternatives:

1. *Continued expansion in the neighborhood.* A building two doors down from Tighe Printing and on the other side of the street was up for either sale or long-term lease. The building was four stories high with a basement, occupying 55,000 square feet. A likely rent would be $2.25 per square foot per year. The asking price for the building was $700,000.

2. *Establishment of a branch plant.* Rather than keep all its production space in close proximity, Tighe Printing could locate a satellite plant elsewhere in the city or in the suburbs. This new branch could house a new press or two and could perhaps concentrate on a certain type of printing (e.g., magazine).

3. *Relocation of the entire operation.* Rather than break up existing operations into two distinct locales or continue a more or less haphazard expansion around the company's main building, Tighe Printing could sell its old holdings and equipment and move the entire operation in one piece to

larger quarters, purchasing new equipment in the process. Exclusive of new machine purchases, a move itself was likely to cost $200,000.

Newly constructed space for either a new branch or a move would cost $18 per square foot or more, depending on location. Rents for suitable, existing space would vary from $2.20 per square foot per year to $3.50 per square foot per year. The higher values would secure space in newer, one-story structures.

As it was now, operations at Tighe Printing left much to be desired. In particular, the movement of goods and information was worsening. The growth of the enterprise through all seven levels of the main building separated departments that logically should have been placed side-by-side. Work-in-process had to be handled almost twice as often as necessary, and, besides being time-consuming, led to more routing errors than Ruth Tighe, at least, felt should be the case. Intrafactory transportation was slow, limited to a single elevator. Because there were only two loading docks, the delivery of paper and other raw materials was often held up to give priority to shipments out of the building. Deliveries often had to be taken at odd hours. In addition, more and more materials and output were being stored outside the plant, sometimes expensively.

The constraints of the building also meant that many of the latest innovations in the printing industry such as computerized typesetting and the faster and larger electronic web presses had to be forgone. Furthermore, space constraints made it impossible to reap the production scheduling advantages of running machines close to one another in tandem and sorting entire magazines or forms on the spot.

DISCUSSION OF TIGHE PRINTING COMPANY

Growth is forcing the Tighe Printing Company to seek more production space, and Ruth Tighe has to choose from among three means of adding that space: expanding locally, placing some operations in a new branch, and relocating to a larger facility. Of these options, expanding locally is the lowest cost one, at least in terms of initial dollar outlay. A building of 55,000 square feet can be purchased for

$700,000 or leased for about $125,000 a year. That much space in new construction would cost about $1 million or more to build and upwards of $200,000 a year to lease. Relocating would cost an additional $200,000.

While a local expansion may be inexpensive in the short run, it may be frightfully expensive in the long run, especially if it locks Tighe Printing to outmoded technology, high materials handling costs, and other detriments to an effective operation. There are indications in the situation that some of this is occurring already. What then are the relative advantages of on-site expansion, new branch establishment, and plant relocation?

The Relative Advantages of On-Site Expansion

On-site expansion is by far the most popular way of adding production space. Its low cost (e.g., often no new land acquisition costs), the relatively short time lag associated with it, and its status as a "known quantity" make it appealing. By expanding on-site a company is assured of keeping its labor force intact and it does not have the difficult task of weeding out products or pieces of the production process for isolation in another plant.

Often, too, on-site expansion is viewed as a way to achieve the benefits of so-called economies of scale. This is a slippery concept, however, and it merits some discussion of its own.

─────────────── ❋ ASIDE ❋ ───────────────

Economies of Scale[4]

It is frequently stated that large companies enjoy a competitive edge over small companies because of the inherent advantages of "economies of scale." The phrase has a strong appeal, and large companies with sizable plants have a certain aura about them. General Motors is no stranger to the observation that its continued cost competitiveness is the result of its size. The phrase draws nods of recognition, yet few people can define it and fewer still have thought critically about it.

All too often you hear a company president nonchalantly say something like, "If we increase the size of our operations in this plant, we'll naturally enjoy some economies of scale." There is nothing natural about economies of scale and certainly nothing to be nonchalant about.

Confusion with the term is understandable since it serves as an umbrella for a number of real but quite distinct concepts. Because it is an umbrella term, "economies of scale" often loses its usefulness in making management decisions on plant size.

Volume, Capacity, and Process Technology

How do economies of scale relate to plant size? The standard definition declares that economies of scale are reaped whenever higher output volumes lead to lower unit costs. However, the definition only seems to be clear.

Consider four different plants, all in the same industry. Plants A and B are physically identical in every respect. They differ only in that Plant B produces just a fraction of the volume of Plant A, perhaps because Company A's marketing efforts are much more effective than Company B's. Plant C is similar to Plant A in layout and equipment but is twice the size. Plant D, on the other hand, incorporates an entirely different process technology from the other three and can produce twice what Plant A can produce.

I draw these examples to distinguish among the concepts of volume, capacity, and process technology. As Table 12-12 shows, Plants A and B share the same capacity and the same process technology, although their actual volumes differ. Plants A and C share the same process technology, although not the same capacity; Plants C and D share the same capacity but not the same process technology.

These concepts of volume, capacity, and process technology are important because they all relate to economies of scale.

Economies of Volume

The higher volume Plant A will enjoy lower unit costs than Plant B because it can spread its fixed costs (e.g., overhead, capital costs, machine setup costs) over a greater number of units. If by "scale" we mean "volume," then the difference in unit

TABLE 12-12 Defining the Differences in Unit Costs

PLANT	CAPACITY	VOLUME PRODUCED	PROCESS TECHNOLOGY	MANUFACTURING COSTS PER UNIT PRODUCED
A	100 ⎤ Difference in capacity; same volume to capacity ratio	100 ⎤ Difference only in volume	Type X	$1/unit
B	100	40 ⎦	Type X	Higher than $1/unit
C	200 ⎦	200	Type X ⎤ Difference only in process technology	Lower than $1/unit
D	200	200	Type Y ⎦	Much lower than $1/unit

SOURCE: Schmenner, "Before You Build a *Big* Factory," p. 102.

costs between Plants A and B can be an economy of scale.

For some people, however, this "spreading of fixed costs" seems too trite an example to be labeled a "scale economy," and so they dismiss it. These people then modify the definition of a scale economy to exclude any economies that are essentially "economies of volume."

Economies of Capacity

As the table shows, Plant C's unit costs are lower than Plant A's and thus much lower than Plant B's. Plant C's increased capacity permits it to carry proportionately less raw materials inventory. This is due to the familiar "economic order quantity" result that optimal inventories need increase only as the square root of volume and not proportionately with volume.

On the other hand, because Plants A and C share the same technology, Plant C is not likely to enjoy a proportionately lower work-in-process inventory, but its finished goods inventories may well be proportionately lower. For example, suppose Plants A and C both make two different products. If Plant A has only one production line that it must change over from one product to the other, it will have to build up proportionately more finished goods inventory to cover its demand than Plant C, which

can afford to manufacture each product on a separate, dedicated line. Plant A needs to carry enough of an inventory of its first product to tide itself over while it makes its second product. Plant C need not worry about this problem.

In addition to these inventory-associated economies, Plant C will have an advantage over the smaller Plant A, as its increased capacity allows the luxury of more spare equipment and maintenance capabilities or of additional and useful overhead functions. If scale means "capacity," then any differences in unit costs between Plants A and C can be appropriately called "economies of scale."

Economies of Process Technology

As we can see, Plant C enjoys some cost advantages over Plant A. However, Plant D enjoys even lower costs—for two major reasons: capital-for-labor substitution and labor specialization. Plant D has automated more (substituted more capital for labor) than Plant C. Using more, better, and different equipment, Plant D has been able to produce as much as Plant C, but it employs fewer workers. As a result, its costs are lower. The increased automation at Plant D may or may not be an advance in the state of technology, but the increase in capital certainly alters the process in Plant D as compared with Plant C. Moreover, often a company cannot make small additions to its plant's stock of equipment and space; large additions (frequently termed "indivisibilities") have to be made and are perhaps the classic explanation for economies of scale. Such indivisibilities are usually substantial alterations to a plant's process technology and so are more than just scale changes. They are changes in process technology, and should be recognized and managed as such.

One particular substitution of capital for labor merits special mention. The geometry of processes that deal with free-flowing materials (e.g., chemicals, molten metals) often permits output to vary according to the volume of its capital equipment, while the costs (construction and/or operating costs) vary according to surface area. This is the frequently quoted "6/10 rule," which argues for large-process technologies. The rule is so named because it was found that for chemical plants a doubling of volume leads only to a 6/10 increase in surface area and thus costs. An oil refinery is one such example. Output depends greatly on the sizes of tanks and pipes, but construction and maintenance costs depend more on surface area of the material that surrounds the oil held inside. For most other (non–free-flowing materials) operations, however, such cost advantages are of much less significance.

Plant D also has lower unit costs because it has altered its process technology to specialize its labor for particular tasks. In order to make its process more continuous, jobs are "deskilled." That is, instead of large numbers of highly skilled workers each doing a number of operations to form the product, the process is organized to link together less skilled workers doing a small number of specific operations. The time and responsibility any one worker devotes to a particular product is reduced in an effort to increase productivity through repetition and specialized competence. The pace of the production process shifts from worker discretion to management option. The automobile assembly line is a classic example of labor specialization and management (e.g., mechanical) pacing.

To reiterate, both capital-for-labor substitution and labor specialization alter process technologies. Thus, if by scale we mean "process technology," then we can appropriately call these two means of cost reduction "economies of scale."

Avoiding Ambiguity

As pointed out in the preceding paragraphs, the term "economies of scale" suffers from irredeemable ambiguity. It can take a variety of meanings depending on one's interpretation of "scale" as volume, capacity, or process technology. Even then, there are a variety of ways to effect the economies. Instead of inviting confusion by using the term "economies of scale," people should think of volume, capacity, and process technology separately.

Plant Size Decisions over Time

The plant size decision depends on the careful balancing of a number of alternative technologies, costs, and risks. Over time, these alternatives become more and more blurred. Technological advance is unpredictable, and it is not clear whether new capital equipment with smaller or with larger break-even volumes will predominate. Lots of new technology is sophisticated, expensive, and large scale; and yet minicomputers and some machine tools are persuasive examples of some small-scale technological change.

In sum, "economies of scale" is vague enough to provide easy justification for any number of decisions on plant capacity. Because it is so vague, its usefulness to managers is minimal. Instead, two areas should be carefully scrutinized: (1) the cost reductions a company can achieve through specific changes in a plant's volume, capacity, or process technology and (2) what those changes mean for management control, logistics, inventories, and the ability to respond to product or process innovations.

---
*

Return to the Issues at Tighe Printing

These cautions about economies of scale notwithstanding, on-site expansion sports some very attractive features. Nevertheless, it is not an all-purpose remedy for production space shortages and there are a host of circumstances where either a new branch or a relocation would be preferred.

The Disadvantages of On-Site Expansion: Building the Case for Branching and Relocation

Although frequently attractive, on-site plant expansion can usher in a host of diseconomies as well, particularly if on-site expansion has been a repeated practice. For example, as more and more production space is added on-site, the layout of the plant typically becomes less and less optimal. Rarely is an entire plant reconfigured during an expansion; rather, only portions of the plant get shifted around. The result, over time, is that departments, once close together, become separated. Materials handling and storage become more difficult, with more chances for delay or error. Managers find themselves isolated from one another and/or from the work groups they are supposed to oversee. In short, intraplant transportation and communication become strained and this strain is likely to have detrimental consequences for product delivery and quality.

Staying at the same site often postpones the introduction of new process technology as well. Old equipment is kept in use, old methods are followed, and the advantages of new equipment and techniques are forgone, with consequences for both future costs and product innovation.

Continued on-site expansion means that more and more workers and, often, more and more products, must be managed. Such a layering of expanded responsibilities creates real complexities for managers at all levels. The existing cadre of managers may be asked to supervise more than they are readily capable of, thus lessening the attention certain problems should receive. With more products and output from the same plant, decisions on the levels, composition, and uses of inventories are likely to become more difficult and prone to error. Decisions on production control—what and when to produce, how to sequence it through the factory—are likely to become vastly more complex as well, just as the cost accounting system is becoming more arbitrary and thus less helpful.

With more products in the plant, management runs the risk not only of complicating supervision, inventory, and production control systems and the like, but also of placing incompatible demands on managers, workers, and systems. For example, products produced in low volumes, but with high quality, demand a different mode of management, worker effort, and control systems than products produced in high volumes with little attention to quality. If both are manufactured in the same facility with common management, workforce, and operating policies and systems, the likely result is that both products will suffer in the individual dimensions (e.g., price, quality, delivery) that make a product competitive.

More than this incompatibility problem, the addition of more workers to an existing site is apt to require the increasing formalization of the workforce-management relationship. The workforce is less apt to identify strongly with the company, and labor relations within the plant may become strained. Old management concessions to the workforce may come back to haunt operations. With increasing size, the plant is more likely to become a target for unionization, if it is not already organized.

For these reasons, continued on-site expansion becomes less and less desirable. The alternatives—new branch establishment and plant relocation—can avoid many of these long-term and frequently subtle pitfalls of on-site expansion, although their abilities to surmount certain of these pitfalls differ. Table 12-13 outlines some of the relative advantages of new branches and relocations.

New branch establishment, for example, is at a relative advantage if the plant's problems run more

TABLE 12-13   Advantages of Branches and Relocations Relative to On-Site Expansion

PROBLEM AREA	NEW BRANCH PLANT	PLANT RELOCATION
Plant layout and materials handling	Radical improvements possible with operations placed in branch; some possibilities of improving base plant as operations are placed in branch	Radical improvements possible
New process technology	New technology for branch possible; likely that base plant will keep much of old technology	Scrapping of old plant, equipment, and methods possible; new technology can supplant it readily
Production and/or inventory control	Can mean radical change to production control procedures and policies in new plant, though not much change to be expected for old plant; inventories can build up by adding branch	Can mean radical changes to production and inventory control; inventory levels not likely to be affected
Managerial impact	Additional managers needed to open and run branch; staff demands increased to coordinate plant interactions	Old set of managers can generally run new plant without stretching themselves too thin
Product proliferation	Can easily manage new products, especially if branch plants are organized as product plants	New products less easily managed
Size of workforce	Keeps workforce levels at all plants under desired ceilings	Little or no effect on workforce size
Financial burdens	Extra overhead demanded to cover more than one location, new plant start-up expenses	Moving costs, new plant start-up expenses
Ease of meeting future growth	Relatively easy; geographic growth met best with new market area plants, product introductions with product plants, and vertical integration with process plants	Not easy; shares many future capacity problems with on-site expansion alternative

to product proliferation, workforce size, or meeting expected future growth. By branching, a company can avoid overloading one plant with either too many products or too many workers. At the same time, the new branch can exploit the latest production technology and the most sensible plant design. The operating policies and systems of the branch can also be meshed carefully with the product(s) chosen for manufacture and with the competitive priorities attached to them.

Plant relocation, on the other hand, is at a relative advantage if the plant's problems are more involved with plant layout, materials handling and storage, new process technology, production and inventory control, and lack of management depth. Relocation, by definition, means closing one facility and opening another at roughly the same time,

which means that relocation can readily scrap old capital, technology, and policies for new. Thus, relocation gains in standing when the plant's problems are less related to large size and more to process technology and control.

Return to Tighe Printing Company

From the description of Tighe Printing's problems, it would seem that relocation is best able to remedy them. The company's present site and building are contributing to poor materials and information flow, excessive outside warehousing, and delayed introduction of production process improvements. The time appears appropriate to abandon the company's history of incremental expansion on site in favor of the more radical approach of relocation. New branch establishment appears to be a less attractive solution since some economies are possible by running nearby machines in tandem. Production scheduling seems to be facilitated by bunching the printing presses at the same site.

Tighe Printing has not performed any quantitative study of the likely opportunity costs of maintaining the existing plant in the face of what the company could do at another location. Some such study would be warranted. However, the implications of the qualitative aspects of the situation, which have already been discussed, are unlikely to be reversed, as the study may show.

SITUATION 12-3

TIGHE PRINTING COMPANY (REPRISE)

After considerable thought, Ruth Tighe decided to relocate her growing printing company. Only by abandoning the old six-story structure the company had grown up in, she reasoned, could the company keep abreast of the latest technological changes that were making over the printing industry. New and sufficient single-story space appeared to be the answer. What remained to decide was where that space ought to be located.

After some preliminary scouting by the company's vice-president for operations, four options presented themselves (excluding, of course, the ever-present option of continuing to search for sites). A summary of site-related costs is included in Table 12-14.

1. Long Wharf Industrial Park in New Haven. Tighe Printing could maintain its home in New Haven proper by moving less than a mile to some vacant land in the nearly complete Long Wharf Industrial Park. Only one parcel of land of suitable size was left, a 5-acre site. Assuming single-story construction, having only 5 acres would restrict the square footage of plant space permitted to 110,000 square feet. (Property covenants in the park restricted plant size to no more than half the area of the site.) Nevertheless, the site provided free parking for Tighe's 220 employees and the certainty that none of the plant's workers would leave as a result of the move. Long Wharf was served as well by bus as was the company's old plant. Construction was likely to take 15 to 18 months.

2. Relocate to an existing plant site in East Haven. In East Haven, about 4 miles east of the old factory, Tighe Printing could move into a factory building that had been vacated 6 months before by a machine tool manufacturer. Some renovation was going to be necessary, estimated at $300,000. The company could move in within 5 months. The plant housed 140,000 square feet on 10 acres of land. Thus, while the plant was more than large enough for the company's needs now, there was also the possibility of expanding on site in the future.

The plant was not served by bus, but parking was ample. Ruth Tighe would have to think about alternative means (company bus, car pools) by which all of the plant's present workers would get to work. Ruth expected that some workers might not make the commute across the Quinnipiac River Bridge to East Haven. The area, however, was as densely populated as most neighborhoods in New Haven itself, and reports indicated that labor availability in the area was excellent.

3. Relocate to available land in Hamden. Another site was available about 11 miles north of the old factory in Hamden. A 12-acre site was available there in the Hamden Industrial Park, with all utilities provided. Construction would take between 12 and 15 months, it was estimated. Bus service was available to the plant, but it was very sporadic, coming only every 60 minutes. Parking would be no problem and the proximity to two expressways in the area would shorten the commute of at least some

TABLE 12-14   Site-Related Costs for Plant Relocation
(Tighe Printing Company)

COST ITEM	SITES			
	LONG WHARF	*EAST HAVEN*	*HAMDEN*	*NEW HAMPSHIRE*
Land price per acre	$70,000/acre (for 5 acres)	$18,000/acre (for 10 acres)	$12,500/acre (for 12 acres)	$6,000/acre (for 12 acres)
Estimated cost of building plus land	$2.8 million (110,000 square feet to be built)	$2.1 million (Asking price for 140,000 square feet)	$2.3 million (110,000 square feet to be built)	$1.9 million (110,000 square feet to be built)
Estimated remodeling costs		$.3 million		
Labor costs		Essentially invariant across sites		
Transportation costs		Essentially invariant across sites		
State income tax	9.1%	9.1%	9.1%	0%
Local property tax (% of real value)	4.0%	3.5%	3.2%	3.3%
Insurance per year—fire, etc. (now $10,000/ year)	$15,000	$15,000	$17,000	$21,500

workers. There was surely a number, say 15 to 25 percent, who would not relocate with the company.

4. Relocate to a 12-acre site near Manchester, New Hampshire. Since most of Tighe Printing's business involved magazine or business forms and catalog contracts with national concerns, and since the transportation involved was the U.S. Mail, the company was not necessarily tied to a location within the New Haven metropolitan area. Of course, the company would lose some of its local clients, but with the continuing growth of southern New Hampshire, there was apt to be enough new business to pick up whatever slack existed.

New Hampshire was alluring for two reasons: (1) New Hampshire levied lower taxes—no income tax and comparable property and other taxes, and (2) New Hampshire was closer to Ruth Tighe's ski lodge and summer home in Vermont.

Picking up stakes and moving so far from New Haven would not be without cost, however. Few of the plant's workers could be expected to move to New Hampshire; some of the plant's managers might also jump ship. Labor was available in southern New Hampshire, but the recent word that Ruth Tighe had heard was that labor was becoming increasingly tight, especially for skilled positions. There certainly were not going to be any labor cost savings.

Moving would not be easy for Ruth Tighe herself or for her family. Her husband, an accountant, could find a new job in New Hampshire fairly easily, but a move could be more disrupting to her two teenaged daughters.

Moving to New Hampshire would probably cost an additional $75,000 over the local move estimate of $200,000. Construction time for the plant was estimated at between 12 and 15 months.

Ruth Tighe wondered which of these four sites, if any, she ought to choose. Net sales in the present year were about $12.7 million and net income before taxes stood at about $675,000. Tighe Printing's present site was valued at roughly $1 million.

TABLE 12-15   Cost Flows and Net Present Values (in millions of dollars)
(Tighe Printing Company)

| SITE | INITIAL INVESTMENT | | | YEARLY EXPENSES THAT DIFFER ACROSS SITES | | | PRESENT VALUE OF COST STREAMS* |
	LAND	BUILDING	OTHER	INCOME TAX	PROPERTY TAX	INSURANCE	
Long Wharf	$.350	$2.8	0	$0.061	$0.126	$0.015	$4.414
East Haven	$.180	$2.1	$0.3†	$0.061	$0.090	$0.015	$3.619
Hamden	$.150	$2.3	0	$0.061	$0.078	$0.017	$3.426
New Hampshire	$.072	$1.9	$ .075‡	0	$0.065	$0.0215	$2.588

*Present value calculations assume a discount rate of 15 percent and a time horizon of 20 years.

†Represents the cost of renovating the available East Haven building.

‡Represents the incremental cost of moving to New Hampshire. All relocations will cost at least $200,000, but the one to New Hampshire will cost $275,000.

DISCUSSION OF TIGHE PRINTING COMPANY
(REPRISE)

The economics of this location decision are very similar to the economics of the Kemper Games situation. The time horizon is long and varying cash flows will be associated with the different years of each of the alternatives. Table 12-15 portrays some cost flows and their illustrative net present values. A time horizon of 20 years is assumed as well as a discount rate of 15 percent. Note that the cost flows represent marginal changes. That is, only costs that differ across locations are included in the calculation. The present values of the cost streams, then, are useful only to compare against one another. A more thorough inclusion of costs and expected revenues could have been done; in that case, the present values could be compared not only against one another but against zero as well, giving some indication of the worth of the investment as well as the relative desirability of each site.

Table 12-11 reveals that New Hampshire would be the lowest cost site by quite a bit, over $800,000 of present value. Ruth Tighe must ask herself whether the abandonment of the company's present workforce and market area would be less costly over the long pull than this site-specific cost advantage. For sure, developing a new workforce and searching out at least some new sales contracts will cost the company something. For example, a training cost of $4000 per employee for each of the company's 200 plus job positions would itself wipe out the cost advantage of the New Hampshire site.

Since Tighe Printing has been thriving in New Haven, there are no strong pressures to cut costs and there is every incentive to keep the company's workforce and customer base intact. There is not much to choose between the East Haven and Hamden sites. Both are measurably cheaper than the Long Wharf site and would retain most of the company's employees. The Hamden site offers potentially more space for expansion, but the East Haven site could be available 7 to 10 months earlier. My own preference would be to move earlier rather than later, but either Hamden or East Haven would be well worth the investment. The Long Wharf site should probably be avoided. Not only is it expensive, but its possibilities for expansion are modest at best, and building on the site would take even longer than building in Hamden.

Tighe Printing Company's situation is representative of many companies, as will be discussed in the next section.

THE NATURE OF LOCATION DECISIONS[5]

Plant relocations are overwhelmingly made by small, growing plants (often independent of particular suppliers, markets, or labor sources) that are pressed for more production space. They move to larger, modern quarters and in the process alter their production technology, sometimes in fundamental ways. The vast majority of relocations are over short distances (less than 20 miles), which help to assure labor force continuity and the retention of customer and supplier contacts. To a lesser degree, relocations also occur to consolidate two or more plants into a single new facility, and to escape from high site costs (wages, land values, taxes). As one might expect, however, it is the plant whose profits are hurting the most that sees relocation chiefly as a means to lower costs. These plants are also the ones who are most likely to move further than 20 miles in search of these lower costs.

Plant relocations are trauma-filled experiences for many managers and so are apt to be avoided if at all possible. Only about a third of the relocations seriously contemplated are actually carried through; actual relocations occur at a rate of only 3 percent per year for manufacturing establishments of all sizes, and less than 1 percent per year for plants of at least 100 employees.

More common, especially within larger companies, is the establishment of new branch plants. Each year, between 3 and 6 percent of the existing stock of plants is added on as new branch plants; of those branches contemplated, more than two-thirds are actually established, double the rate of relocations.

New branches start out small—only 40 percent, on the average, of the size of their sister plants—and are simply organized. They are less apt to be unionized and more likely to enjoy simple logistics. While likely to be located in modern facilities with the latest technology, they are also frequently dependent on the corporate services provided by the plant or plants from which they were spun off. The products they make are commonly mature ones, technically well established, with few engineering changes necessary, although for a quarter to a third of new branches the products and/or technology is brand new.

Multiplant Manufacturing Strategies[6]

Analysis of new branch plants and of the base plants from which they typically spring reveals that the new branch plant fits into a prescribed place in a multiplant company's scheme of things. Four general types of multiplant manufacturing strategies seem to prevail in the operating divisions of large companies. Behind each one are some compelling cost or managerial reasons.

The Product Plant Strategy. Perhaps the most popular strategy is the product plant strategy where distinct products or product lines are manufactured in separate plants, each plant serving the company's entire domestic market area.

The product plant strategy permits each plant to concentrate on a limited set of products, generally within a well-defined market niche. This concentration has the advantage of permitting the plant management to select the process technology, equipment, labor force, manufacturing policies, and organization that are consistent with the particular competitive priorities (e.g., cost, quality, product flexibility, speed of delivery) associated with the plant's products. In this way, the company can avoid much of the complexity and congestion that plague many oversize, multipurpose factories. In addition, if there are any economies of scale to be reaped, a product plant strategy can take advantage of them. Product plants can also take advantage of any raw materials or expertise that are specific to particular geographic areas.

A product plant strategy is likely to correspond to a decentralized manufacturing organization with a relatively small staff at the corporate level. Plant locations may be far-flung, but more often they are clustered within one or two broad regions of the country. Within such a strategy, a significant challenge to management lies in recognizing when a plant has become too large. What constitutes "too large" varies from industry to industry, technology to technology, and company to company; but the most frequently quoted figures lie between 500 and 1000 employees, with few companies stating figures in excess of 2000.

Companies in many industries can divide operations according to a product plant strategy because the products manufactured are many and varied. Colt Industries, Fairchild Industries, and Insilco are large companies whose basic multiplant strategy is product plant. For smaller companies, the product plant strategy is even more prevalent.

The Market Area Plant Strategy. Under this strategy, plants are designated to serve particular subnational market areas. The plants themselves manufacture all or most of the corporation's product line. The market area plant is perhaps the classic notion of the branch plant. When freight costs are important because of high product weight or volume relative to value, it makes sense to spread plants apart geographically. This is all the more true if products are consumed over wide areas, and if the market requires a quick response by manufacturing.

A market area plant strategy is likely to require more corporate coordination than the product plant strategy. The corporate staff is likely to be larger and to carry considerable clout. By the same token, plant managers are less likely to be able to act autonomously. A different management challenge confronts the market area plant—namely, the sequencing and regional authority of new plants. For instance, should an East Coast company's second plant be in the Midwest, West, or South, and how should the market be split between plants? If the second plant is placed in the West, where and when should a third plant be sited?

The national breweries are classic examples of market area plants, as are many glass, can, food, and building products companies. All involve products consumed in quantity everywhere and subject to significant transport costs as a fraction of product value.

The Process Plant Strategy. Rather than separate their products into individual plants, some companies, notably those with complex products, separate their production process into various plants. These plants are often viewed as feeders to one or more final assembly plants. A process plant strategy is less prevalent than the others.

Like the product plant, the process plant exists to simplify an inherently complex and confusing managerial situation. For complex products like automobiles, large machine tools, and computer systems, a number of plants become involved in making components of the completed product. The manufacturer typically faces a rash of make-or-buy choices for many of these components, but to be able to produce one or another of these components competitively may require different raw materials, labor skills, control systems, or management skills and organization. This difficulty, coupled with the already discussed diseconomies introduced by large size, argues for a division of the complete manufacturing process into stages, with separate plants for each stage. For any one stage, however, there may be economies of scale. Diverse manufacturing requirements explain why some plants may be located in the South or the Far East (for lower labor costs), or in resource- or expertise-rich areas (e.g., "Silicon Valley" in California), or merely in a separate location, to provide surrounding plants with a special service that would be uneconomic for them to provide for themselves. This stage-by-stage division may lead to many

feeder plants shipping to one or more assembly plants, or to one or a few feeder plants (for a critical component, say) shipping to many other manufacturing plants. In any event, the concept of plant separation to simplify operations persists.

The process plant strategy is even more demanding of high-level corporate coordination than the market area plant strategy. The process plant strategy is generally accompanied by a manufacturing organization that is highly centralized, technically well versed, and responsible for the control and coordination of materials and product between plants. For this reason, process plants are often located within an easy commute of one another.

The General Purpose Plant Strategy. Some companies do not establish specific plant charters. Rather, plants are prized for their flexibility in adapting to constantly changing product needs. Defense contractors, among others, are typical companies following a general purpose plant strategy.

The general purpose plant strategy demands a considerable degree of centralized control. Coordination of plants is a real management challenge, as is the smooth staging of transitions in plant use and in employee assignments.

Site Selection

Once a multiplant manufacturing strategy has been decided on and plant size picked, site selection follows. The multiplant strategy frequently can say a lot about the choice of region. For example, clustering of plants in a particular region of the country is most apt to occur under the process or general purpose plant strategies and is least likely under the market area strategy. The choice of where within a region to locate, however, is sometimes very straightforward and sometimes baffling.

Many people, including some location consultants, try to simplify the decision making by introducing elaborate rating schemes that quantify everything imaginable about a particular location. To my mind, much of this is false rigor. There are, of course, a number of costs that can usefully be estimated—among them expected labor costs; construction, rental, or remodeling costs; taxes and other government payments; transportation cost savings or penalties for both inputs and finished goods; expenditures for needed services such as energy, pollution control, roads, sewerage, water, and parking; insurance costs; moving costs; and expected plant start-up inefficiencies or time delays due to start-up or to governmental approvals. Often one or just a few of these costs are so important that they can control the entire site selection process. However, while costs such as these may be important to evaluate, they seldom tell the complete story and sometimes they do not differ enough to ground a location choice strictly on their merits. A company should not expect any quantitative analysis to isolate a single area or site that stands alone as clearly optimal. Rather, a company should expect that a number of sites will show more or less the same cost structure.

At the risk of appearing nonscientific, I would argue that the next phase of site selection should be an exploration of the intangible and qualitative features of a location that could be expected to contribute to the company's competitive success. While these factors may be difficult or even impossible to quantify, they are no less real; companies should resist the temptation of letting hard numbers drive out reasoned but qualitative analysis. The intangibles can be of many varieties: risks associated with any of the quantitatively evaluated costs or the sales potential of the site; the area's prevailing "business climate" (which means different things to different people but mainly long-term competitiveness); educational and training strengths of the area; attitudes of the workforce toward productivity, change, and unionization; the aesthetic and cultural attributes of the area (important aspects for attracting and holding managers);

the cooperation of the local and state government for resolving public service or other public matters faced by industry; the commuting distances of workers and managers; and the impact of other, perhaps competitive, industries in the area. Frequently, a careful point-by-point comparison of these difficult-to-quantify factors against the real demands a particular product, area, or process will make on the manufacturing function can argue decisively for a particular site. A site need not rate high on all factors, but it should rate high on those

that truly make a difference for the plant's competitiveness.

The company should be prepared as well for location analyses that, at the end, do not favor one site over another. If careful analysis reveals a toss-up, a company should not feel guilty that a seemingly inconsequential item tips the scale toward one site. After all, in such a case the company stands to gain or lose little by the location choice itself.

QUESTIONS

1. Why is Kemper Games described as being in a joyous predicament? What are some of the tactics Kemper explores for getting out of its predicament? How might Kemper's experience be generalized for other companies' benefit?

2. Define and discuss the following concepts:
   a. net present value
   b. discount rate
   c. the effect of changes in the discount rate and the time horizon on the present value calculation

How do these concepts fit into Kemper's procedure for deciding whether to build or to lease?

3. What role does long-term forecasting play in the capacity plan and its analysis? Compare and contrast two main nonmathematical forecasting techniques and two simple mathematical forecasting techniques.

4. Summarize and discuss the six main lessons that

can be learned from Kemper Games' dilemma.

5. For service industries, what are the main factors involved in decisions about capacity?

6. The term *economies of scale* covers a multitude of concepts. What are some of the more important concepts? How do they relate, if at all, to issues of capacity and expansion?

7. Review three of the relative advantages of branches and relocations vis-a-vis on-site expansion.

8. "Maybe sometimes you can be too successful," comments Ruth Tighe about the progress of her printing company. Are there times when this can be true for a company? In considering the four distinct options, does Tighe look at all aspects of the decision? Support your answer.

9. Summarize and discuss the importance of the various multiplant strategies mentioned in this chapter.

PROBLEMS

1. Hal operates an automotive repair shop. Since the price of gasoline has been predicted to go to $2 per gallon and Detroit is still building fairly large automobiles, many prospective auto buyers are repairing the family car until they see what the price of gasoline will do and what new designs Detroit will generate.

Hal has the opportunity to purchase another auto repair shop across town. This shop has been generating about $60,000 in annual profit after taxes and he feels, with the new demand and better management, he can increase this to $68,000 or $70,000. The present owner is asking $210,000 for the business. Hal has made the following estimates:

Life of the business	20 years
Internal cost of capital	20%

Extra annual expenses
  Hal foresees
	$20,000 for another
	  manager's salary

Analyze Hal's problem and make a recommendation.

2. The Calway Cab Company currently operates a fleet of 27 cabs in a medium-size Midwestern town. The firm is considering expanding the fleet. They feel that each additional cab will generate less clear profit annually than the last additional cab. They have estimated that the twenty-eighth cab will generate $2000 per year and that each additional cab will generate 5 percent less than the previous one. Each cab has a purchase value of $5500 and a trade-in value of $2500 at the end of two years. The company has an internal cost of capital of 15 percent. Ignoring taxes, how many new cabs should they purchase?

3. Amal Gamate owns and operates Consolidated Salvage yards. Amal has a scrap compressor that does not have the capacity to maintain the level of production required. Amal has compiled the following data:

Depreciated value of old compressor	$17,000
Market value of old compressor	$ 1,000
Price of new compressor	$65,000
Installation costs	$ 4,000
Economic life	10 years
Salvage value	$ 1,000
Required rate of return	12%
Estimated annual cost savings	$13,000

Ignoring taxes, answer the following questions:
a. Should Amal purchase the new compressor?
b. What is his actual rate of return?

4. The Carl Bodkin Electronics firm manufactures an assortment of consumer electronics, including C.B. radios. The firm has a standardization program and they have standardized 95 percent of their control knobs. Each of these knobs costs 39¢ when bought at an annual volume of 808,000. The firm's managers have completed a make-or-buy analysis and feel they can make the knobs at a cost savings of 13¢ each. They are currently analyzing two different potential processes:

	Process A	Process B
Installed cost	$35,000	$45,000
Annual operating cost	$ 9,000	$ 6,000
Economic life	4 years	5 years

Ignoring taxes, what is your recommendation and why?

5. Discuss the appropriate management level that should gather information and make the decision regarding the three "brick and mortar" choices for adding capacity presented in the chapter.

6. Discuss the length of the review and planning procedures for various industries. Do those who use longer planning periods have better forecasting methods?

7. What kinds of alternatives should a planning group consider for meeting shortfalls?

SITUATION FOR STUDY

CHEWZEY TOBACCO CO.

The Chewzey Tobacco Co., a manufacturer of chewing tobacco, had its main plant and corporate headquarters in Lakeport, a city situated on Lake Erie. The firm had located in Lakeport, not for the myriad economic factors that are supposed to be considered, but because the late founder lived in Lakeport and had started his small business where he lived. Both the corporate headquarters and the main plant were located in an industrial section of Lakeport about eight blocks from the major downtown business area.

The building was an older five-story building, approximately 80,000 square feet, with 16,000 square feet on each floor. The major materials handling between floors depended on three freight elevators. These elevators were old-style, open cage, rope and pulley actuated, and their maintenance was becoming very expensive. Management estimated that at least one of the three was inoperable two and one-half days per week.

The manufacture of chewing tobacco had originally started with the scrap tobacco left over from the manufacture of cigarettes and cigars. This scrap tobacco was chopped or shredded into strips approximately ¼ inch wide and 4 inches long. The tobacco was mixed with sweeteners and flavoring, such as honey and licorice, to suit the recipes for the various brands sold by the firm. Although the basic processes remained much the same over the years, several factors had led to some changes in materials.

Because chewing tobacco had fallen in respect socially, demand for it had increased somewhat less than the population growth. However, in recent years, aided by media advertisements depicting athletic stars as tobacco chewers and by findings that smoking tobacco may be harmful to health, the consumption of various forms of non-smoking tobacco had shown an increase. The chewing tobacco industry found, as did the brewing and distillery industries, that the "youth" market demanded better and different quality than had the older market. Chewzey had determined that scrap tobacco as raw material was inadequate. Now they had to purchase a low-grade tobacco leaf and strip the stalkier portions out before putting the tobacco through the shredder. They also had to use more sweeteners and more subtle flavorings. The additional sweeteners and flavorings had created no particular difficulty, but the use of low-grade tobacco caused problems. For example, the removal of stalks involved more work and, more importantly, the raw material could no longer be purchased from cigar and cigarette manufacturers; Chewzey had to go directly to the tobacco markets and compete with the cigar and cigarette manufacturers for tobacco.

The firm knew that the five-story building and its location in Lakeport caused them certain inefficiencies, but they wanted to stay in Lakeport because they were comfortable at that location. However, in order to maintain their share of the new demand, management felt it imperative to renovate the old building, including the elevators, and to build an addition to the building. The proposed expansion required the use of half of the present employee parking lot. The proposed expansion was an additional 30,000 square feet at $22.50 per square foot in construction costs. The main fly in the ointment was that the City Planning Board had decreed that any downtown expansion had to include offstreet parking facilities for employees. This, of course, meant the purchase of some very expensive land to be turned into parking spaces.

Chewzey had been in contact with Riverton, Kentucky, a progressive town of 80,000 on the

Ohio River. Riverton had developed an industrial park and was trying to entice industry to locate there. The city was willing to finance the construction of a new plant with municipal bonds and set up a lease/purchase agreement with the tenants. The lease/purchase agreement would entail an attractive interest charge of 7.5 percent per year with the principal to be paid in 20 years.

In the industrial park, Chewzey could have a 10-acre tract at $2500 per acre. Moreover, they could build a one-story building of 125,000 square feet at a construction cost of $15.50 per square foot. In addition, the building code at the industrial park would permit a future expansion of equal size to the proposed building.

Chewzey management felt there were many advantages, as well as disadvantages, to moving to Kentucky. Following are some of the factors they felt they would somehow have to quantify in order to make a decision:

- *Employees.* Some of both the older and newer managers would not leave Lakeport. In addition, several did not want to move to a less cosmopolitan city, as they perceived Riverton to be.

   At the Lakeport facilities the hourly workers were unionized; at Riverton there were few unions. But Chewzey management knew that the union might follow them (albeit, at a later date).

   Although the hourly workers would be offered employment in the new plant, they would not be offered relocation expenses. There was good reason to believe that few of the hourly employees would make the move.

   Riverton had promised aid in recruiting and training new employees.

- *Transportation.* The transportation of finished goods to market was about the same for Riverton as for Lakeport. The tobacco markets were much nearer Riverton than to Lakeport.

- *Cost of capital.* The internal cost of capital that Chewzey had been using was 17 percent. This cost was not thought to be too important to the expansion because the firm felt it was indeed time to move. The forecasted market demand would more than pay for either choice and would also force a panic decision if something were not done soon.

1. What other factors do you think the firm should consider?
2. How would you evaluate the multiple criteria in comparing the alternatives?
3. Are there other alternatives they should consider?

REFERENCE NOTES

1. For an extended description of the decision-making mechanism for capacity expansion or contraction, see Joseph L. Bower, *Managing the Resource Allocation Process* (Homewood, Ill.: Richard D. Irwin, 1972).

2. For examples of more sophisticated forecasting techniques, see Steven C. Wheelwright and Spyros Makridakis, *Forecasting Methods for Management*, 2d ed. (New York: John Wiley & Sons, 1977).

3. These considerations regarding capacity expansions are discussed in Earl Sasser, "Matching Supply and Demand in Service Industries," *Harvard Business Review* 54, no. 6 (November–December 1976), pp. 133–40.

4. This section on economies of scale is adapted from an article of mine entitled "Before You Build a *Big* Factory," *Harvard Business Review* 54, no. 4 (July–August 1976), pp. 100–104.

5. Many of the statistics cited here on location decisions are derived from Roger W. Schmenner, *The Manufacturing Location Decision: Evidence from Cincinnati and New England*, report to the Economic Development Administration, U.S. Department of Commerce, March 1978, 394 pages. See also Schmenner, "Look beyond the Obvious in Plant Location," *Harvard Business Review* 57, no. 1 (January–February 1979).

6. Another useful reference on multiplant manufacturing is F.M. Scherer et al., *The Economics of Multiplant Operation* (Cambridge, Mass.: Harvard University Press, 1975).

13

DEALING WITH TECHNOLOGICAL CHANGE

The management of technological change may well be the least understood aspect of operations management. Companies of wildly different philosophies and organizations have been successful innovators. No one model of technology management has so far been recognized as head and shoulders above the others. And yet everyone realizes that technological advance is critical to a country's continued economic growth. By one estimate, technological innovation was responsible for 45 percent of U.S. economic growth between 1929 and 1969.[1] In addition, high technology companies grow quickly in both sales and employment. At best, this chapter can introduce some of the ideas that people have put forward as important to successful innovation and some of the issues that continue to be debated.

What is technological change? There is debate even on this. Are new products evidence of technological change? How about minor modifications to existing ones? Do new machines constitute technological change? How about bigger (or smaller) revisions of existing ones? We can readily recognize new, far-reaching process technology changes (e.g., Henry Ford's moving assembly line, computer process controls in papermaking), but what about small alterations in an existing process that are more on the scale of line rebalancing? Merely try-

ing to answer these questions can give us some feel for the debate.

The ambiguity associated with technological change is sometimes resolved by recognizing that both product and process changes can be either radical or incremental. The debate itself over which product innovation is significant or which process modification radical is evidence of the belief many share that radical or significant technological change is somehow different and that it demands different modes of thinking and management to make it work. Hence, trying to identify what is or is not radical or significant is a worthwhile endeavor. Even though we may think of technological change as a continuum from "irrelevant" to "momentous," successful innovators, so some people argue, should treat one end of the continuum differently from the other.

Because technological change is a messy topic, this chapter cannot be as neatly or as tightly organized as an author would like. These reservations aside, this chapter focuses on two main themes:

1. The learning curve (sometimes called the experience curve)—a planning tool, heavily dependent on technology, that purportedly shows the relationship between manufacturing costs and

accumulated experience manufacturing an item; usually measured by total units produced to date.

2. Successful versus unsuccessful implementation of technological innovation, including the influences and policies that can affect the introduction of both new products and new production processes.

THE LEARNING CURVE[2]

The notion underlying the learning curve derives from the actual experience of manufacturers in some diverse industries. The learning curve first came to prominence prior to World War II when aircraft manufacturers observed that their costs of assembling an airplane decreased steadily and in a predictable fashion. Since that time the univer-

sality of the learning curve has been demonstrated in a variety of industries, recently and most notably in the electronics industry.

The predictable decline of manufacturing costs is usually expressed in percentage terms that correspond to a doubling of the cumulative volume of the product in question. Thus, an 80 percent learning curve means that as the total number of units produced over time grows to twice any given number, manufacturing costs per unit can be expected to decline to only 80 percent of the cost per unit incurred before the doubling. If 100 airplanes of a new type have been manufactured to date, under an 80 percent learning curve the cost of the two hundredth airplane produced should be only 80 percent of the cost of the hundredth plane. The hundredth, in turn, should have been only 80 percent of the cost of the fiftieth plane, and so on. A 70 percent learning curve shows more cost-cutting

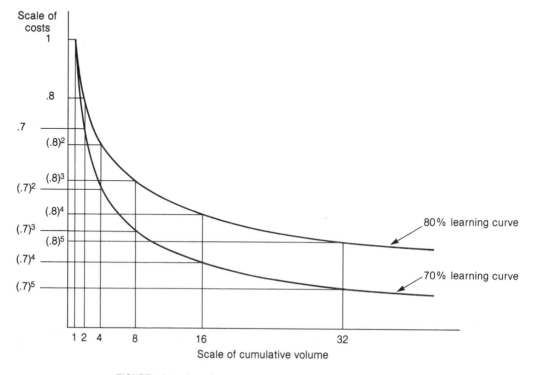

FIGURE 13-1   Learning curves portrayed on a conventional graph.

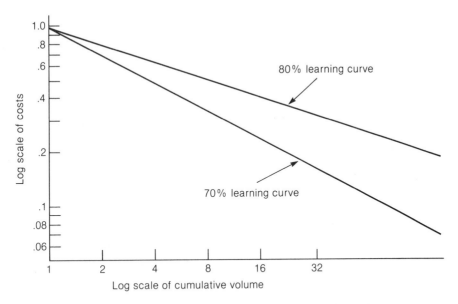

FIGURE 13-2 Learning curves portrayed on a log-log scale graph.

over the doubling of cumulative volume than an 80 percent curve; a 90 percent learning curve shows less.

Because inflation can be markedly erratic, learning curves are usually expressed in real (inflation-adjusted) dollars. Sometimes they are expressed in labor-hours, which gives the same kind of inflation-independent result.

Graphically, an 80 percent learning curve looks like Figure 13-1. This is a logarithmic relationship, which is more commonly portrayed as a straight line on a log-log scale grid such as in Figure 13-2.

For the mathematically inclined, the learning curve relationship can be expressed as

$$(1) \qquad\qquad y = ax^{-b}$$

where x is the cumulative volume of units produced from the first and y is the cost to produce the xth unit. The coefficient "a" represents the cost of the first unit and the exponent "b" indicates the sensitivity of unit cost to cumulative volume.*

The straight line representation of the learning

---

*This exponent b is referred to by economists as the elasticity of unit cost with respect to cumulative volume. The term "elasticity" has special meaning, representing the percent change in one variable for a given percent change in another. The price elasticity of demand is a commonly used example; it indicates the percentage increase in sales that a given percentage decrease in price will stimulate, all other things being equal. That b is in fact an elasticity measure is seen by taking the logarithm of equation 1 and differentiating with respect to $(\ln x)$ as follows:

$$(1) \qquad\qquad y = ax^{-b}$$

$$\ln y = \ln a - b \ln x$$

$$\frac{\partial(\ln y)}{\partial(\ln x)} = -b = \frac{\dfrac{\partial y}{\partial y}}{\dfrac{\partial x}{\partial x}}$$

curve can be seen by taking the logarithm of both sides of equation 1, as follows

(2) $$\ln y = \ln a - b \ln x$$

which is the equation of a straight line on a log-log scale with intercept $\ln a$ and slope $-b$.

It should be made clear that b is not 0.8 for an 80 percent learning curve; there is, however, a relatively simple correspondence between b and the percentage figure that labels the learning curve. This relationship can be derived as follows.

Let $y_1 = ax^{-b}$ and let y_2 be the unit cost for double the cumulative volume of x. The fraction y_2/y_1 would be 0.8 for an 80 percent learning curve, 0.7 for a 70 percent learning curve, and so forth.

(3) $$\frac{y_2}{y_1} = \frac{a(2x)^{-b}}{ax^{-b}} = \frac{a2^{-b}x^{-b}}{ax^{-b}} = 2^{-b}$$

This equation gives the percentage learning curve for every choice of elasticity, b. We can easily turn this equation around to give the elasticity, b, that corresponds to every percentage level of learning curve.

$$\frac{y_2}{y_1} = 2^{-b}$$

$$\ln\left(\frac{y_2}{y_1}\right) = -b \ln 2$$

$$b = \frac{-\ln\left(\frac{y_2}{y_1}\right)}{\ln 2} = \frac{-\ln\left(\frac{y_2}{y_1}\right)}{0.6931}$$

For example, the b corresponding to an 80 percent learning curve is

$$b = \frac{-\ln(.80)}{0.6931} = \frac{+0.2231}{0.6931} = 0.3219$$

This result can be checked in Figure 13-2 as the slope.

So much for the mathematics. What does the learning curve really represent and how can it be of use? An entire legion of factors stands behind the learning curve and all of them can systematically reduce costs over the life cycle of a product. Grouping them into major categories, we have workforce-related factors, process modifications, and product modifications.

WORKFORCE-RELATED FACTORS

- *Worker learning on the job.* This was the initial explanation for the results of the pre-World War II aircraft manufacturers, and for some people, this is what the learning curve represents; for them, it is the so-called "experience curve," which is the broader, more inclusive concept (this text treats both terms as synonyms). Cost decreases attributable to gains in worker efficiency through practice are generally quickly exhausted. That such cost reductions can be sustained over time is dependent on maintaining a stable workforce—high worker turnover can annihilate efficiency gains—and also a workforce that is interested in increasing productivity. As we have discussed before, worker attitudes toward productivity can hang on the compensation program adopted. Some programs, like the Scanlon plan, by purposefully tying compensation to overall productivity gain can do very well at sustaining cost reduction in the workforce.

- *Employee effort and management pressure.* Plain, old-fashioned hard work by workers and managers alike can keep costs down. Sometimes it is overlooked how important management pressure can be not only for worker learning but also for the full exploitation of any of the other factors in this list. Learning curve results frequently have an uncanny knack of matching learning curve expectations, and so we should not discount the impact of management pressure.

- *Workforce organization.* Akin to worker

learning and effort is the organization of the workforce. A systematic training program, a thoughtful division of labor, and a considered plan for job mobility and advancement all have a role to play in lowering costs and in keeping them low over time.

Process Modifications

- *Methods improvements.* Included as methods improvements would be shortcuts in machine setup or operation, changes in the sequencing of a product through the factory, improvements in production and/or inventory control, and the introduction of production aids such as jigs, fixtures, or patterns. These and other changes in methods can sometimes improve the yields of "good product" in the process and reduce the scrap involved.
- *Capital-for-labor substitution.* This is a classic means of lowering costs, substituting machine operations for tasks formerly performed manually.
- *Capital-for-capital substitution.* This means of reducing costs involves the replacement of existing plant and equipment with plant and equipment of more recent vintage. The new equipment is frequently more versatile, faster, more durable, and/or cheaper to operate with capabilities that exceed the existing models. The new equipment may be either larger or smaller than that which it replaces and for this reason more desirable.
- *Vertical integration.* By broadening the span of its process, a manufacturer can often lower its costs, although this is not always the case. This topic is discussed in more detail in the next chapter.
- *"Pure" technological change.* By "pure" technological change I mean the more radical redesigns of the production process that are brought about by breakthroughs in engineering or basic research. Examples abound in almost every industry—continuous casting in steel, computerized typesetting in printing, process control equipment in many industries, freeze drying methods in food processing, to name a few. For these changes new equipment must be designed, and so "pure" technological change usually includes capital-for-labor and capital-for-capital substitution as well. But pure technological change is usually much more than these kinds of substitution, for it involves a rethinking about how a particular product is made. Generally it triggers a host of changes throughout the production process, from changes in worker training and methods and in production and inventory control to changes in the company's handling of capacity requirements.

Pure technological change, in this sense, will be the center of discussion in the second major section of this chapter.

Product Modifications

- *Product redesign.* A frequent source of cost reduction is product redesign. Often a product can be simplified in its design so that its manufacture becomes significantly trouble-free. The term "value engineering" has been coined to describe this critical look at a product's construction and how it can be altered to lower manufacturing costs. Products as diverse as automobiles, television sets, and digital watches have all undergone significant value engineering in recent years.

Not only does product redesign reduce manufacturing cost; it often enhances a product's performance and this, in turn, is valued in the marketplace. If product performance is what the market buys, this kind of product redesign can even be placed in the category of cost re-

SITUATION 13-1

NASHVILLE FIRE EQUIPMENT COMPANY

Mal Getz, President of the Nashville Fire Equipment Company, was in the midst of contract negotiations with the business agent of the union that had recently won the right to represent his company's employees. The union, as one of the points it wanted to negotiate, had broached the concept of regular wage increases as so-called "improvement factors." The union argument was that because workers over time produce more with the same amount of human effort (due to such things as technological progress, better tools, methods, processes, equipment, and worker cooperation), they ought to be rewarded with regular wage increases.

Mal recognized this union point of negotiation as one based on the learning curve principle, and different in character from the typical wage increase to keep up with the cost of living. Mal had to admit to himself that the improvement factor was founded on sound reasoning. Moreover, Nashville Fire Equipment had been benefiting from the learning curve over the last several years, and Mal knew that the union would almost certainly be able to document that fact. It seemed likely then that management would have to agree to negotiate "improvement factors" for the next 3 years, the term of the contract.

The difficulty was that Mal was at a loss as to how to estimate what labor savings the company could legitimately expect over the next 3 years, and thus what improvement factors the company ought to consent to.

The company had recently been rejuvenated by the introduction of an articulating hydraulic boom (known within the industry as a "squirt"), a new product and technique for fire fighting that permitted the quick, pinpoint spraying of water into otherwise inaccessible places. The squirt had been winning increasing acceptance in the fire departments that served as the company's customer base and now accounted for most of the company's sales. Nashville Fire Equipment's squirt was a patentable modification of a similar product that the Seiver Company had licensed Nashville Fire Equipment to make. Table 13-1 documents various times, production volumes, and worker hours associated with the squirt. Over the next year Mal Getz expected to continue to employ 50 workers on the squirt. He wondered whether the table data, coupled with the learning curve concept, could form the basis for a recommendation on suitable improvement factors.

TABLE 13-1 Production Times, Volumes, and Worker Times for the Squirt
(Nashville Fire Equipment Company)

WEEK	CUMULATIVE UNITS PRODUCED AS OF THAT DATE	HOURS NEEDED TO MANUFACTURE FIRST UNIT OF WEEK
2	1	4000
10	7	2550
38	25	1850
70	65	1500
150	180	1170

duction. Semiconductor memory for computers is an example where product performance improvements have been a significant feature in the cost and price decline of the "product" purchased, the storage of a given unit of information in computers and related products.

- *Materials substitution.* Akin to product re-design is the use of different, possibly new, materials in place of other materials in the product. The substitution of aluminum for steel, plastic for glass or metal, metal for wood, and so on can lower the total costs of manufacture with relatively few design changes to many products.

Summary

As the length and breadth of this list makes clear, the learning curve phenomenon is founded on a wealth of strong influences. What is not so clear is how the regularity of the learning curve can be used as a planning and decision tool. Consider Situation 13-1.

Discussion of Nashville Fire Equipment Company

It is easy enough to calculate the learning curve implied by the brief list of data in Table 13-1. The learning curve calculated is depicted in Figure 13-3. Mal Getz could use this finding of an 85 percent learning curve to grant an "improvement factor" to the company's workforce on, say, an annual basis payable at the end of the next year.

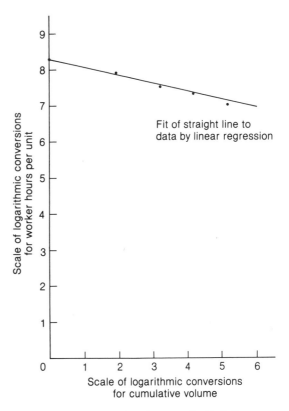

Fit of straight line to data by linear regression

FIGURE 13-3   Learning curve for Nashville Fire Equipment Company's "Squirt."

❋ ASIDE ❋

FITTING A STRAIGHT LINE TO THE COMPANY'S DATA

Fitting a straight line to the data of Table 13-1 involves converting those data to logarithmic form (Table 13-2) and then applying the technique of linear regression to the converted data. Linear re-

TABLE 13-2   Conversion to Logarithms of Data in Table 13-1

CUMULATIVE UNITS PRODUCED	NATURAL LOGARITHM OF CUMULATIVE UNIT PRODUCED	HOURS NEEDED	NATURAL LOGARITHM OF HOURS NEEDED
1	0.00	4000	8.29
7	1.95	2550	7.84
25	3.22	1850	7.52
65	4.17	1500	7.31
180	5.19	1170	7.06

gression, found on many of the calculators currently on the market, is merely a curve fitting procedure for choosing the straight line that minimizes the sum of the squared vertical distances between the data points and the fitted line.*

The equation of the fitted straight line to the converted (natural logarithm) data, as found by linear regression, is

$$\begin{pmatrix} \text{natural} \\ \text{logarithm} \\ \text{of hours} \\ \text{needed} \end{pmatrix} = 8.293 - 0.237 \begin{pmatrix} \text{natural} \\ \text{logarithm of} \\ \text{cumulative units} \\ \text{produced} \end{pmatrix}$$

or put in the nonlogarithmic terms of $y = ax^{-b}$,

$$\text{(hours needed)} = 4000 \cdot \left(\frac{\text{cumulative units}}{\text{produced}} \right)^{-0.237}$$

Converting this estimate of $b(0.237)$ into the appropriate label for the learning curve is accomplished by equation 3 above:

$$\frac{y_2}{y_1} = 2^{-b}, \ 2^{-0.237} = .85$$

Thus, the data of Table 13-1 imply an 85 percent learning curve.

❋

---

*Standard linear regression uses the principle of least squares to select the straight line that best fits a scatter of data in two dimensions. Look at Figure 13-3a, which displays a scatter of points in the xy plane. The point (x_i, y_i) lies above the line $\hat{a} + \hat{b}x$ by the amount e_i. That is,

$$e_i = y_i - \hat{y}_i = y_i - (\hat{a} + \hat{b}x_i)$$

The principle of least squares states that $\hat{a}$ and $\hat{b}$—which determine the positioning and slope of the estimating line—should be chosen so that $\sum_{i=1}^{n} e_i^2$ is as small as possible.

This minimization of the sum of the e_i^2's over all n data points is accomplished when

$$\hat{b} = \frac{\sum_{i=1}^{n}(x_i - \bar{x})(y_i - \bar{y})}{\sum_{i=1}^{n}(x_i - \bar{x})^2}$$

The value of $\hat{a}$ is found as a residual,

$$\hat{a} = \bar{y} - \hat{b}\bar{x}$$

where $\bar{x}$ and $\bar{y}$ are the arithmetic means of the x's and y's in the scatter. It turns out that $\hat{a}$ and $\hat{b}$ share some desirable properties, which are best explored by consulting applied statistics or econometrics texts.

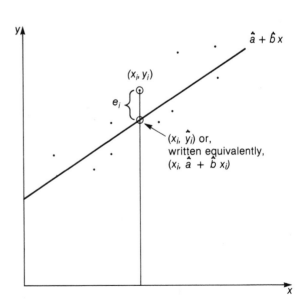

FIGURE 13-3a   Scatter of data and principle of least squares.

Return to Calculating an Improvement Factor

One procedure for calculating an improvement factor is as follows:

1. Calculate how many labor-hours will be spent on the product over the course of the next year.

2. Estimate how many more units of the product are expected to be manufactured during that number of labor-hours.

3. Using the formula, compute the expected labor-hours for the unit that will be manufactured in exactly one year from now.

4. Compare the labor-hours per unit then with the present labor-hours per unit. The labor rate can then be adjusted to reflect the lower labor-hours that will be spent on each unit in a year's time.

For the Nashville Fire Equipment Company, following this procedure entails these calculations:

1. 50 weeks · 50 workers · 40 hours/week = 100,000 labor-hours for the next year

TABLE 13-3 Estimate of Labor-Hours Needed to Produce a Particular Squirt (Nashville Fire Equipment Company)

NUMBER OF UNITS PRODUCED	ESTIMATED LABOR-HOURS NEEDED TO PRODUCE THAT UNIT*
1	4000.0
180	1170.9
181	1169.4
182	1167.9
183	1166.4

*From learning curve estimated in Figure 13-3.

2. To get an estimate of how many more units can be made in 100,000 labor-hours, we have to use the 85 percent learning curve we calculated in Figure 13-3. Each successive unit will require slightly less labor. We could generate a table (Table 13-3) like Table 13-1. Using Table 13-3 we could sum up the individual times, starting with unit 181, until their sum reaches 100,000. By referring to the table, we could then discover the corresponding number unit on which the 100,000th labor-hour was spent.*

---

*Fortunately, we do not have to perform this calculation, although it takes a little integral calculus to avoid it. The labor time spent between the mth unit and the nth unit is approximated by the integral of the learning curve function evaluated between m and n. Since the learning curve function is a monomial, the integral is easily evaluated. In particular, labor time between mth and nth units

(1)
$$= \int_m^n y\,dx$$

where y is the learning curve estimate of labor time needed to produce any unit x. We can then use the formula for the learning curve to substitute for y:

(2)
$$= \int_m^n ax^{-b}dx$$

Then we factor out the constant a:

(3)
$$= a\int_m^n x^{-b}dx$$

Taking the integral, then, yields

(4)
$$= a\frac{x^{1-b}}{1-b}$$

(continues on next page)

If we did this, we would find that the 100,000th labor-hour was spent on the 270th unit. That is, exactly one year from now, if the Nashville Fire Equipment Company continues on its 85 percent learning curve, its workers will be working on the 270th squirt.

3. Over the course of the year it will have produced 90(270 − 180) squirts. The 270th unit will require only

$$y = 4000(270)^{-0.237}$$

$$= 1060 \text{ hours to complete}$$

This situation shows the phenomenal power of the learning curve. It took the Nashville Fire Equipment Company 3 years to produce its first 180 squirts; in a single year's time, if its 85 percent learning curve is maintained, it can expect to produce almost half that amount.

4. At present, 1170 labor-hours are needed to produce the latest unit, the 180th. From the above calculation, in a year's time only 1060 hours will be required, which is only 90.6 percent of the present labor input. With this productivity advance, if the price of the squirt remains the

which can be evaluated at n and m and subtracted to reveal the labor time spent between units.

We can apply this formula to figure out how many squirts the Nashville Fire Equipment Company can be expected to make in a year. We know that 100,000 labor-hours will be spent during the next year. The company has already manufactured 180 squirts according to the learning curve that was derived as

$$y = ax^{-b} = 4000x^{-0.237}$$

Stepping through equation (4), we have

$$100,000 \text{ hours} = \int_{180}^{n} 4000x^{-0.237} dx$$

where n is the as yet unknown number of the unit to be worked on in exactly 1 year's time.

$$= \frac{4000x^{1-0.237}}{1 - 0.237}$$

evaluated at n and 180 and subtracted as follows

$$= \frac{4000n^{0.763}}{0.763} - \frac{4000(180)^{0.763}}{0.763}$$

$$= 5240n^{0.763} - 275,410$$

Rearranging terms and dividing through yields

$$\frac{100,000 + 275,410}{5240} = n^{0.763}$$

$$71.64 = n^{0.763}$$

Taking the natural logarithm of both sides enables us to solve for n:

$$\ln(71.64) = 0.763 \ln n$$

$$\ln n = 5.6$$

which implies

$$n \approx 270$$

same (a rather big if), the company can afford to pay its workers 1.10(1/0.906) times as much in a year's time and still enjoy the same profit margin it now does. This figure of 1.10 thus provides a ceiling on the improvement factor that Mal Getz has to decide upon.

Applying the Learning Curve

The foregoing series of steps demonstrates how the learning curve can be used as a planning device. Here the learning curve was used to calculate an "improvement factor" for labor, but it could also have been used to figure out by what date a given number of units will have been produced or to guide labor hiring practices to fulfill a certain commitment by a given date. The learning curve can be particularly useful in tracking and in planning new product introductions.

However, a larger issue than the mere mechanics of the learning curve is whether the concept can be applied at all to situations like that of the Nashville Fire Equipment Company. What are the weak points in using the learning curve for such situations?

As a glimpse back at Figures 13-1 and 13-2 reveals, the learning curve is keenly sensitive to position and slope, which are determined respectively by the coefficient a in equation 1 and by the exponent b. We ought to ask the question then whether the first squirt made by the company in week 2 of Table 13-1 should be viewed as the absolute first unit or not. As was mentioned in the situation, Nashville's squirt is a patentable modification of a similar product that the Seiver Company had licensed Nashville Fire Equipment to make. It could easily be argued that the first unit should not be the squirt itself but the Seiver Company's licensed product. The impact of such a change can be dramatic. Suppose, for example, that Nashville Fire Equipment's first squirt is viewed as the 31st unit for purposes of computing the learning curve. The latest unit would thus be the 210th. The refigured learning curve would be

$$y = 21{,}850x^{-0.570}$$

which translates to a 67 percent learning curve and drastically different results.

Perhaps the company's early experience with the similar licensed product brought down its labor-hours per unit much more quickly than could otherwise be expected. In that case, the learning curve the company could anticipate over the next year would be much less steep than the presently calculated 85 percent curve. Moreover, what learning curve rate would be appropriate may be very unclear, especially at the outset. Much of the issue of "technological forecasting" revolves around the appropriate choice of the learning curve rate, b, for various new products and which influences on that rate are likely to be important.

These doubts about the position and slope of the learning curve are not easily resolved and argue for great caution. Mal Getz may well be able to grant an "improvement factor" to his workers, but one somewhat less than 110 percent of the current rate seems prudent.

STRATEGIC USE OF THE LEARNING CURVE CONCEPT

This concern for the applicability of the learning curve phenomenon to short-term, tactical decisions of a corporation extends as well to longer term, strategic decisions. The strategic impact of the learning curve is nowhere more evident than in the electronics industry — particularly in the growth and behavior of one company, Texas Instruments. Texas Instruments has the reputation of a tough competitor whose strategy has been to generate huge sales volumes by repeatedly cutting prices. The company has sought the sales leadership in all of the markets it has entered, using low prices to generate volume and using volume, via the learning curve, to generate cost (and price) reductions. Texas Instruments is reputed to relish industry shakeouts, and such companies are generally feared as competitors.

One tactic that some companies have used with success to deter the entry of newcomers to a market and to stimulate a continual shaking out of an industry is preemptive pricing. Preemptive pricing is based on the expectations of the learning curve. Prices are set and announced at low levels, often with slim margins, and it is expected that volume production will stimulate enough cost reduction that total profits will become acceptably high. This kind of pricing is in distinct contrast to the practice of maintaining, for as long as possible, high prices in the face of declining costs, perhaps inviting a massive shakeout as more and more competitors enter the market under the existing price umbrellas.

These divergent strategies are represented pictorially in Figure 13-4. Note that while the initial profits are higher under the price maintenance umbrella strategy, because prices are higher the market is not likely to grow rapidly. Under the preemptive pricing strategy, while margins are often thin, volume is high, sales growth rapid, and total profits can be quite acceptable.

In many industries, preemptive pricing has a distinguished history. For example, all of the so-called "trusts" of the late nineteenth century grew quickly and grew large by keeping prices low and by using technology to cut costs. Rockefeller's Standard Oil refineries were models of the state of the art—the largest and fastest around. Carnegie's Edgar Thomson Steel Works in Pittsburgh was a triumph of rational plant layout and technology. The same stories could be told of sugar and the other trusts. In each of these cases, the first producer to get volume up and to force technological advance in process design was the one that traveled down the learning curve the first, forcing others out of the industry by pricing low and accumulating profits all the while.

It is no coincidence that all of the trusts of the nineteenth century were in commodities. Commodity manufacturers do not have to worry about

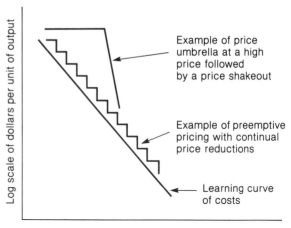

FIGURE 13-4   Pricing strategies and the learning curve.

new product introductions or product modifications undermining sales of their particular products. Commodity manufacturers can concentrate on cost reduction without fearing what competitors will market to counter their own product lines. The power of the learning curve phenomenon is greatly attenuated by continual product model changes or new product introductions. These throw the company onto new learning curves or back up old ones. Consumer taste-sensitive industries are thus much less able to compete successfully with preemptive pricing than are more taste-invariant industries.

This fact suggests that the strategic implications of the learning curve are best exploited by particular classes of companies. Whether a company can adopt preemptive pricing and exploit the learning curve phenomenon successfully depends to a great degree on how it values a dollar received today versus a dollar tomorrow. Preemptive pricing defers its rewards more than traditional price maintenance because it must wait to foster growth in the market and because it stimulates an immediate and ongoing shakeout in the industry. Thus, preemptive pricing is relatively more attractive when some or all of the following features are true:

1. The expected product life is long.
2. The product is standardized, like a commodity, with little risk that consumer tastes will suddenly turn against it.
3. The expected growth of the market is rapid.
4. The apparent slope of the learning curve is steeper, since the learning curve in that instance can constitute a substantial barrier to the entry of other firms into the industry.
5. The product is not patent protected.
6. The company is not particularly strapped for cash.

To the extent these features are true, preemptive pricing (implied by the learning curve) can act to gain market share in a growing market and thereby command considerable profits.

THE DILEMMA OF PRODUCTIVITY INCREASE[3]

Over the decade of the 1970s, productivity, measured as real GNP (gross national product) per worker, has not been advancing at its historical (post–World War II) pace. This falloff in the rate of growth of productivity has puzzled many observers, and no definitive explanation has yet emerged. A number of possible explanations have been advanced, however. Among them:

- Low levels of business investment, caused perhaps by increased uncertainty in the economy.
- The phenomenal increase in energy costs, causing many companies to turn to less energy-intensive production technologies but with no compensating increase in output.
- More pervasive government regulation (e.g., air and water pollution controls), which has required huge "nonproductive" capital outlays for pollution control equipment.

- Shifts in employment away from agriculture and manufacturing and toward the service and government sectors, where productivity increases may be harder to come by.
- Increased reluctance to lay off workers when business turns down.
- Decline in the willingness to work hard, caused perhaps by high marginal income tax rates and/or too "socialist" a welfare system.
- Demographic shifts toward younger, less skilled workers.
- The data themselves are lousy; output is not properly valued.

This list is reminiscent of many of the previously mentioned influences on the learning curve, which itself can be viewed as a measure of productivity. When capital investment, for example, drops we can expect less capital-for-labor or capital-for-capital substitution, and learning curves in general can be expected to flatten out.

This parallelism between the learning curve and the nation's productivity problems can proceed further. As mentioned earlier, companies can be deflected off their learning curves or be forced back up them by product design changes and new product introductions. Often a conflict seems to exist between low costs (riding down the learning curve) and new product innovation. The most dramatic productivity advances associated with the learning curve involve standard products serving mass markets. There is thus a tension between the learning curve (and the productivity advances it represents) and the customization, product variety, and new product introduction that are common to many marketing strategies. At least part of the present decline in the rate of growth of productivity stems from the demands for flexibility that marketing ideas have continued to press upon the production/operations function.

ISSUES IN THE IMPLEMENTATION OF NEW TECHNOLOGY

When we think of technological innovation, we often distinguish between product innovation (new product introductions) and process innovation. While conceptually distinct, the two are often related. Abernathy and Utterback have suggested one such relationship between product and process innovation.[4] Figure 13-5 captures the major points of their idea.

In the early portion of a product's life, product design is critical. A product's early users are almost always more interested in product performance than in price. Considerable product redesign is undertaken to make the product even more useful and desirable for its users. Abernathy has referred to this early phase of product technology as the search for the "dominant design."[5] Dominant designs are those products that "make a market," such as Ford's Model T car, the DC-3 airplane, the Xerox 914 copier, and Kodak's "Brownie" camera. In this early going, the production process is most apt to be a job shop or a near–job shop.

As acceptance of the dominant design proceeds, however, cost reduction becomes increasingly important. Process innovation—geared primarily to lowering costs, increasing yield, and gaining production speed—commands management attention. Changes become less and less radical as the product, the process, and the organization become more and more standardized. The production process edges closer to the continuous flow end of the process spectrum. At the same time, both product and process become increasingly vulnerable to a radically different offering of similar function by some producer outside the traditionally defined industry (e.g., an electronics company like Texas Instruments making watches).

In this view, then, product and process innovation are both aspects of broad technological advance and of the shift in market characteristics, over time, that usually accompanies such advance.

NEW PRODUCT INTRODUCTION

Assessing the Technological Fortunes

Spotting the product designs that will be commercially successful is an uncertain business at best. It has been suggested that a new "technological winner" must score high on a mix of separate criteria:[6]

- *Inventive merit.* How important are the scientific advances in the product?
- *Engineering merit.* Does the engineering of the product fully exploit the scientific advances made? Must many changes be made?
- *Operational merit.* What will the product mean to company operations and organization? Will major revamping be required?
- *Market merit.* Is the product innovation what the market wants and will pay for?

To the extent that a product's inventive merit is strong, its marketing features attractive, and any required engineering and operational changes either slight or fully anticipated, a new product is likely to be a commercial success. A failure in any of these dimensions can spoil an otherwise promising product.

Pinpointing a promising technological advance is unavoidably subjective, but some research suggests that many of the uncertainties involved can be usefully quantified.[7] A number of these approaches to forecasting the success of a new product combine an expert panel with probability measures. Each panel expert is asked to indicate his or her own view of an R&D project's success. These opinions are collected, tabulated, and usually reviewed again by the expert panel, which can then revise its initial probability selections. Such assessments can be made at regular intervals over the years required to research and develop a new product.

Such assessments of the probability for success of various R&D projects can be important inputs to the management of these projects, identifying those that need attention and governing in part

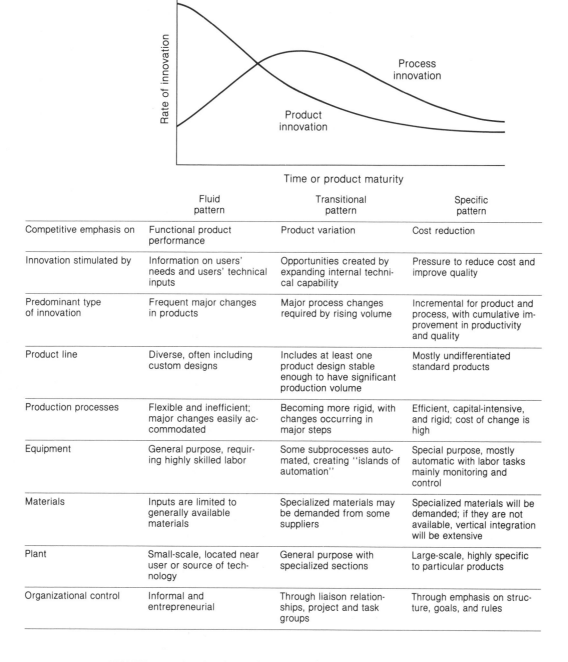

	Fluid pattern	Transitional pattern	Specific pattern
Competitive emphasis on	Functional product performance	Product variation	Cost reduction
Innovation stimulated by	Information on users' needs and users' technical inputs	Opportunities created by expanding internal technical capability	Pressure to reduce cost and improve quality
Predominant type of innovation	Frequent major changes in products	Major process changes required by rising volume	Incremental for product and process, with cumulative improvement in productivity and quality
Product line	Diverse, often including custom designs	Includes at least one product design stable enough to have significant production volume	Mostly undifferentiated standard products
Production processes	Flexible and inefficient; major changes easily accommodated	Becoming more rigid, with changes occurring in major steps	Efficient, capital-intensive, and rigid; cost of change is high
Equipment	General purpose, requiring highly skilled labor	Some subprocesses automated, creating "islands of automation"	Special purpose, mostly automatic with labor tasks mainly monitoring and control
Materials	Inputs are limited to generally available materials	Specialized materials may be demanded from some suppliers	Specialized materials will be demanded; if they are not available, vertical integration will be extensive
Plant	Small-scale, located near user or source of technology	General purpose with specialized sections	Large-scale, highly specific to particular products
Organizational control	Informal and entrepreneurial	Through liaison relationships, project and task groups	Through emphasis on structure, goals, and rules

FIGURE 13-5   Level and type of innovation. (From Abernathy and Utterback, "Patterns of Industrial Innovation," p. 40)

how resources can be controlled and apportioned among projects.

Managing New Product Introduction to the Factory

The search for a dominant design as well as a general broadening of product offerings requires that new product designs be introduced into the factory. Of course, this change is not so wrenching for a job shop process as for a flow process, but in any case it demands special coordination among product engineers, industrial engineers, and operations people. There is as yet no foolproof way of assuring a smooth introduction of a new product to the factory floor, but some general models of new product introduction are worth noting:

1. *Backward integration approach.* In this approach to new product introduction, one or more manufacturing engineers or managers are given the responsibility for introducing a new product to the factory. Their tasks include developing a workable bill-of-materials for purchasing, developing routing and process sheets for work stations within the factory, training labor, deciding on the path of materials movement, devising quality control checks, and constructing fixtures and other worker aids. These manufacturing engineers/managers may also run a "pilot shop" where manufacturing's first tries at making the product are housed before release of the product to the factory floor itself.

   In essence, manufacturing is invited into the product development program, although usually only the later stages of development. With this approach there is the difficult question of how early in the development program manufacturing ought to be called. Too late, and new product introduction to the factory will be either rushed and chaotic, or too much time will be lost in getting the new product to market. Too early, and manufacturing may have to deal with a product that is too "immature" to merit any preparation on manufacturing's part.

2. *Forward integration approach.* As its name implies, this approach reverses the involvement of product development engineers and manufacturing. Here, the engineers who developed the product are invited onto the factory floor to coordinate and guide the development of bills-of-materials, product routing, worker techniques, quality control, and the like. Under this approach, any pilot shop operations are managed by product development engineers.

   In many ways, this is a more intuitively appealing approach to new product introduction—to have the people who developed the product see it through to manufacture. Yet, product design engineers are not manufacturing engineers. This approach risks the development of an expensive production system that would demand the attention of a good manufacturing engineer anyway, sometime later on.

3. *Team approach.* In this approach, neither manufacturing nor engineering is responsible for new product introduction. Rather, a team drawn from both manufacturing and engineering bears the responsibility. This is generally an expensive way to introduce new products, since a number of people have to be released at the same time for membership on the team, but the possibilities for real coordination of product engineering and manufacturing are improved.

None of these three general models of new product introduction dominates the others in all situations; some companies use all three. In broad terms, the team approach becomes relatively more attractive when the product is very complex. The backward integration approach becomes relatively more attractive when the product is simpler and in need of cost reduction in order to compete better on price. The forward integration approach, on the other hand, becomes relatively more attractive when the product is more complex and not threatened with competition based largely on price.

For some new product introductions involving especially complex and uncertain technology, two or more engineering teams are assigned to solve the same problem using fundamentally different means. This kind of "parallel" rather than "sequential" pursuit of new products, while expensive, can cut down on the time it takes to develop a new product. The search for new, more fuel-efficient auto engines is an example of such parallel pursuit, since many ideas are being developed simultaneously.

PROCESS INNOVATION

The introduction of new process innovations is even less well delineated than new product introduction. As mentioned earlier, incremental change is often thought to offer different management problems from radical change. It is frequently felt that continual, small improvements in the process technology can be stimulated by company reward systems or company grants for the pursuit of new ideas, such as are found at companies like 3M. Or, they can be induced by increased management pressure, through work restructuring programs to call forth worker modifications, or by compensation schemes like the Scanlon plan, which ties pay increases to productivity gains. The factors cited earlier as influencing the learning curve can all account for incremental changes in process technology. Further, implementing incremental change can often be done without placing great demands on management's coordinating abilities.

Radical changes to the process technology are more problematic. Bigger bucks and greater risk are involved, as well as the need to coordinate many people in various company departments. What leads to success in such an endeavor is not known with certainty, but analyses of some radical process innovations seem to uphold these general principles:

- The suggested process change must fit the company's business goals and thereby foster the commitment of the company's top management.

- The company must have a realistic idea of what the innovation can do well and should not get swamped by trying to innovate everywhere at once.

- Any test should be made in a setting that is representative of the company's business and environment.

- A strong individual—sometimes termed the "change champion"—should act as both catalyst and critic for the innovation and its implementation.

A flavor for these views on managing innovation can be sampled in the following description of Giant Food Inc. of Landover, Maryland and its leadership position in laser beam scanning at supermarket checkout counters.

Giant Food Inc.: Laser Beam Scanning at the Checkout Counter

Giant Food Inc. was the leading grocery store chain in the Baltimore–Washington area. As of early 1979, it operated about 120 stores in Maryland, Virginia, and the District of Columbia. Only Safeway Stores was in a position to challenge Giant's dominance of this regional market.

Since Giant Food's introduction of self-service grocery shopping to Washington, D.C. in 1936, the company has maintained a reputation for innovation. It was a pioneer in frozen foods in the 1940s and self-service meat departments in the early 1950s. Throughout the late 1950s and the 1960s the chain developed such concepts as combining food and general merchandise and a pharmacy in the same store. Giant Food has also been a leader in consumer advocacy. The company's consumer advisor in the early 1970s was Esther Peterson, the

FIGURE 13-6 A sample universal product code (UPC) symbol. As with all such symbols, the first five digits represent the manufacturer; the second five digits represent the specific item. Price is not included in the symbol.

first appointed Assistant to the President for Consumer Affairs (under Lyndon Johnson). Under Peterson's direction, Giant Food adopted a "consumer bill of rights" and led the way in unit pricing on aisle shelves, calendar dating of perishable commodities, disclosure of nutritional information on the package, and the marketing of recycled paper products. More recently, the company has adopted one of the first semiautomated grocery warehouses to be developed.

Giant Food's tradition of innovation is no more readily appreciated than in its leadership in the application of laser beam scanning to the checkout counter. The company was far and away the nation's technological leader in scanning, having installed it in over 70 stores by the beginning of 1979.

Scanning and Its Benefits. With laser beam scanning the cashier does not have to key in the price of any item that is marked with the special universal product code (UPC) symbol. This symbol, pictured in Figure 13-6, uses bands of lines of varying thickness to represent both the manufacturer and the precise product to be scanned. The product with its attached symbol is drawn over a window in the checkout counter, which houses a low-energy laser beam scanner. This scanner "reads" the UPC, matches the product with its price, which is on file

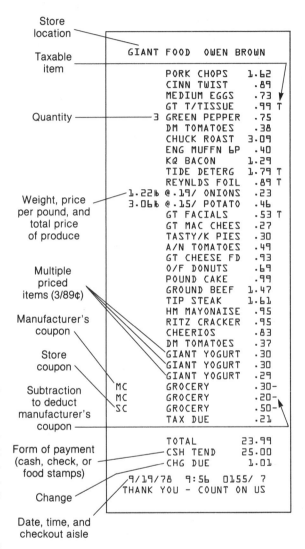

FIGURE 13-7 An annotated sample register tape from a laser beam scanning checkout.

in an in-store minicomputer, and prints out a tape that identifies both product and price (see Figure 13-7).

The now recognized advantages of checkout counter scanning are numerous. These advantages are generally divided into so-called "hard savings" and "soft savings." The hard savings refer to benefits such as:

- Quicker checkout of an order, enabling the store to maintain or improve its checkout service with fewer lanes and cashiers, and better scheduling of both.

- Faster and more accurate end-of-shift balancing of each cash register.

- Elimination of the weighing, bagging, and pricing of produce in the produce department and its transfer to the checkout counter where it can be done more efficiently and more accurately.

- Avoidance of the expense of replacing mechanical cash registers.

- More economical ordering of groceries by stores from headquarters.

These hard savings alone are enough to make scanning very attractive. As of June 1978, Giant Food estimated that these savings total $6634 per month for a store doing $160,000 worth of business each week. This kind of saving is enough to ensure a payback of between 2 and 4 years, depending on the size of the store.

More than this, Giant Food estimated that another $2745 could be saved each month if individual items did not have to be marked with price labels and updated periodically, since a scanning system operates without any keying in of prices. Item price-marking has been the one controversial feature about laser beam scanning. The company, while aware of the savings it could realize if items did not have to be price marked, nevertheless continued to put prices on all its store items in conformance with the demand of some consumer groups.

The soft savings from scanning at the checkout counter refer to some fundamental changes in grocery store management that scanning and the computer system supporting it can foster. Among these soft savings:

- Automatic reordering of certain items in the store without the current need to take physical inventories.

- Reduction in store "shrink" (the loss of what was thought to be received from suppliers) due to errors or theft.

- Monitoring sales, promotions, price discounts, and the like by item and by time period, to permit the store to be more flexible in its response to customer desires and more profitable in the product mix, pricing, and shelf allocation decisions every store must make.

The extent of such soft savings is being explored.

The Genesis of Scanning at Giant Food. Scanning is not a new concept. As long ago as the mid-1960s, an IBM representative discussed the concept of a scanner with Donald R. Buchanan, Giant Food's Vice-President for Data Processing. From a practical standpoint, however, scanning only began to receive the company's serious attention in 1970 when the grocery industry trade associations (retailers, food processors, and wholesalers) began investigating the issue and developing a universal product code symbol. Giant Food was strictly an interested bystander at this time and remained so through the selection of the universal product code symbol design in 1971 and the first test of a scanning system by Kroger in its Kenwood, Ohio store in 1972–73. Buchanan did visit with scanner manufacturers throughout this period, but no commitments were made.

As study results began to appear both from the Kroger test and from tests by the scanner manufacturers, Buchanan began getting a gut feeling that the benefits of scanning would outweigh the costs. On an informal basis, he and selected others from data processing and operations began to study the matter more intensely. In early 1974, Buchanan became convinced that the equipment manufacturers were serious about scanning (IBM had announced its 3660 Supermarket System in November 1973) and that Giant should undertake a study of its own. This view was bolstered by the long-term trend for increasing wages in the industry and thus rewards for those grocery chains that could reduce the labor intensity of store operations. Furthermore, Giant Food's stores were high volume stores, the ones analysis suggested were most favorable to the scanning technology.

Buchanan brought his idea for a test store to the attention of Giant Food's Executive Vice-President, Israel Cohen, and its President, Joseph Danzansky.* After hearing about the proposal and its potential, Cohen and Danzansky approved the test. At this point the informality of the scanning idea gave way to the formality of committing the company's funds to it. Buchanan was given responsibility for the project.

In March 1974, Buchanan appointed a seven-member team, reporting directly to him, and charged them with (1) designing the new "front end" (as the checkout counter area was called), (2) choosing the equipment manufacturer(s) for it, (3) developing the computer software to control the scanning process and the information it provided, and (4) installing the prototype system in the test store. The team leader was recruited from the banking rather than the grocery business and had a strong background in data processing. Four other members of the team had data processing backgrounds, three of them with experience at Giant Food. These technical people included a systems programmer, a senior systems analyst, and two other analysts/programmers. In addition, a store manager and an assistant store manager were assigned permanently to the team.

Buchanan deliberately sought a wide mix of experience for the team and also generous staffing, an indication of Cohen's and Danzansky's commitment to the project. Team motivation was high since the entire team recognized that it had significant control of the direction scanning would take at Giant Food. The team reported each week or so

to Buchanan. It was originally desired to house the team at Giant's headquarters in Landover, Maryland, but space constraints there forced the team to rent some space adjacent to a Giant Food store about 6 to 8 miles from headquarters.

In an associated development, Esther Peterson met with a group of consumers and consumer groups to discuss scanning and its role in a supermarket. The results of these meetings were fed to the team.

Team Operation and the Severna Park Store. Early in the team's deliberations it was decided to use IBM equipment in the test. There were a variety of reasons for the choice. Giant Food was already a satisfied IBM customer, and it was felt that IBM was committed to the scanning technology. It was reasonable to expect that IBM was going to be around for the long pull and, if IBM were true to form, it would place enough people on the project to make it seem as though Giant Food had hired some private consultants. As it turned out, later in the project some IBM people became, in effect, members of the team, although by that time it was clearly a Giant Food operation.

It was decided as well that the test of scanning proceed in a new store so that the project would not disturb in any way existing operations. A new store planned for Severna Park, Maryland (a relatively affluent southern suburb of Baltimore) was chosen. The team trained all of the labor at the new store; Giant Food's operations group assisted the team and was itself trained in this new technology. In fact, the team nearly lived at the store for months, both before and after its opening. The scanning at Severna Park was viewed primarily as a development effort to investigate scanning technology, the systems needed to operate it, the hard cash savings attributable to it, and customer reaction.

---

*Cohen is now President and Chairman. Danzansky is Chairman Emeritus.

The Severna Park store opened in late January 1975. The opening date had been pushed back somewhat by the construction people because the parking lot could not be laid in time. Although the team felt they could have met the original store opening date, they breathed a sigh of relief. Actually, the team was overprepared for the store's opening, having spent nearly a year in planning and preparation.

Most grocery stores enjoy a gala grand opening, preceded by a lot of advertising. In contrast, the Severna Park store opened 10 days prior to its grand opening and with no advertising. The store thus underwent a shakedown with just the people who wandered into it and without the crush and hoopla attending most store openings. The preview opening consisted of a number of media events and a series of explanatory sessions, held three times a day over several days, directed to groups such as the print media, the electronic media, consumer groups, teachers, suppliers, the financial community, Giant Food employees, and labor officials.

The Severna Park store test was designed to be as pure a test of the benefits and operation of scanning as could be devised. The store thus opened without any prices on individual items. Shelves were marked with a new descriptive unit price label and a scanning unit was set up in the front of the store for customers to use. The controversial nature of item pricing was evident soon enough. Even though customer response was enthusiastic, organized consumer groups began to register their complaints, even prior to the store's opening. The store was picketed, and bills were later introduced into the Maryland and Virginia legislatures to require item pricing.

Except for this consumer group reaction, the results from the Severna Park test were promising. Giant officials spent large amounts of time at the store gauging results. Cameras had been mounted to film the checkout process and time-and-motion studies were made of the film.

Taking Scanning past the Test Phase. To this point, no one had given any indication of commitment beyond opening the test store. It was Cohen who announced a few months after the opening of the Severna Park store that a second scanning test installation should be used when the company opened its next store—a unit in Glen Burnie, Maryland in August 1975. It was decided to put prices on all items in the Glen Burnie store. This meant that Cohen's faith in scanning was strong enough not to let the program die in the face of the recession the United States was suffering at the time. This decision also helped set a pattern of placing scanning in the new stores that Giant was scheduling to open.

Cohen's decision to go ahead with scanning in the new Glen Burnie store had an immediate impact on the choice of an equipment manufacturer. At this time, only IBM was offering full-scale scanning equipment. NCR was offering a point-of-sale terminal that could be upgraded at a later time to scanning, but scanning was not yet available. Thus, IBM equipment was chosen for Glen Burnie and would prove to be the model for all of Giant's subsequent scanning stores.

The team responsible for the Severna Park store went ahead with the installation of scanning at Glen Burnie and the training of people there. The experience at Severna Park paid off in an easier and trouble-free installation at Glen Burnie. The benefits seen at the Severna Park test were duplicated at Glen Burnie under its mildly different conditions.

During this time, Giant Food was still somewhat surprised by the extent of consumer group activity against scanning without item pricing. While the company had managed, just barely, to argue the state legislatures of Maryland and Virginia out of mandatory item pricing, management was still very sensitive to consumer reaction. With this in mind, the company agreed to abide by the results of a Michigan State University study of scanning and price recognition. In early 1976, the study reported that there was some loss of price awareness in some consumers when scanning was used without item price marking. Giant Food thereby instituted item pricing in all its planned scanning stores as well as the Severna Park store. This finding was a blow to the company, but Giant publicly stated that they would abide by the results of the study. However, the benefits that Giant Food saw for scanning—both hard and soft savings—appeared to outweigh its costs, even when the savings in item pricing costs are excluded.

As it became more and more clear that scanning at the checkout counter would be a way of life for all of Giant Food's new stores and any that were undergoing extensive remodeling, the company's operations department became more and more involved with this transition in the company.* A point-of-sale installation committee was formed with Buchanan as chairman. The committee consisted of an IBM representative, a manager from the company's construction department, a contract electrician involved in the installation, the vice-president of operations, the company's two zone managers, a personnel manager, and two members of the data processing department. This installation committee was charged with making a smooth transition in all stores and existed apart from the original data processing department team. This committee reviewed time schedules for phases of the installation, reported on installation progress, and ironed out coordination problems among the company departments that were becoming increasingly responsible for individual pieces of the scanner installation program.

At the same time the nature and composition of the original team changed. It dropped from seven members to six, retaining four of the original group, including the team leader. It was now called the data processing department field support team;

its duties became more mechanical, directing and troubleshooting the installation process rather than evaluating it.

A point-of-sale steering committee, chaired by Buchanan, was appointed by Cohen in 1978. This group's purpose was to investigate the soft savings achievable through scanning. Little had been done on this at the beginning of the project, but with an increasing number of stores with scanning and an entire system of information created, it was decided to exploit such possible benefits.

The point-of-sale installation committee met for about 2 years (1976–77) and then disbanded. The field support team and the point-of-sale steering committee continued to operate into 1979. The installation of scanning in Giant Food stores is now routine. A store can now be converted to scanning with only about a week's notice.

With more than 60 percent of its stores using scanning, Giant Food's data processing department was merging the control systems for both scanning and nonscanning stores. As new scanning stores were instituted, separate data files for prices, inventory, costs, and the like were established to support them. As the new scanning system grew, it became more and more desirable to merge it with the former control system. Work continued on this effort into 1979.

Over time there has been a drop in the real costs of installing scanning. Checkout counter stands are no longer the custom products they were in the first scanning stores. The number of grocery items marked with the Universal Product Code symbol has also grown; at the beginning of 1979, 95 percent of dry and frozen goods were marked. Source marking of pharmacy items has lagged behind these other items. Naturally, produce, meats, and seafood must continue to be marked at the store.

Giant Food will probably be the first food chain

*In fact, because of the business advantages that Giant Food saw in scanning, an early commitment was made to install scanning not only in new stores but in all company stores. The first conversion of an existing store occurred in October 1975.

in the United States to be completely converted to point-of-sale scanning.

Lessons from Giant Food

Giant Food Inc. is in no way responsible for the following views and presentation. They remain solely the responsibility of the author.

It is easy to observe how Giant Food's experience clearly reflects the four general principles stated earlier:

1. Laser beam scanning at the checkout was seen early on as fitting particularly well into Giant Food's stores. Those stores were generally large and high volume, and it was in large, high volume stores that the most significant benefits for scanning were expected. Moreover, Giant Food's top managers, Cohen and Danzansky, recognized this affinity and gave the entire project their very strong backing. The company's rich history of innovation no doubt helped establish change as the norm for the company, and so projects like scanning would not be opposed on irrational grounds.

2. Donald Buchanan and the project team did not hold unrealistic ideas about what scanning could do. Nor were all the possible uses of scanning explored at once. Rather, the team's man-

date was a comparatively modest one: to develop a scanning system that worked and to place it in a test store so that some hard savings could be analyzed.

3. Both the Severna Park and Glen Burnie stores used for the tests of scanning were typical of most Giant stores, especially the new ones. The tests were thus as representative as the company could make them.

4. In Donald Buchanan, Giant Food had a strong "change champion" who acted (1) to stimulate the company's thinking about scanning, (2) to organize a diverse project team and give it direction, (3) to isolate the team so that it could do its job without distraction, and (4) to support the team within the company so that team decisions stuck.

These four general principles, of course, may not explain all of Giant Food's success in innovating laser beam scanning at the checkout counter. Other factors may have played an important and as yet undetected role. Nevertheless, these four principles apply to Giant Food; what is more, they seem to carry over from one successful innovator to another. Furthermore, many stalled innovations or outright failures have neglected one or more of these general features of successful innovation. These principles bear careful consideration.

QUESTIONS

1. What do you understand by the term *technological change?* Give three examples of other situations in which the concept would be useful and applicable.

2. What are the mathematical assumptions behind the theory of the learning curve? What does the learning curve represent for manufacturing?

3. What is linear regression and of what relevance is it to the Nashville Fire Equipment Company?

4. What are some uses of the learning curve principle in long-term strategic decisions?

5. Analyze and discuss the relationship between product innovation and process innovation, providing a concrete example from your own reading or experience.

6. Summarize and compare the differences between the three ways of managing the introduction of a new product to a factory.

7. In what ways does Giant Food's introduction of scanning into its grocery stores illustrate the general principles operating behind radical process innovations?

PROBLEMS

1. Summarize the procedure for calculating a learning curve. Of what use is this procedure?

2. It has been observed that preemptive pricing strategies are more useful in certain situations than in others. What are the characteristics of these situations?

3. Select a product that has been introduced to the marketplace within the last 5 years and has proved highly successful. Research the way in which it was developed, and isolate the criteria that led to its successful introduction.

4. How can changing the product design result in a technological change?

5. What level of process change represents a technological change? Explain your answer.

6. Explain how the four criteria for determining a "technological winner" work.

SITUATION FOR STUDY

MEDICAL HOSPITAL

Medical Hospital is a large regional hospital located in Weatherford, Oklahoma. Included in the hospital is a large pharmacy. Recently, the pharmacy has been experiencing long lead times for filling prescriptions, and the pharmacy manager, Patricia Pritchard, is anxious to find a solution to the problem. The main difficulty occurs during night hours and weekends when the regular pharmacists are off duty.

During the evening shifts (3 P.M. to 11 P.M.) and weekends, the pharmacy is staffed by technicians. The technicians are trained in pharmacy procedures but are not pharmacists. They are allowed, however, to fill prescriptions. Due to the time of the shift and the requirement of working every other weekend, it has been very difficult to find highly motivated and trainable people to work full-time. Most people preferred to work days and wanted weekends off. Many who were hired were slow to learn the job.

An alternative to hiring full-time technicians was to hire students from a nearby pharmacy school on a part-time basis. Each student worked about 20 hours a week, and so twice as many employees were needed to fill all of the slots. Most pharmacy students could be expected to work a maximum of two to three years because once they finished their pharmacy program, they were not happy to be just technicians. Also, some of the students would tie their work to the school calendar, and turnover was high in May, August, and December. The result was that from two to five tech-

TABLE 13-A   Orders Filled per Hour
(Medical Hospital)

EMPLOYEE	WEEK 1	WEEK 2	WEEK 3	WEEK 4	WEEK 5	WEEK 6
A	8	12	12	15	18	20
B	6	11	12	14	16	18
C	7	12	14	16	16	16
D	8	10	10	14	14	18
E	12	18	20	21	21	22
F	5	8	10	11	12	14
G	6	8	10	13	15	16
H	8	10	13	15	17	19
I	9	10	12	12	14	16
J	10	12	15	17	19	21

nicians (an average of three) were new every four months. Usually technicians were brought in at a rate of two per week and were trained on the job as well as by a course taught by the pharmacists.

Patricia had noticed not only that productivity was low, but also that the cost of training technicians was high. She had heard that the learning curve concept had been applied in manufacturing and wondered whether it could be applied to the pharmacy's product, a filled order. Pat defined an order as having three medications, the average. If an order had six medications, it was counted as two orders. On an average night 55 orders were processed. The normal maximum speed for an employee was around 20 to 24 orders per hour.

Patricia decided to study, for several weeks, the speed with which 10 technicians filled orders. The shift supervisor collected information on orders filled correctly by these technicians. It was easy to identify each technician's work, as they were required to initial each order filled. Table 13-A shows the results of this study in orders filled per hour, and Figure 13-A shows the learning curves for three of the 10 employees.

Now that Patricia had this information, she was uncertain how it could be used to help reduce the cost of training new employees, and how she could help reduce her turnover problem.

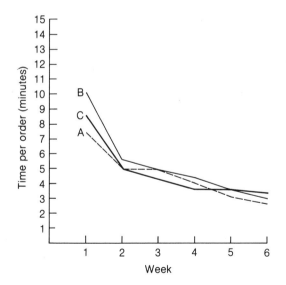

FIGURE 13-A   Learning curves for technicians A, B, and C.

REFERENCE NOTES

1. *Business Week* (July 3, 1978): 47.

2. For some additional information on the learning curve, see David L. Bodde, "Riding the Experience Curve," *Technology Review* 78, no. 5 (March–April 1976), pp. 53–59; Winfred B. Hirschmann, "Profit from the Learning Curve," *Harvard Business Review* 42, no. 1 (January–February 1964), pp. 125–39; William J. Abernathy and Kenneth Wayne, "Limits of the Learning Curve," *Harvard Business Review* 52, no. 5 (September–October 1974), pp. 109–19.

3. Additional sources of information on the dilemma of productivity increase are William J. Abernathy, *The Productivity Dilemma: Roadblock to Innovation in the Automobile Industry* (Baltimore: Johns Hopkins Press, 1978) and Edward Denison, *Effects of Selected Changes in the Institutional and Human Environment upon Output per Unit of Input* (Washington, D.C.: Brookings Institution, 1978).

4. William J. Abernathy and James M. Utterback, "Pattern of Industrial Innovation," *Technology Review* 80, no. 7 (June–July 1978): 40–47.

5. Abernathy, *The Productivity Dilemma*, 1978.

6. George R. White and Margaret B.W. Graham, "How to Spot a Technological Winner," *Harvard Business Review* 56, no. 2 (March–April 1978).

7. H. U. Balthasar, R. A. A. Boschi, and M. M. Menke, "Calling the Shots in R&D," *Harvard Business Review* 56, no. 3 (May–June 1978); William E. Souder, "Analytical Effectiveness of Mathematical Models for R&D Project Selection," *Management Science* (April 1973).

14

DEALING WITH OPPORTUNITIES FOR VERTICAL INTEGRATION

The sequence of activities that bring a good or service into being and then to market is frequently a long one. Very often, the companies involved in the sequence confront some intriguing choices about how much or how little of that sequence to involve themselves with. Take gasoline for example. There are at least six broad stages involved in manufacturing and marketing gasoline: (1) exploring for and purchasing the mineral rights to the land under which the oil lies, (2) drilling the well and pumping oil from it, (3) transporting the crude oil from well to refinery, often by pipeline or tanker, (4) refining the crude oil into a multitude of petroleum products, (5) transporting refined gasoline from refinery to storage tanks (tank farms) and thence to service stations, and (6) selling gasoline at the service station pump. A company can decide to engage in just one of these six activities or to straddle two or more of them. Indeed, there are companies that engage in just one activity and there are companies that engage in all of them.

At issue in this chapter is how to decide the extent of a company's commitment to portions of the full sequence of production and distribution activities for any good or service. In the common terminology, it is a decision about the degree of vertical integration that a company should seek. The decision is complex, influenced by a number of factors.

FACTORS IN THE VERTICAL INTEGRATION DECISION

As an introduction to some of the factors that can guide vertical integration decisions, consider Situation 14-1.

SITUATION 14-1

RICH CLOVER DAIRY

Perhaps it was time to close this chapter in the dairy's history. All Ralph Maynard knew was that it would be an emotional ending, if it came to that. Ralph, president of the Rich Clover Dairy and son of its founder, faced the decision whether to close the dairy's own farm. The farm, located in the lush, rolling countryside north of one of the city's reservoirs, had been the da-

iry's showpiece for over 40 years. Rich Clover's prize herd of guernsey cows were pastured there and the dairy had used this fact to advantage in marketing itself as "the dairy with cows." (Most other dairies had no cows of their own; they bought milk from dairy farmers, processed and bottled it, and then sold it under their brand name.) Many of the area's families had

---

made a point of bringing their children to the dairy to see the cows and bulls, the twice-daily milkings, and the egg-laying chickens. The farm no doubt contributed not only to the dairy's image among local people of being devoted to quality but also its position as the area's second largest dairy.

Times were changing, however, and Rich Clover was not immune. While the dairy's sales had continued to grow with the development of the area, the nature of those sales had changed drastically. Where 20 years ago, fully two-thirds of the dairy's sales were from home deliveries, now they barely accounted for 20 percent. The slack had been taken up by increased sales to grocery stores (Rich Clover was a leading supplier to local chains and Mom-and-Pop independents) and by the founding of the dairy's own convenience stores, which were open from 7 A.M. to 11 P.M. and sold a variety of grocery items in addition to dairy products.

Other changes had some significant implications for the farm itself. The area's continued growth had spread population and housing farther and farther from the downtown. The farm, once a considerable trek out in the country, was now much more within the fringe of the area's growth. Land prices were escalating and the dairy could reap a handsome profit by selling its 1500 acres.

In addition, the farm raised only guernsey cows, which were known for their very rich milk. The dairy's "top-of-the-line" milk (8 percent of sales), "Golden Guernsey," was supplied almost entirely by the farm's herd. With changing lifestyles, however, milk rich in butterfat was steadily losing market share to nonfat and low fat milk. Ralph Maynard could foresee the day when the farm's herd would be forced to supply milk for other than the Golden Guernsey line—the dairy's highest margin product. As it was, 20 years ago the herd had been able to produce only half the dairy's need for guernsey milk; the milk from other guernsey herds had been purchased.

Ralph could foresee other changes at Rich Clover. The dairy's receiving and bottling plant, located in the city, was over 45 years old. Although periodically modernized, the bottling plant was neither as efficient nor as fast as the latest plants other dairies boasted. Moreover, traffic around the plant had become increasingly snarled, in part because the plant's loading operations were more suited to traditional, small milk trucks than to the larger, refrigerated trailers that could better supply grocery and convenience stores. The relocation of the dairy's bottling operations was a choice Ralph could sense he would have to face in the years to come. First, he thought, the farm's future should be addressed.

DISCUSSION OF RICH CLOVER DAIRY

One very important feature of Ralph Maynard's decisions in this situation, as well as in many similar ones, involves the economics of vertical integration. Where in the entire sequence of activities is the rate of return to invested capital high and where is it low? This question is an important one and one that is often very difficult to answer. We can get some handle on it by taking a brief excursion into the realm of economics and the concept of an "economic rent."

✱ ASIDE ✱

ECONOMIC RENTS AND VERTICAL INTEGRATION

A sure way to riches is to offer a product or service that is both in demand and scarce in supply. In such situations the price people are willing to pay is often very much higher than the costs of bringing the product or service to market. The difference between the two is termed an *economic rent*.

Land is the classic example of an economic rent. Certain categories of land, say land with oil underneath it, are in at least relatively fixed supply.

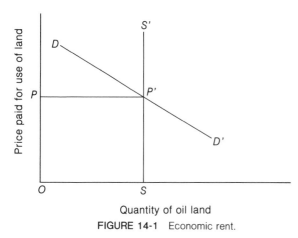

FIGURE 14-1   Economic rent.

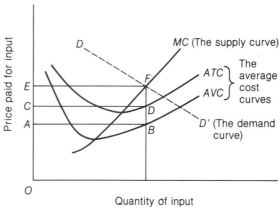

FIGURE 14-2   Economic quasi rent.

That is, even over several years, the known quantity of oil land does not vary greatly (although vary it does). As long as oil companies bid higher for the use of the land than housing developers or commercial interests, owners would be willing to offer their land for drilling. A higher bid brings no further change in behavior from the landowners; all they can say is "Yes, go ahead and drill." What they receive from the oil company is an economic rent.

To aid our understanding, we can graph this situation (Figure 14-1). The quantity OS is the land available. SS' is the supply curve that is vertical, indicating that a higher price offered for the use of the land will not induce more production. Production is fixed at the OS acreage level. DD' is the demand curve, indicating the price the oil company would pay for various quantities of land offered. OP is the per acre price that the company is willing to pay for the services of OS acres of oil land. The OP price is the economic rent in this situation of a production input that is in rigid supply. The landowner reaps a total economic rent of OSP'P, which can be a considerable sum.

Few inputs are in rigid supply, of course, but many come into temporarily rigid supply. Owners of these inputs can in these short-lived cases earn what is called a *quasi rent*. Figure 14-2 illustrates this case. Here, increases in the price offered will induce more of the input to be supplied, as we can tell from the rising supply curve, marked MC because it is really the marginal cost curve for the input. The demand curve intersects the supply curve at F, thus establishing the level OE as the price for the input. The input could be purchased, however, for any price higher than OA, since any price higher than OA would cover the average variable costs of the owner of the input. In the long term, however, we could not count on having the input supplied if the price did not exceed OC, which is the level at which average total costs are covered. The difference, of course, is that some fixed costs must be covered in the longer run, if not in the short run.

Quasi rents are pure rents in the short run, although in the longer run they must go to pay off fixed costs; otherwise the input would have to be withdrawn. In Figure 14-2, the total quasi rent is ABFE. The quantity ABDC represents the fixed costs that must be paid off in the longer run, while CDFE represents pure economic profit.

What do rents and quasi rents have to do with the economics of vertical integration? Rents and quasi rents are important because they often indicate where rates of return are high. Since scarcity brings about rents and quasi rents, it often pays to ask where scarcity lies in an industry. Find scarcity, and you often find a road to riches.

*

RETURNING HOME WITH THE COWS

Back to Ralph Maynard's responsibilities at the Rich Clover Dairy. Where does scarcity exist in dairying? Where do the bucks and the high rates of return lie? According to Maynard, dairy cows are not scarce, and so we should not expect large rates of return from owning a herd of guernsey cows, at least not for their milk production. (Their marketing clout is a different question.) This is an argument then for selling the farm.

If scarcity and high rates of return do not lie with owning cows, where do they lie? The answer to this is less than clear-cut, but the Rich Clover brand name and its quality image appear to be what is "scarce." The industry is one where the retailing end of the business is likely to be a much more important factor than the origin of the milk. Whatever else, a dairy wants to maintain its strength as a bottler and marketer.

This seat-of-the-pants case against a dairy's owning its own herd is insufficient by itself to decide the issue, since the immediate issue is more concerned with whether it is better to hang onto the farm for a few more years in anticipation of even higher land prices in the area or to sell the farm now and invest the cash in some other income-generating alternative. Once again, the decision involves a marginal analysis. Will the land price gains outweigh the expected net benefits of relocating the dairy and adopting a more efficient bottling technology? The strict economics of the decision rest on these calculations, which are less a matter of vertical integration and more a matter of investment analysis.

This divergence of project economics (hold land or relocate) from industry economics (where the economic rents are) is an intriguing one, common to many vertical integration situations. The industry economics are likely to govern the long-run earnings of a company, while individual decisions in the short run are likely to be made on narrower grounds. In this instance, Rich Clover Dairy is likely to be better off without its own guernsey herd in the long run, but land speculation in the short run may well advise keeping the farm at least a few more years. What we need to be vigilant about is that the sequence of short-run decisions we make is consistent with the long-run economics of the industry. We shall return to this theme in further discussions about vertical integration.

Another purely operational concern with implications for vertical integration centers on the balance of capacities between stages of the production process. Over the years at the dairy, the herd of guernsey cows had been insufficient to supply all the Golden Guernsey milk demanded. If recent trends persist, however, the herd will soon provide more than enough milk to meet the declining demand for Golden Guernsey milk. The farm's excess milk would then have to be mixed with other, lower profit margin milk, or else production would have to be cut back. Thus, just because the product mix demanded of the dairy has changed, the attractiveness of vertical integration, already suspect, is eroded further. The capacities of the farm and the bottling plant simply do not match up as well as they used to, and the dairy risks forgoing contribution because of this mismatch.

It was mentioned earlier that the Rich Clover farm had, at least historically, aided the company's marketing efforts and its quality image. This remains an argument for maintaining the farm. There may be other ways, of course, of promoting a quality image. For instance, assuming the dairy is relocated, the sight and advertising of a new bottling plant with all the latest, fastest, and cleanest equipment could well make up for whatever tarnishing occurs to the Rich Clover image as a result of selling the farm.

THE ADVANTAGES OF VERTICAL INTEGRATION

The arguments brought to bear against vertical integration at Rich Clover Dairy notwithstanding, vertical integration can be very attractive. For one thing, integration either backward or forward may lead to the location of the profit-enhancing economic rents in the industry.

Let us pursue our oil industry example further and delve into the history of the industry in the United States.[1] The oil industry did not begin fully integrated but rather integrated backward and forward in piecemeal fashion. In fact, the Standard Oil Company, and later the Standard Oil trust, did not seek vertical integration until it was forced to.

After the discovery of oil in western Pennsylvania in 1859 came a decade of remarkable advance in refining technology that led to low cost, high speed continuous flow refineries. John D. Rockefeller's Standard Oil Company in Cleveland came to the fore in the early 1870s because it was the largest and fastest refinery. At that time, the industry was being racked by excess capacity and price-cutting. Industry associations sprang up but were essentially toothless in enforcing prices on their members.

In trying to add discipline to the loose cartel of refiners, Rockefeller struck a bargain with the railroads that gave Standard Oil and its associates significant price breaks in exchange for the steady use of large numbers of rail tank cars. This arrangement was beneficial to both Standard Oil (lower transport costs) and the railroads (better scheduling of railcars). The lower rail rates were enough to discourage future investments in refineries and to keep existing refiners in the cartel. Rockefeller had succeeded in discovering a way to protect the economic rents he and others in the Standard Oil group enjoyed—namely, by ensuring that refining capacity remained scarce.

Some oil producers soon found a way around Rockefeller's railroad arrangement, however. Via the innovation of the long-distance oil pipeline, some crude oil producers (Standard Oil did not own any crude oil production) in western Pennsylvania were able in the late 1870s to bypass the railroads to bring crude oil to the East Coast for refining, and at a lower cost. These producers then integrated even further forward by building their own refi-

neries since pipelines were even better than railroads at maintaining an even flow of crude into continuously operating refineries. It did not take long for Rockefeller and Standard Oil to realize that the scarcity (and the economic rents) in the industry had shifted. The scarcity of refining capacity was no longer protected. What was scarce was low cost transportation of crude oil from oil field to refinery. Standard Oil moved quickly to build its own pipelines and then to relocate its refinery capacity in the markets that could now be easily served by pipeline. By the early 1880s, low cost crude oil transportation was no longer scarce. Standard Oil's economic rents from refining were once again secure.

In a few years' time, these economic rents were again threatened, this time by the oil wholesalers to whom Standard Oil sold its product. Once small and widely dispersed, the wholesalers began to build large storage facilities, selling large quantities over wider areas for lower unit costs. The larger scale of individual wholesalers gave them increased market power and began shifting the scarcity away from refining capacity to storage and marketing. Again, Standard Oil reacted swiftly to this threat and protected its economic rents by creating its own national sales organization and buying out the wholesalers.

This action brought protection for only a few years until it was realized, with the decline in production in the western Pennsylvania fields, that crude oil production was itself the source of possible scarcities and economic rents. Standard Oil then moved to purchase oil-producing properties to assure itself of crude oil supplies and of any economic rents to be gathered due to periodic constrictions in supply. By the early 1890s then, Standard Oil was a completely integrated company, able to protect itself against the threat of any scarcities.

The point of this brief recapitulation of the fascinating early history of Standard Oil is to spotlight the importance of scarcity and economic rent to vertical integration decisions. So long as no scarcities existed, Standard Oil was content to remain less than fully integrated. But when scarcities arose, Standard Oil was forced to dispell them or face an erosion of its own profitability. Standard Oil's history raises another interesting point: scarcity and economic rents can be tremendously mobile. That fact became painfully obvious in the oil industry once again with the Arab oil embargo of 1973. The Arab oil states reaped stupendous economic rents. Since then, however, there have sometimes been gluts of crude oil, with the likely result of throwing scarcity and economic rents back on refining capacity.

Indeed, Ashland Oil thinks that this is the case. As the chairman of Ashland is quoted in a *Business Week* article (September 4, 1978, p. 99): "If our refineries don't have crude oil, no industry runs in those areas and no commercial enterprises operate.... The government will not allow such a situation to exist." Ashland Oil has been cutting back its oil exploration and production but increasing its refining capacity, precisely because it feels the economic rents lie in refining. Other oil companies disagree, of course, with this assessment and have been stepping up their exploration programs because they feel the economic rents lie in the production of crude oil.

In sum, a major attraction of vertical integration is its ability to control the reaping of economic rents and quasi rents. It does this by assuming all the relevant profit margins in the chain of production and distribution activities that bring a good or service into being and off to market. By controlling the key features of an entire production/distribution system, the vertically integrated company can cut its costs and at the same time control scarcities so as to help maintain prices and reduce the threat of new capacity to the industry.

There are at least two other strong motives for vertically integrating:

1. Providing better control over the quality of suppliers and/or end products.

2. Providing better control over the delivery of supplies and/or end products.

These two motives are defensive ones for a corporation, much as Standard Oil's actions were defensive. Companies that pride themselves on quality or delivery are frequently compelled to provide their own supplies or take their products closer to the consumer. Vertical integration is often seen as one way to maintain reliability in quality or delivery, although it may not be the only way. Maintaining reliability probably contributed to Rich Clover Dairy's establishment of its farm, a motive borne out by the dairy's successful cultivation of a quality image.

THE PERILS OF VERTICAL INTEGRATION

As attractive as vertical integration can be, there are also a host of perils associated with it. The situation at Rich Clover Dairy uncovered a couple of them:

1. Integration into some links of the production/distribution chain may be uneconomic because economic rents are not likely to reside there. For instance, the dairy's backward integration into the ownership of guernsey cows was not likely to provide the dairy with control over scarcities, and so high rates of return on such an investment were unlikely.
2. Vertical integration may induce problems in achieving a balance of capacities among portions of the production process, particularly if the product mix is subject to considerable change. At Rich Clover Dairy, the farm was coming into greater and greater imbalance with the bottling plant since Golden Guernsey milk was passing out of favor.

There are other possible perils with vertical integration, as may surface in Situation 14-2.

SITUATION 14-2

MATHESON SEMICONDUCTOR CORPORATION

Matheson Semiconductor Corporation, located in the "Silicon Valley" of California, was a young but growing firm with a remarkable reputation for innovation. Rod Matheson, the company's founder, was a near-legend in the electronics industry for his ability to crack seemingly impossible engineering problems.

Recently, Matheson had done it again, solving much of the yield problem associated with the "bubble memory," a revolutionary way to store electric charges using layers of garnet crystal. Bubble memory was now a much cheaper way to store charges than RAMs (random access memory silicon chips) or CCDs (charge-coupled devices) and almost as cheap as and certainly much faster to access than magnetic disks, drums, or tapes. Matheson Semiconductor was not the only company working on bubble memories; Texas Instruments, Intel, National Semiconductor, and IBM were among the other, larger companies that had research and development projects devoted to them. With this breakthrough, however, Matheson Semiconductor was clearly in the lead in what promised to be a very large market.

Heretofore, Matheson Semiconductor had been a supplier of semiconductor devices to the original equipment market. It did not manufacture products for the end-user.

The top tier of management at the company was concerned that Matheson Semiconductor keep its lead on bubble memories. Given the well-documented effects of the learning curve, management stressed the importance of quickly establishing sales for the product. At issue was how best to stimulate sales. A substantial number of end-users, to be sure, would order the bubble memory immediately. However, it was not at all evident that the large mainframe computer manufacturers (e.g., IBM, Burroughs, Sperry-Univac) or even the minicomputer makers (e.g., Digital, Data General, Hewlett-Packard) would switch immediately to bubble memories. Some of these companies were tied up with their own R&D projects for bubble memories, CCDs, or RAMs and might be reluctant to jettison them for Matheson Semiconductor's version. Others might want to wait out the technology a while, refraining from redesigns of their own equipment and eagerly awaiting the arrival of still newer technology that might dominate bubble memories.

It had been suggested that Matheson Semiconductor might best help its own cause by going straight to the end-user market with add-on memory units compatible with either IBM or Digital Equipment Corporation computers, or both. This step into forward integration would take some engineering work and some entirely new manufacturing expertise, but the market potential was exceedingly enticing.

Management was split on the issue. Marketing, and to a lesser extent, manufacturing were behind the move to integrate forward. Marketing was eager to conquer new territory; manufacturing, though somewhat cautious about the new demands expected of it, was eager to see costs drop as volume rose. Engineering, on the other hand, was dead set against the proposal, largely because it relished its state-of-the-art position in semiconductor electronics and did not want to be bothered with the more "pedestrian" engineering involved with computer applications.

It looked more and more like the issue was Rod Matheson's alone to resolve.

DISCUSSION OF
MATHESON SEMICONDUCTOR CORPORATION

The allure of high and steady sales volumes for the bubble memory is certainly a strong one. The same sort of allure attracted many semiconductor manufacturers like Texas Instruments, Rockwell International, and National Semiconductor into the hand-held calculator market in the early 1970s. Not all of those companies would admit that the experience was a good one, however. There are many perils to vertical integration, and the type of situation Matheson Semiconductor finds itself in is indicative of many of them.

The prominence of the learning curve concept in industries like electronics has fostered a chicken-egg phenomenon: innovations like the bubble memory cannot break into new markets unless their costs are lower, and their costs will not be lower unless their markets are large. The pressure, then, is to seek out as many applications as possible to get production volumes up. Vertical integration has been among the means employed, despite the fact that the scarcity almost certainly lies in the expertise and production of the innovation (e.g., the bubble memory) and not in the application.

The alternative is to manage around the vertical integration. That is, instead of integrating backward, the company can try to manage its suppliers better; and instead of integrating forward, the company can try to manage its customers better. What does this mean? In the case of Matheson Semiconductor, it might mean a stepped up campaign to locate and to convince a computer hardware manufacturer that the bubble memory would be an ideal means of adding on memory to an existing computer, perhaps enticing the manufacturer more with some of the cost savings from learning curve advances. In the case of backward integration, managing suppliers better might mean deliberately seeking out multiple suppliers to ensure both delivery and reasonable cost. Of course, a company will not be able to manage around vertical integration all the time—companies often have to settle for sole sourcing or for limited product applications—but it is often an attractive alternative.

What about managing vertical integration should a company be sensitive to?

The Flexibility Issue

Vertical integration will almost surely make a company less flexible to react to changes in products, production processes, and production volumes. By layering another full step of production or distribution on the company's existing operations, it is nearly certain that the coordination of change will be more difficult. It is to be expected that as vertical integration broadens, the probability increases that at least some product, process, or volume changes cannot realistically be made at all. The company locks itself in more and more.

At Matheson Semiconductor, for example, forward integration into add-on memory units may constrain the company to produce bubble memories of a certain type for a lot longer than a company so eager to stay on the technological frontier may want to. The classic example of how vertical integration, coupled with a constant drive to lower costs (the learning curve), combined to halt product flexibility is the Model T car of Henry Ford.[2]

Ford was fully integrated in 1927, with processes specifically designed to manufacture almost all of the Model T's parts. From 11¢ of capital investment per sales dollar in 1913, Ford integrated backward and forward to the point where in 1926 each dollar of sales was backed by 33¢ of capital investment, representing such vertical integration as a steel mill, a paper mill, a railroad, a glass plant, and others. Starting in the early twenties, however, car buyer tastes began changing perceptibly. The Model T, an open car design, was being beaten in the marketplace by heavier, more comfortable, closed body cars. Ford tried to modify the Model T to include these features being pioneered by General Motors but could not do so successfully. At last, Ford bit the bullet as its sales shrank. In 1927, it had to close its River Rouge plant for remodeling, but the inflexibility of Ford's process at the time was so great that the remodeling lasted almost a year! From that time on Ford's leadership in the automotive industry was relinquished to General Motors.

Vertical integration can influence process change as well. With so much more invested in the process, integrated producers are less likely to scrap a production technology and somewhat more likely to "patch up" the existing one—not so much because they are ignorant of sunk costs but because individual pieces of the process tend to come up for review and action rather than the entire process itself.

The question for a company contemplating vertical integration is whether inflexibility really matters or not. For many companies, products and demands are standard enough and stable enough that a loss of flexibility is of little concern. For other companies, however, flexibility is of central importance, and for most of these companies significant vertical integration carries with it many perils.

Effect on the "Core" Business

How does a move toward vertical integration affect the nature of the company's "core" business? Increasing the span of production a company takes upon itself raises a couple of questions about the management tasks in operations.

1. Will the move to more vertical integration tend to draw a company out of the particular niche in which it finds itself most competitive? This concern is related to the balance of capacities issue that surfaced in the Rich Clover Dairy situation. Often there exist imbalances in the capacities between stages of a production process. Since management abhors excess capacity almost as much as nature abhors a vacuum, pressure for "doing something" with the excess capacity arises. This "something" may well turn out to be incompatible with the company's core business, the reason for the vertical integration in the first place. For example, a pharmaceutical company's backward integration into chemicals may leave the company with excess chemical production capacity. The company may then seek to sell other chemicals on the side. Over time, the side business may grow, leaving the pharmaceuticals division at odds with the chemicals division for the capacity it was originally supposed to have by right. At this point, the company is no longer a phar-

maceuticals company; it has been pulled out of its niche.

2. Will managing a move toward greater vertical integration place new costs or risks on the company? If so, are these costs or risks acceptable? Often, an increase in vertical integration is quite costly and it raises the level of output at which the company breaks even. With a higher break-even volume, the company faces increased pressure for sales and greater vulnerability to a downturn in the market or to cyclical sales. The company must assess what the higher break-even volume may be and whether it poses any real problems.

Besides financial cost and risk, vertical integration can place strain on a manager's capabilities and on the management organization. The coordination of an integrated operation is frequently different from and more difficult than the coordination of operations within a narrow portion of the process. Concern for production control, logistics, and inventories tends to be much more intense. Authority must cut through all layers of the operation. This typically places managers in roles different from what they are used to and strains the prevailing organization of those managers. Frequently, a different set of managerial skills must be mastered and the organization modified before vertical integration can be made to work well.

To return to Situation 14-2, Matheson Semiconductor has good reason to fear forward integration in this instance. It is probably a company ill-prepared to handle a great deal of coordination across manufacturing, although the engineering-manufacturing coordination is probably well oiled. What is more, vertical integration is likely to weaken its position on the frontier of semiconductor electronics by drawing talent away from the most technically demanding tasks and lessening the company's flexibility. The economics in favor of vertical integration are frequently not compelling, particularly if the vertical integration can be managed around.

A RECAPITULATION

Before making some closing observations about vertical integration, I think it is useful to recapitulate its various attractions and perils.

ATTRACTIONS

1. Can save money by eliminating middleman profits.
2. Can mean better control over deliveries.
3. Can mean better control over quality.
4. Can insulate that which is scarce in the process, and thus what is apt to yield desirable economic rents.

PERILS

1. Can mean an integration move away from scarcity and desirable economic rents into operations with a lower rate of return to invested capital.
2. Can lead to an imbalance of capacities among process stages.
3. Can lead to increasing inflexibility for change in products, process, or production volumes.
4. Can draw a company out of its competitive niche in a market.
5. Can lead to higher break-even volumes that may be susceptible to sales cyclicality.
6. Can strain management talents and organization because of its demands for coordination.
7. Can hide the sometimes equally effective choice of managing suppliers or customers better.

VERTICAL INTEGRATION IN THE LIFE CYCLES OF PRODUCTS AND PROCESSES

When we first examined vertical integration in Segment I of this text, we noted that it is most prevalent in products that are standardized and produced in large volumes by processes that have rigid patterns of flow. In terms of the product-process matrix (Figure 7-1), vertical integration is characteristic of the lower right-hand corner.

In observing the behavior of industries, we should expect to find then that changes which trigger both product standardization and process simplification are apt also to trigger vertical integration in the industry. The firms that are fully integrated are likely to hold a tremendous edge over their nonintegrated competitors.

A fascinating example of this tendency has recently been played out in the watch industry.[3] Historically, the watch industry was extremely fragmented. Separate groups of companies fabricated watch movements, cases, and other components, assembled them into watches, and distributed them. The Swiss watch industry, for example, consisted of many small components fabricators and assemblers.

Enter the age of the quartz movement. This innovation at once improved time-keeping accuracy and simplified watch construction. Quartz movement watches, powered electronically, have fewer parts than mechanical watches. This fact in turn forced watchmaking away from labor-intensive assembly and permitted the introduction of automated equipment. Getting the most from the automated equipment, however, generally meant scheduling longer production runs than the watch industry was used to; this, in turn, meant standardizing designs. There was a risk, of course, that even the modest standardization that occurred would have been resisted by the market, but the advent of the quartz movement electronic watch apparently has been novelty enough. Bulova, for example, reduced the number of basic model series it manufactured from 18 to three.

The acknowledged leader in quartz watches, Seiko of Japan, was a vertically integrated company from the start. It was therefore able to exploit the quartz movement invention (originally Swiss) and develop it further under its own R&D group. Seiko's success has forced a rash of vertical integration moves within the industry that have simplified watchmaking's logistics, cycle times, and labor input. Bulova is integrated and the Swiss industry, historically so fragmented, has clustered into large watch combines.

The Swiss companies like Longines and the U.S. company Bulova still are impressive trademarks in the industry and are relatively the strongest names in jewelry and department store sales. Whether the trademark will remain so influential (that is, whether it will be the source of economic rents) is a matter of some debate. Some believe that the rents are now to be had in production.

QUESTIONS

1. Define and discuss the relationship between vertical integration, economic rents, quasi rents, and scarcity.

2. Summarize and give examples of the main advantages of vertical integration.

3. How does the dilemma of the Matheson Semiconductor Corporation illustrate some of the dangers that can attend vertical integration? Can you think of some of your own examples?

4. Vertical integration almost always affects the nature of a company's core business. Why is this?

5. Think of a life cycle of products and processes similar to that of the watch industry. What part does vertical integration play in that life cycle?

PROBLEMS

1. Many cities in the West and Midwest seem to grow in spurts and jumps. There are patches of city surrounding large tracts of farmland. Discuss the concept of economic rent as related to both land developers who purchase and build on the land and the farmers who continue to farm the land as the cities encroach on it.

2. What market conditions should exist for a firm to consider vertical integration?

3. What are the methods of vertical integration? Discuss the relative merits of each.

4. How does the management coordination task change with greater vertical integration?

5. Give an example of a situation where the reverse of more vertical integration would probably be the better strategy.

6. "Vertical integration will almost surely make a company less flexible to react to changes." Discuss this statement, supporting your points with examples from your reading and/or your own experience.

SITUATION FOR STUDY

CHAR BROYLE BURGER SHOP

Charlene Broyle owned and operated the Char Broyle Burger Shop. Although the shop was not part of a national franchise, its cuisine was similar to that of the many chains such as Burger King and competed directly with them. Charlene was somewhat flamboyant and was known locally as a wheeler-dealer. Her latest two ideas were to supply her own beef and hamburger buns.

For several years, Charlene had been unhappy with the local wholesale butchers from whom she bought ground hamburger. She had found it difficult to negotiate a favorable long-term contract.

Charlene had heard some tales that feedlot operators were making so much money they could not haul it all home in the trunks of their Cadillacs. Some preliminary investigation indicated that for a $200,000 investment, she could start a small feedlot operation that, on an annual average, would supply enough beef for her burger shop.

Much of Charlene's information had come from a casual friend, Tex Wrangler, who was part owner of a feedlot. Tex was first a farmer. He owned two sections of land on which he raised grain crops such as wheat. When it was obvious that his crop would not show a profit, he "turned it in" to a government agency, which paid him a minimum support price for the crop. Rather than plowing the crop under, however, he then took the cattle from the feedlot and let them eat the crop. Thus, Tex was able to use the feedlot to partially ensure his income from his crops.

Other successful feedlots were part of a vertical integration arrangement by some of the well-known animal feed companies.

Charlene knew there were ups and downs in the market, but she felt that most of these were dislocations between supply and demand. As a matter of fact, she felt that these dislocations were the root of her troubles. She therefore concluded that since she would be both demand and supply, there would be no dislocations.

The problem with the hamburger buns was quality and freshness. The shop did not use enough buns for any of the local bakers to make them to Charlene's specifications; so she had to accept "off the shelf" design. At times the buns tasted as if they were made of sawdust, and at other times as if they had not been in the oven long enough. The local bakery would deliver only twice a week. They would not accept the return of unused buns. Charlene always ordered more than enough buns because she felt that it would be the height of ignominy for a burger restaurant to have a stockout on their staple product. The upshot was that many buns had to be discarded because they did not meet Charlene's freshness standards.

After some investigation into this problem Charlene thought she could enlarge the back of the shop and purchase and install a mixer, oven, and assorted equipment for making her own buns. Besides the control of supply and quality, Charlene thought she might be able to use the fact that she made her own buns as an advertising gimmick. It would certainly be possible to incorporate some distinctive innovations into the buns such as flavor, shape, or size. Charlene estimated the cost of setting up her own bakery at $25,000 to $30,000.

1. What do you think of Ms. Broyle's ideas for vertical integration?
2. Are there any important factors that she hasn't considered?
3. Which, if either, alternative would you recommend?

REFERENCE NOTES

1. For the history of the U.S. oil industry, see Alfred Chandler, Jr., *The Visible Hand: The Managerial Revolution in American Business* (Cambridge, Mass.: Harvard University Press, 1977).

2. See William J. Abernathy and Kenneth Wayne, "Limits of the Learning Curve," *Harvard Business Review* 52, no. 5 (September–October 1974), pp. 109–19.

3. See, for example, "Seiko's Smash," *Business Week* (June 5, 1978).

SEGMENT

IV

OPERATIONS STRATEGY AND ORGANIZATION

The last segment of this text pulls together the various elements of operations policy that have been discussed so far and molds them into a view of what constitutes operations strategy. The first chapter of this two-chapter segment deals with the multitude of choices operations managers face and how they can be gathered into a consistent and convincing operations strategy. The second (and last chapter of the book) explores the ever-growing impact of governmental regulation on operations and on operations strategy.

CHAPTER

15

OPERATIONS STRATEGY

It is time to draw together the topics we have discussed so far into a unified view of operations and how operations can be used as an effective competitive weapon for the corporation. It should be clear by now that operations managers have a wealth of choices in the means by which they can influence the manufacture of goods or the delivery of services. It is useful to review these choices, which have been introduced before but in rather piecemeal fashion.

OPERATIONS CHOICES

Operations choices can be segregated into three broad categories: (1) technology and facilities, (2) operating policies, and (3) operations organization. Let us review these categories and choices in turn.

TECHNOLOGY AND FACILITIES

These choices frequently involve large capital expenditures and long periods of time. These are the big decisions that do much to define the type of process employed.

1. *Nature of the process flow.* Is the flow of product through the plant characterized as rigid,

with every product treated in the same way? At the other extreme, is the flow a jumbled one, with products routed in many different ways through the factory? Or, does the flow of product through the process fall somewhere in between?

2. *Degree of vertical integration.* How much of the product's value is a direct result of factory operations? How much backward or forward integration does the company want to engage in?

3. *Type of equipment.* Is the equipment used general purpose in design or special purpose (and thereby constrained to being very effective but in only a limited use)? Is it meant for high speeds and long runs, or not?

4. *Degree of capital or labor intensity in the process.* To what degree has equipment and/or technology permitted labor value to be driven out of the product or service?

5. *Attitude toward new process technology.* To what extent does the company pioneer advances in process technology? Is the company a leader in that regard or a follower? How closely does it track other process improvements?

6. *Attitude toward capacity utilization.* How close to capacity (defined as best as possible) does the company desire to operate? How will-

ing is the company to stock out of a product because of too tight capacity?

7. *Plant size.* How big does the company permit any one plant to grow? To what extent are either economies or diseconomies of scale present?

8. *Plant location and coordination with other plants and/or warehouses.* Where does the company place its operations? How do the locations chosen mesh together into a multiplant operation? What products, processes, or markets are assigned to each plant?

Operating Policies

Once the process technology and facilities have been selected, management must still decide on a host of features concerning how the process technology is used. Two broad segments of such operating policies present themselves: loading the factory and controlling the movement of goods through it.

Loading the Factory

1. *Purchasing.* Given the longer term decision on the plant's degree of vertical integration, what does the plant make for itself and what is purchased from outside suppliers? How are any such suppliers chosen? What kinds of contracts (e.g., long-term versus spot) are sought?

2. *Raw materials inventory system.* How much inventory of raw materials is held? How does that inventory level vary with demand, price discounts, supplier lead time changes, supply uncertainties, or other factors? What triggers the replenishment of the raw materials inventory?

3. *Supply logistics.* How frequently, from where, and by what mode of transportation do raw materials arrive at the plant? How sensitive are costs to changes in these factors? How readily can they be received, inspected, and stored?

4. *Forecasting.* To what degree is the plant's output known with certainty before raw materials must be gathered? To what extent must forecasts be relied on to determine which raw materials ought to be ordered, and how much of each? How beneficial is the use of sophisticated techniques to forecast these materials needs?

Controlling Movement through the Factory

1. *Production planning.* Are goods manufactured to customer order or are they manufactured to stock some finished goods inventory? Is inventory permitted to be built in advance to cover peak period demands or does production try to "chase" demand, with little or no buildup of inventories?

2. *Inventory control and production scheduling.* What triggers the production of goods: orders or reference to a finished goods inventory? How do factors like the pattern of demand and product costs influence any trigger level of finished goods inventory? How is production scheduled and what features of the process, the pattern of demand, or product variations and costs affect the schedule?

3. *Production control.* How much information flows within the production process, both from management to the workforce and from the workforce to management? How easily can product variations, engineering changes, or product mix changes be transmitted to the workforce? How soon can management react to machine breakdowns or other disruptions of the normal flow of product and process on the plant floor?

4. *Pacing of production.* Is the pace of production determined by machine setting, worker effort, management pressure or discretion, or some combination?

5. *Workforce policies.* What are the skill levels required of various jobs throughout the process? Is the work content of the job broad or narrow? Is cross-training of workers desirable? How and how much are workers paid? Are any incen-

tives, wage or otherwise, built into the process? How do workers advance in the factory (e.g., job classifications, different jobs, changes of shift, into management)? How does management feel about unionization?

6. *Quality control.* How is quality checked? How many checks are made at different steps in the process? How much authority is given to quality control personnel?

OPERATIONS ORGANIZATION

1. *Operations control.* Are the major operating decisions made by the company's headquarters staff or are most decisions made by plant personnel acting more autonomously? In other words, is most of the decision-making authority retained centrally or is it dispersed to individual operating units at the plant level?

2. *Talent within the organization.* Where within the organization would the company like to place its best people? Which talents are most prized for the smooth and continued successful operation of the process?

CONSISTENCY IN THESE OPERATIONS CHOICES

These choices—and all operations must make them either explicitly or implicitly—define to a great degree what the corporation's production process looks like and how it operates. Furthermore, these choices are a significant explanation of how well an operation is running or could be expected to run. This is an important point and let us consider it in greater depth.

In Segment I of this text, we discovered that for each broadly defined type of process (e.g., job shop, batch flow, line flow, continuous flow), certain characteristics of the process hang together and define what that process is. For example, one would

expect that a job shop is characterized by such operations choices as general purpose equipment, broad work content of the jobs workers perform, production to order, and lots of information flowing within the shop. If these features were not all present, one would have good reason for suspecting that the particular process being investigated was not a pure job shop. Similarly, one would expect that a continuous flow operation is characterized by operations choices such as special purpose equipment and capital intensity, production to stock rather than to order, machine pacing of production, and at least some dependence on the forecasting of demand. Deviations from this list would also raise questions about the purity of any continuous flow operation.

We can proceed a step further. Not only do certain broad characteristics of any process hang together, but they *should* hang together. The operations choices outlined above should be carefully matched up to be consistent with one another. In most instances, deviations from the model and consistently defined process should be changed because they run a serious risk of acting at cross purposes to the other elements of the process. For example, a "job shop" whose workers are limited by their training or by management edict to perform only a few, very specific tasks (i.e., narrow work content to the job) risks losing a great deal of flexibility and scheduling ease compared to a job shop with broad work contents to the job. Such a process choice risks establishing workers as well as machines as regular bottlenecks to shop capacity. Clearly, in this case, worker tasks ought to be expanded.

To cite another example, a line flow operation that permits many or significant engineering changes on a regular basis risks losing the benefits of production speed, lower labor value in the product, and low work-in-process inventories. The products of a line flow process should be fairly standard; if they cannot be, the other elements chosen for the process ought to be seriously exam-

ined and the process altered to make it less line flow and perhaps more batch flow.

To say that certain broad characteristics of any process should hang together as a consistent whole is not to say that *every* operations choice mentioned above can be unambiguously assigned to a specific process. Picking the process does not at the same time mean that *all* of the operations choices we discussed above are automatically determined. A company typically can exercise a great deal of latitude in selecting the specific elements of its production process. The job shop and the continuous flow process, which lie at either end of the process spectrum, are probably more constrained to specific choices of process elements than are batch or line flow operations. In other words, the job shop and continuous flow processes must, in general, be consistent over a greater range of process element choices than either a batch or line flow process. Nevertheless, considerable choice is possible in defining almost any process.

Recall also from Segment I that different challenges to management are inherent in different types of production processes and in the process elements that make them up. Here, too, the job shop and continuous flow processes are more clearcut in what they demand of management. For the job shop, scheduling workers and machines, bidding for new jobs, handling materials, and maintaining the flexibility to manufacture a great variety of goods are paramount to management. For a continuous flow process, management's challenges are completely different. What is demanded is care with the planning of capacity and new process technology and with the management of materials from suppliers to the plant and from the plant to the customers. The challenges to management for batch or line flow operations are less well delineated, since both must be concerned for the balance of capacities within the process, for product flexibility, for worker motivation and training, and for product design. There are shades of stress on these challenges, but the distinctions between them are more blurred and less clear-cut.

SELECTING CONSISTENT ELEMENTS OF A PRODUCTION PROCESS

Selecting the component elements for a manufacturing or service operations company is not a trivial task. Situations 15-1 and 15-2 offer some practice in describing how an operation ought to be organized.

DISCUSSION OF PORTERFIELD GLASS COMPANY

The previous section on operations choices provided a framework for selecting a production process suitable for Porterfield Glass Company's Glass Container Division. Let us then follow the choices outlined in that section.

Technology and Facilities

While the glass containers made by the division are most likely specialized for the individual customer (e.g., shape, quality glass, color, printing), each bottle goes through the identical steps in the process. Different glass recipes or bottle molds may be used, but the process itself does not vary by customer order in any significant way. The pattern of the process flow can be rather rigid then. As suggested in the situation itself, the equipment is special purpose. Combined with the rather rigid process flow, this feature suggests a considerable degree of capital intensity to the process.

The division could well be vertically integrated to a great degree, with the company owning and controlling its own sand pits and limestone quarries, particularly if demand is large. On the other hand, the raw materials that go into making glass are so common, so readily available, and used in so many other ways that it is hard to believe that backward integration into sand, lime, or soda ash supply would be very attractive. The rate of return to the company's capital is almost certainly as high or higher in bottle-making as in the supply of raw materials for glassmaking. The delivery of such commonly available materials is surely reliable

---

SITUATION 15-1

PORTERFIELD GLASS COMPANY, GLASS CONTAINER DIVISION

The Porterfield Glass Company's Glass Container Division was almost exclusively a manufacturer of bottles for beer, soft drinks, and other beverages. The technology of glass bottle-making was well known and not subject to radical advances. Basically, all that was required to fabricate a bottle was to (1) melt down sand, lime, and soda ash, usually with natural gas, (2) purify the resulting molten glass mixture, (3) suck up a portion of the molten glass into the molds of a rotating bottle-forming machine, (4) treat the molded bottle in a tunnel-like annealing oven, and (5) do any required printing on the bottle. All the equipment was specific to bottle-making.

There were substantial cost advantages with increased size because of energy savings in melting and because larger, more efficient bottle-molding machines could be dedicated to specific bottles without wasting any time with mold resetting. Different colors or glass types had to be manufactured in separate batches.

The company's major customers (breweries and soft-drink bottlers) were scattered across the country but were concentrated in the major metropolitan areas. These bottlers did not like to inventory bottles, primarily because they were bulky, and so demanded at least daily shipments—even shipments three or four times a day to feed their typically multishift bottling operations. For such service these bottlers were willing to enter into long-term contracts and to provide lead time of a month on all orders.

---

enough to remove delivery as an argument for the division's maintaining control over its own raw materials.

The fact that supplies are so readily available and easier to ship than bottles themselves is an argument as well for locating close to customers and not suppliers. Because customers demand a steady stream of bottles into their plants, it is clearly advantageous for the company to locate its plants close to its largest customers, if that can be arranged. Plant size should be determined in large measure by customer needs. The plant should be large enough to incur some of the cost advantages there are in energy savings and mold resetting, but after some threshold level, additional cost advantages from increased size are not likely to be large. As it is, the plant should be constructed purposefully with capacity in excess of long-term customer contracts. Otherwise, the division risks poor delivery performance during a customer's demand peak, which may endanger the entire contract. The division should track customer markets fairly closely so as to anticipate needed capacity expansions. Technological changes are not likely to be important to the industry, as suggested in Situation 15-1; this factor implies that the division can successfully follow rather than lead process innovation.

Operating Policies

The loading of the factory is likely to be dominated by the continual output demands of the long-term customer contracts. Raw materials supplies, which are bulky, are probably best shipped by rail or barge on at least a weekly basis, and perhaps more often. The inventory of raw materials is apt then to be replenished on a regular basis, the quantity of each replenishment being enough to bring the desired buffer stock up to some desired level. The buffer inventory itself is likely to be large since (1) stockouts of materials could jeopardize any contracts and (2) the raw materials are of low value anyway. Heavy investment in forecasting is probably not required; the long-term customer contracts are great aids in determining plant material needs with enough lead time so that deliveries are not jeopardized.

Production should be to customer order and a "chase" type strategy should be followed in planning production over the short term. With long-term customer orders and customer willingness to provide sufficient lead time, production planning of workforce size, hours, and schedule should be fairly straightforward. The schedule, in practice, should not vary much from month to month. There are likely to be advantages in batching orders that use the same glass, though in different shapes or sizes. Changing products—glass or molds—should be a routine matter requiring a very standard directive from management. The quicker and more routine are product changeovers, of course, the more profitable is the entire process. Except for changeover periods, the pace of production is determined solely by machine speeds. Information is largely one-way, from management to the workforce, except for sounding the alarm when a machine breaks down.

The workforce is likely to divide into two skill groups. Highly skilled, highly paid labor is likely to be required for troubleshooting equipment repair, for maintaining the equipment, and perhaps for controlling the glassmaking itself so that it conforms to the "recipe." Other tasks are likely to be unavoidably narrower in content and therefore suitable for lower skilled, lower wage labor. With the equipment largely pacing production, incentive pay schemes are inappropriate. Rather, all workers should be paid by the hour. Opportunities for either cross-training or worker advancement outside the rather narrow and well-defined departments making up the process are relatively scant. Job advancement is likely to be mostly shift changes or relief work. Unionization is likely to make little impact on operations.

Quality of the product is largely a matter of the proper functioning of the equipment. Quality control is best accomplished by sampling output, and using the sample for the identification of problems or potential problems in the process.

Manufacturing Organization

Within a division like the Glass Container Division, authority is best left centralized. Plants are not autonomous, but are much like one another. The central staff should control the larger decisions on technology and facilities, leaving the plant responsible for dealing with day-to-day operating problems, personnel, and equipment maintenance. The plant is best evaluated as a cost center.

Within the plant, management talent in the plant engineering department is critical. At the division level, management talent should be directed to the choice and development of equipment and process technology, since the division's future rests largely on these.

Summary

Glass container manufacture, as should be clear by now, is largely a continuous flow process and it shares a host of traits with other continuous flow or near continuous flow hybrid processes. In fact, the bottle-making process lies very close to the bottling process itself, as the description of the Schlitz brewery process in Chapter 4 makes evident. There simply is not a lot of room in such processes for much deviation in the process characteristics and challenges. More deviation is possible in other types of processes, as Situation 15-2 reveals.

DISCUSSION OF COWLES COMPUTER CORPORATION

Again, using the framework developed in the section on operations choices, the operations at Cowles could be selected, in rough fashion, as will be described.

Technology and Facilities

Compared to Porterfield's Glass Container Division, Cowles confronts a much more jumbled flow to the process, since a certain amount of product

SITUATION 15-2

COWLES COMPUTER CORPORATION

Cowles Computer was a small and very rapidly growing maker of small and medium-size digital computers. Sales were doubling every year and prospects for sales growth in excess of 50 percent per year remained strong. Cowles manufactured computers for so-called end use, that is, for use by customers without any further modification. The end use market could be contrasted with the OEM (original equipment manufacturer) market, which dealt with computers that would be included in other products (e.g., large machine tools). Customers typically wanted different special features added to the basic computer that they purchased. Thus, part of any computer sold looked like all others, and part was unique.

In its product development, Cowles stressed the development of software (e.g., programs, operating language) rather than hardware. Thus, while technically its computers were not particularly advanced or fast, they were extraordinarily versatile and could communicate directly with all other models of Cowles computers. Cowles had been introducing more and more advanced computer systems at a rate of about one new model a year, a fast pace even for the industry.

The assembly of a computer from its component pieces and its subsequent testing, while a complex task, did not require vast scale or particularly sophisticated equipment. The secret to performance lay in the engineering.

customizing must be done. This need for a degree of product variation, coupled with the quick pace of new product introduction, places a premium on Cowles's ability to remain flexible. This product flexibility, in turn, has important implications for the design of the production process. The equipment for the most part should be general purpose and production labor-intensive. Significant vertical integration should be resisted, particularly since the company does not aspire to be a leader in computer hardware. The company ought to be aware of process technology advances in other companies, but need not be a leader itself.

The company's enviable rate of growth will probably keep capacity utilization chronically high, but since a computer is far from being an item one buys off a store shelf, some stockouts can be tolerated. Since there are no real economies of scale, the determination of plant size is more dependent on keeping any plant's operations simple. Where plants are to be located depends on how individual plant charters are established. If the full production process is broken apart in pieces, then it makes sense to locate all the plants close to one another. If, on the other hand, complete, assembled computers of different types are chartered for each plant, then the plants can be located farther away from each other. Given the high degree of new product introduction, however, Cowles may want to keep its plants close together no matter what the charter chosen. In this way, communication and troubleshooting are improved.

Operating Policies

The need for product flexibility carries over to the definition of plant operating policies. The loading of the factory, for example, should reflect the speed at which the market can demand one mix of output rather than another. Long-term supply contracts for all but the most basic and unchanging parts are inappropriate. The raw materials inventory system presents some real challenges. Product obsolescence argues for a low level of raw materials inventory; yet the long manufacturing cycle time one can expect with a complex product like a computer argues for larger inventories to avoid waiting for supplier deliveries. These contrasting forces argue for the importance of forecasting sales. If, in fact, the product customization done involves the latter stages of production, forecasts can be useful in triggering production of the basic component parts of Cowles's computers. Hence, a periodic reorder inventory system may be appropriate. The complexity and ever-changing engineering of computers and the needs of later-stage product customization argue against installing an MRP system to control all of raw materials inventory. Supply logistics can almost certainly be accomplished by truck and air at economical enough rates.

As mentioned above, the manufacturing cycle may be divided between the early stages, where production can be initiated by reference to the forecast and a derived production plan, and the later stages, where the necessary product customization can only be indicated by order. These kinds of separable demands on the production system leave open the possibility of production control through the use of a decoupling inventory. As we discussed, such an inventory has the advantage of shortening the response time of the process by simplifying the flow of information required to meet orders. While the later stages of the process react to individual orders, the process's early stages are initiated by observing the levels of products of different kinds in the work-in-process inventory, which "decouples" the stages. It is the drawing down of inventory that sparks new production in the standard component portion of the process. This procedure smoothes the output rates of the component part of the process, although the customizing stages must still chase demand more. These customizing stages require more information (e.g., product variations to be made, engineering changes). They may also require that information flow back to management from the workforce, since new engineering will need to be evaluated and delivery times adjusted for special orders.

Generally speaking, the workforce will have to be skilled since it will be called upon to perform different and changing tasks on the continually evolving product line. Considerable cross-training is advised. Some standard jobs may permit incentive pay schemes, but for those jobs that are changeable, hourly pay is recommended. Worker advancement to new positions or areas in the factory may be encouraged as a way to spread expertise in the rapidly growing company. Cowles may also be well advised to be wary of possible unionization and to be particularly attentive to worker needs and requests. Unionization may bring an increasing inflexibility to the process, which might handicap future efforts at new product introduction or product mix change.

An important task is the establishment of quality controls and tests. With such a complex product, many things can go wrong. Testing is likely to be time-consuming but it must be done on all units. The series of tests established must shrewdly diagnose problems but with a minimum outlay of time and before large new chunks of value are added to the computers manufactured.

Manufacturing Organization

The company's manufacturing organization is somewhat dependent on the plant charter choice. If plants make their own complete computers themselves, they can be fairly autonomous, with a full resident staff. However, if the plants are feeders to one another, a strong corporate staff must coordinate the activity. Talent within the organization is best centered in engineering (the company's comparative advantage), production control, and quality control.

THE IMPACT OF COMPETITIVE PRIORITIES ON OPERATIONS

Too many managers falsely believe that manufacturing's goal should be low-cost production in every instance. While being the low-cost producer is often a very advantageous position, there are many other ways to compete successfully in most industries. Products can be differentiated from one another too readily and markets have too many niches in which companies can position their products. In one sense, this marketing diversity takes the heat off operations people to cut costs continually; but in another sense, it broadens the role of operations within the company, because operations must now react to different sets of competitive demands.

What is more, the competitive demands that can be placed on manufacturing are diverse and numerous. Consider the following:

1. Cost to produce—the traditional burden on manufacturing to become the low-cost producer.

2. Product performance—whether the product's design or engineering permits it to do more or better than comparable products.

3. Product reliability and workmanship—apart from differences in product design, whether the quality of materials and workmanship enhances the product's value and increases its durability and reliability.

4. Speed of delivery—the time between order taking and customer delivery.

5. Delivery reliability—apart from the speed of delivery, how close actual delivery is to any quoted or anticipated delivery dates.

6. Product customization—how adaptable the operation is to meeting special customer specifications.

7. New product introduction—how readily the operation can bring out product variations or completely new products.

8. Volume flexibility—how readily the operation can switch production rates on some or all of its products.

Which of these competitive demands takes priority at a company depends on several forces: the economics of the industry, particular competitive pressures, government mandates and incentives, the company's own resources, and the company's culture and attitudes. What is important to recognize is that operations can be subject to different, and changing, competitive demands.

THE LIMITS TO OPERATIONS

Some companies compete primarily on each one of these competitive dimensions. Scattered among the low-cost producers are others that emphasize product performance features (e.g., Porsche cars, Hewlett-Packard pocket calculators) or product workmanship (e.g., Rolls Royce cars, Ethan Allen furniture) or any of the other characteristics mentioned. What is crucial to recognize, however, is that no one product and no one production operation can compete across all competitive dimensions with equal vigor. A company must choose which competitive dimensions it wants to rank high and which must necessarily rank lower. A production operation, like anything else, cannot be all things to all people.

To reinforce this truism, consider what it would take to design and operate a manufacturing operation that ranked cost, speed of delivery, and product customization all with the highest priority. One simply cannot concoct an operation that could do justice to even these three competitive dimensions; an internally consistent set of operations choices could not be made that satisfied all three goals. For example, the highly capital-intensive special purpose machinery that could imply low-cost products and speedy deliveries blocks the more labor-intensive, high information needs for a high degree of product customization. By the same token, considerable product customization with rapid delivery could not be accomplished at low cost.

That a production operation cannot perform equally well across all eight of the competitive dimensions listed above may seem to be a totally reasonable, even intuitively obvious, proposition. In a sense it is. However, there are many operations managers for whom the truth of this proposition is not evident. These people like to wear buttons with the word "hero" emblazoned on them; they regularly seek more demands on their operations or at least do not refuse such demands. The following scenario is typical.

The manufacturing operation is humming along nicely until the marketing department starts reciting so-called "customer complaints" about product delivery or quality. The manufacturing manager feels compelled to react quickly to this pressure, and he makes certain adjustments to the process without really examining the longer-term implications of his short-run actions. After a time, the finance department confronts manufacturing with the "corporation's" desire to reduce inventory carrying costs or capital expenditures. In an effort to appease the finance people, manufacturing shaves inventory or tables some spending plans. Step by step, as manufacturing gets tugged and pulled by such forces, whatever consistency existed among the numerous operations choices discussed above starts to unravel. With the introduction of inconsistencies to operations, much of the competitive potency of operations is diluted.

THE CONCEPT OF MANUFACTURING FOCUS

What is needed then is a determination by management of what corporate strategy means for manufacturing—an evaluation of the importance of the eight competitive dimensions cited earlier. Once manufacturing is clear about what is demanded of it, it can go about choosing the technology, facilities, operating policies, and organization that are at once internally consistent and consistent with the declared corporate strategy and competitive priorities. The importance of these consistencies has been argued forcefully and persuasively by Wickham Skinner.[1] Skinner terms this manufacturing "focus." For him, focus is a top-down kind of idea that must start with an explicit state-

ment of the corporation's objectives and strategy. This statement must then be translated into "what it means for manufacturing" and the existing operation examined element by element in a kind of manufacturing audit of the existing facilities, technology, and operating policies. Only then can the corporation think of altering any of the elements that do not mesh with the explicit statements of corporate strategy and its meaning for operations. The goal of factory focus is to have all of the operation—right down to the first line supervisors and all of the workforce—pulling in the same direction, the direction implied by the proclaimed corporate strategy.

Focus is designed to avoid situations where manufacturers have geared up to do well what the corporation does not need done and then do poorly on the task on which the corporation's success really depends. Or, commonly, too many conflicting tasks are asked of the same operation, caused, for example, by product proliferation or by a blind acceptance of "professionalism" in functions like engineering, inventory control, finance, or quality control. The result too often is that no tasks are accomplished very well.

Consider Situation 15-3.

DISCUSSION OF MATTHEW YACHTS

This situation with Matthew Yachts is a common example where product proliferation has begun to sabotage an otherwise smoothly operating production process. How does the apparently innocuous addition of one more type of yacht to a boatyard that makes all kinds of yachts anyway sabotage operations?

To understand this situation, let us trace through some plausible consequences of adding the fixed design yacht to the yard. First of all, we should recognize that the custom work and the fixed design work were very different from one another. The competitive priorities for the two diverge greatly. For the custom work, competitive demands such as

SITUATION 15-3

MATTHEW YACHTS, INC.

Matthew Yachts, located in Montauk, Long Island, manufactured sailing yachts of all descriptions. The company had begun by building custom designed yachts for a largely New York-based clientele. Custom designed yachts still accounted for three-fifths of Matthew's unit sales and four-fifths of its dollar sales and earnings. Over the years, as Matthew Yachts' reputation for quality design and workmanship spread, sales broadened to cover all of the Eastern Seaboard.

In an effort to capitalize on this increased recognition and to secure a piece of the fastest growing market in sailing, Matthew Yachts began manufacturing a standard, fixed design craft. Matthew attacked only the high end of this market, as the boat measured 37 feet in length. Nevertheless, even this end of the market was more price sensitive and less conscious of performance than Matthew Yachts' custom design customers were.

All of the company's yachts were manufactured at the Montauk plant, and shared the same equipment and skilled labor force. Custom designs were given priority in scheduling, and the new boat was only rotated into the schedule whenever demand slackened. As sales of the fixed design boat increased, however,

scheduling the new boat on a regular basis became necessary.

Matthew Yachts were built basically from the bottom up. Fabricating hulls was the first step. Increasingly, fiberglass hulls were demanded for their speed and easy maintenance. Afterward came the below decks woodworking, followed by the fiberglass and woodworking on the deck itself. The masts were turned and drilled separately. Masts and hull were then joined and the finish work completed.

Over the past year, as the fixed design craft continued its steady increase in sales, costs and deliveries began to slide precipitously, especially on the fixed design yachts. During this period, when push came to shove, construction of the fixed design craft always yielded time and resources to the higher profit margin custom designs. As a result, many fixed design yachts were strewn around the yard in various stages of construction. Moreover, space in the existing shipyard was becoming scarce, and a plant expansion of one sort or another appeared inevitable.

The company wondered whether it should stay in the business of building fixed design yachts and, if so, how it should continue.

---

product customization, product performance, and product reliability and workmanship are critical; cost and delivery are much less important. For the fixed design craft, on the other hand, cost and delivery carry relatively more weight, and features like product performance are not nearly so important. These differing competitive priorities place conflicting demands on the production process.

The traditional custom work requires a skilled workforce, broad job content, a tremendous amount of information transmittal through the process, and great attention to the scheduling of work, among other things. The boatyard is a job shop. Into this job shop has been thrown a product that is more standard, sold in higher volumes, and

susceptible to price competition. Ideally, it should not be manufactured with a job shop type of process but with one that is more line flow. Such a process would utilize more and more special purpose equipment, narrower worker tasks balanced against one another to stabilize the pace of work through the yard, a materials inventory and handling system that removes any responsibility for worker ordering or handling of materials, a lower skilled workforce, and more explicit quality checks in the process, among other things.

When the two different kinds of yachts are manufactured in the same boatyard, costs on the fixed design yacht naturally climb over expectations. The workers are obviously treating its construction with the same care and methods that they use for the custom yachts. Deliveries too tend to be long and to grow longer, since the present process is not organized to reduce work-in-process inventories or manufacturing cycle times and the lower margins on the fixed design yachts relegate them to second priority whenever the going gets tough.

The pressing space problem at the boatyard indicates that now is a convenient time for seeking "focus" at the yard by splitting the two product lines and manufacturing them in separate facilities with separate equipment, workforces, and controls. The new, fixed design yacht is probably best produced in a new boatyard, possibly located a considerable distance from Montauk, where a new workforce and more specialized equipment and controls can be devoted to the task. Space problems could be relieved at the same time focus is achieved.

The separation of product lines and manufacturing facilities, so that only one set of competitive demands are addressed at a plant, is a tremendously compelling idea. For Matthew Yachts it means maintaining the match of a job shop process to the custom yachts it was originally designed to manufacture. It also means the match of a new process, more like a line flow, to the standard design, higher volume yachts. In principle, the need for separation to achieve "focus" is clear, and yet there may be good reasons to resist separation, even perhaps in the case of Matthew Yachts. It is to these resistances to focused manufacturing that we now turn.

RESISTANCE TO FOCUSED
MANUFACTURING

While focused manufacturing is an enormously appealing and "clean" concept, it can meet with some resistance. Focus is rooted in the many inevitable trade-offs managers must make about their facilities, technology, and operating policies. It states that there is no one "right" set of policy decisions; choice depends on how one competes.

Focused manufacturing's strength lies in the recognition that production choices abound and in the conviction that they should be tied together for best results. What is often overlooked, however, is that focused manufacturing is itself just one choice among the many that companies confront; while appealing and powerful, it is no cure-all. Like everything else, it is subject to trade-offs.

Consider these cases where focused manufacturing may be resisted by managers, perhaps justly so:

- A single factory produces two distinct product lines, each serving a different type of market. One product line's sales are buoyant and growing, while the other's are shrinking, increasingly vulnerable to competitive attack. Within the factory, minimal separation seems warranted, but splitting the lines cannot be done easily by installing a plant-within-the-plant since (1) production space on site is already cramped and (2) the existing and rampant job bumping between product lines would be difficult, if not impossible, to eliminate without totally disrupting the workforce. Focused manufacturing thus recommends a completely new plant for a product line that is in trouble. Moreover, the new plant will incur some one-time start-up costs and an ongoing overhead structure.

  Here lies the resistance. Do the benefits of focused manufacturing actually outweigh the known costs of new plant construction, start-up, and staffing? And for a product with a possibly shaky future?

- Two different products are manufactured in the same factory. Sales for each are seasonal and offsetting; one product's demand peak nearly matches the other's trough. Nevertheless, the competitive demands on each product are vastly different. One must be produced to rigid specifications, and so worker attention to detail must be paramount. For the other product, quality is not crucial; speed of delivery is. The workforce, inculcated with the importance of caring for product quality, cannot change its ways sufficiently to make the factory a very successful manufacturer of the second product.

Here lies the resistance. Do the benefits of focused manufacturing outweigh the costs not only of establishing a new plant but of carrying seasonally slack capacity in both plants?

- A variation on this theme. Two different product lines are manufactured in the same factory using the same set of very expensive equipment that is now being used significantly below capacity. The labor skills and attitudes required for the two product lines are very different, however; one product therefore is suffering from overattention to quality. Focused manufacturing would split up operations and locations.

  Again, here lies the resistance. Do the benefits of focused manufacturing outweigh the costs of new plant establishment and the carrying costs of expensive and largely idle equipment in both, possibly forgoing economies of scale?

- A new plant is being started up to specialize in the high-volume products of a high-technology company. The plant's capital-intensive component supply department could be constructed specially for the products to be placed in the factory — in a sense, focused for just those products. If this were done, the department would forgo the opportunity to supply other, more sophisticated products of the company. But, a more general purpose design of the department would add 25 percent to capital expenses. Product lives in the industry are short, and nobody knows what the next set of high-volume products will be.

  Here lies the resistance. Do the benefits of designing the plant to be focused, including the capital expense savings, outweigh the technological rigidity that focus may imply for the factory's future?

Similar manufacturing situations are not uncommon, and they offer some perplexing options for managers. Evaluating the forces pushing either for or against focused manufacturing is not a clear-cut endeavor, since a variety of difficult-to-measure factors must be balanced against one another. Nevertheless, merely understanding the pushes and pulls on focused manufacturing may help to ease managers' burdens in confronting this type of situation.

Analyzing Factory Focus

How does focus help? What should a manager look for as predictable consequences of focusing a factory? Focus can help in a variety of ways (although not in all instances):

1. *Improving the flow of materials and product within the company.* Often the first sign of confusion in a factory shows up in plant logistics — late or misdirected materials or product, incorrect order taking or order filling of either materials or product, and increasingly complex production scheduling. In such a situation, focusing by product or product group often makes sense, since by organizing in that way, plant logistics can be simplified and thus improved.

2. *Reducing production cycle times.* Often, by separating out products and at the same time pulling together portions of the production process, a focused factory can reduce its production cycle times. This fact in turn implies reduced work-in-process inventory, fewer rush orders and disruptions to ongoing operations, less expediting asked of suppliers, greater potential capacity, and, perhaps, lower finished goods inventories.

3. *Increasing job specialization and product identification.* By concentrating on a limited number of products or processes, workers and managers may more easily find ways to redefine procedures and methods to smooth the flow of

manufacturing even more. Especially if the workforce can identify with and take pride in the specific product manufactured, the company may benefit from more suggestions for product and cost improvements.

4. *A clearer cost accounting system.* By streamlining operations, the cost accounting for a product or process is simplified, and the simplification often means better pricing decisions and improved capacity utilization.

5. *Better reaction to production gone awry.* Factory focus means ingrained operating routines and corrective measures that can simplify and smooth the factory's reactions to nonstandard, potentially troublesome developments.

In any individual case, of course, these advantages to focus may be present in greater or lesser degree. Furthermore, the ability to measure their impact varies widely. Nevertheless, managers may do well making some estimates of their strength so as not to fall victim to the syndrome of hard numbers driving out reasoned, but qualitative analysis.

As the examples introduced above make clear, there are a number of arguments against focused manufacturing. These, too, vary in the ease by which they can be quantified. A company's ability to focus its manufacturing may be constrained by:

1. *Idle machines.* In separating out products that use the same machinery, a company risks running certain machines at much less than their rated capacities. Thus, a lower volume of output must absorb the fixed costs of the machinery. Fortunately, the sensitivity of total costs and earnings to this increase in fixed cost is relatively easy to calculate.

2. *The savings of placing differently cyclical or seasonal products of diverse characters within the same factory.* As with idle machinery, the costs of focusing operations through product separation, measured in terms of increased inventory building and possibly increased hiring and firing of labor, can frequently be handled quantitatively.

3. *New plant construction with increased overhead.* A more difficult constraint to analyze involves a focusing of operations that, for one reason or another, demand a totally new factory with an accompanying overhead structure rather than the designation of plants-within-plants. Such a radical change is sometimes mandated because of growth of the product lines affected and insufficient room to expand on site. Sometimes it is mandated by the need to develop an entirely different kind of workforce or to get out from under outmoded work rules and practices that could not be modified easily at the old plant. In a sense, then, new plants are mandated generally only when the penalties of maintaining production in a single facility are great.

   Even with the plant-within-a-plant option, overhead will likely increase because of separate supervision, production control, and materials handling. These costs too can be deterrents to focused manufacturing.

4. *"Deserting" an existing workforce.* In separating out products or processes for their own plants, some layoffs of an existing labor force may be necessary, at least temporarily. This is never a happy prospect, even if improvement in workforce practices is one of the reasons behind such a move to focused manufacturing.

5. *Production rigidity.* A more subtle, but nevertheless important, possible constraint on the focusing of manufacturing is the threat of rigidity it poses for production. By segmenting the operations for each of a string of products, for example, one runs the risk of losing the ability to react quickly to some new product or new process innovations. The new independence of each product may lock the company into a much less fluid structure than what it was used to. It makes sense then for companies that expe-

rience a large share of product or process innovation to be leery of a strict segmentation of products or portions of the production process. In fact, focused manufacturing would itself argue for a concentration on the creative, technological function in these kinds of companies anyway, since that is how many such companies compete.

A common thread that emerges from these possible constraints on focused manufacturing is that change — reflected in sales growth, decline, or uncertainty — is an enemy of factory focus. When products are continually introduced or when the mix of products sold frequently shifts or when seasonality or cyclicality abounds, then the costs of complying with factory focus become high and the benefits of focus less clear-cut. Thus, the firm that is growing in sales and product offerings and is in constant need of cash is often the one that confronts the balancing of factory focus against other aspects. Since costs of focused manufacturing may outweigh its benefits, managers must be careful to resist the enticement of hard number costs overshadowing a more nebulous evaluation of benefits. Further, they must be vigilant in continually testing whether focused manufacturing can fit into their situations; for, as easily as focused factories can lose their focus with change, nonfocused factories can acquire the need for it. In our judicial system, we have found that it works best if one is presumed innocent until proven otherwise. In manufacturing, I would argue, it is better to seek focus until proven otherwise.

REVISITING THE PRODUCT-PROCESS MATRIX

These notions of manufacturing focus, change, and resistance to focus can be reinforced by drawing upon the product-process matrix that was introduced in Segment I. As will be recalled, the product-process matrix related the character of a plant's products (e.g., one of a kind vs. commodities) to the character of the process flow (e.g., jumbled vs. rigid). Figure 15-1 reproduces the product-process matrix as it was introduced in Segment I (Figure 7-2).

As it was first discussed, the product-process matrix was devoid of any dynamic features. It was merely a handy box in which to categorize the range of production processes we have considered in this text. As should be evident by now, the typical manufacturing operation must deal constantly with change and with the threat of change. It is natural, then, to expect a number of companies to undergo considerable movement within the product-process matrix. The learning curve, for example, represents a constant pressure to move along the matrix diagonal down and to the right.

Movement within the product-process matrix is not likely, however, to be precisely along the diagonal. Such a smoothly modulated movement is difficult because many process and product changes tend to be abrupt; at least, that has been true of much change in the past, particularly in the continuous flow process industries.[2] A smoothly modulated diagonal movement is also made difficult by the fact that companies tend to concentrate their efforts at any one time on either a large product change or a large process change. Movement along the diagonal requires simultaneous product and process change, which is a complex management enterprise. Thus, rather than smooth movement along the diagonal, companies undergoing change are more apt to demonstrate step-like movements within the matrix, such as depicted in Figure 15-2.

In charting their movement over time within the product-process matrix, companies can generally choose to remain above or below the diagonal, since it is unlikely that they can remain on it. Is a path over time that lies predominantly above the diagonal any better than a path that lies predominantly below it? The question is a meaningful one, and aims at the heart of corporate as well as manufacturing strategy.

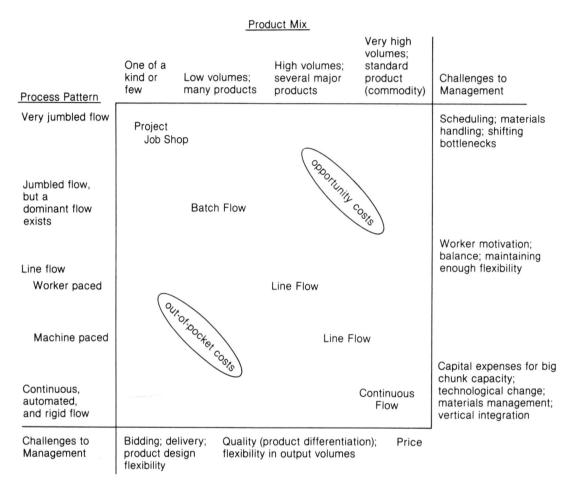

FIGURE 15-1 A product-process matrix.

As noted in Segment I, the area of the product-process matrix that lies below the diagonal is characterized by out-of-pocket expenses. This area is where the rigidity and capital intensity of the process are relatively further advanced than the acceptance (i.e., the increasing commodity aspects) of the process's products. A company whose decisions position it below the diagonal places significant pressure on its marketing people to drum up the sales volume needed to sustain its relatively further advanced process characteristics. Otherwise, the high costs incurred in financing a process change that is significantly capital-intensifying are likely to lower the company's profits. What such a company would like to see is continuing sales growth that brings the company's position within the matrix back to the diagonal, for only the diagonal represents a perfect match of process and product characteristics. In a sense, the diagonal represents those "patches" of the matrix where focused manufacturing is best achieved.

The area above the diagonal, as also noted in Segment I, is characterized not by out-of-pocket expenses, but by opportunity costs. Here, the

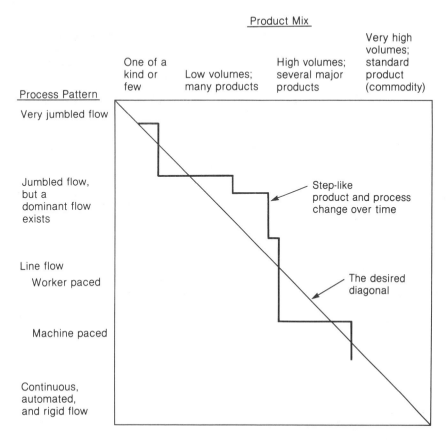

FIGURE 15-2   Movement within the product-process matrix.

process's characteristics are relatively less advanced than is product acceptance. The company's profits suffer, not because high investment in plant and equipment must be paid off, but because process advances could manufacture the product for less. By having its process lag behind its product acceptance, the company forgoes the opportunity to earn more. By positioning itself above the diagonal, the company places pressure on its manufacturing people to lower costs.

A strategy that consistently positions a company above the diagonal of the product-process matrix is essentially a conservative one; the company risks the loss of dollars that could have been made rather than the loss of dollars already earned. As

we observed before, opportunity costs are every bit as real as out-of-pocket ones, but the conservative firm would rather lose potential profits by lagging behind in production technology than incur certain, out-of-pocket expenses for advances in the process. While the road to high profits has no shortcuts and lies in keeping both out-of-pocket and opportunity costs low, the shortcut to bankruptcy lies in incurring out-of-pocket expenditures. Incurring opportunity costs is simply a longer and more tortuous road to bankruptcy, as the company gets left in the dust by faster moving companies.

An analogy to one of my favorite sports may serve as a useful characterization of the "strategy paths" companies can choose to follow. Think of

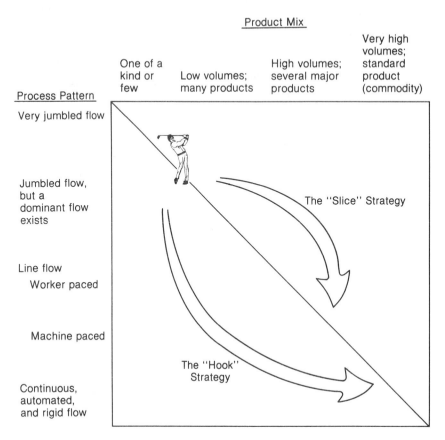

FIGURE 15-3   Strategy paths through the product-process matrix.

the company as a golfer teeing up in the upper left of the matrix (see Figure 15-3). The company/golfer is pondering a shot down the diagonal of the matrix, the center of the fairway for our purposes. Like all golfers, the company/golfer cannot expect to hit the ball straight; he's probably going to put some hook or slice on the ball. Knowing what swinging a certain way will do to the ball, our company/golfer compensates. If he expects to hit a slice, he aims left of the center of the fairway; if he expects to hit a hook, he aims right. It just so happens that the physics of golf dictate that a hook shot is apt to travel further than a slice, since the hook puts an overspin on the ball that makes it roll more when the shot strikes the fairway. In contrast, the slice puts an underspin on the ball that dampens the roll of the ball. The hooked shot, then, is apt to travel further, but it is also more apt to run into the rough if not properly struck. The sliced shot is safer because its roll, once on the fairway, is less, but the shot sacrifices distance.

I hope the analogy is clear. The "slice" is the conservative company's path through the matrix, risking only opportunity costs. The "hook" is the more adventurous path through the matrix, which risks out-of-pocket expenses. Both kinds of "shots" can be successful, ending up with the company/golfer lying on the diagonal (center of the fairway).

The hook, while riskier, is also a more likely way to leave other company/golfers in the dust, far back up the fairway.

ORGANIZING MANUFACTURING[3]

In the foregoing discussion of manufacturing strategy, a recurrent theme has been the search for operations choices that were at once consistent with one another and consistent with the perceived competitive demands that manufacturing must meet if the corporate strategy is to be advanced. A second theme has valued simplicity—no conflicting goals for a factory, single-mindedness of purpose and of worker and management tasks.

These rubrics for the selection of a plant's operating characteristics follow through as well in the definition of the management organization that oversees and coordinates operations. Consistency and simplicity should anchor the manufacturing organization.

How can an organization be consistent and simple? To begin to answer this question, let us analyze two distinct ways to organize an operation's management: the product-centered organization and the process-centered organization.

The Product-Centered Organization

At its simplest, the product-centered organization resembles a traditional plant-with-staff organization, which is repeated at higher and higher levels to control groups of plants and then groups of products and/or product lines. Customarily, individual products or product lines are placed in their own plants and managed exclusively by a product-oriented group of managers. Figure 15-4 offers a schematic representation of a product-centered organization.

Authority in this kind of organization is spread among the products and forced down within each product organization. Each product group is a small but independent company.

So far, this type of organization has been associated exclusively with products and product lines. Equally as valid would be an association with geographic market areas. Here, instead of independent product companies, the company is independent within the boundaries of a certain geographic area. Most commonly, these separate geographic divisions of manufacturing involve foreign operations; but for some companies, domestic operations are organized with considerable authority placed at the regional level. The Burger King organization, as we saw in Segment I, is an example of a market-centered organization. While it is more complete to describe such organization as product/market-centered, for ease of exposition, I will continue to call it a product-centered organization, leaving the market-centered variation implicit.

A product-centered organization is most often found in less complex, perhaps more labor-intensive production processes that do not rely on vast economies of scale nor the latest or most sophisticated equipment. Rather than be dominated by cost reduction, tight controls, and formal planning cycles, the product-centered organization is much more attuned to product mix flexibility and innovation. Consumer goods companies are often product-centered in organization.

The product-centered organization is appealing because it is "clean," responsibilities are well delineated. Performance within the organization is easy to evaluate, since usually product groups are established as profit centers. Plant managers are important in the company and are often charged with responsibility for decisions about process technology, plant equipment, product development, and capacity as well as more routine concerns such as personnel, maintenance, and production control and scheduling.

The product-centered organization demands—and breeds—a special kind of manager: independent, entrepreneurial, well rounded. Junior-level

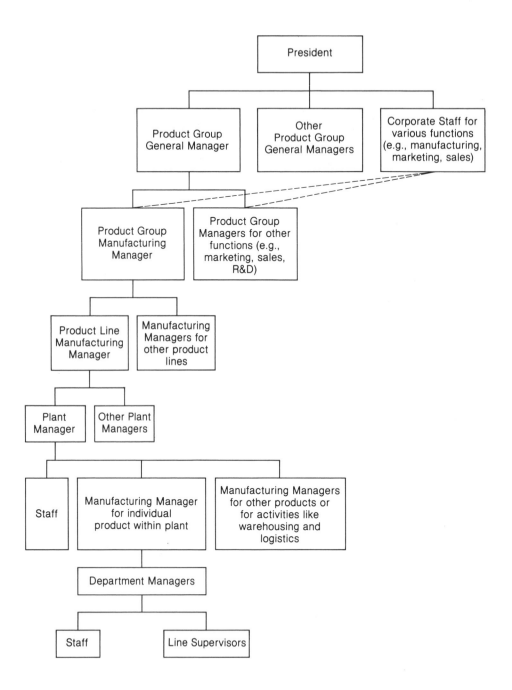

FIGURE 15-4   Organization chart typical of a product-centered manufacturing organization.

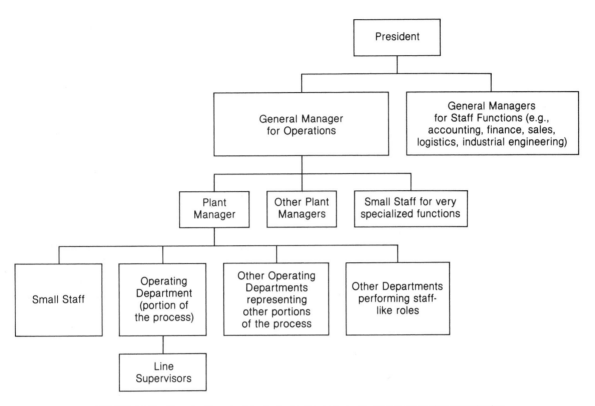

FIGURE 15-5 Organization chart typical of a process-centered manufacturing organization.

managers frequently move within the organization and must be tracked continually as they take on new or different responsibilities.

The corporate staff is relieved of much of its duties, particularly day-to-day operations. The corporate staff in the product-centered organization is often small and left to coordinate policies and personnel across product lines or geographic regions.

THE PROCESS-CENTERED ORGANIZATION

Instead of breaking apart product lines for their own plants and manufacturing staffs, the process-centered organization breaks the process apart into distinct pieces. In this type of organization, most often several plants combine to manufacture the final product although a multiplant operation is not a necessary feature of the organization. What is necessary is that responsibilities in manufacturing are not delineated by product line but rather by segment of the complete manufacturing process. Hence the appellation "process-centered."

Because an entire series of plants or process segments must be coordinated to ensure smooth changes in the mix and quantities of products manufactured, the process-centered organization must be strongly centralized. This centralization of authority contrasts sharply with the decentralization that prevails in the product-centered organization (see Figure 15-5).

In addition to providing coordination, the centralized authority is often absorbed with decisions on needed capacity and its character, on the balance of capacities in the entire process, on logistics, and on technological change and its impact on the process. These decisions are often the key challenges to management when products or processes are complex, as when the company is oriented to particular materials (e.g., oil, chemicals, agricultural products) or to advanced technology (e.g., computers or other electronic products). Because such important decisions are retained centrally, plants within a process-centered organization are nearly always evaluated as cost centers.

Such a centralized, process-centered organization is not conducive to rapid new product introduction nor to vast swings in volume since the pipeline momentum and geographic separation between plants often lead to sluggishness. Nevertheless, if aspects of a process can benefit from large-scale or particularly specialized and rapidly advancing technologies, then a process-centered manufacturing organization offers a substantial contribution.

Because authority in the organization is kept centrally, the character of the managers who "grow up" in such an organization tends to be very different from the character of product-centered managers. Where the product-centered manager is likely to be an entrepreneur and a generalist, the process-centered manager tends to be a technician and a specialist. Because technologies within a process-centered organization are frequently so complex and because decisions involving them are so expensive, the young manager in a process-centered organization is typically removed from the substantial production decisions that are made. Instead, the young manager usually undertakes a rather technical and frequently long apprenticeship. At the end of the apprenticeship, however, lies the opportunity to make decisions of a substantially larger magnitude than most product-centered managers make.

Table 15-1 lists the major operating differences between product-centered and process-centered manufacturing organizations.

There are no strong arguments for consistently favoring one type of organization over the other. In terms of total manufacturing costs, neither organization could always be expected to dominate. The process-centered organization, for example, can best manage economies of scale or situations where tight controls are desirable; but at the same time, the process-centered organization is likely to increase overhead and logistics costs. It may also experience longer production cycle times and larger inventories since it is less flexible in general than the product-centered organization.

Because of the staff specialization within a process-centered organization, technological change is often fostered best under such an organization. The central staff is apt to be highly expert, aware of technological alternatives, trends, research, and the experiences of other companies in the industry. This is a clear advantage of the process-centered organization, since the exploration of technological advance in a product-centered organization may be hit-or-miss. Some corporate staffs may take on the responsibility or a separate research division may sponsor the needed research and development. In any case, major technological issues are often removed from the line operations of the typical product-centered organization.

A process-centered organization may also enjoy a relative advantage when it comes to managing the purchasing function, since such an organization can often win volume discounts. These economies may or may not accrue to a product-centered organization. In some product-centered companies, purchasing is split between the product lines and a central purchasing staff for the very reason of securing volume discounts.

CHOOSING THE ORGANIZATION:
PRODUCT, PROCESS, OR SOME COMBINATION?

As they have been introduced so far, the product- and process-centered organizations are polar op-

TABLE 15-1   Differences between Product-Centered and Process-Centered Manufacturing Organizations

	PRODUCT-CENTERED	PROCESS-CENTERED
Profit or cost responsibility: where located	Product groups	Central organization
Size of corporate staff	Relatively small	Relatively large
Major functions of corporate staff	Review capital appropriation requests	Coordinate decision making with marketing
	Communicate corporate changes and requests	Make facilities decisions
	Act as clearinghouse for personnel information, management recruiting, purchasing, used equipment, management development programs	Set personnel policies
		Set purchasing policies
		Review logistics-inventory management
	Evaluate and reward plant managers	Coordinate production schedules
	Select plant managers and manage career paths—possibly across product group lines	Decide whether to make or buy and whether to vertically integrate
		Recruit future plant managers
		Review plant performance, cost center basis
Major responsibilities of plant organizations	Coordinate decision making with marketing	Use materials and facilities efficiently
	Make facilities decisions (subject to marketing)	Recruit production, clerical, and lower management workers
	Make purchasing and logistics decisions	Train and develop future department and plant managers
	Schedule production and control inventory	Respond to special requests from marketing within limited ranges
	Decide whether to make or buy	
	Recruit management	

SOURCE: Hayes and Schmenner, "How Should You Organize Manufacturing?" p. 112.

posites in some important respects, and they can be expected to place fundamentally different demands on the company—different policies and practices, different measurement and control systems, different managerial attitudes, different kinds of people and career paths. The question arises then in any given situation as to whether a product-centered organization should be put in place, whether a process-centered organization should be preferred, or whether some combination of the two ought to prevail. To explore this question consider Situation 15-4.

DISCUSSION OF STE ELECTRONICS CORPORATION

We can picture the manufacturing organization at STE Electronics as in Figure 15-6. As Rich Charles is only too aware, this kind of organization places distinctly different demands on him and his staff. The profit-center product divisions view the central staff as umpires and as little else. They do not approach the control staff for much day-to-day support, but rather remain in their nearly autonomous worlds. The San Jose plant makes much more use

SITUATION 15-4

STE ELECTRONICS CORPORATION

Rich Charles, Vice-President for Operations at STE Electronics, swore that the San Jose plant was built on quicksand and that any week now, on a visit there, he would be sucked under with no more than a muted gulp for his last breath. It was a constant wonder to him why he wasn't having nightmares about the plant.

STE Electronics Corporation, headquartered in San Francisco, was a small but growing company manufacturing specialty electronics equipment for the process machine industry and for the Department of Defense. The company was organized around two divisions: the Industrial Products Division with its manufacturing facility in Livermore, and the Defense Products Division with its manufacturing facility in Bakersfield. Supplying both of these divisions was the San Jose plant, which made power supplies and printed circuit boards.

As Rich Charles saw it, the San Jose plant was a battleground over which the Industrial Products and Defense Products divisions waged an intermittent war. Charles himself was some sort of umpire who would periodically award the spoils of victory to one division's "army" or the other. There were continual skirmishes between the two divisions concerning the allocation of the San Jose plant's capacity. Each division wanted priority to be given the delivery of its power supplies or printed circuit boards. Both products were critical components of the company's range of electronic equipment, and the failure to deliver on time could seriously interrupt each division's production schedule. Nevertheless, both divisions were playing games with orders on the San Jose plant. In an effort to ensure delivery, both divisions would over-order from San Jose and at the same time pretend they needed every unit they ordered, and quickly at that.

To make matters worse, the Defense Products Division would continually harass San Jose about product quality. This was understandable, too, for the Defense Products Division had to produce to exceedingly precise specifications. The Industrial Products Division was not under as stringent pressure.

Delivery and quality concerns flared up periodically as skirmishes, but there was a pitched battle every year at transfer price setting time. Each division was evaluated as a profit center while the San Jose plant was evaluated as a cost center. Since materials costs were a substantial fraction of product cost, each division had the incentive to keep the transfer prices they paid for their power supplies and printed circuit boards low. But, since San Jose's total costs had to be covered, there were fevered sessions where the allocation of San Jose's overhead expenses were argued over, each division trying to throw them onto the other. Rich Charles did not enjoy these sessions.

Charles had a measure of compassion for the San Jose plant and its management. They were always caught in the crossfire, and it was only the concerted efforts of the cadre of old engineers who ran San Jose that kept things moving as smoothly as they did. However, in not too many years most of the San Jose management were slated for retirement, and Rich Charles was concerned that no young heirs apparent seemed to be rising to take charge of the plant. Charles knew that the young talents in the company were shying away from the San Jose operation, both because of the divisional crossfire and because the product divisions were viewed as the "fast track" within the company. Charles himself had come up mainly through the Industrial Products Division and his predecessor had headed the Defense Products Division. It was no wonder that STE's young managers viewed San Jose as a dead end.

Rich Charles had pondered closing the San Jose operation and spinning off the power supply and printed circuit board production to each division, but he had shied away from this option. San Jose did realize some economies from the scale of its operation and its breakup would be costly and would spread the existing expertise too thin. What Charles really wanted to think about was some alternative organization of manufacturing that might lighten his burden and that of his staff in dealing with San Jose and its interactions with the product divisions. As it was now, San Jose housed only about a quarter of the company's manufacturing employees, but it accounted for well over half of his time and the time of his staff. The plant needed persistent guidance on matters such as forecasts, production control, and inventories.

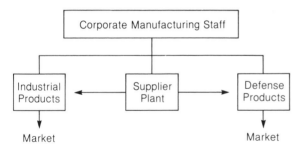

FIGURE 15-6 The manufacturing organization at STE Electronics.

of the central staff, mainly because the central staff cannot afford to risk seeing San Jose "on its own." The plant is too important to the smooth operation of the entire company.

For this kind of situation, Hayes and Schmenner argue for either a product-centered organization or a process-centered one, but not the combination that is evident at STE Electronics. The corporate staff cannot function properly when so many conflicting demands are placed on it. Just as the role or charter for each plant must be clear and simple, so must the role or charter for the central manufacturing staff. Hayes and Schmenner propose a test for such "organizational focus," as they put it: How easy would it be to fragment manufacturing, say, if forced to by the Antitrust Division of the Justice Department? If the operations could be fragmented easily, organizational focus has been achieved. If too many parts of the organization become entangled so that fragmentation is difficult, they argue, the organization is not focused.

What then should Rich Charles do at STE Electronics? It is clear that the suggestion to break up the San Jose plant and to toss a chunk of it to each of the product divisions is sound, at least organizationally. Apart from that, Charles may be well advised to formalize the relationship between San Jose and the product divisions. This organization can be accomplished by insisting that transactions between each product division and the San Jose plant be carried out at "arm's length"; San Jose could enter into contracts with each division and could maintain the right to refuse compliance with a division request, just as the divisions would be free to seek outside suppliers. This approach argues for an organization that is more subsidiary than divisional. To maintain this organizational formality, the corporate staff could be divided into two parts, one aiding and overseeing the San Jose plant and the other coordinating the two product divisions. By seeking this separation, the two organizations assume a more equal status and eliminate the conflicting roles that the corporate manufacturing staff had to play.

A revised organization chart might look like Figure 15-7. As for Rich Charles himself, he might have to choose sides, occupying a role either at the head of the product-centered staff or at the head of the process-centered one. He, too, should not have to occupy the middle ground.

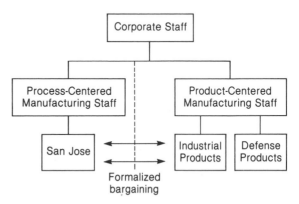

FIGURE 15-7 A revised organization chart for STE Electronics.

QUESTIONS

1. Three categories of decision making or policy making define to a great degree what the corporation's process looks like and how it operates. Summarize the main aspects of each category.

2. Why is consistency valued so highly in the production process choice? Provide your own examples to defend your position.

3. Compare the main operational features of the Porterfield Glass Company with those of Cowles Computer Corporation.

4. What are four of the main competitive demands that can be placed on manufacturing?

5. For a corporation, what are the principal advantages and disadvantages of factory focus? What are the main areas of resistance to focus?

6. "Movement within the product-process matrix is not likely to be precisely along the diagonal." Discuss the theory behind this statement, paying particular attention to what it means to be above or below the diagonal.

7. There are two clear ways to organize an operation's management. What are they? What advantages does each offer and for what kind of operation? How does one choose between the two? Provide a concrete example for your discussions.

8. "Inflexible, special purpose machinery can be as much a part of a flexible manufacturing system as flexible, general purpose machinery." Comment on this statement.

PROBLEMS

1. In what types of situations might it be viable to have a mixture of process characteristics?

2. Discuss the factors or concerns that should be considered in selecting the elements of a production process.

3. Discuss the competitive demands on manufacturing. Can a manufacturing manager expect to perform equally well in all of the demand aspects? Why?

4. What is meant by the term *focused manufacturing* and why is it an important concept?

5. In the situation for study at the end of Chapter 6 Tom Wurkard was attempting to use production and operations management in the house construction industry. Where was his operation located in the product-process matrix? Relate the theoretical concepts of the product-process matrix to Tom's actual process.

6. The home construction industry has for many years tried to get from the top left-hand corner to the bottom right-hand corner of the product-process matrix. What progress in this direction has been made in your local area?

7. Bob Leone's company manufactures a material that significantly lengthens the life of fluorescent lamps. This material is patented, but the patent will run out in 5 years. Demand for the material is growing at a rate of 25 percent a year as the major fluorescent lamp manufacturers use it in more and more of their product offerings. What manufacturing choices would you recommend to Bob to help him cope with this situation?

8. U.S. auto manufacturers are faced with some monumental production challenges—the need to produce more small cars, the need to increase gas mileage on all their cars, and the need to meet

emissions control standards. What kinds of manufacturing changes would you suggest to meet these challenges and still keep autos affordable? Be sure to consider items such as product design, product line breadth, purchasing, vertical integration, process technology, capacity balance, and workforce policies.

9. You are a maker of roller skates, one of the latest crazes of the American public. What manufacturing choices would you make to serve this market, which is expected to grow by 450 percent over the next year? Support your choices. What manufacturing strategy underlies your analysis?

RUCK TRUCK CORPORATION

Tom Horn had just been appointed vice-president of operations for the Ruck Truck Corporation and had moved to the corporate headquarters in Atlanta. Tom had most recently been plant manager of the Ruck Truck plant in Little Rock, Arkansas. The firm had decided to build a new truck plant in the Midwest and had taken an option on 20 acres in an industrial park just outside Dayton, Ohio. Tom's first job as V.P. was to coordinate all the design aspects and managerial concerns to make sure the new plant operated in an efficient and effective manner and made a high contribution to the firm. Tom thought he could rely heavily on his experience at the Little Rock Ruck Truck plant, plus his education, to bring this assignment to a successful conclusion.

The trucks that were built at the Little Rock plant, as well as those to be built at the Dayton plant, were the diesel tractor portion of highway tractor-trailers (the "18-wheelers" of CB and TV renown). The tractors were the "cab over"—flat in front and having no hood. Basic production followed this format:

1. The running gear (including engine, transmission, axles, brakes, and suspension systems) was purchased from name brand suppliers and adapted to suit the particular requirements of the buyer.

2. The frame rails were purchased with prepunched bolt holes in the front. The remaining holes were drilled on semiautomatic machines with patterns, again to suit the configuration ordered by the buyer.

3. The cab was the single component that most distinguished the Ruck Truck from every other manufacturer's. The cab was entirely assembled in the plant from components both made in the plant and purchased.

4. There were a number of variations on the truck design from which a buyer could choose to individualize or customize a truck.

Ruck manufactured to order and felt comfortable with a 90-day backlog—much shorter, and the firm felt uneasy about sales; much longer, and they felt that buyers would go to the competition. Although the firm did occasionally sell trucks to dealers for floor models, the usual sale was to the individual owner/driver through a local dealer. The firm would negotiate lower prices for stripped-down models to fleet operators when necessary to absorb slack capacity. Tom would allow no more than three fleet buyer's trucks to be scheduled in the plant at one time. He thought it best to intersperse these multiple orders in with the typical single unit orders. Ruck Truck's reputation as the "limousine" of trucks was enhanced by the fact that the buyer had such a wide selection of design and accessories from which to choose, as compared to the limited selection offered by larger volume manufacturers. The truck sales price ran from $50,000 to $60,000—typically higher than that of the competition. However, this higher price apparently did not deter buyers.

To get a better grasp of the whole, Tom made the following attempt to identify, define, and categorize the various departments and work centers:

- *Machine shop*—does precision machining of component parts, usually in batches to inventory. Occasionally builds and repairs simple tools, jigs, and fixtures for both itself and other areas. Will also, at times, do precision machining for the maintenance department. Employees are highly skilled machinists.

- *Maintenance department*—keeps the plant and equipment operating; also includes the janitorial function; assembles and installs new machines and processes. With the exception of janitors, the maintenance crew is made up of highly skilled craftsmen such as electricians, maintenance welders, and millwrights. On many of the jobs, more than one trade or skill is involved. Maintenance jobs were scheduled in order of priority: (1) breakdowns priority (2) building or installing a new process (once project funds were approved, the investment was charged to the plant; Tom thought it was not too smart to have a $100,000 machine sitting idle in the receiving area), and (3) preventive maintenance (coordinated with machine/process availability and maintenance department slack).

- *Press department*—contains a variety of brake and punch presses, metal shears, metal rolls, spot welding, metal routers, and metal saws. The machines are used to fabricate a large assortment of component parts from aluminum cab "skin" to support brackets. The parts are made in batches to inventory. The employees are semiskilled machine operators.

- *Production welding area*—assembles and welds various component parts, which are run in batches to inventory requirements. The welders are skilled production welders.

- *Paint areas*—scattered throughout the plant.

  The smaller component parts are hung on a conveyor line, which transports them through an automatic washer and "static" paint process for undercoat paint. The parts are run in batches through the identical process. The one employee required for this process is very low skilled.

  Each finished cab is primed and baked, then given its unique set of colors and trims by painting and baking each color or trim stripe; each color or trim requires a separate trip through the paint booth and oven. Each cab is scheduled to match up with the correct truck chassis.

  The truck wheels are painted in a separate paint booth near the truck line. Again, each set of wheels, usually numbering 10, is painted to order, although white predominates. The wheels are also scheduled to match the production build schedule.

  The chassis or remainder of the truck is painted and baked on the assembly line. The line passes through a paint booth and oven.

  The painters in these operations are skilled production painters.

- *Frame rail drilling*. All the common holes on the front 3-foot portion of the truck rails are prepunched by a vendor. The remainder of the holes (about 75 percent) are drilled on two semiautomatic drilling machines. Both rails of a set of two have the same pattern with the exception of a few holes. The rails are thus clamped together and drilled two at a time. The rails are scheduled and drilled to suit the plant build schedule. The workers are skilled machine operators.

- *Assembly processes*—frame assembly, suspension assembly, transmission to engine assembly, drive shaft assembly, cab assembly, cab trim, door assembly, and wheel tire assembly. These minor assembly operations feed into the major truck assembly operations. Each of these operations performs the same basic set of tasks on each unit, as on an auto assembly line. The major difference at Ruck Truck is the fixtures and tooling that are necessary for each set of possible combinations. For example, the axle/suspension/brake assembly requires an inventory of welding fixtures. Another oddball operation is the drive shaft assembly. The product engineers emphatically declare they could not consider all the variables that would enable them to predetermine drive shaft lengths.

Therefore, each drive shaft is custom fit as the truck chassis is pulled along the assembly line, thus precluding many of the economies that would have been possible otherwise.

Figure 15-A is a schematic representation of most of the productive processes with which Tom must be concerned in trying to design the new plant. Ancillary functions such as shipping, receiving, and materials management Tom neglected for the moment. He felt that if he could get a firm grasp of his problem with the processes described above, then he could fit in the others.

1. What concerns or considerations would you have if you were Tom?
2. What do you suggest that he do?

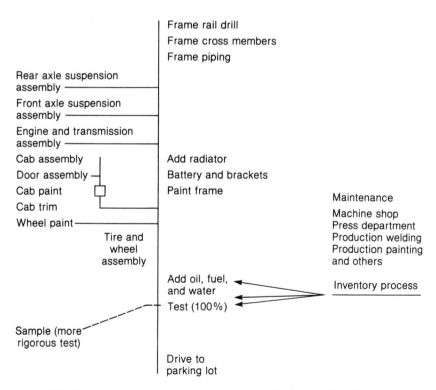

FIGURE 15-A   Major processes to be incorporated into the new Ruck Truck plant.

REFERENCE NOTES

1. See Wickham Skinner, *Manufacturing in the Corporate Strategy* (New York: John Wiley & Sons, 1978), which brings together a number of Skinner's articles that appeared first in the *Harvard Business Review.*

2. See Alfred Chandler Jr., *The Visible Hand: The Managerial Revolution in American Business* (Cambridge, Mass.: Harvard University Press, 1977).

3. This section is based on Robert H. Hayes and Roger W. Schmenner, "How Should You Organize Manufacturing?" *Harvard Business Review* 56, no. 1 (January–February 1978), pp. 105–18.

16

GOVERNMENT REGULATION AND OPERATIONS

Nothing raises the ire of most managers quite like the mention of government regulation. Management jobs ranging from that of the company's chief executive officer down to its first-level supervisors are inescapably touched by the already large, and growing, hand of government intervention. For many, government threatens to "take all the fun out of operating a business." But governmental influence and control is not going to fade away, despite recent and laudable efforts at deregulation. The modern manager will simply have to get along with yet another complexity to be analyzed and acted upon.

To be sure, the price of compliance with government regulation is steep. Companies must hire extra workers simply to handle the paper work. New plant and equipment purchases—often deemed "nonproductive"—must frequently be made. Workers must be hired and trained in particular ways, and specific safety procedures enforced. The list could continue. Periodically, companies report how much they must spend simply to comply. For example, Dow Chemical spent $147 million in 1975 meeting government regulations, $50 million of which it thought excessive. Those figures are peanuts, however, compared to the $80 billion that the automotive companies are expected to spend by 1985 to solve both emissions and energy mandates.[1]

A BRIEF HISTORY OF GOVERNMENT REGULATION

The high cost of compliance notwithstanding, the thoughtful manager is aware that government regulations arose for good and just reasons. The first wave of government regulation swept across the U.S. economy in the 1880s and 1890s, soon after the development of large, integrated corporations. Belief in the inherent virtues of many, small competitors was widely held and it is not surprising that the railroads and the so-called "trusts" were the first to be affected; they were certainly the largest. In 1887, the Interstate Commerce Commission was created to regulate the railroads, which were then engaged in numerous price wars and compensating instances of price discrimination. The ICC acted to stabilize and equalize prices, some say more to the benefit of the railroads themselves than to their customers.

The creation of the ICC was followed in 1890 by the Sherman Antitrust Act, certainly among the most important and (though debatable) best pieces of legislation ever passed by Congress. The Sherman Act followed a couple of decades of unprecedented merger activity that was held to be driving small companies out of business by engaging in so-called "predatory pricing" (temporary pricing under cost). The price discrimination some firms en-

407

gaged in and the conspicuous consumption of some of the nouveau riche swung public opinion and political initiative against monopoly and near-monopoly firms. Although it took a decade for the Sherman Act to catch hold, it is clear that the Act was a significant deterrent to further merger activity. It was invoked on a number of occasions to break up already large firms like American Tobacco, American Can, and Standard Oil. In retrospect, the Sherman Act is often credited with maintaining technological momentum in U.S. industry by avoiding what some consider to be the stifling effects of the cartelization that characterized European industry at the time.

The Sherman Antitrust Act was followed in 1914 by two more pieces of legislation that tried to fill in the gaps of the Sherman Act. One of these, the Clayton Act, addressed mainly price discrimination, tying contracts (e.g., to buy my product A, you must also buy my product B), merger activity, and interlocking directorates. The other, the Federal Trade Commission Act, established that commission both to investigate "unfair methods of competition" and to pass rulings on them that are binding on the companies involved.

While in the years since 1914 there have been some minor changes in antitrust law, plus a host of legal opinions in all its aspects, the foundations of U.S. antitrust law were laid by 1914.

The origins of state regulation of public utilities (electricity, telephone, natural gas, and the like) date from about this time as well. For these industries it has been traditionally recognized that a so-called "natural monopoly" exists. That is to say, over any geographic area there are vast cost reductions to be realized if there is only one supplier. In the case of telephone service, a single supplier eliminates the need for duplicate telephone poles and central office switching equipment and provides all telephones in the area with the same network. The cost of adding an additional subscriber, once the full network is established, is also lower than if multiple suppliers existed. The natural monopoly argument in this case is so intuitively appealing that it is even hard to visualize electricity or telephone service provided in any other way. Still, a monopoly, natural or otherwise, can control price and quantity over considerable ranges, and it is this vulnerability that has argued for regulating public utilities. In most instances, regulation has meant control over prices, price structures, service quality, financial return, accounting principles, and the company's license to operate a particular service. Public utilities, though virtually assured of a reasonable level of earnings over time, are thus regulated in almost all dimensions of their operations.

Much as the turbulent, recession-plagued decades of the 1870s and 1880s spawned antitrust and public utility regulation, the Depression of the 1930s motivated the next significant wave of government intervention in the economy. The federal agencies created in the 1930s were generally more specific in scope than the landmark antitrust legislation that preceded it. Perhaps the most far-reaching piece of legislation in the 1930s was the Wagner Act of 1935, which established the legitimacy of the labor union movement and, in fact, as noted in Chapter 9, was formulated to encourage unionization. As we have already observed, the Wagner Act created the National Labor Relations Board to conduct certification and decertification elections and to rule on unfair labor practices.

Also created in the 1930s were industry-specific agencies such as the Federal Power Commission, the Federal Communications Commission, the Food and Drug Administration, the Civil Aeronautics Board, the Security and Exchange Commission, and several other agencies, many related to banking reform. Considering the deprivation of the times—25 percent unemployment and considerable capital losses—regulation of such basic sectors of the economy as these, mostly designed to protect consumers, is easily understandable.

The latest round of new government intervention, that of the 1970s, is also readily understood mainly as a consequence of the steady post–World War II gains in U.S. affluence and of the massive dislocations in the economy caused by such jolts as wage and price controls (1971) and the Arab oil embargo (1973). Increasing specialization in the economy and numerous social programs have been contributing factors to the economy's marked loss of elasticity or flexibility in recent years. This loss of elasticity has made macroeconomic policy much more complex and frustrating than it appeared to be before the Vietnam War. This complexity and frustration have helped spawn some of the latest federal initiatives dealing with energy, health, and the environment.

Table 16-1 summarizes this brief history of government regulation.

THE ECONOMIC CASE FOR GOVERNMENT INTERVENTION IN THE ECONOMY

The economic rationale for the intervention of government in the economy is to redress what are generally acknowledged to be failures of the unregulated market mechanism. There are a variety of such "market failures," which are really deviations from the conditions that economic theory and practice have established as sufficient to assure Adam Smith's brilliant insight—namely, that everybody working for their own self-interest will, in so doing, work also for society's best interest as if guided by some "invisible hand." Such an insight—that "greed" can actually work toward the common good—provides much of the goal toward which economic policy strives. Indeed, it is hoped that government intervention to remedy one or another market failure will actually rechannel "greed" to everyone's best interest.

Smith's insight was based on a view of the economy as a constant search for new methods and markets. In the years since, his insight has been refined and formalized, with competition seen as a struggle between small firms who must take prices as given and who compete largely on price. This is an obvious simplification to aid the theoretical formality, but many economists feel that Smith's insight can prevail even when some companies are large and powerful, as long as the economy stays dynamic, with constant jostling on price, quality, markets, technology, and products.

Given this kind of dynamic economy, there are three major failures that justify government action. In simplified description, they are:

1. *Monopoly.* A single seller (or, alternatively, a cartel of just a few sellers) can artificially restrict output and thus influence price. By restricting production and raising prices, monopolists can make society as a whole worse off than it would have been if production had not been cut back. It is worse off because more consumers could have used effectively the monopolist's product at prices that would still have given the monopolist profits (although not as much as the monopolist gains from higher prices and restricted output).

   This result of economic theory is the cornerstone to antitrust activity. A corollary result centers on the single buyer, sometimes termed a monopsonist. The monopsonist also exercises market power, in this case by its ability to purchase less of an input than would be best for society as a whole. Antitrust legislation is also aimed at this noncompetitive situation.

2. *Externalities.* When what one consumer or producer does affects directly what other consumers or producers do, apart from the workings of the prices themselves, the market mechanism starts to break down. Pollution is the classic example of such an "externality." For example, one producer may foul a river's water upstream from other producers, imposing extra costs of water filtration on the down-river producers. Or, one plant's air pollution may create health problems for families and firms in

TABLE 16-1 Major Government Regulatory Agencies

AGENCY	FOUNDING	FUNCTION
Regulating Competition		
Interstate Commerce Commission	1887	Regulates route structure and rates for railroads and "common carrier" trucks (i.e., those licensed to carry anything anywhere, as opposed to a company-owned fleet hauling only company goods)
Antitrust Division of the Justice Department	1890 (Sherman Act)	Created to enforce the Sherman Antitrust Act; capable of taking companies to court for civil and criminal conduct in violation of acts; successful in breaking up and in deterring huge size in any one industry
State Public Utility Commissions	Antecedents from 1860s on; electric power companies regulated from 1907 on	Commissions responsible for licenses, rates, earnings targets, accounting practices, quality standards
Federal Trade Commission	1914	Can both investigate and judge "unfair" methods of competition
Federal Power Commission	1930	Sets rates for interstate transmission of electric power; also controls interstate natural gas prices and pipeline routes and rates
Federal Communications Commission	1934	Licenses for broadcasting; regulates interstate rates for telephone and telegraph services
Federal Maritime Commission	1936	The ICC of the seas; charged with price stability for U.S. ocean commerce
Civil Aeronautics Board	1938	The ICC of the skies; regulates routes and rates for airlines; recent scene of considerable deregulation
Worker and Consumer Rights, Health, and Safety		
National Labor Relations Board	1935 (with Wagner Act)	Runs union certification and decertification elections; rules on what constitutes an unfair labor practice
Food and Drug Administration	1931	Regulates parity and labeling of foods and drugs; can ban sale of either
Equal Employment Opportunity Commission	1964	Investigates cases of discrimination in the workplace; can file court cases
National Highway Traffic Safety Administration	1970	Can mandate safety features for autos and other vehicles; can initiate vehicle recalls
Occupational Health and Safety Administration	1971	Can prescribe health and safety rules at virtually all workplaces
Consumer Product Safety Commission	1972	Watchdog for product liability; can mandate product design changes and labeling
Environmental and Energy Matters		
Environmental Protection Agency	1970	Sets standards for pollution control and can enforce them
Federal Energy Administration	1973	Can control domestic oil and gasoline prices; has mandated auto mileage goals

the area. In these cases, pollution imposes costs on society that are not captured fully by the price system. That is to say, the polluter imposes costs on society for which it is not charged.

Government is justified in this case to intervene so that the polluter is charged for the costs its polluting imposes on others. One resolution of this externality is a pollution "tax" on the polluter, levied at a level that reflects the full, social costs of the pollution. Faced with such a tax, the polluter could then "internalize the externality," probably choosing to reduce the level of pollution so as to avoid the tax.

3. *Public goods.* There is a class of goods and services that demonstrates some peculiar properties: (a) one person's enjoyment is not diminished by having another person consume that good or service, and (b) it is difficult to exclude consumers from enjoying the good or service. Think of our national defense. My happiness in our ability to "nuke the Commies" is not diminished at all by your happiness; indeed, once such reassurance is provided, I cannot exclude you from the peace of mind I share, since we both stand under the same nuclear umbrella. These peculiar properties often make it difficult to pay for such goods and services strictly through the private sector. No private company would want to provide our national defense because it is so easy to be a "free rider"; the company simply could not charge for the service and exclude nonpaying individuals from enjoying it. For this reason, then, services like defense, police, traffic and safety, public health, and others have strong claims on public provision and finance. This market failure gives rise to a particular kind of government intervention.

These three market failures constitute the major economic justifications for government intervention in the economy. There are, of course, other political/social reasons for such intervention, but it is these three that are most soundly grounded in economic thinking. Furthermore, the form of government intervention is suggested in each case: (1) proscription of monopolies or cartels or the regulation of their output and prices, (2) taxes or charges for polluters or other initiators of externalities, and (3) public provision of so-called "public goods."

With this discussion as background, we now turn to the major types of existing government regulation.

TYPES OF GOVERNMENT REGULATION

Although the precise ways in which government regulates business vary in almost as many ways as there are government policies, most regulation can be classified into four main types. I will describe these types and offer some examples of their use.

REGULATION OF ENTRY

Entry into an industry, controlled primarily by the issuance of licenses, is a common way to limit what is sometimes thought to be ruinous competition. Licensing is one of the oldest forms of regulation and prevails throughout the transportation, communications, and utilities industries. The ICC, FCC, CAB, and state utilities commissions all possess powers over entry.*

As can be surmised from the brief discussion of the economic rationales for regulation, entry regulations are among the least justified. It has long been argued that the ICC's limitation of entry in

---

*Licensing to limit entry into an industry is to be distinguished from the licensing of individuals into a profession like medicine, based upon some proven level of competence. The entry licensing we are talking about here is not grounded in quality assurance but is done for allegedly economic reasons.

the trucking industry has fostered higher freight rates than would prevail otherwise. In addition, the ICC's sluggishness on railroad innovation and integration with trucking (e.g., piggybacking) has been offered as one explanation for the continuing profitability problems of the railroads. Entry regulations have been a foremost target for deregulation for these reasons. The CAB, under the inventive and energetic chairmanship of Alfred Kahn, has recently turned the airline industry on its ear by deregulating much of that industry. While much of the CAB attention has focused on permitting price competition, other deregulation has focused on permitting change in some of the city pairs that define the markets for the airlines. It is now much easier for one airline to enter another's market, as Dallas-based Braniff International's recent expansions of the routes it flies have clearly demonstrated. The consumer has unarguably been aided by this deregulation; and airline earnings, to the surprise of some airlines, were higher immediately after the deregulation.

Regulation of Price and Earnings

The transportation and utility regulators (e.g., the ICC, CAB, and state utility commissions) have long had the power to fix price and earnings levels for companies. Fixed price levels, as indicated by the recent CAB actions, have also been considered ready targets for deregulation, since price as well as entry regulation is scarcely justified on economic grounds.

Earnings regulation is a more interesting and more defensible means of controlling a company. Used primarily to regulate utilities, the so-called natural monopolies, earnings regulation usually takes the form of permitting a company only a target rate of return on the assets it devotes to providing the service (e.g., telephone, electric power) it is licensed to provide. For example, a telephone company may be permitted to earn a target of, say, 8 percent on its invested capital. What constitutes invested capital is subject to definition by the state regulatory commission as well. Operationally, this limit to the rate of return means that the company's rates/prices can be set only so high, given the expected pattern of demand. Thus, in operation, earnings regulation looks very much like price regulation, but it is price regulation pegged to a company's earnings and subject to annual review by the commission, which dictates the accounting procedures the utility must use.

As one might expect, this kind of rate of return regulation gives the utility the incentive to place considerable assets into its "rate base" since the level of earnings permitted is controlled by the extent of the rate base.

Prescriptive Standards

The fastest growing form of regulation prescribes exactly what the manufacturer may do or must do. An outright ban on production is the bluntest form of this type of regulation; it has existed at the Food and Drug Administration for decades. More recently, the standards prescribed have become more specific—to many managers' minds, nit-picking. Perhaps the most resented new federal agency is the Occupational Safety and Health Administration, which has the authority to insist that businesses adhere to its definition of what is safe and healthful. Needless to say, to some managers the inevitably arbitrary dicta of OSHA have smacked of harassment and bureaucratic inflexibility.

The setting of prescriptive standards has been common to the burgeoning list of agencies attending to safety and health, which include the Consumer Product Safety Commission, the National Highway Traffic Safety Administration, and the Nuclear Regulatory Commission in addition to OSHA and the FDA. Setting such standards makes the most sense when the products or processes threaten to be risky or dangerous, when they are new and relatively unresearched, and when they are complex. They make less sense for more everyday aspects of product or process health and safety.

The unease that many managers and policy-makers alike share about the establishment of prescriptive standards is their arbitrariness and their sluggishness to change. As we have noted in discussing production standards, the march of time and technological progress frequently erode the worth of a standard. Constant vigilance is demanded. Thus, the more standards federal agencies set, the more likely their consequences will run counter to the agencies' initial intentions.

PERFORMANCE-BASED REGULATION

The most easily defended form of regulation — and, ironically, the least prevalent — is based on some measure of performance; it usually levies fines or taxes according to the degree performance deviates from some standard. Pollution control is a classic application of performance-based regulation. Under such a scheme, for example, a plant would be charged a fee for every ton of effluent it dumped back into a river (or into the air). The plant could continue polluting, but the high fee it had to pay would encourage the plant to look for ways to avoid polluting.

The advantage of such a performance-based system is that it gives industry the opportunity to choose among many possible ways to reduce pollution: different inputs (e.g., low sulphur fuel), different processes, different pollution control equipment; a company can choose the cheapest and most efficient way for it to cut back on pollution. A drawback to such effluent fees is the cost of monitoring effluent discharges so that the proper penalty is assessed. Standard-setting is often easier administratively, and easier politically as well.

What is too little realized is that if society still does not like the level of pollution that remains — and under such a scheme, some pollution is likely to go on in those companies for which controlling pollution is more expensive than paying the fee — all that need be done is to raise the fee. That is, if

substantial pollution persists, it is not an indictment of performance-based regulation. Rather, it is an indication that the pollution fee is too low.

The federal standards on automotive fleet average miles per gallon in 1985 is a form of performance-based regulation. Rather than specify the precise way by which increased gas mileage is to be achieved, this requirement has stimulated the auto companies to search for alternative means of raising fleet mileage efficiency — smaller cars, different design and structural materials to reduce weight, more efficient engines.

THE CONSEQUENCES OF REGULATION[2]

From industry's standpoint, while the costs of complying with regulations are high, and often unnecessarily so, the most important competitive consequences lie other than with a company's own costs of compliance. Of course, numerous plants and some companies have had to close principally because the costs of complying with environmental and other regulations became too great. Many of these, to be sure, were only modestly profitable before the advent of environmental regulations, but regulation was the deciding factor in their closing. Nevertheless, the major consequence of regulation for any company is apt to lie in changes to the competitive structure of its industry.

CHANGING THE COMPETITIVE STRUCTURE OF INDUSTRIES

What is important competitively is to recognize how regulation affects particular plants and companies within an industry. As a result of regulations, some plants and companies will be at a competitive advantage. In the parlance we have used before, regulation alters the structure of economic rents in the industry. Thus, some companies that previously enjoyed highly competitive positions may be toppled from them, while other companies gain at their expense.

How does this competitive restructuring occur? How do economic rents get shifted? Consider the following points.

Regulations, particularly environmental regulations, are best met with technologies that are themselves subject to considerable economies of scale. Given, for example, the need to treat a production process's waste water, there are significant cost savings per unit of factory output if the water treatment facility is large rather than small. It is no wonder that International Paper's Androscoggin Mill—large and designed with pollution control in mind—does so well relative to many smaller mills. The environmental control aspects of the process reinforce the papermaking aspects that argue for large size.

This move toward larger scale favors an oligopolistic structure to the industry. The most effective competitors are likely to be those that have continuous flow processes and the latest (and largest) equipment. The costs of compliance thus erect even higher barriers to entry into the industry, effectively muzzling more traditional laws of competition (e.g., competition chiefly on price) and arguably raising the industry's long-term rate of return since entry barriers create economic rents. Of course, in the short term, rates of return are likely to fall as capital resources must be diverted from income-producing projects to pollution control, a non–income-producing alternative. The extent to which rates of return fall or rise naturally differs from company to company and plant to plant.

The dollars spent to meet environmental regulations are typically diverted from projects to increase manufacturing capacity. This fact, coupled with the very large capital costs of adding environmentally approved capacity, has frequently meant that capacity now lags behind demand rather than leading it. That is to say, companies no longer find it advantageous to build up their capacity in anticipation of demand. More and more, they would rather have demand press against existing capacity for a while, even if it means price inflation, before they add to capacity. They want to be sure that the demand will be there for a long time, before they stake their capital on a high-cost addition of capacity. Even then, capacity expansions are likely to be smaller than they would otherwise be, and more frequent.

In this same vein, regulation generally contributes to the lumpiness of the investment decisions of many companies. Lumpy investments are usually to be avoided, if at all possible, since they interrupt smooth additions to capacity. The steel industry is an archetypal example of the problems that investment lumpiness brings about. With current technology, an integrated steel mill, if built from scratch on a so-called "greenfield" site, would have to be huge—about 4.5 million tons per year—in order to be most economical. A steel mill of this size is roughly 4 percent of total U.S. production and more than the yearly growth in demand. Even to U.S. Steel, the industry leader, a plant of this size is an increase of over 10 percent of its capacity. With new capacity implying such tremendous scale, it is no wonder that most steel industry capacity is added by breaking bottlenecks in existing "brownfield" operations. For example, another blast furnace could be added to an existing operation, shifting the bottleneck from the blast furnaces to, say, the hot strip mill. In this way, some of the lumpiness of greenfield site investment is reduced and a more gradual increase made to capacity. At the same time, however, repeated on-site expansion may lead to considerable materials handling difficulties and vast, almost unwieldy management problems. Without a doubt, environmental regulation with its implied lumpiness and uncertainty of investment has slowed the establishment of new sites for heavy industry.

To reiterate, regulation contributes to the competitive restructuring of an industry by altering the distribution of economic rents. This change is done principally by:

- Forcing some plants and companies out of business

- Favoring large-scale (lumpy) operations that can realize the scale advantages of most pollution control technologies (e.g., water treatment)

- Creating uncertainties for investment

- Favoring continuous flow, nonseasonal production

- Raising entry barriers to the industry, possibly leading to increased long-term rates of return after an initial short-term period of lower rates of return

- Favoring capacity expansion that lags behind, rather than leads, demand

The Impact of Regulation on Industry Structure: An Example

As an example of the vast impact government policy can have, consider the recently publicized burgeoning of small, mom-and-pop oil refineries as a consequence of the federal oil entitlements policy. Some paragraphs from a 1978 *Fortune* article on the subject are illuminating.[3]

Some oil experts are predicting that the United States is going to experience a shortage of refinery capacity in a few years. One of the reasons, they add, is that too many refineries are being built. If you think you detect the antic touch of your federal government somewhere in this paradox, you're right. Through some convoluted manipulations of oil-price controls, the government has set off a veritable boom in small refineries. Since 1976, the total number of refining companies in the United States has grown by 41, or more than 31 percent, and the pace seems to be accelerating.

The exploding refinery population consists almost entirely of inefficient, inappropriately designed plants whose main function is to enrich their owners at public expense. Subsidies to small refiners now run well over a billion dollars a year. The government siphons the money away from bigger oil companies, but the consumer ultimately pays.

Few of the subsidized refineries can do what most needs doing. Most are tiny—handling no more than 10,000 barrels of crude oil per day—an anomaly in an industry where standards of efficiency, productivity, and flexibility call for plants with capacities of at least 175,000 barrels per day. And few of these little "teakettles" are capable either of cleaning up the "sour," or high-sulfur, crudes that are relatively plentiful, or of "cracking" the less valuable petroleum fractions into the gasoline and heating oils that the nation most needs.

Out of the Gritty Sediment

Yet, their proliferation has helped discourage investment in bigger, more versatile refineries—the kind that are already severely constrained by environmental regulations. As a result, the United States may in a few years wind up with another refinery bottleneck like the one that led to shortages and price increases in the early 70s, well before OPEC flexed its muscles.

The $2.5-Billion Shuffle

One benefit to small refiners sprang up in the good old days when foreign oil was cheap and the government took pains to keep it out of the country with an import-quota system. All refiners were allowed to import some of their crude oil, but the government allowed small refiners to import proportionately more. The embargo in late 1973 and the subsequent increase in foreign oil prices turned everything on its head. All of a sudden, it was domestic oil, with its cost held down by price controls, that everyone was trying to get his hands on. In an effort to equalize the cost to refiners that processed domestic and foreign oil, the government came up with the so-called entitlements program. Companies that refine relatively large amounts of cheap domestic crude are required to buy entitlements from those refining relatively more imported oil.

The price of each entitlement is the difference in cost between a barrel of imported oil and a barrel of controlled domestic oil. This difference now amounts to $8.35.

At this point (1976) the amount of money that had begun to flow from the big refiners to the small ones began to seem quite interesting. The smallest category of refiners—those running 10,000 barrels per day or less—were allocated 228 "bias" entitlements for every thousand barrels they run. With entitlements now worth about $8.35 a piece, the effect is to hand these refiners a price break of around $2 on each barrel of their raw material—an amount that substantially exceeds their extra costs of refining (a small refinery's costs generally run 50¢ or so a barrel more than a large refinery's).

With that kind of subsidy, it pays to go into the refining business. The cost of building an ultra-simple small refinery lies somewhere in the neighborhood of $1000 per barrel of capacity—and a lot less than that if the operator can scrounge up used equipment or acquire intact an old refinery that some large company previously closed down as uneconomical. Clearing some $20,000 a day before taxes from bias entitlements alone, the 10,000-barrel-a-day teakettle operator could sell his products at cost and still pay for his refinery in somewhere between 8 and 18 months. And from that point on, the gravy would flow in at a rate of around $7 million a year.

The consequences were predictable. In the year prior to the doubling of the subsidy, only three refineries were completed in the United States. In 1976 and 1977, 36 plants were built or spun off and reactivated, 19 of them below 10,000 barrels per day of capacity. Only one—a 126,000-barrel plant—had a capacity over 50,000 barrels a day. Most of the owners of these plants are former petroleum-products jobbers and retailers, and they acknowledge that they wouldn't be in the business if it weren't for the small-refiner bias. Says Lamar Lund, president of Mount Airy Refining Co., whose 11,600-barrel refinery in Louisiana opened last year, "If there weren't the bias or an equivalent benefit, we would have to shut down."

Taken together, the $1.1 billion provided small refiners last year would be enough to build four or five modern 200,000-barrel-a-day plants.

REGULATORY DELAY

Another significant cost of regulation lies in the sometimes massive delays that major capital investment projects often suffer through. A little tinkering with net present value analysis is enough to convince anyone that forestalling the completion of an investment project can seriously undermine that project's economic underpinnings. This is particularly true in our inflationary times when discount rates are higher than those traditionally used and thus more of a penalty to a delayed stream of project revenues.

The regulatory delays involved with the construction of nuclear power generating plants for public utilities are perhaps the most widely known examples of the impact of regulation on construction timetables and costs. Of course, the impact of delay on the economics of a project that has already been started is even more virulent than its impact on projects conceived but not yet begun. Although nuclear power plants are the most widespread example of regulatory delay, many companies (especially in the petroleum, chemicals, primary metals, and pulp and paper industries) have experienced similar kinds of delay in procuring the many permits that must precede the construction of new facilities.

THE IMPACT OF ALTERING REGULATION

The irony of government regulation throughout our history is that, after a while, those regulated often love being regulated and resist any change. Deregulation, or a different kind of regulation (say, a switch from standards-based regulation to performance-based regulation) can be very unsettling to company managements; the familiar status quo is interrupted and risk, especially the kind of competitive restructuring mentioned above, is introduced. As long as rigid regulations are in place, any company knows where it stands and, furthermore, knows where competing companies stand as well. Unloosing such rigid regulations introduces new complexities for managers that only the hearty embrace. Recent efforts at airline, railroad, and trucking deregulation have all experienced industry balking at change for just these reasons.

Technological advance can also create unease with regulation. One of the most salient examples of the impact of technological advance and regulation involves venerable "Ma Bell" (A.T.&T.) herself. Because of technological advances—private microwave transmission lines, computer-to-computer communications—Ma Bell's once monopolistic hold on communications has become fuzzy. Some companies now offer private microwave transmission between cities like Chicago and St. Louis and charge less than A.T.&T. No longer is the Bell System the only permitted entrant to that market. The ongoing computer revolution has also muddied the distinction between what is "computer" and what is the "network" that ties computers together. Various product offerings by computer companies look very much like communications systems, and various communications systems look very much like computers. There are reportedly a number of Justice Department antitrust types who salivate at the thought of IBM and A.T.&T. going at one another for the same markets in the years ahead.

The Bell System's reaction to these developments is that it cannot compete successfully against other firms without being freed from a number of regulatory constraints. Much of the Bell System's service is priced noncompetitively. It is said, for example, that long distance service subsidizes local telephone service, because of the actions of the FCC and the state regulatory commissions. If, indeed, long distance rates are higher than economically justified, regulation does impede the Bell System from competing with microwave transmission companies. In this case, technological advance may have made regulation obsolete. There are many who think so. Interestingly, the entire Bell System has recently undergone a reorganization specifically designed to realign its operations with the marketing opportunities that seem to be budding all around the ever-broadening field of communications.

How these issues of technological advance and regulation will sort themselves out remains largely unclear. It is not easy to decide how much of the Bell System, for example, should still be regulated and in which ways. A great deal remains to be learned.

ESTABLISHING CONFLICTING GOALS

As vexing as any consequence of governmental intervention are the inevitable conflicts that arise from two or more different governmental policies affecting the same operation. The conflicts arising in the automobile industry provide a fruitful example. By the mid-1980s, automobiles must meet two different government standards, one mandated by the Environmental Protection Agency for automotive emissions and the other mandated by the Federal Energy Administration for fleetwide gas mileage. Generally speaking, changes in a car's engineering that lessen auto emissions (e.g., engine modification, certain exhaust systems additions like the catalytic converter) tend to worsen gas mileage. These goals, in themselves admirable, work at cross purposes; if it were not for other attacks on one or another of the problems (e.g., "down-sizing" cars to increase gas mileage), both goals would not be achievable at the same time.

Widespread conflicts may arise from public sector policies that act at cross purposes to one another. Such conflicts can be resolved by an overarching policy. Pollution control is an example. Given that some industrial waste will be generated by any production process, the waste must be disposed of either in the air, in water, or in solid form. Pollution controls must permit one or the other—considering, of course, industry's good faith adoption of the most efficient known technologies for complying with the standards. It seems realistic to acknowledge, however, that air, water, and solid waste pollution cannot all be minimized at the same time. One or more must bend, and it is the function of some overarching policy to decide which. One cannot blithely assume that optimizing each part of a whole will necessarily lead to an optimization of the whole itself; pollution control is but one example of this maxim.

QUESTIONS

1. In your opinion, does any government ever have the right to regulate various aspects of production when those regulations may result in higher costs to consumers? Why or why not?

2. Research the development of three governmental regulatory agencies: one that regulates competition; one that regulates consumer and worker rights; and one that regulates environmental and energy matters.

3. Give a brief review of the development of an-

other nation's governmental regulatory agency or agencies.

4. What are the main points to support the economic case for governmental intervention in the economy? Do you agree with them?

5. Discuss and contrast the four main types of governmental regulation. Provide an example of each.

6. Are all consequences of governmental regulation good? Give concrete examples to support your point of view.

PROBLEMS

1. What was the major thrust of the government regulation started in the 1880s?

2. Government regulation has periods of high activity followed by periods of low activity. Each period also seems to have its own area of emphasis. Describe the time periods and the major emphasis of each. What has been the effect on U.S. industry in each period?

3. Does government regulation ever help industry? Cite some examples.

4. What is the economic justification for allowing monopolies to exist?

5. What influence does society's thoughts have on government regulation of industry?

6. How does government regulation affect the investment of new capital in plant and equipment?

7. Discuss the current regulation of the oil companies and how this regulation has affected new oil exploration within the United States.

8. Explain the managerial thoughts related to deregulation after regulation has been in effect for a number of years.

REFERENCE NOTES

1. *Business Week* (March 26, 1979): 68.

2. Many of these points on the consequences of regulation are due to Robert A. Leone of Harvard University. See also Robert A. Leone and John R. Meyer, "The Economics of V-Shaped Costs," working paper 79-45 of the Harvard Business School, August 1979.

3. Tom Alexander, "How Little Oil Hit a Big Gusher on Capitol Hill," *Fortune* (August 14, 1978): 148–54.

Index